STANDARD NORMAL DISTRIBUTION

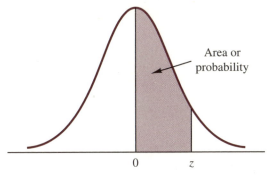

Area or probability

Entries in the table give the area under the curve between the mean and z standard deviations above the mean. For example, for $z = 1.25$ the area under the curve between the mean and z is .3944.

z	.00	.01	.02	.03	.04	.05	.06	.07	.08	.09
.0	.0000	.0040	.0080	.0120	.0160	.0199	.0239	.0279	.0319	.0359
.1	.0398	.0438	.0478	.0517	.0557	.0596	.0636	.0675	.0714	.0753
.2	.0793	.0832	.0871	.0910	.0948	.0987	.1026	.1064	.1103	.1141
.3	.1179	.1217	.1255	.1293	.1331	.1368	.1406	.1443	.1480	.1517
.4	.1554	.1591	.1628	.1664	.1700	.1736	.1772	.1808	.1844	.1879
.5	.1915	.1950	.1985	.2019	.2054	.2088	.2123	.2157	.2190	.2224
.6	.2257	.2291	.2324	.2357	.2389	.2422	.2454	.2486	.2517	.2549
.7	.2580	.2611	.2642	.2673	.2704	.2734	.2764	.2794	.2823	.2852
.8	.2881	.2910	.2939	.2967	.2995	.3023	.3051	.3078	.3106	.3133
.9	.3159	.3186	.3212	.3238	.3264	.3289	.3315	.3340	.3365	.3389
1.0	.3413	.3438	.3461	.3485	.3508	.3531	.3554	.3577	.3599	.3621
1.1	.3643	.3665	.3686	.3708	.3729	.3749	.3770	.3790	.3810	.3830
1.2	.3849	.3869	.3888	.3907	.3925	.3944	.3962	.3980	.3997	.4015
1.3	.4032	.4049	.4066	.4082	.4099	.4115	.4131	.4147	.4162	.4177
1.4	.4192	.4207	.4222	.4236	.4251	.4265	.4279	.4292	.4306	.4319
1.5	.4332	.4345	.4357	.4370	.4382	.4394	.4406	.4418	.4429	.4441
1.6	.4452	.4463	.4474	.4484	.4495	.4505	.4515	.4525	.4535	.4545
1.7	.4554	.4564	.4573	.4582	.4591	.4599	.4608	.4616	.4625	.4633
1.8	.4641	.4649	.4656	.4664	.4671	.4678	.4686	.4693	.4699	.4706
1.9	.4713	.4719	.4726	.4732	.4738	.4744	.4750	.4756	.4761	.4767
2.0	.4772	.4778	.4783	.4788	.4793	.4798	.4803	.4808	.4812	.4817
2.1	.4821	.4826	.4830	.4834	.4838	.4842	.4846	.4850	.4854	.4857
2.2	.4861	.4864	.4868	.4871	.4875	.4878	.4881	.4884	.4887	.4890
2.3	.4893	.4896	.4898	.4901	.4904	.4906	.4909	.4911	.4913	.4916
2.4	.4918	.4920	.4922	.4925	.4927	.4929	.4931	.4932	.4934	.4936
2.5	.4938	.4940	.4941	.4943	.4945	.4946	.4948	.4949	.4951	.4952
2.6	.4953	.4955	.4956	.4957	.4959	.4960	.4961	.4962	.4963	.4964
2.7	.4965	.4966	.4967	.4968	.4969	.4970	.4971	.4972	.4973	.4974
2.8	.4974	.4975	.4976	.4977	.4977	.4978	.4979	.4979	.4980	.4981
2.9	.4981	.4982	.4982	.4983	.4984	.4984	.4985	.4985	.4986	.4986
3.0	.4987	.4987	.4987	.4988	.4988	.4989	.4989	.4989	.4990	.4990

ESSENTIALS OF STATISTICS FOR BUSINESS AND ECONOMICS 4e

David R. Anderson
University of Cincinnati

Dennis J. Sweeney
University of Cincinnati

Thomas A. Williams
Rochester Institute of Technology

THOMSON

SOUTH-WESTERN

Australia · Canada · Mexico · Singapore · Spain · United Kingdom · United States

THOMSON

SOUTH-WESTERN

Essentials of Statistics for Business and Economics, 4e

David R. Anderson, Dennis J. Sweeney, Thomas A. Williams

VP/Editorial Director: Jack W. Calhoun	**Technology Project Editor:** Chris Wittmer	**Production House:** BookMasters, Inc.
Sr. Acquisitions Editor: Charles E. McCormick, Jr.	**Web Coordinator:** Kelly Reid	**Art Director:** Chris Miller
Developmental Editor: Alisa Madden	**Manufacturing Coordinator:** Diane Lohman	**Cover Image:** © Digital Vision
Sr. Marketing Manager: Larry Qualls	**Printer:** R. R. Donnelley Willard, OH	**Photography Manager:** John Hill
Sr. Production Editor: Deanna Quinn		

Library of Congress Control Number:
2004111060

For more information
contact South-Western,
5191 Natorp Boulevard,
Mason, Ohio 45040.
Or you can visit our Internet site at:
http://www.swlearning.com

Dedicated to
Marcia, Cherri, and Robbie

Brief Contents

Contents

Chapter 3   Descriptive Statistics: Numerical Measures   76

Chapter 8 Interval Estimation 293

Chapter 11 Comparisons Involving Proportions and a Test of Independence   **431**

Chapter 12 Simple Linear Regression   **464**

Chapter 13 Multiple Regression 533

The purpose of *ESSENTIALS OF STATISTICS FOR BUSINESS AND ECONOMICS* is to give students, primarily those in the fields of business administration and economics, a conceptual introduction to the field of statistics and its many applications. The text is applications oriented and written with the needs of the nonmathematician in mind; the mathematical prerequisite is knowledge of algebra.

Applications of data analysis and statistical methodology are an integral part of the organization and presentation of the text material. The discussion and development of each technique is presented in an application setting, with the statistical results providing insights to decisions and solutions to problems.

Although the book is applications oriented, we have taken care to provide sound methodological development and to use notation that is generally accepted for the topic being covered. Hence, students will find that this text provides good preparation for the study of more advanced statistical material. A revised and updated bibliography to guide further study is included as an appendix.

Changes in the Fourth Edition

We appreciate the acceptance and positive response to the previous editions of *ESSENTIALS OF STATISTICS FOR BUSINESS AND ECONOMICS*. Accordingly, in making modifications for this new edition, we have maintained the presentation style and readability of those editions. The significant changes in the new edition are summarized here.

Content Revisions

The following list summarizes selected content revisions for the new edition.

- **Interval Estimation:** In past editions, we followed a large sample/small sample approach for interval estimation of a population mean in Chapter 8. In the new edition, we present interval estimation using the σ known and σ unknown paradigm. The standard normal distribution is used in all cases where the population standard deviation can be assumed known. The t distribution is used in all cases where the population standard deviation is estimated by the sample standard deviation. This approach simplifies the methodology for the student and is consistent with computer-based procedures provided by MINITAB and Excel. In the σ unknown case, the new approach provides slightly improved results over the previous large-sample approximation. A t distribution table with up to 100 degrees of freedom is included as Table 2 of Appendix B. This change carries into hypothesis tests about a population mean in Chapter 9 and statistical inferences about two population means in Chapter 10.
- **Hypothesis Testing Using p-Values:** Another change in the new edition is the emphasis on the use of p-values for hypothesis testing. With more and more use of statistical software packages for data analysis, p-values are clearly preferred to the traditional test statistic and rejection region approach. As a result, we now use p-values as the primary method for hypothesis testing applications in Chapters 9 to 13.
- **New Procedure for Two Sample Inferences:** We provide new methodology for inferences about two population means when the population standard deviations are

unknown. The methodology is based on the *t* distribution and is more general in that it can be applied whether or not the population variances are equal. The student no longer has to consider making the equal population variance assumption and making the pooled variance calculation.

- **Descriptive Statistics:** New sections, in Chapters 2 and 3, have been added on the shape of distributions. Skewness is introduced as an important measure of the shape of a distribution. In later chapters, we now mention the need for larger sample sizes in interval estimation and hypothesis testing applications involving a skewed population. Crosstabulation material has been expanded to include more discussion of percentage distributions. Simpson's paradox is used to point out a source of potentially erroneous conclusions when working with crosstabulations.
- **Probability Distributions:** A discussion of the mean, variance, and standard deviation has been added for the Poisson and hypergeometric distributions in Chapter 5 and the exponential distribution in Chapter 6. Chapter 6 also has a new section on the normal approximation of binomial probabilities.

New Examples and Exercises Based on Real Data

We have added approximately 200 new examples and exercises based on real data and recent reference sources of statistical information. Using the *Wall Street Journal, USA Today, Fortune, Barron's,* and a variety of other sources, we have drawn from actual studies to develop explanations and to create exercises that demonstrate many uses of statistics in business and economics. We believe that the use of real data helps generate more student interest in the material and enables the student to learn about both the statistical methodology and its application. The fourth edition of the text contains over 300 examples and exercises based on real data.

New Case Problems

We have added four new case problems to this edition, bringing the total number of case problems in the text to twenty-one. The new case problems appear in the chapters on descriptive statistics, probability distributions, and regression. These case problems provide students with the opportunity to analyze somewhat larger data sets and prepare managerial reports based on the results of the analysis.

New Statistics in Practice

Each chapter begins with a Statistics in Practice article that describes an application of the statistical methodology to be covered in the chapter. Statistics in Practice have been provided by practitioners at companies such as Colgate-Palmolive, Citibank, Procter & Gamble, Monsanto, and others. This edition includes two new Statistics in Practice: Food Lion (Chapter 8) and John Morrell & Company (Chapter 9).

New Materials for MINITAB and Microsoft® Excel

MINITAB and Excel appendixes appear at the end of most chapters. These appendixes provide step-by-step instructions that make it easy for students to use MINITAB or Excel to conduct the statistical analysis presented in the chapter. All appendixes have been updated for the latest versions of MINITAB and Excel. Seven new and/or revised appendixes appear at the end of the chapters on descriptive statistics, interval estimation, hypothesis testing, and regression.

New online resources for students include EASYSTAT: DIGITAL TUTOR FOR MINITAB Release 14 and EASYSTAT: DIGITAL TUTOR FOR MICROSOFT® EXCEL. These focused online tutorials will make it easier for students to learn how to use one of these well-known software products to perform statistical analysis. In each digital video, one of the textbook authors demonstrates how the software can be used to perform a particular statistical procedure.

Students may purchase an online subscription for the MINITAB or the Excel version of EasyStat Digital Tutor at *http://easystat.swlearning.com.*

Features and Pedagogy

We continue many of the features that appeared in previous editions. Some of the important ones are noted here.

Methods Exercises and Applications Exercises

The end-of-section exercises are split into two parts, Methods and Applications. The Methods exercises require students to use the formulas and make the necessary computations. The Applications exercises require students to use the chapter material in real-world situation. Thus, students first focus on the computational "nuts and bolts," then move on to the subtleties of statistical application and interpretation.

Self-Test Exercises

Certain exercises are identified as self-test exercises. Completely worked-out solutions for those exercises are provided in Appendix D at the back of the book. Students can attempt the self-test exercises and immediately check the solution to evaluate their understanding of the concepts presented in the chapter.

Notes and Comments

At the end of many sections, we provide Notes and Comments designed to give the student additional insights about the statistical methodology and its application. Notes and Comments include warnings about or limitations of the methodology, recommendations for application, brief descriptions of additional technical considerations, and other matters.

Data Sets Accompany the Text

Approximately 160 data sets are available on the CD-ROM that is packaged with the text. The data sets are available in both MINITAB and Excel formats. Data set logos are used in the text to identify the data sets that are available on the CD. Data sets for all case problems as well as data sets for larger exercises are included on the CD.

Ancillary Teaching and Learning Materials

Two print ancillaries are available to students either through their bookstore or for direct purchase through the online catalog at *www.swlearning.com.*

- Prepared by Mohammad Ahmadi of the University of Tennessee at Chattanooga, the **Work Book** (ISBN: 0-324-22487-7) will provide the student with significant supplementary study materials. It contains an outline and review, and list of formulas for each text chapter, sample exercises with step-by-step solutions, exercises with answers, and a series of self-testing questions with answers.
- Another student ancillary is the ***Microsoft® Excel Companion for Business Statistics, 3e*** (ISBN: 0-324-22553-9) by David Eldredge of Murray State University. This manual provides step-by-step instructions for using Excel to solve many of the

problems included in introductory business statistics texts. Directions for the latest version of Excel are included.

- WebTutor™, an online ancillary, may be ordered as a package with the new edition of *ESSENTIALS OF STATISTICS FOR BUSINESS AND ECONOMICS*. WebTutor is used by an entire class under the direction of the instructor. It provides Web-based learning resources to students as well as powerful communication and other course management tools including course calendar, chat, online testing, and e-mail for instructors. WebTutor is available with WebCT and Blackboard. See *webtutor. thomsonlearning.com* for more information.

The following instructor support materials are available to adopters from the Thomson Learning™ Academic Resource Center at 800-423-0563 or through **www.swlearning.com.** Some of the materials noted here may also be downloaded from the text's Instructor's Resource page at **asw.swlearning.com.**

Instructor's Resource CD (ISBN: 0-324-22492-3)—All instructor ancillaries are provided on a single CD-ROM. Included in this convenient format are:

- **Solutions Manual**—The Solutions Manual, prepared by the authors, includes solutions for all problems in the text.
- **Solutions to Case Problems**—Also prepared by the authors, solutions to all case problems presented in the text are included here.
- **PowerPoint™ Presentation Slides**—Prepared by John Loucks of St. Edward's University, the presentation slides incorporate graphics to help instructors create even more stimulating lectures. New for the fourth edition, the slides include animation. The slides may be adapted using PowerPoint software to facilitate classroom use.
- **Test Bank** and **ExamView Pro™**—Prepared by Mohammad Ahmadi, the Test Bank includes multiple choice questions and problems for each chapter. ExamView computerized testing software allows instructors to create, edit, store, and print exams.

Acknowledgments

We would like to acknowledge the work of our reviewers who provided comments and suggestions of ways to continue to improve our text. Thanks to:

Michael Broida, Miami University of Ohio

Robert Cochran, University of Wyoming

Doug Dotterweich, East Tennessee State University

Dwight Goehring, California State University–Monterey Bay

Stephen Grubagh, Bentley University

David Keswick, University of Michigan–Flint

Jennifer Kohn, Montclair State University

Rosa Lemel, Kean University

Doug Morris, University of New Hampshire

Kevin Murphy, Oakland University

William Pan, University of New Haven

Carl Poch, Northern Illinois University

Ranga Ramasesh, Texas Christian University

Carolyn Rochelle, East Tennessee State University

Edwin Shapiro, University of San Francisco

Harvey Singer, George Mason University

Minghe Sun, University of Texas–San Antonio

Bill Swank, George Mason University

Geetha Vaidyanathan, University of North Carolina–Greensboro

James Wright, Green Mountain College

Elaine Zanutto, University of Pennsylvania

We continue to owe a debt to our many colleagues and friends for their helpful comments and suggestions in the development of this and earlier editions of our text. Among them are:

Ali Arshad, College of Santa Fe

Timothy M. Bergquist, Northwest Christian College

Habtu Braha, Coppin State College

Robert Cochran, University of Wyoming

Dale DeBoer, University of Colorado–Colorado Springs

Raj Devasagayam, St. Norbert College

Nader D. Ebrahimi, University of New Mexico

H. Robert Gadd, Southern Adventist University

Karen Gutermuth, Virginia Military Institute

Md. Mahbubul Kabir, Lyon College

Gary Nelson, Central Community College–Columbus Campus

Elaine Parks, Laramie County Community College

Charles J. Reichert, University of Wisconsin–Superior

Larry Scheuermann, University of Louisiana, Lafayette

Carlton Scott, University of California–Irvine

Alan D. Smith, Robert Morris College

Stephen L. S. Smith, Gordon College

Wibawa A. Sutanto, Prairie View A&M University

Bennie D. Waller, Francis Marion University

Yan Yu, University of Cincinnati

Zhiwei Zhu, University of Louisiana at Lafayette

Charles Zimmerman, Robert Morris College

A special thanks goes to our associates from business and industry who supplied the Statistics in Practice features. We recognize them individually by a credit line in each of the articles. Finally, we are also indebted to our senior acquisitions editor Charles McCormick, Jr., our senior production editor Deanna Quinn, our senior marketing manager Larry Qualls, and others at Thomson Business and Professional Publishing for their editorial counsel and support during the preparation of this text.

David R. Anderson
Dennis J. Sweeney
Thomas A. Williams

David R. Anderson. David R. Anderson is Professor of Quantitative Analysis in the College of Business Administration at the University of Cincinnati. Born in Grand Forks, North Dakota, he earned his B.S., M.S., and Ph.D. degrees from Purdue University. Professor Anderson has served as Head of the Department of Quantitative Analysis and Operations Management and as Associate Dean of the College of Business Administration. In addition, he was the coordinator of the College's first Executive Program.

At the University of Cincinnati, Professor Anderson has taught introductory statistics for business students as well as graduate-level courses in regression analysis, multivariate analysis, and management science. He has also taught statistical courses at the Department of Labor in Washington, D.C. He has been honored with nominations and awards for excellence in teaching and excellence in service to student organizations.

Professor Anderson has coauthored ten textbooks in the areas of statistics, management science, linear programming, and production and operations management. He is an active consultant in the field of sampling and statistical methods.

Dennis J. Sweeney. Dennis J. Sweeney is Professor of Quantitative Analysis and Founder of the Center for Productivity Improvement at the University of Cincinnati. Born in Des Moines, Iowa, he earned a B.S.B.A. degree from Drake University and his M.B.A. and D.B.A. degrees from Indiana University where he was an NDEA Fellow. During 1978–79, Professor Sweeney worked in the management science group at Procter & Gamble; during 1981–82, he was a visiting professor at Duke University. Professor Sweeney served as Head of the Department of Quantitative Analysis and as Associate Dean of the College of Business Administration at the University of Cincinnati.

Professor Sweeney has published more than thirty articles and monographs in the area of management science and statistics. The National Science Foundation, IBM, Procter & Gamble, Federated Department Stores, Kroger, and Cincinnati Gas & Electric have funded his research, which has been published in *Management Science*, *Operations Research*, *Mathematical Programming*, *Decision Sciences*, and other journals.

Professor Sweeney has coauthored ten textbooks in the areas of statistics, management science, linear programming, and production and operations management.

Thomas A. Williams. Thomas A. Williams is Professor of Management Science in the College of Business at Rochester Institute of Technology. Born in Elmira, New York, he earned his B.S. degree at Clarkson University. He did his graduate work at Rensselaer Polytechnic Institute, where he received his M.S. and Ph.D. degrees.

Before joining the College of Business at RIT, Professor Williams served for seven years as a faculty member in the College of Business Administration at the University of Cincinnati, where he developed the undergraduate program in Information Systems and then served as its coordinator. At RIT he was the first chairman of the Decision Sciences Department. He teaches courses in management science and statistics, as well as graduate courses in regression and decision analysis.

Professor Williams is the coauthor of eleven textbooks in the areas of management science, statistics, production and operations management, and mathematics. He has been a consultant for numerous *Fortune* 500 companies and has worked on projects ranging from the use of data analysis to the development of large-scale regression models.

Data and Statistics

BUSINESS WEEK*
NEW YORK, NEW YORK

With a global circulation of more than 1 million, *Business Week* is the most widely read business magazine in the world. More than 200 dedicated reporters and editors in 26 bureaus worldwide deliver a variety of articles of interest to the business and economic community. Along with feature articles on current topics, the magazine contains regular sections on International Business, Economic Analysis, Information Processing, and Science & Technology. Information in the feature articles and the regular sections helps readers stay abreast of current developments and assess the impact of those developments on business and economic conditions.

Most issues of *Business Week* provide an in-depth report on a topic of current interest. Often, the in-depth reports contain statistical facts and summaries that help the reader understand the business and economic information. For example, the November 11, 2003, issue reported the new momentum for wireless communication; the December 15, 2003, issue reported the best products of 2003; the January 12, 2004, issue described the economic outlook by industry for 2004; and the January 26, 2004, issue provided information about the best mutual funds for the coming year. In addition, the weekly *Business Week Investor* provides statistics about the state of the economy, including production indexes, stock prices, mutual funds, and interest rates.

Business Week also uses statistics and statistical information in managing its own business. For example, an annual survey of subscribers helps the company learn about subscriber demographics, reading habits, likely purchases, lifestyles, and so on. *Business Week* managers use the statistical summaries from the survey to provide better services to subscribers and advertisers.

*The authors are indebted to Charlene Trentham, Research Manager at *Business Week*, for providing this Statistics in Practice.

Business Week uses statistical facts and summaries in many of its articles. © Terri Miller/E-Visual Communications, Inc.

One recent North American subscriber survey indicated that 90% of *Business Week* subscribers use a personal computer at home and that 64% of *Business Week* subscribers are involved with computer purchases at work. Such statistics alert *Business Week* managers to subscriber interest in articles about new developments in computers. The results of the survey are also made available to potential advertisers. The high percentage of subscribers using personal computers at home and the high percentage of subscribers involved with computer purchases at work would be an incentive for a computer manufacturer to consider advertising in *Business Week*.

In this chapter, we discuss the types of data available for statistical analysis and describe how the data are obtained. We introduce descriptive statistics and statistical inference as ways of converting data into meaningful and easily interpreted statistical information.

Frequently, we see the following kinds of statements in newspaper and magazine articles:

- A Jupiter Media survey found that 31% of adult males spend 10 or more hours a week watching television. For adult women, it was 26% (*The Wall Street Journal,* January 26, 2004).
- General Motors, the leader in automotive cash rebates, provided an average cash incentive of $4300 per vehicle during 2003 (*USA Today,* January 23, 2004).
- More than 40% of Marriott International managers work their way up through the ranks (*Fortune,* January 20, 2003).

- Employees in management and finance had a median annual salary of $49,712 for 2003 (*The World Almanac,* 2004).
- Employers plan to hire 12.7% more college graduates in 2004 than they did in 2003 (Collegiate Employment Research Institute, Michigan State University, February 2004).
- The New York Yankees have the highest payroll in major league baseball. In 2003, team payroll was $152,749,814 with a median of $4,575,000 per player (*USA Today,* September 1, 2003).
- The Dow Jones Industrial Average closed at 10,358 on March 31, 2004 (*The Wall Street Journal,* April 1, 2004).

The numerical facts in the preceding statements (31%, 26%, $4300, 40%, $49,712, 12.7%, $152,749,814, $4,575,000, and 10,358) are called statistics. Thus, in everyday usage, the term *statistics* refers to numerical facts. However, the field, or subject, of statistics involves much more than numerical facts. In a broad sense, **statistics** is the art and science of collecting, analyzing, presenting, and interpreting data. Particularly in business and economics, the information provided by collecting, analyzing, presenting, and interpreting data gives managers and decision makers a better understanding of the business and economic environment and thus enables them to make more informed and better decisions. In this text, we emphasize the use of statistics for business and economic decision making.

Chapter 1 begins with some illustrations of the applications of statistics in business and economics. In Section 1.2 we define the term *data* and introduce the concept of a data set. This section also introduces key terms such as *variables* and *observations,* discusses the difference between quantitative and qualitative data, and illustrates the uses of cross-sectional and time series data. Section 1.3 discusses how data can be obtained from existing sources or through survey and experimental studies designed to obtain new data. The important role that the Internet now plays in obtaining data is also highlighted. The uses of data in developing descriptive statistics and in making statistical inferences are described in Sections 1.4 and 1.5.

1.1   Applications in Business and Economics

In today's global business and economic environment, anyone can access vast amounts of statistical information. The most successful managers and decision makers understand the information and know how to use it effectively. In this section, we provide examples that illustrate some of the uses of statistics in business and economics.

Accounting

Public accounting firms use statistical sampling procedures when conducting audits for their clients. For instance, suppose an accounting firm wants to determine whether the amount of accounts receivable shown on a client's balance sheet fairly represents the actual amount of accounts receivable. Usually the large number of individual accounts receivable makes reviewing and validating every account too time-consuming and expensive. As common practice in such situations, the audit staff selects a subset of the accounts called a sample. After reviewing the accuracy of the sampled accounts, the auditors draw a conclusion as to whether the accounts receivable amount shown on the client's balance sheet is acceptable.

Finance

Financial analysts use a variety of statistical information to guide their investment recommendations. In the case of stocks, the analysts review a variety of financial data including price/earnings ratios and dividend yields. By comparing the information for an individual stock with information about the stock market averages, a financial analyst can begin to draw a conclusion as to whether an individual stock is over- or underpriced. For example, *Barron's* (January 6, 2003) reported that the average price/earnings ratio for the 30 stocks in the Dow Jones Industrial Average was 22.36. General Electric showed a price/earnings ratio of 16. In this case, the statistical information on price/earnings ratios indicated a lower price in comparison to earnings for General Electric than the average for the Dow Jones stocks. Therefore, a financial analyst might conclude that General Electric was underpriced. This and other information about General Electric would help the analyst make a buy, sell, or hold recommendation for the stock.

Marketing

Electronic scanners at retail checkout counters collect data for a variety of marketing research applications. For example, data suppliers such as ACNielsen and Information Resources, Inc., purchase point-of-sale scanner data from grocery stores, process the data, and then sell statistical summaries of the data to manufacturers. Manufacturers spend hundreds of thousands of dollars per product category to obtain this type of scanner data. Manufacturers also purchase data and statistical summaries on promotional activities such as special pricing and the use of in-store displays. Brand managers can review the scanner statistics and the promotional activity statistics to gain a better understanding of the relationship between promotional activities and sales. Such analyses often prove helpful in establishing future marketing strategies for the various products.

Production

Today's emphasis on quality makes quality control an important application of statistics in production. A variety of statistical quality control charts are used to monitor the output of a production process. In particular, an x-bar chart can be used to monitor the average output. Suppose, for example, that a machine fills containers with 12 ounces of a soft drink. Periodically, a production worker selects a sample of containers and computes the average number of ounces in the sample. This average, or x-bar value, is plotted on an x-bar chart. A plotted value above the chart's upper control limit indicates overfilling, and a plotted value below the chart's lower control limit indicates underfilling. The process is termed "in control" and allowed to continue as long as the plotted x-bar values fall between the chart's upper and lower control limits. Properly interpreted, an x-bar chart can help determine when adjustments are necessary to correct a production process.

Economics

Economists frequently provide forecasts about the future of the economy or some aspect of it. They use a variety of statistical information in making such forecasts. For instance, in forecasting inflation rates, economists use statistical information on such indicators as the Producer Price Index, the unemployment rate, and manufacturing capacity utilization. Often these statistical indicators are entered into computerized forecasting models that predict inflation rates.

Applications of statistics such as those described in this section are an integral part of this text. Such examples provide an overview of the breadth of statistical applications. To supplement these examples, practitioners in the fields of business and economics provided chapter-opening Statistics in Practice articles that introduce the material covered in each chapter. The Statistics in Practice applications show the importance of statistics in a wide variety of business and economic situations.

1.2   Data

Data are the facts and figures collected, analyzed, and summarized for presentation and interpretation. All the data collected in a particular study are referred to as the **data set** for the study. Table 1.1 shows a data set containing information for 25 of the shadow stocks tracked by the American Association of Individual Investors. Shadow stocks are common stocks of smaller companies that are not closely followed by Wall Street analysts.

Elements, Variables, and Observations

Elements are the entities on which data are collected. For the data set in Table 1.1, each individual company's stock is an element; the element names appear in the first column. With 25 stocks, the data set contains 25 elements.

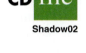

TABLE 1.1 DATA SET FOR 25 SHADOW STOCKS

Company	Exchange	Ticker Symbol	Market Cap ($ millions)	Price/ Earnings Ratio	Gross Profit Margin (%)
DeWolfe Companies	AMEX	DWL	36.4	8.4	36.7
North Coast Energy	OTC	NCEB	52.5	6.2	59.3
Hansen Natural Corp.	OTC	HANS	41.1	14.6	44.8
MarineMax, Inc.	NYSE	HZO	111.5	7.2	23.8
Nanometrics Incorporated	OTC	NANO	228.6	38.0	53.3
TeamStaff, Inc.	OTC	TSTF	92.1	33.5	4.1
Environmental Tectonics	AMEX	ETC	51.1	35.8	35.9
Measurement Specialties	AMEX	MSS	101.8	26.8	37.6
SEMCO Energy, Inc.	NYSE	SEN	193.4	18.7	23.6
Party City Corporation	OTC	PCTY	97.2	15.9	36.4
Embrex, Inc.	OTC	EMBX	136.5	18.9	59.5
Tech/Ops Sevcon, Inc.	AMEX	TO	23.2	20.7	35.7
ARCADIS NV	OTC	ARCAF	173.4	8.8	9.6
Qiao Xing Universal Tele.	OTC	XING	64.3	22.1	30.8
Energy West Incorporated	OTC	EWST	29.1	9.7	16.3
Barnwell Industries, Inc.	AMEX	BRN	27.3	7.4	73.4
Innodata Corporation	OTC	INOD	66.1	11.0	29.6
Medical Action Industries	OTC	MDCI	137.1	26.9	30.6
Instrumentarium Corp.	OTC	INMRY	240.9	3.6	52.1
Petroleum Development	OTC	PETD	95.9	6.1	19.4
Drexler Technology Corp.	OTC	DRXR	233.6	45.6	53.6
Gerber Childrenswear Inc.	NYSE	GCW	126.9	7.9	25.8
Gaiam, Inc.	OTC	GAIA	295.5	68.2	60.7
Artesian Resources Corp.	OTC	ARTNA	62.8	20.5	45.5
York Water Company	OTC	YORW	92.2	22.9	74.2

Source: American Association of Individual Investors, http://www.aaii.com (February 2002).

A **variable** is a characteristic of interest for the elements. The data set in Table 1.1 includes the following five variables:

- *Exchange:* Where the stock is traded—NYSE (New York Stock Exchange), AMEX (American Stock Exchange), and OTC (over-the-counter)
- *Ticker Symbol:* The abbreviation used to identify the stock on the exchange listing
- *Market Cap:* Total value of company (share price multiplied by number of shares outstanding)
- *Price/Earnings Ratio:* Market price per share divided by the most recent 12 months' earnings per share
- *Gross Profit Margin:* Gross profit as a percentage of sales

Measurements collected on each variable for every element in a study provide the data. The set of measurements obtained for a particular element is called an **observation**. Referring to Table 1.1, we see that the set of measurements for the first observation (DeWolfe Companies) is AMEX, DWL, 36.4, 8.4, and 36.7. The set of measurements for the second observation (North Coast Energy) is OTC, NCEB, 52.5, 6.2, and 59.3, and so on. A data set with 25 elements contains 25 observations.

Scales of Measurement

Data collection requires one of the following scales of measurement: nominal, ordinal, interval, or ratio. The scale of measurement determines the amount of information contained in the data and indicates the most appropriate data summarization and statistical analyses.

When the data for a variable consist of labels or names used to identify an attribute of the element, the scale of measurement is considered a **nominal scale**. For example, referring to the data in Table 1.1, we see that the scale of measurement for the exchange variable is nominal because NYSE, AMEX, and OTC are labels used to identify where the company's stock is traded. In cases where the scale of measurement is nominal, a numeric code as well as nonnumeric labels may be used. For example, to facilitate data collection and to prepare the data for entry into a computer database, we might use a numeric code by letting 1 denote the New York Stock Exchange, 2 denote the American Stock Exchange, and 3 denote over-the-counter. In this case the numeric values 1, 2, and 3 provide the labels used to identify where the stock is traded. The scale of measurement is nominal even though the data appear as numeric values.

The scale of measurement for a variable is called an **ordinal scale** if the data exhibit the properties of nominal data and the order or rank of the data is meaningful. For example, Eastside Automotive sends customers a questionnaire designed to obtain data on the quality of its automotive repair service. Each customer provides a repair service rating of excellent, good, or poor. Because the data obtained are the labels—excellent, good, or poor—the data have the properties of nominal data. In addition, the data can be ranked, or ordered, with respect to the service quality. Data recorded as excellent indicate the best service, followed by good and then poor. Thus, the scale of measurement is ordinal. Note that the ordinal data can also be recorded using a numeric code. For example, we could use 1 for excellent, 2 for good, and 3 for poor to maintain the properties of ordinal data. Thus, data for an ordinal scale may be either nonnumeric or numeric.

The scale of measurement for a variable becomes an **interval scale** if the data show the properties of ordinal data and the interval between values is expressed in terms of a fixed unit of measure. Interval data are always numeric. Scholastic Aptitude Test (SAT) scores are an example of interval-scaled data. For example, three students with SAT scores of 1120, 1050, and 970 can be ranked or ordered in terms of best performance to poorest performance. In addition, the differences between the scores are meaningful. For instance, student 1 scored $1120 - 1050 = 70$ points more than student 2, while student 2 scored $1050 - 970 = 80$ points more than student 3.

The scale of measurement for a variable is a **ratio scale** if the data have all the properties of interval data and the ratio of two values is meaningful. Variables such as distance, height, weight, and time use the ratio scale of measurement. This scale requires that a zero value be included to indicate that nothing exists for the variable at the zero point. For example, consider the cost of an automobile. A zero value for the cost would indicate that the automobile has no cost and is free. In addition, if we compare the cost of $30,000 for one automobile to the cost of $15,000 for a second automobile, the ratio property shows that the first automobile is $30,000/$15,000 = 2 times, or twice, the cost of the second automobile.

Qualitative and Quantitative Data

Qualitative data are often referred to as categorical data.

Data can be further classified as either qualitative or quantitative. **Qualitative data** include labels or names used to identify an attribute of each element. Qualitative data use either the nominal or ordinal scale of measurement and may be nonnumeric or numeric. **Quantitative data** require numeric values that indicate how much or how many. Quantitative data are obtained using either the interval or ratio scale of measurement.

The statistical method appropriate for summarizing data depends upon whether the data are qualitative or quantitative.

A **qualitative variable** is a variable with qualitative data, and a **quantitative variable** is a variable with quantitative data. The statistical analysis appropriate for a particular variable depends upon whether the variable is qualitative or quantitative. If the variable is qualitative, the statistical analysis is rather limited. We can summarize qualitative data by counting the number of observations in each qualitative category or by computing the proportion of the observations in each qualitative category. However, even when the qualitative data use a numeric code, arithmetic operations such as addition, subtraction, multiplication, and division do not provide meaningful results. Section 2.1 discusses ways for summarizing qualitative data.

On the other hand, arithmetic operations often provide meaningful results for a quantitative variable. For example, for a quantitative variable, the data may be added and then divided by the number of observations to compute the average value. This average is usually meaningful and easily interpreted. In general, more alternatives for statistical analysis are possible when the data are quantitative. Section 2.2 and Chapter 3 provide ways of summarizing quantitative data.

Cross-Sectional and Time Series Data

For purposes of statistical analysis, distinguishing between cross-sectional data and time series data is important. **Cross-sectional data** are data collected at the same or approximately the same point in time. The data in Table 1.1 are cross-sectional because they describe the five variables for the 25 shadow stocks at the same point in time. **Time series data** are data collected over several time periods. For example, Figure 1.1 provides a graph of the U.S. city average price per gallon for unleaded regular gasoline. The graph shows a sharp increase in the average price per gallon beginning in January 2004. Over a five-month period, the average price per gallon increased from $1.49 to $1.81. Most of the statistical methods presented in this text apply to cross-sectional rather than time series data.

FIGURE 1.1   U.S. CITY AVERAGE PRICE PER GALLON FOR UNLEADED REGULAR GASOLINE

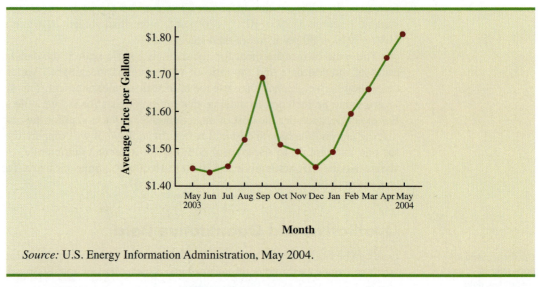

Source: U.S. Energy Information Administration, May 2004.

NOTES AND COMMENTS

1. An observation is the set of measurements obtained for each element in a data set. Hence, the number of observations is always the same as the number of elements. The number of measurements obtained for each element equals the number of variables. Hence, the total number of data items can be determined by multiplying the number of observations by the number of variables.

2. Quantitative data may be discrete or continuous. Quantitative data that measure how many are discrete. Quantitative data that measure how much are continuous because no separation occurs between the possible data values.

1.3   Data Sources

Data can be obtained from existing sources or from surveys and experimental studies designed to collect new data.

Existing Sources

In some cases, data needed for a particular application already exist. Companies maintain a variety of databases about their employees, customers, and business operations. Data on employee salaries, ages, and years of experience can usually be obtained from internal personnel records. Other internal records contain data on sales, advertising expenditures, distribution costs, inventory levels, and production quantities. Most companies also maintain detailed data about their customers. Table 1.2 shows some of the data commonly available from internal company records.

Organizations that specialize in collecting and maintaining data make available substantial amounts of business and economic data. Companies access these external data sources through leasing arrangements or by purchase. Dun & Bradstreet, Bloomberg, and Dow Jones & Company are three firms that provide extensive business database services

TABLE 1.2   EXAMPLES OF DATA AVAILABLE FROM INTERNAL COMPANY RECORDS

Source	Some of the Data Typically Available
Employee records	Name, address, social security number, salary, number of vacation days, number of sick days, and bonus
Production records	Part or product number, quantity produced, direct labor cost, and materials cost
Inventory records	Part or product number, number of units on hand, reorder level, economic order quantity, and discount schedule
Sales records	Product number, sales volume, sales volume by region, and sales volume by customer type
Credit records	Customer name, address, phone number, credit limit, and accounts receivable balance
Customer profile	Age, gender, income level, household size, address, and preferences

to clients. ACNielsen and Information Resources, Inc., built successful businesses collecting and processing data that they sell to advertisers and product manufacturers.

Data are also available from a variety of industry associations and special interest organizations. The Travel Industry Association of America maintains travel-related information such as the number of tourists and travel expenditures by states. Such data would be of interest to firms and individuals in the travel industry. The Graduate Management Admission Council maintains data on test scores, student characteristics, and graduate management education programs. Most of the data from these types of sources are available to qualified users at a modest cost.

The Internet continues to grow as an important source of data and statistical information. Almost all companies maintain Web sites that provide general information about the company as well as data on sales, number of employees, number of products, product prices, and product specifications. In addition, a number of companies now specialize in making information available over the Internet. As a result, one can obtain access to stock quotes, meal prices at restaurants, salary data, and an almost infinite variety of information.

Government agencies are another important source of existing data. For instance, the U.S. Department of Labor maintains considerable data on employment rates, wage rates, size of the labor force, and union membership. Table 1.3 lists selected governmental agencies and some of the data they provide. Most government agencies that collect and process data also make the results available through a Web site. For instance, the U.S. Census Bureau has a wealth of data at its Web site, www.census.gov. Figure 1.2 shows the homepage for the U.S. Census Bureau.

Statistical Studies

Sometimes the data needed for a particular application are not available through existing sources. In such cases, the data can often be obtained by conducting a statistical study. Statistical studies can be classified as either *experimental* or *observational.*

The largest experimental statistical study ever conducted is believed to be the 1954 Public Health Service experiment for the Salk polio vaccine. Nearly 2 million children in grades 1, 2, and 3 were selected from throughout the United States.

In an experimental study, a variable of interest is first identified. Then one or more other variables are identified and controlled so that data can be obtained about how they influence the variable of interest. For example, a pharmaceutical firm might be interested in conducting an experiment to learn about how a new drug affects blood pressure. Blood pressure is the variable of interest in the study. The dosage level of the new drug is another variable that is hoped to have a causal effect on blood pressure. To obtain data about the effect of the new drug, researchers select a sample of individuals. The dosage level of the new drug

TABLE 1.3   EXAMPLES OF DATA AVAILABLE FROM SELECTED GOVERNMENT AGENCIES

Government Agency	Some of the Data Available
Census Bureau *http://www.census.gov*	Population data, number of households, and household income
Federal Reserve Board *http://www.federalreserve.gov*	Data on the money supply, installment credit, exchange rates, and discount rates
Office of Management and Budget *http://www.whitehouse.gov/omb*	Data on revenue, expenditures, and debt of the federal government
Department of Commerce *http://www.doc.gov*	Data on business activity, value of shipments by industry, level of profits by industry, and growing and declining industries
Bureau of Labor Statistics *http://www.bls.gov*	Consumer spending, hourly earnings, unemployment rate, safety records, and international statistics

FIGURE 1.2   U.S. CENSUS BUREAU HOMEPAGE

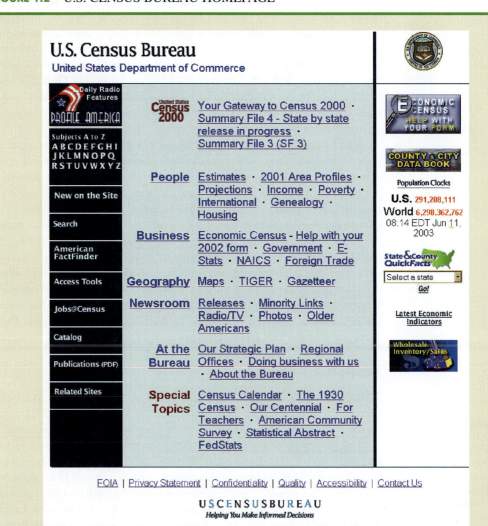

is controlled, as different groups of individuals are given different dosage levels. Before and after data on blood pressure are collected for each group. Statistical analysis of the experimental data can help determine how the new drug affects blood pressure.

Studies of smokers and nonsmokers are observational studies because researchers do not determine or control who will smoke and who will not smoke.

Nonexperimental, or observational, statistical studies make no attempt to control the variables of interest. A survey is perhaps the most common type of observational study. For instance, in a personal interview survey, research questions are first identified. Then a questionnaire is designed and administered to a sample of individuals. Some restaurants use observational studies to obtain data about their customers' opinions of the quality of food, service, atmosphere, and so on. A questionnaire used by the Lobster Pot Restaurant in Redington Shores, Florida, is shown in Figure 1.3. Note that the customers completing the questionnaire are asked to provide ratings for five variables: food quality, friendliness of service, promptness of service, cleanliness, and management. The response categories of excellent, good, satisfactory, and unsatisfactory provide ordinal data that enable Lobster Pot's managers to assess the quality of the restaurant's operation.

Managers wanting to use data and statistical analyses as an aid to decision making must be aware of the time and cost required to obtain the data. The use of existing data sources is desirable when data must be obtained in a relatively short period of time. If important data are not readily available from an existing source, the additional time and cost involved in obtaining the data must be taken into account. In all cases, the decision maker should consider the contribution of the statistical analysis to the decision-making process. The cost

FIGURE 1.3   CUSTOMER OPINION QUESTIONNAIRE USED BY THE LOBSTER POT RESTAURANT, REDINGTON SHORES, FLORIDA

The
LOBSTER
Pot
RESTAURANT

*W*e are happy you stopped by the Lobster Pot Restaurant and want to make sure you will come back. So, if you have a little time, we will really appreciate it if you will fill out this card. Your comments and suggestions are extremely important to us. Thank you!

Server's Name _____

	Excellent	Good	Satisfactory	Unsatisfactory
Food Quality	❏	❏	❏	❏
Friendly Service	❏	❏	❏	❏
Prompt Service	❏	❏	❏	❏
Cleanliness	❏	❏	❏	❏
Management	❏	❏	❏	❏

Comments _____
_____
What prompted your visit to us? _____
_____
Please drop in suggestion box at entrance. Thank you.

of data acquisition and the subsequent statistical analysis should not exceed the savings generated by using the information to make a better decision.

Data Acquisition Errors

Managers should always be aware of the possibility of data errors in statistical studies. Using erroneous data can be worse than not using any data at all. An error in data acquisition occurs whenever the data value obtained is not equal to the true or actual value that would be obtained with a correct procedure. Such errors can occur in a number of ways. For example, an interviewer might make a recording error, such as a transposition in writing the age of a 24-year-old person as 42, or the person answering an interview question might misinterpret the question and provide an incorrect response.

Experienced data analysts take great care in collecting and recording data to ensure that errors are not made. Special procedures can be used to check for internal consistency of the data. For instance, such procedures would indicate that the analyst should review the accuracy of data for a respondent shown to be 22 years of age but reporting 20 years of work experience. Data analysts also review data with unusually large and small values, called outliers, which are candidates for possible data errors. In Chapter 3 we present some of the methods statisticians use to identify outliers.

Errors often occur during data acquisition. Blindly using any data that happen to be available or using data that were acquired with little care can result in misleading information and bad decisions. Thus, taking steps to acquire accurate data can help ensure reliable and valuable decision-making information.

1.4 Descriptive Statistics

Most of the statistical information in newspapers, magazines, company reports, and other publications consists of data that are summarized and presented in a form that is easy for the reader to understand. Such summaries of data, which may be tabular, graphical, or numerical, are referred to as **descriptive statistics**.

Refer again to the data set in Table 1.1 showing data on 25 shadow stocks. Methods of descriptive statistics can be used to provide summaries of the information in this data set. For example, a tabular summary of the data for the qualitative variable Exchange is shown in Table 1.4. A graphical summary of the same data, called a bar graph, is shown in Figure 1.4. These types of tabular and graphical summaries generally make the data easier to interpret. Referring to Table 1.4 and Figure 1.4, we can see easily that the majority of the stocks in the data set are traded over the counter. On a percentage basis, 68% are traded over the counter, 20% are traded on the American Stock Exchange, and 12% are traded on the New York Stock Exchange.

A graphical summary of the data for the quantitative variable Gross Profit Margin for the shadow stocks, called a histogram, is provided in Figure 1.5. The histogram makes it

TABLE 1.4 FREQUENCIES AND PERCENT FREQUENCIES FOR THE EXCHANGE VARIABLE

Exchange	Frequency	Percent Frequency
New York Stock Exchange (NYSE)	3	12
American Stock Exchange (AMEX)	5	20
Over-the-counter (OTC)	17	68
Totals	25	100

FIGURE 1.4   BAR GRAPH FOR THE EXCHANGE VARIABLE

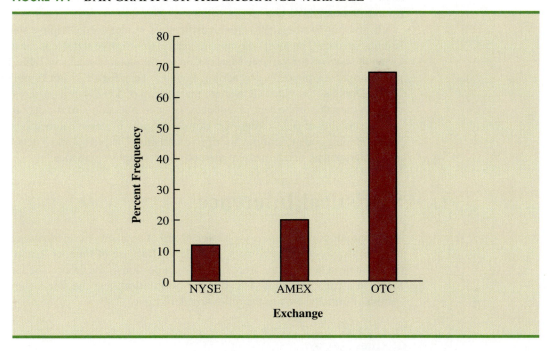

FIGURE 1.5   HISTOGRAM OF GROSS PROFIT MARGIN (%) FOR 25 SHADOW STOCKS

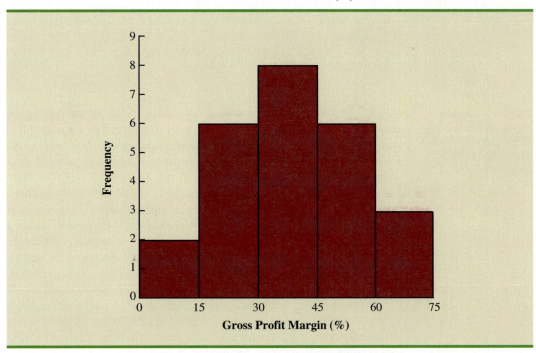

easy to see that the gross profit margins range from 0% to 75%, with the highest concentrations between 30% and 45%.

In addition to tabular and graphical displays, numerical descriptive statistics are used to summarize data. The most common numerical descriptive statistic is the average, or mean. Using the data on the variable Market Cap for the shadow stocks in Table 1.1, we can compute the average market cap by adding the market cap for all 25 stocks and dividing the sum by 25. Doing so provides an average market cap of $112.4 million. This average demonstrates a measure of the central tendency, or central location, of the data for that variable.

In a number of fields, interest continues to grow in statistical methods that can be used for developing and presenting descriptive statistics. Chapters 2 and 3 devote attention to the tabular, graphical, and numerical methods of descriptive statistics.

 ## 1.5 Statistical Inference

Many situations require data for a large group of elements (individuals, companies, voters, households, products, customers, and so on). Because of time, cost, and other considerations, data can be collected from only a small portion of the group. The larger group of elements in a particular study is called the **population**, and the smaller group is called the **sample**. Formally, we use the following definitions.

> **POPULATION**
>
> A population is the set of all elements of interest in a particular study.

> **SAMPLE**
>
> A sample is a subset of the population.

The U.S. government conducts a census every 10 years. Market research firms conduct sample surveys every day.

The process of conducting a survey to collect data for the entire population is called a **census**. The process of conducting a survey to collect data for a sample is called a **sample survey**. As one of its major contributions, statistics uses data from a sample to make estimates and test hypotheses about the characteristics of a population through a process referred to as **statistical inference**.

As an example of statistical inference, let us consider the study conducted by Norris Electronics. Norris manufactures a high-intensity lightbulb used in a variety of electrical products. In an attempt to increase the useful life of the lightbulb, the product design group developed a new lightbulb filament. In this case, the population is defined as all lightbulbs that could be produced with the new filament. To evaluate the advantages of the new filament, 200 bulbs with the new filament were manufactured and tested. Data collected from this sample showed the number of hours each lightbulb operated before filament burnout. See Table 1.5.

Suppose Norris wants to use the sample data to make an inference about the average hours of useful life for the population of all lightbulbs that could be produced with the new filament. Adding the 200 values in Table 1.5 and dividing the total by 200 provides the sample average lifetime for the lightbulbs: 76 hours. We can use this sample result to estimate that the average lifetime for the lightbulbs in the population is 76 hours. Figure 1.6 provides a graphical summary of the statistical inference process for Norris Electronics.

Whenever statisticians use a sample to estimate a population characteristic of interest, they usually provide a statement of the quality, or precision, associated with the

TABLE 1.5   HOURS UNTIL BURNOUT FOR A SAMPLE OF 200 LIGHTBULBS
FOR THE NORRIS ELECTRONICS EXAMPLE

Norris

107	73	68	97	76	79	94	59	98	57
54	65	71	70	84	88	62	61	79	98
66	62	79	86	68	74	61	82	65	98
62	116	65	88	64	79	78	79	77	86
74	85	73	80	68	78	89	72	58	69
92	78	88	77	103	88	63	68	88	81
75	90	62	89	71	71	74	70	74	70
65	81	75	62	94	71	85	84	83	63
81	62	79	83	93	61	65	62	92	65
83	70	70	81	77	72	84	67	59	58
78	66	66	94	77	63	66	75	68	76
90	78	71	101	78	43	59	67	61	71
96	75	64	76	72	77	74	65	82	86
66	86	96	89	81	71	85	99	59	92
68	72	77	60	87	84	75	77	51	45
85	67	87	80	84	93	69	76	89	75
83	68	72	67	92	89	82	96	77	102
74	91	76	83	66	68	61	73	72	76
73	77	79	94	63	59	62	71	81	65
73	63	63	89	82	64	85	92	64	73

estimate. For the Norris example, the statistician might state that the point estimate of the average lifetime for the population of new lightbulbs is 76 hours with a margin of error of ±4 hours. Thus, an interval estimate of the average lifetime for all lightbulbs produced with the new filament is 72 hours to 80 hours. The statistician can also state how confident he or she is that the interval from 72 hours to 80 hours contains the population average.

FIGURE 1.6   THE PROCESS OF STATISTICAL INFERENCE FOR THE NORRIS
ELECTRONICS EXAMPLE

1.6 Computers and Statistical Analysis

Because statistical analysis typically involves large amounts of data, analysts frequently use computer software for this work. For instance, computing the average lifetime for the 200 lightbulbs in the Norris Electronics example (see Table 1.5) would be quite tedious without a computer. To facilitate computer usage, the larger data sets in this book are available on the CD that accompanies the text. A logo in the left margin of the text (e.g., Norris) identifies each of these data sets. The data files are available in both Minitab and Excel formats. In addition, we provide instructions in chapter appendixes for carrying out many of the statistical procedures using Minitab and Excel.

Summary

Statistics is the art and science of collecting, analyzing, presenting, and interpreting data. Nearly every college student majoring in business or economics is required to take a course in statistics. We began the chapter by describing typical statistical applications for business and economics.

Data consist of the facts and figures that are collected and analyzed. Four scales of measurement used to obtain data on a particular variable include nominal, ordinal, interval, and ratio. The scale of measurement for a variable is nominal when the data use labels or names to identify an attribute of an element. The scale is ordinal if the data demonstrate the properties of nominal data and the order or rank of the data is meaningful. The scale is interval if the data demonstrate the properties of ordinal data and the interval between values is expressed in terms of a fixed unit of measure. Finally, the scale of measurement is ratio if the data show all the properties of interval data and the ratio of two values is meaningful.

For purposes of statistical analysis, data can be classified as qualitative or quantitative. Qualitative data use labels or names to identify an attribute of each element. Qualitative data use either the nominal or ordinal scale of measurement and may be nonnumeric or numeric. Quantitative data are numeric values that indicate how much or how many. Quantitative data use either the interval or ratio scale of measurement. Ordinary arithmetic operations are meaningful only if the data are quantitative. Therefore, statistical computations used for quantitative data are not always appropriate for qualitative data.

In Sections 1.4 and 1.5 we introduced the topics of descriptive statistics and statistical inference. Descriptive statistics are the tabular, graphical, and numerical methods used to summarize data. The process of statistical inference uses data obtained from a sample to make estimates or test hypotheses about the characteristics of a population. In the last section of the chapter we noted that computers facilitate statistical analysis. The larger data sets contained in Minitab and Excel files can be found on the CD that accompanies the text.

Glossary

Statistics The art and science of collecting, analyzing, presenting, and interpreting data.
Data The facts and figures collected, analyzed, and summarized for presentation and interpretation.
Data set All the data collected in a particular study.
Elements The entities on which data are collected.
Variable A characteristic of interest for the elements.
Observation The set of measurements obtained for a particular element.

Nominal scale The scale of measurement for a variable when the data use labels or names to identify an attribute of an element. Nominal data may be nonnumeric or numeric.

Ordinal scale The scale of measurement for a variable if the data exhibit the properties of nominal data and the order or rank of the data is meaningful. Ordinal data may be nonnumeric or numeric.

Interval scale The scale of measurement for a variable if the data demonstrate the properties of ordinal data and the interval between values is expressed in terms of a fixed unit of measure. Interval data are always numeric.

Ratio scale The scale of measurement for a variable if the data demonstrate all the properties of interval data and the ratio of two values is meaningful. Ratio data are always numeric.

Qualitative data Labels or names used to identify an attribute of each element. Qualitative data use either the nominal or ordinal scale of measurement and may be nonnumeric or numeric.

Quantitative data Numeric values that indicate how much or how many of something. Quantitative data are obtained using either the interval or ratio scale of measurement.

Qualitative variable A variable with qualitative data.

Quantitative variable A variable with quantitative data.

Cross-sectional data Data collected at the same or approximately the same point in time.

Time series data Data collected over several time periods.

Descriptive statistics Tabular, graphical, and numerical summaries of data.

Population The set of all elements of interest in a particular study.

Sample A subset of the population.

Census A survey to collect data on the entire population.

Sample survey A survey to collect data on a sample.

Statistical inference The process of using data obtained from a sample to make estimates or test hypotheses about the characteristics of a population.

Exercises

1. Discuss the differences between statistics as numerical facts and statistics as a discipline or field of study.

2. *Condé Nast Traveler* magazine conducts an annual survey of subscribers in order to determine the best places to stay throughout the world. Table 1.6 shows a sample of nine European hotels (*Condé Nast Traveler,* January 2000). The price of a standard double room during the hotel's high season ranges from $ (lowest price) to $$$$ (highest price). The overall score includes subscribers' evaluations of each hotel's rooms, service, restaurants, location/atmosphere, and public areas; a higher overall score corresponds to a higher level of satisfaction.
   a. How many elements are in this data set?
   b. How many variables are in this data set?
   c. Which variables are qualitative and which variables are quantitative?
   d. What type of measurement scale is used for each of the variables?

3. Refer to Table 1.6.
   a. What is the average number of rooms for the nine hotels?
   b. Compute the average overall score.
   c. What is the percentage of hotels located in England?
   d. What is the percentage of hotels with a room rate of $$?

4. All-in-one sound systems, called minisystems, typically include an AM/FM tuner, a dual-cassette tape deck, and a CD changer in a book-sized box with two separate speakers. The data in Table 1.7 show the retail price, sound quality, CD capacity, FM tuning sensitivity and selectivity, and the number of tape decks for a sample of 10 minisystems (*Consumer Reports Buying Guide 2002*).

TABLE 1.6   RATINGS FOR NINE PLACES TO STAY IN EUROPE

Hotel

Name of Property	Country	Room Rate	Number of Rooms	Overall Score
Graveteye Manor	England	$$	18	83.6
Villa d'Este	Italy	$$$$	166	86.3
Hotel Prem	Germany	$	54	77.8
Hotel d'Europe	France	$$	47	76.8
Palace Luzern	Switzerland	$$	326	80.9
Royal Crescent Hotel	England	$$$	45	73.7
Hotel Sacher	Austria	$$$	120	85.5
Duc de Bourgogne	Belgium	$	10	76.9
Villa Gallici	France	$$	22	90.6

Source: Condé Nast Traveler, January 2000.

TABLE 1.7   A SAMPLE OF 10 MINISYSTEMS

Minisystems

Brand and Model	Price ($)	Sound Quality	CD Capacity	FM Tuning	Tape Decks
Aiwa NSX-AJ800	250	Good	3	Fair	2
JVC FS-SD1000	500	Good	1	Very Good	0
JVC MX-G50	200	Very Good	3	Excellent	2
Panasonic SC-PM11	170	Fair	5	Very Good	1
RCA RS 1283	170	Good	3	Poor	0
Sharp CD-BA2600	150	Good	3	Good	2
Sony CHC-CL1	300	Very Good	3	Very Good	1
Sony MHC-NX1	500	Good	5	Excellent	2
Yamaha GX-505	400	Very Good	3	Excellent	1
Yamaha MCR-E100	500	Very Good	1	Excellent	0

    a.   How many elements does this data set contain?

    b.   What is the population?

    c.   Compute the average price for the sample.

    d.   Using the results in part (c), estimate the average price for the population.

5.   Consider the data set for the sample of 10 minisystems in Table 1.7.

    a.   How many variables are in the data set?

    b.   Which of the variables are quantitative and which are qualitative?

    c.   What is the average CD capacity for the sample?

    d.   What percentage of the minisystems provides an FM tuning rating of very good or excellent?

    e.   What percentage of the minisystems includes two tape decks?

6.   Columbia House provides CDs to its mail-order club members. A Columbia House Music Survey asked new club members to complete an 11-question survey. Some of the questions asked were:

    a.   How many CDs have you bought in the last 12 months?

    b.   Are you currently a member of a national mail-order book club? (Yes or No)

    c.   What is your age?

    d.   Including yourself, how many people (adults and children) are in your household?

    e.   What kind of music are you interested in buying? (15 categories were listed, including hard rock, soft rock, adult contemporary, heavy metal, rap, and country.)

Comment on whether each question provides qualitative or quantitative data.

7. A *Barron's* subscriber survey (September 15, 2000) asked subscribers to indicate their employment status. The data were recorded with 1 denoting employed full-time, 2 denoting employed part-time, 3 denoting retired, and 4 denoting unemployed (homemaker, student, etc.).
   a. The variable is employment status. Is it a qualitative or quantitative variable?
   b. What type of measurement scale is being used for this variable?

8. The Gallup organization conducted a telephone survey with a randomly selected national sample of 1005 adults, 18 years and older. The survey asked the respondents, "How would you describe your own physical health at this time?" (http://www.gallup.com, February 7, 2002). Response categories were Excellent, Good, Only Fair, Poor, and No opinion.
   a. What was the sample size for this survey?
   b. Are the data qualitative or quantitative?
   c. Would it make more sense to use averages or percentages as a summary of the data for this question?
   d. Of the respondents, 29% said their personal health was excellent. How many individuals provided this response?

9. The Commerce Department reported receiving the following applications for the Malcolm Baldrige National Quality Award: 23 from large manufacturing firms, 18 from large service firms, and 30 from small businesses.
   a. Is type of business a qualitative or quantitative variable?
   b. What percentage of the applications came from small businesses?

10. *The Wall Street Journal* subscriber survey (October 13, 2003) asked 46 questions about subscriber characteristics and interests. State whether each of the following questions provided qualitative or quantitative data and indicate the measurement scale appropriate for each.
    a. What is your age?
    b. Are you male or female?
    c. When did you first start reading the *WSJ*? High school, college, early career, mid-career, late career, or retirement?
    d. How long have you been in your present job or position?
    e. What type of vehicle are you considering for your next purchase? Nine response categories include sedan, sports car, SUV, minivan, and so on.

11. State whether each of the following variables is qualitative or quantitative and indicate its measurement scale.
    a. Annual sales
    b. Soft-drink size (small, medium, large)
    c. Employee classification (GS1 through GS18)
    d. Earnings per share
    e. Method of payment (cash, check, credit card)

12. The Hawaii Visitors Bureau collects data on visitors to Hawaii. The following questions were among 16 asked in a questionnaire handed out to passengers during incoming airline flights in June 2003.
    - This trip to Hawaii is my: 1st, 2nd, 3rd, 4th, etc.
    - The primary reason for this trip is: (10 categories including vacation, convention, honeymoon)
    - Where I plan to stay: (11 categories including hotel, apartment, relatives, camping)
    - Total days in Hawaii
    a. What is the population being studied?
    b. Is the use of a questionnaire a good way to reach the population of passengers on incoming airline flights?
    c. Comment on each of the four questions in terms of whether it will provide qualitative or quantitative data.

FIGURE 1.7   EARNINGS FOR VOLKSWAGEN

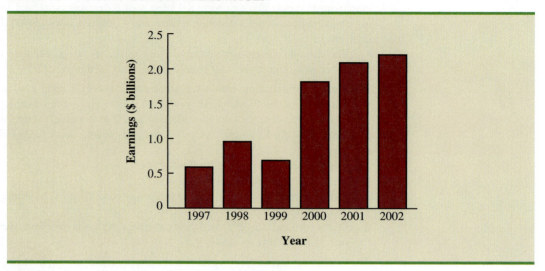

13. Figure 1.7 provides a bar graph summarizing the earnings for Volkswagen for the years 1997 to 2002 (*Business Week,* July 23, 2001).
    a. Are the data qualitative or quantitative?
    b. Are the data time series or cross-sectional?
    c. What is the variable of interest?
    d. Comment on the trend in Volkswagen's earnings over time. Would you expect to see an increase or decrease in 2003?

14. The Recording Industry of America keeps track of recorded music sales by type of music, format, and age group. The following data show the percentage of music sales by type (*The New York Times 2002 Almanac*).

Type	1996	1997	1998	1999	2000
Rock	32.6	32.5	25.7	25.2	24.8
Country	12.1	11.2	12.8	10.8	10.7
R&B	12.1	11.2	12.8	10.5	9.7
Pop	9.3	9.4	10.0	10.3	11.0
Rap	8.9	10.1	9.7	10.8	12.9
Gospel	4.3	4.5	6.3	5.1	4.8
Classical	3.4	2.8	3.3	3.5	2.7
Jazz	3.3	2.8	1.9	3.0	2.9
Other	14.0	15.5	17.5	20.8	20.5

    a. Is the type of music a qualitative or quantitative variable?
    b. Construct a graph of rock music sales over the five-year period; use the horizontal axis to display the year and the vertical axis to display the percentage of music sales. Is this graph based on cross-sectional data or time series data?
    c. Construct a bar graph for type of music sales in 2000. Is this graph based on cross-sectional data or time series data?

15. The Food and Drug Administration (FDA) reported the number of new drugs approved over an eight-year period (*The Wall Street Journal,* January 12, 2004). Figure 1.8 provides a bar graph summarizing the number of new drugs approved each year.
    a. Are the data qualitative or quantitative?
    b. Are the data time series or cross-sectional?
    c. How many new drugs were approved in 2003?

FIGURE 1.8   NUMBER OF NEW DRUGS APPROVED BY THE FOOD AND DRUG
ADMINISTRATION

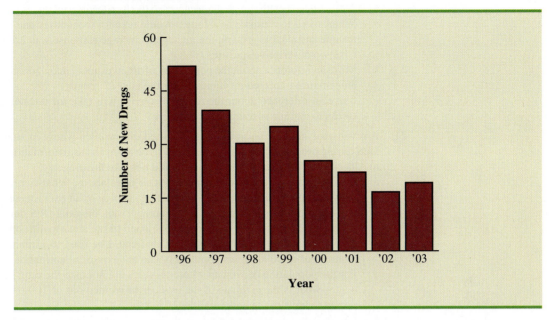

d. What year had the fewest new drugs approved? How many?

e. Comment on the trend in the number of new drugs approved by the FDA over the eight-year period.

16. The marketing group at your company developed a new diet soft drink that it claims will capture a large share of the young adult market.

    a. What data would you want to see before deciding to invest substantial funds in introducing the new product into the marketplace?

    b. How would you expect the data mentioned in part (a) to be obtained?

17. A manager of a large corporation recommends a $10,000 raise be given to keep a valued subordinate from moving to another company. What internal and external sources of data might be used to decide whether such a salary increase is appropriate?

18. A survey of 430 business travelers found 155 business travelers used a travel agent to make the travel arrangements (*USA Today,* November 20, 2003).

    a. Develop a descriptive statistic that can be used to estimate the percentage of all business travelers who use a travel agent to make travel arrangements.

    b. The survey reported that the most frequent way business travelers make travel arrangements is by using an online travel site. If 44% of business travelers surveyed made their arrangements this way, how many of the 430 business travelers used an online travel site?

    c. Are the data on how travel arrangements are made qualitative or quantitative?

19. A *Business Week* North American subscriber study collected data from a sample of 2861 subscribers. Fifty-nine percent of the respondents indicated an annual income of $75,000 or more, and 50% reported having an American Express credit card.

    a. What is the population of interest in this study?

    b. Is annual income a qualitative or quantitative variable?

    c. Is ownership of an American Express card a qualitative or quantitative variable?

    d. Does this study involve cross-sectional or time series data?

    e. Describe any statistical inferences *Business Week* might make on the basis of the survey.

20. A survey of 131 investment managers in *Barron's* Big Money poll revealed the following (*Barron's,* October 28, 2002):

- 43% of managers classified themselves as bullish or very bullish on the stock market.
- The average expected return over the next 12 months for equities was 11.2%.
- 21% selected health care as the sector most likely to lead the market in the next 12 months.
- When asked to estimate how long it would take for technology and telecom stocks to resume sustainable growth, the managers' average response was 2.5 years.

a. Cite two descriptive statistics.
b. Make an inference about the population of all investment managers concerning the average return expected on equities over the next 12 months.
c. Make an inference about the length of time it will take for technology and telecom stocks to resume sustainable growth.

21. A seven-year medical research study reported that women whose mothers took the drug DES during pregnancy were *twice* as likely to develop tissue abnormalities that might lead to cancer as were women whose mothers did not take the drug.
a. This study involved the comparison of two populations. What were the populations?
b. Do you suppose the data were obtained in a survey or an experiment?
c. For the population of women whose mothers took the drug DES during pregnancy, a sample of 3980 women showed 63 developed tissue abnormalities that might lead to cancer. Provide a descriptive statistic that could be used to estimate the number of women out of 1000 in this population who have tissue abnormalities.
d. For the population of women whose mothers did not take the drug DES during pregnancy, what is the estimate of the number of women out of 1000 who would be expected to have tissue abnormalities?
e. Medical studies often use a relatively large sample (in this case, 3980). Why?

22. In the fall of 2003, Arnold Schwarzenegger challenged Governor Gray Davis for the governorship of California. A Policy Institute of California survey of registered voters reported Arnold Schwarzenegger in the lead with an estimated 54% of the vote (*Newsweek,* September 8, 2003).
a. What was the population for this survey?
b. What was the sample for this survey?
c. Why was a sample used in this situation? Explain.

23. Nielsen Media Research conducts weekly surveys of television viewing throughout the United States, publishing both rating and market share data. The Nielsen rating is the percentage of households with televisions watching a program, while the Nielsen share is the percentage of households watching a program among those households with televisions in use. For example, Nielsen Media Research results for the 2003 Baseball World Series between the New York Yankees and the Florida Marlins showed a rating of 12.8% and a share of 22% (Associated Press, October 27, 2003). Thus, 12.8% of households with televisions were watching the World Series and 22% of households with televisions in use were watching the World Series. Based on the rating and share data for major television programs, Nielsen publishes a weekly ranking of television programs as well as a weekly ranking of the four major networks: ABC, CBS, NBC, and Fox.
a. What is Nielsen Media Research attempting to measure?
b. What is the population?
c. Why would a sample be used in this situation?
d. What kinds of decisions or actions are based on the Nielsen rankings?

24. A sample of midterm grades for five students showed the following results: 72, 65, 82, 90, 76. Which of the following statements are correct, and which should be challenged as being too generalized?
a. The average midterm grade for the sample of five students is 77.
b. The average midterm grade for all students who took the exam is 77.
c. An estimate of the average midterm grade for all students who took the exam is 77.
d. More than half of the students who take this exam will score between 70 and 85.
e. If five other students are included in the sample, their grades will be between 65 and 90.

CHAPTER 2

Descriptive Statistics: Tabular and Graphical Presentations

STATISTICS *in* PRACTICE

COLGATE-PALMOLIVE COMPANY*
NEW YORK, NEW YORK

The Colgate-Palmolive Company started as a small soap and candle shop in New York City in 1806. Today, Colgate-Palmolive employs more than 40,000 people working in more than 200 countries and territories around the world. Although best known for its brand names of Colgate, Palmolive, Ajax, and Fab, the company also markets Mennen, Hill's Science Diet, and Hill's Prescription Diet products.

The Colgate-Palmolive Company uses statistics in its quality assurance program for home laundry detergent products. One concern is customer satisfaction with the quantity of detergent in a carton. Every carton in each size category is filled with the same amount of detergent by weight, but the volume of detergent is affected by the density of the detergent powder. For instance, if the powder density is on the heavy side, a smaller volume of detergent is needed to reach the carton's specified weight. As a result, the carton may appear to be underfilled when opened by the consumer.

To control the problem of heavy detergent powder, limits are placed on the acceptable range of powder density. Statistical samples are taken periodically, and the density of each powder sample is measured. Data summaries are then provided for operating personnel so that corrective action can be taken if necessary to keep the density within the desired quality specifications.

A frequency distribution for the densities of 150 samples taken over a one-week period and a histogram are shown in the accompanying table and figure. Density levels above .40 are unacceptably high. The frequency distribution and histogram show that the operation is meeting its quality guidelines with all of the densities less than or equal to .40. Managers viewing these statistical summaries would be pleased with the quality of the detergent production process.

In this chapter, you will learn about tabular and graphical methods of descriptive statistics such as frequency distributions, bar graphs, histograms, stem-and-leaf displays, crosstabulations, and others. The goal of these methods is to summarize data so that the data can be easily understood and interpreted.

*The authors are indebted to William R. Fowle, Manager of Quality Assurance, Colgate-Palmolive Company, for providing this Statistics in Practice.

Statistical summaries help maintain the quality of these Colgate-Palmolive products. © Joe Higgins/South-Western.

Frequency Distribution of Density Data

Density	Frequency
.29–.30	30
.31–.32	75
.33–.34	32
.35–.36	9
.37–.38	3
.39–.40	1
Total	150

Histogram of Density Data

Less than 1% of samples near the undesirable .40 level

As indicated in Chapter 1, data can be classified as either qualitative or quantitative. **Qualitative data** use labels or names to identify categories of like items. **Quantitative data** are numerical values that indicate how much or how many.

This chapter introduces tabular and graphical methods commonly used to summarize both qualitative and quantitative data. Tabular and graphical summaries of data can be found in annual reports, newspaper articles, and research studies. Everyone is exposed to these types of presentations. Hence, it is important to understand how they are prepared and how they should be interpreted. We begin with tabular and graphical methods for summarizing data concerning a single variable. The last section introduces methods for summarizing data when the relationship between two variables is of interest.

Modern statistical software packages provide extensive capabilities for summarizing data and preparing graphical presentations. Minitab and Excel are two packages that are widely available. In the chapter appendixes, we show some of their capabilities.

2.1 Summarizing Qualitative Data

Frequency Distribution

We begin the discussion of how tabular and graphical methods can be used to summarize qualitative data with the definition of a **frequency distribution**.

> **FREQUENCY DISTRIBUTION**
>
> A frequency distribution is a tabular summary of data showing the number (frequency) of items in each of several nonoverlapping classes.

Let us use the following example to demonstrate the construction and interpretation of a frequency distribution for qualitative data. Coke Classic, Diet Coke, Dr. Pepper, Pepsi-Cola, and Sprite are five popular soft drinks. Assume that the data in Table 2.1 show the soft drink selected in a sample of 50 soft drink purchases.

TABLE 2.1   DATA FROM A SAMPLE OF 50 SOFT DRINK PURCHASES

SoftDrink

Coke Classic	Sprite	Pepsi-Cola
Diet Coke	Coke Classic	Coke Classic
Pepsi-Cola	Diet Coke	Coke Classic
Diet Coke	Coke Classic	Coke Classic
Coke Classic	Diet Coke	Pepsi-Cola
Coke Classic	Coke Classic	Dr. Pepper
Dr. Pepper	Sprite	Coke Classic
Diet Coke	Pepsi-Cola	Diet Coke
Pepsi-Cola	Coke Classic	Pepsi-Cola
Pepsi-Cola	Coke Classic	Pepsi-Cola
Coke Classic	Coke Classic	Pepsi-Cola
Dr. Pepper	Pepsi-Cola	Pepsi-Cola
Sprite	Coke Classic	Coke Classic
Coke Classic	Sprite	Dr. Pepper
Diet Coke	Dr. Pepper	Pepsi-Cola
Coke Classic	Pepsi-Cola	Sprite
Coke Classic	Diet Coke	

TABLE 2.2

FREQUENCY
DISTRIBUTION OF
SOFT DRINK
PURCHASES

Soft Drink	Frequency
Coke Classic	19
Diet Coke	8
Dr. Pepper	5
Pepsi-Cola	13
Sprite	5
Total	50

To develop a frequency distribution for these data, we count the number of times each soft drink appears in Table 2.1. Coke Classic appears 19 times, Diet Coke appears 8 times, Dr. Pepper appears 5 times, Pepsi-Cola appears 13 times, and Sprite appears 5 times. These counts are summarized in the frequency distribution in Table 2.2.

This frequency distribution provides a summary of how the 50 soft drink purchases are distributed across the five soft drinks. This summary offers more insight than the original data shown in Table 2.1. Viewing the frequency distribution, we see that Coke Classic is the leader, Pepsi-Cola is second, Diet Coke is third, and Sprite and Dr. Pepper are tied for fourth. The frequency distribution summarizes information about the popularity of the five best-selling soft drinks.

Relative Frequency and Percent Frequency Distributions

A frequency distribution shows the number (frequency) of items in each of several nonoverlapping classes. However, we are often interested in the proportion, or percentage, of items in each class. The *relative frequency* of a class equals the fraction or proportion of items belonging to a class. For a data set with n observations, the relative frequency of each class can be determined as follows:

RELATIVE FREQUENCY

$$\text{Relative frequency of a class} = \frac{\text{Frequency of the class}}{n} \qquad (2.1)$$

The *percent frequency* of a class is the relative frequency multiplied by 100.

A **relative frequency distribution** gives a tabular summary of data showing the relative frequency for each class. A **percent frequency distribution** summarizes the percent frequency of the data for each class. Table 2.3 shows a relative frequency distribution and a percent frequency distribution for the soft drink data. In Table 2.3 we see that the relative frequency for Coke Classic is 19/50 = .38, the relative frequency for Diet Coke is 8/50 = .16, and so on. From the percent frequency distribution, we see that 38% of the purchases were Coke Classic, 16% of the purchases were Diet Coke, and so on. We can also note that 38% + 26% + 16% = 80% of the purchases were the top three soft drinks.

Bar Graphs and Pie Charts

A **bar graph**, or bar chart, is a graphical device for depicting qualitative data summarized in a frequency, relative frequency, or percent frequency distribution. On one axis of the graph (usually the horizontal axis), we specify the labels that are used for the classes (categories). A frequency, relative frequency, or percent frequency scale can be used for the other axis of

TABLE 2.3 RELATIVE AND PERCENT FREQUENCY DISTRIBUTIONS
OF SOFT DRINK PURCHASES

Soft Drink	Relative Frequency	Percent Frequency
Coke Classic	.38	38
Diet Coke	.16	16
Dr. Pepper	.10	10
Pepsi-Cola	.26	26
Sprite	.10	10
Total	1.00	100

FIGURE 2.1   BAR GRAPH OF SOFT DRINK PURCHASES

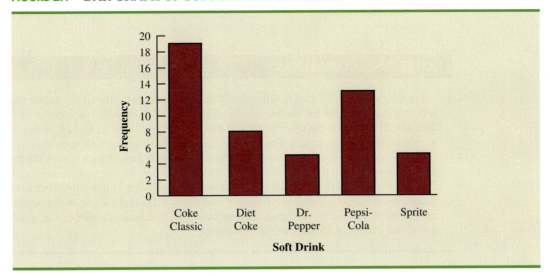

In quality control applications, bar graphs are used to identify the most important causes of problems. When the bars are arranged in descending order of height from left to right with the most frequently occurring cause appearing first, the bar graph is called a pareto diagram. *This diagram is named for its founder, Vilfredo Pareto, an Italian economist.*

the graph (usually the vertical axis). Then, using a bar of fixed width drawn above each class label, we extend the length of the bar until we reach the frequency, relative frequency, or percent frequency of the class. For qualitative data, the bars should be separated to emphasize the fact that each class is separate. Figure 2.1 shows a bar graph of the frequency distribution for the 50 soft drink purchases. Note how the graphical presentation shows Coke Classic, Pepsi-Cola, and Diet Coke to be the most preferred brands.

The **pie chart** provides another graphical device for presenting relative frequency and percent frequency distributions for qualitative data. To construct a pie chart, we first draw a circle to represent all of the data. Then we use the relative frequencies to subdivide the circle into sectors, or parts, that correspond to the relative frequency for each class. For example, because a circle contains 360 degrees and Coke Classic shows a relative frequency of .38, the sector of the pie chart labeled Coke Classic consists of .38(360) = 136.8 degrees. The sector of the pie chart labeled Diet Coke consists of .16(360) = 57.6 degrees. Similar calculations for the other classes yield the pie chart in Figure 2.2. The

FIGURE 2.2   PIE CHART OF SOFT DRINK PURCHASES

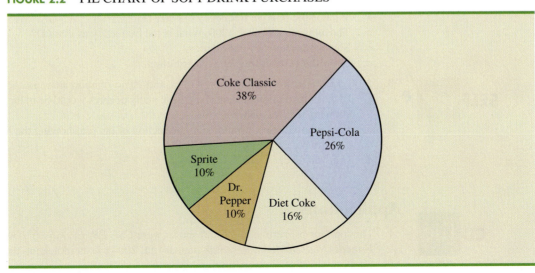

numerical values shown for each sector can be frequencies, relative frequencies, or percent frequencies.

1. Often the number of classes in a frequency distribution is the same as the number of categories found in the data, as is the case for the soft drink purchase data in this section. The data involve only five soft drinks, and a separate frequency distribution class was defined for each one. Data that included all soft drinks would require many categories, most of which would have a small number of purchases. Most statisticians recommend that classes with smaller frequencies be grouped into an aggregate class called "other." Classes with frequencies of 5% or less would most often be treated in this fashion.

2. The sum of the frequencies in any frequency distribution always equals the number of observations. The sum of the relative frequencies in any relative frequency distribution always equals 1.00, and the sum of the percentages in a percent frequency distribution always equals 100.

Exercises

Methods

1. The response to a question has three alternatives: A, B, and C. A sample of 120 responses provides 60 A, 24 B, and 36 C. Show the frequency and relative frequency distributions.

2. A partial relative frequency distribution is given.

Class	Relative Frequency
A	.22
B	.18
C	.40
D	

   a. What is the relative frequency of class D?
   b. The total sample size is 200. What is the frequency of class D?
   c. Show the frequency distribution.
   d. Show the percent frequency distribution.

3. A questionnaire provides 58 Yes, 42 No, and 20 no-opinion answers.
   a. In the construction of a pie chart, how many degrees would be in the section of the pie showing the Yes answers?
   b. How many degrees would be in the section of the pie showing the No answers?
   c. Construct a pie chart.
   d. Construct a bar graph.

Applications

4. The top four primetime television shows were *CSI, ER, Everybody Loves Raymond,* and *Friends* (*Nielsen Media Research,* January 11, 2004). Data indicating the preferred shows for a sample of 50 viewers follow.

CSI	Friends	CSI	CSI	CSI
CSI	CSI	Raymond	ER	ER
Friends	CSI	ER	Friends	CSI
ER	ER	Friends	CSI	Raymond
CSI	Friends	CSI	CSI	Friends
ER	ER	ER	Friends	Raymond
CSI	Friends	Friends	CSI	Raymond
Friends	Friends	Raymond	Friends	CSI
Raymond	Friends	ER	Friends	CSI
CSI	ER	CSI	Friends	ER

a.   Are these data qualitative or quantitative?
b.   Provide frequency and percent frequency distributions.
c.   Construct a bar graph and a pie chart.
d.   On the basis of the sample, which television show has the largest viewing audience? Which one is second?

5.   In alphabetical order, the six most common last names in the United States are Brown, Davis, Johnson, Jones, Smith, and Williams (*Time Almanac 2001*). Assume that a sample of 50 individuals with one of these last names provided the following data.

Brown	Williams	Williams	Williams	Brown
Smith	Jones	Smith	Johnson	Smith
Davis	Smith	Brown	Williams	Johnson
Johnson	Smith	Smith	Johnson	Brown
Williams	Davis	Johnson	Williams	Johnson
Williams	Johnson	Jones	Smith	Brown
Johnson	Smith	Smith	Brown	Jones
Jones	Jones	Smith	Smith	Davis
Davis	Jones	Williams	Davis	Smith
Jones	Johnson	Brown	Johnson	Davis

Summarize the data by constructing the following:
a.   Relative and percent frequency distributions
b.   A bar graph
c.   A pie chart
d.   Based on these data, what are the three most common last names?

6.   The eight best-selling paperback business books are listed in Table 2.4 (*Business Week,* April 3, 2000). Suppose a sample of book purchases provided the following data:

7 Habits	Dad	7 Habits	Millionaire	Millionaire	WSJ Guide
Motley	Millionaire	Tax Guide	7 Habits	Dad	Dummies
Millionaire	Motley	Dad	Dad	Parachute	Dad
Dad	7 Habits	WSJ Guide	WSJ Guide	WSJ Guide	7 Habits
Motley	WSJ Guide	Millionaire	7 Habits	Millionaire	Millionaire
Millionaire	7 Habits	Millionaire	7 Habits	Motley	Motley
Motley	7 Habits	Dad	Dad	Dad	Dad
7 Habits	WSJ Guide	Tax Guide	Millionaire	Motley	Tax Guide
Motley	Motley	Millionaire	Millionaire	Dad	Dummies
Millionaire	Millionaire	Millionaire	Dad	Millionaire	Dad

a.   Construct frequency and percent frequency distributions for the data. Group any books with a frequency of 5% or less in an "other" category.
b.   Rank the best-selling books.
c.   What percentage of the sales are represented by *The Millionaire Next Door* and *Rich Dad, Poor Dad*?

Names

TABLE 2.4

THE EIGHT
BEST-SELLING
PAPERBACK
BUSINESS BOOKS

- *The 7 Habits of Highly Effective People*
- *Investing for Dummies*
- *The Ernst & Young Tax Guide 2000*
- *The Millionaire Next Door*
- *The Motley Fool Investment Guide*
- *Rich Dad, Poor Dad*
- *The Wall Street Journal Guide to Understanding Money and Investing*
- *What Color Is Your Parachute? 2000*

BWBooks

30   ESSENTIALS OF STATISTICS FOR BUSINESS AND ECONOMICS

7. Leverock's Waterfront Steakhouse in Maderia Beach, Florida, uses a questionnaire to ask customers how they rate the server, food quality, cocktails, prices, and atmosphere at the restaurant. Each characteristic is rated on a scale of outstanding (O), very good (V), good (G), average (A), and poor (P). Use descriptive statistics to summarize the following data collected on food quality. What is your feeling about the food quality ratings at the restaurant?

G	O	V	G	A	O	V	O	V	G	O	V	A
V	O	P	V	O	G	A	O	O	O	G	O	V
V	A	G	O	V	P	V	O	O	G	O	O	V
O	G	A	O	V	O	O	G	V	A	G		

8. Data for a sample of 55 members of the Baseball Hall of Fame in Cooperstown, New York, are shown here. Each observation indicates the primary position played by the Hall of Famers: pitcher (P), catcher (H), 1st base (1), 2nd base (2), 3rd base (3), shortstop (S), left field (L), center field (C), and right field (R).

L	P	C	H	2	P	R	1	S	S	1	L	P	R	P
P	P	P	R	C	S	L	R	P	C	C	P	P	R	P
2	3	P	H	L	P	1	C	P	P	P	S	1	L	R
R	1	2	H	S	3	H	2	L	P					

a. Use frequency and relative frequency distributions to summarize the data.
b. What position provides the most Hall of Famers?
c. What position provides the fewest Hall of Famers?
d. What outfield position (L, C, or R) provides the most Hall of Famers?
e. Compare infielders (1, 2, 3, and S) to outfielders (L, C, and R).

9. About 60% of small and medium-sized businesses are family-owned. A TEC International Inc. survey asked the chief executive officers (CEOs) of family-owned businesses how they became the CEO (*The Wall Street Journal,* December 16, 2003). Responses were that the CEO inherited the business, the CEO built the business, or the CEO was hired by the family-owned firm. A sample of 26 CEOs of family-owned businesses provided the following data on how each became the CEO.

CEOs

Built	Built	Built	Inherited
Inherited	Built	Inherited	Built
Inherited	Built	Built	Built
Built	Hired	Hired	Hired
Inherited	Inherited	Inherited	Built
Built	Built	Built	Hired
Built	Inherited		

a. Provide a frequency distribution.
b. Provide a percent frequency distribution.
c. Construct a bar graph.
d. What percentage of CEOs of family-owned businesses became the CEO because they inherited the business? What is the primary reason a person becomes the CEO of a family-owned business?

10. A 2001 Merrill Lynch Client Satisfaction Survey asked clients to indicate how satisfied they were with their financial consultant. Client responses were coded 1 to 7, with 1 indicating "not at all satisfied" and 7 indicating "extremely satisfied." Assume that the following data are from a sample of 60 responses for a particular financial consultant.

Client

5	7	6	6	7	5	5	7	3	6
7	7	6	6	6	5	5	6	7	7
6	6	4	4	7	6	7	6	7	6
5	7	5	7	6	4	7	5	7	6
6	5	3	7	7	6	6	6	6	5
5	6	6	7	7	5	6	4	6	6

a. Comment on why these data are qualitative.
b. Provide a frequency distribution and a relative frequency distribution for the data.
c. Provide a bar graph.
d. On the basis of your summaries, comment on the clients' overall evaluation of the financial consultant.

2.2 Summarizing Quantitative Data

Frequency Distribution

TABLE 2.5

YEAR-END AUDIT TIMES (IN DAYS)

12	14	19	18
15	15	18	17
20	27	22	23
22	21	33	28
14	18	16	13

As defined in Section 2.1, a frequency distribution is a tabular summary of data showing the number (frequency) of items in each of several nonoverlapping classes. This definition holds for quantitative as well as qualitative data. However, with quantitative data we must be more careful in defining the nonoverlapping classes to be used in the frequency distribution.

For example, consider the quantitative data in Table 2.5. These data show the time in days required to complete year-end audits for a sample of 20 clients of Sanderson and Clifford, a small public accounting firm. The three steps necessary to define the classes for a frequency distribution with quantitative data are:

1. Determine the number of nonoverlapping classes.
2. Determine the width of each class.
3. Determine the class limits.

Let us demonstrate these steps by developing a frequency distribution for the audit time data in Table 2.5.

Audit

Number of classes Classes are formed by specifying ranges that will be used to group the data. As a general guideline, we recommend using between 5 and 20 classes. For a small number of data items, as few as five or six classes may be used to summarize the data. For a larger number of data items, a larger number of classes is usually required. The goal is to use enough classes to show the variation in the data, but not so many classes that some contain only a few data items. Because the number of data items in Table 2.5 is relatively small ($n = 20$), we chose to develop a frequency distribution with five classes.

Making the classes the same width reduces the chance of inappropriate interpretations by the user.

Width of the classes The second step in constructing a frequency distribution for quantitative data is to choose a width for the classes. As a general guideline, we recommend that the width be the same for each class. Thus the choices of the number of classes and the width of classes are not independent decisions. A larger number of classes means a smaller class width, and vice versa. To determine an approximate class width, we begin by identifying the largest and smallest data values. Then, with the desired number of classes specified, we can use the following expression to determine the approximate class width.

$$\text{Approximate class width} = \frac{\text{Largest data value} - \text{Smallest data value}}{\text{Number of classes}} \tag{2.2}$$

The approximate class width given by equation (2.2) can be rounded to a more convenient value based on the preference of the person developing the frequency distribution. For example, an approximate class width of 9.28 might be rounded to 10 simply because 10 is a more convenient class width to use in presenting a frequency distribution.

For the data involving the year-end audit times, the largest data value is 33 and the smallest data value is 12. Because we decided to summarize the data with five classes, using equation (2.2) provides an approximate class width of $(33 - 12)/5 = 4.2$. We therefore decided to round up and use a class width of five days in the frequency distribution.

No single frequency distribution is best for a data set. Different people may construct different, but equally acceptable, frequency distributions. The goal is to reveal the natural grouping and variation in the data.

In practice, the number of classes and the appropriate class width are determined by trial and error. Once a possible number of classes is chosen, equation (2.2) is used to find the approximate class width. The process can be repeated for a different number of classes. Ultimately, the analyst uses judgment to determine the combination of the number of classes and class width that provides the best frequency distribution for summarizing the data.

For the audit time data in Table 2.5, after deciding to use five classes, each with a width of five days, the next task is to specify the class limits for each of the classes.

Class limits   Class limits must be chosen so that each data item belongs to one and only one class. The *lower class limit* identifies the smallest possible data value assigned to the class. The *upper class limit* identifies the largest possible data value assigned to the class. In developing frequency distributions for qualitative data, we did not need to specify class limits because each data item naturally fell into a separate class. But with quantitative data, such as the audit times in Table 2.5, class limits are necessary to determine where each data value belongs.

Using the audit time data in Table 2.5, we selected 10 days as the lower class limit and 14 days as the upper class limit for the first class. This class is denoted 10–14 in Table 2.6. The smallest data value, 12, is included in the 10–14 class. We then selected 15 days as the lower class limit and 19 days as the upper class limit of the next class. We continued defining the lower and upper class limits to obtain a total of five classes: 10–14, 15–19, 20–24, 25–29, and 30–34. The largest data value, 33, is included in the 30–34 class. The difference between the lower class limits of adjacent classes is the class width. Using the first two lower class limits of 10 and 15, we see that the class width is $15 - 10 = 5$.

With the number of classes, class width, and class limits determined, a frequency distribution can be obtained by counting the number of data values belonging to each class. For example, the data in Table 2.5 show that four values—12, 14, 14, and 13—belong to the 10–14 class. Thus, the frequency for the 10–14 class is 4. Continuing this counting process for the 15–19, 20–24, 25–29, and 30–34 classes provides the frequency distribution in Table 2.6. Using this frequency distribution, we can observe the following:

1. The most frequently occurring audit times are in the class of 15–19 days. Eight of the 20 audit times belong to this class.
2. Only one audit required 30 or more days.

Other conclusions are possible, depending on the interests of the person viewing the frequency distribution. The value of a frequency distribution is that it provides insights about the data that are not easily obtained by viewing the data in their original unorganized form.

Class midpoint   In some applications, we want to know the midpoints of the classes in a frequency distribution for quantitative data. The **class midpoint** is the value halfway between the lower and upper class limits. For the audit time data, the five class midpoints are 12, 17, 22, 27, and 32.

Relative Frequency and Percent Frequency Distributions

We define the relative frequency and percent frequency distributions for quantitative data in the same manner as for qualitative data. First, recall that the relative frequency is the proportion of the observations belonging to a class. With n observations,

$$\text{Relative frequency of class} = \frac{\text{Frequency of the class}}{n}$$

The percent frequency of a class is the relative frequency multiplied by 100.

Based on the class frequencies in Table 2.6 and with $n = 20$, Table 2.7 shows the relative frequency distribution and percent frequency distribution for the audit time data. Note that .40 of the audits, or 40%, required from 15 to 19 days. Only .05 of the audits, or 5%, required 30 or more days. Again, additional interpretations and insights can be obtained by using Table 2.7.

TABLE 2.6

FREQUENCY DISTRIBUTION FOR THE AUDIT TIME DATA

Audit Time (days)	Frequency
10–14	4
15–19	8
20–24	5
25–29	2
30–34	1
Total	20

TABLE 2.7   RELATIVE AND PERCENT FREQUENCY DISTRIBUTIONS FOR THE AUDIT
TIME DATA

Audit Time (days)	Relative Frequency	Percent Frequency
10–14	.20	20
15–19	.40	40
20–24	.25	25
25–29	.10	10
30–34	.05	5
Total	1.00	100

Dot Plot

One of the simplest graphical summaries of data is a **dot plot**. A horizontal axis shows the range for the data. Each data value is represented by a dot placed above the axis. Figure 2.3 is the dot plot for the audit time data in Table 2.5. The three dots located above 18 on the horizontal axis indicate that an audit time of 18 days occurred three times. Dot plots show the details of the data and are useful for comparing the distribution of the data for two or more variables.

Histogram

A common graphical presentation of quantitative data is a **histogram**. This graphical summary can be prepared for data previously summarized in either a frequency, relative frequency, or percent frequency distribution. A histogram is constructed by placing the variable of interest on the horizontal axis and the frequency, relative frequency, or percent frequency on the vertical axis. The frequency, relative frequency, or percent frequency of each class is shown by drawing a rectangle whose base is determined by the class limits on the horizontal axis and whose height is the corresponding frequency, relative frequency, or percent frequency.

Figure 2.4 is a histogram for the audit time data. Note that the class with the greatest frequency is shown by the rectangle appearing above the class of 15–19 days. The height of the rectangle shows that the frequency of this class is 8. A histogram for the relative or percent frequency distribution of these data would look the same as the histogram in Figure 2.4 with the exception that the vertical axis would be labeled with relative or percent frequency values.

As Figure 2.4 shows, the adjacent rectangles of a histogram touch one another. Unlike a bar graph, a histogram contains no natural separation between the rectangles of adjacent classes. This format is the usual convention for histograms. Because the classes for the audit time data are stated as 10–14, 15–19, 20–24, 25–29, and 30–34, one-unit spaces of 14 to 15, 19 to 20, 24 to 25, and 29 to 30 would seem to be needed between the classes. These spaces are eliminated when constructing a histogram. Eliminating the spaces

FIGURE 2.3   DOT PLOT FOR THE AUDIT TIME DATA

FIGURE 2.4 HISTOGRAM FOR THE AUDIT TIME DATA

between classes in a histogram for the audit time data helps show that all values between the lower limit of the first class and the upper limit of the last class are possible.

One of the most important uses of a histogram is to provide information about the shape, or form, of a distribution. Figure 2.5 contains four histograms constructed from relative frequency distributions. Panel A shows the histogram for a set of data moderately skewed to the left. A histogram is said to be skewed to the left if its tail extends farther to the left. This histogram is typical for exam scores, with no scores above 100%, most of the scores above 70%, and only a few really low scores. Panel B shows the histogram for a set of data moderately skewed to the right. A histogram is said to be skewed to the right if its tail extends farther to the right. An example of this type of histogram would be for data such as housing prices; a few very expensive houses create the skewness in the right tail.

Panel C shows a symmetric histogram. In a symmetric histogram, the left tail mirrors the shape of the right tail. Histograms for data found in applications are never perfectly symmetric, but the histogram for many applications may be roughly symmetric. Data for SAT scores, heights and weights of people, and so on lead to histograms that are roughly symmetric. Panel D shows a histogram highly skewed to the right. This histogram was constructed from data on the amount of customer purchases over one day at a women's apparel store. Data from applications in business and economics often lead to histograms that are skewed to the right. For instance, data on housing prices, salaries, purchase amounts, and so on often result in histograms skewed to the right.

Cumulative Distributions

A variation of the frequency distribution that provides another tabular summary of quantitative data is the **cumulative frequency distribution**. The cumulative frequency distribution uses the number of classes, class widths, and class limits developed for the frequency distribution. However, rather than showing the frequency of each class, the cumulative frequency distribution shows the number of data items with values *less than or equal to the upper class limit* of each class. The first two columns of Table 2.8 provide the cumulative frequency distribution for the audit time data.

To understand how the cumulative frequencies are determined, consider the class with the description "less than or equal to 24." The cumulative frequency for this class is simply

FIGURE 2.5   HISTOGRAMS SHOWING DIFFERING LEVELS OF SKEWNESS

the sum of the frequencies for all classes with data values less than or equal to 24. For the frequency distribution in Table 2.6, the sum of the frequencies for classes 10–14, 15–19, and 20–24 indicates that $4 + 8 + 5 = 17$ data values are less than or equal to 24. Hence, the cumulative frequency for this class is 17. In addition, the cumulative frequency distribution in Table 2.8 shows that four audits were completed in 14 days or less and 19 audits were completed in 29 days or less.

As a final point, we note that a **cumulative relative frequency distribution** shows the proportion of data items, and a **cumulative percent frequency distribution** shows the percentage of data items with values less than or equal to the upper limit of each class. The cumulative relative frequency distribution can be computed either by summing the relative frequencies in the relative frequency distribution or by dividing the cumulative frequencies by the total number of items. Using the latter approach, we found the cumulative relative frequencies in column 3 of Table 2.8 by dividing the cumulative frequencies in column 2 by the total number of items ($n = 20$). The cumulative percent frequencies were again computed by multiplying the relative frequencies by 100. The cumulative relative and percent frequency distributions show that .85 of the audits, or 85%, were completed in 24 days or less, .95 of the audits, or 95%, were completed in 29 days or less, and so on.

TABLE 2.8   CUMULATIVE FREQUENCY, CUMULATIVE RELATIVE FREQUENCY, AND CUMULATIVE PERCENT FREQUENCY DISTRIBUTIONS FOR THE AUDIT TIME DATA

Audit Time (days)	Cumulative Frequency	Cumulative Relative Frequency	Cumulative Percent Frequency
Less than or equal to 14	4	.20	20
Less than or equal to 19	12	.60	60
Less than or equal to 24	17	.85	85
Less than or equal to 29	19	.95	95
Less than or equal to 34	20	1.00	100

Ogive

A graph of a cumulative distribution, called an **ogive**, shows data values on the horizontal axis and either the cumulative frequencies, the cumulative relative frequencies, or the cumulative percent frequencies on the vertical axis. Figure 2.6 illustrates an ogive for the cumulative frequencies of the audit time data in Table 2.8.

The ogive is constructed by plotting a point corresponding to the cumulative frequency of each class. Because the classes for the audit time data are 10–14, 15–19, 20–24, and so on, one-unit gaps appear from 14 to 15, 19 to 20, and so on. These gaps are eliminated by plotting points halfway between the class limits. Thus, 14.5 is used for the 10–14 class, 19.5 is used for the 15–19 class, and so on. The "less than or equal to 14" class with a cumulative frequency of 4 is shown on the ogive in Figure 2.6 by the point located at 14.5 on the horizontal axis and 4 on the vertical axis. The "less than or equal to 19" class with a cumulative frequency of 12 is shown by the point located at 19.5 on the horizontal axis and 12 on the vertical axis. Note that one additional point is plotted at the left end of the ogive. This point starts the ogive by showing that no data values fall below the 10–14 class. It is plotted at 9.5 on the horizontal axis and 0 on the vertical axis. The plotted points are connected by straight lines to complete the ogive.

FIGURE 2.6   OGIVE FOR THE AUDIT TIME DATA

NOTES AND COMMENTS

1. A bar graph and a histogram are essentially the same thing; both are graphical presentations of the data in a frequency distribution. A histogram is just a bar graph with no separation between bars. For some discrete quantitative data, a separation between bars is also appropriate. Consider, for example, the number of classes in which a college student is enrolled. The data may only assume integer values. Intermediate values such as 1.5, 2.73, and so on are not possible. With continuous quantitative data, however, such as the audit times in Table 2.5, a separation between bars is not appropriate.

2. The appropriate values for the class limits with quantitative data depend on the level of accuracy of the data. For instance, with the audit time data of Table 2.5 the limits used were integer values. If the data were rounded to the nearest tenth of a day (e.g., 12.3, 14.4, and so on), then the limits would be stated in tenths of days. For instance, the first class would be 10.0–14.9. If the data were recorded to the nearest hundredth

of a day (e.g., 12.34, 14.45, and so on), the limits would be stated in hundredths of days. For instance, the first class would be 10.00–14.99.

3. An *open-end* class requires only a lower class limit or an upper class limit. For example, in the audit time data of Table 2.5, suppose two of the audits had taken 58 and 65 days. Rather than continue with the classes of width 5 with classes 35–39, 40–44, 45–49, and so on, we could simplify the frequency distribution to show an open-end class of "35 or more." This class would have a frequency of 2. Most often the open-end class appears at the upper end of the distribution. Sometimes an open-end class appears at the lower end of the distribution, and occasionally such classes appear at both ends.

4. The last entry in a cumulative frequency distribution always equals the total number of observations. The last entry in a cumulative relative frequency distribution always equals 1.00 and the last entry in a cumulative percent frequency distribution always equals 100.

Exercises

Methods

11. Consider the following data.

14	21	23	21	16
19	22	25	16	16
24	24	25	19	16
19	18	19	21	12
16	17	18	23	25
20	23	16	20	19
24	26	15	22	24
20	22	24	22	20

Frequency

a. Develop a frequency distribution using classes of 12–14, 15–17, 18–20, 21–23, and 24–26.
b. Develop a relative frequency distribution and a percent frequency distribution using the classes in part (a).

12. Consider the following frequency distribution.

Class	Frequency
10–19	10
20–29	14
30–39	17
40–49	7
50–59	2

Construct a cumulative frequency distribution and a cumulative relative frequency distribution.

13. Construct a histogram and an ogive for the data in exercise 12.

14. Consider the following data.

8.9	10.2	11.5	7.8	10.0	12.2	13.5	14.1	10.0	12.2
6.8	9.5	11.5	11.2	14.9	7.5	10.0	6.0	15.8	11.5

   a. Construct a dot plot.
   b. Construct a frequency distribution.
   c. Construct a percent frequency distribution.

Applications

15. A doctor's office staff studied the waiting times for patients who arrive at the office with a request for emergency service. The following data with waiting times in minutes were collected over a one-month period.

2   5   10   12   4   4   5   17   11   8   9   8   12   21   6   8   7   13   18   3

   Use classes of 0–4, 5–9, and so on in the following:
   a. Show the frequency distribution.
   b. Show the relative frequency distribution.
   c. Show the cumulative frequency distribution.
   d. Show the cumulative relative frequency distribution.
   e. What proportion of patients needing emergency service wait 9 minutes or less?

16. Consider the following two frequency distributions. The first frequency distribution provides an approximation of the annual adjusted gross income in the United States (Internal Revenue Service, March 2003). The second frequency distribution shows exam scores for students in a college statistics course.

Income ($1000s)	Frequency (millions)	Exam Score	Frequency
0–24	60	Below 30	2
25–49	33	30–39	5
50–74	20	40–49	6
75–99	6	50–59	13
100–124	4	60–69	32
125–149	2	70–79	78
150–174	1	80–89	43
175–199	1	90–99	21
Total	127	Total	200

   a. Develop a histogram for the annual income data. What evidence of skewness does it show? Does this skewness make sense? Explain.
   b. Develop a histogram for the exam score data. What evidence of skewness does it show? Explain.
   c. Develop a histogram for the data in exercise 11. What evidence of skewness does it show? What is the general shape of the distribution?

17. Mendelsohn Media Research provided survey data on the annual amount of household purchases by families with an annual income of $75,000 or more (*Money*, 2001). Assume that the following data from a sample of 25 households show the dollars spent in the past year on books and magazines.

CD file

Spending

280	496	382	202	287
266	119	10	385	135
475	255	379	267	24
42	25	283	110	423
160	123	16	243	363

a. Construct a frequency distribution and relative frequency distribution for the data.
b. Provide a histogram. Comment on the shape of the distribution.
c. Comment on the annual spending on books and magazines for families in the sample.

18. Wageweb conducts surveys of salary data and presents summaries on its Web site. Wageweb reported annual salaries of marketing vice presidents ranged from $85,090 to $190,054 (Wageweb.com, April 12, 2000). Assume the following data come from a sample of the annual salaries for 50 marketing vice presidents. Data are in thousands of dollars.

CD file

Wageweb

145	95	148	112	132
140	162	118	170	144
145	127	148	165	138
173	113	104	141	142
116	178	123	141	138
127	143	134	136	137
155	93	102	154	142
134	165	123	124	124
138	160	157	138	131
114	135	151	138	157

a. What are the lowest and highest salaries?
b. Use a class width of $15,000 and prepare tabular summaries of the annual salary data.
c. What proportion of the annual salaries are $135,000 or less?
d. What percentage of the annual salaries are more than $150,000?
e. Prepare a histogram. Comment on the shape of the distribution.

19. Sorting through unsolicited e-mail and spam affects the productivity of office workers. An InsightExpress survey monitored office workers to determine the unproductive time per day devoted to unsolicited e-mail and spam (*USA Today,* November 13, 2003). The following data show a sample of time in minutes devoted to this task.

2	4	8	4
8	1	2	32
12	1	5	7
5	5	3	4
24	19	4	14

Summarize the data by constructing the following:
a. A frequency distribution (Classes 1–5, 6–10, 11–15, 16–20, and so on)
b. A relative frequency distribution
c. A cumulative frequency distribution
d. A cumulative relative frequency distribution
e. An ogive
f. What percentage of office workers spend 5 minutes or less on unsolicited e-mail and spam? What percentage of office workers spend more than 10 minutes a day on this task?

20. The top 20 concert tours and their average ticket price for shows in North America are shown here. The list is based on data provided to the trade publication *Pollstar* by concert promoters and venue managers (*Associated Press,* November 21, 2003).

CD file

Concerts

Concert Tour	Ticket Price	Concert Tour	Ticket Price
Bruce Springsteen	$72.40	Toby Keith	$37.76
Dave Matthews Band	44.11	James Taylor	44.93
Aerosmith/KISS	69.52	Alabama	40.83
Shania Twain	61.80	Harper/Johnson	33.70
Fleetwood Mac	78.34	50 Cent	38.89
Radiohead	39.50	Steely Dan	36.38
Cher	64.47	Red Hot Chili Peppers	56.82
Counting Crows	36.48	R.E.M.	46.16
Timberlake/Aguilera	74.43	American Idols Live	39.11
Mana	46.48	Mariah Carey	56.08

Summarize the data by constructing the following:
a.   A frequency distribution and a percent frequency distribution
b.   A histogram
c.   What concert had the most expensive average ticket price? What concert had the least expensive average ticket price?
d.   Comment on what the data indicate about the average ticket prices of the top concert tours.

21.   The *Nielsen Home Technology Report* provided information about home technology and its usage by persons age 12 and older. The following data are the hours of personal computer usage during one week for a sample of 50 persons.

Computer

4.1	1.5	10.4	5.9	3.4	5.7	1.6	6.1	3.0	3.7
3.1	4.8	2.0	14.8	5.4	4.2	3.9	4.1	11.1	3.5
4.1	4.1	8.8	5.6	4.3	3.3	7.1	10.3	6.2	7.6
10.8	2.8	9.5	12.9	12.1	0.7	4.0	9.2	4.4	5.7
7.2	6.1	5.7	5.9	4.7	3.9	3.7	3.1	6.1	3.1

Summarize the data by constructing the following:
a.   A frequency distribution (use a class width of three hours)
b.   A relative frequency distribution
c.   A histogram
d.   An ogive
e.   Comment on what the data indicate about personal computer usage at home.

2.3   Exploratory Data Analysis: The Stem–and–Leaf Display

The techniques of **exploratory data analysis** consist of simple arithmetic and easy-to-draw graphs that can be used to summarize data quickly. One technique—referred to as a **stem-and-leaf display**—can be used to show both the rank order and shape of a data set simultaneously.

To illustrate the use of a stem-and-leaf display, consider the data in Table 2.9. These data result from a 150-question aptitude test given to 50 individuals recently interviewed for a position at Haskens Manufacturing. The data indicate the number of questions answered correctly.

To develop a stem-and-leaf display, we first arrange the leading digits of each data value to the left of a vertical line. To the right of the vertical line, we record the last digit for each

TABLE 2.9   NUMBER OF QUESTIONS ANSWERED CORRECTLY ON AN APTITUDE TEST

ApTest

112	72	69	97	107
73	92	76	86	73
126	128	118	127	124
82	104	132	134	83
92	108	96	100	92
115	76	91	102	81
95	141	81	80	106
84	119	113	98	75
68	98	115	106	95
100	85	94	106	119

data value. Based on the top row of data in Table 2.9 (112, 72, 69, 97, and 107), the first five entries in constructing a stem-and-leaf display would be as follows:

```
 6 | 9
 7 | 2
 8 |
 9 | 7
10 | 7
11 | 2
12 |
13 |
14 |
```

For example, the data value 112 shows the leading digits 11 to the left of the line and the last digit 2 to the right of the line. Similarly, the data value 72 shows the leading digit 7 to the left of the line and last digit 2 to the right of the line. Continuing to place the last digit of each data value on the line corresponding to its leading digit(s) provides the following:

```
 6 | 9  8
 7 | 2  3  6  3  6  5
 8 | 6  2  3  1  1  0  4  5
 9 | 7  2  2  6  2  1  5  8  8  5  4
10 | 7  4  8  0  2  6  6  0  6
11 | 2  8  5  9  3  5  9
12 | 6  8  7  4
13 | 2  4
14 | 1
```

With this organization of the data, sorting the digits on each line into rank order is simple. Doing so provides the stem-and-leaf display shown here.

```
 6 | 8  9
 7 | 2  3  3  5  6  6
 8 | 0  1  1  2  3  4  5  6
 9 | 1  2  2  2  4  5  5  6  7  8  8
10 | 0  0  2  4  6  6  6  7  8
11 | 2  3  5  5  8  9  9
12 | 4  6  7  8
13 | 2  4
14 | 1
```

The numbers to the left of the vertical line (6, 7, 8, 9, 10, 11, 12, 13, and 14) form the *stem,* and each digit to the right of the vertical line is a *leaf.* For example, consider the first row with a stem value of 6 and leaves of 8 and 9.

```
6 | 8   9
```

This indicates that two data values have a first digit of six. The leaves show that the data values are 68 and 69. Similarly, the second row

$$7 \mid 2 \quad 3 \quad 3 \quad 5 \quad 6 \quad 6$$

indicates that six data values have a first digit of seven. The leaves show that the data values are 72, 73, 73, 75, 76, and 76.

To focus on the shape indicated by the stem-and-leaf display, let us use a rectangle to contain the leaves of each stem. Doing so, we obtain the following.

```
 6 | 8  9
 7 | 2  3  3  5  6  6
 8 | 0  1  1  2  3  4  5  6
 9 | 1  2  2  2  4  5  5  6  7  8  8
10 | 0  0  2  4  6  6  6  7  8
11 | 2  3  5  5  8  9  9
12 | 4  6  7  8
13 | 2  4
14 | 1
```

Rotating this page counterclockwise onto its side provides a picture of the data that is similar to a histogram with classes of 60–69, 70–79, 80–89, and so on.

Although the stem-and-leaf display may appear to offer the same information as a histogram, it has two primary advantages.

1. The stem-and-leaf display is easier to construct by hand.
2. Within a class interval, the stem-and-leaf display provides more information than the histogram because the stem-and-leaf shows the actual data.

In a stretched stem-and-leaf display, whenever a stem value is stated twice, the first value corresponds to leaf values of 0–4, and the second value corresponds to leaf values of 5–9.

Just as a frequency distribution or histogram has no absolute number of classes, neither does a stem-and-leaf display have an absolute number of rows or stems. If we believe that our original stem-and-leaf display condensed the data too much, we can easily stretch the display by using two or more stems for each leading digit. For example, to use two stems for each leading digit, we would place all data values ending in 0, 1, 2, 3, and 4 in one row and all values ending in 5, 6, 7, 8, and 9 in a second row. The following stretched stem-and-leaf display illustrates this approach.

```
 6 | 8  9
 7 | 2  3  3
 7 | 5  6  6
 8 | 0  1  1  2  3  4
 8 | 5  6
 9 | 1  2  2  2  4
 9 | 5  5  6  7  8  8
10 | 0  0  2  4
10 | 6  6  6  7  8
11 | 2  3
11 | 5  5  8  9  9
12 | 4
12 | 6  7  8
13 | 2  4
13 |
14 | 1
```

Note that values 72, 73, and 73 have leaves in the 0–4 range and are shown with the first stem value of 7. The values 75, 76, and 76 have leaves in the 5–9 range and are shown with the second stem value of 7. This stretched stem-and-leaf display is similar to a frequency distribution with intervals of 65–69, 70–74, 75–79, and so on.

The preceding example showed a stem-and-leaf display for data with as many as three digits. Stem-and-leaf displays for data with more than three digits are possible. For example, consider the following data on the number of hamburgers sold by a fast-food restaurant for each of 15 weeks.

1565	1852	1644	1766	1888	1912	2044	1812
1790	1679	2008	1852	1967	1954	1733	

A stem-and-leaf display of these data follows.

Leaf unit = 10

```
15 | 6
16 | 4  7
17 | 3  6  9
18 | 1  5  5  8
19 | 1  5  6
20 | 0  4
```

A single digit is used to define each leaf in a stem-and-leaf display. The leaf unit indicates how to multiply the stem-and-leaf numbers in order to approximate the original data. Leaf units may be 100, 10, 1, 0.1, and so on.

Note that a single digit is used to define each leaf and that only the first three digits of each data value have been used to construct the display. At the top of the display we have specified Leaf unit = 10. To illustrate how to interpret the values in the display, consider the first stem, 15, and its associated leaf, 6. Combining these numbers, we obtain 156. To reconstruct an approximation of the original data value, we must multiply this number by 10, the value of the *leaf unit*. Thus, 156 × 10 = 1560 is an approximation of the original data value used to construct the stem-and-leaf display. Although it is not possible to reconstruct the exact data value from this stem-and-leaf display, the convention of using a single digit for each leaf enables stem-and-leaf displays to be constructed for data having a large number of digits. For stem-and-leaf displays where the leaf unit is not shown, the leaf unit is assumed to equal 1.

Exercises

Methods

22. Construct a stem-and-leaf display for the following data.

70	72	75	64	58	83	80	82
76	75	68	65	57	78	85	72

23. Construct a stem-and-leaf display for the following data.

11.3	9.6	10.4	7.5	8.3	10.5	10.0
9.3	8.1	7.7	7.5	8.4	6.3	8.8

24. Construct a stem-and-leaf display for the following data. Use a leaf unit of 10.

1161	1206	1478	1300	1604	1725	1361	1422
1221	1378	1623	1426	1557	1730	1706	1689

Applications

25. A psychologist developed a new test of adult intelligence. The test was administered to 20 individuals, and the following data were obtained.

114	99	131	124	117	102	106	127	119	115
98	104	144	151	132	106	125	122	118	118

Construct a stem-and-leaf display for the data.

26. The American Association of Individual Investors conducts an annual survey of discount brokers. The following prices charged are from a sample of 24 discount brokers (*AAII Journal,* January 2003). The two types of trades are a broker-assisted trade of 100 shares at $50 per share and an online trade of 500 shares at $50 per share.

Broker

Broker	Broker-Assisted 100 Shares at $50/Share	Online 500 Shares at $50/Share	Broker	Broker-Assisted 100 Shares at $50/Share	Online 500 Shares at $50/Share
Accutrade	30.00	29.95	Merrill Lynch Direct	50.00	29.95
Ameritrade	24.99	10.99	Muriel Siebert	45.00	14.95
Banc of America	54.00	24.95	NetVest	24.00	14.00
Brown & Co.	17.00	5.00	Recom Securities	35.00	12.95
Charles Schwab	55.00	29.95	Scottrade	17.00	7.00
CyberTrader	12.95	9.95	Sloan Securities	39.95	19.95
E*TRADE Securities	49.95	14.95	Strong Investments	55.00	24.95
First Discount	35.00	19.75	TD Waterhouse	45.00	17.95
Freedom Investments	25.00	15.00	T. Rowe Price	50.00	19.95
Harrisdirect	40.00	20.00	Vanguard	48.00	20.00
Investors National	39.00	62.50	Wall Street Discount	29.95	19.95
MB Trading	9.95	10.55	York Securities	40.00	36.00

a. Round the trading prices to the nearest dollar and develop a stem-and-leaf display for 100 shares at $50 per share. Comment on what you learned about broker-assisted trading prices.

b. Round the trading prices to the nearest dollar and develop a stretched stem-and-leaf display for 500 shares online at $50 per share. Comment on what you learned about online trading prices.

27. The prices per share for the 30 companies making up the Dow Jones Industrial Average are shown below (*The Wall Street Journal,* April 9, 2004).

StockPrices

Company	$/Share	Company	$/Share
Alcoa	$34	Honeywell	$35
Altria Group	55	IBM	93
American Express	52	Intel	27
American International	76	Johnson & Johnson	51
Boeing	41	J.P. Morgan Chase	41
Caterpillar	82	McDonald's	29
Citigroup	52	Merck	45
Coca-Cola	51	Microsoft	25
Disney	26	Pfizer	36
DuPont	43	Procter & Gamble	106
ExxonMobil	42	SBE Communications	24
General Electric	31	3M	82
General Motors	47	United Technologies	90
Hewlett-Packard	23	Verizon	37
Home Depot	36	Wal-Mart Stores	57

a. Develop a stem-and-leaf display.
b. Use the stem-and-leaf display to answer the following questions:
   - What does the grouping of the data in the stem-and-leaf display tell you about the prices per share for the 30 Dow Jones companies?
   - What is the price-per-share range for the majority of the companies?
   - How many companies have a price per share of $36?
   - What is the most frequently appearing price per share?
   - What should be considered a relatively high price per share? What percentage of the companies have a price per share in this range? Which companies have a price per share in this range, and what is the price per share for each?
c. Use *The Wall Street Journal* or another business publication to find the current price per share for each of the 30 Dow Jones Industrial Average companies. Construct a stem-and-leaf display for these data and use the display to comment on any changes in the prices per share since April 2004.

28. The 2004 Naples, Florida, mini marathon (13.1 miles) had 1228 registrants (*The Naples Daily News,* January 17, 2004). Competition was held in six age groups. The following data show the ages for a sample of 40 individuals who participated in the marathon.

Marathon

49	33	40	37	56
44	46	57	55	32
50	52	43	64	40
46	24	30	37	43
31	43	50	36	61
27	44	35	31	43
52	43	66	31	50
72	26	59	21	47

a. Show a stretched stem-and-leaf display.
b. What age group had the largest number of runners?
c. What age occurred most frequently?
d. A *Naples Daily News* feature article emphasized the number of runners who were "20-something." What percentage of the runners were in the 20-something age group? What do you suppose was the focus of the article?

2.4   Crosstabulations and Scatter Diagrams

Crosstabulations and scatter diagrams are used to summarize data in a way that reveals the relationship between two variables.

Thus far in this chapter, we focused on tabular and graphical methods used to summarize the data for *one variable at a time.* Often a manager or decision maker requires tabular and graphical methods that will assist in the understanding of the *relationship between two variables.* Crosstabulation and scatter diagrams are two such methods.

Crosstabulation

A **crosstabulation** is a tabular summary of data for two variables. Let us illustrate the use of a crosstabulation by considering the following application based on data from Zagat's Restaurant Review. The quality rating and the meal price data were collected for a sample of 300 restaurants located in the Los Angeles area. Table 2.10 shows the data for the first 10 restaurants. Data on a restaurant's quality rating and typical meal price are reported. Quality rating is a qualitative variable with rating categories of good, very good, and excellent. Meal price is a quantitative variable that ranges from $10 to $49.

A crosstabulation of the data for this application is shown in Table 2.11. The left and top margin labels define the classes for the two variables. In the left margin, the row labels (good, very good, and excellent) correspond to the three classes of the quality rating variable. In the top margin, the column labels ($10–19, $20–29, $30–39, and $40–49) correspond to the four classes of the meal price variable. Each restaurant in the sample provides a quality

TABLE 2.10   QUALITY RATING AND MEAL PRICE FOR 300 LOS ANGELES RESTAURANTS

Restaurant

Restaurant	Quality Rating	Meal Price ($)
1	Good	18
2	Very Good	22
3	Good	28
4	Excellent	38
5	Very Good	33
6	Good	28
7	Very Good	19
8	Very Good	11
9	Very Good	23
10	Good	13
.	.	.
.	.	.
.	.	.

rating and a meal price. Thus, each restaurant in the sample is associated with a cell appearing in one of the rows and one of the columns of the crosstabulation. For example, restaurant 5 is identified as having a very good quality rating and a meal price of $33. This restaurant belongs to the cell in row 2 and column 3 of Table 2.11. In constructing a crosstabulation, we simply count the number of restaurants that belong to each of the cells in the crosstabulation table.

In reviewing Table 2.11, we see that the greatest number of restaurants in the sample (64) have a very good rating and a meal price in the $20–29 range. Only two restaurants have an excellent rating and a meal price in the $10–19 range. Similar interpretations of the other frequencies can be made. In addition, note that the right and bottom margins of the crosstabulation provide the frequency distributions for quality rating and meal price separately. From the frequency distribution in the right margin, we see that data on quality ratings show 84 good restaurants, 150 very good restaurants, and 66 excellent restaurants. Similarly, the bottom margin shows the frequency distribution for the meal price variable.

Dividing the totals in the right margin of the crosstabulation by the total for that column provides a relative and percent frequency distribution for the quality rating variable.

Quality Rating	Relative Frequency	Percent Frequency
Good	.28	28
Very Good	.50	50
Excellent	.22	22
Total	1.00	100

TABLE 2.11   CROSSTABULATION OF QUALITY RATING AND MEAL PRICE FOR 300 LOS ANGELES RESTAURANTS

Quality Rating	Meal Price				
	$10–19	$20–29	$30–39	$40–49	Total
Good	42	40	2	0	84
Very Good	34	64	46	6	150
Excellent	2	14	28	22	66
Total	78	118	76	28	300

From the percent frequency distribution we see that 28% of the restaurants were rated good, 50% were rated very good, and 22% were rated excellent.

Dividing the totals in the bottom row of the crosstabulation by the total for that row provides a relative and percent frequency distribution for the meal price variable.

Meal Price	Relative Frequency	Percent Frequency
$10–19	.26	26
$20–29	.39	39
$30–39	.25	25
$40–49	.09	9
Total	1.00	100

Note that the sum of the values in each column do not add exactly to the column total, because the values being summed are rounded. From the percent frequency distribution we see that 26% of the meal prices are in the lowest price class ($10–19), 39% are in the next higher class, and so on.

The frequency and relative frequency distributions constructed from the margins of a crosstabulation provide information about each of the variables individually, but they do not shed any light on the relationship between the variables. The primary value of a crosstabulation lies in the insight it offers about the relationship between the variables. A review of the crosstabulation in Table 2.11 reveals that higher meal prices are associated with the higher quality restaurants, and the lower meal prices are associated with the lower quality restaurants.

Converting the entries in a crosstabulation into row percentages or column percentages can provide more insight into the relationship between the two variables. For row percentages, the results of dividing each frequency in Table 2.11 by its corresponding row total are shown in Table 2.12. Each row of Table 2.12 is a percent frequency distribution of meal price for one of the quality rating categories. Of the restaurants with the lowest quality rating (good), we see that the greatest percentages are for the less expensive restaurants (50% have $10–19 meal prices and 47.6% have $20–29 meal prices). Of the restaurants with the highest quality rating (excellent), we see that the greatest percentages are for the more expensive restaurants (42.4% have $30–39 meal prices and 33.4% have $40–49 meal prices). Thus, we continue to see that the more expensive meals are associated with the higher quality restaurants.

Crosstabulation is widely used for examining the relationship between two variables. In practice, the final reports for many statistical studies include a large number of crosstabulation tables. In the Los Angeles restaurant survey, the crosstabulation is based on one qualitative variable (quality rating) and one quantitative variable (meal price). Crosstabulations can also be developed when both variables are qualitative and when both variables are quantitative. When quantitative variables are used, however, we must first create classes for the values of the variable. For instance, in the restaurant example we grouped the meal prices into four classes ($10–19, $20–29, $30–39, and $40–49).

TABLE 2.12   ROW PERCENTAGES FOR EACH QUALITY RATING CATEGORY

Quality Rating	Meal Price $10–19	$20–29	$30–39	$40–49	Total
Good	50.0	47.6	2.4	0.0	100
Very Good	22.7	42.7	30.6	4.0	100
Excellent	3.0	21.2	42.4	33.4	100

Simpson's Paradox

The data in two or more crosstabulations are often combined or aggregated to produce a summary crosstabulation showing how two variables are related. In such cases, we must be careful in drawing conclusions about the relationship between the two variables in the aggregated crosstabulation. In some cases the conclusions based upon the aggregated crosstabulation can be completely reversed if we look at the unaggregated data, an occurrence known as **Simpson's paradox**. To provide an illustration of Simpson's paradox we consider an example involving the analysis of verdicts for two judges in two types of courts.

Judges Ron Luckett and Dennis Kendall presided over cases in Common Pleas Court and Municipal Court during the past three years. Some of the verdicts they rendered were appealed. In most of these cases the appeals court upheld the original verdicts, but in some cases those verdicts were reversed. For each judge a crosstabulation was developed based upon two variables: Verdict (upheld or reversed) and Type of Court (Common Pleas and Municipal). Suppose that the two crosstabulations were then combined by aggregating the type of court data. The resulting aggregated crosstabulation contains two variables: Verdict (upheld or reversed) and Judge (Luckett or Kendall). This crosstabulation shows the number of appeals in which the verdict was upheld and the number in which the verdict was reversed for both judges. The following crosstabulation shows these results along with the column percentages in parentheses next to each value.

Verdict	Judge		Total
	Luckett	**Kendall**	
Upheld	129 (86%)	110 (88%)	239
Reversed	21 (14%)	15 (12%)	36
Total (%)	150 (100%)	125 (100%)	275

A review of the column percentages shows that 14% of the verdicts were reversed for Judge Luckett, but only 12% of the verdicts were reversed for Judge Kendall. Thus, we might conclude that Judge Kendall is doing a better job because a higher percentage of his verdicts are being upheld. A problem arises with this conclusion, however.

The following crosstabulations show the cases tried by Luckett and Kendall in the two courts; column percentages are also shown in parentheses next to each value.

	Judge Luckett				Judge Kendall		
Verdict	**Common Pleas**	**Municipal Court**	**Total**	**Verdict**	**Common Pleas**	**Municipal Court**	**Total**
Upheld	29 (91%)	100 (85%)	129	**Upheld**	90 (90%)	20 (80%)	110
Reversed	3 (9%)	18 (15%)	21	**Reversed**	10 (10%)	5 (20%)	15
Total (%)	32 (100%)	118 (100%)	150	**Total (%)**	100 (100%)	25 (100%)	125

From the crosstabulation and column percentages for Luckett, we see that his verdicts were upheld in 91% of the Common Pleas Court cases and in 85% of the Municipal Court cases. From the crosstabulation and column percentages for Kendall, we see that his verdicts were upheld in 90% of the Common Pleas Court cases and in 80% of the Municipal Court cases. Comparing the column percentages for the two judges, we see that Judge Luckett demonstrates a better record than Judge Kendall in both courts. This result contradicts the conclusion we reached when we aggregated the data across both courts for the original crosstabulation. It appeared then that Judge Kendall had the better record. This example illustrates Simpson's paradox.

The original crosstabulation was obtained by aggregating the data in the separate crosstabulations for the two courts. Note that for both judges the percentage of appeals that resulted in reversals was much higher in Municipal Court than in Common Pleas Court. Because Judge Luckett tried a much higher percentage of his cases in Municipal Court, the aggregated data favored Judge Kendall. When we look at the crosstabulations for the two courts separately, however, Judge Luckett clearly shows the better record. Thus, for the original crosstabulation, we see that the *type of court* is a hidden variable that cannot be ignored when evaluating the records of the two judges.

Because of Simpson's paradox, we need to be especially careful when drawing conclusions using aggregated data. Before drawing any conclusions about the relationship between two variables shown for a crosstabulation involving aggregated data, you should investigate whether any hidden variables could affect the results.

Scatter Diagram and Trendline

A **scatter diagram** is a graphical presentation of the relationship between two quantitative variables, and a **trendline** is a line that provides an approximation of the relationship. As an illustration, consider the advertising/sales relationship for a stereo and sound equipment store in San Francisco. On 10 occasions during the past three months, the store used weekend television commercials to promote sales at its stores. The managers want to investigate whether a relationship exists between the number of commercials shown and sales at the store during the following week. Sample data for the 10 weeks with sales in hundreds of dollars are shown in Table 2.13.

Figure 2.7 shows the scatter diagram and the trendline* for the data in Table 2.13. The number of commercials (x) is shown on the horizontal axis and the sales (y) are shown on the vertical axis. For week 1, $x = 2$ and $y = 50$. A point with those coordinates is plotted on the scatter diagram. Similar points are plotted for the other nine weeks. Note that during two of the weeks one commercial was shown, during two of the weeks two commercials were shown, and so on.

The completed scatter diagram in Figure 2.7 indicates a positive relationship between the number of commercials and sales. Higher sales are associated with a higher number of commercials. The relationship is not perfect in that all points are not on a straight line. However, the general pattern of the points and the trendline suggest that the overall relationship is positive.

Some general scatter diagram patterns and the types of relationships they suggest are shown in Figure 2.8. The top left panel depicts a positive relationship similar to the one for

TABLE 2.13   SAMPLE DATA FOR THE STEREO AND SOUND EQUIPMENT STORE

Week	Number of Commercials x	Sales ($100s) y
1	2	50
2	5	57
3	1	41
4	3	54
5	4	54
6	1	38
7	5	63
8	3	48
9	4	59
10	2	46

*The equation of the trendline is $y = 4.95x + 36.15$. The slope of the trendline is 4.95 and the y-intercept (the point where the line intersects the y axis) is 36.15. We will discuss in detail the interpretation of the slope and y-intercept for a linear trendline in Chapter 12 when we study simple linear regression.

FIGURE 2.7   SCATTER DIAGRAM AND TRENDLINE FOR THE STEREO AND SOUND
EQUIPMENT STORE

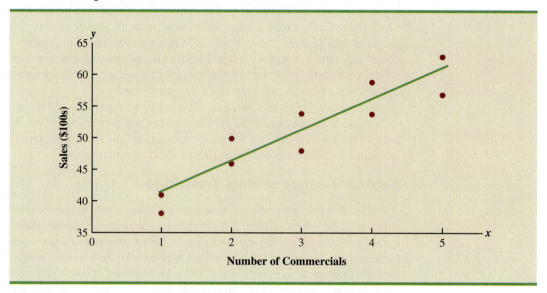

FIGURE 2.8   TYPES OF RELATIONSHIPS DEPICTED BY SCATTER DIAGRAMS

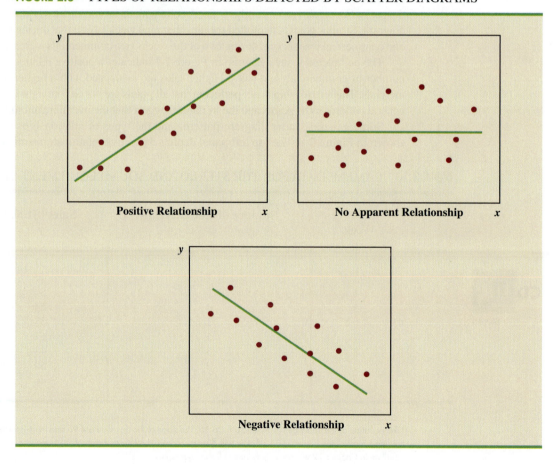

the number of commercials and sales example. In the top right panel, the scatter diagram shows no apparent relationship between the variables. The bottom panel depicts a negative relationship where y tends to decrease as x increases.

Exercises

Methods

Crosstab

29. The following data are for 30 observations involving two qualitative variables, x and y. The categories for x are A, B, and C; the categories for y are 1 and 2.

Observation	x	y	Observation	x	y
1	A	1	16	B	2
2	B	1	17	C	1
3	B	1	18	B	1
4	C	2	19	C	1
5	B	1	20	B	1
6	C	2	21	C	2
7	B	1	22	B	1
8	C	2	23	C	2
9	A	1	24	A	1
10	B	1	25	B	1
11	A	1	26	C	2
12	B	1	27	C	2
13	C	2	28	A	1
14	C	2	29	B	1
15	C	2	30	B	2

a. Develop a crosstabulation for the data, with x as the row variable and y as the column variable.
b. Compute the row percentages.
c. Compute the column percentages.
d. What is the relationship, if any, between x and y?

30. The following 20 observations are for two quantitative variables, x and y.

Scatter

Observation	x	y	Observation	x	y
1	−22	22	11	−37	48
2	−33	49	12	34	−29
3	2	8	13	9	−18
4	29	−16	14	−33	31
5	−13	10	15	20	−16
6	21	−28	16	−3	14
7	−13	27	17	−15	18
8	−23	35	18	12	17
9	14	−5	19	−20	−11
10	3	−3	20	−7	−22

a. Develop a scatter diagram for the relationship between x and y.
b. What is the relationship, if any, between x and y?

Applications

31. The following crosstabulation shows household income by educational level of the head of household (*Statistical Abstract of the United States: 2002*).

| | Household Income ($1000s) | | | | | |
Educational Level	Under 25	25.0–49.9	50.0–74.9	75.0–99.9	100 or more	Total
Not H.S. graduate	9285	4093	1589	541	354	15862
H.S. graduate	10150	9821	6050	2737	2028	30786
Some college	6011	8221	5813	3215	3120	26380
Bachelor's degree	2138	3985	3952	2698	4748	17521
Beyond bach. deg.	813	1497	1815	1589	3765	9479
Total	28397	27617	19219	10780	14015	100028

   a. Compute the row percentages and identify the percent frequency distributions of income for households in which the head is a high school graduate and in which the head holds a bachelor's degree.

   b. What percentage of households headed by high school graduates earn $75,000 or more? What percentage of households headed by bachelor's degree recipients earn $75,000 or more?

   c. Construct percent frequency histograms of income for households headed by persons with a high school degree and for those headed by persons with a bachelor's degree. Is any relationship evident between household income and educational level?

32. Refer again to the crosstabulation of household income by educational level shown in exercise 31.

   a. Compute column percentages and identify the percent frequency distributions displayed. What percentage of the heads of households did not graduate from high school?

   b. What percentage of the households earning $100,000 or more were headed by a person having schooling beyond a bachelor's degree? What percentage of the households headed by a person with schooling beyond a bachelor's degree earned over $100,000? Why are these two percentages different?

   c. Compare the percent frequency distributions for those households earning "Under 25," "100 or more," and for "Total." Comment on the relationship between household income and educational level of the head of household.

33. Recently, management at Oak Tree Golf Course received a few complaints about the condition of the greens. Several players complained that the greens are too fast. Rather than react to the comments of just a few, the Golf Association conducted a survey of 100 male and 100 female golfers. The survey results are summarized here.

Male Golfers

| | Greens Condition | |
Handicap	Too Fast	Fine
Under 15	10	40
15 or more	25	25

Female Golfers

| | Greens Condition | |
Handicap	Too Fast	Fine
Under 15	1	9
15 or more	39	51

   a. Combine these two crosstabulations into one with Male, Female as the row labels and the column labels Too Fast and Fine. Which group shows the highest percentage saying that the greens are too fast?

b. Refer to the initial crosstabulations. For those players with low handicaps (better players), which group (male or female) shows the highest percentage saying the greens are too fast?

c. Refer to the initial crosstabulations. For those players with higher handicaps, which group (male or female) shows the highest percentage saying the greens are too fast?

d. What conclusions can you draw about the preferences of men and women concerning the speed of the greens? Are the conclusions you draw from part (a) as compared with parts (b) and (c) consistent? Explain any apparent inconsistencies.

34. Table 2.14 provides financial data for a sample of 36 companies whose stock trades on the New York Stock Exchange (*Investor's Business Daily,* April 7, 2000). The data on Sales/Margins/ROE are a composite rating based on a company's sales growth rate, its profit margins, and its return on equity (ROE). EPS Rating is a measure of growth in earnings per share for the company.

TABLE 2.14   FINANCIAL DATA FOR A SAMPLE OF 36 COMPANIES

Company	EPS Rating	Relative Price Strength	Industry Group Relative Strength	Sales/Margins/ROE
Advo	81	74	B	A
Alaska Air Group	58	17	C	B
Alliant Tech	84	22	B	B
Atmos Energy	21	9	C	E
Bank of Am.	87	38	C	A
Bowater PLC	14	46	C	D
Callaway Golf	46	62	B	E
Central Parking	76	18	B	C
Dean Foods	84	7	B	C
Dole Food	70	54	E	C
Elec. Data Sys.	72	69	A	B
Fed. Dept. Store	79	21	D	B
Gateway	82	68	A	A
Goodyear	21	9	E	D
Hanson PLC	57	32	B	B
ICN Pharm.	76	56	A	D
Jefferson Plt.	80	38	D	C
Kroger	84	24	D	A
Mattel	18	20	E	D
McDermott	6	6	A	C
Monaco	97	21	D	A
Murphy Oil	80	62	B	B
Nordstrom	58	57	B	C
NYMAGIC	17	45	D	D
Office Depot	58	40	B	B
Payless Shoes	76	59	B	B
Praxair	62	32	C	B
Reebok	31	72	C	E
Safeway	91	61	D	A
Teco Energy	49	48	D	B
Texaco	80	31	D	C
US West	60	65	B	A
United Rental	98	12	C	A
Wachovia	69	36	E	B
Winnebago	83	49	D	A
York International	28	14	D	B

Source: Investor's Business Daily, April 7, 2000.

   a.   Prepare a crosstabulation of the data on Sales/Margins/ROE (rows) and EPS Rating (columns). Use classes of 0–19, 20–39, 40–59, 60–79, and 80–99 for EPS Rating.
   b.   Compute row percentages and comment on any relationship between the variables.

35.   Refer to the data in Table 2.14.
   a.   Prepare a crosstabulation of the data on Sales/Margins/ROE and Industry Group Relative Strength.
   b.   Prepare a frequency distribution for the data on Sales/Margins/ROE.
   c.   Prepare a frequency distribution for the data on Industry Group Relative Strength.
   d.   How has the crosstabulation helped in preparing the frequency distributions in parts (b) and (c)?

36.   Refer to the data in Table 2.14.
   a.   Prepare a scatter diagram of the data on EPS Rating and Relative Price Strength.
   b.   Comment on the relationship, if any, between the variables. (The meaning of the EPS Rating is described in exercise 34. Relative Price Strength is a measure of the change in the stock's price over the past 12 months. Higher values indicate greater strength.)

37.   The National Football League rates prospects position by position on a scale that ranges from 5 to 9. The ratings are interpreted as follows: 8–9 should start the first year; 7.0–7.9 should start; 6.0–6.9 will make the team as a backup; and 5.0–5.9 can make the club and contribute. Table 2.15 shows the position, weight, speed (seconds for 40 yards), and ratings for 40 NFL prospects (*USA Today*, April 14, 2000).
   a.   Prepare a crosstabulation of the data on Position (rows) and Speed (columns). Use classes of 4.00–4.49, 4.50–4.99, 5.00–5.49, and 5.50–5.99 for speed.
   b.   Comment on the relationship between Position and Speed based upon the crosstabulation developed in part (a).
   c.   Develop a scatter diagram of the data on Speed and Rating. Use the vertical axis for Rating.
   d.   Comment on the relationship, if any, between Speed and Rating.

Summary

A set of data, even if modest in size, is often difficult to interpret directly in the form in which it is gathered. Tabular and graphical methods provide procedures for organizing and summarizing data so that patterns are revealed and the data are more easily interpreted. Frequency distributions, relative frequency distributions, percent frequency distributions, bar graphs, and pie charts were presented as tabular and graphical procedures for summarizing qualitative data. Frequency distributions, relative frequency distributions, percent frequency distributions, histograms, cumulative frequency distributions, cumulative relative frequency distributions, cumulative percent frequency distributions, and ogives were presented as ways of summarizing quantitative data. A stem-and-leaf display provides an exploratory data analysis technique that can be used to summarize quantitative data. Crosstabulation was presented as a tabular method for summarizing data for two variables. The scatter diagram was introduced as a graphical method for showing the relationship between two quantitative variables. Figure 2.9 shows the tabular and graphical methods presented in this chapter.

With large data sets, computer software packages are essential in constructing tabular and graphical summaries of data. In the two chapter appendixes, we show how Minitab and Excel can be used for this purpose.

TABLE 2.15   NATIONAL FOOTBALL LEAGUE RATINGS FOR 40 DRAFT PROSPECTS

CD file

NFL

Observation	Name	Position	Weight	Speed	Rating
1	Peter Warrick	Wide receiver	194	4.53	9
2	Plaxico Burress	Wide receiver	231	4.52	8.8
3	Sylvester Morris	Wide receiver	216	4.59	8.3
4	Travis Taylor	Wide receiver	199	4.36	8.1
5	Laveranues Coles	Wide receiver	192	4.29	8
6	Dez White	Wide receiver	218	4.49	7.9
7	Jerry Porter	Wide receiver	221	4.55	7.4
8	Ron Dugans	Wide receiver	206	4.47	7.1
9	Todd Pinkston	Wide receiver	169	4.37	7
10	Dennis Northcutt	Wide receiver	175	4.43	7
11	Anthony Lucas	Wide receiver	194	4.51	6.9
12	Darrell Jackson	Wide receiver	197	4.56	6.6
13	Danny Farmer	Wide receiver	217	4.6	6.5
14	Sherrod Gideon	Wide receiver	173	4.57	6.4
15	Trevor Gaylor	Wide receiver	199	4.57	6.2
16	Cosey Coleman	Guard	322	5.38	7.4
17	Travis Claridge	Guard	303	5.18	7
18	Kaulana Noa	Guard	317	5.34	6.8
19	Leander Jordan	Guard	330	5.46	6.7
20	Chad Clifton	Guard	334	5.18	6.3
21	Manula Savea	Guard	308	5.32	6.1
22	Ryan Johanningmeir	Guard	310	5.28	6
23	Mark Tauscher	Guard	318	5.37	6
24	Blaine Saipaia	Guard	321	5.25	6
25	Richard Mercier	Guard	295	5.34	5.8
26	Damion McIntosh	Guard	328	5.31	5.3
27	Jeno James	Guard	320	5.64	5
28	Al Jackson	Guard	304	5.2	5
29	Chris Samuels	Offensive tackle	325	4.95	8.5
30	Stockar McDougle	Offensive tackle	361	5.5	8
31	Chris McIngosh	Offensive tackle	315	5.39	7.8
32	Adrian Klemm	Offensive tackle	307	4.98	7.6
33	Todd Wade	Offensive tackle	326	5.2	7.3
34	Marvel Smith	Offensive tackle	320	5.36	7.1
35	Michael Thompson	Offensive tackle	287	5.05	6.8
36	Bobby Williams	Offensive tackle	332	5.26	6.8
37	Darnell Alford	Offensive tackle	334	5.55	6.4
38	Terrance Beadles	Offensive tackle	312	5.15	6.3
39	Tutan Reyes	Offensive tackle	299	5.35	6.1
40	Greg Robinson-Ran	Offensive tackle	333	5.59	6

FIGURE 2.9   TABULAR AND GRAPHICAL METHODS FOR SUMMARIZING DATA

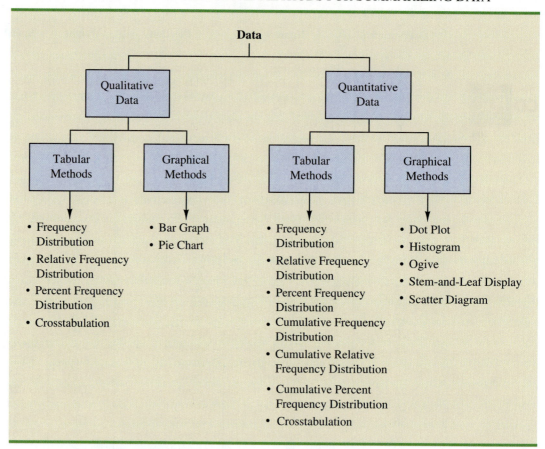

Glossary

Qualitative data Labels or names used to identify categories of like items.

Quantitative data Numerical values that indicate how much or how many.

Frequency distribution A tabular summary of data showing the number (frequency) of data values in each of several nonoverlapping classes.

Relative frequency distribution A tabular summary of data showing the fraction or proportion of data values in each of several nonoverlapping classes.

Percent frequency distribution A tabular summary of data showing the percentage of data values in each of several nonoverlapping classes.

Bar graph A graphical device for depicting qualitative data that have been summarized in a frequency, relative frequency, or percent frequency distribution.

Pie chart A graphical device for presenting data summaries based on subdivision of a circle into sectors that correspond to the relative frequency for each class.

Class midpoint The value halfway between the lower and upper class limits.

Dot plot A graphical device that summarizes data by the number of dots above each data value on the horizontal axis.

Histogram A graphical presentation of a frequency distribution, relative frequency distribution, or percent frequency distribution of quantitative data constructed by placing the class intervals on the horizontal axis and the frequencies, relative frequencies, or percent frequencies on the vertical axis.

Cumulative frequency distribution A tabular summary of quantitative data showing the number of data values that are less than or equal to the upper class limit of each class.

Cumulative relative frequency distribution A tabular summary of quantitative data showing the fraction or proportion of data values that are less than or equal to the upper class limit of each class.

Cumulative percent frequency distribution A tabular summary of quantitative data showing the percentage of data values that are less than or equal to the upper class limit of each class.

Ogive A graph of a cumulative distribution.

Exploratory data analysis Methods that use simple arithmetic and easy-to-draw graphs to summarize data quickly.

Stem-and-leaf display An exploratory data analysis technique that simultaneously rank orders quantitative data and provides insight about the shape of the distribution.

Crosstabulation A tabular summary of data for two variables. The classes for one variable are represented by the rows; the classes for the other variable are represented by the columns.

Simpson's paradox Conclusions drawn from two or more separate crosstabulations that can be reversed when the data are aggregated into a single crosstabulation.

Scatter diagram A graphical presentation of the relationship between two quantitative variables. One variable is shown on the horizontal axis and the other variable is shown on the vertical axis.

Trendline A line that provides an approximation of the relationship between two variables.

Key Formulas

Relative Frequency

$$\frac{\text{Frequency of the class}}{n} \qquad \textbf{(2.1)}$$

Approximate Class Width

$$\frac{\text{Largest data value} - \text{Smallest data value}}{\text{Number of classes}} \qquad \textbf{(2.2)}$$

Supplementary Exercises

38. The five top-selling vehicles during 2003 were the Chevrolet Silverado/C/K pickup, Dodge Ram pickup, Ford F-Series pickup, Honda Accord, and Toyota Camry (*Motor Trend*, 2003). Data from a sample of 50 vehicle purchases are presented in Table 2.16.

TABLE 2.16   DATA FOR 50 VEHICLE PURCHASES

CD file
AutoData

Silverado	Ram	Accord	Camry	Camry
Silverado	Silverado	Camry	Ram	F-Series
Ram	F-Series	Accord	Ram	Ram
Silverado	F-Series	F-Series	Silverado	Ram
Ram	Ram	Accord	Silverado	Camry
F-Series	Ram	Silverado	Accord	Silverado
Camry	F-Series	F-Series	F-Series	Silverado
F-Series	Silverado	F-Series	F-Series	Ram
Silverado	Silverado	Camry	Camry	F-Series
Silverado	F-Series	F-Series	Accord	Accord

a. Develop a frequency and percent frequency distribution.
b. What is the best-selling pickup truck, and what is the best-selling passenger car?
c. Show a pie chart.

39. Each of the *Fortune* 1000 companies belongs to one of several industry classifications (*Fortune,* April 17, 2000). A sample of 20 companies with their corresponding industry classification follows.

Company	Industry Classification	Company	Industry Classification
IBP	Food	Borden	Food
Intel	Electronics	McDonnell Douglas	Aerospace
Coca-Cola	Beverage	Morton International	Chemicals
Union Carbide	Chemicals	Quaker Oats	Food
General Electric	Electronics	PepsiCo	Beverage
Motorola	Electronics	Maytag	Electronics
Kellogg	Food	Textron	Aerospace
Dow Chemical	Chemicals	Sara Lee	Food
Campbell Soup	Food	Harris	Electronics
Ralston Purina	Food	Eaton	Electronics

a. Provide a frequency distribution showing the number of companies in each industry.
b. Provide a percent frequency distribution.
c. Provide a bar graph for the data.

40. *Golf Magazine*'s Top 100 Teachers were asked the question, "What is the most critical area that prevents golfers from reaching their potential?" The possible responses were lack of accuracy, poor approach shots, poor mental approach, lack of power, limited practice, poor putting, poor short game, and poor strategic decisions. The data obtained follow (*Golf Magazine,* February 2002):

Golf

Mental approach	Mental approach	Short game	Short game	Short game
Practice	Accuracy	Mental approach	Accuracy	Putting
Power	Approach shots	Accuracy	Short game	Putting
Accuracy	Mental approach	Mental approach	Accuracy	Power
Accuracy	Accuracy	Short game	Power	Short game
Accuracy	Putting	Mental approach	Strategic decisions	Accuracy
Short game	Power	Mental approach	Approach shots	Short game
Practice	Practice	Mental approach	Power	Power
Mental approach	Short game	Mental approach	Short game	Strategic decisions
Accuracy	Short game	Accuracy	Mental approach	Short game
Mental approach	Putting	Mental approach	Mental approach	Putting
Practice	Putting	Practice	Short game	Putting
Power	Mental approach	Short game	Practice	Strategic decisions
Accuracy	Short game	Accuracy	Practice	Putting
Accuracy	Short game	Accuracy	Short game	Putting
Accuracy	Approach shots	Short game	Mental approach	Practice
Short game	Short game	Strategic decisions	Short game	Short game
Practice	Practice	Short game	Practice	Strategic decisions
Mental approach	Strategic decisions	Strategic decisions	Power	Short game
Accuracy	Practice	Practice	Practice	Accuracy

a. Develop a frequency and percent frequency distribution.
b. Which four critical areas most often prevent golfers from reaching their potential?

TABLE 2.17   BOOK VALUE PER SHARE FOR DOW JONES INDUSTRIAL AVERAGE STOCKS

Dow

Company	Book Value per Share	Company	Book Value per Share
AT&T	14.59	Home Depot	7.71
Alcoa	12.30	Honeywell	11.25
Altria Group	8.96	IBM	13.37
American Express	9.04	Intel	5.39
Boeing	12.92	International Paper	21.37
Caterpillar	16.18	Johnson & Johnson	7.79
Citigroup	15.09	J.P. Morgan Chase	20.31
Coca-Cola	4.57	McDonald's	7.30
Disney	11.28	Merck	6.89
Du Pont	14.17	Microsoft	8.49
Eastman Kodak	9.93	Procter & Gamble	8.80
ExxonMobil	10.62	SBE Communications	9.69
General Electric	5.43	3M	14.93
General Motors	35.15	United Technologies	17.36
Hewlett-Packard	7.33	Wal-Mart Stores	7.85

41. The data in Table 2.17 show the book value per share for the 30 stocks that compose the Dow Jones Industrial Average (*Barron's,* March 10, 2003).
    a. Construct a frequency distribution to summarize the data. Use a class width of 6.00.
    b. Develop a relative frequency distribution.
    c. Construct a cumulative frequency distribution.
    d. Construct a cumulative relative frequency distribution.
    e. Construct a histogram as a graphical representation of the data. Comment on the shape of the distribution.

42. The closing prices of 40 common stocks follow (*Barron's,* March 10, 2003).

Comstock

29.63	34.00	43.25	8.75	37.88	8.63	7.63	30.38	35.25	19.38
9.25	16.50	38.00	53.38	16.63	1.25	48.38	18.00	9.38	9.25
10.00	25.02	18.00	8.00	28.50	24.25	21.63	18.50	33.63	31.13
32.25	29.63	79.38	11.38	38.88	11.50	52.00	14.00	9.00	33.50

   a. Construct frequency and relative frequency distributions.
   b. Construct cumulative frequency and cumulative relative frequency distributions.
   c. Construct a histogram.
   d. Using your summaries, make comments and observations about the price of common stock.

43. Ninety-four shadow stocks were reported by the American Association of Individual Investors. The term *shadow* indicates stocks for small to medium-sized firms not followed closely by the major brokerage houses. Information on where the stock was traded—New York Stock Exchange (NYSE), American Stock Exchange (AMEX), and over-the-counter (OTC)—the earnings per share, and the price/earnings ratio was provided for the following sample of 20 shadow stocks.

Shadow

Stock	Exchange	Earnings per Share ($)	Price/Earnings Ratio
Chemi-Trol	OTC	.39	27.30
Candie's	OTC	.07	36.20
TST/Impreso	OTC	.65	12.70

(continued)

Stock	Exchange	Earnings per Share ($)	Price/Earnings Ratio
Unimed Pharm.	OTC	.12	59.30
Skyline Chili	AMEX	.34	19.30
Cyanotech	OTC	.22	29.30
Catalina Light.	NYSE	.15	33.20
DDL Elect.	NYSE	.10	10.20
Euphonix	OTC	.09	49.70
Mesa Labs	OTC	.37	14.40
RCM Tech.	OTC	.47	18.60
Anuhco	AMEX	.70	11.40
Hello Direct	OTC	.23	21.10
Hilite Industries	OTC	.61	7.80
Alpha Tech.	OTC	.11	34.60
Wegener Group	OTC	.16	24.50
U.S. Home & Garden	OTC	.24	8.70
Chalone Wine	OTC	.27	44.40
Eng. Support Sys.	OTC	.89	16.70
Int. Remote Imaging	AMEX	.86	4.70

a. Provide frequency and relative frequency distributions for the exchange data. Where are most shadow stocks listed?

b. Provide frequency and relative frequency distributions for the earnings per share and price/earnings ratio data. Use classes of 0.00–0.19, 0.20–0.39, and so on, for the earnings per share data and classes of 0.0–9.9, 10.0–19.9, and so on for the price/earnings ratio data. What observations and comments can you make about the shadow stocks?

44. A state-by-state listing of per capita personal income follows (Bureau of Economic Analysis, *Current Population Survey,* March 2000).

CD file

Income

Ala.	21,500	Ky.	21,551	N.D.	21,708
Alaska	25,771	La.	21,385	Ohio	25,239
Ariz.	23,152	Maine	23,002	Okla.	21,056
Ark.	20,393	Md.	30,023	Ore.	24,775
Calif.	27,579	Mass.	32,902	Penn.	26,889
Colo.	28,821	Mich.	25,979	R.I.	26,924
Conn.	37,700	Minn.	27,667	S.C.	21,387
Del.	29,932	Miss.	18,998	S.D.	22,201
D.C.	37,325	Mo.	24,447	Tenn.	23,615
Fla.	25,922	Mont.	20,427	Texas	25,028
Ga.	25,106	Neb.	24,786	Utah	21,096
Hawaii	26,210	Nev.	27,360	Vt.	24,217
Idaho	21,080	N.H.	29,219	Va.	27,489
Ill.	28,976	N.J.	33,953	Wash.	28,066
Ind.	24,302	N.M.	20,008	W. Va.	19,373
Iowa	24,007	N.Y.	31,679	Wis.	25,184
Kan.	25,049	N.C.	24,122	Wyo.	23,225

Develop a frequency distribution, a relative frequency distribution, and a histogram.

45. *Drug Store News* (September 2002) provided data on annual pharmacy sales for the leading pharmacy retailers in the United States. The following data are annual sales in millions.

Retailer	Sales	Retailer	Sales
Ahold USA	$ 1700	Medicine Shoppe	$ 1757
CVS	12700	Rite-Aid	8637
Eckerd	7739	Safeway	2150
Kmart	1863	Walgreens	11660
Kroger	3400	Wal-Mart	7250

a. Show a stem-and-leaf display.
b. Identify the annual sales levels for the smallest, medium, and largest drug retailers.
c. What are the two largest drug retailers?

46. The daily high and low temperatures for 20 cities follow (*USA Today,* May 9, 2000).

HighLow

City	High	Low	City	High	Low
Athens	75	54	Melbourne	66	50
Bangkok	92	74	Montreal	64	52
Cairo	84	57	Paris	77	55
Copenhagen	64	39	Rio de Janeiro	80	61
Dublin	64	46	Rome	81	54
Havana	86	68	Seoul	64	50
Hong Kong	81	72	Singapore	90	75
Johannesburg	61	50	Sydney	68	55
London	73	48	Tokyo	79	59
Manila	93	75	Vancouver	57	43

a. Prepare a stem-and-leaf display for the high temperatures.
b. Prepare a stem-and-leaf display for the low temperatures.
c. Compare the stem-and-leaf displays from parts (a) and (b), and make some comments about the differences between daily high and low temperatures.
d. Use the stem-and-leaf display from part (a) to determine the number of cities having a high temperature of 80 degrees or above.
e. Provide frequency distributions for both high and low temperature data.

47. Refer to the data set for high and low temperatures for 20 cities in exercise 46.
a. Develop a scatter diagram to show the relationship between the two variables, high temperature and low temperature.
b. Comment on the relationship between high and low temperature.

48. A study of job satisfaction was conducted for four occupations. Job satisfaction was measured using an 18-item questionnaire with each question receiving a response score of 1 to 5 with higher scores indicating greater satisfaction. The sum of the 18 scores provides the job satisfaction score for each individual in the sample. The data are as follow.

OccupSat

Occupation	Satisfaction Score	Occupation	Satisfaction Score	Occupation	Satisfaction Score
Lawyer	42	Physical Therapist	78	Systems Analyst	60
Physical Therapist	86	Systems Analyst	44	Physical Therapist	59
Lawyer	42	Systems Analyst	71	Cabinetmaker	78
Systems Analyst	55	Lawyer	50	Physical Therapist	60

(continued)

Occupation	Satisfaction Score	Occupation	Satisfaction Score	Occupation	Satisfaction Score
Lawyer	38	Lawyer	48	Physical Therapist	50
Cabinetmaker	79	Cabinetmaker	69	Cabinetmaker	79
Lawyer	44	Physical Therapist	80	Systems Analyst	62
Systems Analyst	41	Systems Analyst	64	Lawyer	45
Physical Therapist	55	Physical Therapist	55	Cabinetmaker	84
Systems Analyst	66	Cabinetmaker	64	Physical Therapist	62
Lawyer	53	Cabinetmaker	59	Systems Analyst	73
Cabinetmaker	65	Cabinetmaker	54	Cabinetmaker	60
Lawyer	74	Systems Analyst	76	Lawyer	64
Physical Therapist	52				

a.   Provide a crosstabulation of occupation and job satisfaction score.

b.   Compute the row percentages for your crosstabulation in part (a).

c.   What observations can you make concerning the level of job satisfaction for these occupations?

49.   Do larger companies generate more revenue? The following data show the number of employees and annual revenue for a sample of 20 *Fortune* 1000 companies (*Fortune, April 17, 2000*).

CD file

RevEmps

Company	Employees	Revenue ($ millions)	Company	Employees	Revenue ($ millions)
Sprint	77,600	19,930	American Financial	9,400	3,334
Chase Manhattan	74,801	33,710	Fluor	53,561	12,417
Computer Sciences	50,000	7,660	Phillips Petroleum	15,900	13,852
Wells Fargo	89,355	21,795	Cardinal Health	36,000	25,034
Sunbeam	12,200	2,398	Borders Group	23,500	2,999
CBS	29,000	7,510	MCI Worldcom	77,000	37,120
Time Warner	69,722	27,333	Consolidated Edison	14,269	7,491
Steelcase	16,200	2,743	IBP	45,000	14,075
Georgia-Pacific	57,000	17,796	Super Value	50,000	17,421
Toro	1,275	4,673	H&R Block	4,200	1,669

a.   Prepare a scatter diagram to show the relationship between the variables Revenue and Employees.

b.   Comment on any relationship between the variables.

50.   A survey of commercial buildings served by the Cincinnati Gas & Electric Company asked what main heating fuel was used and what year the building was constructed. A partial crosstabulation of the findings follows.

Year Constructed	Fuel Type				
	Electricity	Natural Gas	Oil	Propane	Other
1973 or before	40	183	12	5	7
1974–1979	24	26	2	2	0
1980–1986	37	38	1	0	6
1987–1991	48	70	2	0	1

a. Complete the crosstabulation by showing the row totals and column totals.
b. Show the frequency distributions for year constructed and for fuel type.
c. Prepare a crosstabulation showing column percentages.
d. Prepare a crosstabulation showing row percentages.
e. Comment on the relationship between year constructed and fuel type.

51. Table 2.18 contains a portion of the data on the file named Fortune on the CD that accompanies the text. It provides data on stockholders' equity, market value, and profits for a sample of 50 *Fortune* 500 companies.

TABLE 2.18 DATA FOR A SAMPLE OF 50 *FORTUNE 500* COMPANIES

Fortune

Company	Stockholders' Equity ($1000s)	Market Value ($1000s)	Profit ($1000s)
AGCO	982.1	372.1	60.6
AMP	2698.0	12017.6	2.0
Apple Computer	1642.0	4605.0	309.0
Baxter International	2839.0	21743.0	315.0
Bergen Brunswick	629.1	2787.5	3.1
Best Buy	557.7	10376.5	94.5
Charles Schwab	1429.0	35340.6	348.5
.	.	.	.
.	.	.	.
.	.	.	.
Walgreen	2849.0	30324.7	511.0
Westvaco	2246.4	2225.6	132.0
Whirlpool	2001.0	3729.4	325.0
Xerox	5544.0	35603.7	395.0

a. Prepare a crosstabulation for the variables Stockholders' Equity and Profit. Use classes of 0–200, 200–400, . . . , 1000–1200 for Profit, and classes of 0–1200, 1200–2400, . . . , 4800–6000 for Stockholders' Equity.
b. Compute the row percentages for your crosstabulation in part (a).
c. What relationship, if any, do you notice between Profit and Stockholders' Equity?

52. Refer to the data set in Table 2.18.
a. Prepare a crosstabulation for the variables Market Value and Profit.
b. Compute the row percentages for your crosstabulation in part (a).
c. Comment on any relationship between the variables.

53. Refer to the data set in Table 2.18.
a. Prepare a scatter diagram to show the relationship between the variables Profit and Stockholders' Equity.
b. Comment on any relationship between the variables.

54. Refer to the data set in Table 2.18.
a. Prepare a scatter diagram to show the relationship between the variables Market Value and Stockholders' Equity.
b. Comment on any relationship between the variables.

Case Problem # Pelican Stores

Pelican Stores is a chain of women's apparel stores operating throughout the country. The chain recently ran a promotion in which discount coupons were sent to customers of related stores. Data collected for a sample of 100 in-store credit card transactions during one day

TABLE 2.19   DATA FOR A SAMPLE OF 100 CREDIT CARD PURCHASES AT PELICAN STORES

Pelican

Customer	Method of Payment	Items	Discount Amount	Sales	Gender	Marital Status	Age
1	Discover	1	0.00	39.50	Male	Married	32
2	Proprietary Card	1	25.60	102.40	Female	Married	36
3	Proprietary Card	1	0.00	22.50	Female	Married	32
4	Proprietary Card	5	121.10	100.40	Female	Married	28
5	Mastercard	2	0.00	54.00	Female	Married	34
.	.	.	.	.	.	.	.
.	.	.	.	.	.	.	.
.	.	.	.	.	.	.	.
96	Mastercard	1	0.00	39.50	Female	Married	44
97	Proprietary Card	9	82.75	253.00	Female	Married	30
98	Proprietary Card	10	18.00	287.59	Female	Married	52
99	Proprietary Card	2	31.40	47.60	Female	Married	30
100	Proprietary Card	1	11.06	28.44	Female	Married	44

in November 2002 are contained in the file named Pelican. Table 2.19 shows a portion of the data set. A nonzero amount for the Discount variable indicates that the customer brought in the promotional coupons and used them. For a very few customers, the discount amount is actually greater than the sales amount (see customer 4). The sales amount is net of discounts and returns.

Pelican's management would like to use this sample data to learn about its customer base and to evaluate the promotion involving discount coupons.

Managerial Report

Use the tabular and graphical methods of descriptive statistics to help management develop a customer profile and to evaluate the promotional campaign. At a minimum, your report should include the following.

1. Percent frequency distributions for key variables.
2. A bar graph or pie chart showing the percentage of customer purchases attributable to the promotional campaign.
3. A crosstabulation of type of customer (regular or promotional) versus sales. Comment on any similarities or differences present.
4. A scatter diagram of sales versus discount for only those customers responding to the promotion. Comment on any relationship apparent between sales and discount.
5. A scatter diagram to explore the relationship between sales and customer age.

Appendix 2.1   Using Minitab for Tabular and Graphical Presentations

Minitab offers extensive capabilities for constructing tabular and graphical summaries of data. In this appendix we show how Minitab can be used to construct several graphical summaries and the tabular summary of a crosstabulation. The graphical methods presented include the dot plot, the histogram, the stem-and-leaf display, and the scatter diagram.

Dot Plot

Audit

We use the audit time data in Table 2.5 to demonstrate. The data are in column C1 of a Minitab worksheet. The following steps will generate a dot plot.

Step 1. Select the **Graph** menu and choose **Dotplot**
Step 2. Select **One Y, Simple** and click **OK**
Step 3. When the Dotplot-One Y, Simple dialog box appears:
      Enter C1 in the **Graph Variables** box
      Click **OK**

Histogram

Audit

We show how to construct a histogram with frequencies on the vertical axis using the audit time data in Table 2.5. The data are in column C1 of a Minitab worksheet. The following steps will generate a histogram for audit times.

Step 1. Select the **Graph** menu
Step 2. Choose **Histogram**
Step 3. Select **Simple** and click **OK**
Step 4. When the Histogram-Simple dialog box appears:
      Enter C1 in the **Graph Variables** box
      Click **OK**
Step 5. When the Histogram appears:
      Position the mouse pointer over any one of the bars
      Double-click
Step 6. When the Edit Bars dialog box appears:
      Click on the **Binning** tab
      Select **Midpoint** for Interval Type
      Select **Midpoint/Cutpoint positions** for Interval Definition
      Enter 12:32/5 in the **Midpoint/Cutpoint positions** box*
      Click **OK**

Stem-and-Leaf Display

ApTest

We use the aptitude test data in Table 2.9 to demonstrate the construction of a stem-and-leaf display. The data are in column C1 of a Minitab worksheet. The following steps will generate the stretched stem-and-leaf display shown in Section 2.3.

Step 1. Select the **Graph** menu
Step 2. Choose **Stem-and-Leaf**
Step 3. When the Stem-and-Leaf dialog box appears:
      Enter C1 in the **Graph Variables** box
      Click **OK**

Scatter Diagram

Stereo

We use the stereo and sound equipment store data in Table 2.13 to demonstrate the construction of a scatter diagram. The weeks are numbered from 1 to 10 in column C1, the data for number of commercials are in column C2, and the data for sales are in column C3 of a Minitab worksheet. The following steps will generate the scatter diagram shown in Figure 2.7.

---

*The entry 12:35/5 indicates that 12 is the midpoint of the first class, 35 is the midpoint of the last class, and 5 is the class width.

Step 1. Select the **Graph** menu
Step 2. Choose **Scatterplot**
Step 3. Select **Simple** and click **OK**
Step 4. When the Scatterplot-Simple dialog box appears:
   Enter C3 under **Y variables** and C2 under **X variables**
   Click **OK**

Crosstabulation

Restaurant

We use the data from Zagat's restaurant review, part of which is shown in Table 2.10, to demonstrate. The restaurants are numbered from 1 to 300 in column C1 of the Minitab worksheet. The quality ratings are in column C2, and the meal prices are in column C3.

Minitab can only create a crosstabulation for qualitative variables and meal price is a quantitative variable: So we need to first code the meal price data by specifying the class to which each meal price belongs. The following steps will code the meal price data to create four classes of meal price in column C4: $10–19, $20–29, $30–39, and $40–49.

Step 1. Select the **Data** menu
Step 2. Choose **Code**
Step 3. Choose **Numeric to Text**
Step 4. When the Code-Numeric to Text dialog box appears:
   Enter C3 in the **Code data from columns** box
   Enter C4 in the **Into columns** box
   Enter 10:19 in the first **Original values** box and $10–19 in the adjacent **New** box
   Enter 20:29 in the second **Original values** box and $20–29 in the adjacent **New** box
   Enter 30:39 in the third **Original values** box and $30–39 in the adjacent **New** box
   Enter 40:49 in the fourth **Original values** box and $40–49 in the adjacent **New** box
   Click **OK**

For each meal price in column C3 the associated meal price category will now appear in column C4. We can now develop a crosstabulation for quality rating and the meal price categories by using the data in columns C2 and C4. The following steps will create a crosstabulation containing the same information as shown in Table 2.11.

Step 1. Select the **Stat** menu
Step 2. Choose **Tables**
Step 3. Choose **Cross Tabulation and Chi-Square**
Step 4. When the Cross Tabulation and Chi-Square dialog box appears:
   Enter C2 in the **For rows** box and C4 in the **For columns** box
   Select **Counts** under Display
   Click **OK**

Appendix 2.2 # Using Excel for Tabular and Graphical Presentations

Excel offers extensive capabilities for constructing tabular and graphical summaries of data. Three of the most powerful tools available are the Insert Function tool, the Chart Wizard, and the PivotTable Report.

Functions and the Insert Function Tool

Excel provides a variety of functions that are useful for statistical analysis. If we know what function we want and how to use it, we can simply enter the function directly into a cell of an Excel worksheet. If not, Excel provides an Insert Function tool to help in identifying the functions available and in using them.

Insert Function tool To access the Insert Function tool, click f_x on the formula bar or select the **Insert** menu and choose f_x **Function.** The **Insert Function** dialog box will then appear (see Figure 2.10). The **Or select a category box** shows a list of the categories of Excel functions; we selected **Statistical** in Figure 2.10. With **Statistical** selected, a list of all the statistical functions available is displayed in the **Select a function** box. Here, we highlight the **COUNTIF** function. Once a function is highlighted, the proper form for the function along with a brief description appears below the **Select a function** box. To obtain assistance in properly using the function, click **OK.**

SoftDrink

Frequency distributions We show how the COUNTIF function can be used to construct a frequency distribution for the data on soft drink purchases in Table 2.1. Refer to Figure 2.11 as we describe the tasks involved. The formula worksheet (shows the functions and formulas used) is set in the background, and the value worksheet (shows the results obtained using the functions and formulas) appears in the foreground.

The label "Brand Purchased" and the data for the 50 soft drink purchases are in cells A1:A51. We also entered labels in cells C1:D1 and the soft drink names into cells C2:C6. Excel's COUNTIF function can be used to count the number of times each soft drink appears

FIGURE 2.10   EXCEL'S INSERT FUNCTION DIALOG BOX

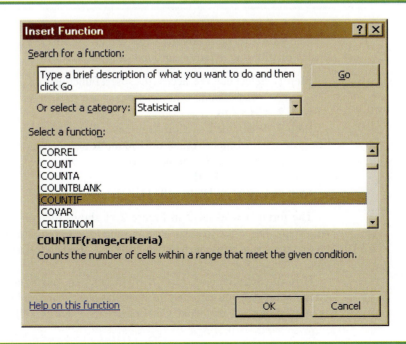

FIGURE 2.11   FREQUENCY DISTRIBUTION FOR SOFT DRINK PURCHASES
CONSTRUCTED USING EXCEL'S COUNTIF FUNCTION

	A	B	C	D	E
1	**Brand Purchased**		**Soft Drink**	**Frequency**	
2	Coke Classic		Coke Classic	=COUNTIF($A$2:$A$51,C2)	
3	Diet Coke		Diet Coke	=COUNTIF($A$2:$A$51,C3)	
4	Pepsi-Cola		Dr. Pepper	=COUNTIF($A$2:$A$51,C4)	
5	Diet Coke		Pepsi-Cola	=COUNTIF($A$2:$A$51,C5)	
6	Coke Classic		Sprite	=COUNTIF($A$2:$A$51,C6)	
7	Coke Classic				
8	Dr. Pepper				
9	Diet Coke				
10	Pepsi-Cola				
45	Pepsi-Cola				
46	Pepsi-Cola				
47	Pepsi-Cola				
48	Coke Classic				
49	Dr. Pepper				
50	Pepsi-Cola				
51	Sprite				
52					

Note: Rows 11–44 are hidden.

	A	B	C	D	E
1	**Brand Purchased**		**Soft Drink**	**Frequency**	
2	Coke Classic		Coke Classic	19	
3	Diet Coke		Diet Coke	8	
4	Pepsi-Cola		Dr. Pepper	5	
5	Diet Coke		Pepsi-Cola	13	
6	Coke Classic		Sprite	5	
7	Coke Classic				
8	Dr. Pepper				
9	Diet Coke				
10	Pepsi-Cola				
45	Pepsi-Cola				
46	Pepsi-Cola				
47	Pepsi-Cola				
48	Coke Classic				
49	Dr. Pepper				
50	Pepsi-Cola				
51	Sprite				
52					

in cells A2:A51. The following steps utilize the Insert Function tool to produce the frequency distribution in the foreground of Figure 2.11.

Step 1. Select cell **D2**, access the Insert Function tool, and choose **COUNTIF** from the list of statistical functions

Step 2. Click **OK**

Step 3. When the Function Arguments dialog box appears:
Enter $A$2:$A$51 in the **Range** box
Enter C2 in the **Criteria** box
Click **OK**

Step 4. Copy cell D2 to cells D3:D6

The formula worksheet in Figure 2.11 shows the cell formulas inserted by applying these steps. The value worksheet shows the values computed using these cell formulas; we see that the Excel worksheet shows the same frequency distribution that we developed in Table 2.2.

If you are familiar with the COUNTIF function, and do not need the assistance of the Insert Function tool, you can enter the formulas directly into cells D2:D6. For instance, to count the number of times that Coke Classic appears, enter the following formula into cell D2:

=COUNTIF($A$2:$A$51,C2)

To count the number of times the other soft drinks appear, copy this formula into cells D3:D6.

Many more of Excel's functions will be demonstrated in future chapter appendixes. Depending on the complexity of the function, we will either enter it directly into the appropriate cell or utilize the Insert Function tool.

Chart Wizard

Excel's Chart Wizard provides extensive capabilities for developing graphical presentations. This tool allows us to go beyond what can be done with functions and formulas alone. We show how it can be used to construct bar graphs, histograms, and scatter diagrams.

Bar graphs and histograms Here we show how the Chart Wizard can be used to construct bar graphs and histograms. Let us start by developing a bar graph for the soft drink data; we constructed a frequency distribution in Figure 2.11. The chart we are going to develop is an extension of that worksheet. Refer to Figure 2.12 as we describe the tasks involved. The value worksheet from Figure 2.11 is set in the background; the chart developed using the Chart Wizard appears in the foreground.

The following steps describe how to use Excel's Chart Wizard to construct a bar graph for the soft drink data using the frequency distribution appearing in cells C1:D6.

Step 1. Select cells C1:D6
Step 2. Select the **Chart Wizard** button on the Standard toolbar (or select the **Insert** menu and choose the **Chart** option)

FIGURE 2.12   BAR GRAPH OF SOFT DRINK PURCHASES CONSTRUCTED USING EXCEL'S CHART WIZARD

	A	B	C	D	E	F	G	H	I
1	Brand Purchased		Soft Drink	Frequency					
2	Coke Classic		Coke Classic	19					
3	Diet Coke		Diet Coke	8					
4	Pepsi-Cola		Dr. Pepper	5					
5	Diet Coke		Pepsi-Cola	13					
6	Coke Classic		Sprite	5					
7	Coke Classic								
8	Dr. Pepper								
9	Diet Coke								
10	Pepsi-Cola								
45	Pepsi-Cola								
46	Pepsi-Cola								
47	Pepsi-Cola								
48	Coke Classic								
49	Dr. Pepper								
50	Pepsi-Cola								
51	Sprite								
52									
53									
54									
55									
56									
57									

Bar Graph of Soft Drink Purchases

Step 3. When the Chart Wizard—Step 1 of 4—Chart Type dialog box appears:
Choose **Column** in the **Chart type** list
Choose **Clustered Column** from the **Chart sub-type** display
Click **Next**

Step 4. When the Chart Wizard—Step 2 of 4—Chart Source Data dialog box appears:
Click **Next**

Step 5. When the Chart Wizard—Step 3 of 4—Chart Options dialog box appears:
Select the **Titles** tab
Enter Bar Graph of Soft Drink Purchases in the **Chart title** box
Enter Soft Drink in the **Category (X) axis** box
Enter Frequency in the **Values (Y) axis** box
Select the **Legend** tab and then
Remove the check in the **Show legend** box
Click **Next**

Step 6. When the Chart Wizard—Step 4 of 4—Chart Location dialog box appears:
Specify a location for the new chart (We used the current worksheet by selecting **As object in**)
Click **Finish**

The resulting bar graph (chart) is shown in Figure 2.12.*

Excel's Chart Wizard can produce a pie chart for the soft drink data in a similar fashion. To develop a pie chart, choose Pie in the Chart type list in step 3.

As we stated in a note and comment at the end of Section 2.2, a histogram is essentially the same as a bar graph with no separation between the bars. Figure 2.13 shows the audit time data with a frequency distribution in the background and a bar graph developed using the Chart Wizard (using the same steps just described) in the foreground. Because the adjacent bars in a histogram must touch, we need to edit the column chart (the bar graph) in order to eliminate the gap between each of the bars. The following steps accomplish this process.

Step 1. Right-click on any bar in the column chart to produce a list of options
Step 2. Choose **Format Data Series**
Step 3. When the Format Data Series dialog box appears:
Select the **Options** tab
Enter 0 in the **Gap width** box
Click **OK**

Scatter diagram   We use the stereo and sound equipment store data in Table 2.13 to demonstrate the use of Excel's Chart Wizard to construct a scatter diagram. Refer to Figure 2.14 as we describe the tasks involved. The value worksheet is set in the background, and the scatter diagram produced by the Chart Wizard appears in the foreground. The following steps will produce the scatter diagram.

Step 1. Select cells B1:C11
Step 2. Select the **Chart Wizard** button on the standard toolbar (or select the **Insert** menu and choose the **Chart** option)
Step 3. When the Chart Wizard—Step 1 of 4—Chart Type dialog box appears:
Choose **XY (Scatter)** in the **Chart type:** display
Click **Next**
Step 4. When the Chart Wizard—Step 2 of 4—Chart Source Data dialog box appears:
Click **Next**

---

*Resizing an Excel chart is not difficult. First, select the chart. Small block squares, called sizing handles, will appear on the chart border. Click on the sizing handles and drag them to resize the figure to your preference.

FIGURE 2.13   HISTOGRAM CONSTRUCTED USING EXCEL FOR THE AUDIT TIME DATA

	A	B	C	D	E	F	G	H	I	J	K
1	Audit Time		Audit Time	Frequency							
2	12		10-14	4							
3	15		15-19	8							
4	20		20-24	5							
5	22		25-29	2							
6	14		30-34	1							
7	14										
8	15										
9	27										
10	21										
11	18										
12	19										
13	18										
14	22										
15	33										
16	16										
17	18										
18	17										
19	23										
20	28										
21	13										
22											
23											

FIGURE 2.14   SCATTER DIAGRAM FOR STEREO AND SOUND EQUIPMENT STORE
USING EXCEL'S CHART WIZARD

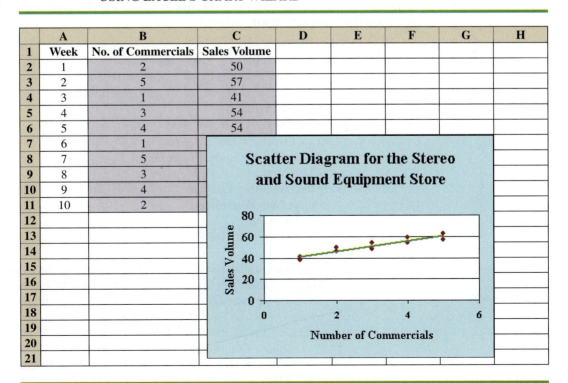

	A	B	C	D	E	F	G	H
1	Week	No. of Commercials	Sales Volume					
2	1	2	50					
3	2	5	57					
4	3	1	41					
5	4	3	54					
6	5	4	54					
7	6	1						
8	7	5						
9	8	3						
10	9	4						
11	10	2						
12								
13								
14								
15								
16								
17								
18								
19								
20								
21								

Step 5. When the Chart Wizard—Step 3 of 4—Chart Options dialog box appears:

         Select the **Titles** tab

         Enter Scatter Diagram for the Stereo and Sound Equipment Store in the **Chart title** box

         Enter Commercials in the **Value (X) axis** box

         Enter Sales Volume in the **Value (Y) axis** box

         Select the **Legend** tab

         Remove the check in the **Show legend** box

         Click **Next**

Step 6. When the Chart Wizard—Step 4 of 4—Chart Location dialog box appears:

         Specify a location for the new chart (We used the current worksheet by selecting **As object in**)

         Click **Finish**

It is easy to now add a trendline to the scatter diagram.

Step 1. Position the mouse pointer over any data point in the scatter diagram and right-click to display a list of options

Step 2. Choose **Add Trendline**

Step 3. When the Add Trendline dialog box appears:

         Select the **Type** tab

         Choose **Linear** from the **Trend/Regression type** display

         Click **OK**

PivotTable Report

Excel's PivotTable Report provides a valuable tool for managing data sets involving more than one variable. We will illustrate its use by showing how to develop a crosstabulation.

Crosstabulation We illustrate the construction of a crosstabulation using the restaurant data in Figure 2.15. Labels are entered in row 1, and the data for each of the 300 restaurants are entered into cells A2:C301.

Step 1. Select the **Data** menu

Step 2. Choose **PivotTable and PivotChart Report**

Step 3. When the PivotTable and PivotChart Wizard—Step 1 of 3—dialog box appears:

         Choose **Microsoft Office Excel list or database**

         Choose **PivotTable**

         Click **Next**

Step 4. When the PivotTable and PivotChart Wizard—Step 2 of 3—dialog box appears:

         Enter A1:C301 in the **Range** box

         Click **Next**

Step 5. When the PivotTable and PivotChart Wizard—Step 3 of 3—dialog box appears:

         Select **New Worksheet**

         Click **Layout**

Step 6. When the PivotTable and PivotChart Wizard—Layout diagram appears (see Figure 2.16):

         Drag the **Quality Rating** field button to the **ROW** section of the diagram

         Drag the **Meal Price ($)** field button to the **COLUMN** section of the diagram

         Drag the **Restaurant** field button to the **DATA** section of the diagram

         Double-click the **Sum of Restaurant** field button in the DATA section

         When the PivotTable Field dialog box appears:

             Choose **Count** under **Summarize by**

             Click **OK** (Figure 2.17 shows the completed layout diagram)

         Click **OK**

FIGURE 2.15   EXCEL WORKSHEET CONTAINING RESTAURANT DATA

Restaurant

Note: Rows 12–291 are hidden.

	A	B	C	D
	Restaurant	**Quality Rating**	**Meal Price ($)**	
1				
2	1	Good	18	
3	2	Very Good	22	
4	3	Good	28	
5	4	Excellent	38	
6	5	Very Good	33	
7	6	Good	28	
8	7	Very Good	19	
9	8	Very Good	11	
10	9	Very Good	23	
11	10	Good	13	
292	291	Very Good	23	
293	292	Very Good	24	
294	293	Excellent	45	
295	294	Good	14	
296	295	Good	18	
297	296	Good	17	
298	297	Good	16	
299	298	Good	15	
300	299	Very Good	38	
301	300	Very Good	31	
302				

FIGURE 2.16   PIVOTTABLE AND PIVOTCHART WIZARD—LAYOUT DIAGRAM

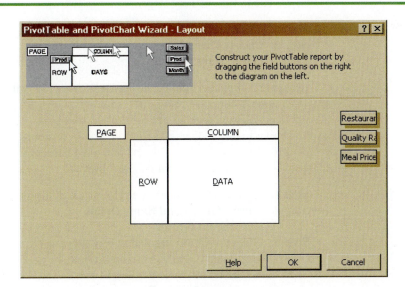

FIGURE 2.17   COMPLETED LAYOUT DIAGRAM

Step 7. When the PivotTable and PivotChart Wizard—Step 3 of 3—dialog box reappears:
Click **Finish**

A portion of the output generated by Excel is shown in Figure 2.18. Note that the output that appears in columns D through AK is hidden so the results can be shown in a reasonably sized figure. The row labels (Excellent, Good, and Very Good) and row totals (66, 84, 150, and 300) that appear in Figure 2.18 are the same as the row labels and row totals shown in Table 2.11. But they are in a different order. To put them in the order Good, Very Good, Excellent, follow these steps.

Step 1. Right-click on Excellent in cell A5
Step 2. Choose **Order**
Step 3. Select **Move to End**

In Figure 2.18, one column is designated for each possible value of meal price. For example, column B contains a count of restaurants with a $10 meal price, column C contains a count of restaurants with an $11 meal price, and so on. To view the PivotTable Report in a form similar to that shown in Table 2.11, we must group the columns into four price categories: $10–19, $20–29, $30–39, and $40–49. The steps necessary to group the columns for the worksheet shown in Figure 2.18 follow.

Step 1. Right-click on Meal Price ($) in cell B3 of the PivotTable
Step 2. Choose **Group and Show Detail**
　　　　　　Choose **Group**
Step 3. When the **Grouping** dialog box appears
　　　　　　Enter 10 in the **Starting at** box
　　　　　　Enter 49 in the **Ending at** box
　　　　　　Enter 10 in the **By** box
　　　　　　Click **OK**

The revised PivotTable output is shown in Figure 2.19. It is the final PivotTable. Note that it provides the same information as the crosstabulation shown in Table 2.11.

FIGURE 2.18   INITIAL PIVOTTABLE REPORT OUTPUT (COLUMNS D:AK ARE HIDDEN)

	A	B	C	AL	AM	AN	AO
1							
2							
3	Count of Restaurant	Meal Price ($) ▼					
4	Quality Rating ▼	10	11	47	48	Grand Total	
5	Excellent			2	2	66	
6	Good	6	4			84	
7	Very Good	1	4		1	150	
8	Grand Total	7	8	2	3	300	
9							
10							
11							
12							
13							
14							
15							
16							
17							
18							
19							
20							

FIGURE 2.19   FINAL PIVOTTABLE REPORT FOR RESTAURANT DATA

	A	B	C	D	E	F	G
1							
2							
3	Count of Restaurant	Meal Price ($) ▼					
4	Quality Rating ▼	10-19	20-29	30-39	40-49	Grand Total	
5	Good	42	40	2		84	
6	Very Good	34	64	46	6	150	
7	Excellent	2	14	28	22	66	
8	Grand Total	78	118	76	28	300	
9							
10							
11							
12							
13							
14							
15							
16							
17							
18							
19							
20							

CHAPTER 3

Descriptive Statistics: Numerical Measures

SMALL FRY DESIGN*
SANTA ANA, CALIFORNIA

Founded in 1997, Small Fry Design is a toy and accessory company that designs and imports products for infants. The company's product line includes teddy bears, mobiles, musical toys, rattles, and security blankets and features high-quality soft toy designs with an emphasis on color, texture, and sound. The products are designed in the United States and manufactured in China.

Small Fry Design uses independent representatives to sell the products to infant furnishing retailers, children's accessory and apparel stores, gift shops, upscale department stores, and major catalog companies. Currently, Small Fry Design products are distributed in more than 1000 retail outlets throughout the United States.

Cash flow management is one of the most critical activities in the day-to-day operation of this company. Ensuring sufficient incoming cash to meet both current and ongoing debt obligations can mean the difference between business success and failure. A critical factor in cash flow management is the analysis and control of accounts receivable. By measuring the average age and dollar value of outstanding invoices, management can predict cash availability and monitor changes in the status of accounts receivable. The company set the following goals: the average age for outstanding invoices should not exceed 45 days, and the dollar value of invoices more than 60 days old should not exceed 5% of the dollar value of all accounts receivable.

In a recent summary of accounts receivable status, the following descriptive statistics were provided for the age of outstanding invoices:

Mean	40 days
Median	35 days
Mode	31 days

A new Small Fry Design mobile. © Photo courtesy of Small Fry Design, Inc.

Interpretation of these statistics shows that the mean or average age of an invoice is 40 days. The median shows that half of the invoices remain outstanding 35 days or more. The mode of 31 days, the most frequent invoice age, indicates that the most common length of time an invoice is outstanding is 31 days. The statistical summary also showed that only 3% of the dollar value of all accounts receivable was more than 60 days old. Based on the statistical information, management was satisfied that accounts receivable and incoming cash flow were under control.

In this chapter, you will learn how to compute and interpret some of the statistical measures used by Small Fry Design. In addition to the mean, median, and mode, you will learn about other descriptive statistics such as the range, variance, standard deviation, percentiles, and correlation. These numerical measures will assist in the understanding and interpretation of data.

*The authors are indebted to John A. McCarthy, President of Small Fry Design, for providing this Statistics in Practice.

In Chapter 2 we discussed tabular and graphical presentations used to summarize data. In this chapter, we present several numerical measures that provide additional alternatives for summarizing data.

We start by developing numerical summary measures for data sets consisting of a single variable. When a data set contains more than one variable, the same numerical measures can be computed separately for each variable. However, in the two-variable case, we will also develop measures of the relationship between the variables.

Numerical measures of location, dispersion, shape, and association are introduced. If the measures are computed for data from a sample, they are called **sample statistics**. If the measures are computed for data from a population, they are called **population parameters**. In statistical inference, a sample statistic is referred to as the **point estimator** of the corresponding population parameter. In Chapter 7 we will discuss in more detail the process of point estimation.

In the two chapter appendixes we show how Minitab and Excel can be used to compute many of the numerical measures described in the chapter.

3.1 Measures of Location

Mean

Perhaps the most important measure of location is the **mean**, or average value, for a variable. The mean provides a measure of central location for the data. If the data are from a sample, the mean is denoted by $\bar{x}$; if the data are from a population, the mean is denoted by the Greek letter μ.

In statistical formulas, it is customary to denote the value of variable x for the first observation by x_1, the value of variable x for the second observation by x_2, and so on. In general, the value of variable x for the ith observation is denoted by x_i. For a sample with n observations, the formula for the sample mean is as follows.

The sample mean $\bar{x}$ is a sample statistic.

> SAMPLE MEAN
>
> $$\bar{x} = \frac{\Sigma x_i}{n} \tag{3.1}$$

In the preceding formula, the numerator is the sum of the values of the n observations. That is,

$$\Sigma x_i = x_1 + x_2 + \cdots + x_n$$

The Greek letter Σ is the summation sign.

To illustrate the computation of a sample mean, let us consider the following class size data for a sample of five college classes.

$$46 \quad 54 \quad 42 \quad 46 \quad 32$$

We use the notation x_1, x_2, x_3, x_4, x_5 to represent the number of students in each of the five classes.

$$x_1 = 46 \qquad x_2 = 54 \qquad x_3 = 42 \qquad x_4 = 46 \qquad x_5 = 32$$

Hence, to compute the sample mean, we can write

$$\bar{x} = \frac{\Sigma x_i}{n} = \frac{x_1 + x_2 + x_3 + x_4 + x_5}{5} = \frac{46 + 54 + 42 + 46 + 32}{5} = 44$$

The sample mean class size is 44 students.

Another illustration of the computation of a sample mean is given in the following situation. Suppose that a college placement office sent a questionnaire to a sample of business school graduates requesting information on monthly starting salaries. Table 3.1 shows the

TABLE 3.1   MONTHLY STARTING SALARIES FOR A SAMPLE OF 12 BUSINESS SCHOOL
GRADUATES

Salary

Graduate	Monthly Starting Salary ($)	Graduate	Monthly Starting Salary ($)
1	2850	7	2890
2	2950	8	3130
3	3050	9	2940
4	2880	10	3325
5	2755	11	2920
6	2710	12	2880

collected data. The mean monthly starting salary for the sample of 12 business college
graduates is computed as

$$\bar{x} = \frac{\Sigma x_i}{n} = \frac{x_1 + x_2 + \cdots + x_{12}}{12}$$

$$= \frac{2850 + 2950 + \cdots + 2880}{12}$$

$$= \frac{35{,}280}{12} = 2940$$

Equation (3.1) shows how the mean is computed for a sample with n observations. The
formula for computing the mean of a population remains the same, but we use different notation to indicate that we are working with the entire population. The number of observations in a population is denoted by N and the symbol for a population mean is μ.

*The sample mean $\bar{x}$ is a
point estimator of the
population mean μ.*

POPULATION MEAN

$$\mu = \frac{\Sigma x_i}{N} \qquad\qquad\qquad \textbf{(3.2)}$$

Median

The **median** is another measure of central location for a variable. The median is the value
in the middle when the data are arranged in ascending order (smallest value to largest
value). With an odd number of observations, the median is the middle value. An even number of observations has no single middle value. In this case, we follow convention and define the median as the average of the values for the middle two observations. For
convenience the definition of the median is restated as follows.

MEDIAN

Arrange the data in ascending order (smallest value to largest value).

(a) For an odd number of observations, the median is the middle value.
(b) For an even number of observations, the median is the average of the two middle values.

Let us apply this definition to compute the median class size for the sample of five college classes. Arranging the data in ascending order provides the following list.

$$32 \quad 42 \quad 46 \quad 46 \quad 54$$

Because $n = 5$ is odd, the median is the middle value. Thus the median class size is 46 students. Even though this data set contains two observations with values of 46, each observation is treated separately when we arrange the data in ascending order.

Suppose we also compute the median starting salary for the 12 business college graduates in Table 3.1. We first arrange the data in ascending order.

$$2710 \quad 2755 \quad 2850 \quad 2880 \quad 2880 \quad \underbrace{2890 \quad 2920}_{\text{Middle Two Values}} \quad 2940 \quad 2950 \quad 3050 \quad 3130 \quad 3325$$

Because $n = 12$ is even, we identify the middle two values: 2890 and 2920. The median is the average of these values.

$$\text{Median} = \frac{2890 + 2920}{2} = 2905$$

The median is the measure of location most often reported for annual income and property value data because a few extremely large incomes or property values can inflate the mean. In such cases, the median is the preferred measure of central location.

Although the mean is the more commonly used measure of central location, in some situations the median is preferred. The mean is influenced by extremely small and large data values. For instance, suppose that one of the graduates (see Table 3.1) had a starting salary of $10,000 per month (maybe the individual's family owns the company). If we change the highest monthly starting salary in Table 3.1 from $3325 to $10,000 and recompute the mean, the sample mean changes from $2940 to $3496. The median of $2905, however, is unchanged, because $2890 and $2920 are still the middle two values. With the extremely high starting salary included, the median provides a better measure of central location than the mean. We can generalize to say that whenever a data set contains extreme values, the median is often the preferred measure of central location.

Mode

A third measure of location is the **mode**. The mode is defined as follows.

> **MODE**
>
> The mode is the value that occurs with greatest frequency.

To illustrate the identification of the mode, consider the sample of five class sizes. The only value that occurs more than once is 46. Because this value, occurring with a frequency of 2, has the greatest frequency, it is the mode. As another illustration, consider the sample of starting salaries for the business school graduates. The only monthly starting salary that occurs more than once is $2880. Because this value has the greatest frequency, it is the mode.

Situations can arise for which the greatest frequency occurs at two or more different values. In these instances more than one mode exists. If the data contain exactly two modes, we say that the data are *bimodal.* If data contain more than two modes, we say that the data are *multimodal.* In multimodal cases the mode is almost never reported because listing three or more modes would not be particularly helpful in describing a location for the data.

The mode is an important measure of location for qualitative data. For example, the qualitative data set in Table 2.2 resulted in the following frequency distribution for soft drink purchases.

Soft Drink	Frequency
Coke Classic	19
Diet Coke	8
Dr. Pepper	5
Pepsi-Cola	13
Sprite	5
Total	50

The mode, or most frequently purchased soft drink, is Coke Classic. For this type of data it obviously makes no sense to speak of the mean or median. The mode provides the information of interest, the most frequently purchased soft drink.

Percentiles

A **percentile** provides information about how the data are spread over the interval from the smallest value to the largest value. For data that do not contain numerous repeated values, the pth percentile divides the data into two parts. Approximately p percent of the observations have values less than the pth percentile; approximately $(100 - p)$ percent of the observations have values greater than the pth percentile. The pth percentile is formally defined as follows.

> PERCENTILE
>
> The pth percentile is a value such that *at least p* percent of the observations are less than or equal to this value and *at least* $(100 - p)$ percent of the observations are greater than or equal to this value.

Colleges and universities frequently report admission test scores in terms of percentiles. For instance, suppose an applicant obtains a raw score of 54 on the verbal portion of an admission test. How this student performed in relation to other students taking the same test may not be readily apparent. However, if the raw score of 54 corresponds to the 70th percentile, we know that approximately 70% of the students scored lower than this individual and approximately 30% of the students scored higher than this individual.

The following procedure can be used to compute the pth percentile.

> CALCULATING THE pTH PERCENTILE
>
> *Following these steps makes it easy to calculate percentiles.*
>
> **Step 1.** Arrange the data in ascending order (smallest value to largest value).
> **Step 2.** Compute an index i
>
> $$i = \left(\frac{p}{100} \right) n$$
>
> where p is the percentile of interest and n is the number of observations.

Step 3. (a) If *i is not an integer, round up.* The next integer *greater* than *i* denotes the position of the *p*th percentile.
(b) If *i is an integer,* the *p*th percentile is the average of the values in positions *i* and *i* + 1.

As an illustration of this procedure, let us determine the 85th percentile for the starting salary data in Table 3.1.

Step 1. Arrange the data in ascending order.

2710   2755   2850   2880   2880   2890   2920   2940   2950   3050   3130   3325

Step 2.

$$i = \left(\frac{p}{100}\right)n = \left(\frac{85}{100}\right)12 = 10.2$$

Step 3. Because *i* is not an integer, *round up.* The position of the 85th percentile is the next integer greater than 10.2, the 11th position.

Returning to the data, we see that the 85th percentile is the data value in the 11th position, or 3130.

As another illustration of this procedure, let us consider the calculation of the 50th percentile for the starting salary data. Applying step 2, we obtain

$$i = \left(\frac{50}{100}\right)12 = 6$$

Because *i* is an integer, step 3(b) states that the 50th percentile is the average of the sixth and seventh data values; thus the 50th percentile is (2890 + 2920)/2 = 2905. Note that the *50th percentile is also the median.*

Quartiles

Quartiles are just specific percentiles; thus, the steps for computing percentiles can be applied directly in the computation of quartiles.

It is often desirable to divide data into four parts, with each part containing approximately one-fourth, or 25% of the observations. Figure 3.1 shows a data distribution divided into four parts. The division points are referred to as the **quartiles** and are defined as

Q_1 = first quartile, or 25th percentile

Q_2 = second quartile, or 50th percentile (also the median)

Q_3 = third quartile, or 75th percentile.

The starting salary data are again arranged in ascending order. We already identified Q_2, the second quartile (median), as 2905.

2710   2755   2850   2880   2880   2890   2920   2940   2950   3050   3130   3325

The computations of quartiles Q_1 and Q_3 require the use of the rule for finding the 25th and 75th percentiles. These calculations follow.

For Q_1,

$$i = \left(\frac{p}{100}\right)n = \left(\frac{25}{100}\right)12 = 3$$

FIGURE 3.1   LOCATION OF THE QUARTILES

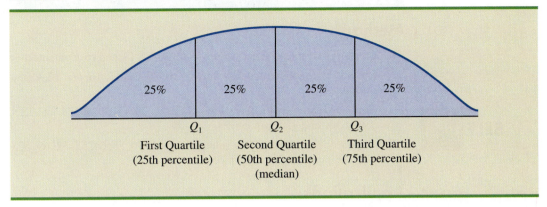

Because i is an integer, step 3(b) indicates that the first quartile, or 25th percentile, is the average of the third and fourth data values; thus, $Q_1 = (2850 + 2880)/2 = 2865$.

For Q_3,

$$i = \left(\frac{p}{100}\right)n = \left(\frac{75}{100}\right)12 = 9$$

Again, because i is an integer, step 3(b) indicates that the third quartile, or 75th percentile, is the average of the ninth and tenth data values; thus, $Q_3 = (2950 + 3050)/2 = 3000$.

The quartiles divide the starting salary data into four parts, with each part containing 25% of the observations.

2710   2755   2850 | 2880   2880   2890 | 2920   2940   2950 | 3050   3130   3325

$Q_1 = 2865$ $Q_2 = 2905$ $Q_3 = 3000$

(Median)

We defined the quartiles as the 25th, 50th, and 75th percentiles. Thus, we computed the quartiles in the same way as percentiles. However, other conventions are sometimes used to compute quartiles, and the actual values reported for quartiles may vary slightly depending on the convention used. Nevertheless, the objective of all procedures for computing quartiles is to divide the data into four equal parts.

NOTES AND COMMENTS

It is better to use the median than the mean as a measure of central location when a data set contains extreme values. Another measure, sometimes used when extreme values are present, is the *trimmed mean*. It is obtained by deleting a percentage of the smallest and largest values from a data set and then computing the mean of the remaining values. For example, the 5% trimmed mean is obtained by re-moving the smallest 5% and the largest 5% of the data values and then computing the mean of the remaining values. Using the sample with $n = 12$ starting salaries, $0.05(12) = 0.6$. Rounding this value to 1 indicates that the 5% trimmed mean would remove the 1 smallest data value and the 1 largest data value. The 5% trimmed mean using the 10 re-maining observations is 2924.50.

Exercises

Methods

1. Consider a sample with data values of 10, 20, 12, 17, and 16. Compute the mean and median.
2. Consider a sample with data values of 10, 20, 21, 17, 16, and 12. Compute the mean and median.

3. Consider a sample with data values of 27, 25, 20, 15, 30, 34, 28, and 25. Compute the 20th, 25th, 65th, and 75th percentiles.
4. Consider a sample with data values of 53, 55, 70, 58, 64, 57, 53, 69, 57, 68, and 53. Compute the mean, median, and mode.

Applications

5. The Dow Jones Travel Index reported what business travelers pay for hotel rooms per night in major U.S. cities (*The Wall Street Journal*, January 16, 2004). The average hotel room rates for 20 cities are as follows:

Atlanta	$163	Minneapolis	$125
Boston	177	New Orleans	167
Chicago	166	New York	245
Cleveland	126	Orlando	146
Dallas	123	Phoenix	139
Denver	120	Pittsburgh	134
Detroit	144	San Francisco	167
Houston	173	Seattle	162
Los Angeles	160	St. Louis	145
Miami	192	Washington, D.C.	207

a. What is the mean hotel room rate?
b. What is the median hotel room rate?
c. What is the mode?
d. What is the first quartile?
e. What is the third quartile?

6. J. D. Powers and Associates surveyed cell phone users in order to learn about the minutes of cell phone usage per month (Associated Press, June 2002). Minutes per month for a sample of 15 cell phone users are shown here.

615	135	395
430	830	1180
690	250	420
265	245	210
180	380	105

a. What is the mean number of minutes of usage per month?
b. What is the median number of minutes of usage per month?
c. What is the 85th percentile?
d. J. D. Powers and Associates reported that the average wireless subscriber plan allows up to 750 minutes of usage per month. What do the data suggest about cell phone subscribers' utilization of their monthly plan?

7. The American Association of Individual Investors conducted an annual survey of discount brokers (*AAII Journal*, January 2003). The commissions charged by 24 discount brokers for two types of trades, a broker-assisted trade of 100 shares at $50 per share and an online trade of 500 shares at $50 per share, are shown in Table 3.2.

TABLE 3.2   COMMISSIONS CHARGED BY DISCOUNT BROKERS

Broker

Broker	Broker-Assisted 100 Shares at $50/Share	Online 500 Shares at $50/Share	Broker	Broker-Assisted 100 Shares at $50/Share	Online 500 Shares at $50/Share
Accutrade	30.00	29.95	Merrill Lynch Direct	50.00	29.95
Ameritrade	24.99	10.99	Muriel Siebert	45.00	14.95
Banc of America	54.00	24.95	NetVest	24.00	14.00
Brown & Co.	17.00	5.00	Recom Securities	35.00	12.95
Charles Schwab	55.00	29.95	Scottrade	17.00	7.00
CyberTrader	12.95	9.95	Sloan Securities	39.95	19.95
E*TRADE Securities	49.95	14.95	Strong Investments	55.00	24.95
First Discount	35.00	19.75	TD Waterhouse	45.00	17.95
Freedom Investments	25.00	15.00	T. Rowe Price	50.00	19.95
Harrisdirect	40.00	20.00	Vanguard	48.00	20.00
Investors National	39.00	62.50	Wall Street Discount	29.95	19.95
MB Trading	9.95	10.55	York Securities	40.00	36.00

Source: AAII Journal, January 2003.

a. Compute the mean, median, and mode for the commission charged on a broker-assisted trade of 100 shares at $50 per share.
b. Compute the mean, median, and mode for the commission charged on an online trade of 500 shares at $50 per share.
c. Which costs more, a broker-assisted trade of 100 shares at $50 per share or an online trade of 500 shares at $50 per share?
d. Is the cost of a transaction related to the amount of the transaction?

8. Millions of Americans get up each morning and telecommute to work from offices in their home. Following is a sample of age data for individuals working at home.

| 18 | 54 | 20 | 46 | 25 | 48 | 53 | 27 | 26 | 37 |
| 40 | 36 | 42 | 25 | 27 | 33 | 28 | 40 | 45 | 25 |

a. Compute the mean and mode.
b. The median age of the population of all adults is 35.5 years (*The World Almanac,* 2004). Use the median age of the preceding data to comment on whether the at-home workers tend to be younger or older than the population of all adults.
c. Compute the first and third quartiles.
d. Compute and interpret the 32nd percentile.

9. Media Matrix collected data showing the most popular Web sites when browsing at home and at work (*Business 2.0,* January 2000). The following data show the number of unique visitors (thousands) for the top 25 Web sites when browsing at home.

Websites

Web Site	Unique Visitors (1000s)
about.com	5538
altavista.com	7391
amazon.com	7986
angelfire.com	8917
aol.com	23863
bluemountainarts.com	6786

(*continued*)

Web Site	Unique Visitors (1000s)
ebay.com	8296
excite.com	10479
geocities.com	15321
go.com	14330
hotbot.com	5760
hotmail.com	11791
icq.com	5052
looksmart.com	5984
lycos.com	9950
microsoft.com	15593
msn.com	23505
netscape.com	14470
passport.com	11299
real.com	6785
snap.com	5730
tripod.com	7970
xoom.com	5652
yahoo.com	26796
zdnet.com	5133

a. Compute the mean and median.
b. Do you think it would be better to use the mean or the median as the measure of central location for these data? Explain.
c. Compute the first and third quartiles.
d. Compute and interpret the 85th percentile.

10. An American Hospital Association survey found that most hospital emergency rooms are operating at full capacity (Associated Press, April 9, 2002). The survey collected data on the emergency room waiting times for hospitals where the emergency room is operating at full capacity and for hospitals where the emergency room is in balance and rarely operates at capacity. Sample data showing waiting times in minutes are as follows.

ER Waiting Times for Hospitals at Full Capacity		ER Waiting Times for Hospitals in Balance	
87	59	60	39
80	110	54	32
47	83	18	56
73	79	29	26
50	50	45	37
93	66	34	38
72	115		

a. Compute the mean and median emergency room waiting times for hospitals operating at full capacity.
b. Compute the mean and median emergency room waiting times for hospitals operating in balance.
c. What observations can you make about emergency room waiting times based on these results? Would the American Hospital Association express concern with the statistical results shown here?

11. In automobile mileage and gasoline-consumption testing, 13 automobiles were road tested for 300 miles in both city and highway driving conditions. The following data were recorded for miles-per-gallon performance.

City: 16.2 16.7 15.9 14.4 13.2 15.3 16.8 16.0 16.1 15.3 15.2 15.3 16.2
Highway: 19.4 20.6 18.3 18.6 19.2 17.4 17.2 18.6 19.0 21.1 19.4 18.5 18.7

Use the mean, median, and mode to make a statement about the difference in performance for city and highway driving.

12. The following data show the price, picture capacity, and battery life (minutes) for 20 digital cameras (*PC World,* January 2000).

Cameras

Camera	Price ($)	Picture Capacity	Battery Life (minutes)
Agfa Ephoto CL30	349	36	25
Canon PowerShot A50	499	106	75
Canon PowerShot Pro70	999	96	118
Epson PhotoPC 800	699	120	99
Fujifilm DX-10	299	30	229
Fujifilm MX-2700	699	141	124
Fujifilm MX-2900 Zoom	899	141	88
HP PhotoSmart C200	299	80	68
Kodak DC215 Zoom	399	54	159
Kodak DC265 Zoom	899	180	186
Kodak DC280 Zoom	799	245	143
Minolta Dimage EX Zoom 1500	549	105	38
Nikon Coolpix 950	999	32	88
Olympus D-340R	299	122	161
Olympus D-450 Zoom	499	122	62
Ricoh RDC-500	699	99	56
Sony Cybershot DSC-F55	699	63	69
Sony Mavica MVC-FD73	599	40	186
Sony Mavica MVC-FD88	999	40	88
Toshiba PDR-M4	599	124	142

a. Compute the mean price.
b. Compute the mean picture capacity.
c. Compute the mean battery life.
d. If you had to select one camera from this list, which camera would you choose? Explain.

3.2 Measures of Variability

In addition to measures of location, it is often desirable to consider measures of variability, or dispersion. For example, suppose that you are a purchasing agent for a large manufacturing firm and that you regularly place orders with two different suppliers. After several months of operation, you find that the mean number of days required to fill orders is 10 days for both of the suppliers. The histograms summarizing the number of working days required to fill orders from the suppliers are shown in Figure 3.2. Although the mean number of days is 10 for both suppliers, do the two suppliers demonstrate the same degree of reliability in terms of making deliveries on schedule? Note the dispersion, or variability, in delivery times indicated by the histograms. Which supplier would you prefer?

For most firms, receiving materials and supplies on schedule is important. The seven- or eight-day deliveries shown for J.C. Clark Distributors might be viewed favorably;

FIGURE 3.2   HISTORICAL DATA SHOWING THE NUMBER OF DAYS REQUIRED TO FILL ORDERS

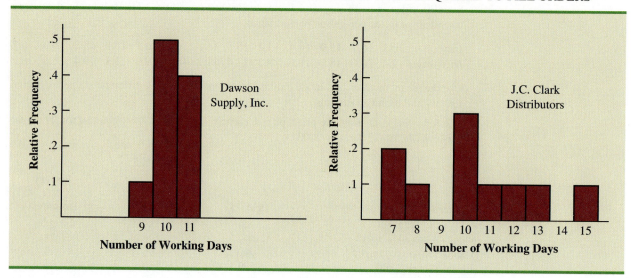

however, a few of the slow 13- to 15-day deliveries could be disastrous in terms of keeping a workforce busy and production on schedule. This example illustrates a situation in which the variability in the delivery times may be an overriding consideration in selecting a supplier. For most purchasing agents, the lower variability shown for Dawson Supply, Inc., would make Dawson the preferred supplier.

We turn now to a discussion of some commonly used measures of variability.

Range

The simplest measure of variability is the **range**.

> RANGE
>
> $$\text{Range} = \text{Largest value} - \text{Smallest value}$$

Let us refer to the data on starting salaries for business school graduates in Table 3.1. The largest starting salary is 3325 and the smallest is 2710. The range is $3325 - 2710 = 615$.

Although the range is the easiest of the measures of variability to compute, it is seldom used as the only measure. The reason is that the range is based on only two of the observations and thus is highly influenced by extreme values. Suppose one of the graduates received a starting salary of $10,000 per month. In this case, the range would be $10,000 - 2710 = 7290$ rather than 615. This large value for the range would not be especially descriptive of the variability in the data because 11 of the 12 starting salaries are closely grouped between 2710 and 3130.

Interquartile Range

A measure of variability that overcomes the dependency on extreme values is the **interquartile range (IQR)**. This measure of variability is the difference between the third quartile, Q_3, and the first quartile, Q_1. In other words, the interquartile range is the range for the middle 50% of the data.

> **INTERQUARTILE RANGE**
>
> $$\text{IQR} = Q_3 - Q_1 \tag{3.3}$$

For the data on monthly starting salaries, the quartiles are $Q_3 = 3000$ and $Q_1 = 2865$. Thus, the interquartile range is $3000 - 2865 = 135$.

Variance

The **variance** is a measure of variability that utilizes all the data. The variance is based on the difference between the value of each observation (x_i) and the mean. The difference between each x_i and the mean ($\bar{x}$ for a sample, μ for a population) is called a *deviation about the mean*. For a sample, a deviation about the mean is written $(x_i - \bar{x})$; for a population, it is written $(x_i - \mu)$. In the computation of the variance, the deviations about the mean are *squared*.

If the data are for a population, the average of the squared deviations is called the *population variance*. The population variance is denoted by the Greek symbol σ^2. For a population of N observations and with μ denoting the population mean, the definition of the population variance is as follows.

> **POPULATION VARIANCE**
>
> $$\sigma^2 = \frac{\Sigma(x_i - \mu)^2}{N} \tag{3.4}$$

In most statistical applications, the data being analyzed are for a sample. When we compute a sample variance, we are often interested in using it to estimate the population variance σ^2. Although a detailed explanation is beyond the scope of this text, it can be shown that if the sum of the squared deviations about the sample mean is divided by $n - 1$, and not n, the resulting sample variance provides an unbiased estimate of the population variance. For this reason, the *sample variance,* denoted by s^2, is defined as follows.

The sample variance s^2 is the estimator of the population variance σ^2.

> **SAMPLE VARIANCE**
>
> $$s^2 = \frac{\Sigma(x_i - \bar{x})^2}{n - 1} \tag{3.5}$$

To illustrate the computation of the sample variance, we will use the data on class size for the sample of five college classes as presented in Section 3.1. A summary of the data, including the computation of the deviations about the mean and the squared deviations about the mean, is shown in Table 3.3. The sum of squared deviations about the mean is $\Sigma(x_i - \bar{x})^2 = 256$. Hence, with $n - 1 = 4$, the sample variance is

$$s^2 = \frac{\Sigma(x_i - \bar{x})^2}{n - 1} = \frac{256}{4} = 64$$

Before moving on, let us note that the units associated with the sample variance often cause confusion. Because the values being summed in the variance calculation, $(x_i - \bar{x})^2$, are squared, the units associated with the sample variance are also *squared*. For instance, the

TABLE 3.3   COMPUTATION OF DEVIATIONS AND SQUARED DEVIATIONS ABOUT THE MEAN FOR THE CLASS SIZE DATA

Number of Students in Class (x_i)	Mean Class Size ($\bar{x}$)	Deviation About the Mean ($x_i - \bar{x}$)	Squared Deviation About the Mean ($x_i - \bar{x})^2$
46	44	2	4
54	44	10	100
42	44	−2	4
46	44	2	4
32	44	−12	144
		0	256
		$\Sigma(x_i - \bar{x})$	$\Sigma(x_i - \bar{x})^2$

The variance is useful in comparing the variability of two or more variables.

sample variance for the class size data is $s^2 = 64$ (students)^2. The squared units associated with variance make it difficult to obtain an intuitive understanding and interpretation of the numerical value of the variance. We recommend that you think of the variance as a measure useful in comparing the amount of variability for two or more variables. In a comparison of the variables, the one with the largest variance shows the most variability. Further interpretation of the value of the variance may not be necessary.

As another illustration of computing a sample variance, consider the starting salaries listed in Table 3.1 for the 12 business school graduates. In Section 3.1, we showed that the sample mean starting salary was 2940. The computation of the sample variance ($s^2 = 27,440.91$) is shown in Table 3.4.

TABLE 3.4   COMPUTATION OF THE SAMPLE VARIANCE FOR THE STARTING SALARY DATA

Monthly Salary (x_i)	Sample Mean ($\bar{x}$)	Deviation About the Mean ($x_i - \bar{x}$)	Squared Deviation About the Mean ($x_i - \bar{x})^2$
2850	2940	−90	8,100
2950	2940	10	100
3050	2940	110	12,100
2880	2940	−60	3,600
2755	2940	−185	34,225
2710	2940	−230	52,900
2890	2940	−50	2,500
3130	2940	190	36,100
2940	2940	0	0
3325	2940	385	148,225
2920	2940	−20	400
2880	2940	−60	3,600
		0	301,850
		$\Sigma(x_i - \bar{x})$	$\Sigma(x_i - \bar{x})^2$

Using equation (3.5),

$$s^2 = \frac{\Sigma(x_i - \bar{x})^2}{n - 1} = \frac{301,850}{11} = 27,440.91$$

In Tables 3.3 and 3.4 we show both the sum of the deviations about the mean and the sum of the squared deviations about the mean. For any data set, the sum of the deviations about the mean will *always equal zero*. Note that in Tables 3.3 and 3.4, $\Sigma(x_i - \bar{x}) = 0$. The positive deviations and negative deviations cancel each other, causing the sum of the deviations about the mean to equal zero.

Standard Deviation

The **standard deviation** is defined to be the positive square root of the variance. Following the notation we adopted for a sample variance and a population variance, we use s to denote the sample standard deviation and σ to denote the population standard deviation. The standard deviation is derived from the variance in the following way.

The sample standard deviation s is the estimator of the population standard deviation σ.

> **STANDARD DEVIATION**
>
> $$\text{Sample standard deviation} = s = \sqrt{s^2} \qquad (3.6)$$
> $$\text{Population standard deviation} = \sigma = \sqrt{\sigma^2} \qquad (3.7)$$

Recall that the sample variance for the sample of class sizes in five college classes is $s^2 = 64$. Thus, the sample standard deviation is $s = \sqrt{64} = 8$. For the data on starting salaries, the sample standard deviation is $s = \sqrt{27{,}440.91} = 165.65$.

The standard deviation is easier to interpret than the variance because the standard deviation is measured in the same units as the data.

What is gained by converting the variance to its corresponding standard deviation? Recall that the units associated with the variance are squared. For example, the sample variance for the starting salary data of business school graduates is $s^2 = 27{,}440.91$ (dollars)^2. Because the standard deviation is the square root of the variance, the units of the variance, dollars squared, are converted to dollars in the standard deviation. Thus, the standard deviation of the starting salary data is $165.65. In other words, the standard deviation is measured in the same units as the original data. For this reason the standard deviation is more easily compared to the mean and other statistics that are measured in the same units as the original data.

Coefficient of Variation

The coefficient of variation is a relative measure of variability; it measures the standard deviation relative to the mean.

In some situations we may be interested in a descriptive statistic that indicates how large the standard deviation is relative to the mean. This measure is called the **coefficient of variation** and is usually expressed as a percentage.

> **COEFFICIENT OF VARIATION**
>
> $$\left(\frac{\text{Standard deviation}}{\text{Mean}} \times 100 \right)\% \qquad (3.8)$$

For the class size data, we found a sample mean of 44 and a sample standard deviation of 8. The coefficient of variation is $[(8/44) \times 100]\% = 18.2\%$. In words, the coefficient of variation tells us that the sample standard deviation is 18.2% of the value of the sample mean. For the starting salary data with a sample mean of 2940 and a sample standard deviation of 165.65, the coefficient of variation, $[(165.65/2940) \times 100]\% = 5.6\%$, tells us the sample standard deviation is only 5.6% of the value of the sample mean. In general, the coefficient of variation is a useful statistic for comparing the variability of variables that have different standard deviations and different means.

NOTES AND COMMENTS

1. Statistical software packages and spreadsheets can be used to develop the descriptive statistics presented in this chapter. After the data are entered into a worksheet, a few simple commands can be used to generate the desired output. In Appendixes 3.1 and 3.2, we show how Minitab and Excel can be used to develop descriptive statistics.

2. The standard deviation is a commonly used measure of the risk associated with investing in stock and stock funds (*Business Week,* January 17, 2000). It provides a measure of how monthly returns fluctuate around the long-run average return.

3. Rounding the value of the sample mean $\bar{x}$ and the values of the squared deviations $(x_i - \bar{x})^2$ may introduce errors when a calculator is used in the computation of the variance and standard deviation. To reduce rounding errors, we recommend carrying at least six significant digits during intermediate calculations. The resulting variance or standard deviation can then be rounded to fewer digits.

4. An alternative formula for the computation of the sample variance is

$$s^2 = \frac{\Sigma x_i^2 - n\bar{x}^2}{n - 1}$$

where $\Sigma x_i^2 = x_1^2 + x_2^2 + \cdots + x_n^2$.

Exercises

Methods

13. Consider a sample with data values of 10, 20, 12, 17, and 16. Compute the range and interquartile range.

14. Consider a sample with data values of 10, 20, 12, 17, and 16. Compute the variance and standard deviation.

15. Consider a sample with data values of 27, 25, 20, 15, 30, 34, 28, and 25. Compute the range, interquartile range, variance, and standard deviation.

Applications

16. A bowler's scores for six games were 182, 168, 184, 190, 170, and 174. Using these data as a sample, compute the following descriptive statistics.
    a. Range   c. Standard deviation
    b. Variance   d. Coefficient of variation

17. A home theater in a box is the easiest and cheapest way to provide surround sound for a home entertainment center. A sample of prices is shown here (*Consumer Reports Buying Guide,* 2004). The prices are for models with a DVD player and for models without a DVD player.

Models with DVD Player	Price	Models without DVD Player	Price
Sony HT-1800DP	$450	Pioneer HTP-230	$300
Pioneer HTD-330DV	300	Sony HT-DDW750	300
Sony HT-C800DP	400	Kenwood HTB-306	360
Panasonic SC-HT900	500	RCA RT-2600	290
Panasonic SC-MTI	400	Kenwood HTB-206	300

     a. Compute the mean price for models with a DVD player and the mean price for models without a DVD player. What is the additional price paid to have a DVD player included in a home theater unit?
     b. Compute the range, variance, and standard deviation for the two samples. What does this information tell you about the prices for models with and without a DVD player?

18. Car rental rates per day for a sample of seven Eastern U.S. cities are as follows (*The Wall Street Journal*, January 16, 2004).

City	Daily Rate
Boston	$43
Atlanta	35
Miami	34
New York	58
Orlando	30
Pittsburgh	30
Washington, D.C.	36

   a. Compute the mean, variance, and standard deviation for the car rental rates.
   b. A similar sample of seven Western U.S. cities showed a sample mean car rental rate of $38 per day. The variance and standard deviation were 12.3 and 3.5, respectively. Discuss any difference between the car rental rates in Eastern and Western U.S. cities.

19. The *Los Angeles Times* regularly reports the air quality index for various areas of Southern California. A sample of air quality index values for Pomona provided the following data: 28, 42, 58, 48, 45, 55, 60, 49, and 50.
   a. Compute the range and interquartile range.
   b. Compute the sample variance and sample standard deviation.
   c. A sample of air quality index readings for Anaheim provided a sample mean of 48.5, a sample variance of 136, and a sample standard deviation of 11.66. What comparisons can you make between the air quality in Pomona and that in Anaheim on the basis of these descriptive statistics?

20. The following data were used to construct the histograms of the number of days required to fill orders for Dawson Supply, Inc., and J.C. Clark Distributors (see Figure 3.2).

Dawson Supply Days for Delivery: 11   10   9   10   11   11   10   11   10   10
Clark Distributors Days for Delivery: 8   10   13   7   10   11   10   7   15   12

Use the range and standard deviation to support the previous observation that Dawson Supply provides the more consistent and reliable delivery times.

21. How do grocery costs compare across the country? Using a market basket of 10 items including meat, milk, bread, eggs, coffee, potatoes, cereal, and orange juice, *Where to Retire* magazine calculated the cost of the market basket in six cities and in six retirement areas across the country (*Where to Retire*, November/December 2003). The data with market basket cost to the nearest dollar are as follows:

City	Cost	Retirement Area	Cost
Buffalo, NY	$33	Biloxi-Gulfport, MS	$29
Des Moines, IA	27	Asheville, NC	32
Hartford, CT	32	Flagstaff, AZ	32
Los Angeles, CA	38	Hilton Head, SC	34
Miami, FL	36	Fort Myers, FL	34
Pittsburgh, PA	32	Santa Fe, NM	31

   a. Compute the mean, variance, and standard deviation for the sample of cities and the sample of retirement areas.
   b. What observations can be made based on the two samples?

Broker

22. The American Association of Individual Investors conducted an annual survey of discount brokers (*AAII Journal,* January 2003). The commissions charged by 24 discount brokers for two types of trades, a broker-assisted trade of 100 shares at $50 per share and an on-line trade of 500 shares at $50 per share, are shown in Table 3.2.
    a. Compute the range and interquartile range for each type of trade.
    b. Compute the variance and standard deviation for each type of trade.
    c. Compute the coefficient of variation for each type of trade.
    d. Compare the variability of cost for the two types of trades.

23. *PC World* provided ratings for 15 notebook PCs (*PC World,* February 2000). A 100-point scale was used to provide an overall rating for each notebook. A score in the 90s is exceptional, while one in the 70s is good. The overall ratings for the 15 notebooks are shown here.

Notebook

Notebook	Overall Rating
AMS Tech Roadster 15CTA380	67
Compaq Armada M700	78
Compaq Prosignia Notebook 150	79
Dell Inspiron 3700 C466GT	80
Dell Inspiron 7500 R500VT	84
Dell Latitude Cpi A366XT	76
Enpower ENP-313 Pro	77
Gateway Solo 9300LS	92
HP Pavilion Notebook PC	83
IBM ThinkPad I Series 1480	78
Micro Express NP7400	77
Micron TransPort NX PII-400	78
NEC Versa SX	78
Sceptre Soundx 5200	73
Sony VAIO PCG-F340	77

Compute the range, interquartile range, variance, and standard deviation for this sample of notebook PCs.

24. The following times were recorded by the quarter-mile and mile runners of a university track team (times are in minutes).

Quarter-Mile Times:	.92	.98	1.04	.90	.99
Mile Times:	4.52	4.35	4.60	4.70	4.50

After viewing this sample of running times, one of the coaches commented that the quarter-milers turned in the more consistent times. Use the standard deviation and the coefficient of variation to summarize the variability in the data. Does the use of the coefficient of variation indicate that the coach's statement should be qualified?

3.3 Measures of Distribution Shape, Relative Location, and Detecting Outliers

We have described several measures of location and variability for data. In addition, it is often important to have a measure of the shape of a distribution. In Chapter 2 we noted that a histogram provides a graphical display showing the shape of a distribution. An important numerical measure of the shape of a distribution is called **skewness**.

Distribution Shape

Shown in Figure 3.3 are four histograms constructed from relative frequency distributions. The histograms in Panels A and B are moderately skewed. The one in Panel A is skewed to the left; its skewness is $-.85$. The histogram in Panel B is skewed to the right; its skew-

FIGURE 3.3   HISTOGRAMS SHOWING THE SKEWNESS FOR FOUR DISTRIBUTIONS

ness is +.85. The histogram in Panel C is symmetric; its skewness is zero. The histogram in Panel D is highly skewed to the right; its skewness is 1.62. The formula used to compute skewness is somewhat complex.* However, the skewness can be easily computed using statistical software (see Appendixes 3.1 and 3.2). For data skewed to the left, the skewness is negative; for data skewed to the right, the skewness is positive. If the data are symmetric, the skewness is zero.

For a symmetric distribution, the mean and the median are equal. When the data are positively skewed, the mean will usually be greater than the median; when the data are negatively skewed, the mean will usually be less than the median. The data used to construct the histogram in Panel D are customer purchases at a women's apparel store. The mean purchase amount is $77.60 and the median purchase amount is $59.70. The relatively few large purchase amounts tend to increase the mean, while the median remains unaffected by the large purchase amounts. The median provides the preferred measure of location when the data are highly skewed.

---

*The formula for the skewness of sample data:

$$\text{Skewness} = \frac{n}{(n-1)(n-2)} \sum \left(\frac{x_i - \bar{x}}{s} \right)^3$$

z-Scores

In addition to measures of location, variability, and shape, we are also interested in the relative location of values within a data set. Measures of relative location help us determine how far a particular value is from the mean.

By using both the mean and standard deviation, we can determine the relative location of any observation. Suppose we have a sample of n observations, with the values denoted by $x_1, x_2, \ldots, x_n$. In addition, assume that the sample mean, $\bar{x}$, and the sample standard deviation, s, are already computed. Associated with each value, x_i, is another value called its **z-score**. Equation (3.9) shows how the z-score is computed for each x_i.

z-SCORE

$$z_i = \frac{x_i - \bar{x}}{s} \tag{3.9}$$

where

z_i = the z-score for x_i
$\bar{x}$ = the sample mean
s = the sample standard deviation

The z-score is often called the *standardized value.* The z-score, z_i, can be interpreted as the *number of standard deviations x_i is from the mean $\bar{x}$*. For example, $z_1 = 1.2$ would indicate that x_1 is 1.2 standard deviations greater than the sample mean. Similarly, $z_2 = -.5$ would indicate that x_2 is .5, or 1/2, standard deviation less than the sample mean. A z-score greater than zero occurs for observations with a value greater than the mean, and a z-score less than zero occurs for observations with a value less than the mean. A z-score of zero indicates that the value of the observation is equal to the mean.

The z-score for any observation can be interpreted as a measure of the relative location of the observation in a data set. Thus, observations in two different data sets with the same z-score can be said to have the same relative location in terms of being the same number of standard deviations from the mean.

The z-scores for the class size data are computed in Table 3.5. Recall the previously computed sample mean, $\bar{x} = 44$, and sample standard deviation, $s = 8$. The z-score of -1.50 for the fifth observation shows it is farthest from the mean; it is 1.50 standard deviations below the mean.

TABLE 3.5 z-SCORES FOR THE CLASS SIZE DATA

Number of Students in Class (x_i)	Deviation About the Mean ($x_i - \bar{x}$)	z-score $\left(\dfrac{x_i - \bar{x}}{s} \right)$
46	2	2/8 = .25
54	10	10/8 = 1.25
42	-2	$-2/8 = -.25$
46	2	2/8 = .25
32	-12	$-12/8 = -1.50$

Chebyshev's Theorem

Chebyshev's theorem enables us to make statements about the proportion of data values that must be within a specified number of standard deviations of the mean.

CHEBYSHEV'S THEOREM

At least $(1 - 1/z^2)$ of the data values must be within z standard deviations of the mean, where z is any value greater than 1.

Some of the implications of this theorem, with $z = 2, 3,$ and 4 standard deviations, follow.

- At least .75, or 75%, of the data values must be within $z = 2$ standard deviations of the mean.
- At least .89, or 89%, of the data values must be within $z = 3$ standard deviations of the mean.
- At least .94, or 94%, of the data values must be within $z = 4$ standard deviations of the mean.

For an example using Chebyshev's theorem, suppose that the midterm test scores for 100 students in a college business statistics course had a mean of 70 and a standard deviation of 5. How many students had test scores between 60 and 80? How many students had test scores between 58 and 82?

For the test scores between 60 and 80, we note that 60 is two standard deviations below the mean and 80 is two standard deviations above the mean. Using Chebyshev's theorem, we see that at least .75, or at least 75%, of the observations must have values within two standard deviations of the mean. Thus, at least 75% of the students must have scored between 60 and 80.

Chebyshev's theorem requires z > 1; but z need not be an integer.

For the test scores between 58 and 82, we see that $(58 - 70)/5 = -2.4$ indicates 58 is 2.4 standard deviations below the mean and that $(82 - 70)/5 = +2.4$ indicates 82 is 2.4 standard deviations above the mean. Applying Chebyshev's theorem with $z = 2.4$, we have

$$\left(1 - \frac{1}{z^2}\right) = \left(1 - \frac{1}{(2.4)^2}\right) = .826$$

At least 82.6% of the students must have test scores between 58 and 82.

Empirical Rule

The empirical rule is based on the normal probability distribution, which will be discussed in Chapter 6. The normal distribution is used extensively throughout the text.

One of the advantages of Chebyshev's theorem is that it applies to any data set regardless of the shape of the distribution of the data. Indeed, it could be used with any of the distributions in Figure 3.3. In many practical applications, however, data sets exhibit a symmetric mound-shaped or bell-shaped distribution like the one shown in Figure 3.4. When the data are believed to approximate this distribution, the **empirical rule** can be used to determine the percentage of data values that must be within a specified number of standard deviations of the mean.

EMPIRICAL RULE

For data having a bell-shaped distribution:

- Approximately 68% of the data values will be within one standard deviation of the mean.
- Approximately 95% of the data values will be within two standard deviations of the mean.
- Almost all of the data values will be within three standard deviations of the mean.

FIGURE 3.4   A SYMMETRIC MOUND-SHAPED OR BELL-SHAPED DISTRIBUTION

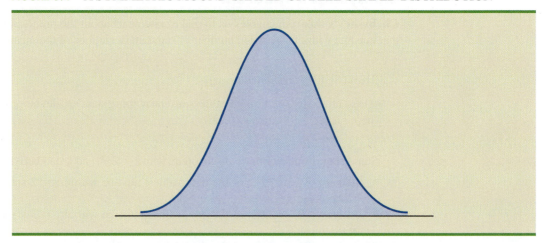

For example, liquid detergent cartons are filled automatically on a production line. Filling weights frequently have a bell-shaped distribution. If the mean filling weight is 16 ounces and the standard deviation is .25 ounces, we can use the empirical rule to draw the following conclusions.

- Approximately 68% of the filled cartons will have weights between 15.75 and 16.25 ounces (within one standard deviation of the mean).
- Approximately 95% of the filled cartons will have weights between 15.50 and 16.50 ounces (within two standard deviations of the mean).
- Almost all filled cartons will have weights between 15.25 and 16.75 ounces (within three standard deviations of the mean).

Detecting Outliers

Sometimes a data set will have one or more observations with unusually large or unusually small values. These extreme values are called **outliers**. Experienced statisticians take steps to identify outliers and then review each one carefully. An outlier may be a data value that has been incorrectly recorded. If so, it can be corrected before further analysis. An outlier may also be from an observation that was incorrectly included in the data set; if so, it can be removed. Finally, an outlier may be an unusual data value that has been recorded correctly and belongs in the data set. In such cases it should remain.

It is a good idea to check for outliers before making decisions based on data analysis. Errors are often made in recording data and entering data into the computer. Outliers should not necessarily be deleted, but their accuracy and appropriateness should be verified.

Standardized values (z-scores) can be used to identify outliers. Recall that the empirical rule allows us to conclude that for data with a bell-shaped distribution, almost all the data values will be within three standard deviations of the mean. Hence, in using z-scores to identify outliers, we recommend treating any data value with a z-score less than -3 or greater than $+3$ as an outlier. Such data values can then be reviewed for accuracy and to determine whether they belong in the data set.

Refer to the z-scores for the class size data in Table 3.5. The z-score of -1.50 shows the fifth class size is farthest from the mean. However, this standardized value is well within the -3 to $+3$ guideline for outliers. Thus, the z-scores do not indicate that outliers are present in the class size data.

NOTES AND COMMENTS

1. Chebyshev's theorem is applicable for any data set and can be used to state the minimum number of data values that will be within a certain number of standard deviations of the mean. If the data are known to be approximately bell-shaped, more can be said. For instance, the empirical rule allows us to say that *approximately* 95% of the data values will be within two standard deviations of the mean; Chebyshev's theorem allows us to conclude only that at least 75% of the data values will be in that interval.

2. Before analyzing a data set, statisticians usually make a variety of checks to ensure the validity of data. In a large study it is not uncommon for errors to be made in recording data values or in entering the values into a computer. Identifying outliers is one tool used to check the validity of the data.

Exercises

Methods

25. Consider a sample with data values of 10, 20, 12, 17, and 16. Compute the z-score for each of the five observations.

26. Consider a sample with a mean of 500 and a standard deviation of 100. What are the z-scores for the following data values: 520, 650, 500, 450, and 280?

27. Consider a sample with a mean of 30 and a standard deviation of 5. Use Chebyshev's theorem to determine the percentage of the data within each of the following ranges.
    a.   20 to 40
    b.   15 to 45
    c.   22 to 38
    d.   18 to 42
    e.   12 to 48

28. Suppose the data have a bell-shaped distribution with a mean of 30 and a standard deviation of 5. Use the empirical rule to determine the percentage of data within each of the following ranges.
    a.   20 to 40
    b.   15 to 45
    c.   25 to 35

Applications

29. The results of a national survey showed that on average, adults sleep 6.9 hours per night (2000 Omnibus Sleep in America Poll). Suppose that the standard deviation is 1.2 hours.
    a.   Use Chebyshev's theorem to calculate the percentage of individuals who sleep between 4.5 and 9.3 hours.
    b.   Use Chebyshev's theorem to calculate the percentage of individuals who sleep between 3.9 and 9.9 hours.
    c.   Assume that the number of hours of sleep follows a bell-shaped distribution. Use the empirical rule to calculate the percentage of individuals who sleep between 4.5 and 9.3 hours per day. How does this result compare to the value that you obtained using Chebyshev's theorem in part (a)?

30. The Energy Information Administration reported that the mean retail price per gallon of regular grade gasoline was $1.47 (*The Wall Street Journal,* January 30, 2003). Suppose that the standard deviation was $.08 and that the retail price per gallon has a bell-shaped distribution.
    a.   What percentage of regular grade gasoline sold between $1.39 and $1.55 per gallon?
    b.   What percentage of regular grade gasoline sold between $1.39 and $1.63 per gallon?
    c.   What percentage of regular grade gasoline sold for more than $1.63 per gallon?

31. The national average for the verbal portion of the College Board's Scholastic Aptitude Test (SAT) is 507 (*The World Almanac,* 2004). The College Board periodically rescales the test scores such that the standard deviation is approximately 100. Answer the following questions using a bell-shaped distribution and the empirical rule for the verbal test scores.

a. What percentage of students have an SAT verbal score greater than 607?
b. What percentage of students have an SAT verbal score greater than 707?
c. What percentage of students have an SAT verbal score between 407 and 507?
d. What percentage of students have an SAT verbal score between 307 and 607?

32. The high costs in the California real estate market have caused families who cannot afford to buy bigger homes to consider backyard sheds as an alternative form of housing expansion. Many are using the backyard structures for home offices, art studios, and hobby areas as well as for additional storage. The mean price of a customized wooden, shingled backyard structure is $3100 (*Newsweek*, September 29, 2003). Assume that the standard deviation is $1200.
a. What is the *z*-score for a backyard structure costing $2300?
b. What is the *z*-score for a backyard structure costing $4900?
c. Interpret the *z*-scores in parts (a) and (b). Comment on whether either should be considered an outlier.
d. The *Newsweek* article described a backyard shed-office combination built in Albany, California, for $13,000. Should this structure be considered an outlier? Explain.

33. Wageweb conducts surveys of salary data and presents summaries on its Web site. Salaries reported for benefits managers ranged from $50,935 to $79,577 (Wageweb.com, April 12, 2000). Assume the following data are a sample of the annual salaries for 30 benefits managers. Data are in thousands of dollars.

WageWeb

57.7	64.4	62.1	59.1	71.1
63.0	64.7	61.2	66.8	61.8
64.2	63.3	62.2	61.2	59.4
63.0	66.7	60.3	74.0	62.8
68.7	63.8	59.2	60.3	56.6
59.3	69.5	61.7	58.9	63.1

a. Compute the mean and standard deviation for the sample data.
b. Using the mean and standard deviation computed in part (a) as estimates of the mean and standard deviation of salary for the population of benefits managers, use Chebyshev's theorem to determine the percentage of benefits managers with an annual salary between $55,000 and $71,000.
c. Develop a histogram for the sample data. Computer software provides .97 as the measure of skewness. Does it appear reasonable to assume that the distribution of annual salary can be approximated by a bell-shaped distribution?
d. Assume that the distribution of annual salary is bell-shaped. Using the mean and standard deviation computed in part (a) as estimates of the mean and standard deviation of salary for the population of benefits managers, use the empirical rule to determine the percentage of benefits managers with an annual salary between $55,000 and $71,000. Compare your answer with the value computed in part (b).
e. Do the sample data contain any outliers?

34. A sample of 10 NCAA college basketball game scores provided the following data (*USA Today*, January 26, 2004).

NCAA

Winning Team	Points	Losing Team	Points	Winning Margin
Arizona	90	Oregon	66	24
Duke	85	Georgetown	66	19
Florida State	75	Wake Forest	70	5
Kansas	78	Colorado	57	21
Kentucky	71	Notre Dame	63	8
Louisville	65	Tennessee	62	3
Oklahoma State	72	Texas	66	6

Winning Team	Points	Losing Team	Points	Winning Margin
Purdue	76	Michigan State	70	6
Stanford	77	Southern Cal	67	10
Wisconsin	76	Illinois	56	20

    a.   Compute the mean and standard deviation for the points scored by the winning team.

    b.   Assume that the points scored by the winning teams for all NCAA games follow a bell-shaped distribution. Using the mean and standard deviation found in part (a), estimate the percentage of all NCAA games in which the winning team scores 84 or more points. Estimate the percentage of NCAA games in which the winning team scores more than 90 points.

    c.   Compute the mean and standard deviation for the winning margin. Do the data contain outliers? Explain.

35. *Consumer Review* posts reviews and ratings of a variety of products on the Internet. The following is a sample of 20 speaker systems and their ratings (http://www.audioreview.com). The ratings are on a scale of 1 to 5, with 5 being best.

Speakers

Speaker	Rating	Speaker	Rating
Infinity Kappa 6.1	4.00	ACI Sapphire III	4.67
Allison One	4.12	Bose 501 Series	2.14
Cambridge Ensemble II	3.82	DCM KX-212	4.09
Dynaudio Contour 1.3	4.00	Eosone RSF1000	4.17
Hsu Rsch. HRSW12V	4.56	Joseph Audio RM7si	4.88
Legacy Audio Focus	4.32	Martin Logan Aerius	4.26
Mission 73li	4.33	Omni Audio SA 12.3	2.32
PSB 400i	4.50	Polk Audio RT12	4.50
Snell Acoustics D IV	4.64	Sunfire True Subwoofer	4.17
Thiel CS1.5	4.20	Yamaha NS-A636	2.17

    a.   Compute the mean and the median.

    b.   Compute the first and third quartiles.

    c.   Compute the standard deviation.

    d.   The skewness of this data is -1.67. Comment on the shape of the distribution.

    e.   What are the z-scores associated with Allison One and Omni Audio?

    f.   Do the data contain any outliers? Explain.

3.4   Exploratory Data Analysis

In Chapter 2 we introduced the stem-and-leaf display as a technique of exploratory data analysis. Recall that exploratory data analysis enables us to use simple arithmetic and easy-to-draw pictures to summarize data. In this section we continue exploratory data analysis by considering five-number summaries and box plots.

Five-Number Summary

In a **five-number summary**, the following five numbers are used to summarize the data.

    1. Smallest value

    2. First quartile (Q_1)

    3. Median (Q_2)

4. Third quartile (Q_3)
5. Largest value

The easiest way to develop a five-number summary is to first place the data in ascending order. Then it is easy to identify the smallest value, the three quartiles, and the largest value. The monthly starting salaries shown in Table 3.1 for a sample of 12 business school graduates are repeated here in ascending order.

2710   2755   2850 | 2880   2880   2890 | 2920   2940   2950 | 3050   3130   3325

$Q_1 = 2865$ $Q_2 = 2905$ $Q_3 = 3000$
                         (Median)

The median of 2905 and the quartiles $Q_1 = 2865$ and $Q_3 = 3000$ were computed in Section 3.1. Reviewing the data shows a smallest value of 2710 and a largest value of 3325. Thus the five-number summary for the salary data is 2710, 2865, 2905, 3000, 3325. Approximately one-fourth, or 25%, of the observations are between adjacent numbers in a five-number summary.

Box Plot

A **box plot** is a graphical summary of data that is based on a five-number summary. A key to the development of a box plot is the computation of the median and the quartiles, Q_1 and Q_3. The interquartile range, IQR = $Q_3 - Q_1$, is also used. Figure 3.5 is the box plot for the monthly starting salary data. The steps used to construct the box plot follow.

Box plots provide another way to identify outliers. But they do not necessarily identify the same values as those with a z-score less than −3 or greater than +3. Either or both procedures may be used.

1. A box is drawn with the ends of the box located at the first and third quartiles. For the salary data, $Q_1 = 2865$ and $Q_3 = 3000$. This box contains the middle 50% of the data.
2. A vertical line is drawn in the box at the location of the median (2905 for the salary data).
3. By using the interquartile range, IQR = $Q_3 - Q_1$, *limits* are located. The limits for the box plot are 1.5(IQR) below Q_1 and 1.5(IQR) above Q_3. For the salary data, IQR = $Q_3 - Q_1 = 3000 - 2865 = 135$. Thus, the limits are 2865 − 1.5(135) = 2662.5 and 3000 + 1.5(135) = 3202.5. Data outside these limits are considered *outliers*.
4. The dashed lines in Figure 3.5 are called *whiskers*. The whiskers are drawn from the ends of the box to the smallest and largest values *inside the limits* computed in step 3. Thus, the whiskers end at salary values of 2710 and 3130.
5. Finally, the location of each outlier is shown with the symbol *. In Figure 3.5 we see one outlier, 3325.

FIGURE 3.5   BOX PLOT OF THE STARTING SALARY DATA WITH LINES SHOWING THE LOWER AND UPPER LIMITS

In Figure 3.5 we included lines showing the location of the upper and lower limits. These lines were drawn to show how the limits are computed and where they are located for the salary data. Although the limits are always computed, generally they are not drawn on the box plots. Figure 3.6 shows the usual appearance of a box plot for the salary data.

FIGURE 3.6   BOX PLOT OF THE STARTING SALARY DATA

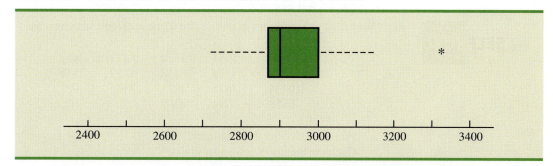

NOTES AND COMMENTS

1. An advantage of the exploratory data analysis procedures is that they are easy to use; few numerical calculations are necessary. We simply sort the data values into ascending order and identify the five-number summary. The box plot can then be constructed. It is not necessary to compute the mean and the standard deviation for the data.

2. In Appendix 3.1, we show how to construct a box plot for the starting salary data using Minitab. The box plot obtained looks just like the one in Figure 3.6, but turned on its side.

Exercises

Methods

36. Consider a sample with data values of 27, 25, 20, 15, 30, 34, 28, and 25. Provide the five-number summary for the data.

37. Show the box plot for the data in exercise 36.

38. Show the five-number summary and the box plot for the following data: 5, 15, 18, 10, 8, 12, 16, 10, 6.

39. A data set has a first quartile of 42 and a third quartile of 50. Compute the lower and upper limits for the corresponding box plot. Should a data value of 65 be considered an outlier?

Applications

40. Ebby Halliday Realtors provide advertisements for distinctive properties and estates located throughout the United States. The prices listed for 22 distinctive properties and estates are shown here (*The Wall Street Journal,* January 16, 2004). Prices are in thousands.

Property

1500	700	2995
895	619	880
719	725	3100
619	739	1699
625	799	1120
4450	2495	1250
2200	1395	912
1280		

a. Provide a five-number summary.
b. Compute the lower and upper limits.
c. The highest priced property, $4,450,000, is listed as an estate overlooking White Rock Lake in Dallas, Texas. Should this property be considered an outlier? Explain.
d. Should the second highest priced property listed for $3,100,000 be considered an outlier? Explain.
e. Show a box plot.

41. Annual sales, in millions of dollars, for 21 pharmaceutical companies follow.

8408	1374	1872	8879	2459	11413
608	14138	6452	1850	2818	1356
10498	7478	4019	4341	739	2127
3653	5794	8305			

a. Provide a five-number summary.
b. Compute the lower and upper limits.
c. Do the data contain any outliers?
d. Johnson & Johnson's sales are the largest on the list at $14,138 million. Suppose a data entry error (a transposition) had been made and the sales had been entered as $41,138 million. Would the method of detecting outliers in part (c) identify this problem and allow for correction of the data entry error?
e. Show a box plot.

42. Major League Baseball payrolls continue to escalate. Team payrolls in millions are as follows (*The Miami Herald*, May 22, 2002).

CD file

Payroll

Team	Payroll	Team	Payroll
Anaheim	$ 62	Milwaukee	$ 50
Arizona	103	Minnesota	40
Atlanta	93	Montreal	39
Baltimore	60	NY Mets	95
Boston	108	NY Yankees	126
Chi Cubs	76	Oakland	40
Chi White Sox	57	Philadelphia	58
Cincinnati	45	Pittsburgh	42
Cleveland	79	San Diego	41
Colorado	57	San Francisco	78
Detroit	55	Seattle	90
Florida	42	St. Louis	74
Houston	63	Tampa Bay	34
Kansas City	47	Texas	105
Los Angeles	95	Toronto	77

a. What is the median team payroll?
b. Provide a five-number summary.
c. Is the $126 million payroll for the New York Yankees an outlier? Explain.
d. Show a box plot.

43. New York Stock Exchange (NYSE) Chairman Richard Grasso and NYSE Board of Directors came under fire for the large compensation package being paid to Grasso. When it comes to salary plus bonus, Grasso's $8.5 million out-earned the top executives of all major financial services companies. The data that follow show total annual salary plus bonus paid

to the top executives of 14 financial services companies (*The Wall Street Journal,* September 17, 2003). Data are in millions.

Company	Salary/Bonus	Company	Salary/Bonus
Aetna	$3.5	Fannie Mae	$4.3
AIG	6.0	Federal Home Loan	0.8
Allstate	4.1	Fleet Boston	1.0
American Express	3.8	Freddie Mac	1.2
Chubb	2.1	Mellon Financial	2.0
Cigna	1.0	Merrill Lynch	7.7
Citigroup	1.0	Wells Fargo	8.0

a. What is the median annual salary plus bonus paid to the top executive of the 14 financial service companies?
b. Provide a five-number summary.
c. Should Grasso's $8.5 million annual salary plus bonus be considered an outlier for this group of top executives? Explain.
d. Show a box plot.

44. A listing of 46 mutual funds and their 12-month total return percentage is shown in Table 3.6 (*Smart Money,* February 2004).

Mutual

a. What are the mean and median return percentages for these mutual funds?
b. What are the first and third quartiles?
c. Provide a five-number summary.
d. Do the data contain any outliers? Show a box plot.

TABLE 3.6   TWELVE-MONTH RETURN FOR MUTUAL FUNDS

Mutual Fund	Return (%)	Mutual Fund	Return (%)
Alger Capital Appreciation	23.5	Nations Small Company	21.4
Alger LargeCap Growth	22.8	Nations SmallCap Index	24.5
Alger MidCap Growth	38.3	Nations Strategic Growth	10.4
Alger SmallCap	41.3	Nations Value Inv	10.8
AllianceBernstein Technology	40.6	One Group Diversified Equity	10.0
Federated American Leaders	15.6	One Group Diversified Int'l	10.9
Federated Capital Appreciation	12.4	One Group Diversified Mid Cap	15.1
Federated Equity-Income	11.5	One Group Equity Income	6.6
Federated Kaufmann	33.3	One Group Int'l Equity Index	13.2
Federated Max-Cap Index	16.0	One Group Large Cap Growth	13.6
Federated Stock	16.9	One Group Large Cap Value	12.8
Janus Adviser Int'l Growth	10.3	One Group Mid Cap Growth	18.7
Janus Adviser Worldwide	3.4	One Group Mid Cap Value	11.4
Janus Enterprise	24.2	One Group Small Cap Growth	23.6
Janus High-Yield	12.1	PBHG Growth	27.3
Janus Mercury	20.6	Putnam Europe Equity	20.4
Janus Overseas	11.9	Putnam Int'l Capital Opportunity	36.6
Janus Worldwide	4.1	Putnam International Equity	21.5
Nations Convertible Securities	13.6	Putnam Int'l New Opportunity	26.3
Nations Int'l Equity	10.7	Strong Advisor Mid Cap Growth	23.7
Nations LargeCap Enhd. Core	13.2	Strong Growth 20	11.7
Nations LargeCap Index	13.5	Strong Growth Inv	23.2
Nation MidCap Index	19.5	Strong Large Cap Growth	14.5

3.5 Measures of Association Between Two Variables

Thus far we examined numerical methods used to summarize the data for *one variable at a time*. Often a manager or decision maker is interested in the *relationship between two variables*. In this section we present covariance and correlation as descriptive measures of the relationship between two variables.

We begin by reconsidering the application concerning a stereo and sound equipment store in San Francisco as presented in Section 2.4. The store's manager wants to determine the relationship between the number of weekend television commercials shown and the sales at the store during the following week. Sample data with sales expressed in hundreds of dollars are provided in Table 3.7. It shows 10 observations ($n = 10$), one for each week. The scatter diagram in Figure 3.7 shows a positive relationship, with higher sales (y) associated with a greater number of commercials (x). In fact, the scatter diagram suggests that a straight line could be used as an approximation of the relationship. In the following discussion, we introduce **covariance** as a descriptive measure of the linear association between two variables.

Covariance

For a sample of size n with the observations (x_1, y_1), (x_2, y_2), and so on, the sample covariance is defined as follows:

SAMPLE COVARIANCE

$$s_{xy} = \frac{\Sigma(x_i - \bar{x})(y_i - \bar{y})}{n - 1} \tag{3.10}$$

This formula pairs each x_i with a y_i. We then sum the products obtained by multiplying the deviation of each x_i from its sample mean $\bar{x}$ by the deviation of the corresponding y_i from its sample mean $\bar{y}$; this sum is then divided by $n - 1$.

TABLE 3.7 SAMPLE DATA FOR THE STEREO AND SOUND EQUIPMENT STORE

Week	Number of Commercials x	Sales Volume ($100s) y
1	2	50
2	5	57
3	1	41
4	3	54
5	4	54
6	1	38
7	5	63
8	3	48
9	4	59
10	2	46

FIGURE 3.7   SCATTER DIAGRAM FOR THE STEREO AND SOUND EQUIPMENT STORE

To measure the strength of the linear relationship between the number of commercials x and the sales volume y in the stereo and sound equipment store problem, we use equation (3.10) to compute the sample covariance. The calculations in Table 3.8 show the computation of $\Sigma(x_i - \bar{x})(y_i - \bar{y})$. Note that $\bar{x} = 30/10 = 3$ and $\bar{y} = 510/10 = 51$. Using equation (3.10), we obtain a sample covariance of

$$s_{xy} = \frac{\Sigma(x_i - \bar{x})(y_i - \bar{y})}{n - 1} = \frac{99}{9} = 11$$

TABLE 3.8   CALCULATIONS FOR THE SAMPLE COVARIANCE

x_i	y_i	$x_i - \bar{x}$	$y_i - \bar{y}$	$(x_i - \bar{x})(y_i - \bar{y})$
2	50	−1	−1	1
5	57	2	6	12
1	41	−2	−10	20
3	54	0	3	0
4	54	1	3	3
1	38	−2	−13	26
5	63	2	12	24
3	48	0	−3	0
4	59	1	8	8
2	46	−1	−5	5
Totals 30	510	0	0	99

$$s_{xy} = \frac{\Sigma(x_i - \bar{x})(y_i - \bar{y})}{n - 1} = \frac{99}{10 - 1} = 11$$

The formula for computing the covariance of a population of size N is similar to equation (3.10), but we use different notation to indicate that we are working with the entire population.

POPULATION COVARIANCE

$$\sigma_{xy} = \frac{\Sigma(x_i - \mu_x)(y_i - \mu_y)}{N}$$

(3.11)

In equation (3.11) we use the notation μ_x for the population mean of the variable x and μ_y for the population mean of the variable y. The population covariance σ_{xy} is defined for a population of size N.

Interpretation of the Covariance

The covariance is a measure of the linear association between two variables.

To aid in the interpretation of the sample covariance, consider Figure 3.8. It is the same as the scatter diagram of Figure 3.7 with a vertical dashed line at $\bar{x} = 3$ and a horizontal dashed line at $\bar{y} = 51$. The lines divide the graph into four quadrants. Points in quadrant I correspond to x_i greater than $\bar{x}$ and y_i greater than $\bar{y}$, points in quadrant II correspond to x_i less than $\bar{x}$ and y_i greater than $\bar{y}$, and so on. Thus, the value of $(x_i - \bar{x})(y_i - \bar{y})$ must be positive for points in quadrant I, negative for points in quadrant II, positive for points in quadrant III, and negative for points in quadrant IV.

If the value of s_{xy} is positive, the points with the greatest influence on s_{xy} must be in quadrants I and III. Hence, a positive value for s_{xy} indicates a positive linear association between x and y; that is, as the value of x increases, the value of y increases. If the value of s_{xy} is negative, however, the points with the greatest influence on s_{xy} are in quadrants II and IV. Hence, a negative value for s_{xy} indicates a negative linear association between x and y; that is, as the value of x increases, the value of y decreases. Finally, if the points are evenly distributed across all four quadrants, the value of s_{xy} will be close to zero, indicating no linear association between x and y. Figure 3.9 shows the values of s_{xy} that can be expected with three different types of scatter diagrams.

FIGURE 3.8   PARTITIONED SCATTER DIAGRAM FOR THE STEREO AND SOUND EQUIPMENT STORE

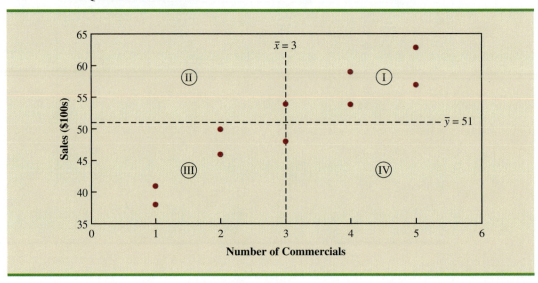

FIGURE 3.9   INTERPRETATION OF SAMPLE COVARIANCE

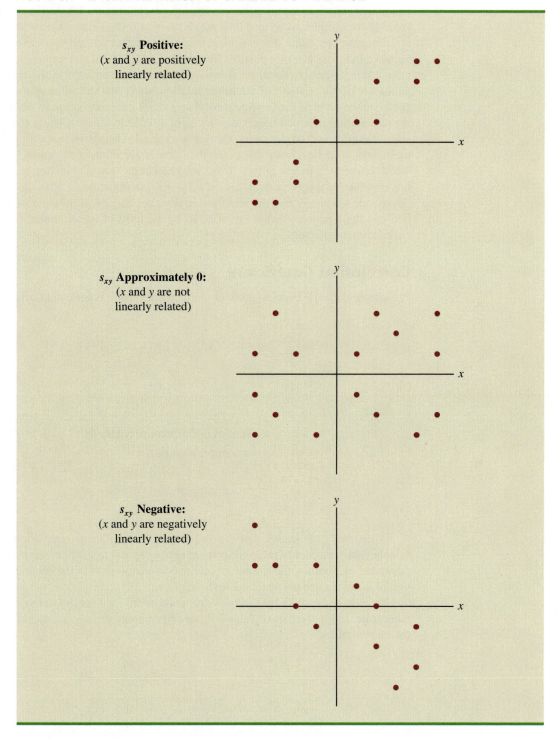

Referring again to Figure 3.8, we see that the scatter diagram for the stereo and sound equipment store follows the pattern in the top panel of Figure 3.9. As we should expect, the value of the sample covariance indicates a positive linear relationship with $s_{xy} = 11$.

From the preceding discussion, it might appear that a large positive value for the covariance indicates a strong positive linear relationship and that a large negative value indicates a strong negative linear relationship. However, one problem with using covariance as a measure of the strength of the linear relationship is that the value of the covariance depends on the units of measurement for x and y. For example, suppose we are interested in the relationship between height x and weight y for individuals. Clearly the strength of the relationship should be the same whether we measure height in feet or inches. Measuring the height in inches, however, gives us much larger numerical values for $(x_i - \bar{x})$ than when we measure height in feet. Thus, with height measured in inches, we would obtain a larger value for the numerator $\Sigma(x_i - \bar{x})(y_i - \bar{y})$ in equation (3.10)—and hence a larger covariance—when in fact the relationship does not change. A measure of the relationship between two variables that is not affected by the units of measurement for x and y is the **correlation coefficient**.

Correlation Coefficient

For sample data, the Pearson product moment correlation coefficient is defined as follows.

PEARSON PRODUCT MOMENT CORRELATION COEFFICIENT: SAMPLE DATA

$$r_{xy} = \frac{s_{xy}}{s_x s_y} \qquad (3.12)$$

where

r_{xy} = sample correlation coefficient
s_{xy} = sample covariance
s_x = sample standard deviation of x
s_y = sample standard deviation of y

Equation (3.12) shows that the Pearson product moment correlation coefficient for sample data (commonly referred to more simply as the *sample correlation coefficient*) is computed by dividing the sample covariance by the product of the sample standard deviation of x and the sample standard deviation of y.

Let us now compute the sample correlation coefficient for the stereo and sound equipment store. Using the data in Table 3.8, we can compute the sample standard deviations for the two variables.

$$s_x = \sqrt{\frac{\Sigma(x_i - \bar{x})^2}{n - 1}} = \sqrt{\frac{20}{9}} = 1.49$$

$$s_y = \sqrt{\frac{\Sigma(y_i - \bar{y})^2}{n - 1}} = \sqrt{\frac{566}{9}} = 7.93$$

Now, because $s_{xy} = 11$, the sample correlation coefficient equals

$$r_{xy} = \frac{s_{xy}}{s_x s_y} = \frac{11}{(1.49)(7.93)} = +.93$$

The formula for computing the correlation coefficient for a population, denoted by the Greek letter ρ_{xy} (rho, pronounced "row"), follows.

PEARSON PRODUCT MOMENT CORRELATION COEFFICIENT: POPULATION DATA

The sample correlation coefficient r_{xy} is the estimator of the population correlation coefficient ρ_{xy}.

$$\rho_{xy} = \frac{\sigma_{xy}}{\sigma_x \sigma_y}$$

(3.13)

where

ρ_{xy} = population correlation coefficient
σ_{xy} = population covariance
σ_x = population standard deviation for x
σ_y = population standard deviation for y

The sample correlation coefficient r_{xy} provides an estimate of the population correlation coefficient ρ_{xy}.

Interpretation of the Correlation Coefficient

First let us consider a simple example that illustrates the concept of a perfect positive linear relationship. The scatter diagram in Figure 3.10 depicts the relationship between x and y based on the following sample data.

x_i	y_i
5	10
10	30
15	50

FIGURE 3.10   SCATTER DIAGRAM DEPICTING A PERFECT POSITIVE LINEAR RELATIONSHIP

The straight line drawn through each of the three points shows a perfect linear relationship between x and y. In order to apply equation (3.12) to compute the sample correlation we must first compute s_{xy}, s_x, and s_y. Some of the computations are shown in Table 3.9. Using the results in Table 3.9, we find

$$s_{xy} = \frac{\Sigma(x_i - \bar{x})(y_i - \bar{y})}{n - 1} = \frac{200}{2} = 100$$

$$s_x = \sqrt{\frac{\Sigma(x_i - \bar{x})^2}{n - 1}} = \sqrt{\frac{50}{2}} = 5$$

$$s_y = \sqrt{\frac{\Sigma(y_i - \bar{y})^2}{n - 1}} = \sqrt{\frac{800}{2}} = 20$$

$$r_{xy} = \frac{s_{xy}}{s_x s_y} = \frac{100}{5(20)} = 1$$

The correlation coefficient ranges from −1 to +1. Values close to −1 or +1 indicate a strong linear relationship. The closer the correlation is to zero, the weaker the relationship.

Thus, we see that the value of the sample correlation coefficient is 1.

In general, it can be shown that if all the points in a data set fall on a positively sloped straight line, the value of the sample correlation coefficient is +1; that is, a sample correlation coefficient of +1 corresponds to a perfect positive linear relationship between x and y. Moreover, if the points in the data set fall on a straight line having negative slope, the value of the sample correlation coefficient is −1; that is, a sample correlation coefficient of −1 corresponds to a perfect negative linear relationship between x and y.

Let us now suppose that a certain data set indicates a positive linear relationship between x and y but that the relationship is not perfect. The value of r_{xy} will be less than 1, indicating that the points in the scatter diagram are not all on a straight line. As the points deviate more and more from a perfect positive linear relationship, the value of r_{xy} becomes smaller and smaller. A value of r_{xy} equal to zero indicates no linear relationship between x and y, and values of r_{xy} near zero indicate a weak linear relationship.

For the data involving the stereo and sound equipment store, recall that $r_{xy} = +.93$. Therefore, we conclude that a strong positive linear relationship occurs between the number of commercials and sales. More specifically, an increase in the number of commercials is associated with an increase in sales.

In closing, we note that correlation provides a measure of linear association and not necessarily causation. A high correlation between two variables does not mean that changes in one variable will cause changes in the other variable. For example, we may find that the quality rating and the typical meal price of restaurants are positively correlated. However, simply increasing the meal price at a restaurant will not cause the quality rating to increase.

TABLE 3.9   COMPUTATIONS USED IN CALCULATING THE SAMPLE CORRELATION COEFFICIENT

	x_i	y_i	$x_i - \bar{x}$	$(x_i - \bar{x})^2$	$y_i - \bar{y}$	$(y_i - \bar{y})^2$	$(x_i - \bar{x})(y_i - \bar{y})$
	5	10	−5	25	−20	400	100
	10	30	0	0	0	0	0
	15	50	5	25	20	400	100
Totals	30	90	0	50	0	800	200

$\bar{x} = 10$ $\bar{y} = 30$

Exercises

Methods

45. Five observations taken for two variables follow.

x_i	4	6	11	3	16
y_i	50	50	40	60	30

a. Develop a scatter diagram with x on the horizontal axis.
b. What does the scatter diagram developed in part (a) indicate about the relationship between the two variables?
c. Compute and interpret the sample covariance.
d. Compute and interpret the sample correlation coefficient.

46. Five observations taken for two variables follow.

x_i	6	11	15	21	27
y_i	6	9	6	17	12

a. Develop a scatter diagram for these data.
b. What does the scatter diagram indicate about a relationship between x and y?
c. Compute and interpret the sample covariance.
d. Compute and interpret the sample correlation coefficient.

Applications

47. Nielsen Media Research provides two measures of the television viewing audience: a television program *rating*, which is the percentage of households with televisions watching a program, and a television program *share*, which is the percentage of households watching a program among those with televisions in use. The following data show the Nielsen television ratings and share data for the Major League Baseball World Series over a nine-year period (Associated Press, October 27, 2003).

Rating	19	17	17	14	16	12	15	12	13
Share	32	28	29	24	26	20	24	20	22

a. Develop a scatter diagram with rating on the horizontal axis.
b. What is the relationship between rating and share? Explain.
c. Compute and interpret the sample covariance.
d. Compute the sample correlation coefficient. What does this value tell us about the relationship between rating and share?

48. A department of transportation's study on driving speed and mileage for midsize automobiles resulted in the following data.

Driving Speed	30	50	40	55	30	25	60	25	50	55
Mileage	28	25	25	23	30	32	21	35	26	25

Compute and interpret the sample correlation coefficient.

49. *PC World* provided ratings for 15 notebook PCs (*PC World,* February 2000). The performance score is a measure of how fast a PC can run a mix of common business applications as compared to a baseline machine. For example, a PC with a performance score of 200 is twice as fast as the baseline machine. A 100-point scale was used to provide an overall rating for each notebook tested in the study. A score in the 90s is exceptional, while one in the 70s is good. Table 3.10 shows the performance scores and the overall ratings for the 15 notebooks.

TABLE 3.10   PERFORMANCE SCORES AND OVERALL RATINGS FOR 15 NOTEBOOK PCs

PCs

Notebook	Performance Score	Overall Rating
AMS Tech Roadster 15CTA380	115	67
Compaq Armada M700	191	78
Compaq Prosignia Notebook 150	153	79
Dell Inspiron 3700 C466GT	194	80
Dell Inspiron 7500 R500VT	236	84
Dell Latitude Cpi A366XT	184	76
Enpower ENP-313 Pro	184	77
Gateway Solo 9300LS	216	92
HP Pavilion Notebook PC	185	83
IBM ThinkPad I Series 1480	183	78
Micro Express NP7400	189	77
Micron TransPort NX PII-400	202	78
NEC Versa SX	192	78
Sceptre Soundx 5200	141	73
Sony VAIO PCG-F340	187	77

a.   Compute the sample correlation coefficient.
b.   What does the sample correlation coefficient tell about the relationship between the performance score and the overall rating?

50.   The Dow Jones Industrial Average (DJIA) and the Standard & Poor's (S&P) 500 Index are both used as measures of overall movement in the stock market. The DJIA is based on the price movements of 30 large companies; the S&P 500 is an index composed of 500 stocks. Some say the S&P 500 is a better measure of stock market performance because it is broader based. The closing price for the DJIA and the S&P 500 for 10 weeks, beginning with February 11, 2000, are shown (*Barron's,* April 17, 2000).

DowS&P

Date	Dow Jones	S&P 500	Date	Dow Jones	S&P 500
February 11	10425	1387	March 17	10595	1464
February 18	10220	1346	March 24	11113	1527
February 25	9862	1333	March 31	10922	1499
March 3	10367	1409	April 7	11111	1516
March 10	9929	1395	April 14	10306	1357

a.   Compute the sample correlation coefficient for these data.
b.   Discuss the association between the DJIA and the S&P 500 Index.

51.   The daily high and low temperatures for 12 U.S. cities are as follows (Weather Channel, January 25, 2004).

Temperature

City	High	Low	City	High	Low
Albany	9	−8	Los Angeles	62	47
Boise	32	26	New Orleans	71	55
Cleveland	21	19	Portland	43	36
Denver	37	10	Providence	18	8
Des Moines	24	16	Raleigh	28	24
Detroit	20	17	Tulsa	55	38

a.   What is the sample mean daily high temperature?
b.   What is the sample mean daily low temperature?
c.   What is the correlation between the high and low temperatures?

3.6   The Weighted Mean and Working with Grouped Data

In Section 3.1, we presented the mean as one of the most important measures of central location. The formula for the mean of a sample with n observations is restated as follows.

$$\bar{x} = \frac{\Sigma x_i}{n} = \frac{x_1 + x_2 + \cdots + x_n}{n} \qquad \textbf{(3.14)}$$

In this formula, each x_i is given equal importance or weight. Although this practice is most common, in some instances, the mean is computed by giving each observation a weight that reflects its importance. A mean computed in this manner is referred to as a **weighted mean**.

Weighted Mean

The weighted mean is computed as follows:

WEIGHTED MEAN

$$\bar{x} = \frac{\Sigma w_i x_i}{\Sigma w_i} \qquad \textbf{(3.15)}$$

where

x_i = value of observation i
w_i = weight for observation i

When the data are from a sample, equation (3.15) provides the weighted sample mean. When the data are from a population, μ replaces $\bar{x}$ and equation (3.15) provides the weighted population mean.

   As an example of the need for a weighted mean, consider the following sample of five purchases of a raw material over the past three months.

Purchase	Cost per Pound ($)	Number of Pounds
1	3.00	1200
2	3.40	500
3	2.80	2750
4	2.90	1000
5	3.25	800

Note that the cost per pound varies from $2.80 to $3.40, and the quantity purchased varies from 500 to 2750 pounds. Suppose that a manager asked for information about the mean cost per pound of the raw material. Because the quantities ordered vary, we must use the formula for a weighted mean. The five cost-per-pound data values are $x_1 = 3.00, x_2 = 3.40, x_3 = 2.80$, $x_4 = 2.90$, and $x_5 = 3.25$. The weighted mean cost per pound is found by weighting each cost by its corresponding quantity. For this example, the weights are $w_1 = 1200$, $w_2 = 500$, $w_3 = 2750$, $w_4 = 1000$, and $w_5 = 800$. Using equation (3.15), the weighted mean is calculated as follows:

$$\bar{x} = \frac{1200(3.00) + 500(3.40) + 2750(2.80) + 1000(2.90) + 800(3.25)}{1200 + 500 + 2750 + 1000 + 800}$$

$$= \frac{18,500}{6250} = 2.96$$

Thus, the weighted mean computation shows that the mean cost per pound for the raw material is $2.96. Note that using equation (3.14) rather than the weighted mean formula would have provided misleading results. In this case, the mean of the five cost-per-pound values is $(3.00 + 3.40 + 2.80 + 2.90 + 3.25)/5 = 15.35/5 = \$3.07$, which overstates the actual mean cost per pound purchased.

The choice of weights for a particular weighted mean computation depends upon the application. An example that is well known to college students is the computation of a grade point average (GPA). In this computation, the data values generally used are 4 for an A grade, 3 for a B grade, 2 for a C grade, 1 for a D grade, and 0 for an F grade. The weights are the number of credits hours earned for each grade. Exercise 54 at the end of this section provides an example of this weighted mean computation. In other weighted mean computations, quantities such as pounds, dollars, or volume are frequently used as weights. In any case, when observations vary in importance, the analyst must choose the weight that best reflects the importance of each observation in the determination of the mean.

Computing a grade point average is a good example of the use of a weighted mean.

Grouped Data

In most cases, measures of location and variability are computed by using the individual data values. Sometimes, however, data are available only in a grouped or frequency distribution form. In the following discussion, we show how the weighted mean formula can be used to obtain approximations of the mean, variance, and standard deviation for **grouped data**.

In Section 2.2 we provided a frequency distribution of the time in days required to complete year-end audits for the public accounting firm of Sanderson and Clifford. The frequency distribution of audit times based on a sample of 20 clients is shown again in Table 3.11. Based on this frequency distribution, what is the sample mean audit time?

To compute the mean using only the grouped data, we treat the midpoint of each class as being representative of the items in the class. Let M_i denote the midpoint for class i and let f_i denote the frequency of class i. The weighted mean formula (3.15) is then used with the data values denoted as M_i and the weights given by the frequencies f_i. In this case, the denominator of equation (3.15) is the sum of the frequencies, which is the

TABLE 3.11   FREQUENCY DISTRIBUTION OF AUDIT TIMES

Audit Time (days)	Frequency
10–14	4
15–19	8
20–24	5
25–29	2
30–34	1
Total	20

sample size n. That is, $\Sigma f_i = n$. Thus, the equation for the sample mean for grouped data is as follows.

SAMPLE MEAN FOR GROUPED DATA

$$\bar{x} = \frac{\Sigma f_i M_i}{n} \qquad \qquad \textbf{(3.16)}$$

where

$$M_i = \text{the midpoint for class } i$$
$$f_i = \text{the frequency for class } i$$
$$n = \text{the sample size}$$

With the class midpoints, M_i, halfway between the class limits, the first class of 10–14 in Table 3.11 has a midpoint at $(10 + 14)/2 = 12$. The five class midpoints and the weighted mean computation for the audit time data are summarized in Table 3.12. As can be seen, the sample mean audit time is 19 days.

To compute the variance for grouped data, we use a slightly altered version of the formula for the variance provided in equation (3.5). In equation (3.5), the squared deviations of the data about the sample mean $\bar{x}$ were written $(x_i - \bar{x})^2$. However, with grouped data, the values are not known. In this case, we treat the class midpoint, M_i, as being representative of the x_i values in the corresponding class. Thus, the squared deviations about the sample mean, $(x_i - \bar{x})^2$, are replaced by $(M_i - \bar{x})^2$. Then, just as we did with the sample mean calculations for grouped data, we weight each value by the frequency of the class, f_i. The sum of the squared deviations about the mean for all the data is approximated by $\Sigma f_i (M_i - \bar{x})^2$. The term $n - 1$ rather than n appears in the denominator in order to make the sample variance the estimate of the population variance. Thus, the following formula is used to obtain the sample variance for grouped data.

SAMPLE VARIANCE FOR GROUPED DATA

$$s^2 = \frac{\Sigma f_i (M_i - \bar{x})^2}{n - 1} \qquad \qquad \textbf{(3.17)}$$

TABLE 3.12   COMPUTATION OF THE SAMPLE MEAN AUDIT TIME FOR GROUPED DATA

Audit Time (days)	Class Midpoint (M_i)	Frequency (f_i)	$f_i M_i$
10–14	12	4	48
15–19	17	8	136
20–24	22	5	110
25–29	27	2	54
30–34	32	1	32
		20	380

$$\text{Sample mean } \bar{x} = \frac{\Sigma f_i M_i}{n} = \frac{380}{20} = 19 \text{ days}$$

TABLE 3.13 COMPUTATION OF THE SAMPLE VARIANCE OF AUDIT TIMES
FOR GROUPED DATA (SAMPLE MEAN $\bar{x} = 19$)

Audit Time (days)	Class Midpoint (M_i)	Frequency (f_i)	Deviation $(M_i - \bar{x})$	Squared Deviation $(M_i - \bar{x})^2$	$f_i(M_i - \bar{x})^2$
10–14	12	4	−7	49	196
15–19	17	8	−2	4	32
20–24	22	5	3	9	45
25–29	27	2	8	64	128
30–34	32	1	13	169	169
		20			570

$$\Sigma f_i(M_i - \bar{x})^2$$

$$\text{Sample variance } s^2 = \frac{\Sigma f_i(M_i - \bar{x})^2}{n - 1} = \frac{570}{19} = 30$$

The calculation of the sample variance for audit times based on the grouped data from Table 3.11 is shown in Table 3.13. As can be seen, the sample variance is 30.

The standard deviation for grouped data is simply the square root of the variance for grouped data. For the audit time data, the sample standard deviation is $s = \sqrt{30} = 5.48$.

Before closing this section on computing measures of location and dispersion for grouped data, we note that formulas (3.16) and (3.17) are for a sample. Population summary measures are computed similarly. The grouped data formulas for a population mean and variance follow.

POPULATION MEAN FOR GROUPED DATA

$$\mu = \frac{\Sigma f_i M_i}{N} \tag{3.18}$$

POPULATION VARIANCE FOR GROUPED DATA

$$\sigma^2 = \frac{\Sigma f_i(M_i - \mu)^2}{N} \tag{3.19}$$

NOTES AND COMMENTS

In computing descriptive statistics for grouped data, the class midpoints are used to approximate the data values in each class. As a result, the descriptive statistics for grouped data approximate the descriptive statistics that would result from using the original data directly. We therefore recommend computing descriptive statistics from the original data rather than from grouped data whenever possible.

Exercises

Methods

52. Consider the following data and corresponding weights.

x_i	Weight (w_i)
3.2	6
2.0	3
2.5	2
5.0	8

a. Compute the weighted mean.
b. Compute the sample mean of the four data values without weighting. Note the difference in the results provided by the two computations.

53. Consider the sample data in the following frequency distribution.

Class	Midpoint	Frequency
3–7	5	4
8–12	10	7
13–17	15	9
18–22	20	5

a. Compute the sample mean.
b. Compute the sample variance and sample standard deviation.

Applications

54. The grade point average for college students is based on a weighted mean computation. For most colleges, the grades are given the following data values: A (4), B (3), C (2), D (1), and F (0). After 60 credit hours of course work, a student at State University earned 9 credit hours of A, 15 credit hours of B, 33 credit hours of C, and 3 credit hours of D.
a. Compute the student's grade point average.
b. Students at State University must maintain a 2.5 grade point average for their first 60 credit hours of course work in order to be admitted to the business college. Will this student be admitted?

55. *Bloomberg Personal Finance* (July/August 2001) included the following companies in its recommended investment portfolio. For a portfolio value of $25,000, the recommended dollar amounts allocated to each stock are shown.

Company	Portfolio ($)	Estimated Growth Rate (%)	Dividend Yield (%)
Citigroup	3000	15	1.21
General Electric	5500	14	1.48
Kimberly-Clark	4200	12	1.72
Oracle	3000	25	0.00
Pharmacia	3000	20	0.96
SBC Communications	3800	12	2.48
WorldCom	2500	35	0.00

a. Using the portfolio dollar amounts as the weights, what is the weighted average estimated growth rate for the portfolio?
b. What is the weighted average dividend yield for the portfolio?

56. A service station recorded the following frequency distribution for the number of gallons of gasoline sold per car in a sample of 680 cars.

Gasoline (gallons)	Frequency
0–4	74
5–9	192
10–14	280
15–19	105
20–24	23
25–29	6
Total	680

Compute the mean, variance, and standard deviation for these grouped data. If the service station expects to service about 120 cars on a given day, estimate the total number of gallons of gasoline that will be sold.

57. A survey of subscribers to *Fortune* magazine asked the following question: "How many of the last four issues have you read?" Suppose that the following frequency distribution summarizes 500 responses.

Number Read	Frequency
0	15
1	10
2	40
3	85
4	350
Total	500

a. What is the mean number of issues read by a *Fortune* subscriber?
b. What is the standard deviation of the number of issues read?

Summary

In this chapter we introduced several descriptive statistics that can be used to summarize the location, variability, and shape of a data distribution. Unlike the tabular and graphical procedures introduced in Chapter 2, the measures introduced in this chapter summarize the data in terms of numerical values. When the numerical values obtained are for a sample, they are called sample statistics. When the numerical values obtained are for a population, they are called population parameters. Some of the notation used for sample statistics and population parameters follow.

In statistical inference, the sample statistic is referred to as the point estimator of the population parameter.

	Sample Statistic	Population Parameter
Mean	$\bar{x}$	μ
Variance	s^2	σ^2
Standard deviation	s	σ
Covariance	s_{xy}	σ_{xy}
Correlation	r_{xy}	ρ_{xy}

As measures of central location, we defined the mean, median, and mode. Then the concept of percentiles was used to describe other locations in the data set. Next, we presented the range, interquartile range, variance, standard deviation, and coefficient of variation as measures of variability or dispersion. Our primary measure of the shape of a data distribution was the skewness. Negative values indicate a data distribution skewed to the left. Positive values indicate a data distribution skewed to the right. We then described how the mean and standard deviation could be used, applying Chebyshev's theorem and the empirical rule, to provide more information about the distribution of data and to identify outliers.

In Section 3.4 we showed how to develop a five-number summary and a box plot to provide simultaneous information about the location, variability, and shape of the distribution. In Section 3.5 we introduced covariance and the correlation coefficient as measures of association between two variables. In the final section, we showed how to compute a weighted mean and how to calculate a mean, variance, and standard deviation for grouped data.

The descriptive statistics we discussed can be developed using statistical software packages and spreadsheets. In Appendix 3.1 we show how to develop most of the descriptive statistics introduced in the chapter using Minitab. In Appendix 3.2, we demonstrate the use of Excel for the same purpose.

Glossary

Sample statistic A numerical value used as a summary measure for a sample (e.g., the sample mean, $\bar{x}$, the sample variance, s^2, and the sample standard deviation, s).

Population parameter A numerical value used as a summary measure for a population (e.g., the population mean, μ, the population variance, σ^2, and the population standard deviation, σ).

Point estimator The sample statistic, such as $\bar{x}$, s^2, and s, when used to estimate the corresponding population parameter.

Mean A measure of central location computed by summing the data values and dividing by the number of observations.

Median A measure of central location provided by the value in the middle when the data are arranged in ascending order.

Mode A measure of location, defined as the value that occurs with greatest frequency.

Percentile A value such that at least p percent of the observations are less than or equal to this value and at least $(100 - p)$ percent of the observations are greater than or equal to this value. The 50th percentile is the median.

Quartiles The 25th, 50th, and 75th percentiles, referred to as the first quartile, the second quartile (median), and third quartile, respectively. The quartiles can be used to divide a data set into four parts, with each part containing approximately 25% of the data.

Range A measure of variability, defined to be the largest value minus the smallest value.

Interquartile range (IQR) A measure of variability, defined to be the difference between the third and first quartiles.

Variance A measure of variability based on the squared deviations of the data values about the mean.

Standard deviation A measure of variability computed by taking the positive square root of the variance.

Coefficient of variation A measure of relative variability computed by dividing the standard deviation by the mean and multiplying by 100.

Skewness A measure of the shape of a data distribution. Data skewed to the left result in negative skewness; a symmetric data distribution results in zero skewness; and data skewed to the right result in positive skewness.

z-**score** A value computed by dividing the deviation about the mean $(x_i - \bar{x})$ by the standard deviation *s*. A *z*-score is referred to as a standardized value and denotes the number of standard deviations x_i is from the mean.

Chebyshev's theorem A theorem that can be used to make statements about the proportion of data values that must be within a specified number of standard deviations of the mean.

Empirical rule A rule that can be used to compute the percentage of data values that must be within one, two, and three standard deviations of the mean for data that exhibit a bell-shaped distribution.

Outlier An unusually small or unusually large data value.

Five-number summary An exploratory data analysis technique that uses five numbers to summarize the data: smallest value, first quartile, median, third quartile, and largest value.

Box plot A graphical summary of data based on a five-number summary.

Covariance A measure of linear association between two variables. Positive values indicate a positive relationship; negative values indicate a negative relationship.

Correlation coefficient A measure of linear association between two variables that takes on values between -1 and $+1$. Values near $+1$ indicate a strong positive linear relationship; values near -1 indicate a strong negative linear relationship; and values near zero indicate the lack of a linear relationship.

Weighted mean The mean obtained by assigning each observation a weight that reflects its importance.

Grouped data Data available in class intervals as summarized by a frequency distribution. Individual values of the original data are not available.

Key Formulas

Sample Mean

$$\bar{x} = \frac{\Sigma x_i}{n} \tag{3.1}$$

Population Mean

$$\mu = \frac{\Sigma x_i}{N} \tag{3.2}$$

Interquartile Range

$$\text{IQR} = Q_3 - Q_1 \tag{3.3}$$

Population Variance

$$\sigma^2 = \frac{\Sigma(x_i - \mu)^2}{N} \tag{3.4}$$

Sample Variance

$$s^2 = \frac{\Sigma(x_i - \bar{x})^2}{n - 1} \tag{3.5}$$

Standard Deviation

$$\text{Sample standard deviation} = s = \sqrt{s^2} \tag{3.6}$$

$$\text{Population standard deviation} = \sigma = \sqrt{\sigma^2} \tag{3.7}$$

Coefficient of Variation

$$\left(\frac{\text{Standard deviation}}{\text{Mean}} \times 100\right)\%$$

(3.8)

z-Score

$$z_i = \frac{x_i - \bar{x}}{s}$$

(3.9)

Sample Covariance

$$s_{xy} = \frac{\Sigma(x_i - \bar{x})(y_i - \bar{y})}{n - 1}$$

(3.10)

Population Covariance

$$\sigma_{xy} = \frac{\Sigma(x_i - \mu_x)(y_i - \mu_y)}{N}$$

(3.11)

Pearson Product Moment Correlation Coefficient: Sample Data

$$r_{xy} = \frac{s_{xy}}{s_x s_y}$$

(3.12)

Pearson Product Moment Correlation Coefficient: Population Data

$$\rho_{xy} = \frac{\sigma_{xy}}{\sigma_x \sigma_y}$$

(3.13)

Weighted Mean

$$\bar{x} = \frac{\Sigma w_i x_i}{\Sigma w_i}$$

(3.15)

Sample Mean for Grouped Data

$$\bar{x} = \frac{\Sigma f_i M_i}{n}$$

(3.16)

Sample Variance for Grouped Data

$$s^2 = \frac{\Sigma f_i (M_i - \bar{x})^2}{n - 1}$$

(3.17)

Population Mean for Grouped Data

$$\mu = \frac{\Sigma f_i M_i}{N}$$

(3.18)

Population Variance for Grouped Data

$$\sigma^2 = \frac{\Sigma f_i (M_i - \mu)^2}{N}$$

(3.19)

Supplementary Exercises

58. According to the 2003 Annual Consumer Spending Survey, the average monthly Bank of America Visa credit card charge was $1838 (*U.S. Airways Attaché Magazine,* December 2003). A sample of monthly credit card charges provides the following data.

CD file

Visa

236	1710	1351	825	7450
316	4135	1333	1584	387
991	3396	170	1428	1688

a. Compute the mean and median.
b. Compute the first and third quartiles.
c. Compute the range and interquartile range.
d. Compute the variance and standard deviation.
e. The skewness measure for these data is 2.12. Comment on the shape of this distribution. Is it the shape you would expect? Why or why not?
f. Do the data contain outliers?

59. The total annual compensation for a board member at one of the nation's 100 biggest public companies is based in part on the cash retainer, an annual payment for serving on the board. In addition to the cash retainer, a board member may receive a stock retainer, a stock grant, a stock option, and a fee for attending board meetings. The total compensation can easily exceed $100,000 even with an annual retainer as low as $15,000. The following data show the cash retainer (in $1000s) for a sample of 20 of the nation's biggest public companies (*USA Today,* April 17, 2000).

CD file

Retainer

Company	Cash Retainer
American Express	64
Bank of America	36
Boeing	26
Chevron	35
Dell Computer	40
DuPont	35
ExxonMobil	40
Ford Motor	30
General Motors	60
International Paper	36
Kroger	28
Lucent Technologies	50
Motorola	20
Procter & Gamble	55
Raytheon	40
Sears Roebuck	30
Texaco	15
United Parcel Service	55
Wal-Mart Stores	25
Xerox	40

Compute the following descriptive statistics.
a. Mean, median, and mode
b. The first and third quartiles
c. The range and interquartile range
d. The variance and the standard deviation
e. Coefficient of variation

60. Dividend yield is the annual dividend per share a company pays divided by the current market price per share expressed as a percentage. A sample of 10 large companies provided the following dividend yield data (*The Wall Street Journal,* January 16, 2004).

Company	Yield %	Company	Yield %
Altria Group	5.0	General Motors	3.7
American Express	0.8	JPMorgan Chase	3.5
Caterpillar	1.8	McDonald's	1.6
Eastman Kodak	1.9	United Technology	1.5
ExxonMobil	2.5	Wal-Mart Stores	0.7

a. What are the mean and median dividend yields?
b. What are the variance and standard deviation?
c. Which company provides the highest dividend yield?
d. What is the z-score for McDonald's? Interpret this z-score.
e. What is the z-score for General Motors? Interpret this z-score.
f. Based on z-scores, do the data contain any outliers?

61. According to Forrester Research, Inc., approximately 19% of Internet users play games online. The following data show the number of unique users (in thousands) for the month of March for 10 game sites (*The Wall Street Journal,* April 17, 2000).

Site	Unique Users
aolgames.com	9416
extremelotto.com	3955
freelotto.com	12901
gamesville.com	4844
iwin.com	7410
prizecentral.com	4899
shockwave.com	5582
speedyclick.com	6628
uproar.com	8821
webstakes.com	7499

Using these data, compute the mean, median, variance, and standard deviation.

62. The typical household income for a sample of 20 cities follows (*Places Rated Almanac,* 2000). Data are in thousands of dollars.

Income

City	Income
Akron, OH	74.1
Atlanta, GA	82.4
Birmingham, AL	71.2
Bismark, ND	62.8
Cleveland, OH	79.2
Columbia, SC	66.8
Danbury, CT	132.3
Denver, CO	82.6
Detroit, MI	85.3
Fort Lauderdale, FL	75.8

(continued)

City	Income
Hartford, CT	89.1
Lancaster, PA	75.2
Madison, WI	78.8
Naples, FL	100.0
Nashville, TN	77.3
Philadelphia, PA	87.0
Savannah, GA	67.8
Toledo, OH	71.2
Trenton, NJ	106.4
Washington, DC	97.4

a. Compute the mean and standard deviation for the sample data.
b. Using the mean and standard deviation computed in part (a) as estimates of the mean and standard deviation of household income for the population of all cities, use Chebyshev's theorem to determine the range within which 75% of the household incomes for the population of all cities must fall.
c. Assume that the distribution of household income is bell-shaped. Using the mean and standard deviation computed in part (a) as estimates of the mean and standard deviation of household income for the population of all cities, use the empirical rule to determine the range within which 95% of the household incomes for the population of all cities must fall. Compare your answer with the value in part (b).
d. Do the sample data contain any outliers?

63. Public transportation and the automobile are two methods an employee can use to get to work each day. Samples of times recorded for each method are shown. Times are in minutes.

Public Transportation:	28	29	32	37	33	25	29	32	41	34
Automobile:	29	31	33	32	34	30	31	32	35	33

a. Compute the sample mean time to get to work for each method.
b. Compute the sample standard deviation for each method.
c. On the basis of your results from parts (a) and (b), which method of transportation should be preferred? Explain.
d. Develop a box plot for each method. Does a comparison of the box plots support your conclusion in part (c)?

64. The typical household income and typical home price for a sample of 20 cities follow (*Places Rated Almanac,* 2000). Data are in thousands of dollars.

CD file

Cities

City	Income	Home Price
Bismark, ND	62.8	92.8
Columbia, SC	66.8	116.7
Savannah, GA	67.8	108.1
Birmingham, AL	71.2	130.9
Toledo, OH	71.2	101.1
Akron, OH	74.1	114.9
Lancaster, PA	75.2	125.9
Fort Lauderdale, FL	75.8	145.3
Nashville, TN	77.3	125.9
Madison, WI	78.8	145.2

City	Income	Home Price
Cleveland, OH	79.2	135.8
Atlanta, GA	82.4	126.9
Denver, CO	82.6	161.9
Detroit, MI	85.3	145.0
Philadelphia, PA	87.0	151.5
Hartford, CT	89.1	162.1
Washington, DC	97.4	191.9
Naples, FL	100.0	173.6
Trenton, NJ	106.4	168.1
Danbury, CT	132.3	234.1

    a.   What is the value of the sample covariance? Does it indicate a positive or a negative linear relationship?

    b.   What is the sample correlation coefficient?

65.   The following data show the media expenditures ($ millions) and shipments in millions of barrels (bbls.) for 10 major brands of beer.

CD file

Beer

Brand	Media Expenditures ($ millions)	Shipments in bbls. (millions)
Budweiser	120.0	36.3
Bud Light	68.7	20.7
Miller Lite	100.1	15.9
Coors Light	76.6	13.2
Busch	8.7	8.1
Natural Light	0.1	7.1
Miller Genuine Draft	21.5	5.6
Miller High Life	1.4	4.4
Busch Lite	5.3	4.3
Milwaukee's Best	1.7	4.3

    a.   What is the sample covariance? Does it indicate a positive or negative relationship?

    b.   What is the sample correlation coefficient?

66.   *Road & Track* provided the following sample of the tire ratings and load-carrying capacity of automobiles tires.

Tire Rating	Load-Carrying Capacity
75	853
82	1047
85	1135
87	1201
88	1235
91	1356
92	1389
93	1433
105	2039

a. Develop a scatter diagram for the data with tire rating on the x-axis.
b. What is the sample correlation coefficient, and what does it tell you about the relationship between tire rating and load-carrying capacity?

67. The following data show the trailing 52-weeks primary share earnings and book values as reported by 10 companies (*The Wall Street Journal*, March 13, 2000).

Company	Book Value	Earnings
Am Elec	25.21	2.69
Columbia En	23.20	3.01
Con Ed	25.19	3.13
Duke Energy	20.17	2.25
Edison Int'l	13.55	1.79
Enron Cp.	7.44	1.27
Peco	13.61	3.15
Pub Sv Ent	21.86	3.29
Southn Co.	8.77	1.86
Unicom	23.22	2.74

a. Develop a scatter diagram for the data with book value on the x-axis.
b. What is the sample correlation coefficient, and what does it tell you about the relationship between the earnings per share and the book value?

68. A forecasting technique referred to as moving averages uses the average or mean of the most recent n periods to forecast the next value for time series data. With a three-period moving average, the most recent three periods of data are used in the forecast computation. Consider a product with the following demand for the first three months of the current year: January (800 units), February (750 units), and March (900 units).
a. What is the three-month moving average forecast for April?
b. A variation of this forecasting technique is called weighted moving averages. The weighting allows the more recent time series data to receive more weight or more importance in the computation of the forecast. For example, a weighted three-month moving average might give a weight of 3 to data one month old, a weight of 2 to data two months old, and a weight of 1 to data three months old. Use the data given to provide a three-month weighted moving average forecast for April.

69. The days to maturity for a sample of five money market funds are shown here. The dollar amounts invested in the funds are provided. Use the weighted mean to determine the mean number of days to maturity for dollars invested in these five money market funds.

Days to Maturity	Dollar Value ($ millions)
20	20
12	30
7	10
5	15
6	10

70. Automobiles traveling on a road with a posted speed limit of 55 miles per hour are checked for speed by a state police radar system. Following is a frequency distribution of speeds.

Speed (miles per hour)	Frequency
45–49	10
50–54	40
55–59	150
60–64	175
65–69	75
70–74	15
75–79	10
Total	475

a. What is the mean speed of the automobiles traveling on this road?
b. Compute the variance and the standard deviation.

Case Problem 1   Pelican Stores

Pelican Stores, a chain of women's apparel stores operating throughout the country, recently ran a promotion in which discount coupons were sent to customers of related stores. Data collected for a sample of 100 in-store credit card transactions during one day in November 2002 are contained in the file named Pelican. Table 3.14 shows a portion of the data set. A nonzero amount for the Discount variable indicates that the customer brought in the promotional coupons and used them. For a few customers, the discount amount is greater than the sales amount (see customer 4). The sales amount is net of returns.

TABLE 3.14   SAMPLE DATA FOR 100 CREDIT CARD PURCHASES AT PELICAN STORES

Pelican

Customer	Method of Payment	Items	Discount Amount	Sales	Gender	Marital Status	Age
1	Discover	1	0.00	39.50	Male	Married	32
2	Proprietary Card	1	25.60	102.40	Female	Married	36
3	Proprietary Card	1	0.00	22.50	Female	Married	32
4	Proprietary Card	5	121.10	100.40	Female	Married	28
5	Mastercard	2	0.00	54.00	Female	Married	34
.	.	.	.	.	.	.	.
.	.	.	.	.	.	.	.
96	Mastercard	1	0.00	39.50	Female	Married	44
97	Proprietary Card	9	82.75	253.00	Female	Married	30
98	Proprietary Card	10	18.00	287.59	Female	Married	52
99	Proprietary Card	2	31.40	47.60	Female	Married	30
100	Proprietary Card	1	11.06	28.44	Female	Married	44

Pelican's management wants to use this sample data to learn about its customer base and to evaluate the promotion involving discount coupons.

Managerial Report

Use the methods of descriptive statistics presented in this chapter to summarize the data and comment on your findings. At a minimum, your report should include the following.

1. Descriptive statistics on sales and descriptive statistics on sales by various classifications of customers.
2. Descriptive statistics on the relationship between discount amount and sales for those customers responding to the promotion.
3. Descriptive statistics concerning the relationship between age and sales.

Comment on any findings that appear interesting and of potential value to management.

Case Problem 2   National Health Care Association

The National Health Care Association is concerned about the shortage of nurses the health care profession is projecting for the future. To learn the current degree of job satisfaction among nurses, the association sponsored a study of hospital nurses throughout the country. As part of this study, 50 nurses in a sample indicated their degree of satisfaction with their work, their pay, and their opportunities for promotion. Each of the three aspects of satisfaction was measured on a scale from 0 to 100, with larger values indicating higher degrees of satisfaction. The data collected also showed the type of hospital employing the nurses. The types of hospitals were Private, Veterans Administration (VA), and University. A portion of the data is shown in Table 3.15. The complete data set can be found on the CD accompanying the text in the file named Health.

TABLE 3.15   SATISFACTION SCORE DATA FOR A SAMPLE OF 50 NURSES

Health

Nurse	Hospital	Work	Pay	Promotion
1	Private	74	47	63
2	VA	72	76	37
3	University	75	53	92
4	Private	89	66	62
5	University	69	47	16
6	Private	85	56	64
7	University	89	80	64
8	Private	88	36	47
9	University	88	55	52
10	Private	84	42	66
.	.	.	.	.
.	.	.	.	.
.	.	.	.	.
45	University	79	59	41
46	University	84	53	63
47	University	87	66	49
48	VA	84	74	37
49	VA	95	66	52
50	Private	72	57	40

Managerial Report

Use methods of descriptive statistics to summarize the data. Present the summaries that will be beneficial in communicating the results to others. Discuss your findings. Specifically, comment on the following questions.

1. On the basis of the entire data set and the three job satisfaction variables, what aspect of the job is most satisfying for the nurses? What appears to be the least satisfying? In what area(s), if any, do you feel improvements should be made? Discuss.
2. On the basis of descriptive measures of variability, what measure of job satisfaction appears to generate the greatest difference of opinion among the nurses? Explain.
3. What can be learned about the types of hospitals? Does any particular type of hospital seem to have better levels of job satisfaction than the other types? Do your results suggest any recommendations for learning about and improving job satisfaction? Discuss.
4. What additional descriptive statistics and insights can you use to learn about and possibly improve job satisfaction?

Case Problem 3   # Business Schools of Asia-Pacific

Asian

The pursuit of a higher education degree in business is now international. A survey shows that more and more Asians choose the Master of Business Administration degree route to corporate success (*Asia, Inc.,* September 1997). The number of applicants for MBA courses at Asia-Pacific schools continues to increase about 30% a year. In 1997, the 74 business schools in the Asia-Pacific region reported a record 170,000 applications for the 11,000 full-time MBA degrees to be awarded in 1999. A main reason for the surge in demand is that an MBA can greatly enhance earning power.

Across the region, thousands of Asians show an increasing willingness to temporarily shelve their careers and spend two years in pursuit of a theoretical business qualification. Courses in these schools are notoriously tough and include economics, banking, marketing, behavioral sciences, labor relations, decision making, strategic thinking, business law, and more. *Asia, Inc.* provided the data set in Table 3.16, which shows some of the characteristics of the leading Asia-Pacific business schools.

Managerial Report

Use the methods of descriptive statistics to summarize the data in Table 3.16. Discuss your findings.

1. Include a summary for each variable in the data set. Make comments and interpretations based on maximums and minimums, as well as the appropriate means and proportions. What new insights do these descriptive statistics provide concerning Asia-Pacific business schools?
2. Summarize the data to compare the following:
   a. Any difference between local and foreign tuition costs.
   b. Any difference between mean starting salaries for schools requiring and not requiring work experience.
   c. Any difference between starting salaries for schools requiring and not requiring English tests.
3. Do starting salaries appear to be related to tuition?
4. Present any additional graphical and numerical summaries that will be beneficial in communicating the data in Table 3.16 to others.

TABLE 3.16 DATA FOR 25 ASIA-PACIFIC BUSINESS SCHOOLS

Business School	Full-Time Enrollment	Students per Faculty	Local Tuition ($)	Foreign Tuition ($)	Age	% Foreign	GMAT	English Test	Work Experience	Starting Salary ($)
Melbourne Business School	200	5	24,420	29,600	28	47	Yes	No	Yes	71,400
University of New South Wales (Sydney)	228	4	19,993	32,582	29	28	Yes	No	Yes	65,200
Indian Institute of Management (Ahmedabad)	392	5	4,300	4,300	22	0	No	No	No	7,100
Chinese University of Hong Kong	90	5	11,140	11,140	29	10	Yes	No	No	31,000
International University of Japan (Niigata)	126	4	33,060	33,060	28	60	Yes	Yes	No	87,000
Asian Institute of Management (Manila)	389	5	7,562	9,000	25	50	Yes	No	Yes	22,800
Indian Institute of Management (Bangalore)	380	5	3,935	16,000	23	1	Yes	No	No	7,500
National University of Singapore	147	6	6,146	7,170	29	51	Yes	Yes	Yes	43,300
Indian Institute of Management (Calcutta)	463	8	2,880	16,000	23	0	No	No	No	7,400
Australian National University (Canberra)	42	2	20,300	20,300	30	80	Yes	Yes	Yes	46,600
Nanyang Technological University (Singapore)	50	5	8,500	8,500	32	20	Yes	No	Yes	49,300
University of Queensland (Brisbane)	138	17	16,000	22,800	32	26	No	No	Yes	49,600
Hong Kong University of Science and Technology	60	2	11,513	11,513	26	37	Yes	No	Yes	34,000
Macquarie Graduate School of Management (Sydney)	12	8	17,172	19,778	34	27	No	No	Yes	60,100
Chulalongkorn University (Bangkok)	200	7	17,355	17,355	25	6	Yes	No	Yes	17,600
Monash Mt. Eliza Business School (Melbourne)	350	13	16,200	22,500	30	30	Yes	Yes	Yes	52,500
Asian Institute of Management (Bangkok)	300	10	18,200	18,200	29	90	No	Yes	Yes	25,000
University of Adelaide	20	19	16,426	23,100	30	10	No	No	Yes	66,000
Massey University (Palmerston North, New Zealand)	30	15	13,106	21,625	37	35	No	Yes	Yes	41,400
Royal Melbourne Institute of Technology Business Graduate School	30	7	13,880	17,765	32	30	No	Yes	Yes	48,900
Jamnalal Bajaj Institute of Management Studies (Bombay)	240	9	1,000	1,000	24	0	No	No	Yes	7,000
Curtin Institute of Technology (Perth)	98	15	9,475	19,097	29	43	Yes	No	Yes	55,000
Lahore University of Management Sciences	70	14	11,250	26,300	23	2.5	No	No	No	7,500
Universiti Sains Malaysia (Penang)	30	5	2,260	2,260	32	15	No	Yes	Yes	16,000
De La Salle University (Manila)	44	17	3,300	3,600	28	3.5	Yes	No	Yes	13,100

Appendix 3.1 Descriptive Statistics Using Minitab

In this appendix, we describe how to use Minitab to develop descriptive statistics. Table 3.1 listed the starting salaries for 12 business school graduates. Panel A of Figure 3.11 shows the descriptive statistics obtained by using Minitab to summarize these data. Definitions of the headings in Panel A follow.

N	number of data values
N*	number of missing data values
Mean	mean
SE Mean	standard error of mean
StDev	standard deviation
Minimum	minimum data value
Q1	first quartile
Median	median
Q3	third quartile
Maximum	maximum data value

The label SE Mean refers to the *standard error of the mean.* It is computed by dividing the standard deviation by the square root of N. The interpretation and use of this measure are discussed in Chapter 7 when we introduce the topics of sampling and sampling distributions.

Although the numerical measures of range, interquartile range, variance, and coefficient of variation do not appear on the Minitab output, these values can be easily computed from the results in Figure 3.11 as follows.

$$\text{Range} = \text{Maximum} - \text{Minimum}$$
$$\text{IQR} = Q_3 - Q_1$$
$$\text{Variance} = (\text{StDev})^2$$
$$\text{Coefficient of Variation} = (\text{StDev}/\text{Mean}) \times 100$$

Finally, note that Minitab's quartiles $Q_1 = 2857.5$ and $Q_3 = 3025$ are slightly different from the quartiles $Q_1 = 2865$ and $Q_3 = 3000$ computed in Section 3.1. The different conventions* used to identify the quartiles explain this variation. Hence, the values of Q_1 and Q_3 provided by one convention may not be identical to the values of Q_1 and Q_3 provided by another convention. Any differences tend to be negligible, however, and the results provided should not mislead the user in making the usual interpretations associated with quartiles.

Let us now see how the statistics in Figure 3.11 are generated. The starting salary data are in column C2 of a Minitab worksheet. The following steps can then be used to generate the descriptive statistics.

Salary

Step 1. Select the **Stat** menu
Step 2. Choose **Basic Statistics**
Step 3. Choose **Display Descriptive Statistics**
Step 4. When the Display Descriptive Statistics dialog box appears:
       Enter C2 in the **Variables** box
       Click **OK**

---

*With the n observations arranged in ascending order (smallest value to largest value), Minitab uses the positions given by $(n + 1)/4$ and $3(n + 1)/4$ to locate Q_1 and Q_3, respectively. When a position is fractional, Minitab interpolates between the two adjacent ordered data values to determine the corresponding quartile.

FIGURE 3.11   DESCRIPTIVE STATISTICS AND BOX PLOT PROVIDED BY MINITAB

Panel A: Descriptive Statistics

N	N*	Mean	SEMean	StDev
12	0	2940.0	47.8	165.7

Minimum	Q1	Median	Q3	Maximum
2710.0	2857.5	2905.0	3025.0	3325.0

Panel B: Box Plot

Panel B of Figure 3.11 is a box plot provided by Minitab. The box drawn from the first to third quartiles contains the middle 50% of the data. The line within the box locates the median. The asterisk indicates an outlier at 3325.

The following steps generate the box plot shown in Panel B of Figure 3.11.

Step 1. Select the **Graph** menu
Step 2. Choose **Boxplot**
Step 3. Select **Simple** and click **OK**
Step 4. When the Boxplot-One Y, Simple dialog box appears:
　　　　Enter C2 in the **Graph variables** box
　　　　Click **OK**

The skewness measure also does not appear as part of Minitab's standard descriptive statistics output. However, we can include it in the descriptive statistics display by following these steps.

Step 1. Select the **Stat** menu
Step 2. Choose **Basic Statistics**
Step 3. Choose **Display Descriptive Statistics**
Step 4. When the Display Descriptive Statistics dialog box appears:
　　　　Click **Statistics**
　　　　Select **Skewness**
　　　　Click **OK**
　　　　Click **OK**

The skewness measure of 1.09 will then appear in your worksheet.

Stereo

Figure 3.12 shows the covariance and correlation output that Minitab provided for the stereo and sound equipment store data in Table 3.7. In the covariance portion of the figure, No. of Comme denotes the number of weekend television commercials and Sales Volume denotes the sales during the following week. The value in column No. of Comme and row Sales Volume, 11, is the sample covariance as computed in Section 3.5. The value in column No. of Comme and row No. of Comme, 2.22222, is the sample variance for the number of

FIGURE 3.12   COVARIANCE AND CORRELATION PROVIDED BY MINITAB
FOR THE NUMBER OF COMMERCIALS AND SALES DATA

```
Covariances: No. of Commercials, Sales Volume

               No. of Comme   Sales Volume
No. of Comme       2.22222
Sales Volume      11.00000        62.88889


Correlations: No. of Commercials, Sales Volume

Pearson correlation of No. of Commercials and Sales Volume = 0.930
P-Value = 0.000
```

commercials, and the value in column Sales Volume and row Sales Volume, 62.88889, is
the sample variance for sales. The sample correlation coefficient, 0.930, is shown in the correlation portion of the output. Note: The interpretation of the *p*-value = 0.000 is discussed
in Chapter 9.

Let us now describe how to obtain the information in Figure 3.12. We entered the data
for the number of commercials into column C2 and the data for sales volume into column C3 of a Minitab worksheet. The steps necessary to generate the covariance output
in the first three rows of Figure 3.12 follow.

Step 1. Select the **Stat** menu
Step 2. Choose **Basic Statistics**
Step 3. Choose **Covariance**
Step 4. When the Covariance dialog box appears:
        Enter C2 C3 in the **Variables** box
        Click **OK**

To obtain the correlation output in Figure 3.12, only one change is necessary in the steps
for obtaining the covariance. In step 3, the **Correlation** option is selected.

Appendix 3.2   Descriptive Statistics Using Excel

Excel can be used to generate the descriptive statistics discussed in this chapter. We show
how Excel can be used to generate several measures of location and variability for a single
variable and to generate the covariance and correlation coefficient as measures of association between two variables.

Using Excel Functions

Salary

Excel provides functions for computing the mean, median, mode, sample variance, and sample
standard deviation. We illustrate the use of these Excel functions by computing the mean, median,
mode, sample variance, and sample standard deviation for the starting salary data in Table 3.1.
Refer to Figure 3.13 as we describe the steps involved. The data are entered in column B.

Excel's AVERAGE function can be used to compute the mean by entering the following formula into cell E1:

$$=AVERAGE(B2:B13)$$

Similarly, the formulas =MEDIAN(B2:B13), =MODE(B2:B13), =VAR(B2:B13), and
=STDEV(B2:B13) are entered into cells E2:E5, respectively, to compute the median,

FIGURE 3.13   USING EXCEL FUNCTIONS FOR COMPUTING THE MEAN, MEDIAN, MODE, VARIANCE, AND STANDARD DEVIATION

	A	B	C	D	E	F
1	Graduate	Starting Salary		Mean	=AVERAGE(B2:B13)	
2	1	2850		Median	=MEDIAN(B2:B13)	
3	2	2950		Mode	=MODE(B2:B13)	
4	3	3050		Variance	=VAR(B2:B13)	
5	4	2880		Standard Deviation	=STDEV(B2:B13)	
6	5	2755				
7	6	2710				
8	7	2890				
9	8	3130				
10	9	2940				
11	10	3325				
12	11	2920				
13	12	2880				
14						

	A	B	C	D	E	F
1	Graduate	Starting Salary		Mean	2940	
2	1	2850		Median	2905	
3	2	2950		Mode	2880	
4	3	3050		Variance	27440.91	
5	4	2880		Standard Deviation	165.65	
6	5	2755				
7	6	2710				
8	7	2890				
9	8	3130				
10	9	2940				
11	10	3325				
12	11	2920				
13	12	2880				
14						

mode, variance, and standard deviation. The worksheet in the foreground shows that the values computed using the Excel functions are the same as we computed earlier in the chapter.

Excel also provides functions that can be used to compute the covariance and correlation coefficient. You must be careful when using these functions because the covariance function treats the data as a population and the correlation function treats the data as a sample. Thus, the result obtained using Excel's covariance function must be adjusted to provide the sample covariance. We show here how these functions can be used to compute the sample covariance and the sample correlation coefficient for the stereo and sound equipment store data in Table 3.7. Refer to Figure 3.14 as we present the steps involved.

Excel's covariance function, COVAR, can be used to compute the population covariance by entering the following formula into cell F1:

Stereo

$$=COVAR(B2:B11,C2:C11)$$

Similarly, the formula =CORREL(B2:B11,C2:C11) is entered into cell F2 to compute the sample correlation coefficient. The worksheet in the foreground shows the values computed using the Excel functions. Note that the value of the sample correlation coefficient (.93) is the same as computed using equation (3.12). However, the result provided by the Excel COVAR function, 9.9, was obtained by treating the data as a population. Thus, we must adjust the Excel result of 9.9 to obtain the sample covariance. The adjustment is rather simple. First, note that the formula for the population covariance, equation (3.11), requires dividing by the total number of observations in the data set. But the formula for the sample covariance, equation (3.10), requires dividing by the total number of observations minus 1.

FIGURE 3.14   USING EXCEL FUNCTIONS FOR COMPUTING COVARIANCE AND CORRELATION

	A	B	C	D	E	F	G
1	Week	Commercials	Sales		Population Covariance	=COVAR(B2:B11:C2:C11)	
2	1	2	50		Sample Correlation	=CORREL(B2:B11,C2:C11)	
3	2	5	57				
4	3	1	41				
5	4	3	54				
6	5	4	54				
7	6	1	38				
8	7	5	63				
9	8	3	48				
10	9	4	59				
11	10	2	46				
12							

	A	B	C	D	E	F	G
1	Week	Commercials	Sales		Population Covariance	9.90	
2	1	2	50		Sample Correlation	0.93	
3	2	5	57				
4	3	1	41				
5	4	3	54				
6	5	4	54				
7	6	1	38				
8	7	5	63				
9	8	3	48				
10	9	4	59				
11	10	2	46				
12							

So, to use the Excel result of 9.9 to compute the sample covariance, we simply multiply 9.9 by $n/(n-1)$. Because $n = 10$, we obtain

$$s_{xy} = \left(\frac{10}{9}\right)9.9 = 11$$

Thus, the sample covariance for the stereo and sound equipment data is 11.

Using Excel's Descriptive Statistics Tool

As we already demonstrated, Excel provides statistical functions to compute descriptive statistics for a data set. These functions can be used to compute one statistic at a time (e.g., mean, variance, etc.). Excel also provides a variety of Data Analysis Tools. One of these tools, called Descriptive Statistics, allows the user to compute a variety of descriptive statistics at once. We show here how it can be used to compute descriptive statistics for the starting salary data in Table 3.1. Refer to Figure 3.15 as we describe the steps involved.

Salary

Step 1. Select the **Tools** menu
Step 2. Choose **Data Analysis**
Step 3. When the Data Analysis dialog box appears:
    Choose **Descriptive Statistics**
    Click **OK**
Step 4. When the Descriptive Statistics dialog box appears:
    Enter B1:B13 in the **Input Range** box
    Select **Grouped By Columns**
    Select **Labels in First Row**
    Select **Output Range**

FIGURE 3.15   EXCEL'S DESCRIPTIVE STATISTICS TOOL OUTPUT

	A	B	C	D	E	F
1	Graduate	Starting Salary		*Starting Salary*		
2	1	2850				
3	2	2950		Mean	2940	
4	3	3050		Standard Error	47.82	
5	4	2880		Median	2905	
6	5	2755		Mode	2880	
7	6	2710		Standard Deviation	165.65	
8	7	2890		Sample Variance	27440.91	
9	8	3130		Kurtosis	1.7189	
10	9	2940		Skewness	1.0911	
11	10	3325		Range	615	
12	11	2920		Minimum	2710	
13	12	2880		Maximum	3325	
14				Sum	35280	
15				Count	12	
16						

> Enter D1 in the **Output Range** box (to identify the upper left-hand corner of the section of the worksheet where the descriptive statistics will appear)
> Select **Summary statistics**
> Click **OK**

Cells D1:E15 of Figure 3.15 show the descriptive statistics provided by Excel. The boldface entries are the descriptive statistics we covered in this chapter. The descriptive statistics that are not boldface are either covered subsequently in the text or discussed in more advanced texts.

CHAPTER 4

Introduction to Probability

CONTENTS

STATISTICS IN PRACTICE:
MORTON INTERNATIONAL

MORTON INTERNATIONAL*
CHICAGO, ILLINOIS

Morton International is a company with businesses in salt, household products, rocket motors, and specialty chemicals. Carstab Corporation, a subsidiary of Morton International, produces specialty chemicals and offers a variety of chemicals designed to meet the unique specifications of its customers. For one particular customer, Carstab produced an expensive catalyst used in chemical processing. Some, but not all, of the lots produced by Carstab met the customer's specifications for the product.

Carstab's customer agreed to test each lot after receiving it and determine whether the catalyst would perform the desired function. Lots that did not pass the customer's test would be returned to Carstab. Over time, Carstab found that the customer was accepting 60% of the lots and returning 40%. In probability terms, each Carstab shipment to the customer had a .60 probability of being accepted and a .40 probability of being returned.

Neither Carstab nor its customer was pleased with these results. In an effort to improve service, Carstab explored the possibility of duplicating the customer's test prior to shipment. However, the high cost of the special testing equipment made that alternative infeasible. Carstab's chemists then proposed a new, relatively low-cost test designed to indicate whether a lot would pass the customer's test. The probability question of interest was: What is the probability that a lot will pass the customer's test if it has passed the new Carstab test?

Morton Salt: "When It Rains It Pours." © Joe Higgins/ South-Western.

A sample of lots was produced and subjected to the new Carstab test. Only lots that passed the new test were sent to the customer. Probability analysis of the data indicated that if a lot passed the Carstab test, it had a .909 probability of passing the customer's test and being accepted. Alternatively, if a lot passed the Carstab test, it had only a .091 probability of being returned. The probability analysis provided key supporting evidence for the adoption and implementation of the new testing procedure at Carstab. The new test resulted in an immediate improvement in customer service and a substantial reduction in shipping and handling costs for returned lots.

The probability of a lot being accepted by the customer after passing the new Carstab test is called a conditional probability. In this chapter, you will learn how to compute this and other probabilities that are helpful in decision making.

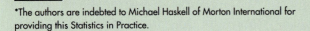

*The authors are indebted to Michael Haskell of Morton International for providing this Statistics in Practice.

Managers often base their decisions on an analysis of uncertainties such as the following:

1. What are the chances that sales will decrease if we increase prices?
2. What is the likelihood a new assembly method will increase productivity?
3. How likely is it that the project will be finished on time?
4. What is the chance that a new investment will be profitable?

Some of the earliest work on probability originated in a series of letters between Pierre de Fermat and Blaise Pascal in the 1650s.

Probability is a numerical measure of the likelihood that an event will occur. Thus, probabilities can be used as measures of the degree of uncertainty associated with the four events previously listed. If probabilities are available, we can determine the likelihood of each event occurring.

Probability values are always assigned on a scale from 0 to 1. A probability near zero indicates an event is unlikely to occur; a probability near 1 indicates an event is almost certain to occur. Other probabilities between 0 and 1 represent degrees of likelihood that an event will occur. For example, if we consider the event "rain tomorrow," we understand that when the weather report indicates "a near-zero probability of rain," it means almost no chance of rain. However, if a .90 probability of rain is reported, we know that rain is likely to occur. A .50 probability indicates that rain is just as likely to occur as not. Figure 4.1 depicts the view of probability as a numerical measure of the likelihood of an event occurring.

4.1 Experiments, Counting Rules, and Assigning Probabilities

In discussing probability, we define an **experiment** as a process that generates well-defined outcomes. On any single repetition of an experiment, one and only one of the possible experimental outcomes will occur. Several examples of experiments and their associated outcomes follow.

Experiment	Experimental Outcomes
Toss a coin	Head, tail
Select a part for inspection	Defective, nondefective
Conduct a sales call	Purchase, no purchase
Roll a die	1, 2, 3, 4, 5, 6
Play a football game	Win, lose, tie

By specifying all possible experimental outcomes, we identify the **sample space** for an experiment.

SAMPLE SPACE

The sample space for an experiment is the set of all experimental outcomes.

Experimental outcomes are also called sample points.

An experimental outcome is also called a **sample point** to identify it as an element of the sample space.

FIGURE 4.1   PROBABILITY AS A NUMERICAL MEASURE OF THE LIKELIHOOD OF AN EVENT OCCURRING

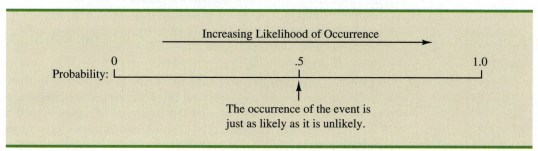

Consider the first experiment in the preceding table—tossing a coin. The upward face of the coin—a head or a tail—determines the experimental outcomes (sample points). If we let S denote the sample space, we can use the following notation to describe the sample space.

$$S = \{\text{Head, Tail}\}$$

The sample space for the second experiment in the table—selecting a part for inspection—can be described as follows:

$$S = \{\text{Defective, Nondefective}\}$$

Both of the experiments just described have two experimental outcomes (sample points). However, suppose we consider the fourth experiment listed in the table—rolling a die. The possible experimental outcomes, defined as the number of dots appearing on the upward face of the die, are the six points in the sample space for this experiment.

$$S = \{1, 2, 3, 4, 5, 6\}$$

Counting Rules, Combinations, and Permutations

Being able to identify and count the experimental outcomes is a necessary step in assigning probabilities. We now discuss three useful counting rules.

Multiple-step experiments The first counting rule applies to multiple-step experiments. Consider the experiment of tossing two coins. Let the experimental outcomes be defined in terms of the pattern of heads and tails appearing on the upward faces of the two coins. How many experimental outcomes are possible for this experiment? The experiment of tossing two coins can be thought of as a two-step experiment in which step 1 is the tossing of the first coin and step 2 is the tossing of the second coin. If we use H to denote a head and T to denote a tail, (H, H) indicates the experimental outcome with a head on the first coin and a head on the second coin. Continuing this notation, we can describe the sample space (S) for this coin-tossing experiment as follows:

$$S = \{(H, H), (H, T), (T, H), (T, T)\}$$

Thus, we see that four experimental outcomes are possible. In this case, we can easily list all of the experimental outcomes.

The counting rule for multiple-step experiments makes it possible to determine the number of experimental outcomes without listing them.

COUNTING RULE FOR MULTIPLE-STEP EXPERIMENTS

If an experiment can be described as a sequence of k steps with n_1 possible outcomes on the first step, n_2 possible outcomes on the second step, and so on, then the total number of experimental outcomes is given by $(n_1)(n_2) \ldots (n_k)$.

Viewing the experiment of tossing two coins as a sequence of first tossing one coin ($n_1 = 2$) and then tossing the other coin ($n_2 = 2$), we can see from the counting rule that there are $(2)(2) = 4$ distinct experimental outcomes. As shown, they are $S = \{(H, H), (H, T), (T, H), (T, T)\}$. The number of experimental outcomes in an experiment involving tossing six coins is $(2)(2)(2)(2)(2)(2) = 64$.

Without the tree diagram, one might think only three experimental outcomes are possible for two tosses of a coin: 0 heads, 1 head, and 2 heads.

A **tree diagram** is a graphical representation that helps in visualizing a multiple-step experiment. Figure 4.2 shows a tree diagram for the experiment of tossing two coins. The sequence of steps moves from left to right through the tree. Step 1 corresponds to tossing the first coin, and step 2 corresponds to tossing the second coin. For each step, the two possible outcomes are head or tail. Note that for each possible outcome at step 1 two branches correspond to the two possible outcomes at step 2. Each of the points on the right end of the tree corresponds to an experimental outcome. Each path through the tree from the leftmost node to one of the nodes at the right side of the tree corresponds to a unique sequence of outcomes.

Let us now see how the counting rule for multiple-step experiments can be used in the analysis of a capacity expansion project for the Kentucky Power & Light Company (KP&L). KP&L is starting a project designed to increase the generating capacity of one of its plants in northern Kentucky. The project is divided into two sequential stages or steps: stage 1 (design) and stage 2 (construction). Even though each stage will be scheduled and controlled as closely as possible, management cannot predict beforehand the exact time required to complete each stage of the project. An analysis of similar construction projects revealed possible completion times for the design stage of 2, 3, or 4 months and possible completion times for the construction stage of 6, 7, or 8 months. In addition, because of the critical need for additional electrical power, management set a goal of 10 months for the completion of the entire project.

Because this project has three possible completion times for the design stage (step 1) and three possible completion times for the construction stage (step 2), the counting rule for multiple-step experiments can be applied here to determine a total of $(3)(3) = 9$ experimental outcomes. To describe the experimental outcomes, we use a two-number notation; for instance, (2, 6) indicates that the design stage is completed in 2 months and the construction stage is completed in 6 months. This experimental outcome results in a total of $2 + 6 = 8$ months to complete the entire project. Table 4.1 summarizes the nine experimental outcomes for the KP&L problem. The tree diagram in Figure 4.3 shows how the nine outcomes (sample points) occur.

The counting rule and tree diagram help the project manager identify the experimental outcomes and determine the possible project completion times. From the information in

FIGURE 4.2 TREE DIAGRAM FOR THE EXPERIMENT OF TOSSING TWO COINS

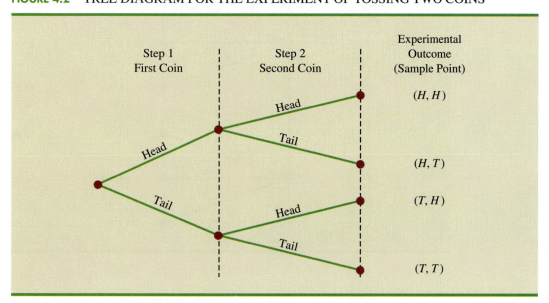

TABLE 4.1   EXPERIMENTAL OUTCOMES (SAMPLE POINTS) FOR THE KP&L PROJECT

Completion Time (months)

Stage 1 Design	Stage 2 Construction	Notation for Experimental Outcome	Total Project Completion Time (months)
2	6	(2, 6)	8
2	7	(2, 7)	9
2	8	(2, 8)	10
3	6	(3, 6)	9
3	7	(3, 7)	10
3	8	(3, 8)	11
4	6	(4, 6)	10
4	7	(4, 7)	11
4	8	(4, 8)	12

FIGURE 4.3   TREE DIAGRAM FOR THE KP&L PROJECT

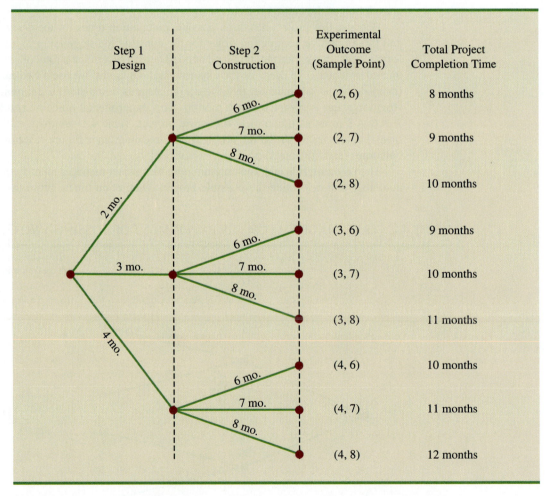

Figure 4.3, we see that the project will be completed in 8 to 12 months, with six of the nine experimental outcomes providing the desired completion time of 10 months or less. Even though identifying the experimental outcomes may be helpful, we need to consider how probability values can be assigned to the experimental outcomes before making an assessment of the probability that the project will be completed within the desired 10 months.

Combinations A second useful counting rule allows one to count the number of experimental outcomes when the experiment involves selecting n objects from a (usually larger) set of N objects. It is called the counting rule for combinations.

COUNTING RULE FOR COMBINATIONS

The number of combinations of N objects taken n at a time is

$$C_n^N = \binom{N}{n} = \frac{N!}{n!(N-n)!} \tag{4.1}$$

where

$$N! = N(N-1)(N-2)\cdots(2)(1)$$
$$n! = n(n-1)(n-2)\cdots(2)(1)$$

and, by definition,

$$0! = 1$$

The notation ! means *factorial;* for example, 5 factorial is $5! = (5)(4)(3)(2)(1) = 120$.

In sampling from a finite population of size N, the counting rule for combinations is used to find the number of different samples of size n that can be selected.

As an illustration of the counting rule for combinations, consider a quality control procedure in which an inspector randomly selects two of five parts to test for defects. In a group of five parts, how many combinations of two parts can be selected? The counting rule in equation (4.1) shows that with $N = 5$ and $n = 2$, we have

$$C_2^5 = \binom{5}{2} = \frac{5!}{2!(5-2)!} = \frac{(5)(4)(3)(2)(1)}{(2)(1)(3)(2)(1)} = \frac{120}{12} = 10$$

Thus, 10 outcomes are possible for the experiment of randomly selecting two parts from a group of five. If we label the five parts as A, B, C, D, and E, the 10 combinations or experimental outcomes can be identified as AB, AC, AD, AE, BC, BD, BE, CD, CE, and DE.

As another example, consider that the Ohio lottery system uses the random selection of six integers from a group of 47 to determine the weekly lottery winner. The counting rule for combinations, equation (4.1), can be used to determine the number of ways six different integers can be selected from a group of 47.

$$\binom{47}{6} = \frac{47!}{6!(47-6)!} = \frac{47!}{6!41!} = \frac{(47)(46)(45)(44)(43)(42)}{(6)(5)(4)(3)(2)(1)} = 10,737,573$$

The counting rule for combinations shows that the chance of winning the lottery is very unlikely.

The counting rule for combinations tells us that more than 10 million experimental outcomes are possible in the lottery drawing. An individual who buys a lottery ticket has 1 chance in 10,737,573 of winning.

Permutations A third counting rule that is sometimes useful is the counting rule for permutations. It allows one to compute the number of experimental outcomes when n objects are to be selected from a set of N objects where the order of selection is important. The same n objects selected in a different order is considered a different experimental outcome.

COUNTING RULE FOR PERMUTATIONS

The number of permutations of N objects taken n at a time is given by

$$P_n^N = n!\binom{N}{n} = \frac{N!}{(N-n)!} \qquad (4.2)$$

The counting rule for permutations closely relates to the one for combinations; however, an experiment results in more permutations than combinations for the same number of objects because every selection of n objects can be ordered in $n!$ different ways.

As an example, consider again the quality control process in which an inspector selects two of five parts to inspect for defects. How many permutations may be selected? The counting rule in equation (4.2) shows that with $N = 5$ and $n = 2$, we have

$$P_2^5 = \frac{5!}{(5-2)!} = \frac{5!}{3!} = \frac{(5)(4)(3)(2)(1)}{(3)(2)(1)} = \frac{120}{6} = 20$$

Thus, 20 outcomes are possible for the experiment of randomly selecting two parts from a group of five when the order of selection must be taken into account. If we label the parts A, B, C, D, and E, the 20 permutations are AB, BA, AC, CA, AD, DA, AE, EA, BC, CB, BD, DB, BE, EB, CD, DC, CE, EC, DE, and ED.

Assigning Probabilities

Now let us see how probabilities can be assigned to experimental outcomes. The three approaches most frequently used are the classical, relative frequency, and subjective methods. Regardless of the method used, two **basic requirements for assigning probabilities** must be met.

BASIC REQUIREMENTS FOR ASSIGNING PROBABILITIES

1. The probability assigned to each experimental outcome must be between 0 and 1, inclusively. If we let E_i denote the ith experimental outcome and $P(E_i)$ its probability, then this requirement can be written as

$$0 \leq P(E_i) \leq 1 \text{ for all } i \qquad (4.3)$$

2. The sum of the probabilities for all the experimental outcomes must equal 1.0. For n experimental outcomes, this requirement can be written as

$$P(E_1) + P(E_2) + \cdots + P(E_n) = 1 \qquad (4.4)$$

The **classical method** of assigning probabilities is appropriate when all the experimental outcomes are equally likely. If n experimental outcomes are possible, a probability of $1/n$ is assigned to each experimental outcome. When using this approach, the two basic requirements for assigning probabilities are automatically satisfied.

For an example, consider the experiment of tossing a fair coin; the two experimental outcomes—head and tail—are equally likely. Because one of the two equally likely outcomes is a head, the probability of observing a head is 1/2, or .50. Similarly, the probability of observing a tail is also 1/2, or .50.

As another example, consider the experiment of rolling a die. It would seem reasonable to conclude that the six possible outcomes are equally likely, and hence each outcome is assigned a probability of 1/6. If $P(1)$ denotes the probability that one dot appears on the upward face of the die, then $P(1) = 1/6$. Similarly, $P(2) = 1/6$, $P(3) = 1/6$, $P(4) = 1/6$, $P(5) = 1/6$, and $P(6) = 1/6$. Note that these probabilities satisfy the two basic requirements of equations (4.3) and (4.4) because each of the probabilities is greater than or equal to zero and they sum to 1.0.

The **relative frequency method** of assigning probabilities is appropriate when data are available to estimate the proportion of the time the experimental outcome will occur if the experiment is repeated a large number of times. As an example consider a study of waiting times in the X-ray department for a local hospital. A clerk recorded the number of patients waiting for service at 9:00 A.M. on 20 successive days and obtained the following results.

Number Waiting	Number of Days Outcome Occurred
0	2
1	5
2	6
3	4
4	3
Total	20

These data show that on 2 of the 20 days, zero patients were waiting for service; on 5 of the days, one patient was waiting for service; and so on. Using the relative frequency method, we would assign a probability of 2/20 = .10 to the experimental outcome of zero patients waiting for service, 5/20 = .25 to the experimental outcome of one patient waiting, 6/20 = .30 to two patients waiting, 4/20 = .20 to three patients waiting, and 3/20 = .15 to four patients waiting. As with the classical method, using the relative frequency method automatically satisfies the two basic requirements of equations (4.3) and (4.4).

The **subjective method** of assigning probabilities is most appropriate when one cannot realistically assume that the experimental outcomes are equally likely and when little relevant data are available. When the subjective method is used to assign probabilities to the experimental outcomes, we may use any information available, such as our experience or intuition. After considering all available information, a probability value that expresses our *degree of belief* (on a scale from 0 to 1) that the experimental outcome will occur is specified. Because subjective probability expresses a person's degree of belief, it is personal. Using the subjective method, different people can be expected to assign different probabilities to the same experimental outcome.

The subjective method requires extra care to ensure that the two basic requirements of equations (4.3) and (4.4) are satisfied. Regardless of a person's degree of belief, the probability value assigned to each experimental outcome must be between 0 and 1, inclusive, and the sum of all the probabilities for the experimental outcomes must equal 1.0.

Consider the case in which Tom and Judy Elsbernd make an offer to purchase a house. Two outcomes are possible:

$$E_1 = \text{their offer is accepted}$$
$$E_2 = \text{their offer is rejected}$$

Judy believes that the probability their offer will be accepted is .8; thus, Judy would set $P(E_1) = .8$ and $P(E_2) = .2$. Tom, however, believes that the probability that their offer will be accepted is .6; hence, Tom would set $P(E_1) = .6$ and $P(E_2) = .4$. Note that Tom's probability estimate for E_1 reflects a greater pessimism that their offer will be accepted.

Both Judy and Tom assigned probabilities that satisfy the two basic requirements. The fact that their probability estimates are different emphasizes the personal nature of the subjective method.

Even in business situations where either the classical or the relative frequency approach can be applied, managers may want to provide subjective probability estimates. In such cases, the best probability estimates often are obtained by combining the estimates from the classical or relative frequency approach with subjective probability estimates.

Bayes' theorem (see Section 4.5) provides a means for combining subjectively determined prior probabilities with probabilities obtained by other means to obtain revised, or posterior, probabilities.

Probabilities for the KP&L Project

To perform further analysis on the KP&L project, we must develop probabilities for each of the nine experimental outcomes listed in Table 4.1. On the basis of experience and judgment, management concluded that the experimental outcomes were not equally likely. Hence, the classical method of assigning probabilities could not be used. Management then decided to conduct a study of the completion times for similar projects undertaken by KP&L over the past three years. The results of a study of 40 similar projects are summarized in Table 4.2.

After reviewing the results of the study, management decided to employ the relative frequency method of assigning probabilities. Management could have provided subjective probability estimates, but felt that the current project was quite similar to the 40 previous projects. Thus, the relative frequency method was judged best.

In using the data in Table 4.2 to compute probabilities, we note that outcome (2, 6)—stage 1 completed in 2 months and stage 2 completed in 6 months—occurred six times in the 40 projects. We can use the relative frequency method to assign a probability of $6/40 = .15$ to this outcome. Similarly, outcome (2, 7) also occurred in six of the 40 projects, providing a $6/40 = .15$ probability. Continuing in this manner, we obtain the probability assignments for the sample points of the KP&L project shown in Table 4.3. Note that $P(2, 6)$ represents the probability of the sample point (2, 6), $P(2, 7)$ represents the probability of the sample point (2, 7), and so on.

TABLE 4.2   COMPLETION RESULTS FOR 40 KP&L PROJECTS

Completion Time (months)		Sample Point	Number of Past Projects Having These Completion Times
Stage 1 Design	**Stage 2 Construction**		
2	6	(2, 6)	6
2	7	(2, 7)	6
2	8	(2, 8)	2
3	6	(3, 6)	4
3	7	(3, 7)	8
3	8	(3, 8)	2
4	6	(4, 6)	2
4	7	(4, 7)	4
4	8	(4, 8)	6
		Total	40

TABLE 4.3   PROBABILITY ASSIGNMENTS FOR THE KP&L PROJECT BASED
ON THE RELATIVE FREQUENCY METHOD

Sample Point	Project Completion Time	Probability of Sample Point
(2, 6)	8 months	$P(2, 6) = 6/40 = .15$
(2, 7)	9 months	$P(2, 7) = 6/40 = .15$
(2, 8)	10 months	$P(2, 8) = 2/40 = .05$
(3, 6)	9 months	$P(3, 6) = 4/40 = .10$
(3, 7)	10 months	$P(3, 7) = 8/40 = .20$
(3, 8)	11 months	$P(3, 8) = 2/40 = .05$
(4, 6)	10 months	$P(4, 6) = 2/40 = .05$
(4, 7)	11 months	$P(4, 7) = 4/40 = .10$
(4, 8)	12 months	$P(4, 8) = 6/40 = \underline{.15}$
		Total 1.00

NOTES AND COMMENTS

1. In statistics, the notion of an experiment differs somewhat from the notion of an experiment in the physical sciences. In the physical sciences, researchers usually conduct an experiment in a laboratory or a controlled environment in order to learn about cause and effect. In statistical experiments, probability determines outcomes. Even though the experiment is repeated in exactly the same way, an entirely different outcome may occur. Because of this influence of probability on the outcome, the experiments of statistics are sometimes called *random experiments.*

2. When drawing a random sample without replacement from a population of size N, the counting rule for combinations is used to find the number of different samples of size n that can be selected.

Exercises

Methods

1. An experiment has three steps with three outcomes possible for the first step, two outcomes possible for the second step, and four outcomes possible for the third step. How many experimental outcomes exist for the entire experiment?

2. How many ways can three items be selected from a group of six items? Use the letters A, B, C, D, E, and F to identify the items, and list each of the different combinations of three items.

3. How many permutations of three items can be selected from a group of six? Use the letters A, B, C, D, E, and F to identify the items, and list each of the permutations of items B, D, and F.

4. Consider the experiment of tossing a coin three times.
   a. Develop a tree diagram for the experiment.
   b. List the experimental outcomes.
   c. What is the probability for each experimental outcome?

5. Suppose an experiment has five equally likely outcomes: E_1, E_2, E_3, E_4, E_5. Assign probabilities to each outcome and show that the requirements in equations (4.3) and (4.4) are satisfied. What method did you use?

6. An experiment with three outcomes has been repeated 50 times, and it was learned that E_1 occurred 20 times, E_2 occurred 13 times, and E_3 occurred 17 times. Assign probabilities to the outcomes. What method did you use?

7. A decision maker subjectively assigned the following probabilities to the four outcomes of an experiment: $P(E_1) = .10$, $P(E_2) = .15$, $P(E_3) = .40$, and $P(E_4) = .20$. Are these probability assignments valid? Explain.

Applications

8. In the city of Milford, applications for zoning changes go through a two-step process: a review by the planning commission and a final decision by the city council. At step 1 the planning commission reviews the zoning change request and makes a positive or negative recommendation concerning the change. At step 2 the city council reviews the planning commission's recommendation and then votes to approve or to disapprove the zoning change. Suppose the developer of an apartment complex submits an application for a zoning change. Consider the application process as an experiment.
    a. How many sample points are there for this experiment? List the sample points.
    b. Construct a tree diagram for the experiment.

9. Simple random sampling uses a sample of size n from a population of size N to obtain data that can be used to make inferences about the characteristics of a population. Suppose that, from a population of 50 bank accounts, we want to take a random sample of four accounts in order to learn about the population. How many different random samples of four accounts are possible?

10. Venture capital can provide a big boost in funds available to companies. According to Venture Economics (*Investor's Business Daily*, April 28, 2000), of 2374 venture capital disbursements, 1434 were to companies in California, 390 were to companies in Massachusetts, 217 were to companies in New York, and 112 were to companies in Colorado. Twenty-two percent of the companies receiving funds were in the early stages of development and 55% of the companies were in an expansion stage. Suppose you want to randomly choose one of these companies to learn about how venture capital funds are used.
    a. What is the probability the company chosen will be from California?
    b. What is the probability the company chosen will not be from one of the four states mentioned?
    c. What is the probability the company will not be in the early stages of development?
    d. Assuming the companies in the early stages of development were evenly distributed across the country, how many Massachusetts companies receiving venture capital funds were in their early stages of development?
    e. The total amount of funds invested was $32.4 billion. Estimate the amount that went to Colorado.

11. The National Highway Traffic Safety Administration (NHTSA) conducted a survey to learn about how drivers throughout the United States are using seat belts (Associated Press, August 25, 2003). Sample data consistent with the NHTSA survey are as follows.

	Driver Using Seat Belt?	
Region	**Yes**	**No**
Northeast	148	52
Midwest	162	54
South	296	74
West	252	48
Total	858	228

    a. For the United States, what is the probability that a driver is using a seat belt?
    b. The seat belt usage probability for a U.S. driver a year earlier was .75. NHTSA chief Dr. Jeffrey Runge had hoped for a .78 probability in 2003. Would he have been pleased with the 2003 survey results?

    c.   What is the probability of seat belt usage by region of the country? What region has the highest seat belt usage?

    d.   What proportion of the drivers in the sample came from each region of the country? What region had the most drivers selected? What region had the second most drivers selected?

    e.   Assuming the total number of drivers in each region is the same, do you see any reason why the probability estimate in part (a) might be too high? Explain.

12.   The Powerball lottery is played twice each week in 23 states, the Virgin Islands, and the District of Columbia. To play Powerball a participant must purchase a ticket for $1 and then select five numbers from the digits 1 through 53 and a Powerball number from the digits 1 through 42. To determine the winning numbers for each game, lottery officials draw five white balls out of a drum with 53 white balls, and one red ball out of a drum with 42 red balls. To win the jackpot, a participant's numbers must match the numbers on the five white balls in any order and the number on the red Powerball. In August 2001, four winners shared a jackpot of $295 million by matching the numbers 8-17-22-42-47 plus Powerball number 21. In addition to the jackpot, a variety of other prizes are awarded each time the game is played. For instance, a prize of $100,000 is paid if the participant's five numbers match the numbers on the five white balls (www.powerball.com, March 25, 2003).

    a.   Compute the number of ways the first five numbers can be selected.

    b.   What is the probability of winning a prize of $100,000 by matching the numbers on the five white balls?

    c.   What is the probability of winning the Powerball jackpot?

13.   A company that manufactures toothpaste is studying five different package designs. Assuming that one design is just as likely to be selected by a consumer as any other design, what selection probability would you assign to each of the package designs? In an actual experiment, 100 consumers were asked to pick the design they preferred. The following data were obtained. Do the data confirm the belief that one design is just as likely to be selected as another? Explain.

Design	Number of Times Preferred
1	5
2	15
3	30
4	40
5	10

Events and Their Probabilities

In the introduction to this chapter we used the term *event* much as it would be used in everyday language. Then, in Section 4.1 we introduced the concept of an experiment and its associated experimental outcomes or sample points. Sample points and events provide the foundation for the study of probability. As a result, we must now introduce the formal definition of an **event** as it relates to sample points. Doing so will provide the basis for determining the probability of an event.

> EVENT
>
> An event is a collection of sample points.

For an example, let us return to the KP&L project and assume that the project manager is interested in the event that the entire project can be completed in 10 months or less. Referring to Table 4.3, we see that six sample points—(2, 6), (2, 7), (2, 8), (3, 6), (3, 7), and (4, 6)—provide a project completion time of 10 months or less. Let C denote the event that the project is completed in 10 months or less; we write

$$C = \{(2, 6), (2, 7), (2, 8), (3, 6), (3, 7), (4, 6)\}$$

Event C is said to occur if *any one* of these six sample points appears as the experimental outcome.

Other events that might be of interest to KP&L management include the following.

L = The event that the project is completed in *less* than 10 months

M = The event that the project is completed in *more* than 10 months

Using the information in Table 4.3, we see that these events consist of the following sample points.

$$L = \{(2, 6), (2, 7), (3, 6)\}$$
$$M = \{(3, 8), (4, 7), (4, 8)\}$$

A variety of additional events can be defined for the KP&L project, but in each case the event must be identified as a collection of sample points for the experiment.

Given the probabilities of the sample points shown in Table 4.3, we can use the following definition to compute the probability of any event that KP&L management might want to consider.

PROBABILITY OF AN EVENT

The probability of any event is equal to the sum of the probabilities of the sample points in the event.

Using this definition, we calculate the probability of a particular event by adding the probabilities of the sample points (experimental outcomes) that make up the event. We can now compute the probability that the project will take 10 months or less to complete. Because this event is given by $C = \{(2, 6), (2, 7), (2, 8), (3, 6), (3, 7), (4, 6)\}$, the probability of event C, denoted $P(C)$, is given by

$$P(C) = P(2, 6) + P(2, 7) + P(2, 8) + P(3, 6) + P(3, 7) + P(4, 6)$$

Refer to the sample point probabilities in Table 4.3; we have

$$P(C) = .15 + .15 + .05 + .10 + .20 + .05 = .70$$

Similarly, because the event that the project is completed in less than 10 months is given by $L = \{(2, 6), (2, 7), (3, 6)\}$, the probability of this event is given by

$$P(L) = P(2, 6) + P(2, 7) + P(3, 6)$$
$$= .15 + .15 + .10 = .40$$

Finally, for the event that the project is completed in more than 10 months, we have $M = \{(3, 8), (4, 7), (4, 8)\}$ and thus

$$P(M) = P(3, 8) + P(4, 7) + P(4, 8)$$
$$= .05 + .10 + .15 = .30$$

Using these probability results, we can now tell KP&L management that there is a .70 probability that the project will be completed in 10 months or less, a .40 probability that the project will be completed in less than 10 months, and a .30 probability that the project will be completed in more than 10 months. This procedure of computing event probabilities can be repeated for any event of interest to the KP&L management.

Any time that we can identify all the sample points of an experiment and assign probabilities to each, we can compute the probability of an event using the definition. However, in many experiments the large number of sample points makes the identification of the sample points, as well as the determination of their associated probabilities, extremely cumbersome, if not impossible. In the remaining sections of this chapter, we present some basic probability relationships that can be used to compute the probability of an event without knowledge of all the sample point probabilities.

NOTES AND COMMENTS

1. The sample space, S, is an event. Because it contains all the experimental outcomes, it has a probability of 1; that is, $P(S) = 1$.
2. When the classical method is used to assign probabilities, the assumption is that the experimental outcomes are equally likely. In such cases, the probability of an event can be computed by counting the number of experimental outcomes in the event and dividing the result by the total number of experimental outcomes.

Exercises

Methods

14. An experiment has four equally likely outcomes: E_1, E_2, E_3, and E_4.
    a. What is the probability that E_2 occurs?
    b. What is the probability that any two of the outcomes occur (e.g., E_1 or E_3)?
    c. What is the probability that any three of the outcomes occur (e.g., E_1 or E_2 or E_4)?

15. Consider the experiment of selecting a playing card from a deck of 52 playing cards. Each card corresponds to a sample point with a 1/52 probability.
    a. List the sample points in the event an ace is selected.
    b. List the sample points in the event a club is selected.
    c. List the sample points in the event a face card (jack, queen, or king) is selected.
    d. Find the probabilities associated with each of the events in parts (a), (b), and (c).

16. Consider the experiment of rolling a pair of dice. Suppose that we are interested in the sum of the face values showing on the dice.
    a. How many sample points are possible? (*Hint:* Use the counting rule for multiple-step experiments.)
    b. List the sample points.
    c. What is the probability of obtaining a value of 7?
    d. What is the probability of obtaining a value of 9 or greater?
    e. Because each roll has six possible even values (2, 4, 6, 8, 10, and 12) and only five possible odd values (3, 5, 7, 9, and 11), the dice should show even values more often than odd values. Do you agree with this statement? Explain.
    f. What method did you use to assign the probabilities requested?

Applications

17. Refer to the KP&L sample points and sample point probabilities in Tables 4.2 and 4.3.
    a. The design stage (stage 1) will run over budget if it takes 4 months to complete. List the sample points in the event the design stage is over budget.
    b. What is the probability that the design stage is over budget?
    c. The construction stage (stage 2) will run over budget if it takes 8 months to complete. List the sample points in the event the construction stage is over budget.
    d. What is the probability that the construction stage is over budget?
    e. What is the probability that both stages are over budget?

18. Suppose that a manager of a large apartment complex provides the following subjective probability estimates about the number of vacancies that will exist next month.

Vacancies	Probability
0	.05
1	.15
2	.35
3	.25
4	.10
5	.10

Provide the probability of each of the following events.
    a. No vacancies
    b. At least four vacancies
    c. Two or fewer vacancies

19. The National Sporting Goods Association conducted a survey of persons 7 years of age or older about participation in sports activities (*Statistical Abstract of the United States: 2002*). The total population in this age group was reported at 248.5 million, with 120.9 million male and 127.6 million female. The number of participants for the top five sports activities appears here.

Activity	Participants (millions)	
	Male	**Female**
Bicycle riding	22.2	21.0
Camping	25.6	24.3
Exercise walking	28.7	57.7
Exercising with equipment	20.4	24.4
Swimming	26.4	34.4

    a. For a randomly selected female, estimate the probability of participation in each of the sports activities.
    b. For a randomly selected male, estimate the probability of participation in each of the sports activities.
    c. For a randomly selected person, what is the probability the person participates in exercise walking?
    d. Suppose you just happen to see an exercise walker going by. What is the probability the walker is a woman? What is the probability the walker is a man?

20. *Fortune* magazine publishes an annual issue containing information on *Fortune* 500 companies. The following data show the six states with the largest number of *Fortune* 500 companies as well as the number of companies headquartered in those states (*Fortune*, April 17, 2000).

State	Number of Companies
New York	56
California	53
Texas	43
Illinois	37
Ohio	28
Pennsylvania	28

Suppose a *Fortune* 500 company is chosen for a follow-up questionnaire. What are the probabilities of the following events?
a.   Let N be the event the company is headquartered in New York. Find $P(N)$.
b.   Let T be the event the company is headquartered in Texas. Find $P(T)$.
c.   Let B be the event the company is headquartered in one of these six states. Find $P(B)$.

21. The U.S. population by age is as follows (*The World Almanac 2004*). The data are in millions of people.

Age	Number
19 and under	80.5
20 to 24	19.0
25 to 34	39.9
35 to 44	45.2
45 to 54	37.7
55 to 64	24.3
65 and over	35.0

Assume that a person will be randomly chosen from this population.
a.   What is the probability the person is 20 to 24 years old?
b.   What is the probability the person is 20 to 34 years old?
c.   What is the probability the person is 45 years or older?

 4.3

Some Basic Relationships of Probability

Complement of an Event

Given an event A, the **complement of A** is defined to be the event consisting of all sample points that are *not* in A. The complement of A is denoted by A^c. Figure 4.4 is a diagram, known as a **Venn diagram**, which illustrates the concept of a complement. The rectangular area represents the sample space for the experiment and as such contains all possible sample points. The circle represents event A and contains only the sample points that belong to A. The shaded region of the rectangle contains all sample points not in event A and is by definition the complement of A.

In any probability application, either event A or its complement A^c must occur. Therefore, we have

$$P(A) + P(A^c) = 1$$

FIGURE 4.4   COMPLEMENT OF EVENT *A* IS SHADED

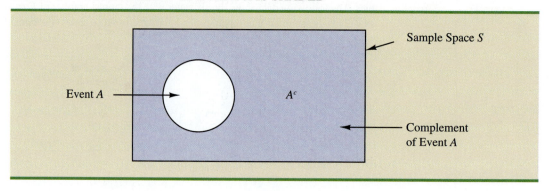

Solving for *P*(*A*), we obtain the following result.

> COMPUTING PROBABILITY USING THE COMPLEMENT
>
> $$P(A) = 1 - P(A^c) \tag{4.5}$$

Equation (4.5) shows that the probability of an event *A* can be computed easily if the probability of its complement, $P(A^c)$, is known.

As an example, consider the case of a sales manager who, after reviewing sales reports, states that 80% of new customer contacts result in no sale. By allowing *A* to denote the event of a sale and A^c to denote the event of no sale, the manager is stating that $P(A^c) = .80$. Using equation (4.5), we see that

$$P(A) = 1 - P(A^c) = 1 - .80 = .20$$

We can conclude that a new customer contact has a .20 probability of resulting in a sale.

In another example, a purchasing agent states a .90 probability that a supplier will send a shipment that is free of defective parts. Using the complement, we can conclude that there is a $1 - .90 = .10$ probability that the shipment will contain defective parts.

Addition Law

The addition law is helpful when we are interested in knowing the probability that at least one of two events occurs. That is, with events *A* and *B* we are interested in knowing the probability that event *A* or event *B* or both occur.

Before we present the addition law, we need to discuss two concepts related to the combination of events: the *union* of events and the *intersection* of events. Given two events *A* and *B*, the **union of *A* and *B*** is defined as follows.

> UNION OF TWO EVENTS
>
> The *union* of *A* and *B* is the event containing *all* sample points belonging to *A or B or both*. The union is denoted by $A \cup B$.

The Venn diagram in Figure 4.5 depicts the union of events *A* and *B*. Note that the two circles contain all the sample points in event *A* as well as all the sample points in event *B*.

FIGURE 4.5   UNION OF EVENTS *A* AND *B* IS SHADED

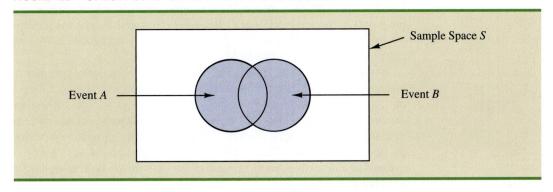

The fact that the circles overlap indicates that some sample points are contained in both *A* and *B*.

The definition of the **intersection of *A* and *B*** follows.

INTERSECTION OF TWO EVENTS

Given two events *A* and *B*, the *intersection* of *A* and *B* is the event containing the sample points belonging to *both A and B*. The intersection is denoted by $A \cap B$.

The Venn diagram depicting the intersection of events *A* and *B* is shown in Figure 4.6. The area where the two circles overlap is the intersection; it contains the sample points that are in both *A* and *B*.

Let us now continue with a discussion of the addition law. The **addition law** provides a way to compute the probability that event *A* or event *B* or both occur. In other words, the addition law is used to compute the probability of the union of two events. The addition law is written as follows.

ADDITION LAW

$$P(A \cup B) = P(A) + P(B) - P(A \cap B)$$ **(4.6)**

FIGURE 4.6   INTERSECTION OF EVENTS *A* AND *B* IS SHADED

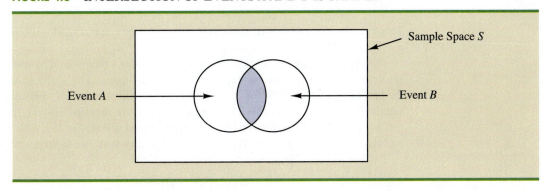

To understand the addition law intuitively, note that the first two terms in the addition law, $P(A) + P(B)$, account for all the sample points in $A \cup B$. However, because the sample points in the intersection $A \cap B$ are in both A and B, when we compute $P(A) + P(B)$, we are in effect counting each of the sample points in $A \cap B$ twice. We correct for this overcounting by subtracting $P(A \cap B)$.

As an example of an application of the addition law, let us consider the case of a small assembly plant with 50 employees. Each worker is expected to complete work assignments on time and in such a way that the assembled product will pass a final inspection. On occasion, some of the workers fail to meet the performance standards by completing work late or assembling a defective product. At the end of a performance evaluation period, the production manager found that 5 of the 50 workers completed work late, 6 of the 50 workers assembled a defective product, and 2 of the 50 workers both completed work late *and* assembled a defective product.

Let

$$L = \text{the event that the work is completed late}$$
$$D = \text{the event that the assembled product is defective}$$

The relative frequency information leads to the following probabilities.

$$P(L) = \frac{5}{50} = .10$$

$$P(D) = \frac{6}{50} = .12$$

$$P(L \cap D) = \frac{2}{50} = .04$$

After reviewing the performance data, the production manager decided to assign a poor performance rating to any employee whose work was either late or defective; thus the event of interest is $L \cup D$. What is the probability that the production manager assigned an employee a poor performance rating?

Note that the probability question is about the union of two events. Specifically, we want to know $P(L \cup D)$. Using equation (4.6), we have

$$P(L \cup D) = P(L) + P(D) - P(L \cap D)$$

Knowing values for the three probabilities on the right side of this expression, we can write

$$P(L \cup D) = .10 + .12 - .04 = .18$$

This calculation tells us that there is a .18 probability that a randomly selected employee received a poor performance rating.

As another example of the addition law, consider a recent study conducted by the personnel manager of a major computer software company. The study showed that 30% of the employees who left the firm within two years did so primarily because they were dissatisfied with their salary, 20% left because they were dissatisfied with their work assignments, and 12% of the former employees indicated dissatisfaction with *both* their salary and their work assignments. What is the probability that an employee who leaves within two years does so because of dissatisfaction with salary, dissatisfaction with the work assignment, or both?

Let

$$S = \text{the event that the employee leaves because of salary}$$
$$W = \text{the event that the employee leaves because of work assignment}$$

We have $P(S) = .30$, $P(W) = .20$, and $P(S \cap W) = .12$. Using equation (4.6), the addition law, we have

$$P(S \cup W) = P(S) + P(W) - P(S \cap W) = .30 + .20 - .12 = .38.$$

We find a .38 probability that an employee leaves for salary or work assignment reasons.

Before we conclude our discussion of the addition law, let us consider a special case that arises for **mutually exclusive events**.

MUTUALLY EXCLUSIVE EVENTS

Two events are said to be mutually exclusive if the events have no sample points in common.

Events A and B are mutually exclusive if, when one event occurs, the other cannot occur. Thus, a requirement for A and B to be mutually exclusive is that their intersection must contain no sample points. The Venn diagram depicting two mutually exclusive events A and B is shown in Figure 4.7. In this case $P(A \cap B) = 0$ and the addition law can be written as follows.

ADDITION LAW FOR MUTUALLY EXCLUSIVE EVENTS
$$P(A \cup B) = P(A) + P(B)$$

FIGURE 4.7   MUTUALLY EXCLUSIVE EVENTS

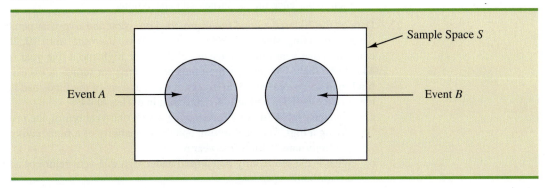

Exercises

Methods

22. Suppose that we have a sample space with five equally likely experimental outcomes: E_1, E_2, E_3, E_4, E_5. Let

$$A = \{E_1, E_2\}$$
$$B = \{E_3, E_4\}$$
$$C = \{E_2, E_3, E_5\}$$

a. Find $P(A)$, $P(B)$, and $P(C)$.
b. Find $P(A \cup B)$. Are A and B mutually exclusive?
c. Find A^c, C^c, $P(A^c)$, and $P(C^c)$.
d. Find $A \cup B^c$ and $P(A \cup B^c)$.
e. Find $P(B \cup C)$.

23. Suppose that we have a sample space $S = \{E_1, E_2, E_3, E_4, E_5, E_6, E_7\}$, where $E_1, E_2, \ldots,$ E_7 denote the sample points. The following probability assignments apply: $P(E_1) = .05$, $P(E_2) = .20$, $P(E_3) = .20$, $P(E_4) = .25$, $P(E_5) = .15$, $P(E_6) = .10$, and $P(E_7) = .05$. Let

$$A = \{E_1, E_4, E_6\}$$
$$B = \{E_2, E_4, E_7\}$$
$$C = \{E_2, E_3, E_5, E_7\}$$

a. Find $P(A)$, $P(B)$, and $P(C)$.
b. Find $A \cup B$ and $P(A \cup B)$.
c. Find $A \cap B$ and $P(A \cap B)$.
d. Are events A and C mutually exclusive?
e. Find B^c and $P(B^c)$.

Applications

24. Clarkson University surveyed alumni to learn more about what they think of Clarkson. One part of the survey asked respondents to indicate whether their overall experience at Clarkson fell short of expectations, met expectations, or surpassed expectations. The results showed that 4% of the respondents did not provide a response, 26% said that their experience fell short of expectations, and 65% of the respondents said that their experience met expectations (*Clarkson Magazine,* Summer 2001).
a. If we chose an alumnus at random, what is the probability that the alumnus would say their experience surpassed expectations?
b. If we chose an alumnus at random, what is the probability that the alumnus would say their experience met or surpassed expectations?

25. Data on the 30 largest bond funds provided one-year and five-year percentage returns for the period ending March 31, 2000 (*The Wall Street Journal,* April 10, 2000). Suppose we consider a one-year return in excess of 2% to be high and a five-year return in excess of 44% to be high. One-half of the funds had a one-year return in excess of 2%, 12 of the funds had a five-year return in excess of 44%, and six of the funds had both a one-year return in excess of 2% and a five-year return in excess of 44%.
a. Find the probability of a fund having a high one-year return, the probability of a fund having a high five-year return, and the probability of a fund having both a high one-year return and a high five-year return.
b. What is the probability that a fund had a high one-year return or a high five-year return or both?
c. What is the probability that a fund had neither a high one-year return nor a high five-year return?

26. Data on the 30 largest stock and balanced funds provided one-year and five-year percentage returns for the period ending March 31, 2000 (*The Wall Street Journal,* April 10, 2000). Suppose we consider a one-year return in excess of 50% to be high and a five-year return in excess of 300% to be high. Nine of the funds had one-year returns in excess of 50%, seven of the funds had five-year returns in excess of 300%, and five of the funds had both one-year returns in excess of 50% and five-year returns in excess of 300%.
    a. What is the probability of a high one-year return, and what is the probability of a high five-year return?
    b. What is the probability of both a high one-year return and a high five-year return?
    c. What is the probability of neither a high one-year return nor a high five-year return?

27. A 2001 preseason NCAA football poll asked respondents to answer the question, "Will the Big Ten or the Pac-10 have a team in this year's national championship game, the Rose Bowl?" Of the 13,429 respondents, 2961 said the Big Ten would, 4494 said the Pac-10 would, and 6823 said neither the Big Ten nor the Pac-10 would have a team in the Rose Bowl (www.yahoo.com, August 30, 2001).
    a. What is the probability that a respondent said neither the Big Ten nor the Pac-10 will have a team in the Rose Bowl?
    b. What is the probability that a respondent said either the Big Ten or the Pac-10 will have a team in the Rose Bowl?
    c. Find the probability that a respondent said both the Big Ten and the Pac-10 would have a team in the Rose Bowl.

28. A survey of magazine subscribers showed that 45.8% rented a car during the past 12 months for business reasons, 54% rented a car during the past 12 months for personal reasons, and 30% rented a car during the past 12 months for both business and personal reasons.
    a. What is the probability that a subscriber rented a car during the past 12 months for business or personal reasons?
    b. What is the probability that a subscriber did not rent a car during the past 12 months for either business or personal reasons?

29. High school seniors with strong academic records apply to the nation's most selective colleges in greater numbers each year. Because the number of slots remains relatively stable, some colleges reject more early applicants. The University of Pennsylvania received 2851 applications for early admission. Of this group, it admitted 1033 students, rejected 854 outright, and deferred 964 to the regular admissions pool. Penn admitted about 18% of the applicants in the regular admissions pool for a total class size (number of early admissions plus number of regular admissions) of 2375 students (*USA Today,* January 24, 2001). Let E, R, and D represent the events that a student who applies for early admission is admitted, rejected outright, or deferred to the regular admissions pool; and let A represent the event that a student in the regular admissions pool is admitted.
    a. Use the data to estimate $P(E)$, $P(R)$, and $P(D)$.
    b. Are events E and D mutually exclusive? Find $P(E \cap D)$.
    c. For the 2375 students admitted to Penn, what is the probability that a randomly selected student was accepted for early admission?
    d. Suppose a student applies to Penn for early admission. What is the probability the student will be admitted for early admission or be accepted for admission in the regular admissions pool?

4.4 Conditional Probability

Often, the probability of an event is influenced by whether a related event already occurred. Suppose we have an event A with probability $P(A)$. If we obtain new information and learn that a related event, denoted by B, already occurred, we will want to take advantage of this information by calculating a new probability for event A. This new probability of event A is called a **conditional probability** and is written $P(A \mid B)$. We use the notation | to indicate that we are considering the probability of event A *given* the condition that event B has occurred. Hence, the notation $P(A \mid B)$ reads "the probability of A given B."

As an illustration of the application of conditional probability, consider the situation of the promotion status of male and female officers of a major metropolitan police force in the eastern United States. The police force consists of 1200 officers, 960 men and 240 women. Over the past two years, 324 officers on the police force received promotions. The specific breakdown of promotions for male and female officers is shown in Table 4.4.

After reviewing the promotion record, a committee of female officers raised a discrimination case on the basis that 288 male officers had received promotions but only 36 female officers had received promotions. The police administration argued that the relatively low number of promotions for female officers was due not to discrimination, but to the fact that relatively few females are members of the police force. Let us show how conditional probability could be used to analyze the discrimination charge.

Let

$$M = \text{event an officer is a man}$$
$$W = \text{event an officer is a woman}$$
$$A = \text{event an officer is promoted}$$
$$A^c = \text{event an officer is not promoted}$$

Dividing the data values in Table 4.4 by the total of 1200 officers enables us to summarize the available information with the following probability values.

$P(M \cap A) = 288/1200 = .24 =$ probability that a randomly selected officer is a man *and* is promoted

$P(M \cap A^c) = 672/1200 = .56 =$ probability that a randomly selected officer is a man *and* is not promoted

$P(W \cap A) = 36/1200 = .03 =$ probability that a randomly selected officer is a woman *and* is promoted

$P(W \cap A^c) = 204/1200 = .17 =$ probability that a randomly selected officer is a woman *and* is not promoted

Because each of these values gives the probability of the intersection of two events, the probabilities are called **joint probabilities**. Table 4.5, which provides a summary of the probability information for the police officer promotion situation, is referred to as a *joint probability table*.

The values in the margins of the joint probability table provide the probabilities of each event separately. That is, $P(M) = .80$, $P(W) = .20$, $P(A) = .27$, and $P(A^c) = .73$. These

TABLE 4.4   PROMOTION STATUS OF POLICE OFFICERS OVER THE PAST TWO YEARS

	Men	Women	Total
Promoted	288	36	324
Not Promoted	672	204	876
Total	960	240	1200

TABLE 4.5   JOINT PROBABILITY TABLE FOR PROMOTIONS

Joint probabilities appear in the body of the table.

	Men (M)	Women (W)	Total
Promoted (A)	.24	.03	.27
Not Promoted (A^c)	.56	.17	.73
Total	.80	.20	1.00

Marginal probabilities appear in the margins of the table.

probabilities are referred to as **marginal probabilities** because of their location in the margins of the joint probability table. We note that the marginal probabilities are found by summing the joint probabilities in the corresponding row or column of the joint probability table. For instance, the marginal probability of being promoted is $P(A) = P(M \cap A) + P(W \cap A) = .24 + .03 = .27$. From the marginal probabilities, we see that 80% of the force is male, 20% of the force is female, 27% of all officers received promotions, and 73% were not promoted.

Let us begin the conditional probability analysis by computing the probability that an officer is promoted given that the officer is a man. In conditional probability notation, we are attempting to determine $P(A \mid M)$. To calculate $P(A \mid M)$, we first realize that this notation simply means that we are considering the probability of the event A (promotion) given that the condition designated as event M (the officer is a man) is known to exist. Thus $P(A \mid M)$ tells us that we are now concerned only with the promotion status of the 960 male officers. Because 288 of the 960 male officers received promotions, the probability of being promoted given that the officer is a man is 288/960 = .30. In other words, given that an officer is a man, that officer had a 30% chance of receiving a promotion over the past two years.

This procedure was easy to apply because the values in Table 4.4 show the number of officers in each category. We now want to demonstrate how conditional probabilities such as $P(A \mid M)$ can be computed directly from related event probabilities rather than the frequency data of Table 4.4.

We have shown that $P(A \mid M) = 288/960 = .30$. Let us now divide both the numerator and denominator of this fraction by 1200, the total number of officers in the study.

$$P(A \mid M) = \frac{288}{960} = \frac{288/1200}{960/1200} = \frac{.24}{.80} = .30$$

We now see that the conditional probability $P(A \mid M)$ can be computed as .24/.80. Refer to the joint probability table (Table 4.5). Note in particular that .24 is the joint probability of A and M; that is, $P(A \cap M) = .24$. Also note that .80 is the marginal probability that a randomly selected officer is a man; that is, $P(M) = .80$. Thus, the conditional probability $P(A \mid M)$ can be computed as the ratio of the joint probability $P(A \cap M)$ to the marginal probability $P(M)$.

$$P(A \mid M) = \frac{P(A \cap M)}{P(M)} = \frac{.24}{.80} = .30$$

The fact that conditional probabilities can be computed as the ratio of a joint probability to a marginal probability provides the following general formula for conditional probability calculations for two events A and B.

CONDITIONAL PROBABILITY

$$P(A \mid B) = \frac{P(A \cap B)}{P(B)} \qquad (4.7)$$

or

$$P(B \mid A) = \frac{P(A \cap B)}{P(A)} \qquad (4.8)$$

The Venn diagram in Figure 4.8 is helpful in obtaining an intuitive understanding of conditional probability. The circle on the right shows that event B has occurred; the portion of the circle that overlaps with event A denotes the event $(A \cap B)$. We know that once event B has occurred, the only way that we can also observe event A is for the event $(A \cap B)$ to occur. Thus, the ratio $P(A \cap B)/P(B)$ provides the conditional probability that we will observe event A given that event B has already occurred.

Let us return to the issue of discrimination against the female officers. The marginal probability in row 1 of Table 4.5 shows that the probability of promotion of an officer is $P(A) = .27$ (regardless of whether that officer is male or female). However, the critical issue in the discrimination case involves the two conditional probabilities $P(A \mid M)$ and $P(A \mid W)$. That is, what is the probability of a promotion *given* that the officer is a man, and what is the probability of a promotion *given* that the officer is a woman? If these two probabilities are equal, a discrimination argument has no basis because the chances of a promotion are the same for male and female officers. However, a difference in the two conditional probabilities will support the position that male and female officers are treated differently in promotion decisions.

We already determined that $P(A \mid M) = .30$. Let us now use the probability values in Table 4.5 and the basic relationship of conditional probability in equation (4.7) to compute

FIGURE 4.8   CONDITIONAL PROBABILITY $P(A \mid B) = P(A \cap B)/P(B)$

the probability that an officer is promoted given that the officer is a woman; that is, $P(A \mid W)$. Using equation (4.7), with W replacing B, we obtain

$$P(A \mid W) = \frac{P(A \cap W)}{P(W)} = \frac{.03}{.20} = .15$$

What conclusion do you draw? The probability of a promotion given that the officer is a man is .30, twice the .15 probability of a promotion given that the officer is a woman. Although the use of conditional probability does not in itself prove that discrimination exists in this case, the conditional probability values support the argument presented by the female officers.

Independent Events

In the preceding illustration, $P(A) = .27$, $P(A \mid M) = .30$, and $P(A \mid W) = .15$. We see that the probability of a promotion (event A) is affected or influenced by whether the officer is a man or a woman. Particularly, because $P(A \mid M) \neq P(A)$, we would say that events A and M are dependent events. That is, the probability of event A (promotion) is altered or affected by knowing that event M (the officer is a man) exists. Similarly, with $P(A \mid W) \neq P(A)$, we would say that events A and W are *dependent events*. However, if the probability of event A is not changed by the existence of event M—that is, $P(A \mid M) = P(A)$—we would say that events A and M are **independent events**. This situation leads to the following definition of the independence of two events.

INDEPENDENT EVENTS

Two events A and B are independent if

$$P(A \mid B) = P(A) \tag{4.9}$$

or

$$P(B \mid A) = P(B) \tag{4.10}$$

Otherwise, the events are dependent.

Multiplication Law

Whereas the addition law of probability is used to compute the probability of a union of two events, the multiplication law is used to compute the probability of the intersection of two events. The multiplication law is based on the definition of conditional probability. Using equations (4.7) and (4.8) and solving for $P(A \cap B)$, we obtain the **multiplication law**.

MULTIPLICATION LAW

$$P(A \cap B) = P(B)P(A \mid B) \tag{4.11}$$

or

$$P(A \cap B) = P(A)P(B \mid A) \tag{4.12}$$

To illustrate the use of the multiplication law, consider a newspaper circulation department where it is known that 84% of the households in a particular neighborhood subscribe to the daily edition of the paper. If we let D denote the event that a household subscribes to the daily edition, $P(D) = .84$. In addition, it is known that the probability that a household that already holds a daily subscription also subscribes to the Sunday edition (event S) is .75; that is, $P(S \mid D) = .75$.

What is the probability that a household subscribes to both the Sunday and daily editions of the newspaper? Using the multiplication law, we compute the desired $P(S \cap D)$ as

$$P(S \cap D) = P(D)P(S \mid D) = .84(.75) = .63$$

We now know that 63% of the households subscribe to both the Sunday and daily editions.

Before concluding this section, let us consider the special case of the multiplication law when the events involved are independent. Recall that events A and B are independent whenever $P(A \mid B) = P(A)$ or $P(B \mid A) = P(B)$. Hence, using equations (4.11) and (4.12) for the special case of independent events, we obtain the following multiplication law.

MULTIPLICATION LAW FOR INDEPENDENT EVENTS

$$P(A \cap B) = P(A)P(B) \qquad \textbf{(4.13)}$$

To compute the probability of the intersection of two independent events, we simply multiply the corresponding probabilities. Note that the multiplication law for independent events provides another way to determine whether A and B are independent. That is, if $P(A \cap B) = P(A)P(B)$, then A and B are independent; if $P(A \cap B) \neq P(A)P(B)$, then A and B are dependent.

As an application of the multiplication law for independent events, consider the situation of a service station manager who knows from past experience that 80% of the customers use a credit card when they purchase gasoline. What is the probability that the next two customers purchasing gasoline will each use a credit card? If we let

A = the event that the first customer uses a credit card

B = the event that the second customer uses a credit card

then the event of interest is $A \cap B$. Given no other information, we can reasonably assume that A and B are independent events. Thus,

$$P(A \cap B) = P(A)P(B) = (.80)(.80) = .64$$

To summarize this section, we note that our interest in conditional probability is motivated by the fact that events are often related. In such cases, we say the events are dependent and the conditional probability formulas in equations (4.7) and (4.8) must be used to compute the event probabilities. If two events are not related, they are independent; in this case neither event's probability is affected by whether the other event occurred.

NOTES AND COMMENTS

Do not confuse the notion of mutually exclusive events with that of independent events. Two events with nonzero probabilities cannot be both mutually exclusive and independent. If one mutually exclusive event is known to occur, the other cannot occur; thus, the probability of the other event occurring is reduced to zero. They are therefore dependent.

Exercises

Methods

30. Suppose that we have two events, A and B, with $P(A) = .50$, $P(B) = .60$, and $P(A \cap B) = .40$.
    a. Find $P(A \mid B)$.
    b. Find $P(B \mid A)$.
    c. Are A and B independent? Why or why not?

31. Assume that we have two events, A and B, that are mutually exclusive. Assume further that we know $P(A) = .30$ and $P(B) = .40$.
    a. What is $P(A \cap B)$?
    b. What is $P(A \mid B)$?
    c. A student in statistics argues that the concepts of mutually exclusive events and independent events are really the same, and that if events are mutually exclusive they must be independent. Do you agree with this statement? Use the probability information in this problem to justify your answer.
    d. What general conclusion would you make about mutually exclusive and independent events given the results of this problem?

Applications

32. Due to rising health insurance costs, 43 million people in the United States go without health insurance (*Time,* December 1, 2003). Sample data representative of the national health insurance coverage for individuals 18 years of age and older are shown here.

		Health Insurance	
		Yes	**No**
Age	**18 to 34**	750	170
	35 and over	950	130

    a. Develop a joint probability table for these data and use the table to answer the remaining questions.
    b. What do the marginal probabilities tell you about the age of the U.S. population?
    c. What is the probability that a randomly selected individual does not have health insurance coverage?
    d. If the individual is between the ages of 18 and 34, what is the probability that the individual does not have health insurance coverage?
    e. If the individual is age 35 or over, what is the probability that the individual does not have health insurance coverage?
    f. If the individual does not have health insurance, what is the probability that the individual is in the 18 to 34 age group?
    g. What does the probability information tell you about health insurance coverage in the United States?

33. In a survey of MBA students, the following data were obtained on "students' first reason for application to the school in which they matriculated."

		Reason for Application			
		School Quality	**School Cost or Convenience**	**Other**	**Totals**
Enrollment Status	**Full Time**	421	393	76	890
	Part Time	400	593	46	1039
	Totals	821	986	122	1929

    a. Develop a joint probability table for these data.
    b. Use the marginal probabilities of school quality, school cost or convenience, and other to comment on the most important reason for choosing a school.

c. If a student goes full time, what is the probability that school quality is the first reason for choosing a school?

d. If a student goes part time, what is the probability that school quality is the first reason for choosing a school?

e. Let A denote the event that a student is full time and let B denote the event that the student lists school quality as the first reason for applying. Are events A and B independent? Justify your answer.

34. The following table shows the probabilities of blood types in the general population (Hoxworth Blood Center, Cincinnati, Ohio, March 2003).

	A	B	AB	O
Rh+	.34	.09	.04	.38
Rh−	.06	.02	.01	.06

a. What is the probability a person will have type O blood?
b. What is the probability a person will be Rh−?
c. What is the probability a person will be Rh− given he or she has type O blood?
d. What is the probability a person will have type B blood given he or she is Rh+?
e. What is the probability a married couple will both be Rh−?
f. What is the probability a married couple will both have type AB blood?

35. The U.S. Bureau of Labor Statistics collected data on the occupations of workers 25 to 64 years old. The following table shows the number of male and female workers (in millions) in each occupation category (*Statistical Abstract of the United States: 2002*).

Occupation	Male	Female
Managerial/Professional	19079	19021
Tech./Sales/Administrative	11079	19315
Service	4977	7947
Precision Production	11682	1138
Operators/Fabricators/Labor	10576	3482
Farming/Forestry/Fishing	1838	514

a. Develop a joint probability table.
b. What is the probability of a female worker being a manager or professional?
c. What is the probability of a male worker being in precision production?
d. Is occupation independent of gender? Justify your answer with a probability calculation.

36. Reggie Miller of the Indiana Pacers is the National Basketball Association's best career free throw shooter, making 89% of his shots (*USA Today*, January 22, 2004). Assume that late in a basketball game, Reggie Miller is fouled and is awarded two shots.
a. What is the probability that he will make both shots?
b. What is the probability that he will make at least one shot?
c. What is the probability that he will miss both shots?
d. Late in a basketball game, a team often intentionally fouls an opposing player in order to stop the game clock. The usual strategy is to intentionally foul the other team's worst free throw shooter. Assume that the Indiana Pacers' center makes 58% of his free throw shots. Calculate the probabilities for the center as shown in parts (a), (b), and (c), and show that intentionally fouling the Indiana Pacers' center is a better strategy than intentionally fouling Reggie Miller.

37. A purchasing agent placed rush orders for a particular raw material with two different suppliers, *A* and *B*. If neither order arrives in four days, the production process must be shut down until at least one of the orders arrives. The probability that supplier *A* can deliver the material in four days is .55. The probability that supplier *B* can deliver the material in four days is .35.

   a. What is the probability that both suppliers will deliver the material in four days? Because two separate suppliers are involved, we are willing to assume independence.
   b. What is the probability that at least one supplier will deliver the material in four days?
   c. What is the probability that the production process will be shut down in four days because of a shortage of raw material (that is, both orders are late)?

38. The Minneapolis Heart Institute Foundation conducted a study to determine the benefit of follow-up care for patients discharged from a hospital after treatment for a heart attack (*The Wall Street Journal,* November 11, 2002). Out of 2060 patients, 1070 did not return for follow-up treatment and 990 did. Within 24 months, 14 of the patients receiving follow-up treatment died, and 29 of the patients not receiving follow-up treatment died. Within 54 months, 20 of the patients receiving follow-up treatment died, and 49 of the patients not receiving follow-up treatment died.

   a. What is the probability of a patient dying within 24 months of being discharged after treatment for a heart attack?
   b. Using the data for 24 months after discharge, compute the conditional probabilities of dying for patients receiving and not receiving follow-up treatment.
   c. Is the probability of dying within 24 months of discharge independent of whether the person receives follow-up treatment? Explain.
   d. Using the data for 54 months after discharge, compute the conditional probabilities of dying for patients receiving and not receiving follow-up treatment.
   e. Would you recommend enrolling in a follow-up treatment program to a friend?

Bayes' Theorem

In the discussion of conditional probability, we indicated that revising probabilities when new information is obtained is an important phase of probability analysis. Often, we begin the analysis with initial or **prior probability** estimates for specific events of interest. Then, from sources such as a sample, a special report, or a product test, we obtain additional information about the events. Given this new information, we update the prior probability values by calculating revised probabilities, referred to as **posterior probabilities**. **Bayes' theorem** provides a means for making these probability calculations. The steps in this probability revision process are shown in Figure 4.9.

As an application of Bayes' theorem, consider a manufacturing firm that receives shipments of parts from two different suppliers. Let A_1 denote the event that a part is from supplier 1 and A_2 denote the event that a part is from supplier 2. Currently, 65% of the parts purchased by the company are from supplier 1 and the remaining 35% are from supplier 2. Hence, if a part is selected at random, we would assign the prior probabilities $P(A_1) = .65$ and $P(A_2) = .35$.

FIGURE 4.9   PROBABILITY REVISION USING BAYES' THEOREM

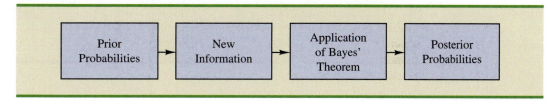

TABLE 4.6   HISTORICAL QUALITY LEVELS OF TWO SUPPLIERS

	Percentage Good Parts	Percentage Bad Parts
Supplier 1	98	2
Supplier 2	95	5

The quality of the purchased parts varies with the source of supply. Historical data suggest that the quality ratings of the two suppliers are as shown in Table 4.6. If we let G denote the event that a part is good and B denote the event that a part is bad, the information in Table 4.6 provides the following conditional probability values.

$$P(G \mid A_1) = .98 \quad P(B \mid A_1) = .02$$
$$P(G \mid A_2) = .95 \quad P(B \mid A_2) = .05$$

The tree diagram in Figure 4.10 depicts the process of the firm receiving a part from one of the two suppliers and then discovering that the part is good or bad as a two-step experiment. We see that four experimental outcomes are possible; two correspond to the part being good and two correspond to the part being bad.

Each of the experimental outcomes is the intersection of two events, so we can use the multiplication rule to compute the probabilities. For instance,

$$P(A_1, G) = P(A_1 \cap G) = P(A_1)P(G \mid A_1)$$

The process of computing these joint probabilities can be depicted in what is called a probability tree (see Figure 4.11). From left to right through the tree, the probabilities

FIGURE 4.10   TREE DIAGRAM FOR TWO-SUPPLIER EXAMPLE

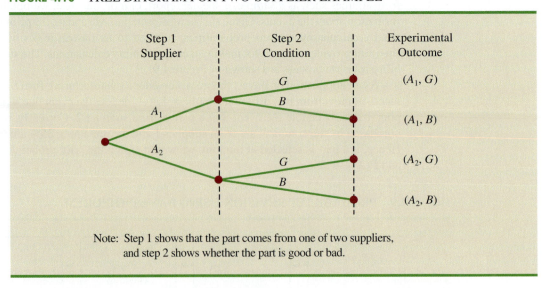

Note: Step 1 shows that the part comes from one of two suppliers, and step 2 shows whether the part is good or bad.

FIGURE 4.11   PROBABILITY TREE FOR TWO-SUPPLIER EXAMPLE

for each branch at step 1 are prior probabilities and the probabilities for each branch at step 2 are conditional probabilities. To find the probabilities of each experimental outcome, we simply multiply the probabilities on the branches leading to the outcome. Each of these joint probabilities is shown in Figure 4.11 along with the known probabilities for each branch.

Suppose now that the parts from the two suppliers are used in the firm's manufacturing process and that a machine breaks down because it attempts to process a bad part. Given the information that the part is bad, what is the probability that it came from supplier 1 and what is the probability that it came from supplier 2? With the information in the probability tree (Figure 4.11), Bayes' theorem can be used to answer these questions.

Letting B denote the event that the part is bad, we are looking for the posterior probabilities $P(A_1 \mid B)$ and $P(A_2 \mid B)$. From the law of conditional probability, we know that

$$P(A_1 \mid B) = \frac{P(A_1 \cap B)}{P(B)}$$

(4.14)

Referring to the probability tree, we see that

$$P(A_1 \cap B) = P(A_1)P(B \mid A_1)$$

(4.15)

To find $P(B)$, we note that event B can occur in only two ways: $(A_1 \cap B)$ and $(A_2 \cap B)$. Therefore, we have

$$\begin{aligned} P(B) &= P(A_1 \cap B) + P(A_2 \cap B) \\ &= P(A_1)P(B \mid A_1) + P(A_2)P(B \mid A_2) \end{aligned}$$

(4.16)

Substituting from equations (4.15) and (4.16) into equation (4.14) and writing a similar result for $P(A_2 \mid B)$, we obtain Bayes' theorem for the case of two events.

The Reverend Thomas Bayes (1702–1761), a Presbyterian minister, is credited with the original work leading to the version of Bayes' theorem in use today.

BAYES' THEOREM (TWO-EVENT CASE)

$$P(A_1 \mid B) = \frac{P(A_1)P(B \mid A_1)}{P(A_1)P(B \mid A_1) + P(A_2)P(B \mid A_2)} \qquad (4.17)$$

$$P(A_2 \mid B) = \frac{P(A_2)P(B \mid A_2)}{P(A_1)P(B \mid A_1) + P(A_2)P(B \mid A_2)} \qquad (4.18)$$

Using equation (4.17) and the probability values provided in the example, we have

$$P(A_1 \mid B) = \frac{P(A_1)P(B \mid A_1)}{P(A_1)P(B \mid A_1) + P(A_2)P(B \mid A_2)}$$

$$= \frac{(.65)(.02)}{(.65)(.02) + (.35)(.05)} = \frac{.0130}{.0130 + .0175}$$

$$= \frac{.0130}{.0305} = .4262$$

In addition, using equation (4.18), we find $P(A_2 \mid B)$.

$$P(A_2 \mid B) = \frac{(.35)(.05)}{(.65)(.02) + (.35)(.05)}$$

$$= \frac{.0175}{.0130 + .0175} = \frac{.0175}{.0305} = .5738$$

Note that in this application we started with a probability of .65 that a part selected at random was from supplier 1. However, given information that the part is bad, the probability that the part is from supplier 1 drops to .4262. In fact, if the part is bad, it has better than a 50–50 chance that it came from supplier 2; that is, $P(A_2 \mid B) = .5738$.

Bayes' theorem is applicable when the events for which we want to compute posterior probabilities are mutually exclusive and their union is the entire sample space.* For the case of n mutually exclusive events $A_1, A_2, \ldots, A_n$, whose union is the entire sample space, Bayes' theorem can be used to compute any posterior probability $P(A_i \mid B)$ as shown here.

BAYES' THEOREM

$$P(A_i \mid B) = \frac{P(A_i)P(B \mid A_i)}{P(A_1)P(B \mid A_1) + P(A_2)P(B \mid A_2) + \cdots + P(A_n)P(B \mid A_n)} \qquad (4.19)$$

*If the union of events is the entire sample space, the events are said to be *collectively exhaustive*.

With prior probabilities $P(A_1)$, $P(A_2)$, ..., $P(A_n)$ and the appropriate conditional probabilities $P(B \mid A_1)$, $P(B \mid A_2)$, ..., $P(B \mid A_n)$, equation (4.19) can be used to compute the posterior probability of the events $A_1, A_2, \ldots, A_n$.

Tabular Approach

A tabular approach is helpful in conducting the Bayes' theorem calculations. Such an approach is shown in Table 4.7 for the parts supplier problem. The computations shown there are done in the following steps.

Step 1. Prepare the following three columns:
Column 1—The mutually exclusive events A_i for which posterior probabilities are desired
Column 2—The prior probabilities $P(A_i)$ for the events
Column 3—The conditional probabilities $P(B \mid A_i)$ of the new information B given each event

Step 2. In column 4, compute the joint probabilities $P(A_i \cap B)$ for each event and the new information B by using the multiplication law. These joint probabilities are found by multiplying the prior probabilities in column 2 by the corresponding conditional probabilities in column 3; that is, $P(A_i \cap B) = P(A_i)P(B \mid A_i)$.

Step 3. Sum the joint probabilities in column 4. The sum is the probability of the new information, $P(B)$. Thus we see in Table 4.7 that there is a .0130 probability that the part came from supplier 1 and is bad and a .0175 probability that the part came from supplier 2 and is bad. Because these are the only two ways in which a bad part can be obtained, the sum .0130 + .0175 shows an overall probability of .0305 of finding a bad part from the combined shipments of the two suppliers.

Step 4. In column 5, compute the posterior probabilities using the basic relationship of conditional probability.

$$P(A_i \mid B) = \frac{P(A_i \cap B)}{P(B)}$$

Note that the joint probabilities $P(A_i \cap B)$ are in column 4 and the probability $P(B)$ is the sum of column 4.

TABLE 4.7 TABULAR APPROACH TO BAYES' THEOREM CALCULATIONS FOR THE TWO-SUPPLIER PROBLEM

(1) Events A_i	(2) Prior Probabilities $P(A_i)$	(3) Conditional Probabilities $P(B \mid A_i)$	(4) Joint Probabilities $P(A_i \cap B)$	(5) Posterior Probabilities $P(A_i \mid B)$
A_1	.65	.02	.0130	.0130/.0305 = .4262
A_2	.35	.05	.0175	.0175/.0305 = .5738
	1.00		$P(B) = .0305$	1.0000

NOTES AND COMMENTS

1. Bayes' theorem is used extensively in decision analysis. The prior probabilities are often subjective estimates provided by a decision maker. Sample information is obtained and posterior probabilities are computed for use in choosing the best decision.

2. An event and its complement are mutually exclusive, and their union is the entire sample space. Thus, Bayes' theorem is always applicable for computing posterior probabilities of an event and its complement.

Exercises

Methods

39. The prior probabilities for events A_1 and A_2 are $P(A_1) = .40$ and $P(A_2) = .60$. It is also known that $P(A_1 \cap A_2) = 0$. Suppose $P(B \mid A_1) = .20$ and $P(B \mid A_2) = .05$.
    a. Are A_1 and A_2 mutually exclusive? Explain.
    b. Compute $P(A_1 \cap B)$ and $P(A_2 \cap B)$.
    c. Compute $P(B)$.
    d. Apply Bayes' theorem to compute $P(A_1 \mid B)$ and $P(A_2 \mid B)$.

40. The prior probabilities for events A_1, A_2, and A_3 are $P(A_1) = .20$, $P(A_2) = .50$, and $P(A_3) = .30$. The conditional probabilities of event B given A_1, A_2, and A_3 are $P(B \mid A_1) = .50$, $P(B \mid A_2) = .40$, and $P(B \mid A_3) = .30$.
    a. Compute $P(B \cap A_1)$, $P(B \cap A_2)$, and $P(B \cap A_3)$.
    b. Apply Bayes' theorem, equation (4.19), to compute the posterior probability $P(A_2 \mid B)$.
    c. Use the tabular approach to applying Bayes' theorem to compute $P(A_1 \mid B)$, $P(A_2 \mid B)$, and $P(A_3 \mid B)$.

Applications

41. A consulting firm submitted a bid for a large research project. The firm's management initially felt they had a 50–50 chance of getting the project. However, the agency to which the bid was submitted subsequently requested additional information on the bid. Past experience indicates that for 75% of the successful bids and 40% of the unsuccessful bids the agency requested additional information.
    a. What is the prior probability of the bid being successful (that is, prior to the request for additional information)?
    b. What is the conditional probability of a request for additional information given that the bid will ultimately be successful?
    c. Compute the posterior probability that the bid will be successful given a request for additional information.

42. A local bank reviewed its credit card policy with the intention of recalling some of its credit cards. In the past approximately 5% of cardholders defaulted, leaving the bank unable to collect the outstanding balance. Hence, management established a prior probability of .05 that any particular cardholder will default. The bank also found that the probability of missing a monthly payment is .20 for customers who do not default. Of course, the probability of missing a monthly payment for those who default is 1.
    a. Given that a customer missed one or more monthly payments, compute the posterior probability that the customer will default.
    b. The bank would like to recall its card if the probability that a customer will default is greater than .20. Should the bank recall its card if the customer misses a monthly payment? Why or why not?

43. Small cars get better gas mileage, but they are not as safe as bigger cars. Small cars accounted for 18% of the vehicles on the road, but accidents involving small cars led to 11,898 fatalities during a recent year (*Reader's Digest,* May 2000). Assume the probability a small car is involved in an accident is .18. The probability of an accident involving a small car leading to a fatality is .128 and the probability of an accident not involving a small car leading to a fatality is .05. Suppose you learn of an accident involving a fatality. What is the probability a small car was involved? Assume that the likelihood of getting into an accident is independent of car size.

44. The American Council of Education reported that 47% of college freshmen earn a degree and graduate within five years (Associated Press, May 6, 2002). Assume that graduation records show women make up 50% of the students who graduated within five years, but only 45% of the students who did not graduate within five years. The students who had not graduated within five years either dropped out or were still working on their degrees.
    a. Let A_1 = the student graduated within five years
       A_2 = the student did not graduate within five years
       W = the student is a female student
       Using the given information, what are the values for $P(A_1)$, $P(A_2)$, $P(W \mid A_1)$, and $P(W \mid A_2)$?
    b. What is the probability that a female student will graduate within five years?
    c. What is the probability that a male student will graduate within five years?
    d. Given the preceding results, what are the percentage of women and the percentage of men in the entering freshman class?

45. In an article about investment growth, *Money* magazine reported that drug stocks show powerful long-term trends and offer investors unparalleled potential for strong and steady gains. The federal Health Care Financing Administration supports this conclusion through its forecast that annual prescription drug expenditures will reach $366 billion by 2010, up from $117 billion in 2000. Many individuals age 65 and older rely heavily on prescription drugs. For this group, 82% take prescription drugs regularly, 55% take three or more prescriptions regularly, and 40% currently use five or more prescriptions. In contrast, 49% of people under age 65 take prescriptions regularly, with 17% taking three or more prescriptions regularly and 28% using five or more prescriptions (*Money,* September 2001). The U.S. Census Bureau reports that of the 281,421,906 people in the United States, 34,991,753 are age 65 years and older (U.S. Census Bureau, *Census 2000*).
    a. Compute the probability that a person in the United States is age 65 or older.
    b. Compute the probability that a person takes prescription drugs regularly.
    c. Compute the probability that a person is age 65 or older and takes five or more prescriptions.
    d. Given a person uses five or more prescriptions, compute the probability that the person is age 65 or older.

Summary

In this chapter we introduced basic probability concepts and illustrated how probability analysis can be used to provide helpful information for decision making. We described how probability can be interpreted as a numerical measure of the likelihood that an event will occur. In addition, we saw that the probability of an event can be computed either by summing the probabilities of the experimental outcomes (sample points) comprising the event or by using the relationships established by the addition, conditional probability, and multiplication laws of probability. For cases in which additional information is available, we showed how Bayes' theorem can be used to obtain revised or posterior probabilities.

Glossary

Probability A numerical measure of the likelihood that an event will occur.
Experiment A process that generates well-defined outcomes.

Sample space The set of all experimental outcomes.

Sample point An element of the sample space. A sample point represents an experimental outcome.

Tree diagram A graphical representation that helps in visualizing a multiple-step experiment.

Basic requirements for assigning probabilities Two requirements that restrict the manner in which probability assignments can be made: (1) for each experimental outcome E_i we must have $0 \leq P(E_i) \leq 1$; (2) considering all experimental outcomes, we must have $P(E_1) + P(E_2) + \cdots + P(E_n) = 1.0$.

Classical method A method of assigning probabilities that is appropriate when all the experimental outcomes are equally likely.

Relative frequency method A method of assigning probabilities that is appropriate when data are available to estimate the proportion of the time the experimental outcome will occur if the experiment is repeated a large number of times.

Subjective method A method of assigning probabilities on the basis of judgment.

Event A collection of sample points.

Complement of A The event consisting of all sample points that are not in A.

Venn diagram A graphical representation for showing symbolically the sample space and operations involving events in which the sample space is represented by a rectangle and events are represented as circles within the sample space.

Union of A and B The event containing all sample points belonging to A or B or both. The union is denoted $A \cup B$.

Intersection of A and B The event containing the sample points belonging to both A and B. The intersection is denoted $A \cap B$.

Addition law A probability law used to compute the probability of the union of two events. It is $P(A \cup B) = P(A) + P(B) - P(A \cap B)$. For mutually exclusive events, $P(A \cap B) = 0$; in this case the addition law reduces to $P(A \cup B) = P(A) + P(B)$.

Mutually exclusive events Events that have no sample points in common; that is, $A \cap B$ is empty and $P(A \cap B) = 0$.

Conditional probability The probability of an event given that another event already occurred. The conditional probability of A given B is $P(A \mid B) = P(A \cap B)/P(B)$.

Joint probability The probability of two events both occurring; that is, the probability of the intersection of two events.

Marginal probability The values in the margins of a joint probability table that provide the probabilities of each event separately.

Independent events Two events A and B where $P(A \mid B) = P(A)$ or $P(B \mid A) = P(B)$; that is, the events have no influence on each other.

Multiplication law A probability law used to compute the probability of the intersection of two events. It is $P(A \cap B) = P(B)P(A \mid B)$ or $P(A \cap B) = P(A)P(B \mid A)$. For independent events it reduces to $P(A \cap B) = P(A)P(B)$.

Prior probabilities Initial estimates of the probabilities of events.

Posterior probabilities Revised probabilities of events based on additional information.

Bayes' theorem A method used to compute posterior probabilities.

Key Formulas

Counting Rule for Combinations

$$C_n^N = \binom{N}{n} = \frac{N!}{n!(N-n)!} \tag{4.1}$$

Counting Rule for Permutations

$$P_n^N = n!\binom{N}{n} = \frac{N!}{(N-n)!} \qquad \textbf{(4.2)}$$

Computing Probability Using the Complement

$$P(A) = 1 - P(A^c) \qquad \textbf{(4.5)}$$

Addition Law

$$P(A \cup B) = P(A) + P(B) - P(A \cap B) \qquad \textbf{(4.6)}$$

Conditional Probability

$$P(A \mid B) = \frac{P(A \cap B)}{P(B)} \qquad \textbf{(4.7)}$$

$$P(B \mid A) = \frac{P(A \cap B)}{P(A)} \qquad \textbf{(4.8)}$$

Multiplication Law

$$P(A \cap B) = P(B)P(A \mid B) \qquad \textbf{(4.11)}$$

$$P(A \cap B) = P(A)P(B \mid A) \qquad \textbf{(4.12)}$$

Multiplication Law for Independent Events

$$P(A \cap B) = P(A)P(B) \qquad \textbf{(4.13)}$$

Bayes' Theorem

$$P(A_i \mid B) = \frac{P(A_i)P(B \mid A_i)}{P(A_1)P(B \mid A_1) + P(A_2)P(B \mid A_2) + \cdots + P(A_n)P(B \mid A_n)} \qquad \textbf{(4.19)}$$

Supplementary Exercises

46. In a *Business Week*/Harris Poll, 1035 adults were asked about their attitudes toward business (*Business Week,* September 11, 2000). One question asked: "How would you rate large U.S. companies on making good products and competing in a global environment?" The responses were: excellent—18%, pretty good—50%, only fair—26%, poor—5%, and don't know/no answer—1%.
    a. What is the probability that a respondent rated U.S. companies pretty good or excellent?
    b. How many respondents rated U.S. companies poor?
    c. How many respondents did not know or did not answer?

47. A financial manager made two new investments—one in the oil industry and one in municipal bonds. After a one-year period, each of the investments will be classified as either successful or unsuccessful. Consider the making of the two investments as an experiment.
    a. How many sample points exist for this experiment?
    b. Show a tree diagram and list the sample points.
    c. Let $O =$ the event that the oil industry investment is successful and $M =$ the event that the municipal bond investment is successful. List the sample points in O and in M.
    d. List the sample points in the union of the events $(O \cup M)$.
    e. List the sample points in the intersection of the events $(O \cap M)$.
    f. Are events O and M mutually exclusive? Explain.

48. In early 2003, President Bush proposed eliminating the taxation of dividends to share-holders on the grounds that it was double taxation. Corporations pay taxes on the earnings that are later paid out in dividends. In a poll of 671 Americans, TechnoMetrica Market Intelligence found that 47% favored the proposal, 44% opposed it, and 9% were not sure (*Investor's Business Daily,* January 13, 2003). In looking at the responses across party lines the poll showed that 29% of Democrats were in favor, 64% of Republicans were in favor, and 48% of Independents were in favor.
    a. How many of those polled favored elimination of the tax on dividends?
    b. What is the conditional probability in favor of the proposal given the person polled is a Democrat?
    c. Is party affiliation independent of whether one is in favor of the proposal?
    d. If we assume people's responses were consistent with their own self-interest, which group do you believe will benefit most from passage of the proposal?

49. A study of 31,000 hospital admissions in New York State found that 4% of the admissions led to treatment–caused injuries. One-seventh of these treatment–caused injuries resulted in death, and one-fourth were caused by negligence. Malpractice claims were filed in one out of 7.5 cases involving negligence, and payments were made in one out of every two claims.
    a. What is the probability a person admitted to the hospital will suffer a treatment–caused injury due to negligence?
    b. What is the probability a person admitted to the hospital will die from a treatment-caused injury?
    c. In the case of a negligent treatment–caused injury, what is the probability a malpractice claim will be paid?

50. A telephone survey to determine viewer response to a new television show obtained the following data.

Rating	Frequency
Poor	4
Below average	8
Average	11
Above average	14
Excellent	13

    a. What is the probability that a randomly selected viewer will rate the new show as average or better?
    b. What is the probability that a randomly selected viewer will rate the new show below average or worse?

51. The following crosstabulation shows household income by educational level of the head of household (*Statistical Abstract of the United States: 2002*).

	Household Income ($1000s)					
Education Level	**Under 25**	**25.0– 49.9**	**50.0– 74.9**	**75.0– 99.9**	**100 or more**	**Total**
Not H.S. Graduate	9,285	4,093	1,589	541	354	15,862
H.S. Graduate	10,150	9,821	6,050	2,737	2,028	30,786
Some College	6,011	8,221	5,813	3,215	3,120	26,380
Bachelor's Degree	2,138	3,985	3,952	2,698	4,748	17,521
Beyond Bach. Deg.	813	1,497	1,815	1,589	3,765	9,479
Total	28,397	27,617	19,219	10,780	14,015	100,028

a. Develop a joint probability table.
b. What is the probability of a head of household not being a high school graduate?
c. What is the probability of a head of household having a bachelor's degree or more education?
d. What is the probability of a household headed by someone with a bachelor's degree earning $100,000 or more?
e. What is the probability of a household having income below $25,000?
f. What is the probability of a household headed by someone with a bachelor's degree earning less than $25,000?
g. Is household income independent of educational level?

52. A GMAC MBA new-matriculants survey provided the following data for 2018 students.

		Applied to More Than One School	
		Yes	No
Age Group	23 and under	207	201
	24–26	299	379
	27–30	185	268
	31–35	66	193
	36 and over	51	169

a. For a randomly selected MBA student, prepare a joint probability table for the experiment consisting of observing the student's age and whether the student applied to one or more schools.
b. What is the probability that a randomly selected applicant is 23 or under?
c. What is the probability that a randomly selected applicant is older than 26?
d. What is the probability that a randomly selected applicant applied to more than one school?

53. Refer again to the data from the GMAC new-matriculants survey in exercise 52.
a. Given that a person applied to more than one school, what is the probability that the person is 24–26 years old?
b. Given that a person is in the 36-and-over age group, what is the probability that the person applied to more than one school?
c. What is the probability that a person is 24–26 years old or applied to more than one school?
d. Suppose a person is known to have applied to only one school. What is the probability that the person is 31 or more years old?
e. Is the number of schools applied to independent of age? Explain.

54. An IBD/TIPP poll conducted to learn about attitudes toward investment and retirement (*Investor's Business Daily*, May 5, 2000) asked male and female respondents how important they felt level of risk was in choosing a retirement investment. The following joint probability table was constructed from the data provided. "Important" means the respondent said level of risk was either important or very important.

	Male	Female	Total
Important	.22	.27	.49
Not Important	.28	.23	.51
Total	.50	.50	1.00

a. What is the probability a survey respondent will say level of risk is important?
b. What is the probability a male respondent will say level of risk is important?
c. What is the probability a female respondent will say level of risk is important?
d. Is the level of risk independent of the gender of the respondent? Why or why not?
e. Do male and female attitudes toward risk differ?

55. A large consumer goods company ran a television advertisement for one of its soap products. On the basis of a survey that was conducted, probabilities were assigned to the following events.

$$B = \text{individual purchased the product}$$
$$S = \text{individual recalls seeing the advertisement}$$
$$B \cap S = \text{individual purchased the product and recalls seeing the advertisement}$$

The probabilities assigned were $P(B) = .20$, $P(S) = .40$, and $P(B \cap S) = .12$.
a. What is the probability of an individual's purchasing the product given that the individual recalls seeing the advertisement? Does seeing the advertisement increase the probability that the individual will purchase the product? As a decision maker, would you recommend continuing the advertisement (assuming that the cost is reasonable)?
b. Assume that individuals who do not purchase the company's soap product buy from its competitors. What would be your estimate of the company's market share? Would you expect that continuing the advertisement will increase the company's market share? Why or why not?
c. The company also tested another advertisement and assigned it values of $P(S) = .30$ and $P(B \cap S) = .10$. What is $P(B \mid S)$ for this other advertisement? Which advertisement seems to have had the bigger effect on customer purchases?

56. Cooper Realty is a small real estate company located in Albany, New York, specializing primarily in residential listings. They recently became interested in determining the likelihood of one of their listings being sold within a certain number of days. An analysis of company sales of 800 homes in previous years produced the following data.

		Days Listed Until Sold			
		Under 30	31–90	Over 90	Total
Initial Asking Price	Under $150,000	50	40	10	100
	$150,000–$199,999	20	150	80	250
	$200,000–$250,000	20	280	100	400
	Over $250,000	10	30	10	50
	Total	100	500	200	800

a. If A is defined as the event that a home is listed for more than 90 days before being sold, estimate the probability of A.
b. If B is defined as the event that the initial asking price is under $150,000, estimate the probability of B.
c. What is the probability of $A \cap B$?
d. Assuming that a contract was just signed to list a home with an initial asking price of less than $150,000, what is the probability that the home will take Cooper Realty more than 90 days to sell?
e. Are events A and B independent?

57. A company studied the number of lost-time accidents occurring at its Brownsville, Texas, plant. Historical records show that 6% of the employees suffered lost-time accidents last year. Management believes that a special safety program will reduce such accidents to 5% during the current year. In addition, it estimates that 15% of employees who had lost-time accidents last year will experience a lost-time accident during the current year.
     a. What percentage of the employees will experience lost-time accidents in both years?
     b. What percentage of the employees will suffer at least one lost-time accident over the two-year period?

58. The Dallas IRS auditing staff, concerned with identifying potentially fraudulent tax returns, believes that the probability of finding a fraudulent return given that the return contains deductions for contributions exceeding the IRS standard is .20. Given that the deductions for contributions do not exceed the IRS standard, the probability of a fraudulent return decreases to .02. If 8% of all returns exceed the IRS standard for deductions due to contributions, what is the best estimate of the percentage of fraudulent returns?

59. An oil company purchased an option on land in Alaska. Preliminary geologic studies assigned the following prior probabilities.

$$P(\text{high-quality oil}) = .50$$
$$P(\text{medium-quality oil}) = .20$$
$$P(\text{no oil}) = .30$$

     a. What is the probability of finding oil?
     b. After 200 feet of drilling on the first well, a soil test is taken. The probabilities of finding the particular type of soil identified by the test follow.

$$P(\text{soil} \mid \text{high-quality oil}) = .20$$
$$P(\text{soil} \mid \text{medium-quality oil}) = .80$$
$$P(\text{soil} \mid \text{no oil}) = .20$$

     How should the firm interpret the soil test? What are the revised probabilities, and what is the new probability of finding oil?

60. Companies that do business over the Internet can often obtain probability information about Web site visitors from previous Web sites visited. The article "Internet Marketing" (*Interfaces,* March/April 2001) described how clickstream data on Web sites visited could be used in conjunction with a Bayesian updating scheme to determine the gender of a Web site visitor. Par Fore created a Web site to market golf equipment and apparel. Management would like a certain offer to appear for female visitors and a different offer to appear for male visitors. From a sample of past Web site visits, management learned that 60% of the visitors to ParFore.com are male and 40% are female.
     a. What is the prior probability that the next visitor to the Web site will be female?
     b. Suppose you know that the current visitor to ParFore.com previously visited the Dillard's Web site, and that women are three times as likely to visit the Dillard's Web site as men. What is the revised probability that the current visitor to ParFore.com is female? Should you display the offer that appeals more to female visitors or the one that appeals more to male visitors?

Case Problem   Hamilton County Judges

Hamilton County judges try thousands of cases per year. In an overwhelming majority of the cases disposed, the verdict stands as rendered. However, some cases are appealed, and of those appealed, some of the cases are reversed. Kristen DelGuzzi of *The Cincinnati Enquirer* conducted a study of cases handled by Hamilton County judges over a three-year period. Shown in Table 4.8 are the results for 182,908 cases handled (disposed) by 38 judges

TABLE 4.8   TOTAL CASES DISPOSED, APPEALED, AND REVERSED IN HAMILTON COUNTY COURTS

CD file

Judge

Common Pleas Court

Judge	Total Cases Disposed	Appealed Cases	Reversed Cases
Fred Cartolano	3,037	137	12
Thomas Crush	3,372	119	10
Patrick Dinkelacker	1,258	44	8
Timothy Hogan	1,954	60	7
Robert Kraft	3,138	127	7
William Mathews	2,264	91	18
William Morrissey	3,032	121	22
Norbert Nadel	2,959	131	20
Arthur Ney, Jr.	3,219	125	14
Richard Niehaus	3,353	137	16
Thomas Nurre	3,000	121	6
John O'Connor	2,969	129	12
Robert Ruehlman	3,205	145	18
J. Howard Sundermann	955	60	10
Ann Marie Tracey	3,141	127	13
Ralph Winkler	3,089	88	6
Total	43,945	1762	199

Domestic Relations Court

Judge	Total Cases Disposed	Appealed Cases	Reversed Cases
Penelope Cunningham	2,729	7	1
Patrick Dinkelacker	6,001	19	4
Deborah Gaines	8,799	48	9
Ronald Panioto	12,970	32	3
Total	30,499	106	17

Municipal Court

Judge	Total Cases Disposed	Appealed Cases	Reversed Cases
Mike Allen	6,149	43	4
Nadine Allen	7,812	34	6
Timothy Black	7,954	41	6
David Davis	7,736	43	5
Leslie Isaiah Gaines	5,282	35	13
Karla Grady	5,253	6	0
Deidra Hair	2,532	5	0
Dennis Helmick	7,900	29	5
Timothy Hogan	2,308	13	2
James Patrick Kenney	2,798	6	1
Joseph Luebbers	4,698	25	8
William Mallory	8,277	38	9
Melba Marsh	8,219	34	7
Beth Mattingly	2,971	13	1
Albert Mestemaker	4,975	28	9
Mark Painter	2,239	7	3
Jack Rosen	7,790	41	13
Mark Schweikert	5,403	33	6
David Stockdale	5,371	22	4
John A. West	2,797	4	2
Total	108,464	500	104

in Common Pleas Court, Domestic Relations Court, and Municipal Court. Two of the judges (Dinkelacker and Hogan) did not serve in the same court for the entire three-year period.

The purpose of the newspaper's study was to evaluate the performance of the judges. Appeals are often the result of mistakes made by judges, and the newspaper wanted to know which judges were doing a good job and which were making too many mistakes. You are called in to assist in the data analysis. Use your knowledge of probability and conditional probability to help with the ranking of the judges. You also may be able to analyze the likelihood of appeal and reversal for cases handled by different courts.

Managerial Report

Prepare a report with your rankings of the judges. Also, include an analysis of the likelihood of appeal and case reversal in the three courts. At a minimum, your report should include the following:

1. The probability of cases being appealed and reversed in the three different courts.
2. The probability of a case being appealed for each judge.
3. The probability of a case being reversed for each judge.
4. The probability of reversal given an appeal for each judge.
5. Rank the judges within each court. State the criteria you used and provide a rationale for your choice.

CHAPTER 5

Discrete Probability Distributions

CONTENTS

STATISTICS IN PRACTICE:
CITIBANK

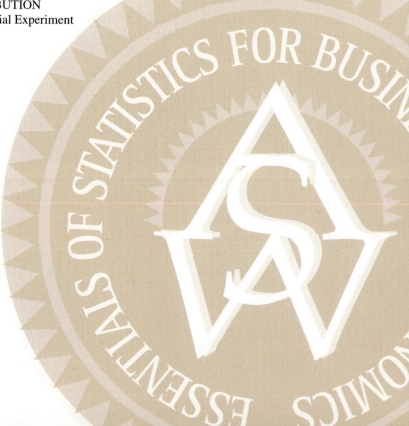

CITIBANK*
LONG ISLAND CITY, NEW YORK

Citibank, a division of Citigroup, makes available a wide range of financial services, including checking and savings accounts, loans and mortgages, insurance, and investment services, within the framework of a unique strategy for delivering those services called Citibanking. Citibanking entails a consistent brand identity all over the world, consistent product offerings, and high-level customer service. Citibanking lets you manage your money anytime, anywhere, anyway you choose. Whether you need to save for the future or borrow for today, you can do it all at Citibank.

Citibanking's state-of-the-art automatic teller machines (ATMs) located in Citicard Banking Centers (CBCs) let customers do all their banking in one place with the touch of a finger, 24 hours a day, 7 days a week. More than 150 different banking functions from deposits to managing investments can be performed with ease. Citibanking ATMs are so much more than just cash machines that customers today use them for 80% of their transactions.

Each Citibank CBC operates as a waiting line system with randomly arriving customers seeking service at one of the ATMs. If all ATMs are busy, the arriving customers wait in line. Periodic CBC capacity studies are used to analyze customer waiting times and to determine whether additional ATMs are needed.

Data collected by Citibank showed that the random customer arrivals followed a probability distribution known as the Poisson distribution. Using the Poisson distribution, Citibank can compute probabilities for the number of customers arriving at a CBC during any time period and make decisions concern-

A Citibank ATM in Manhattan. © PhotoDisc/Getty Images.

ing the number of ATMs needed. For example, let x = the number of customers arriving during a one-minute period. Assuming that a particular CBC has a mean arrival rate of two customers per minute, the following table shows the probabilities for the number of customers arriving during a one-minute period.

x	Probability
0	.1353
1	.2707
2	.2707
3	.1804
4	.0902
5 or more	.0527

Discrete probability distributions, such as the one used by Citibank, are the topic of this chapter. In addition to the Poisson distribution, you will learn about the binomial and hypergeometric distributions and how they can be used to provide helpful probability information.

*The authors are indebted to Ms. Stacey Karter, Citibank, for providing this Statistics in Practice.

In this chapter we continue the study of probability by introducing the concepts of random variables and probability distributions. The focus of this chapter is discrete probability distributions. Three special discrete probability distributions—the binomial, Poisson, and hypergeometric—are covered.

5.1   Random Variables

In Chapter 4 we defined the concept of an experiment and its associated experimental outcomes. A random variable provides a means for describing experimental outcomes using numerical values. Random variables must assume numerical values.

Random variables must assume numerical values.

> **RANDOM VARIABLE**
>
> A **random variable** is a numerical description of the outcome of an experiment.

In effect, a random variable associates a numerical value with each possible experimental outcome. The particular numerical value of the random variable depends on the outcome of the experiment. A random variable can be classified as being either *discrete* or *continuous* depending on the numerical values it assumes.

Discrete Random Variables

A random variable that may assume either a finite number of values or an infinite sequence of values such as 0, 1, 2, . . . is referred to as a **discrete random variable**. For example, consider the experiment of an accountant taking the certified public accountant (CPA) examination. The examination has four parts. We can define a random variable as $x =$ the number of parts of the CPA examination passed. It is a discrete random variable because it may assume the finite number of values 0, 1, 2, 3, or 4.

As another example of a discrete random variable, consider the experiment of cars arriving at a tollbooth. The random variable of interest is $x =$ the number of cars arriving during a one-day period. The possible values for x come from the sequence of integers 0, 1, 2, and so on. Hence, x is a discrete random variable assuming one of the values in this infinite sequence.

Although the outcomes of many experiments can naturally be described by numerical values, others cannot. For example, a survey question might ask an individual to recall the message in a recent television commercial. This experiment would have two possible outcomes: the individual cannot recall the message and the individual can recall the message. We can still describe these experimental outcomes numerically by defining the discrete random variable x as follows: let $x = 0$ if the individual cannot recall the message and $x = 1$ if the individual can recall the message. The numerical values for this random variable are arbitrary (we could use 5 and 10), but they are acceptable in terms of the definition of a random variable—namely, x is a random variable because it provides a numerical description of the outcome of the experiment.

Table 5.1 provides some additional examples of discrete random variables. Note that in each example the discrete random variable assumes a finite number of values or an infinite sequence of values such as 0, 1, 2, ... These types of discrete random variables are discussed in detail in this chapter.

TABLE 5.1   EXAMPLES OF DISCRETE RANDOM VARIABLES

Experiment	Random Variable (x)	Possible Values for the Random Variable
Contact five customers	Number of customers who place an order	0, 1, 2, 3, 4, 5
Inspect a shipment of 50 radios	Number of defective radios	0, 1, 2, $\cdots$, 49, 50
Operate a restaurant for one day	Number of customers	0, 1, 2, 3, $\cdots$
Sell an automobile	Gender of the customer	0 if male; 1 if female

Continuous Random Variables

A random variable that may assume any numerical value in an interval or collection of intervals is called a **continuous random variable**. Experimental outcomes based on measurement scales such as time, weight, distance, and temperature can be described by continuous random variables. For example, consider an experiment of monitoring incoming telephone calls to the claims office of a major insurance company. Suppose the random variable of interest is x = the time between consecutive incoming calls in minutes. This random variable may assume any value in the interval $x \geq 0$. Actually, an infinite number of values are possible for x, including values such as 1.26 minutes, 2.751 minutes, 4.3333 minutes, and so on. As another example, consider a 90-mile section of interstate highway I-75 north of Atlanta, Georgia. For an emergency ambulance service located in Atlanta, we might define the random variable as x = number of miles to the location of the next traffic accident along this section of I-75. In this case, x would be a continuous random variable assuming any value in the interval $0 \leq x \leq 90$. Additional examples of continuous random variables are listed in Table 5.2. Note that each example describes a random variable that may assume any value in an interval of values. Continuous random variables and their probability distributions will be the topic of Chapter 6.

TABLE 5.2 EXAMPLES OF CONTINUOUS RANDOM VARIABLES

Experiment	Random Variable (x)	Possible Values for the Random Variable
Operate a bank	Time between customer arrivals in minutes	$x \geq 0$
Fill a soft drink can (max = 12.1 ounces)	Number of ounces	$0 \leq x \leq 12.1$
Construct a new library	Percentage of project complete after six months	$0 \leq x \leq 100$
Test a new chemical process	Temperature when the desired reaction takes place (min 150° F; max 212° F)	$150 \leq x \leq 212$

NOTES AND COMMENTS

One way to determine whether a random variable is discrete or continuous is to think of the values of the random variable as points on a line segment. Choose two points representing values of the random variable. If the entire line segment between the two points also represents possible values for the random variable, then the random variable is continuous.

Exercises

Methods

1. Consider the experiment of tossing a coin twice.
    a. List the experimental outcomes.
    b. Define a random variable that represents the number of heads occurring on the two tosses.
    c. Show what value the random variable would assume for each of the experimental outcomes.
    d. Is this random variable discrete or continuous?

2. Consider the experiment of a worker assembling a product.
    a. Define a random variable that represents the time in minutes required to assemble the product.
    b. What values may the random variable assume?
    c. Is the random variable discrete or continuous?

Applications

3. Three students scheduled interviews for summer employment at the Brookwood Institute. In each case the interview results in either an offer for a position or no offer. Experimental outcomes are defined in terms of the results of the three interviews.
    a. List the experimental outcomes.
    b. Define a random variable that represents the number of offers made. Is the random variable continuous?
    c. Show the value of the random variable for each of the experimental outcomes.

4. Suppose we know home mortgage rates for 12 Florida lending institutions. Assume that the random variable of interest is the number of lending institutions in this group that offers a 30-year fixed rate of 8.5% or less. What values may this random variable assume?

5. To perform a certain type of blood analysis, lab technicians must perform two procedures. The first procedure requires either one or two separate steps, and the second procedure requires either one, two, or three steps.
    a. List the experimental outcomes associated with performing the blood analysis.
    b. If the random variable of interest is the total number of steps required to do the complete analysis (both procedures), show what value the random variable will assume for each of the experimental outcomes.

6. Listed is a series of experiments and associated random variables. In each case, identify the values that the random variable can assume and state whether the random variable is discrete or continuous.

Experiment	Random Variable (x)
a. Take a 20-question examination	Number of questions answered correctly
b. Observe cars arriving at a tollbooth for 1 hour	Number of cars arriving at tollbooth
c. Audit 50 tax returns	Number of returns containing errors
d. Observe an employee's work	Number of nonproductive hours in an eight-hour workday
e. Weigh a shipment of goods	Number of pounds

5.2 Discrete Probability Distributions

The **probability distribution** for a random variable describes how probabilities are distributed over the values of the random variable. For a discrete random variable x, the probability distribution is defined by a **probability function**, denoted by $f(x)$. The probability function provides the probability for each value of the random variable.

As an illustration of a discrete random variable and its probability distribution, consider the sales of automobiles at DiCarlo Motors in Saratoga, New York. Over the past 300 days of operation, sales data show 54 days with no automobiles sold, 117 days with 1 automobile sold, 72 days with 2 automobiles sold, 42 days with 3 automobiles sold, 12 days with 4 automobiles sold, and 3 days with 5 automobiles sold. Suppose we consider the experiment of selecting a day of operation at DiCarlo Motors and define the random variable of interest as x = the number of automobiles sold during a day. From historical data, we know

x is a discrete random variable that can assume the values 0, 1, 2, 3, 4, or 5. In probability function notation, $f(0)$ provides the probability of 0 automobiles sold, $f(1)$ provides the probability of 1 automobile sold, and so on. Because historical data show 54 of 300 days with 0 automobiles sold, we assign the value 54/300 = .18 to $f(0)$, indicating that the probability of 0 automobiles being sold during a day is .18. Similarly, because 117 of 300 days had 1 automobile sold, we assign the value 117/300 = .39 to $f(1)$, indicating that the probability of exactly 1 automobile being sold during a day is .39. Continuing in this way for the other values of the random variable, we compute the values for $f(2), f(3), f(4),$ and $f(5)$ as shown in Table 5.3, the probability distribution for the number of automobiles sold during a day at DiCarlo Motors.

A primary advantage of defining a random variable and its probability distribution is that once the probability distribution is known, it is relatively easy to determine the probability of a variety of events that may be of interest to a decision maker. For example, using the probability distribution for DiCarlo Motors as shown in Table 5.3, we see that the most probable number of automobiles sold during a day is 1 with a probability of $f(1) = .39$. In addition, there is an $f(3) + f(4) + f(5) = .14 + .04 + .01 = .19$ probability of selling three or more automobiles during a day. These probabilities, plus others the decision maker may ask about, provide information that can help the decision maker understand the process of selling automobiles at DiCarlo Motors.

In the development of a probability function for any discrete random variable, the following two conditions must be satisfied.

These conditions are the analogs to the two basic requirements for assigning probabilities to experimental outcomes presented in Chapter 4.

REQUIRED CONDITIONS FOR A DISCRETE PROBABILITY FUNCTION

$$f(x) \geq 0 \tag{5.1}$$
$$\Sigma f(x) = 1 \tag{5.2}$$

Table 5.3 shows that the probabilities for the random variable x satisfy equation (5.1); $f(x)$ is greater than or equal to 0 for all values of x. In addition, because the probabilities sum to 1, equation (5.2) is satisfied. Thus, the DiCarlo Motors probability function is a valid discrete probability function.

We can also present probability distributions graphically. In Figure 5.1 the values of the random variable x for DiCarlo Motors are shown on the horizontal axis and the probability associated with these values is shown on the vertical axis.

In addition to tables and graphs, a formula that gives the probability function, $f(x)$, for every value of x is often used to describe probability distributions. The simplest example of

TABLE 5.3   PROBABILITY DISTRIBUTION FOR THE NUMBER OF AUTOMOBILES SOLD DURING A DAY AT DICARLO MOTORS

x	$f(x)$
0	.18
1	.39
2	.24
3	.14
4	.04
5	.01
Total	1.00

FIGURE 5.1   GRAPHICAL REPRESENTATION OF THE PROBABILITY DISTRIBUTION
FOR THE NUMBER OF AUTOMOBILES SOLD DURING A DAY AT
DICARLO MOTORS

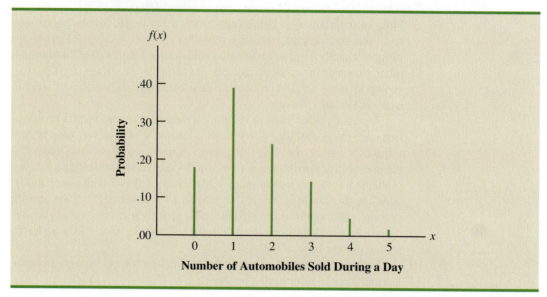

a discrete probability distribution given by a formula is the **discrete uniform probability
distribution**. Its probability function is defined by equation (5.3).

DISCRETE UNIFORM PROBABILITY FUNCTION

$$f(x) = 1/n \qquad\qquad (5.3)$$

where

$n = $ the number of values the random variable may assume

For example, suppose that for the experiment of rolling a die we define the random
variable x to be the number of dots on the upward face. For this experiment, $n = 6$ values
are possible for the random variable; $x = 1, 2, 3, 4, 5, 6$. Thus, the probability function for
this discrete uniform random variable is

$$f(x) = 1/6 \qquad x = 1, 2, 3, 4, 5, 6$$

The possible values of the random variable and the associated probabilities are shown.

x	$f(x)$
1	1/6
2	1/6
3	1/6
4	1/6
5	1/6
6	1/6

As another example, consider the random variable x with the following discrete probability distribution.

x	$f(x)$
1	1/10
2	2/10
3	3/10
4	4/10

This probability distribution can be defined by the formula

$$f(x) = \frac{x}{10} \quad \text{for } x = 1, 2, 3, \text{ or } 4$$

Evaluating $f(x)$ for a given value of the random variable will provide the associated probability. For example, using the preceding probability function, we see that $f(2) = 2/10$ provides the probability that the random variable assumes a value of 2.

The more widely used discrete probability distributions generally are specified by formulas. Three important cases are the binomial, Poisson, and hypergeometric distributions; these distributions are discussed later in the chapter.

Exercises

Methods

7.   The probability distribution for the random variable x follows.

x	$f(x)$
20	.20
25	.15
30	.25
35	.40

    a.   Is this probability distribution valid? Explain.
    b.   What is the probability that $x = 30$?
    c.   What is the probability that x is less than or equal to 25?
    d.   What is the probability that x is greater than 30?

Applications

8.   The following data were collected by counting the number of operating rooms in use at Tampa General Hospital over a 20-day period: On three of the days only one operating room was used, on five of the days two were used, on eight of the days three were used, and on four days all four of the hospital's operating rooms were used.
    a.   Use the relative frequency approach to construct a probability distribution for the number of operating rooms in use on any given day.
    b.   Draw a graph of the probability distribution.
    c.   Show that your probability distribution satisfies the required conditions for a valid discrete probability distribution.

9. Nationally, 38% of fourth-graders cannot read an age-appropriate book. The following data show the number of children, by age, identified as learning disabled under special education. Most of these children have reading problems that should be identified and corrected before third grade. Current federal law prohibits most children from receiving extra help from special education programs until they fall behind by approximately two years' worth of learning, and that typically means third grade or later (*USA Today*, September 6, 2001).

Age	Number of Children
6	37,369
7	87,436
8	160,840
9	239,719
10	286,719
11	306,533
12	310,787
13	302,604
14	289,168

Suppose that we want to select a sample of children identified as learning disabled under special education for a program designed to improve reading ability. Let x be a random variable indicating the age of one randomly selected child.

a. Use the data to develop a probability distribution for x. Specify the values for the random variable and the corresponding values for the probability function $f(x)$.
b. Draw a graph of the probability distribution.
c. Show that the probability distribution satisfies equations (5.1) and (5.2).

10. Table 5.4 shows the percent frequency distributions of job satisfaction scores for a sample of information systems (IS) senior executives and IS middle managers. The scores range from a low of 1 (very dissatisfied) to a high of 5 (very satisfied).

TABLE 5.4 PERCENT FREQUENCY DISTRIBUTION OF JOB SATISFACTION SCORES FOR INFORMATION SYSTEMS EXECUTIVES AND MIDDLE MANAGERS

Job Satisfaction Score	IS Senior Executives (%)	IS Middle Managers (%)
1	5	4
2	9	10
3	3	12
4	42	46
5	41	28

a. Develop a probability distribution for the job satisfaction score of a senior executive.
b. Develop a probability distribution for the job satisfaction score of a middle manager.
c. What is the probability a senior executive will report a job satisfaction score of 4 or 5?
d. What is the probability a middle manager is very satisfied?
e. Compare the overall job satisfaction of senior executives and middle managers.

11. A technician services mailing machines at companies in the Phoenix area. Depending on the type of malfunction, the service call can take 1, 2, 3, or 4 hours. The different types of malfunctions occur at about the same frequency.

    a.   Develop a probability distribution for the duration of a service call.

    b.   Draw a graph of the probability distribution.

    c.   Show that your probability distribution satisfies the conditions required for a discrete probability function.

    d.   What is the probability a service call will take three hours?

    e.   A service call has just come in, but the type of malfunction is unknown. It is 3:00 P.M. and service technicians usually get off at 5:00 P.M. What is the probability the service technician will have to work overtime to fix the machine today?

12.   The director of admissions at Lakeville Community College subjectively assessed a probability distribution for x, the number of entering students, as follows.

x	$f(x)$
1000	.15
1100	.20
1200	.30
1300	.25
1400	.10

    a.   Is this probability distribution valid? Explain.

    b.   What is the probability of 1200 or fewer entering students?

13.   A psychologist determined that the number of sessions required to obtain the trust of a new patient is either 1, 2, or 3. Let x be a random variable indicating the number of sessions required to gain the patient's trust. The following probability function has been proposed.

$$f(x) = \frac{x}{6} \qquad \text{for } x = 1, 2, \text{ or } 3$$

    a.   Is this probability function valid? Explain.

    b.   What is the probability that it takes exactly 2 sessions to gain the patient's trust?

    c.   What is the probability that it takes at least 2 sessions to gain the patient's trust?

14.   The following table is a partial probability distribution for the MRA Company's projected profits (x = profit in \$1000s) for the first year of operation (the negative value denotes a loss).

x	$f(x)$
−100	.10
0	.20
50	.30
100	.25
150	.10
200	

    a.   What is the proper value for $f(200)$? What is your interpretation of this value?

    b.   What is the probability that MRA will be profitable?

    c.   What is the probability that MRA will make at least \$100,000?

5.3 **Expected Value and Variance**

Expected Value

The **expected value**, or mean, of a random variable is a measure of the central location for the random variable. The formula for the expected value of a discrete random variable x follows.

The expected value is a weighted average of the values the random variable may assume. The weights are the probabilities.

EXPECTED VALUE OF A DISCRETE RANDOM VARIABLE

$$E(x) = \mu = \Sigma x f(x) \qquad \textbf{(5.4)}$$

Both the notations $E(x)$ and μ are used to denote the expected value of a random variable.

Equation (5.4) shows that to compute the expected value of a discrete random variable, we must multiply each value of the random variable by the corresponding probability $f(x)$ and then add the resulting products. Using the DiCarlo Motors automobile sales example from Section 5.2, we show the calculation of the expected value for the number of automobiles sold during a day in Table 5.5. The sum of the entries in the $xf(x)$ column shows that the expected value is 1.50 automobiles per day. We therefore know that although sales of 0, 1, 2, 3, 4, or 5 automobiles are possible on any one day, over time DiCarlo can anticipate selling an average of 1.50 automobiles per day. Assuming 30 days of operation during a month, we can use the expected value of 1.50 to forecast average monthly sales of $30(1.50) = 45$ automobiles.

The expected value does not have to be a value the random variable can assume.

Variance

Even though the expected value provides the mean value for the random variable, we often need a measure of variability, or dispersion. Just as we used the variance in Chapter 3 to summarize the variability in data, we now use **variance** to summarize the variability in the values of a random variable. The formula for the variance of a discrete random variable follows.

The variance is a weighted average of the squared deviations of a random variable from its mean. The weights are the probabilities.

VARIANCE OF A DISCRETE RANDOM VARIABLE

$$\text{Var}(x) = \sigma^2 = \Sigma(x - \mu)^2 f(x) \qquad \textbf{(5.5)}$$

TABLE 5.5 CALCULATION OF THE EXPECTED VALUE FOR THE NUMBER OF AUTOMOBILES SOLD DURING A DAY AT DICARLO MOTORS

x	$f(x)$	$xf(x)$
0	.18	$0(.18) = $ .00
1	.39	$1(.39) = $ .39
2	.24	$2(.24) = $ .48
3	.14	$3(.14) = $ .42
4	.04	$4(.04) = $ .16
5	.01	$5(.01) = $ .05
		1.50

$$E(x) = \mu = \Sigma x f(x)$$

TABLE 5.6   CALCULATION OF THE VARIANCE FOR THE NUMBER OF AUTOMOBILES SOLD DURING A DAY AT DICARLO MOTORS

x	$x - \mu$	$(x - \mu)^2$	$f(x)$	$(x - \mu)^2 f(x)$
0	$0 - 1.50 = -1.50$	2.25	.18	$2.25(.18) = .4050$
1	$1 - 1.50 = -.50$	.25	.39	$.25(.39) = .0975$
2	$2 - 1.50 = .50$	.25	.24	$.25(.24) = .0600$
3	$3 - 1.50 = 1.50$	2.25	.14	$2.25(.14) = .3150$
4	$4 - 1.50 = 2.50$	6.25	.04	$6.25(.04) = .2500$
5	$5 - 1.50 = 3.50$	12.25	.01	$12.25(.01) = \underline{.1225}$
				1.2500

$$\sigma^2 = \Sigma(x - \mu)^2 f(x)$$

As equation (5.5) shows, an essential part of the variance formula is the deviation, $x - \mu$, which measures how far a particular value of the random variable is from the expected value, or mean, μ. In computing the variance of a random variable, the deviations are squared and then weighted by the corresponding value of the probability function. The sum of these weighted squared deviations for all values of the random variable is referred to as the *variance*. The notations Var(x) and σ^2 are both used to denote the variance of a random variable.

The calculation of the variance for the probability distribution of the number of automobiles sold during a day at DiCarlo Motors is summarized in Table 5.6. We see that the variance is 1.25. The **standard deviation**, σ, is defined as the positive square root of the variance. Thus, the standard deviation for the number of automobiles sold during a day is

$$\sigma = \sqrt{1.25} = 1.118$$

The standard deviation is measured in the same units as the random variable ($\sigma = 1.118$ automobiles) and therefore is often preferred in describing the variability of a random variable. The variance σ^2 is measured in squared units and is thus more difficult to interpret.

Exercises

Methods

15. The following table provides a probability distribution for the random variable x.

x	$f(x)$
3	.25
6	.50
9	.25

a. Compute $E(x)$, the expected value of x.
b. Compute σ^2, the variance of x.
c. Compute σ, the standard deviation of x.

16. The following table provides a probability distribution for the random variable y.

y	$f(y)$
2	.20
4	.30
7	.40
8	.10

a. Compute $E(y)$.
b. Compute Var(y) and σ.

Applications

17. A volunteer ambulance service handles 0 to 5 service calls on any given day. The probability distribution for the number of service calls is as follows.

Number of Service Calls	Probability	Number of Service Calls	Probability
0	.10	3	.20
1	.15	4	.15
2	.30	5	.10

a. What is the expected number of service calls?
b. What is the variance in the number of service calls? What is the standard deviation?

18. The American Housing Survey reported the following data on the number of bedrooms in owner-occupied and renter-occupied houses in central cities (http://www.census.gov, March 31, 2003).

	Number of Houses (1000s)	
Bedrooms	Renter-Occupied	Owner-Occupied
0	547	23
1	5012	541
2	6100	3832
3	2644	8690
4 or more	557	3783

a. Define a random variable x = number of bedrooms in renter-occupied houses and develop a probability distribution for the random variable. (Let $x = 4$ represent 4 or more bedrooms.)
b. Compute the expected value and variance for the number of bedrooms in renter-occupied houses.
c. Define a random variable y = number of bedrooms in owner-occupied houses and develop a probability distribution for the random variable. (Let $y = 4$ represent 4 or more bedrooms.)
d. Compute the expected value and variance for the number of bedrooms in owner-occupied houses.
e. What observations can you make from a comparison of the number of bedrooms in renter-occupied versus owner-occupied homes?

19. The National Basketball Association (NBA) records a variety of statistics for each team. Two of these statistics are the percentage of field goals made by the team and the percentage of three-point shots made by the team. For a portion of the 2004 season, the shooting records of the 29 teams in the NBA showed the probability of scoring two points by mak-

ing a field goal was .44, and the probability of scoring three points by making a three-point shot was .34 (http://www.nba.com, January 3, 2004).

a. What is the expected value of a two-point shot for these teams?

b. What is the expected value of a three-point shot for these teams?

c. If the probability of making a two-point shot is greater than the probability of making a three-point shot, why do coaches allow some players to shoot the three-point shot if they have the opportunity? Use expected value to explain your answer.

20. The probability distribution for damage claims paid by the Newton Automobile Insurance Company on collision insurance follows.

Payment ($)	Probability
0	.90
400	.04
1000	.03
2000	.01
4000	.01
6000	.01

a. Use the expected collision payment to determine the collision insurance premium that would enable the company to break even.

b. The insurance company charges an annual rate of $260 for the collision coverage. What is the expected value of the collision policy for a policyholder? (*Hint:* It is the expected payments from the company minus the cost of coverage.) Why does the policyholder purchase a collision policy with this expected value?

21. The following probability distributions of job satisfaction scores for a sample of information systems (IS) senior executives and IS middle managers range from a low of 1 (very dissatisfied) to a high of 5 (very satisfied).

Job Satisfaction Score	Probability	
	IS Senior Executives	IS Middle Managers
1	.05	.04
2	.09	.10
3	.03	.12
4	.42	.46
5	.41	.28

a. What is the expected value of the job satisfaction score for senior executives?

b. What is the expected value of the job satisfaction score for middle managers?

c. Compute the variance of job satisfaction scores for executives and middle managers.

d. Compute the standard deviation of job satisfaction scores for both probability distributions.

e. Compare the overall job satisfaction of senior executives and middle managers.

22. The demand for a product of Carolina Industries varies greatly from month to month. The probability distribution in the following table, based on the past two years of data, shows the company's monthly demand.

Unit Demand	Probability
300	.20
400	.30
500	.35
600	.15

a. If the company bases monthly orders on the expected value of the monthly demand, what should Carolina's monthly order quantity be for this product?

b. Assume that each unit demanded generates $70 in revenue and that each unit ordered costs $50. How much will the company gain or lose in a month if it places an order based on your answer to part (a) and the actual demand for the item is 300 units?

23. The 2002 New York City Housing and Vacancy Survey showed a total of 59,324 rent-controlled housing units and 236,263 rent-stabilized units built in 1947 or later. For these rental units, the probability distributions for the number of persons living in the unit are given (http://www.census.gov, January 12, 2004).

Number of Persons	Rent-Controlled	Rent-Stabilized
1	.61	.41
2	.27	.30
3	.07	.14
4	.04	.11
5	.01	.03
6	.00	.01

a. What is the expected value of the number of persons living in each type of unit?

b. What is the variance of the number of persons living in each type of unit?

c. Make some comparisons between the number of persons living in rent-controlled units and the number of persons living in rent-stabilized units.

24. The J. R. Ryland Computer Company is considering a plant expansion to enable the company to begin production of a new computer product. The company's president must determine whether to make the expansion a medium- or large-scale project. Demand for the new product is uncertain, which for planning purposes may be low demand, medium demand, or high demand. The probability estimates for demand are .20, .50, and .30, respectively. Letting x and y indicate the annual profit in thousands of dollars, the firm's planners developed the following profit forecasts for the medium- and large-scale expansion projects.

		Medium-Scale Expansion Profit		Large-Scale Expansion Profit	
		x	$f(x)$	y	$f(y)$
	Low	50	.20	0	.20
Demand	Medium	150	.50	100	.50
	High	200	.30	300	.30

a. Compute the expected value for the profit associated with the two expansion alternatives. Which decision is preferred for the objective of maximizing the expected profit?

b. Compute the variance for the profit associated with the two expansion alternatives. Which decision is preferred for the objective of minimizing the risk or uncertainty?

5.4 Binomial Probability Distribution

The binomial probability distribution is a discrete probability distribution that provides many applications. It is associated with a multiple-step experiment that we call the binomial experiment.

A Binomial Experiment

A **binomial experiment** exhibits the following four properties.

PROPERTIES OF A BINOMIAL EXPERIMENT

1. The experiment consists of a sequence of n identical trials.
2. Two outcomes are possible on each trial. We refer to one outcome as a *success* and the other outcome as a *failure*.
3. The probability of a success, denoted by p, does not change from trial to trial. Consequently, the probability of a failure, denoted by $1 - p$, does not change from trial to trial.
4. The trials are independent.

Jakob Bernoulli (1654–1705), the first of the Bernoulli family of Swiss mathematicians, published a treatise on probability that contained the theory of permutations and combinations, as well as the binomial theorem.

If properties 2, 3, and 4 are present, we say the trials are generated by a Bernoulli process. If, in addition, property 1 is present, we say we have a binomial experiment. Figure 5.2 depicts one possible sequence of successes and failures for a binomial experiment involving eight trials.

In a binomial experiment, our interest is in the *number of successes occurring in the n trials*. If we let x denote the number of successes occurring in the n trials, we see that x can assume the values of 0, 1, 2, 3, . . . , n. Because the number of values is finite, x is a *discrete* random variable. The probability distribution associated with this random variable is called the **binomial probability distribution**. For example, consider the experiment of tossing a coin five times and on each toss observing whether the coin lands with a head or a tail on its upward face. Suppose we want to count the number of heads appearing over the five tosses. Does this experiment show the properties of a binomial experiment? What is the random variable of interest? Note that:

1. The experiment consists of five identical trials; each trial involves the tossing of one coin.
2. Two outcomes are possible for each trial: a head or a tail. We can designate head a success and tail a failure.
3. The probability of a head and the probability of a tail are the same for each trial, with $p = .5$ and $1 - p = .5$.
4. The trials or tosses are independent because the outcome on any one trial is not affected by what happens on other trials or tosses.

FIGURE 5.2 ONE POSSIBLE SEQUENCE OF SUCCESSES AND FAILURES FOR AN EIGHT-TRIAL BINOMIAL EXPERIMENT

Property 1: The experiment consists of $n = 8$ identical trials.

Property 2: Each trial results in either success (S) or failure (F).

Trials ⟶ 1 2 3 4 5 6 7 8

Outcomes ⟶ S F F S S F S S

Thus, the properties of a binomial experiment are satisfied. The random variable of interest is x = the number of heads appearing in the five trials. In this case, x can assume the values of 0, 1, 2, 3, 4, or 5.

As another example, consider an insurance salesperson who visits 10 randomly selected families. The outcome associated with each visit is classified as a success if the family purchases an insurance policy and a failure if the family does not. From past experience, the salesperson knows the probability that a randomly selected family will purchase an insurance policy is .10. Checking the properties of a binomial experiment, we observe that:

1. The experiment consists of 10 identical trials; each trial involves contacting one family.
2. Two outcomes are possible on each trial: the family purchases a policy (success) or the family does not purchase a policy (failure).
3. The probabilities of a purchase and a nonpurchase are assumed to be the same for each sales call, with p = .10 and $1 - p$ = .90.
4. The trials are independent because the families are randomly selected.

Because the four assumptions are satisfied, this example is a binomial experiment. The random variable of interest is the number of sales obtained in contacting the 10 families. In this case, x can assume the values of 0, 1, 2, 3, 4, 5, 6, 7, 8, 9, and 10.

Property 3 of the binomial experiment is called the *stationarity assumption* and is sometimes confused with property 4, independence of trials. To see how they differ, consider again the case of the salesperson calling on families to sell insurance policies. If, as the day wore on, the salesperson got tired and lost enthusiasm, the probability of success (selling a policy) might drop to .05, for example, by the tenth call. In such a case, property 3 (stationarity) would not be satisfied, and we would not have a binomial experiment. Even if property 4 held—that is, the purchase decisions of each family were made independently—it would not be a binomial experiment if property 3 was not satisfied.

In applications involving binomial experiments, a special mathematical formula, called the *binomial probability function,* can be used to compute the probability of x successes in the n trials. Using probability concepts introduced in Chapter 4, we will show in the context of an illustrative problem how the formula can be developed.

Martin Clothing Store Problem

Let us consider the purchase decisions of the next three customers who enter the Martin Clothing Store. On the basis of past experience, the store manager estimates the probability that any one customer will make a purchase is .30. What is the probability that two of the next three customers will make a purchase?

Using a tree diagram (Figure 5.3), we can see that the experiment of observing the three customers each making a purchase decision has eight possible outcomes. Using S to denote success (a purchase) and F to denote failure (no purchase), we are interested in experimental outcomes involving two successes in the three trials (purchase decisions). Next, let us verify that the experiment involving the sequence of three purchase decisions can be viewed as a binomial experiment. Checking the four requirements for a binomial experiment, we note that:

1. The experiment can be described as a sequence of three identical trials, one trial for each of the three customers who will enter the store.
2. Two outcomes—the customer makes a purchase (success) or the customer does not make a purchase (failure)—are possible for each trial.
3. The probability that the customer will make a purchase (.30) or will not make a purchase (.70) is assumed to be the same for all customers.
4. The purchase decision of each customer is independent of the decisions of the other customers.

FIGURE 5.3   TREE DIAGRAM FOR THE MARTIN CLOTHING STORE PROBLEM

			Experimental	
First	Second	Third		
Customer	Customer	Customer	Outcome	Value of x

Outcomes (read from diagram):

Experimental Outcome	Value of x
(S, S, S)	3
(S, S, F)	2
(S, F, S)	2
(S, F, F)	1
(F, S, S)	2
(F, S, F)	1
(F, F, S)	1
(F, F, F)	0

S = Purchase
F = No purchase
x = Number of customers making a purchase

Hence, the properties of a binomial experiment are present.

The number of experimental outcomes resulting in exactly x successes in n trials can be computed using the following formula.*

NUMBER OF EXPERIMENTAL OUTCOMES PROVIDING EXACTLY x SUCCESSES IN n TRIALS

$$\binom{n}{x} = \frac{n!}{x!(n-x)!} \tag{5.6}$$

where

$$n! = n(n-1)(n-2)\cdots(2)(1)$$

and, by definition,

$$0! = 1$$

Now let us return to the Martin Clothing Store experiment involving three customer purchase decisions. Equation (5.6) can be used to determine the number of experimental

---

*This formula, introduced in Chapter 4, determines the number of combinations of n objects selected x at a time. For the binomial experiment, this combinatorial formula provides the number of experimental outcomes (sequences of n trials) resulting in x successes.

outcomes involving two purchases; that is, the number of ways of obtaining $x = 2$ successes in the $n = 3$ trials. From equation (5.6) we have

$$\binom{n}{x} = \binom{3}{2} = \frac{3!}{2!(3-2)!} = \frac{(3)(2)(1)}{(2)(1)(1)} = \frac{6}{2} = 3$$

Equation (5.6) shows that three of the experimental outcomes yield two successes. From Figure 5.3 we see these three outcomes are denoted by (S, S, F), (S, F, S), and (F, S, S).

Using equation (5.6) to determine how many experimental outcomes have three successes (purchases) in the three trials, we obtain

$$\binom{n}{x} = \binom{3}{3} = \frac{3!}{3!(3-3)!} = \frac{3!}{3!0!} = \frac{(3)(2)(1)}{3(2)(1)(1)} = \frac{6}{6} = 1$$

From Figure 5.3 we see that the one experimental outcome with three successes is identified by (S, S, S).

We know that equation (5.6) can be used to determine the number of experimental outcomes that result in x successes. If we are to determine the probability of x successes in n trials, however, we must also know the probability associated with each of these experimental outcomes. Because the trials of a binomial experiment are independent, we can simply multiply the probabilities associated with each trial outcome to find the probability of a particular sequence of successes and failures.

The probability of purchases by the first two customers and no purchase by the third customer, denoted (S, S, F), is given by

$$pp(1 - p)$$

With a .30 probability of a purchase on any one trial, the probability of a purchase on the first two trials and no purchase on the third is given by

$$(.30)(.30)(.70) = (.30)^2(.70) = .063$$

Two other experimental outcomes also result in two successes and one failure. The probabilities for all three experimental outcomes involving two successes follow.

| Trial Outcomes | | | | Probability of |
1st Customer	2nd Customer	3rd Customer	Experimental Outcome	Experimental Outcome
Purchase	Purchase	No purchase	(S, S, F)	$pp(1-p) = p^2(1-p)$ $= (.30)^2(.70) = .063$
Purchase	No purchase	Purchase	(S, F, S)	$p(1-p)p = p^2(1-p)$ $= (.30)^2(.70) = .063$
No purchase	Purchase	Purchase	(F, S, S)	$(1-p)pp = p^2(1-p)$ $= (.30)^2(.70) = .063$

Observe that all three experimental outcomes with two successes have exactly the same probability. This observation holds in general. In any binomial experiment, all sequences of trial outcomes yielding x successes in n trials have the *same probability* of occurrence. The probability of each sequence of trials yielding x successes in n trials follows.

Probability of a particular
sequence of trial outcomes $= p^x(1 - p)^{(n-x)}$ **(5.7)**
with x successes in n trials

For the Martin Clothing Store, this formula shows that any experimental outcome with two successes has a probability of $p^2(1 - p)^{(3-2)} = p^2(1 - p)^1 = (.30)^2(.70)^1 = .063$.

Because equation (5.6) shows the number of outcomes in a binomial experiment with x successes and equation (5.7) gives the probability for each sequence involving x successes, we combine equations (5.6) and (5.7) to obtain the following **binomial probability function**.

BINOMIAL PROBABILITY FUNCTION

$$f(x) = \binom{n}{x} p^x(1 - p)^{(n-x)}$$ **(5.8)**

where

$$f(x) = \text{the probability of } x \text{ successes in } n \text{ trials}$$
$$n = \text{the number of trials}$$
$$\binom{n}{x} = \frac{n!}{x!(n - x)!}$$
$$p = \text{the probability of a success on any one trial}$$
$$1 - p = \text{the probability of a failure on any one trial}$$

In the Martin Clothing Store example, let us compute the probability that no customer makes a purchase, exactly one customer makes a purchase, exactly two customers make a purchase, and all three customers make a purchase. The calculations are summarized in Table 5.7, which gives the probability distribution of the number of customers making a purchase. Figure 5.4 is a graph of this probability distribution.

The binomial probability function can be applied to *any* binomial experiment. If we are satisfied that a situation demonstrates the properties of a binomial experiment and if we know the values of n and p, we can use equation (5.8) to compute the probability of x successes in the n trials.

TABLE 5.7   PROBABILITY DISTRIBUTION FOR THE NUMBER OF CUSTOMERS
MAKING A PURCHASE

x	$f(x)$
0	$\dfrac{3!}{0!3!} (.30)^0(.70)^3 = .343$
1	$\dfrac{3!}{1!2!} (.30)^1(.70)^2 = .441$
2	$\dfrac{3!}{2!1!} (.30)^2(.70)^1 = .189$
3	$\dfrac{3!}{3!0!} (.30)^3(.70)^0 = \underline{.027}$
	1.000

FIGURE 5.4   GRAPHICAL REPRESENTATION OF THE PROBABILITY DISTRIBUTION FOR THE NUMBER OF CUSTOMERS MAKING A PURCHASE

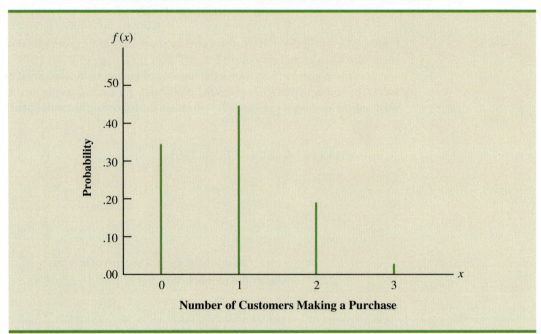

If we consider variations of the Martin experiment, such as 10 customers rather than three entering the store, the binomial probability function given by equation (5.8) is still applicable. Suppose we have a binomial experiment with $n = 10$, $x = 4$, and $p = .30$. The probability of making exactly four sales to 10 customers entering the store is

$$f(4) = \frac{10!}{4!6!} (.30)^4(.70)^6 = .2001$$

Using Tables of Binomial Probabilities

Tables have been developed that give the probability of x successes in n trials for a binomial experiment. The tables are generally easy to use and quicker than equation (5.8). Table 5 of Appendix B provides such a table of binomial probabilities. A portion of this table appears in Table 5.8. To use this table, we must specify the values of n, p, and x for the binomial experiment of interest. In the example at the top of Table 5.8, we see that the probability of $x = 3$ successes in a binomial experiment with $n = 10$ and $p = .40$ is .2150. You can use equation (5.8) to verify that you would obtain the same answer if you used the binomial probability function directly.

Now let us use Table 5.8 to verify the probability of four successes in 10 trials for the Martin Clothing Store problem. Note that the value of $f(4) = .2001$ can be read directly from the table of binomial probabilities, with $n = 10$, $x = 4$, and $p = .30$.

With modern calculators, these tables are almost unnecessary. It is easy to evaluate equation (5.8) directly.

Even though the tables of binomial probabilities are relatively easy to use, it is impossible to have tables that show all possible values of n and p that might be encountered in a binomial experiment. However, with today's calculators, using equation (5.8) to calculate the desired probability is not difficult, especially if the number of trials is not large. In the exercises, you should practice using equation (5.8) to compute the binomial probabilities unless the problem specifically requests that you use the binomial probability table.

TABLE 5.8   SELECTED VALUES FROM THE BINOMIAL PROBABILITY TABLE
EXAMPLE: $n = 10$, $x = 3$, $p = .40$; $f(3) = .2150$

						p					
n	x	.05	.10	.15	.20	.25	.30	.35	.40	.45	.50
9	0	.6302	.3874	.2316	.1342	.0751	.0404	.0207	.0101	.0046	.0020
	1	.2985	.3874	.3679	.3020	.2253	.1556	.1004	.0605	.0339	.0176
	2	.0629	.1722	.2597	.3020	.3003	.2668	.2162	.1612	.1110	.0703
	3	.0077	.0446	.1069	.1762	.2336	.2668	.2716	.2508	.2119	.1641
	4	.0006	.0074	.0283	.0661	.1168	.1715	.2194	.2508	.2600	.2461
	5	.0000	.0008	.0050	.0165	.0389	.0735	.1181	.1672	.2128	.2461
	6	.0000	.0001	.0006	.0028	.0087	.0210	.0424	.0743	.1160	.1641
	7	.0000	.0000	.0000	.0003	.0012	.0039	.0098	.0212	.0407	.0703
	8	.0000	.0000	.0000	.0000	.0001	.0004	.0013	.0035	.0083	.0176
	9	.0000	.0000	.0000	.0000	.0000	.0000	.0001	.0003	.0008	.0020
10	0	.5987	.3487	.1969	.1074	.0563	.0282	.0135	.0060	.0025	.0010
	1	.3151	.3874	.3474	.2684	.1877	.1211	.0725	.0403	.0207	.0098
	2	.0746	.1937	.2759	.3020	.2816	.2335	.1757	.1209	.0763	.0439
	3	.0105	.0574	.1298	.2013	.2503	.2668	.2522	**.2150**	.1665	.1172
	4	.0010	.0112	.0401	.0881	.1460	.2001	.2377	.2508	.2384	.2051
	5	.0001	.0015	.0085	.0264	.0584	.1029	.1536	.2007	.2340	.2461
	6	.0000	.0001	.0012	.0055	.0162	.0368	.0689	.1115	.1596	.2051
	7	.0000	.0000	.0001	.0008	.0031	.0090	.0212	.0425	.0746	.1172
	8	.0000	.0000	.0000	.0001	.0004	.0014	.0043	.0106	.0229	.0439
	9	.0000	.0000	.0000	.0000	.0000	.0001	.0005	.0016	.0042	.0098
	10	.0000	.0000	.0000	.0000	.0000	.0000	.0000	.0001	.0003	.0010

Statistical software packages such as Minitab and spreadsheet packages such as Excel also provide a capability for computing binomial probabilities. Consider the Martin Clothing Store example with $n = 10$ and $p = .30$. Figure 5.5 shows the binomial probabilities generated by Minitab for all possible values of x. Note that these values are the same as those found in the $p = .30$ column of Table 5.8. Appendix 5.1 gives the step-by-step procedure for using Minitab to generate the output in Figure 5.5. Appendix 5.2 describes how Excel can be used to compute binomial probabilities.

Expected Value and Variance for the Binomial Distribution

In Section 5.3 we provided formulas for computing the expected value and variance of a discrete random variable. In the special case where the random variable has a binomial distribution with a known number of trials n and a known probability of success p, the general formulas for the expected value and variance can be simplified. The results follow.

EXPECTED VALUE AND VARIANCE FOR THE BINOMIAL DISTRIBUTION

$$E(x) = \mu = np \tag{5.9}$$

$$\text{Var}(x) = \sigma^2 = np(1 - p) \tag{5.10}$$

FIGURE 5.5 MINITAB OUTPUT SHOWING BINOMIAL PROBABILITIES FOR THE MARTIN CLOTHING STORE PROBLEM

x	P(X = x)
0.00	0.0282
1.00	0.1211
2.00	0.2335
3.00	0.2668
4.00	0.2001
5.00	0.1029
6.00	0.0368
7.00	0.0090
8.00	0.0014
9.00	0.0001
10.00	0.0000

For the Martin Clothing Store problem with three customers, we can use equation (5.9) to compute the expected number of customers who will make a purchase.

$$E(x) = np = 3(.30) = .9$$

Suppose that for the next month the Martin Clothing Store forecasts 1000 customers will enter the store. What is the expected number of customers who will make a purchase? The answer is $\mu = np = (1000)(.3) = 300$. Thus, to increase the expected number of purchases, Martin's must induce more customers to enter the store and/or somehow increase the probability that any individual customer will make a purchase after entering.

For the Martin Clothing Store problem with three customers, we see that the variance and standard deviation for the number of customers who will make a purchase are

$$\sigma^2 = np(1 - p) = 3(.3)(.7) = .63$$
$$\sigma = \sqrt{.63} = .79$$

For the next 1000 customers entering the store, the variance and standard deviation for the number of customers who will make a purchase are

$$\sigma^2 = np(1 - p) = 1000(.3)(.7) = 210$$
$$\sigma = \sqrt{210} = 14.49$$

NOTES AND COMMENTS

1. The binomial tables in Appendix B show values of p only up to and including $p = .50$. It would appear that such tables cannot be used when the probability of success exceeds $p = .50$. However, they can be used by noting that the probability of $n - x$ failures is also the probability of x successes. When the probability of success is greater than $p = .50$, one can compute the probability of $n - x$ failures instead. The probability of failure, $1 - p$, will be less than .50 when $p > .50$.

2. Some sources present binomial tables in a cumulative form. In using such tables, one must subtract to find the probability of x successes in n trials. For example, $f(2) = P(x \leq 2) - P(x \leq 1)$. Our tables provide these probabilities directly. To compute cumulative probabilities using our tables, one simply sums the individual probabilities. For example, to compute $P(x \leq 2)$ using our tables, we sum $f(0) + f(1) + f(2)$.

Exercises

Methods

25. Consider a binomial experiment with two trials and $p = .4$.
    a. Draw a tree diagram for this experiment (see Figure 5.3).
    b. Compute the probability of one success, $f(1)$.
    c. Compute $f(0)$.
    d. Compute $f(2)$.
    e. Compute the probability of at least one success.
    f. Compute the expected value, variance, and standard deviation.

26. Consider a binomial experiment with $n = 10$ and $p = .10$.
    a. Compute $f(0)$.
    b. Compute $f(2)$.
    c. Compute $P(x \leq 2)$.
    d. Compute $P(x \geq 1)$.
    e. Compute $E(x)$.
    f. Compute $Var(x)$ and σ.

27. Consider a binomial experiment with $n = 20$ and $p = .70$.
    a. Compute $f(12)$.
    b. Compute $f(16)$.
    c. Compute $P(x \geq 16)$.
    d. Compute $P(x \leq 15)$.
    e. Compute $E(x)$.
    f. Compute $Var(x)$ and σ.

Applications

28. A Harris Interactive survey for InterContinental Hotels & Resorts asked respondents, "When traveling internationally, do you generally venture out on your own to experience culture, or stick with your tour group and itineraries?" The survey found that 23% of the respondents stick with their tour group (*USA Today,* January 21, 2004).
    a. In a sample of six international travelers, what is the probability that two will stick with their tour group?
    b. In a sample of six international travelers, what is the probability that at least two will stick with their tour group?
    c. In a sample of 10 international travelers, what is the probability that none will stick with the tour group?

29. According to a *Business Week*/Harris Poll of 1035 adults, 40% of those surveyed agreed strongly with the proposition that business has too much power over American life (*Business Week,* September 11, 2000). Assume this percentage is representative of the American population. In a sample of 20 individuals taken from a cross-section of the American population, what is the probability that at least five of these individuals will feel that business has too much power over American life?

30. When a new machine is functioning properly, only 3% of the items produced are defective. Assume that we will randomly select two parts produced on the machine and that we are interested in the number of defective parts found.
    a. Describe the conditions under which this situation would be a binomial experiment.
    b. Draw a tree diagram similar to Figure 5.3 showing this problem as a two-trial experiment.
    c. How many experimental outcomes result in exactly one defect being found?
    d. Compute the probabilities associated with finding no defects, exactly one defect, and two defects.

31. Nine percent of undergraduate students carry credit card balances greater than $7000 (*Reader's Digest,* July 2002). Suppose 10 undergraduate students are selected randomly to be interviewed about credit card usage.
    a. Is the selection of 10 students a binomial experiment? Explain.
    b. What is the probability that two of the students will have a credit card balance greater than $7000?
    c. What is the probability that none will have a credit card balance greater than $7000?
    d. What is the probability that at least three will have a credit card balance greater than $7000?

32. Military radar and missile detection systems are designed to warn a country of an enemy attack. A reliability question is whether a detection system will be able to identify an attack and issue a warning. Assume that a particular detection system has a .90 probability of detecting a missile attack. Use the binomial probability distribution to answer the following questions.
    a. What is the probability that a single detection system will detect an attack?
    b. If two detection systems are installed in the same area and operate independently, what is the probability that at least one of the systems will detect the attack?
    c. If three systems are installed, what is the probability that at least one of the systems will detect the attack?
    d. Would you recommend that multiple detection systems be used? Explain.

33. Fifty percent of Americans believed the country was in a recession, even though technically the economy had not shown two straight quarters of negative growth (*Business Week,* July 30, 2001). For a sample of 20 Americans, make the following calculations.
    a. Compute the probability that exactly 12 people believed the country was in a recession.
    b. Compute the probability that no more than five people believed the country was in a recession.
    c. How many people would you expect to say the country was in a recession?
    d. Compute the variance and standard deviation of the number of people who believed the country was in a recession.

34. Forty percent of business travelers carry either a cell phone or a laptop (*USA Today,* September 12, 2000). For a sample of 15 business travelers, make the following calculations.
    a. Compute the probability that three of the travelers carry a cell phone or laptop.
    b. Compute the probability that 12 of the travelers carry neither a cell phone nor a laptop.
    c. Compute the probability that at least three of the travelers carry a cell phone or a laptop.

35. A university found that 20% of its students withdraw without completing the introductory statistics course. Assume that 20 students registered for the course.
    a. Compute the probability that two or fewer will withdraw.
    b. Compute the probability that exactly four will withdraw.
    c. Compute the probability that more than three will withdraw.
    d. Compute the expected number of withdrawals.

36. For the special case of a binomial random variable, we stated that the variance could be computed using the formula $\sigma^2 = np(1 - p)$. For the Martin Clothing Store problem with $n = 3$ and $p = .3$ we found $\sigma^2 = np(1 - p) = 3(.3)(.7) = .63$. Use the general definition of variance for a discrete random variable, equation (5.5), and the probabilities in Table 5.7 to verify that the variance is in fact .63.

37. Seventy-two percent of Americans have online access (*CNBC,* December 3, 2001). In a random sample of 30 people, what is the expected number of persons with online access? What are the variance and standard deviation?

5.5 Poisson Probability Distribution

In this section we consider a discrete random variable that is often useful in estimating the number of occurrences over a specified interval of time or space. For example, the random variable of interest might be the number of arrivals at a car wash in one hour, the number

The Poisson probability distribution is often used to model random arrivals in waiting line situations.

of repairs needed in 10 miles of highway, or the number of leaks in 100 miles of pipeline. If the following two properties are satisfied, the number of occurrences is a random variable described by the **Poisson probability distribution**.

PROPERTIES OF A POISSON EXPERIMENT

1. The probability of an occurrence is the same for any two intervals of equal length.
2. The occurrence or nonoccurrence in any interval is independent of the occurrence or nonoccurrence in any other interval.

The **Poisson probability function** is defined by equation (5.11).

POISSON PROBABILITY FUNCTION

$$f(x) = \frac{\mu^x e^{-\mu}}{x!} \qquad\qquad \textbf{(5.11)}$$

where

$$f(x) = \text{the probability of } x \text{ occurrences in an interval}$$
$$\mu = \text{expected value or mean number of occurrences in an interval}$$
$$e = 2.71828$$

Siméon Poisson taught mathematics at the Ecole Polytechnique in Paris from 1802 to 1808. In 1837, he published a work entitled, "Researches on the Probability of Criminal and Civil Verdicts," which includes a discussion of what later became known as the Poisson distribution.

Before we consider a specific example to see how the Poisson distribution can be applied, note that the number of occurrences, x, has no upper limit. It is a discrete random variable that may assume an infinite sequence of values ($x = 0, 1, 2, \ldots$).

An Example Involving Time Intervals

Bell Labs uses the Poisson distribution to model the arrival of phone calls.

Suppose that we are interested in the number of arrivals at the drive-up teller window of a bank during a 15-minute period on weekday mornings. If we can assume that the probability of a car arriving is the same for any two time periods of equal length and that the arrival or nonarrival of a car in any time period is independent of the arrival or nonarrival in any other time period, the Poisson probability function is applicable. Suppose these assumptions are satisfied and an analysis of historical data shows that the average number of cars arriving in a 15-minute period of time is 10; in this case, the following probability function applies.

$$f(x) = \frac{10^x e^{-10}}{x!}$$

The random variable here is $x = $ number of cars arriving in any 15-minute period.

If management wanted to know the probability of exactly five arrivals in 15 minutes, we would set $x = 5$ and thus obtain

$$\begin{array}{c}\text{Probability of exactly}\\ \text{5 arrivals in 15 minutes}\end{array} = f(5) = \frac{10^5 e^{-10}}{5!} = .0378$$

Although this probability was determined by evaluating the probability function with $\mu = 10$ and $x = 5$, it is often easier to refer to a table for the Poisson distribution. The table provides probabilities for specific values of x and μ. We included such a table as Table 7 of Appendix B. For convenience, we reproduced a portion of this table as Table 5.9. Note that to use the table of Poisson probabilities, we need know only the values of x and μ. From Table 5.9

TABLE 5.9   SELECTED VALUES FROM THE POISSON PROBABILITY TABLES
EXAMPLE: $\mu = 10$, $x = 5$; $f(5) = .0378$

					μ					
x	9.1	9.2	9.3	9.4	9.5	9.6	9.7	9.8	9.9	10
0	.0001	.0001	.0001	.0001	.0001	.0001	.0001	.0001	.0001	.0000
1	.0010	.0009	.0009	.0008	.0007	.0007	.0006	.0005	.0005	.0005
2	.0046	.0043	.0040	.0037	.0034	.0031	.0029	.0027	.0025	.0023
3	.0140	.0131	.0123	.0115	.0107	.0100	.0093	.0087	.0081	.0076
4	.0319	.0302	.0285	.0269	.0254	.0240	.0226	.0213	.0201	.0189
5	.0581	.0555	.0530	.0506	.0483	.0460	.0439	.0418	.0398	**.0378**
6	.0881	.0851	.0822	.0793	.0764	.0736	.0709	.0682	.0656	.0631
7	.1145	.1118	.1091	.1064	.1037	.1010	.0982	.0955	.0928	.0901
8	.1302	.1286	.1269	.1251	.1232	.1212	.1191	.1170	.1148	.1126
9	.1317	.1315	.1311	.1306	.1300	.1293	.1284	.1274	.1263	.1251
10	.1198	.1210	.1219	.1228	.1235	.1241	.1245	.1249	.1250	.1251
11	.0991	.1012	.1031	.1049	.1067	.1083	.1098	.1112	.1125	.1137
12	.0752	.0776	.0799	.0822	.0844	.0866	.0888	.0908	.0928	.0948
13	.0526	.0549	.0572	.0594	.0617	.0640	.0662	.0685	.0707	.0729
14	.0342	.0361	.0380	.0399	.0419	.0439	.0459	.0479	.0500	.0521
15	.0208	.0221	.0235	.0250	.0265	.0281	.0297	.0313	.0330	.0347
16	.0118	.0127	.0137	.0147	.0157	.0168	.0180	.0192	.0204	.0217
17	.0063	.0069	.0075	.0081	.0088	.0095	.0103	.0111	.0119	.0128
18	.0032	.0035	.0039	.0042	.0046	.0051	.0055	.0060	.0065	.0071
19	.0015	.0017	.0019	.0021	.0023	.0026	.0028	.0031	.0034	.0037
20	.0007	.0008	.0009	.0010	.0011	.0012	.0014	.0015	.0017	.0019
21	.0003	.0003	.0004	.0004	.0005	.0006	.0006	.0007	.0008	.0009
22	.0001	.0001	.0002	.0002	.0002	.0002	.0003	.0003	.0004	.0004
23	.0000	.0001	.0001	.0001	.0001	.0001	.0001	.0001	.0002	.0002
24	.0000	.0000	.0000	.0000	.0000	.0000	.0000	.0001	.0001	.0001

we see that the probability of five arrivals in a 15-minute period is found by locating the value in the row of the table corresponding to $x = 5$ and the column of the table corresponding to $\mu = 10$. Hence, we obtain $f(5) = .0378$.

In the preceding example, the mean of the Poisson distribution is $\mu = 10$ arrivals per 15-minute period. A property of the Poisson distribution is that the mean of the distribution and the variance of the distribution are *equal*. Thus, the variance for the number of arrivals during 15-minute periods is $\sigma^2 = 10$. The standard deviation is $\sigma = \sqrt{10} = 3.16$.

A property of the Poisson distribution is that the mean and variance are equal.

Our illustration involves a 15-minute period, but other time periods can be used. Suppose we want to compute the probability of one arrival in a three-minute period. Because 10 is the expected number of arrivals in a 15-minute period, we see that $10/15 = 2/3$ is the expected number of arrivals in a one-minute period and that $(2/3)(3 \text{ minutes}) = 2$ is the expected number of arrivals in a three-minute period. Thus, the probability of x arrivals in a three-minute time period with $\mu = 2$ is given by the following Poisson probability function.

$$f(x) = \frac{2^x e^{-2}}{x!}$$

The probability of one arrival in a three-minute period is calculated as follows:

$$\text{Probability of exactly} \atop \text{1 arrival in 3 minutes} = f(1) = \frac{2^1 e^{-2}}{1!} = .2707$$

Earlier we computed the probability of five arrivals in a 15-minute period; it was .0378. Note that the probability of one arrival in a three-minute period (.2707) is not the same. When computing a Poisson probability for a different time interval, we must first convert the mean arrival rate to the time period of interest and then compute the probability.

An Example Involving Length or Distance Intervals

Let us illustrate an application not involving time intervals in which the Poisson distribution is useful. Suppose we are concerned with the occurrence of major defects in a highway one month after resurfacing. We will assume that the probability of a defect is the same for any two highway intervals of equal length and that the occurrence or nonoccurrence of a defect in any one interval is independent of the occurrence or nonoccurrence of a defect in any other interval. Hence, the Poisson distribution can be applied.

Suppose we learn that major defects one month after resurfacing occur at the average rate of two per mile. Let us find the probability of no major defects in a particular three-mile section of the highway. Because we are interested in an interval with a length of three miles, $\mu = $ (2 defects/mile)(3 miles) $= 6$ represents the expected number of major defects over the three-mile section of highway. Using equation (5.11), the probability of no major defects is $f(0) = 6^0 e^{-6}/0! = .0025$. Thus, it is unlikely that no major defects will occur in the three-mile section. In fact, this example indicates a $1 - .0025 = .9975$ probability of at least one major defect in the three-mile highway section.

Exercises

Methods

38. Consider a Poisson distribution with $\mu = 3$.
     a.   Write the appropriate Poisson probability function.
     b.   Compute $f(2)$.
     c.   Compute $f(1)$.
     d.   Compute $P(x \geq 2)$.

39. Consider a Poisson distribution with a mean of two occurrences per time period.
     a.   Write the appropriate Poisson probability function.
     b.   What is the expected number of occurrences in three time periods?
     c.   Write the appropriate Poisson probability function to determine the probability of x occurrences in three time periods.
     d.   Compute the probability of two occurrences in one time period.
     e.   Compute the probability of six occurrences in three time periods.
     f.   Compute the probability of five occurrences in two time periods.

Applications

40. Phone calls arrive at the rate of 48 per hour at the reservation desk for Regional Airways.
     a.   Compute the probability of receiving three calls in a five-minute interval of time.
     b.   Compute the probability of receiving exactly 10 calls in 15 minutes.
     c.   Suppose no calls are currently on hold. If the agent takes five minutes to complete the current call, how many callers do you expect to be waiting by that time? What is the probability that none will be waiting?
     d.   If no calls are currently being processed, what is the probability that the agent can take three minutes for personal time without being interrupted by a call?

41. During the period of time that a local university takes phone-in registrations, calls come in at the rate of one every two minutes.
    a. What is the expected number of calls in one hour?
    b. What is the probability of three calls in five minutes?
    c. What is the probability of no calls in a five-minute period?

42. More than 50 million guests stayed at bed and breakfasts (B&Bs) last year. The Web site for the Bed and Breakfast Inns of North America (www.bestinns.net), which averages approximately seven visitors per minute, enables many B&Bs to attract guests without waiting years to be mentioned in guidebooks (*Time,* September 2001).
    a. Compute the probability of no Web site visitors in a one-minute period.
    b. Compute the probability of two or more Web site visitors in a one-minute period.
    c. Compute the probability of one or more Web site visitors in a 30-second period.
    d. Compute the probability of five or more Web site visitors in a one-minute period.

43. Airline passengers arrive randomly and independently at the passenger-screening facility at a major international airport. The mean arrival rate is 10 passengers per minute.
    a. Compute the probability of no arrivals in a one-minute period.
    b. Compute the probability that three or fewer passengers arrive in a one-minute period.
    c. Compute the probability of no arrivals in a 15-second period.
    d. Compute the probability of at least one arrival in a 15-second period.

44. From 1990 through 1999, an average of approximately 26 aircraft accidents per year involved one or more passenger fatalities. Since 2000, the average decreased to 15 accidents per year (*The World Almanac and Book of Facts,* 2004). Assume that aircraft accidents continue to occur at the rate of 15 per year.
    a. Compute the mean number of aircraft accidents per month.
    b. Compute the probability of no accidents during a month.
    c. Compute the probability of exactly one accident during a month.
    d. Compute the probability of more than one accident during a month.

45. The National Safety Council reported that air bag–related fatalities dropped to 18 in the year 2000 (http://www.nsc.org).
    a. Compute the expected number of air bag–related fatalities per month.
    b. Compute the probability of no air bag–related fatalities in a month.
    c. Compute the probability of two or more air bag–related fatalities in a month.

 5.6 # Hypergeometric Probability Distribution

The **hypergeometric probability distribution** is closely related to the binomial distribution. The two probability distributions differ in two key ways. With the hypergeometric distribution, the trials are not independent; and the probability of success changes from trial to trial.

In the usual notation for the hypergeometric distribution, r denotes the number of elements in the population of size N labeled success, and $N - r$ denotes the number of elements in the population labeled failure. The **hypergeometric probability function** is used to compute the probability that in a random selection of n elements, selected without replacement, we obtain x elements labeled success and $n - x$ elements labeled failure. For this outcome to occur, we must obtain x successes from the r successes in the population and $n - x$ failures from the $N - r$ failures. The following hypergeometric probability function provides $f(x)$, the probability of obtaining x successes in a sample of size n.

HYPERGEOMETRIC PROBABILITY FUNCTION

$$f(x) = \frac{\binom{r}{x}\binom{N-r}{n-x}}{\binom{N}{n}} \qquad \text{for } 0 \leq x \leq r \qquad \text{(5.12)}$$

where

$f(x) = $ probability of x successes in n trials
$n = $ number of trials
$N = $ number of elements in the population
$r = $ number of elements in the population labeled success

Note that $\binom{N}{n}$ represents the number of ways a sample of size n can be selected from a population of size N; $\binom{r}{x}$ represents the number of ways that x successes can be selected from a total of r successes in the population; and $\binom{N-r}{n-x}$ represents the number of ways that $n - x$ failures can be selected from a total of $N - r$ failures in the population.

To illustrate the computations involved in using equation (5.12), let us consider the following quality control application. Electric fuses produced by Ontario Electric are packaged in boxes of 12 units each. Suppose an inspector randomly selects three of the 12 fuses in a box for testing. If the box contains exactly five defective fuses, what is the probability that the inspector will find exactly one of the three fuses defective? In this application, $n = 3$ and $N = 12$. With $r = 5$ defective fuses in the box the probability of finding $x = 1$ defective fuse is

$$f(1) = \frac{\binom{5}{1}\binom{7}{2}}{\binom{12}{3}} = \frac{\left(\frac{5!}{1!4!}\right)\left(\frac{7!}{2!5!}\right)}{\left(\frac{12!}{3!9!}\right)} = \frac{(5)(21)}{220} = .4773$$

Now suppose that we wanted to know the probability of finding *at least* 1 defective fuse. The easiest way to answer this question is to first compute the probability that the inspector does not find any defective fuses. The probability of $x = 0$ is

$$f(0) = \frac{\binom{5}{0}\binom{7}{3}}{\binom{12}{3}} = \frac{\left(\frac{5!}{0!5!}\right)\left(\frac{7!}{3!4!}\right)}{\left(\frac{12!}{3!9!}\right)} = \frac{(1)(35)}{220} = .1591$$

With a probability of zero defective fuses $f(0) = .1591$, we conclude that the probability of finding at least one defective fuse must be $1 - .1591 = .8409$. Thus, there is a reasonably high probability that the inspector will find at least 1 defective fuse.

The mean and variance of a hypergeometric distribution are as follows.

$$E(x) = \mu = n\left(\frac{r}{N}\right) \tag{5.13}$$

$$\text{Var}(x) = \sigma^2 = n\left(\frac{r}{N}\right)\left(1 - \frac{r}{N}\right)\left(\frac{N-n}{N-1}\right) \tag{5.14}$$

In the preceding example $n = 3$, $r = 5$, and $N = 12$. Thus, the mean and variance for the number of defective fuses is

$$\mu = n\left(\frac{r}{N}\right) = 3\left(\frac{5}{12}\right) = 1.25$$

$$\sigma^2 = n\left(\frac{r}{N}\right)\left(1 - \frac{r}{N}\right)\left(\frac{N-n}{N-1}\right) = 3\left(\frac{5}{12}\right)\left(1 - \frac{5}{12}\right)\left(\frac{12-3}{12-1}\right) = .60$$

The standard deviation is $\sigma = \sqrt{.60} = .77$.

NOTES AND COMMENTS

Consider a hypergeometric distribution with n trials. Let $p = (r/N)$ denote the probability of a success on the first trial. If the population size is large, the term $(N - n)/(N - 1)$ in equation (5.14) approaches 1. As a result, the expected value and variance can be written $E(x) = np$ and $\text{Var}(x) = np(1 - p)$. Note that these expressions are the same as the expressions used to compute the expected value and variance of a binomial distribution, as in equations (5.9) and (5.10). When the population size is large, a hypergeometric distribution can be approximated by a binomial distribution with n trials and a probability of success $p = (r/N)$.

Exercises

Methods

46. Suppose $N = 10$ and $r = 3$. Compute the hypergeometric probabilities for the following values of n and x.
    a. $n = 4, x = 1$.
    b. $n = 2, x = 2$.
    c. $n = 2, x = 0$.
    d. $n = 4, x = 2$.

47. Suppose $N = 15$ and $r = 4$. What is the probability of $x = 3$ for $n = 10$?

Applications

48. In a survey conducted by the Gallup Organization, respondents were asked, "What is your favorite sport to watch?" Football and basketball ranked number one and two in terms of preference (http://www.gallup.com, January 3, 2004). Assume that in a group of 10 individuals, seven preferred football and three preferred basketball. A random sample of three of these individuals is selected.
    a. What is the probability that exactly two preferred football?
    b. What is the probability that the majority (either two or three) preferred football?

49. Blackjack, or twenty-one as it is frequently called, is a popular gambling game played in Las Vegas casinos. A player is dealt two cards. Face cards (jacks, queens, and kings) and tens have a point value of 10. Aces have a point value of 1 or 11. A 52-card deck contains 16 cards with a point value of 10 (jacks, queens, kings, and tens) and four aces.

a. What is the probability that both cards dealt are aces or 10-point cards?
b. What is the probability that both of the cards are aces?
c. What is the probability that both of the cards have a point value of 10?
d. A blackjack is a 10-point card and an ace for a value of 21. Use your answers to parts (a), (b), and (c) to determine the probability that a player is dealt blackjack. (*Hint:* Part (d) is not a hypergeometric problem. Develop your own logical relationship as to how the hypergeometric probabilities from parts (a), (b), and (c) can be combined to answer this question.)

50. Axline Computers manufactures personal computers at two plants, one in Texas and the other in Hawaii. The Texas plant has 40 employees; the Hawaii plant has 20. A random sample of 10 employees is to be asked to fill out a benefits questionnaire.

a. What is the probability that none of the employees in the sample work at the plant in Hawaii?
b. What is the probability that one of the employees in the sample works at the plant in Hawaii?
c. What is the probability that two or more of the employees in the sample work at the plant in Hawaii?
d. What is the probability that nine of the employees in the sample work at the plant in Texas?

51. The *2003 Zagat Restaurant Survey* provides food, decor, and service ratings for some of the top restaurants across the United States. For 15 top-ranking restaurants located in Boston, the average price of a dinner, including one drink and tip, was $48.60. You are leaving for a business trip to Boston and will eat dinner at three of these restaurants. Your company will reimburse you for a maximum of $50 per dinner. Business associates familiar with these restaurants have told you that the meal cost at one-third of these restaurants will exceed $50. Suppose that you randomly select three of these restaurants for dinner.
a. What is the probability that none of the meals will exceed the cost covered by your company?
b. What is the probability that one of the meals will exceed the cost covered by your company?
c. What is the probability that two of the meals will exceed the cost covered by your company?
d. What is the probability that all three of the meals will exceed the cost covered by your company?

52. A shipment of 10 items has two defective and eight nondefective items. In the inspection of the shipment, a sample of items will be selected and tested. If a defective item is found, the shipment of 10 items will be rejected.
a. If a sample of three items is selected, what is the probability that the shipment will be rejected?
b. If a sample of four items is selected, what is the probability that the shipment will be rejected?
c. If a sample of five items is selected, what is the probability that the shipment will be rejected?
d. If management would like a .90 probability of rejecting a shipment with two defective and eight nondefective items, how large a sample would you recommend?

Summary

A random variable provides a numerical description of the outcome of an experiment. The probability distribution for a random variable describes how the probabilities are distributed over the values the random variable can assume. For any discrete random variable x, the probability distribution is defined by a probability function, denoted by $f(x)$, which provides the probability associated with each value of the random variable. Once the probability function is defined, we can compute the expected value, variance, and standard deviation for the random variable.

The binomial distribution can be used to determine the probability of x successes in n trials whenever the experiment has the following properties:

1. The experiment consists of a sequence of n identical trials.
2. Two outcomes are possible on each trial, one called success and the other failure.
3. The probability of a success p does not change from trial to trial. Consequently, the probability of failure, $1 - p$, does not change from trial to trial.
4. The trials are independent.

When the four properties hold, the binomial probability function can be used to determine the probability of obtaining x successes in n trials. Formulas were also presented for the mean and variance of the binomial distribution.

The Poisson distribution is used when it is desirable to determine the probability of obtaining x occurrences over an interval of time or space. The following assumptions are necessary for the Poisson distribution to be applicable.

1. The probability of an occurrence of the event is the same for any two intervals of equal length.
2. The occurrence or nonoccurrence of the event in any interval is independent of the occurrence or nonoccurrence of the event in any other interval.

A third discrete probability distribution, the hypergeometric, was introduced in Section 5.6. Like the binomial, it is used to compute the probability of x successes in n trials. But, in contrast to the binomial, the probability of success changes from trial to trial.

Glossary

Random variable A numerical description of the outcome of an experiment.

Discrete random variable A random variable that may assume either a finite number of values or an infinite sequence of values.

Continuous random variable A random variable that may assume any numerical value in an interval or collection of intervals.

Probability distribution A description of how the probabilities are distributed over the values of the random variable.

Probability function A function, denoted by $f(x)$, that provides the probability that x assumes a particular value for a discrete random variable.

Discrete uniform probability distribution A probability distribution for which each possible value of the random variable has the same probability.

Expected value A measure of the central location of a random variable.

Variance A measure of the variability, or dispersion, of a random variable.

Standard deviation The positive square root of the variance.

Binomial experiment An experiment having the four properties stated at the beginning of Section 5.4.

Binomial probability distribution A probability distribution showing the probability of x successes in n trials of a binomial experiment.

Binomial probability function The function used to compute binomial probabilities.

Poisson probability distribution A probability distribution showing the probability of x occurrences of an event over a specified interval of time or space.

Poisson probability function The function used to compute Poisson probabilities.

Hypergeometric probability distribution A probability distribution showing the probability of x successes in n trials from a population with r successes and $N - r$ failures.

Hypergeometric probability function The function used to compute hypergeometric probabilities.

Key Formulas

Discrete Uniform Probability Function

$$f(x) = 1/n \tag{5.3}$$

where

$$n = \text{the number of values the random variable may assume}$$

Expected Value of a Discrete Random Variable

$$E(x) = \mu = \Sigma x f(x) \tag{5.4}$$

Variance of a Discrete Random Variable

$$\text{Var}(x) = \sigma^2 = \Sigma(x - \mu)^2 f(x) \tag{5.5}$$

Number of Experimental Outcomes Providing Exactly x Successes in n Trials

$$\binom{n}{x} = \frac{n!}{x!(n-x)!} \tag{5.6}$$

Binomial Probability Function

$$f(x) = \binom{n}{x} p^x (1-p)^{(n-x)} \tag{5.8}$$

Expected Value for the Binomial Distribution

$$E(x) = \mu = np \tag{5.9}$$

Variance for the Binomial Distribution

$$\text{Var}(x) = \sigma^2 = np(1-p) \tag{5.10}$$

Poisson Probability Function

$$f(x) = \frac{\mu^x e^{-\mu}}{x!} \tag{5.11}$$

Hypergeometric Probability Function

$$f(x) = \frac{\binom{r}{x}\binom{N-r}{n-x}}{\binom{N}{n}} \quad \text{for } 0 \le x \le r \tag{5.12}$$

Expected Value for the Hypergeometric Distribution

$$E(x) = \mu = n\left(\frac{r}{N}\right) \tag{5.13}$$

Variance for the Hypergeometric Distribution

$$\text{Var}(x) = \sigma^2 = n\left(\frac{r}{N}\right)\left(1 - \frac{r}{N}\right)\left(\frac{N - n}{N - 1}\right) \tag{5.14}$$

Supplementary Exercises

53. The *Barron's* Big Money Poll asked 131 investment managers across the United States about their short-term investment outlook (*Barron's,* October 28, 2002). Their responses showed 4% were very bullish, 39% were bullish, 29% were neutral, 21% were bearish, and 7% were very bearish. Let x be the random variable reflecting the level of optimism about the market. Set $x = 5$ for very bullish down through $x = 1$ for very bearish.
    a. Develop a probability distribution for the level of optimism of investment managers.
    b. Compute the expected value for the level of optimism.
    c. Compute the variance and standard deviation for the level of optimism.
    d. Comment on what your results imply about the level of optimism and its variability.

54. The American Association of Individual Investors publishes an annual guide to the top mutual funds (*The Individual Investor's Guide to the Top Mutual Funds,* 22e, American Association of Individual Investors, 2003). Table 5.10 contains their ratings of the total risk for 29 categories of mutual funds.
    a. Let $x = 1$ for low risk up through $x = 5$ for high risk, and develop a probability distribution for level of risk.
    b. What are the expected value and variance for total risk?
    c. It turns out that 11 of the fund categories were bond funds. For the bond funds, seven categories were rated low and four were rated below average. Compare the total risk of the bond funds with the 18 categories of stock funds.

TABLE 5.10   RISK RATING FOR 29 CATEGORIES OF MUTUAL FUNDS

Total Risk	Number of Fund Categories
Low	7
Below Average	6
Average	3
Above Average	6
High	7

55. The budgeting process for a midwestern college resulted in expense forecasts for the coming year (in $ millions) of $9, $10, $11, $12, and $13. Because the actual expenses are unknown, the following respective probabilities are assigned: .3, .2, .25, .05, and .2.
    a. Show the probability distribution for the expense forecast.
    b. What is the expected value of the expense forecast for the coming year?
    c. What is the variance of the expense forecast for the coming year?
    d. If income projections for the year are estimated at $12 million, comment on the financial position of the college.

56. A survey conducted by the Bureau of Transportation Statistics (BTS) showed that the average commuter spends about 26 minutes on a one-way door-to-door trip from home to work. In addition, 5% of commuters reported a one-way commute of more than one hour (http://www.bts.gov, January 12, 2004).

a.   If 20 commuters are surveyed on a particular day, what is the probability that three will report a one-way commute of more than one hour?

b.   If 20 commuters are surveyed on a particular day, what is the probability that none will report a one-way commute of more than one hour?

c.   If a company has 2000 employees, what is the expected number of employees that have a one-way commute of more than one hour?

d.   If a company has 2000 employees, what is the variance and standard deviation of the number of employees that have a one-way commute of more than one hour?

57.   A company is planning to interview Internet users to learn how its proposed Web site will be received by different age groups. According to the Census Bureau, 40% of individuals ages 18 to 54 and 12% of individuals age 55 and over use the Internet (*Statistical Abstract of the United States,* 2000).

a.   How many people from the 18–54 age group must be contacted to find an expected number of at least 10 Internet users?

b.   How many people from the age group 55 and over must be contacted to find an expected number of at least 10 Internet users?

c.   If you contact the number of 18- to 54-year-old people suggested in part (a), what is the standard deviation of the number who will be Internet users?

d.   If you contact the number of people age 55 and older suggested in part (b), what is the standard deviation of the number who will be Internet users?

58.   Many companies use a quality control technique called acceptance sampling to monitor incoming shipments of parts, raw materials, and so on. In the electronics industry, component parts are commonly shipped from suppliers in large lots. Inspection of a sample of *n* components can be viewed as the *n* trials of a binomial experiment. The outcome for each component tested (trial) will be that the component is classified as good or defective. Reynolds Electronics accepts a lot from a particular supplier if the defective components in the lot do not exceed 1%. Suppose a random sample of five items from a recent shipment is tested.

a.   Assume that 1% of the shipment is defective. Compute the probability that no items in the sample are defective.

b.   Assume that 1% of the shipment is defective. Compute the probability that exactly one item in the sample is defective.

c.   What is the probability of observing one or more defective items in the sample if 1% of the shipment is defective?

d.   Would you feel comfortable accepting the shipment if one item was found to be defective? Why or why not?

59.   The unemployment rate is 4.1% (*Barron's,* September 4, 2000). Assume that 100 employable people are selected randomly.

a.   What is the expected number of people who are unemployed?

b.   What are the variance and standard deviation of the number of people who are unemployed?

60.   A poll conducted by Zogby International showed that of those Americans who said music plays a "very important" role in their lives, 30% said their local radio stations "always" play the kind of music they like (http://www.zogby.com, January 12, 2004). Suppose a sample of 800 people who say music plays an important role in their lives is taken.

a.   How many would you expect to say that their local radio stations always play the kind of music they like?

b.   What is the standard deviation of the number of respondents who think their local radio stations always play the kind of music they like?

c.   What is the standard deviation of the number of respondents who do not think their local radio stations always play the kind of music they like?

61.   Cars arrive at a car wash randomly and independently; the probability of an arrival is the same for any two time intervals of equal length. The mean arrival rate is 15 cars per hour. What is the probability that 20 or more cars will arrive during any given hour of operation?

62. A new automated production process averages 1.5 breakdowns per day. Because of the cost associated with a breakdown, management is concerned about the possibility of having three or more breakdowns during a day. Assume that breakdowns occur randomly, that the probability of a breakdown is the same for any two time intervals of equal length, and that breakdowns in one period are independent of breakdowns in other periods. What is the probability of having three or more breakdowns during a day?

63. A regional director responsible for business development in the state of Pennsylvania is concerned about the number of small business failures. If the mean number of small business failures per month is 10, what is the probability that exactly four small businesses will fail during a given month? Assume that the probability of a failure is the same for any two months and that the occurrence or nonoccurrence of a failure in any month is independent of failures in any other month.

64. Customer arrivals at a bank are random and independent; the probability of an arrival in any one-minute period is the same as the probability of an arrival in any other one-minute period. Answer the following questions, assuming a mean arrival rate of three customers per minute.
    a. What is the probability of exactly three arrivals in a one-minute period?
    b. What is the probability of at least three arrivals in a one-minute period?

65. A deck of playing cards contains 52 cards, four of which are aces. What is the probability that the deal of a five-card hand provides:
    a. A pair of aces?
    b. Exactly one ace?
    c. No aces?
    d. At least one ace?

66. Through the week ending September 16, 2001, Tiger Woods was the leading money winner on the PGA Tour, with total earnings of $5,517,777. Of the top 10 money winners, seven players used a Titleist brand golf ball (http://www.pgatour.com). Suppose that we randomly select two of the top 10 money winners.
    a. What is the probability that exactly one uses a Titleist golf ball?
    b. What is the probability that both use Titleist golf balls?
    c. What is the probability that neither uses a Titleist golf ball?

Appendix 5.1   Discrete Probability Distributions with Minitab

Statistical packages such as Minitab offer a relatively easy and efficient procedure for computing binomial probabilities. In this appendix, we show the step-by-step procedure for determining the binomial probabilities for the Martin Clothing Store problem in Section 5.4. Recall that the desired binomial probabilities are based on $n = 10$ and $p = .30$. Before beginning the Minitab routine, the user must enter the desired values of the random variable x into a column of the worksheet. We entered the values 0, 1, 2, . . . , 10 in column 1 (see Figure 5.5) to generate the entire binomial probability distribution. The Minitab steps to obtain the desired binomial probabilities follow.

Step 1. Select the **Calc** menu
Step 2. Choose **Probability Distributions**
Step 3. Choose **Binomial**
Step 4. When the Binomial Distribution dialog box appears:
    Select **Probability**
    Enter 10 in the **Number of trials** box
    Enter .3 in the **Probability of success** box
    Enter C1 in the **Input column** box
    Click **OK**

The Minitab output with the binomial probabilities will appear as shown in Figure 5.5.

Minitab provides Poisson and hypergeometric probabilities in a similar manner. For instance, to compute Poisson probabilities the only differences are in step 3, where the **Poisson** option would be selected, and step 4, where the **Mean** would be entered rather than the number of trials and the probability of success.

Appendix 5.2 Discrete Probability Distributions with Excel

Excel provides functions for computing probabilities for the binomial, Poisson, and hypergeometric distributions introduced in this chapter. The Excel function for computing binomial probabilities is BINOMDIST. It has four arguments: x (the number of successes), n (the number of trials), p (the probability of success), and cumulative. FALSE is used for the fourth argument (cumulative) if we want the probability of x successes, and TRUE is used for the fourth argument if we want the cumulative probability of x or fewer successes. Here we show how to compute the probabilities of 0 through 10 successes for the Martin Clothing Store problem in Section 5.4 (see Figure 5.5).

As we describe the worksheet development refer to Figure 5.6; the formula worksheet is set in the background, and the value worksheet appears in the foreground. We entered

FIGURE 5.6   EXCEL WORKSHEET FOR COMPUTING BINOMIAL PROBABILITIES

	A	B	C	D
1	Number of Trials (*n*)	10		
2	Probability of Success (*p*)	0.3		
3				
4		*x*	*f(x)*	
5		0	=BINOMDIST(B5,$B$1,$B$2,FALSE)	
6		1	=BINOMDIST(B6,$B$1,$B$2,FALSE)	
7		2	=BINOMDIST(B7,$B$1,$B$2,FALSE)	
8		3	=BINOMDIST(B8,$B$1,$B$2,FALSE)	
9		4	=BINOMDIST(B9,$B$1,$B$2,FALSE)	
10		5	=BINOMDIST(B10,$B$1,$B$2,FALSE)	
11		6	=BINOMDIST(B11,$B$1,$B$2,FALSE)	
12		7	=BINOMDIST(B12,$B$1,$B$2,FALSE)	
13		8	=BINOMDIST(B13,$B$1,$B$2,FALSE)	
14		9	=BINOMDIST(B14,$B$1,$B$2,FALSE)	
15		10	=BINOMDIST(B15,$B$1,$B$2,FALSE)	
16				

	A	B	C	D
1	Number of Trials (*n*)	10		
2	Probability of Success (*p*)	0.3		
3				
4		*x*	*f(x)*	
5		0	0.0282	
6		1	0.1211	
7		2	0.2335	
8		3	0.2668	
9		4	0.2001	
10		5	0.1029	
11		6	0.0368	
12		7	0.0090	
13		8	0.0014	
14		9	0.0001	
15		10	0.0000	
16				

the number of trials (10) into cell B1, the probability of success into cell B2, and the values for the random variable into cells B5:B15. The following steps will generate the desired probabilities:

Step 1. Use the BINOMDIST function to compute the probability of $x = 0$ by entering the following formula into cell C5:

$$=\text{BINOMDIST(B5,\$B\$1,\$B\$2,FALSE)}$$

Step 2. Copy the formula in cell C5 into cells C6:C15.

The value worksheet in Figure 5.6 shows that the probabilities obtained are the same as in Figure 5.5. Poisson and hypergeometric probabilities can be computed in a similar fashion. The POISSON and HYPERGEOMDIST functions are used. Excel's Insert Function tool can help the user in entering the proper arguments for these functions (see Appendix 2.2).

CHAPTER 6

Continuous Probability Distributions

CONTENTS

STATISTICS *in* PRACTICE

PROCTER & GAMBLE*
CINCINNATI, OHIO

Procter & Gamble (P&G) produces and markets such products as detergents, disposable diapers, over-the-counter pharmaceuticals, dentifrices, bar soaps, mouthwashes, and paper towels. Worldwide, it has the leading brand in more categories than any other consumer products company.

As a leader in the application of statistical methods in decision making, P&G employs people with diverse academic backgrounds: engineering, statistics, operations research, and business. The major quantitative technologies for which these people provide support are probabilistic decision and risk analysis, advanced simulation, quality improvement, and quantitative methods (e.g., linear programming, regression analysis, probability analysis).

The Industrial Chemicals Division of P&G is a major supplier of fatty alcohols derived from natural substances such as coconut oil and from petroleum-based derivatives. The division wanted to know the economic risks and opportunities of expanding its fatty-alcohol production facilities, so it called in P&G's experts in probabilistic decision and risk analysis to help. After structuring and modeling the problem, they determined that the key to profitability was the cost difference between the petroleum- and coconut-based raw materials. Future costs were unknown, but the analysts were able to represent them with the following continuous random variables.

x = the coconut oil price per pound of fatty alcohol

and

y = the petroleum raw material price per pound of fatty alcohol

Because the key to profitability was the difference between these two random variables, a third random variable, $d = x - y$, was used in the analysis. Experts were interviewed to determine

Some of Procter & Gamble's many well-known products. © Joe Higgins/South-Western.

the probability distribution for x and y. In turn, this information was used to develop a probability distribution for the difference in prices d. This continuous probability distribution showed a .90 probability that the price difference would be \$.0655 or less and a .50 probability that the price difference would be \$.035 or less. In addition, there was only a .10 probability that the price difference would be \$.0045 or less.[†]

The Industrial Chemicals Division thought that being able to quantify the impact of raw material price differences was key to reaching a consensus. The probabilities obtained were used in a sensitivity analysis of the raw material price difference. The analysis yielded sufficient insight to form the basis for a recommendation to management.

The use of continuous random variables and their probability distributions was helpful to P&G in analyzing the economic risks associated with its fatty-alcohol production. In this chapter, you will gain an understanding of continuous random variables and their probability distributions including one of the most important probability distributions in statistics, the normal distribution.

---

*The authors are indebted to Joel Kahn of Procter & Gamble for providing this Statistics in Practice.

[†]The price differences stated here have been modified to protect proprietary data.

In the preceding chapter we discussed discrete random variables and their probability distributions. In this chapter we turn to the study of continuous random variables. Specifically, we discuss three continuous probability distributions: the uniform, the normal, and the exponential.

A fundamental difference separates discrete and continuous random variables in terms of how probabilities are computed. For a discrete random variable, the probability function $f(x)$ provides the probability that the random variable assumes a particular value. With continuous random variables, the counterpart of the probability function is the **probability density function**, also denoted by $f(x)$. The difference is that the probability density function does not directly provide probabilities. However, the area under the graph of $f(x)$ corresponding to a given interval does provide the probability that the continuous random variable x assumes a value in that interval. So when we compute probabilities for continuous random variables we are computing the probability that the random variable assumes any value in an interval.

One of the implications of the definition of probability for continuous random variables is that the probability of any particular value of the random variable is zero, because the area under the graph of $f(x)$ at any particular point is zero. In Section 6.1 we demonstrate these concepts for a continuous random variable that has a uniform distribution.

Much of the chapter is devoted to describing and showing applications of the normal distribution. The normal distribution is of major importance because of its wide applicability and its extensive use in statistical inference. The chapter closes with a discussion of the exponential distribution.

6.1   Uniform Probability Distribution

Consider the random variable x representing the flight time of an airplane traveling from Chicago to New York. Suppose the flight time can be any value in the interval from 120 minutes to 140 minutes. Because the random variable x can assume any value in that interval, x is a continuous rather than a discrete random variable. Let us assume that sufficient actual flight data are available to conclude that the probability of a flight time within any 1-minute interval is the same as the probability of a flight time within any other 1-minute interval contained in the larger interval from 120 to 140 minutes. With every 1-minute interval being equally likely, the random variable x is said to have a **uniform probability distribution**. The probability density function, which defines the uniform distribution for the flight-time random variable, is

Whenever the probability is proportional to the length of the interval, the random variable is uniformly distributed.

$$f(x) = \begin{cases} 1/20 & \text{for } 120 \leq x \leq 140 \\ 0 & \text{elsewhere} \end{cases}$$

Figure 6.1 is a graph of this probability density function. In general, the uniform probability density function for a random variable x is defined by the following formula.

> **UNIFORM PROBABILITY DENSITY FUNCTION**
>
> $$f(x) = \begin{cases} \dfrac{1}{b-a} & \text{for } a \leq x \leq b \\ 0 & \text{elsewhere} \end{cases} \tag{6.1}$$

For the flight-time random variable, $a = 120$ and $b = 140$.

FIGURE 6.1   UNIFORM PROBABILITY DENSITY FUNCTION FOR FLIGHT TIME

As noted in the introduction, for a continuous random variable, we consider probability only in terms of the likelihood that a random variable assumes a value within a specified interval. In the flight time example, an acceptable probability question is: What is the probability that the flight time is between 120 and 130 minutes? That is, what is $P(120 \leq x \leq 130)$? Because the flight time must be between 120 and 140 minutes and because the probability is described as being uniform over this interval, we feel comfortable saying $P(120 \leq x \leq 130) = .50$. In the following subsection we show that this probability can be computed as the area under the graph of $f(x)$ from 120 to 130 (see Figure 6.2).

Area as a Measure of Probability

Let us make an observation about the graph in Figure 6.2. Consider the area under the graph of $f(x)$ in the interval from 120 to 130. The area is rectangular, and the area of a rectangle is simply the width multiplied by the height. With the width of the interval equal to $130 - 120 = 10$ and the height equal to the value of the probability density function $f(x) = 1/20$, we have area = width $\times$ height = $10(1/20) = 10/20 = .50$.

FIGURE 6.2   AREA PROVIDES PROBABILITY OF FLIGHT TIME BETWEEN 120
AND 130 MINUTES

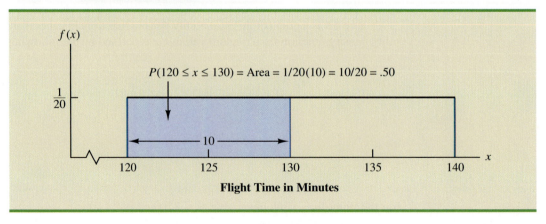

What observation can you make about the area under the graph of $f(x)$ and probability? They are identical! Indeed, this observation is valid for all continuous random variables. Once a probability density function $f(x)$ is identified, the probability that x takes a value between some lower value x_1 and some higher value x_2 can be found by computing the area under the graph of $f(x)$ over the interval from x_1 to x_2.

Given the uniform distribution for flight time and using the interpretation of area as probability, we can answer any number of probability questions about flight times. For example, what is the probability of a flight time between 128 and 136 minutes? The width of the interval is $136 - 128 = 8$. With the uniform height of $f(x) = 1/20$, we see that $P(128 \leq x \leq 136) = 8(1/20) = .40$.

Note that $P(120 \leq x \leq 140) = 20(1/20) = 1$; that is, the total area under the graph of $f(x)$ is equal to 1. This property holds for all continuous probability distributions and is the analog of the condition that the sum of the probabilities must equal 1 for a discrete probability function. For a continuous probability density function, we must also require that $f(x) \geq 0$ for all values of x. This requirement is the analog of the requirement that $f(x) \geq 0$ for discrete probability functions.

Two major differences stand out between the treatment of continuous random variables and the treatment of their discrete counterparts.

To see that the probability of any single point is 0, refer to Figure 6.2 and compute the probability of a single point, say, x = 125. P(x = 125) = P(125 ≤ x ≤ 125) = 0(1/20) = 0.

1. We no longer talk about the probability of the random variable assuming a particular value. Instead, we talk about the probability of the random variable assuming a value within some given interval.
2. The probability of a continuous random variable assuming a value within some given interval from x_1 to x_2 is defined to be the area under the graph of the probability density function between x_1 and x_2. Because a single point is an interval of zero width, this implies that the probability of a continuous random variable assuming any particular value exactly is zero. It also means that the probability of a continuous random variable assuming a value in any interval is the same whether or not the endpoints are included.

The calculation of the expected value and variance for a continuous random variable is analogous to that for a discrete random variable. However, because the computational procedure involves integral calculus, we leave the derivation of the appropriate formulas to more advanced texts.

For the uniform continuous probability distribution introduced in this section, the formulas for the expected value and variance are

$$E(x) = \frac{a + b}{2}$$

$$\text{Var}(x) = \frac{(b - a)^2}{12}$$

In these formulas, a is the smallest value and b is the largest value that the random variable may assume.

Applying these formulas to the uniform distribution for flight times from Chicago to New York, we obtain

$$E(x) = \frac{(120 + 140)}{2} = 130$$

$$\text{Var}(x) = \frac{(140 - 120)^2}{12} = 33.33$$

The standard deviation of flight times can be found by taking the square root of the variance. Thus, $\sigma = 5.77$ minutes.

NOTES AND COMMENTS

To see more clearly why the height of a probability density function is not a probability, think about a random variable with the following uniform probability distribution.

$$f(x) = \begin{cases} 2 & \text{for } 0 \leq x \leq .5 \\ 0 & \text{elsewhere} \end{cases}$$

The height of the probability density function, $f(x)$, is 2 for values of x between 0 and .5. However, we know probabilities can never be greater than 1. Thus, we see that $f(x)$ cannot be interpreted as the probability of x.

Exercises

Methods

1. The random variable x is known to be uniformly distributed between 1.0 and 1.5.
   a. Show the graph of the probability density function.
   b. Compute $P(x = 1.25)$.
   c. Compute $P(1.0 \leq x \leq 1.25)$.
   d. Compute $P(1.20 < x < 1.5)$.

2. The random variable x is known to be uniformly distributed between 10 and 20.
   a. Show the graph of the probability density function.
   b. Compute $P(x < 15)$.
   c. Compute $P(12 \leq x \leq 18)$.
   d. Compute $E(x)$.
   e. Compute $\text{Var}(x)$.

Applications

3. Delta Airlines quotes a flight time of 2 hours, 5 minutes for its flights from Cincinnati to Tampa. Suppose we believe that actual flight times are uniformly distributed between 2 hours and 2 hours, 20 minutes.
   a. Show the graph of the probability density function for flight time.
   b. What is the probability that the flight will be no more than 5 minutes late?
   c. What is the probability that the flight will be more than 10 minutes late?
   d. What is the expected flight time?

4. Most computer languages include a function that can be used to generate random numbers. In Excel, the RAND function can be used to generate random numbers between 0 and 1. If we let x denote a random number generated using RAND, then x is a continuous random variable with the following probability density function.

$$f(x) = \begin{cases} 1 & \text{for } 0 \leq x \leq 1 \\ 0 & \text{elsewhere} \end{cases}$$

   a. Graph the probability density function.
   b. What is the probability of generating a random number between .25 and .75?
   c. What is the probability of generating a random number with a value less than or equal to .30?
   d. What is the probability of generating a random number with a value greater than .60?

5. The driving distance for the top 100 golfers on the PGA tour is between 284.7 and 310.6 yards (*Golfweek,* March 29, 2003). Assume that the driving distance for these golfers is uniformly distributed over this interval.
   a. Give a mathematical expression for the probability density function of driving distance.
   b. What is the probability the driving distance for one of these golfers is less than 290 yards?
   c. What is the probability the driving distance for one of these golfers is at least 300 yards?
   d. What is the probability the driving distance for one of these golfers is between 290 and 305 yards?
   e. How many of these golfers drive the ball at least 290 yards?

6. The label on a bottle of liquid detergent shows the contents to be 12 ounces per bottle. The production operation fills the bottle uniformly according to the following probability density function.

$$f(x) = \begin{cases} 8 & \text{for } 11.975 \le x \le 12.100 \\ 0 & \text{elsewhere} \end{cases}$$

   a. What is the probability that a bottle will be filled with between 12 and 12.05 ounces?
   b. What is the probability that a bottle will be filled with 12.02 or more ounces?
   c. Quality control accepts a bottle that is filled to within .02 ounces of the number of ounces shown on the container label. What is the probability that a bottle of this liquid detergent will fail to meet the quality control standard?

7. Suppose we are interested in bidding on a piece of land and we know one other bidder is interested.* The seller announced that the highest bid in excess of $10,000 will be accepted. Assume that the competitor's bid x is a random variable that is uniformly distributed between $10,000 and $15,000.
   a. Suppose you bid $12,000. What is the probability that your bid will be accepted?
   b. Suppose you bid $14,000. What is the probability that your bid will be accepted?
   c. What amount should you bid to maximize the probability that you get the property?
   d. Suppose you know someone who is willing to pay you $16,000 for the property. Would you consider bidding less than the amount in part (c)? Why or why not?

6.2   Normal Probability Distribution

The most important probability distribution for describing a continuous random variable is the **normal probability distribution**. The normal distribution has been used in a wide variety of practical applications in which the random variables are heights and weights of people, test scores, scientific measurements, amounts of rainfall, and other similar values. It is also widely used in statistical inference, which is the major topic of the remainder of this book. In such applications, the normal distribution provides a description of the likely results obtained through sampling.

Abraham de Moivre, a French mathematician, published The Doctrine of Chances *in 1733. He derived the normal distribution.*

Normal Curve

The form, or shape, of the normal distribution is illustrated by the bell-shaped normal curve in Figure 6.3. The probability density function that defines the bell-shaped curve of the normal distribution follows.

---

*This exercise is based on a problem suggested to us by Professor Roger Myerson of Northwestern University.

FIGURE 6.3   BELL-SHAPED CURVE FOR THE NORMAL DISTRIBUTION

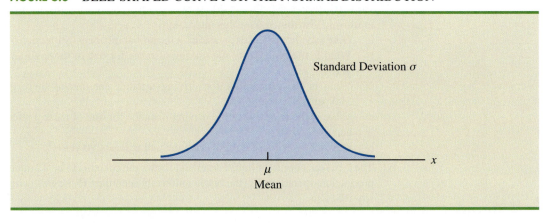

NORMAL PROBABILITY DENSITY FUNCTION

$$f(x) = \frac{1}{\sigma\sqrt{2\pi}} e^{-(x-\mu)^2/2\sigma^2}$$ **(6.2)**

where

μ = mean
σ = standard deviation
π = 3.14159
e = 2.71828

We make several observations about the characteristics of the normal distribution.

The normal curve has two parameters, μ and σ. They determine the location and shape of the normal distribution.

1. The entire family of normal distributions is differentiated by two parameters: its mean μ and its standard deviation σ.
2. The highest point on the normal curve is at the mean, which is also the median and mode of the distribution.
3. The mean of the distribution can be any numerical value: negative, zero, or positive. Three normal distributions with the same standard deviation but three different means (-10, 0, and 20) are shown here.

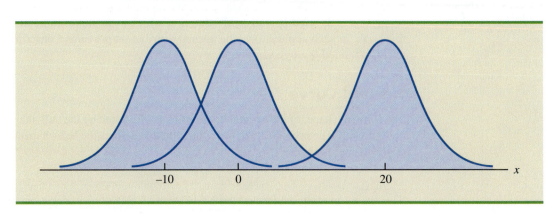

4. The normal distribution is symmetric, with the shape of the curve to the left of the mean a mirror image of the shape of the curve to the right of the mean. The tails of the curve extend to infinity in both directions and theoretically never touch the horizontal axis. Because it is symmetric, the normal distribution is not skewed; its skewness measure is zero.
5. The standard deviation determines how flat and wide the curve is. Larger values of the standard deviation result in wider, flatter curves, showing more variability in the data. Two normal distributions with the same mean but with different standard deviations are shown here.

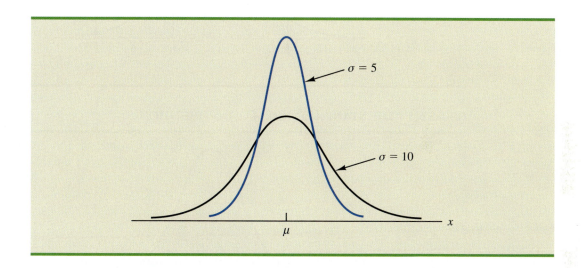

6. Probabilities for the normal random variable are given by areas under the curve. The total area under the curve for the normal distribution is 1. Because the distribution is symmetric, the area under the curve to the left of the mean is .50 and the area under the curve to the right of the mean is .50.
7. The percentage of values in some commonly used intervals are:
    a. 68.3% of the values of a normal random variable are within plus or minus one standard deviation of its mean.
    b. 95.4% of the values of a normal random variable are within plus or minus two standard deviations of its mean.
    c. 99.7% of the values of a normal random variable are within plus or minus three standard deviations of its mean.

These percentages are the basis for the empirical rule introduced in Section 3.3.

Figure 6.4 shows properties (a), (b), and (c) graphically.

Standard Normal Probability Distribution

A random variable that has a normal distribution with a mean of zero and a standard deviation of one is said to have a **standard normal probability distribution**. The letter z is commonly used to designate this particular normal random variable. Figure 6.5 is the graph of the standard normal distribution. It has the same general appearance as other normal distributions, but with the special properties of $\mu = 0$ and $\sigma = 1$.

FIGURE 6.4   AREAS UNDER THE CURVE FOR ANY NORMAL DISTRIBUTION

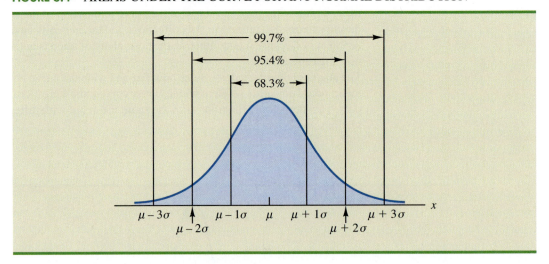

FIGURE 6.5   THE STANDARD NORMAL DISTRIBUTION

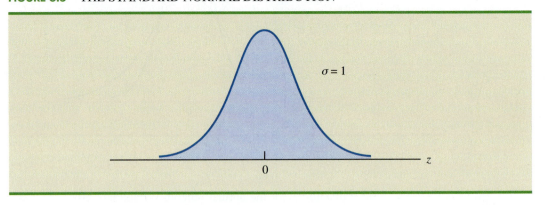

Because $\mu = 0$ and $\sigma = 1$, the formula for the standard normal probability density function is a simpler version of equation (6.2).

STANDARD NORMAL DENSITY FUNCTION

$$f(x) = \frac{1}{\sqrt{2\pi}} e^{-z^2/2}$$

For the normal probability density function, the height of the curve varies and more advanced mathematics is required to compute the areas that represent probability.

As with other continuous random variables, probability calculations with any normal distribution are made by computing areas under the graph of the probability density function. Thus, to find the probability that a normal random variable is within any specific interval, we must compute the area under the normal curve over that interval. For the standard normal distribution, areas under the normal curve have been computed and are available in tables that can be used in computing probabilities. Table 6.1 is such a table; it is also available as Table 1 of Appendix B and inside the front cover of this text.

To see how the table of areas under the curve for the standard normal distribution (Table 6.1) can be used to find probabilities, let us consider some examples. Later, we will see how this same table can be used to compute probabilities for any normal distribution.

TABLE 6.1   AREAS, OR PROBABILITIES, FOR THE STANDARD NORMAL DISTRIBUTION

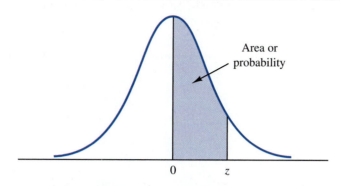

z	.00	.01	.02	.03	.04	.05	.06	.07	.08	.09
.0	.0000	.0040	.0080	.0120	.0160	.0199	.0239	.0279	.0319	.0359
.1	.0398	.0438	.0478	.0517	.0557	.0596	.0636	.0675	.0714	.0753
.2	.0793	.0832	.0871	.0910	.0948	.0987	.1026	.1064	.1103	.1141
.3	.1179	.1217	.1255	.1293	.1331	.1368	.1406	.1443	.1480	.1517
.4	.1554	.1591	.1628	.1664	.1700	.1736	.1772	.1808	.1844	.1879
.5	.1915	.1950	.1985	.2019	.2054	.2088	.2123	.2157	.2190	.2224
.6	.2257	.2291	.2324	.2357	.2389	.2422	.2454	.2486	.2517	.2549
.7	.2580	.2611	.2642	.2673	.2704	.2734	.2764	.2794	.2823	.2852
.8	.2881	.2910	.2939	.2967	.2995	.3023	.3051	.3078	.3106	.3133
.9	.3159	.3186	.3212	.3238	.3264	.3289	.3315	.3340	.3365	.3389
1.0	.3413	.3438	.3461	.3485	.3508	.3531	.3554	.3577	.3599	.3621
1.1	.3643	.3665	.3686	.3708	.3729	.3749	.3770	.3790	.3810	.3830
1.2	.3849	.3869	.3888	.3907	.3925	.3944	.3962	.3980	.3997	.4015
1.3	.4032	.4049	.4066	.4082	.4099	.4115	.4131	.4147	.4162	.4177
1.4	.4192	.4207	.4222	.4236	.4251	.4265	.4279	.4292	.4306	.4319
1.5	.4332	.4345	.4357	.4370	.4382	.4394	.4406	.4418	.4429	.4441
1.6	.4452	.4463	.4474	.4484	.4495	.4505	.4515	.4525	.4535	.4545
1.7	.4554	.4564	.4573	.4582	.4591	.4599	.4608	.4616	.4625	.4633
1.8	.4641	.4649	.4656	.4664	.4671	.4678	.4686	.4693	.4699	.4706
1.9	.4713	.4719	.4726	.4732	.4738	.4744	.4750	.4756	.4761	.4767
2.0	.4772	.4778	.4783	.4788	.4793	.4798	.4803	.4808	.4812	.4817
2.1	.4821	.4826	.4830	.4834	.4838	.4842	.4846	.4850	.4854	.4857
2.2	.4861	.4864	.4868	.4871	.4875	.4878	.4881	.4884	.4887	.4890
2.3	.4893	.4896	.4898	.4901	.4904	.4906	.4909	.4911	.4913	.4916
2.4	.4918	.4920	.4922	.4925	.4927	.4929	.4931	.4932	.4934	.4936
2.5	.4938	.4940	.4941	.4943	.4945	.4946	.4948	.4949	.4951	.4952
2.6	.4953	.4955	.4956	.4957	.4959	.4960	.4961	.4962	.4963	.4964
2.7	.4965	.4966	.4967	.4968	.4969	.4970	.4971	.4972	.4973	.4974
2.8	.4974	.4975	.4976	.4977	.4977	.4978	.4979	.4979	.4980	.4981
2.9	.4981	.4982	.4982	.4983	.4984	.4984	.4985	.4985	.4986	.4986
3.0	.4987	.4987	.4987	.4988	.4988	.4989	.4989	.4989	.4990	.4990

To begin, let us see how we can compute the probability that the z value for the standard normal random variable will be between .00 and 1.00; that is, $P(.00 \leq z \leq 1.00)$. The darkly shaded region in the following graph shows this probability.

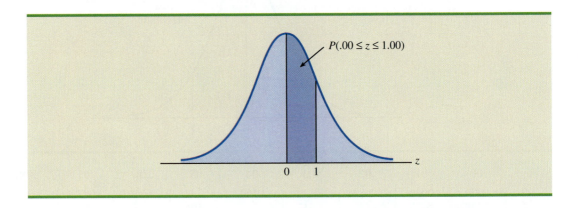

The entries in Table 6.1 give the area under the standard normal curve between the mean, $z = 0$, and a specified value of z (see the graph at the top of the table). In this case, we are interested in the area between $z = 0$ and $z = 1.00$. Thus, we must find the entry in the table corresponding to $z = 1.00$. First we find 1.0 in the left column of the table and then find .00 in the top row of the table. By looking in the body of the table, we find that the 1.0 row and the .00 column intersect at the value of .3413, which gives us the desired probability: $P(.00 \leq z \leq 1.00) = .3413$. A portion of Table 6.1 showing these steps follows.

z	.00	.01	.02
.			
.			
.			
.9	.3159	.3186	.3212
1.0	.3413	.3438	.3461
1.1	.3643	.3665	.3686
1.2	.3849	.3869	.3888
.			
.			
.			

$P(.00 \leq z \leq 1.00)$

Using the same approach, we can find $P(.00 \leq z \leq 1.25)$. By first locating the 1.2 row and then moving across to the .05 column, we find $P(.00 \leq z \leq 1.25) = .3944$.

As another example of the use of the table of areas for the standard normal distribution, we compute the probability of obtaining a z value between $z = -1.00$ and $z = 1.00$; that is, $P(-1.00 \leq z \leq 1.00)$.

Note that we already used Table 6.1 to show that the probability of a z value between $z = .00$ and $z = 1.00$ is .3413, and recall that the normal distribution is *symmetric*. Thus, the probability of a z value between $z = .00$ and $z = -1.00$ is the same as the probability of a z value between $z = .00$ and $z = +1.00$. Hence, the probability of a z value between $z = -1.00$ and $z = +1.00$ is

$$P(-1.00 \leq z \leq .00) + P(.00 \leq z \leq 1.00) = .3413 + .3413 = .6826$$

FIGURE 6.6   GREAR TIRE COMPANY MILEAGE DISTRIBUTION

Let us now assume that Grear is considering a guarantee that will provide a discount on replacement tires if the original tires do not exceed the mileage stated in the guarantee. What should the guaranteed mileage be if Grear wants no more than 10% of the tires to be eligible for the discount guarantee? This question is interpreted graphically in Figure 6.7.

According to Figure 6.7, 40% of the area must be between the mean and the unknown guarantee mileage. We look up .4000 in the body of Table 6.1. By symmetry, the area sought is at approximately 1.28 standard deviations to the left of the mean. That is, $z = -1.28$ is the value of the standard normal random variable corresponding to the desired mileage

FIGURE 6.7   GREAR'S DISCOUNT GUARANTEE

guarantee on the Grear Tire normal distribution. To find the value of x corresponding to $z = -1.28$, we have

$$z = \frac{x - \mu}{\sigma} = -1.28$$
$$x - \mu = -1.28\sigma$$
$$x = \mu - 1.28\sigma$$

With $\mu = 36,500$ and $\sigma = 5000$,

$$x = 36,500 - 1.28(5000) = 30,100$$

With the guarantee set at 30,000 miles, the actual percentage eligible for the guarantee will be 9.68%.

Thus, a guarantee of 30,100 miles will meet the requirement that approximately 10% of the tires will be eligible for the guarantee. Perhaps, with this information, the firm will set its tire mileage guarantee at 30,000 miles.

Again, we see the important role that probability distributions play in providing decision-making information. Namely, once a probability distribution is established for a particular application, it can be used quickly and easily to obtain probability information about the problem. Probability does not establish a decision recommendation directly, but it provides information that helps the decision maker better understand the risks and uncertainties associated with the problem. Ultimately, this information may assist the decision maker in reaching a good decision.

Exercises

Methods

8. Using Figure 6.4 as a guide, sketch a normal curve for a random variable x that has a mean of $\mu = 100$ and a standard deviation of $\sigma = 10$. Label the horizontal axis with values of 70, 80, 90, 100, 110, 120, and 130.

9. A random variable is normally distributed with a mean of $\mu = 50$ and a standard deviation of $\sigma = 5$.
   a. Sketch a normal curve for the probability density function. Label the horizontal axis with values of 35, 40, 45, 50, 55, 60, and 65. Figure 6.4 shows that the normal curve almost touches the horizontal axis at three standard deviations below and at three standard deviations above the mean (in this case at 35 and 65).
   b. What is the probability the random variable will assume a value between 45 and 55?
   c. What is the probability the random variable will assume a value between 40 and 60?

10. Draw a graph for the standard normal distribution. Label the horizontal axis at values of $-3, -2, -1, 0, 1, 2,$ and 3. Then use the table of probabilities for the standard normal distribution to compute the following probabilities.
   a. $P(0 \leq z \leq 1)$
   b. $P(0 \leq z \leq 1.5)$
   c. $P(0 < z < 2)$
   d. $P(0 < z < 2.5)$

11. Given that z is a standard normal random variable, compute the following probabilities.
   a. $P(-1 \leq z \leq 0)$
   b. $P(-1.5 \leq z \leq 0)$
   c. $P(-2 < z < 0)$
   d. $P(-2.5 \leq z \leq 0)$
   e. $P(-3 \leq z \leq 0)$

12. Given that z is a standard normal random variable, compute the following probabilities.
    a. $P(0 \leq z \leq .83)$
    b. $P(-1.57 \leq z \leq 0)$
    c. $P(z > .44)$
    d. $P(z \geq -.23)$
    e. $P(z < 1.20)$
    f. $P(z \leq -.71)$

13. Given that z is a standard normal random variable, compute the following probabilities.
    a. $P(-1.98 \leq z \leq .49)$
    b. $P(.52 \leq z \leq 1.22)$
    c. $P(-1.75 \leq z \leq -1.04)$

14. Given that z is a standard normal random variable, find z for each situation.
    a. The area between 0 and z is .4750.
    b. The area between 0 and z is .2291.
    c. The area to the right of z is .1314.
    d. The area to the left of z is .6700.

15. Given that z is a standard normal random variable, find z for each situation.
    a. The area to the left of z is .2119.
    b. The area between $-z$ and z is .9030.
    c. The area between $-z$ and z is .2052.
    d. The area to the left of z is .9948.
    e. The area to the right of z is .6915.

16. Given that z is a standard normal random variable, find z for each situation.
    a. The area to the right of z is .01.
    b. The area to the right of z is .025.
    c. The area to the right of z is .05.
    d. The area to the right of z is .10.

Applications

17. The average amount parents and children spent per child on back-to-school clothes in Autumn 2001 was $527 (*CNBC*, September 5, 2001). Assume the standard deviation is $160 and that the amount spent is normally distributed.
    a. What is the probability that the amount spent on a randomly selected child is more than $700?
    b. What is the probability that the amount spent on a randomly selected child is less than $100?
    c. What is the probability that the amount spent on a randomly selected child is between $450 and $700?
    d. What is the probability that the amount spent on a randomly selected child is no more than $300?

18. The average stock price for companies making up the S&P 500 is $30, and the standard deviation is $8.20 (*Business Week*, Special Annual Issue, Spring 2003). Assume the stock prices are normally distributed.
    a. What is the probability a company will have a stock price of at least $40?
    b. What is the probability a company will have a stock price no higher than $20?
    c. How high does a stock price have to be to put a company in the top 10%?

19. The average amount of precipitation in Dallas, Texas, during the month of April is 3.5 inches (*The World Almanac*, 2000). Assume that a normal distribution applies and that the standard deviation is .8 inches.
    a. What percentage of the time does the amount of rainfall in April exceed 5 inches?
    b. What percentage of the time is the amount of rainfall in April less than 3 inches?
    c. A month is classified as extremely wet if the amount of rainfall is in the upper 10% for that month. How much precipitation must fall before a month of April is classified as extremely wet?

20. In January 2003, the American worker spent an average of 77 hours logged on to the Internet while at work (*CNBC,* March 15, 2003). Assume the times are normally distributed and that the standard deviation is 20 hours.
    a. What is the probability a randomly selected worker spent fewer than 50 hours logged on to the Internet?
    b. What percentage of workers spent more than 100 hours logged on to the Internet?
    c. A person is classified as a heavy user if he or she is in the upper 20% of usage. How many hours must a worker have logged on to the Internet to be considered a heavy user?

21. A person must score in the upper 2% of the population on an IQ test to qualify for membership in Mensa, the international high-IQ society (*US Airways Attaché,* September 2000). If IQ scores are normally distributed with a mean of 100 and a standard deviation of 15, what score must a person have to qualify for Mensa?

22. According to the Bureau of Labor Statistics, the average weekly pay for a U.S. production worker was $441.84 (*The World Almanac,* 2000). Assume that available data indicate that production worker wages were normally distributed with a standard deviation of $90.
    a. What is the probability that a worker earned between $400 and $500?
    b. How much did a production worker have to earn to be in the top 20% of wage earners?
    c. For a randomly selected production worker, what is the probability the worker earned less than $250 per week?

23. The time needed to complete a final examination in a particular college course is normally distributed with a mean of 80 minutes and a standard deviation of 10 minutes. Answer the following questions.
    a. What is the probability of completing the exam in one hour or less?
    b. What is the probability that a student will complete the exam in more than 60 minutes but less than 75 minutes?
    c. Assume that the class has 60 students and that the examination period is 90 minutes in length. How many students do you expect will be unable to complete the exam in the allotted time?

24. The daily trading volumes (millions of shares) for stocks traded on the New York Stock Exchange for 12 days in August and September are shown here (*Barron's,* August 7, 2000, September 4, 2000, and September 11, 2000).

917	983	1046
944	723	783
813	1057	766
836	992	973

The probability distribution of trading volume is approximately normal.
    a. Compute the mean and standard deviation for the daily trading volume to use as estimates of the population mean and standard deviation.
    b. What is the probability that on a particular day the trading volume will be less than 800 million shares?
    c. What is the probability that trading volume will exceed 1 billion shares?
    d. If the exchange wants to issue a press release on the top 5% of trading days, what volume will trigger a release?

25. The average ticket price for a Washington Redskins football game was $81.89 for the 2001 season (*USA Today,* September 6, 2001). With the additional costs of parking, food, drinks, and souvenirs, the average cost for a family of four to attend a game totaled $442.54. Assume the normal distribution applies and that the standard deviation is $65.
    a. What is the probability that a family of four will spend more than $400?
    b. What is the probability that a family of four will spend $300 or less?
    c. What is the probability that a family of four will spend between $400 and $500?

Normal Approximation of Binomial Probabilities

In Section 5.4 we presented the discrete binomial distribution. Recall that a binomial experiment consists of a sequence of n identical independent trials with each trial having two possible outcomes, a success or a failure. The probability of a success on a trial is the same for all trials and is denoted by p. The binomial random variable is the number of successes in the n trials, and probability questions pertain to the probability of x successes in the n trials.

When the number of trials becomes large, evaluating the binomial probability function by hand or with a calculator is difficult. In cases where $np \geq 5$, and $n(1 - p) \geq 5$, the normal distribution provides an easy-to-use approximation of binomial probabilities. When using the normal approximation to the binomial, we set $\mu = np$ and $\sigma = \sqrt{np(1 - p)}$ in the definition of the normal curve.

Let us illustrate the normal approximation to the binomial by supposing that a particular company has a history of making errors in 10% of its invoices. A sample of 100 invoices has been taken, and we want to compute the probability that 12 invoices contain errors. That is, we want to find the binomial probability of 12 successes in 100 trials. In applying the normal approximation in this case, we set $\mu = np = (100)(.1) = 10$ and $\sigma = \sqrt{np(1 - p)} = \sqrt{(100)(.1)(.9)} = 3$. A normal distribution with $\mu = 10$ and $\sigma = 3$ is shown in Figure 6.8.

Recall that, with a continuous probability distribution, probabilities are computed as areas under the probability density function. As a result, the probability of any single value for the random variable is zero. Thus to approximate the binomial probability of 12 successes, we compute the area under the corresponding normal curve between 11.5 and 12.5. The .5 that we add and subtract from 12 is called a **continuity correction factor**. It is introduced because a continuous distribution is being used to approximate a discrete distribution. Thus, $P(x = 12)$ for the *discrete* binomial distribution is approximated by $P(11.5 \leq x \leq 12.5)$ for the *continuous* normal distribution.

FIGURE 6.8   NORMAL APPROXIMATION TO A BINOMIAL PROBABILITY DISTRIBUTION WITH $n = 100$ AND $p = .10$ SHOWING THE PROBABILITY OF 12 ERRORS

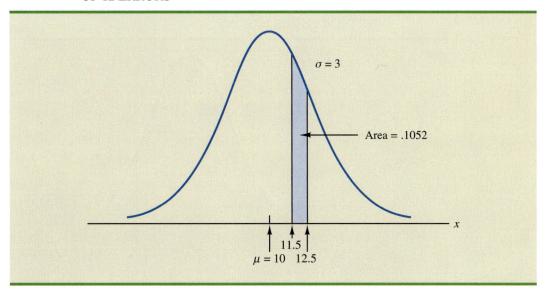

Converting to the standard normal distribution to compute $P(11.5 \leq x \leq 12.5)$, we have

$$z = \frac{x - \mu}{\sigma} = \frac{12.5 - 10.0}{3} = .83 \quad \text{at } x = 12.5$$

and

$$z = \frac{x - \mu}{\sigma} = \frac{11.5 - 10.0}{3} = .50 \quad \text{at } x = 11.5$$

From Table 6.1 we find that the area under the curve (in Figure 6.8) between 10 and 12.5 is .2967. Similarly, the area under the curve between 10 and 11.5 is .1915. Therefore, the area between 11.5 and 12.5 is .2967 − .1915 = .1052. The normal approximation to the probability of 12 successes in 100 trials is .1052.

For another illustration, suppose we want to compute the probability of 13 or fewer errors in the sample of 100 invoices. Figure 6.9 shows the area under the normal curve that approximates this probability. Note that the use of the continuity correction factor results in the value of 13.5 being used to compute the desired probability. The z value corresponding to $x = 13.5$ is

$$z = \frac{13.5 - 10.0}{3.0} = 1.17$$

Table 6.1 shows that the area under the standard normal curve between 0 and 1.17 is .3790. The area under the normal curve approximating the probability of 13 or fewer errors is given by the shaded portion of the graph in Figure 6.9. The probability is .3790 + .5000 = .8790.

FIGURE 6.9 NORMAL APPROXIMATION TO A BINOMIAL PROBABILITY DISTRIBUTION WITH $n = 100$ AND $p = .10$ SHOWING THE PROBABILITY OF 13 OR FEWER ERRORS

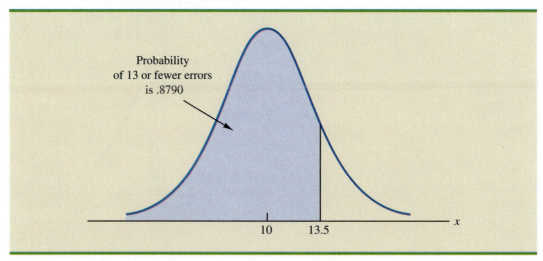

Probability of 13 or fewer errors is .8790

Exercises

Methods

26. A binomial probability distribution has $p = .20$ and $n = 100$.
    a. What are the mean and standard deviation?
    b. Is this situation one in which binomial probabilities can be approximated by the normal probability distribution? Explain.
    c. What is the probability of exactly 24 successes?
    d. What is the probability of 18 to 22 successes?
    e. What is the probability of 15 or fewer successes?

27. Assume a binomial probability distribution has $p = .60$ and $n = 200$.
    a. What are the mean and standard deviation?
    b. Is this situation one in which binomial probabilities can be approximated by the normal probability distribution? Explain.
    c. What is the probability of 100 to 110 successes?
    d. What is the probability of 130 or more successes?
    e. What is the advantage of using the normal probability distribution to approximate the binomial probabilities? Use part (d) to explain the advantage.

Applications

28. President Bush proposed the elimination of taxes on dividends paid to shareholders on the grounds that they result in double taxation. The earnings used to pay dividends are already taxed to the corporation. A survey on this issue revealed that 47% of Americans favor the proposal. By political party, 64% of Republicans and 29% of Democrats favor the proposal (*Investor's Business Daily,* January 13, 2003). Suppose a group of 250 Americans gather to hear a speech about the proposal.
    a. What is the probability at least half of the group is in favor of the proposal?
    b. You later find out 150 Republicans and 100 Democrats are present. Now what is your estimate of the expected number in favor of the proposal?
    c. Will a speaker in favor of the proposal be better received by this group than one against the proposal?

29. The unemployment rate is 5.8% (*Bureau of Labor Statistics,* http://www.bls.gov, April 3, 2003). Suppose that 100 employable people are selected randomly.
    a. What is the expected number who are unemployed?
    b. What are the variance and standard deviation of the number who are unemployed?
    c. What is the probability that exactly six are unemployed?
    d. What is the probability that at least four are unemployed?

30. When you sign up for a credit card, do you read the contract carefully? In a FindLaw.com survey, individuals were asked, "How closely do you read a contract for a credit card?" (*USA Today,* October 16, 2003). The findings were that 44% read every word, 33% read enough to understand the contract, 11% just glance at it, and 4% don't read it at all.
    a. For a sample of 500 people, how many would you expect to say that they read every word of a credit card contract?
    b. For a sample of 500 people, what is the probability that 200 or fewer will say they read every word of a credit card contract?
    c. For a sample of 500 people, what is the probability that at least 15 say they don't read credit card contracts?

31. A Myrtle Beach resort hotel has 120 rooms. In the spring months, hotel room occupancy is approximately 75%.
    a. What is the probability that at least half of the rooms are occupied on a given day?
    b. What is the probability that 100 or more rooms are occupied on a given day?
    c. What is the probability that 80 or fewer rooms are occupied on a given day?

6.4 Exponential Probability Distribution

The **exponential probability distribution** may be used for random variables such as the time between arrivals at a car wash, the time required to load a truck, the distance between major defects in a highway, and so on. The exponential probability density function follows.

EXPONENTIAL PROBABILITY DENSITY FUNCTION

$$f(x) = \frac{1}{\mu} e^{-x/\mu} \qquad \text{for } x \geq 0, \mu > 0 \tag{6.4}$$

As an example of the exponential distribution, suppose that x represents the loading time for a truck at the Schips loading dock and follows such a distribution. If the mean, or average, loading time is 15 minutes ($\mu = 15$), the appropriate probability density function is

$$f(x) = \frac{1}{15} e^{-x/15}$$

Figure 6.10 is the graph of this probability density function.

Computing Probabilities for the Exponential Distribution

In waiting line applications, the exponential distribution is often used for service time.

As with any continuous probability distribution, the area under the curve corresponding to an interval provides the probability that the random variable assumes a value in that interval. In the Schips loading dock example, the probability that loading a truck will take six minutes or less ($x \leq 6$) is defined to be the area under the curve in Figure 6.10 from $x = 0$ to $x = 6$. Similarly, the probability that the loading time will be 18 minutes or less ($x \leq 18$)

FIGURE 6.10   EXPONENTIAL DISTRIBUTION FOR THE SCHIPS LOADING DOCK EXAMPLE is the area under the curve from $x = 0$ to $x = 18$. Note also that the probability that the loading time will be between six minutes and 18 minutes ($6 \leq x \leq 18$) is given by the area under the curve from $x = 6$ to $x = 18$.

To compute exponential probabilities such as those just described, we use the following formula. It provides the cumulative probability of obtaining a value for the exponential random variable of less than or equal to some specific value denoted by x_0.

EXPONENTIAL DISTRIBUTION: CUMULATIVE PROBABILITIES

$$P(x \leq x_0) = 1 - e^{-x_0/\mu} \tag{6.5}$$

For the Schips loading dock example, $x =$ loading time and $\mu = 15$, which gives us

$$P(x \leq x_0) = 1 - e^{-x_0/15}$$

Hence, the probability that loading a truck will take six minutes or less is

$$P(x \leq 6) = 1 - e^{-6/15} = .3297$$

Figure 6.11 shows the area or probability for a loading time of six minutes or less.

Using equation (6.5), we calculate the probability of loading a truck in 18 minutes or less.

$$P(x \leq 18) = 1 - e^{-18/15} = .6988$$

Thus, the probability that loading a truck will take between six minutes and 18 minutes is equal to $.6988 - .3297 = .3691$. Probabilities for any other interval can be computed similarly.

FIGURE 6.11   PROBABILITY OF A LOADING TIME OF 6 MINUTES OR LESS

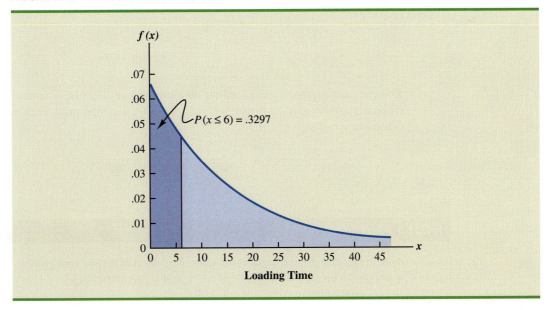

A property of the exponential distribution is that the mean and standard deviation are equal.

In the preceding example, the mean time it takes to load a truck is $\mu = 15$ minutes. A property of the exponential distribution is that the mean of the distribution and the standard deviation of the distribution are *equal*. Thus, the standard deviation for the time it takes to load a truck is $\sigma = 15$ minutes. The variance is $\sigma^2 = (15)^2 = 225$.

Relationship Between the Poisson and Exponential Distributions

In Section 5.5 we introduced the Poisson distribution as a discrete probability distribution that is often useful in examining the number of occurrences of an event over a specified interval of time or space. Recall that the Poisson probability function is

$$f(x) = \frac{\mu^x e^{-\mu}}{x!}$$

where

$$\mu = \text{expected value or mean number of occurrences over a specified interval}$$

If arrivals follow a Poisson distribution, the time between arrivals must follow an exponential distribution.

The continuous exponential probability distribution is related to the discrete Poisson distribution. If the Poisson distribution provides an appropriate description of the number of occurrences per interval, the exponential distribution provides a description of the length of the interval between occurrences.

To illustrate this relationship, suppose the number of cars that arrive at a car wash during one hour is described by a Poisson probability distribution with a mean of 10 cars per hour. The Poisson probability function that gives the probability of x arrivals per hour is

$$f(x) = \frac{10^x e^{-10}}{x!}$$

Because the average number of arrivals is 10 cars per hour, the average time between cars arriving is

$$\frac{1 \text{ hour}}{10 \text{ cars}} = .1 \text{ hour/car}$$

Thus, the corresponding exponential distribution that describes the time between the arrivals has a mean of $\mu = .1$ hour per car; as a result, the appropriate exponential probability density function is

$$f(x) = \frac{1}{.1} e^{-x/.1} = 10e^{-10x}$$

NOTES AND COMMENTS

As we can see in Figure 6.10, the exponential distribution is skewed to the right. Indeed, the skewness measure for exponential distributions is 2. The exponential distribution gives us a good idea what a skewed distribution looks like.

Exercises

Methods

32. Consider the following exponential probability density function.

$$f(x) = \frac{1}{8}\,e^{-x/8} \qquad \text{for } x \geq 0$$

    a.   Find $P(x \leq 6)$.
    b.   Find $P(x \leq 4)$.
    c.   Find $P(x \geq 6)$.
    d.   Find $P(4 \leq x \leq 6)$.

33. Consider the following exponential probability density function.

$$f(x) = \frac{1}{3}\,e^{-x/3} \qquad \text{for } x \geq 0$$

    a.   Write the formula for $P(x \leq x_0)$.
    b.   Find $P(x \leq 2)$.
    c.   Find $P(x \geq 3)$.
    d.   Find $P(x \leq 5)$.
    e.   Find $P(2 \leq x \leq 5)$.

Applications

34. *Internet Magazine* monitors Internet service providers (ISPs) and provides statistics on their performance. The average time to download a Web page for free ISPs is approximately 20 seconds for European Web pages (*Internet Magazine,* January 2000). Assume the time to download a Web page follows an exponential distribution.
    a.   What is the probability it will take less than 10 seconds to download a Web page?
    b.   What is the probability it will take more than 30 seconds to download a Web page?
    c.   What is the probability it will take between 10 and 30 seconds to download a Web page?

35. The time between arrivals of vehicles at a particular intersection follows an exponential probability distribution with a mean of 12 seconds.
    a.   Sketch this exponential probability distribution.
    b.   What is the probability that the arrival time between vehicles is 12 seconds or less?
    c.   What is the probability that the arrival time between vehicles is 6 seconds or less?
    d.   What is the probability of 30 or more seconds between vehicle arrivals?

36. The lifetime (hours) of an electronic device is a random variable with the following exponential probability density function.

$$f(x) = \frac{1}{50}\,e^{-x/50} \qquad \text{for } x \geq 0$$

    a.   What is the mean lifetime of the device?
    b.   What is the probability that the device will fail in the first 25 hours of operation?
    c.   What is the probability that the device will operate 100 or more hours before failure?

37. Sparagowski & Associates conducted a study of service times at the drive-up window of fast-food restaurants. The average time between placing an order and receiving the order at McDonald's restaurants was 2.78 minutes (*The Cincinnati Enquirer,* July 9, 2000). Waiting times, such as these, frequently follow an exponential distribution.
    a.   What is the probability that a customer's service time is less than 2 minutes?
    b.   What is the probability that a customer's service time is more than 5 minutes?
    c.   What is the probability that a customer's service time is more than 2.78 minutes?

38. According to a *Barron's* Primary Reader Survey, the average annual number of investment transactions for a subscriber is 30 (http://www.barronsmag.com, July 28, 2000). Suppose the number of transactions in a year follows the Poisson probability distribution.
    a. Show the probability distribution for the time between investment transactions.
    b. What is the probability of no transactions during the month of January for a particular subscriber?
    c. What is the probability that the next transaction will occur within the next half month for a particular subscriber?

Summary

This chapter extended the discussion of probability distributions to the case of continuous random variables. The major conceptual difference between discrete and continuous probability distributions involves the method of computing probabilities. With discrete distributions, the probability function $f(x)$ provides the probability that the random variable x assumes various values. With continuous distributions, the probability density function $f(x)$ does not provide probability values directly. Instead, probabilities are given by areas under the curve or graph of the probability density function $f(x)$. Because the area under the curve above a single point is zero, we observe that the probability of any particular value is zero for a continuous random variable.

Three continuous probability distributions—the uniform, normal, and exponential distributions—were treated in detail. The normal distribution is used widely in statistical inference and will be used extensively throughout the remainder of the text.

Glossary

Probability density function A function used to compute probabilities for a continuous random variable. The area under the graph of a probability density function over an interval represents probability.

Uniform probability distribution A continuous probability distribution for which the probability that the random variable will assume a value in any interval is the same for each interval of equal length.

Normal probability distribution A continuous probability distribution. Its probability density function is bell-shaped and determined by its mean μ and standard deviation σ.

Standard normal probability distribution A normal distribution with a mean of zero and a standard deviation of one.

Continuity correction factor A value of .5 that is added to or subtracted from a value of x when the continuous normal distribution is used to approximate the discrete binomial distribution.

Exponential probability distribution A continuous probability distribution that is useful in computing probabilities for the time it takes to complete a task.

Key Formulas

Uniform Probability Density Function

$$f(x) = \begin{cases} \dfrac{1}{b-a} & \text{for } a \leq x \leq b \\ 0 & \text{elsewhere} \end{cases} \tag{6.1}$$

Normal Probability Density Function

$$f(x) = \frac{1}{\sigma \sqrt{2\pi}} e^{-(x-\mu)^2/2\sigma^2}$$

(6.2)

Converting to the Standard Normal Distribution

$$z = \frac{x - \mu}{\sigma}$$

(6.3)

Exponential Probability Density Function

$$f(x) = \frac{1}{\mu} e^{-x/\mu} \qquad \text{for } x \geq 0, \mu > 0$$

(6.4)

Exponential Distribution: Cumulative Probabilities

$$P(x \leq x_0) = 1 - e^{-x_0/\mu}$$

(6.5)

Supplementary Exercises

39. A business executive, transferred from Chicago to Atlanta, needs to sell her house in Chicago quickly. The executive's employer has offered to buy the house for $210,000, but the offer expires at the end of the week. The executive does not currently have a better offer, but can afford to leave the house on the market for another month. From conversations with her realtor, the executive believes the price she will get by leaving the house on the market for another month is uniformly distributed between $200,000 and $225,000.
    a. If she leaves the house on the market for another month, what is the mathematical expression for the probability density function of the sales price?
    b. If she leaves it on the market for another month, what is the probability she will get at least $215,000 for the house?
    c. If she leaves it on the market for another month, what is the probability she will get less than $210,000?
    d. Should the executive leave the house on the market for another month? Why or why not?

40. The U.S. Bureau of Labor Statistics reports that the average annual expenditure on food and drink for all families is $5700 (*Money,* December 2003). Assume that annual expenditure on food and drink is normally distributed and that the standard deviation is $1500.
    a. How much do the 10% of families with the lowest expenditure level spend annually on food and drink?
    b. What percentage of families spend more than $7000 annually on food and drink?
    c. How much do the 5% of the families with the highest expenditure level spend annually on food and drink?

41. Motorola used the normal distribution to determine the probability of defects and the number of defects expected in a production process. Assume a production process produces items with a mean weight of 10 ounces. Calculate the probability of a defect and the expected number of defects for a 1000-unit production run in the following situations.
    a. The process standard deviation is .15, and the process control is set at plus or minus one standard deviation. Units with weights less than 9.85 or greater than 10.15 ounces will be classified as defects.
    b. Through process design improvements, the process standard deviation can be reduced to .05. Assume the process control remains the same, with weights less than 9.85 or greater than 10.15 ounces being classified as defects.
    c. What is the advantage of reducing process variation, thereby setting process control limits at a greater number of standard deviations from the mean?

42. The average annual amount American households spend for daily transportation is $6312 (*Money,* August 2001). Assume that the amount spent is normally distributed.
    a. Suppose you learn that 5% of American households spend less than $1000 for daily transportation. What is the standard deviation of the amount spent?
    b. What is the probability that a household spends between $4000 and $6000?
    c. What is the amount spent by the 3% of households with the highest daily transportation cost?

43. *Condé Nast Traveler* publishes a Gold List of the top hotels all over the world. The Broadmoor Hotel in Colorado Springs contains 700 rooms and is on the 2004 Gold List (*Condé Nast Traveler,* January 2004). Suppose Broadmoor's marketing group forecasts a demand of 670 rooms for the coming weekend. Assume that demand for the upcoming weekend is normally distributed with a standard deviation of 30.
    a. What is the probability all the hotel's room will be rented?
    b. What is the probability 50 or more rooms will not be rented?
    c. Would you recommend the hotel consider offering a promotion to increase demand? What considerations would be important?

44. Ward Doering Auto Sales is considering offering a special service contract that will cover the total cost of any service work required on leased vehicles. From experience, the company manager estimates that yearly service costs are approximately normally distributed, with a mean of $150 and a standard deviation of $25.
    a. If the company offers the service contract to customers for a yearly charge of $200, what is the probability that any one customer's service costs will exceed the contract price of $200?
    b. What is Ward's expected profit per service contract?

45. Is lack of sleep causing traffic fatalities? A study conducted under the auspices of the National Highway Traffic Safety Administration found that the average number of fatal crashes caused by drowsy drivers each year was 1550 (*Business Week,* January 26, 2004). Assume the annual number of fatal crashes per year is normally distributed with a standard deviation of 300.
    a. What is the probability of fewer than 1000 fatal crashes in a year?
    b. What is the probability the number of fatal crashes will be between 1000 and 2000 for a year?
    c. For a year to be in the upper 5% with respect to the number of fatal crashes, how many fatal crashes would have to occur?

46. Assume that the test scores from a college admissions test are normally distributed, with a mean of 450 and a standard deviation of 100.
    a. What percentage of the people taking the test score between 400 and 500?
    b. Suppose someone receives a score of 630. What percentage of the people taking the test score better? What percentage score worse?
    c. If a particular university will not admit anyone scoring below 480, what percentage of the persons taking the test would be acceptable to the university?

47. According to *Advertising Age,* the average base salary for women working as copywriters in advertising firms is higher than the average base salary for men. The average base salary for women is $67,000 and the average base salary for men is $65,500 (*Working Woman,* July/August 2000). Assume salaries are normally distributed and that the standard deviation is $7000 for both men and women.
    a. What is the probability of a woman receiving a salary in excess of $75,000?
    b. What is the probability of a man receiving a salary in excess of $75,000?
    c. What is the probability of a woman receiving a salary below $50,000?
    d. How much would a woman have to make to have a higher salary than 99% of her male counterparts?

48. A machine fills containers with a particular product. The standard deviation of filling weights is known from past data to be .6 ounce. If only 2% of the containers hold less than 18 ounces, what is the mean filling weight for the machine? That is, what must μ equal? Assume the filling weights have a normal distribution.

49. Consider a multiple-choice examination with 50 questions. Each question has four possible answers. Assume that a student who has done the homework and attended lectures has a 75% probability of answering any question correctly.
    a. A student must answer 43 or more questions correctly to obtain a grade of A. What percentage of the students who have done their homework and attended lectures will obtain a grade of A on this multiple-choice examination?
    b. A student who answers 35 to 39 questions correctly will receive a grade of C. What percentage of students who have done their homework and attended lectures will obtain a grade of C on this multiple-choice examination?
    c. A student must answer 30 or more questions correctly to pass the examination. What percentage of the students who have done their homework and attended lectures will pass the examination?
    d. Assume that a student has not attended class and has not done the homework for the course. Furthermore, assume that the student will simply guess at the answer to each question. What is the probability that this student will answer 30 or more questions correctly and pass the examination?

50. A blackjack player at a Las Vegas casino learned that the house will provide a free room if play is for four hours at an average bet of $50. The player's strategy provides a probability of .49 of winning on any one hand, and the player knows that there are 60 hands per hour. Suppose the player plays for four hours at a bet of $50 per hand.
    a. What is the player's expected payoff?
    b. What is the probability the player loses $1000 or more?
    c. What is the probability the player wins?
    d. Suppose the player starts with $1500. What is the probability of going broke?

51. The time in minutes for which a student uses a computer terminal at the computer center of a major university follows an exponential probability distribution with a mean of 36 minutes. Assume a student arrives at the terminal just as another student is beginning to work on the terminal.
    a. What is the probability that the wait for the second student will be 15 minutes or less?
    b. What is the probability that the wait for the second student will be between 15 and 45 minutes?
    c. What is the probability that the second student will have to wait an hour or more?

52. The Web site for the Bed and Breakfast Inns of North America (http://www.bestinns.net) gets approximately seven visitors per minute (*Time,* September 2001). Suppose the number of Web site visitors per minute follows a Poisson probability distribution.
    a. What is the mean time between visits to the Web site?
    b. Show the exponential probability density function for the time between Web site visits.
    c. What is the probability no one will access the Web site in a 1-minute period?
    d. What is the probability no one will access the Web site in a 12-second period?

53. The average travel time to work for New York City residents is 36.5 minutes (*Time Almanac,* 2001).
    a. Assume the exponential probability distribution is applicable and show the probability density function for the travel time to work for a typical New Yorker.
    b. What is the probability it will take a typical New Yorker between 20 and 40 minutes to travel to work?
    c. What is the probability it will take a typical New Yorker more than 40 minutes to travel to work?

54. The time (in minutes) between telephone calls at an insurance claims office has the following exponential probability distribution.

$$f(x) = .50e^{-.50x} \qquad \text{for } x \geq 0$$

a. What is the mean time between telephone calls?
b. What is the probability of having 30 seconds or less between telephone calls?
c. What is the probability of having 1 minute or less between telephone calls?
d. What is the probability of having 5 or more minutes without a telephone call?

Case Problem   ## Specialty Toys

Specialty Toys, Inc., sells a variety of new and innovative children's toys. Management learned that the preholiday season is the best time to introduce a new toy, because many families use this time to look for new ideas for December holiday gifts. When Specialty discovers a new toy with good market potential, it chooses an October market entry date.

In order to get toys in its stores by October, Specialty places one-time orders with its manufacturers in June or July of each year. Demand for children's toys can be highly volatile. If a new toy catches on, a sense of shortage in the marketplace often increases the demand to high levels and large profits can be realized. However, new toys can also flop, leaving Specialty stuck with high levels of inventory that must be sold at reduced prices. The most important question the company faces is deciding how many units of a new toy should be purchased to meet anticipated sales demand. If too few are purchased, sales will be lost; if too many are purchased, profits will be reduced because of low prices realized in clearance sales.

For the coming season, Specialty plans to introduce a new product called Weather Teddy. This variation of a talking teddy bear is made by a company in Taiwan. When a child presses Teddy's hand, the bear begins to talk. A built-in barometer selects one of five responses that predict the weather conditions. The responses range from "It looks to be a very nice day! Have fun" to "I think it may rain today. Don't forget your umbrella." Tests with the product show that, even though it is not a perfect weather predictor, its predictions are surprisingly good. Several of Specialty's managers claimed Teddy gave predictions of the weather that were as good as many local television weather forecasters.

As with other products, Specialty faces the decision of how many Weather Teddy units to order for the coming holiday season. Members of the management team suggested order quantities of 15,000, 18,000, 24,000, or 28,000 units. The wide range of order quantities suggested indicate considerable disagreement concerning the market potential. The product management team asks you for an analysis of the stock-out probabilities for various order quantities, an estimate of the profit potential, and to help make an order quantity recommendation. Specialty expects to sell Weather Teddy for $24 based on a cost of $16 per unit. If inventory remains after the holiday season, Specialty will sell all surplus inventory for $5 per unit. After reviewing the sales history of similar products, Specialty's senior sales forecaster predicted an expected demand of 20,000 units with a 0.90 probability that demand would be between 10,000 units and 30,000 units.

Managerial Report

Prepare a managerial report that addresses the following issues and recommends an order quantity for the Weather Teddy product.

1. Use the sales forecaster's prediction to describe a normal probability distribution that can be used to approximate the demand distribution. Sketch the distribution and show its mean and standard deviation.

2. Compute the probability of a stock-out for the order quantities suggested by members of the management team.
3. Compute the projected profit for the order quantities suggested by the management team under three scenarios: worst case in which sales = 10,000 units, most likely case in which sales = 20,000 units, and best case in which sales = 30,000 units.
4. One of Specialty's managers felt that the profit potential was so great that the order quantity should have a 70% chance of meeting demand and only a 30% chance of any stock-outs. What quantity would be ordered under this policy, and what is the projected profit under the three sales scenarios?
5. Provide your own recommendation for an order quantity and note the associated profit projections. Provide a rationale for your recommendation.

Appendix 6.1   Continuous Probability Distributions with Minitab

Let us demonstrate the Minitab procedure for computing continuous probabilities by referring to the Grear Tire Company problem where tire mileage was described by a normal distribution with $\mu = 36{,}500$ and $\sigma = 5000$. One question asked was: What is the probability that the tire mileage will exceed 40,000 miles?

For continuous probability distributions, Minitab gives a cumulative probability; that is, Minitab gives the probability that the random variable will assume a value less than or equal to a specified constant. For the Grear tire mileage question, Minitab can be used to determine the cumulative probability that the tire mileage will be less than or equal to 40,000 miles. (The specified constant in this case is 40,000.) After obtaining the cumulative probability from Minitab, we must subtract it from 1 to determine the probability that the tire mileage will exceed 40,000 miles.

Prior to using Minitab to compute a probability, one must enter the specified constant into a column of the worksheet. For the Grear tire mileage question we entered the specified constant of 40,000 into column C1 of the Minitab worksheet. The steps in using Minitab to compute the cumulative probability of the normal random variable assuming a value less than or equal to 40,000 follow.

Step 1. Select the **Calc** menu
Step 2. Choose **Probability Distributions**
Step 3. Choose **Normal**
Step 4. When the Normal Distribution dialog box appears:
  Select **Cumulative probability**
  Enter 36500 in the **Mean** box
  Enter 5000 in the **Standard deviation** box
  Enter C1 in the **Input column** box (the column containing 40,000)
  Click **OK**

After the user clicks **OK,** Minitab prints the cumulative probability that the normal random variable assumes a value less than or equal to 40,000. Minitab shows that this probability is .7580. Because we are interested in the probability that the tire mileage will be greater than 40,000, the desired probability is $1 - .7580 = .2420$.

A second question in the Grear Tire Company problem was: What mileage guarantee should Grear set to ensure that no more than 10% of the tires qualify for the guarantee? Here we are given a probability and want to find the corresponding value for the random variable. Minitab uses an inverse calculation routine to find the value of the random variable associated with a given cumulative probability. First, we must enter the cumulative probability into a column of the Minitab worksheet (say, C1). In this case, the desired cumulative probability is .10. Then, the first three steps of the Minitab procedure are as already listed. In step 4, we select **Inverse cumulative probability** instead of **Cumulative probability** and complete the remaining parts of the step. Minitab then displays the mileage guarantee of 30,092 miles.

Minitab is capable of computing probabilities for other continuous probability distributions, including the exponential probability distribution. To compute exponential probabilities, follow the procedure shown previously for the normal probability distribution and choose the **Exponential** option in step 3. Step 4 is as shown, with the exception that entering the standard deviation is not required. Output for cumulative probabilities and inverse cumulative probabilities is identical to that described for the normal probability distribution.

Appendix 6.2 Continuous Probability Distributions with Excel

Excel provides the capability for computing probabilities for several continuous probability distributions, including the normal and exponential probability distributions. In this appendix, we describe how Excel can be used to compute probabilities for any normal distribution. The procedures for the exponential and other continuous distributions are similar to the one we describe for the normal distribution.

Let us return to the Grear Tire Company problem where the tire mileage was described by a normal distribution with $\mu = 36{,}500$ and $\sigma = 5000$. Assume we are interested in the probability that tire mileage will exceed 40,000 miles.

Excel's NORMDIST function provides cumulative probabilities for a normal distribution. The general form of the function is NORMDIST $(x, \mu, \sigma,$ cumulative). For the fourth argument, TRUE is specified if a cumulative probability is desired. Thus, to compute the cumulative probability that the tire mileage will be less than or equal to 40,000 miles we would enter the following formula into any cell of an Excel worksheet:

$$=\text{NORMDIST}(40000,36500,5000,\text{TRUE})$$

At this point, .7580 will appear in the cell where the formula was entered, indicating that the probability of tire mileage being less than or equal to 40,000 miles is .7580. Therefore, the probability that tire mileage will exceed 40,000 miles is $1 - .7580 = .2420$.

Excel's NORMINV function uses an inverse computation to find the x value corresponding to a given cumulative probability. For instance, suppose we want to find the guaranteed mileage Grear should offer so that no more than 10% of the tires will be eligible for the guarantee. We would enter the following formula into any cell of an Excel worksheet:

$$=\text{NORMINV}(.1,36500,5000)$$

At this point, 30092 will appear in the cell where the formula was entered indicating that the probability of a tire lasting 30,092 miles or less is .10.

The Excel function for computing exponential probabilities is EXPONDIST. Using it is straightforward. But if one needs help specifying the proper values for the arguments, Excel's Insert Function tool can be used (see Appendix 2.2).

CHAPTER 7

Sampling and Sampling Distributions

CONTENTS

STATISTICS *in* PRACTICE

MEADWESTVACO CORPORATION*
STAMFORD, CONNECTICUT

MeadWestvaco Corporation, a leading producer of packaging, coated and specialty papers, consumer and office products, and specialty chemicals, employs more than 30,000 people. It operates worldwide in 33 countries and serves customers located in approximately 100 countries. MeadWestvaco holds a leading position in paper production, with an annual capacity of 1.8 million tons. The company's products include textbook paper, glossy magazine paper, beverage packaging systems, and office products. MeadWestvaco's internal consulting group uses sampling to provide a variety of information that enables the company to obtain significant productivity benefits and remain competitive.

For example, MeadWestvaco maintains large woodland holdings, which supply the trees, or raw material, for many of the company's products. Managers need reliable and accurate information about the timberlands and forests to evaluate the company's ability to meet its future raw material needs. What is the present volume in the forests? What is the past growth of the forests? What is the projected future growth of the forests? With answers to these important questions MeadWestvaco's managers can develop plans for the future, including long-term planting and harvesting schedules for the trees.

How does MeadWestvaco obtain the information it needs about its vast forest holdings? Data collected from sample plots throughout the forests are the basis for learning about the population of trees owned by the company. To identify the sample plots, the timberland holdings are first divided into three sections based on location and types of trees. Using maps and random numbers, MeadWestvaco analysts identify random samples of $\frac{1}{5}$- to $\frac{1}{7}$-acre plots in each section of the for-

*The authors are indebted to Dr. Edward P. Winkofsky for providing this Statistics in Practice.

Random sampling of its forest holdings enables MeadWestvaco Corporation to meet future raw material needs. © Walter Hodges/Corbis.

est. MeadWestvaco foresters collect data from these sample plots to learn about the forest population.

Foresters throughout the organization participate in the field data collection process. Periodically, two-person teams gather information on each tree in every sample plot. The sample data are entered into the company's continuous forest inventory (CFI) computer system. Reports from the CFI system include a number of frequency distribution summaries containing statistics on types of trees, present forest volume, past forest growth rates, and projected future forest growth and volume. Sampling and the associated statistical summaries of the sample data provide the reports essential for the effective management of MeadWestvaco's forests and timberlands.

In this chapter you will learn about simple random sampling and the sample selection process. In addition, you will learn how statistics such as the sample mean and sample proportion are used to estimate the population mean and population proportion. The important concept of a sampling distribution is also introduced.

In Chapter 1, we defined a *population* and a *sample.* The definitions are restated here.

1. A *population* is the set of all the elements of interest in a study.
2. A *sample* is a subset of the population.

Numerical characteristics of a population, such as the mean and standard deviation, are called **parameters**. A primary purpose of statistical inference is to develop estimates and test hypotheses about population parameters using information contained in a sample.

Let us begin by citing two situations in which samples provide estimates of population parameters.

1. A tire manufacturer developed a new tire designed to provide an increase in mileage over the firm's current line of tires. To estimate the mean number of miles provided by the new tires, the manufacturer selected a sample of 120 new tires for testing. The test results provided a sample mean of 36,500 miles. Hence, an estimate of the mean tire mileage for the population of new tires was 36,500 miles.
2. Members of a political party were considering supporting a particular candidate for election to the U.S. Senate, and party leaders wanted an estimate of the proportion of registered voters favoring the candidate. The time and cost associated with contacting every individual in the population of registered voters were prohibitive. Hence, a sample of 400 registered voters was selected and 160 of the 400 voters indicated a preference for the candidate. An estimate of the proportion of the population of registered voters favoring the candidate was 160/400 = .40.

These two examples illustrate some of the reasons why samples are used. Note that in the tire mileage example, collecting the data on tire life involves wearing out each tire tested. Clearly it is not feasible to test every tire in the population; a sample is the only realistic way to obtain the desired tire mileage data. In the example involving the election, contacting every registered voter in the population is theoretically possible, but the time and cost in doing so are prohibitive; thus, a sample of registered voters is preferred.

A sample mean provides an estimate of a population mean, and a sample proportion provides an estimate of a population proportion. With estimates such as these, some estimation error can be expected. This chapter provides the basis for determining how large that error might be.

It is important to realize that sample results provide only *estimates* of the values of the population characteristics. We do not expect the sample mean of 36,500 miles to exactly equal the mean mileage for all tires in the population, nor do we expect exactly .40, or 40%, of the population of registered voters to favor the candidate. The reason is simply that the sample contains only a portion of the population. With proper sampling methods, the sample results will provide "good" estimates of the population parameters. But how good can we expect the sample results to be? Fortunately, statistical procedures are available for answering this question.

In this chapter we show how simple random sampling can be used to select a sample from a population. We then show how data obtained from a simple random sample can be used to compute estimates of a population mean, a population standard deviation, and a population proportion. In addition, we introduce the important concept of a sampling distribution. As we show, knowledge of the appropriate sampling distribution is what enables us to make statements about how close the sample estimates are to the corresponding population parameters. The last section discusses some alternatives to simple random sampling that are often employed in practice.

7.1 The Electronics Associates Sampling Problem

The director of personnel for Electronics Associates, Inc. (EAI), has been assigned the task of developing a profile of the company's 2500 managers. The characteristics to be identified include the mean annual salary for the managers and the proportion of managers having completed the company's management training program.

CD file

EAI

Using the 2500 managers as the population for this study, we can find the annual salary and the training program status for each individual by referring to the firm's personnel records. The data file containing this information for all 2500 managers in the population is on the CD that accompanies the text.

Using the EAI data set and the formulas presented in Chapter 3, we compute the population mean and the population standard deviation for the annual salary data.

$$\text{Population mean:} \quad \mu = \$51,800$$
$$\text{Population standard deviation:} \quad \sigma = \$4000$$

The data for the training program status show that 1500 of the 2500 managers completed the training program. Letting p denote the proportion of the population that completed the training program, we see that $p = 1500/2500 = .60$. The population mean annual salary ($\mu = \$51,800$), the population standard deviation of annual salary ($\sigma = \$4000$), and the population proportion that completed the training program ($p = .60$) are parameters of the population of EAI managers.

Now, suppose that the necessary information on all the EAI managers was not readily available in the company's database. The question we now consider is how the firm's director of personnel can obtain estimates of the population parameters by using a sample of managers rather than all 2500 managers in the population. Suppose that a sample of 30 managers will be used. Clearly, the time and the cost of developing a profile would be substantially less for 30 managers than for the entire population. If the personnel director could be assured that a sample of 30 managers would provide adequate information about the population of 2500 managers, working with a sample would be preferable to working with the entire population. Let us explore the possibility of using a sample for the EAI study by first considering how we can identify a sample of 30 managers.

Often the cost of collecting information from a sample is substantially less than from a population, especially when personal interviews must be conducted to collect the information.

7.2   Simple Random Sampling

Several methods can be used to select a sample from a population; one of the most common is **simple random sampling**. The definition of a simple random sample and the process of selecting a simple random sample depend on whether the population is *finite* or *infinite*. Because the EAI sampling problem involves a finite population of 2500 managers, we first consider sampling from a finite population.

Sampling from a Finite Population

A simple random sample of size n from a finite population of size N is defined as follows.

> **SIMPLE RANDOM SAMPLE (FINITE POPULATION)**
>
> A simple random sample of size n from a finite population of size N is a sample selected such that each possible sample of size n has the same probability of being selected.

One procedure for selecting a simple random sample from a finite population is to choose the elements for the sample one at a time in such a way that, at each step, each of the elements remaining in the population has the same probability of being selected. Sampling n elements in this way will satisfy the definition of a simple random sample from a finite population.

Computer-generated random numbers can also be used to implement the random sample selection process. Excel provides a function for generating random numbers in its worksheets.

To select a simple random sample from the finite population of EAI managers, we first assign each manager a number. For example, we can assign the managers the numbers 1 to 2500 in the order that their names appear in the EAI personnel file. Next, we refer to the table of random numbers shown in Table 7.1. Using the first row of the table, each digit, 6, 3, 2, . . . , is a random digit having an equal chance of occurring. Because the largest number in the population list of EAI managers, 2500, has four digits, we will select random numbers from the table in sets or groups of four digits. Even though we may start the selection of random numbers anywhere in the table and move systematically in a direction of our choice, we will use the first row of Table 7.1 and move from left to right. The first 7 four-digit random numbers are

The random numbers in the table are shown in groups of five for readability.

6327   1599   8671   7445   1102   1514   1807

Because the numbers in the table are random, these four-digit numbers are equally likely.

TABLE 7.1   RANDOM NUMBERS

63271	59986	71744	51102	15141	80714	58683	93108	13554	79945
88547	09896	95436	79115	08303	01041	20030	63754	08459	28364
55957	57243	83865	09911	19761	66535	40102	26646	60147	15702
46276	87453	44790	67122	45573	84358	21625	16999	13385	22782
55363	07449	34835	15290	76616	67191	12777	21861	68689	03263
69393	92785	49902	58447	42048	30378	87618	26933	40640	16281
13186	29431	88190	04588	38733	81290	89541	70290	40113	08243
17726	28652	56836	78351	47327	18518	92222	55201	27340	10493
36520	64465	05550	30157	82242	29520	69753	72602	23756	54935
81628	36100	39254	56835	37636	02421	98063	89641	64953	99337
84649	48968	75215	75498	49539	74240	03466	49292	36401	45525
63291	11618	12613	75055	43915	26488	41116	64531	56827	30825
70502	53225	03655	05915	37140	57051	48393	91322	25653	06543
06426	24771	59935	49801	11082	66762	94477	02494	88215	27191
20711	55609	29430	70165	45406	78484	31639	52009	18873	96927
41990	70538	77191	25860	55204	73417	83920	69468	74972	38712
72452	36618	76298	26678	89334	33938	95567	29380	75906	91807
37042	40318	57099	10528	09925	89773	41335	96244	29002	46453
53766	52875	15987	46962	67342	77592	57651	95508	80033	69828
90585	58955	53122	16025	84299	53310	67380	84249	25348	04332
32001	96293	37203	64516	51530	37069	40261	61374	05815	06714
62606	64324	46354	72157	67248	20135	49804	09226	64419	29457
10078	28073	85389	50324	14500	15562	64165 ·	06125	71353	77669
91561	46145	24177	15294	10061	98124	75732	00815	83452	97355
13091	98112	53959	79607	52244	63303	10413	63839	74762	50289

We can now use these four-digit random numbers to give each manager in the population an equal chance of being included in the random sample. The first number, 6327, is greater than 2500. It does not correspond to one of the numbered managers in the population, and hence is discarded. The second number, 1599, is between 1 and 2500. Thus the first manager selected for the random sample is number 1599 on the list of EAI managers. Continuing this process, we ignore the numbers 8671 and 7445 before identifying managers number 1102, 1514, and 1807 to be included in the random sample. This process continues until the simple random sample of 30 EAI managers has been obtained.

In implementing this simple random sample selection process, it is possible that a random number used previously may appear again in the table before the sample of 30 EAI managers has been selected. Because we do not want to select a manager more than one time, any previously used random numbers are ignored because the corresponding manager is already included in the sample. Selecting a sample in this manner is referred to as **sampling without replacement**. If we selected a sample such that previously used random numbers are acceptable and specific managers could be included in the sample two or more times, we would be **sampling with replacement**. Sampling with replacement is a valid way of identifying a simple random sample. However, sampling without replacement is the sampling procedure used most often. When we refer to simple random sampling, we will assume that the sampling is without replacement.

Sampling from an Infinite Population

In practice, a population being studied is usually considered infinite if it involves an ongoing process that makes listing or counting every element in the population impossible.

In some situations, the population is either infinite or so large that for practical purposes it must be treated as infinite. For example, suppose that a fast-food restaurant would like to obtain a profile of its customers by selecting a simple random sample of customers and asking each customer to complete a short questionnaire. In such situations, the ongoing process of customer visits to the restaurant can be viewed as coming from an infinite population. The definition of a simple random sample from an infinite population follows.

SIMPLE RANDOM SAMPLE (INFINITE POPULATION)

A simple random sample from an infinite population is a sample selected such that the following conditions are satisfied.

1. Each element selected comes from the population.
2. Each element is selected independently.

For infinite populations, a sample selection procedure must be specially devised to select the items independently and thus avoid a selection bias that gives higher selection probabilities to certain types of elements.

For the example of selecting a simple random sample of customers at a fast-food restaurant, the first requirement is satisfied by any customer who comes into the restaurant. The second requirement is satisfied by selecting customers independently. The purpose of the second requirement is to prevent selection bias. Selection bias would occur if, for instance, five consecutive customers selected were all friends who arrived together. We might expect these customers to exhibit similar profiles. Selection bias can be avoided by ensuring that the selection of a particular customer does not influence the selection of any other customer. In other words, the customers must be selected independently.

McDonald's, the fast-food restaurant leader, implemented a simple random sampling procedure for just such a situation. The sampling procedure was based on the fact that some customers presented discount coupons. Whenever a customer presented a discount coupon, the next customer served was asked to complete a customer profile questionnaire. Because arriving customers presented discount coupons randomly, and independently, this sampling plan ensured that customers were selected independently. Thus, the two requirements for a simple random sample from an infinite population were satisfied.

Infinite populations are often associated with an ongoing process that operates continuously over time. For example, parts being manufactured on a production line, transactions occurring at a bank, telephone calls arriving at a technical support center, and customers entering stores may all be viewed as coming from an infinite population. In such cases, a creative sampling procedure ensures that no selection bias occurs and that the sample elements are selected independently.

NOTES AND COMMENTS

1. The number of different simple random samples of size n that can be selected from a finite population of size N is

$$\frac{N!}{n!(N-n)!}$$

In this formula, $N!$ and $n!$ are the factorial computations discussed in Chapter 4. For the EAI problem with $N = 2500$ and $n = 30$, this expression can be used to show that approximately 2.75×10^{69} different simple random samples of 30 EAI managers can be obtained.

2. Computer software packages can be used to select a random sample. In the chapter appendixes, we show how Minitab and Excel can be used to select a simple random sample from a finite population.

Exercises

Methods

1. Consider a finite population with five elements labeled A, B, C, D, and E. Ten possible simple random samples of size 2 can be selected.
   a. List the 10 samples beginning with AB, AC, and so on.
   b. Using simple random sampling, what is the probability that each sample of size 2 is selected?
   c. Assume the number 1 corresponds to A, the number 2 corresponds to B, and so on. List the simple random sample of size 2 that will be selected by using the random digits 8 0 5 7 5 3 2.

2. Assume a finite population has 350 elements. Using the last three digits of each of the five-digit random numbers below (601, 022, 448, . . .), determine the first four elements that will be selected for the simple random sample.

   98601   73022   83448   02147   34229   27553   84147   93289   14209

Applications

3. *Fortune* publishes data on sales, profits, assets, stockholders' equity, market value, and earnings per share for the 500 largest U.S. industrial corporations (*Fortune* 500, 2003). Assume that you want to select a simple random sample of 10 corporations from the *Fortune* 500 list. Use the last three digits in column 9 of Table 7.1, beginning with 554. Read down the column and identify the numbers of the 10 corporations that would be selected.

4. The 10 most active securities on the New York (NYSE), Nasdaq, and American (AMEX) exchanges with market caps greater than $500 million are as follows (*The Wall Street Journal,* February 21, 2003):

Applied Materials	Nasdaq 100
Cisco Systems	Nextel
Intel	Oracle
Lucent Technologies	SPDR
Microsoft	Sun Microsystems

   a. Assume that a random sample of five securities will be selected for an in-depth study of trading behavior. Beginning with the first random digit in Table 7.1 and reading down the column, use the single-digit random numbers to select a simple random sample of five securities to be used in this study.
   b. According to the Notes and Comments information, how many different simple random samples of size 5 can be selected from the list of 10 securities?

5. A student government organization is interested in estimating the proportion of students who favor a mandatory "pass-fail" grading policy for elective courses. A list of names and addresses of the 645 students enrolled during the current quarter is available from the registrar's office. Using three-digit random numbers in row 10 of Table 7.1 and moving across the row from left to right, identify the first 10 students who would be selected using simple random sampling. The three-digit random numbers begin with 816, 283, and 610.

6. The *County and City Data Book,* published by the Census Bureau, lists information on 3139 counties throughout the United States. Assume that a national study will collect data from 30 randomly selected counties. Use four-digit random numbers from the last column of Table 7.1 to identify the numbers corresponding to the first five counties selected for the sample. Ignore the first digits and begin with the four-digit random numbers 9945, 8364, 5702, and so on.

7. Assume that we want to identify a simple random sample of 12 of the 372 doctors practicing in a particular city. The doctors' names are available from a local medical organization. Use the eighth column of five-digit random numbers in Table 7.1 to identify the 12 doctors for the sample. Ignore the first two random digits in each five-digit grouping of the random numbers. This process begins with random number 108 and proceeds down the column of random numbers.

8. The following list provides the NCAA top 25 football teams for the 2002 season (*NCAA News*, January 4, 2003). Use the ninth column of the random numbers in Table 7.1, beginning with 13554, to select a simple random sample of six football teams. Begin with team 13 and use the first two digits in each row of the ninth column for your selection process. Which six football teams are selected for the simple random sample?

1. Ohio State	14. Virginia Tech
2. Miami	15. Penn State
3. Georgia	16. Auburn
4. Southern California	17. Notre Dame
5. Oklahoma	18. Pittsburgh
6. Kansas State	19. Marshall
7. Texas	20. West Virginia
8. Iowa	21. Colorado
9. Michigan	22. TCU
10. Washington State	23. Florida State
11. North Carolina State	24. Florida
12. Boise State	25. Virginia
13. Maryland	

9. *The Wall Street Journal* provides the net asset value, the year-to-date percent return, and the three-year percent return for 555 mutual funds (*The Wall Street Journal*, April 25, 2003). Assume that a simple random sample of 12 of the 555 mutual funds will be selected for a follow-up study on the size and performance of mutual funds. Use the fourth column of the random numbers in Table 7.1, beginning with 51102, to select the simple random sample of 12 mutual funds. Begin with mutual fund 102 and use the *last* three digits in each row of the fourth column for your selection process. What are the numbers of the 12 mutual funds in the simple random sample?

10. Indicate whether the following populations should be considered finite or infinite.
    a. All registered voters in the state of California.
    b. All television sets that could be produced by the Allentown, Pennsylvania, plant of the TV-M Company.
    c. All orders that could be processed by a mail-order firm.
    d. All emergency telephone calls that could come into a local police station.
    e. All components that Fibercon, Inc., produced on the second shift on May 17.

 # 7.3 Point Estimation

Now that we described how to select a simple random sample, let us return to the EAI problem. A simple random sample of 30 managers and the corresponding data on annual salary and management training program participation are as shown in Table 7.2. The notation x_1, x_2, and so on is used to denote the annual salary of the first manager in the sample, the annual salary of the second manager in the sample, and so on. Participation in the management training program is indicated by Yes in the management training program column.

To estimate the value of a population parameter, we compute a corresponding characteristic of the sample, referred to as a **sample statistic**. For example, to estimate the population mean μ and the population standard deviation σ for the annual salary of EAI

TABLE 7.2   ANNUAL SALARY AND TRAINING PROGRAM STATUS FOR A SIMPLE
RANDOM SAMPLE OF 30 EAI MANAGERS

Annual Salary (\$)	Management Training Program	Annual Salary (\$)	Management Training Program
$x_1 = 49{,}094.30$	Yes	$x_{16} = 51{,}766.00$	Yes
$x_2 = 53{,}263.90$	Yes	$x_{17} = 52{,}541.30$	No
$x_3 = 49{,}643.50$	Yes	$x_{18} = 44{,}980.00$	Yes
$x_4 = 49{,}894.90$	Yes	$x_{19} = 51{,}932.60$	Yes
$x_5 = 47{,}621.60$	No	$x_{20} = 52{,}973.00$	Yes
$x_6 = 55{,}924.00$	Yes	$x_{21} = 45{,}120.90$	Yes
$x_7 = 49{,}092.30$	Yes	$x_{22} = 51{,}753.00$	Yes
$x_8 = 51{,}404.40$	Yes	$x_{23} = 54{,}391.80$	No
$x_9 = 50{,}957.70$	Yes	$x_{24} = 50{,}164.20$	No
$x_{10} = 55{,}109.70$	Yes	$x_{25} = 52{,}973.60$	No
$x_{11} = 45{,}922.60$	Yes	$x_{26} = 50{,}241.30$	No
$x_{12} = 57{,}268.40$	No	$x_{27} = 52{,}793.90$	No
$x_{13} = 55{,}688.80$	Yes	$x_{28} = 50{,}979.40$	Yes
$x_{14} = 51{,}564.70$	No	$x_{29} = 55{,}860.90$	Yes
$x_{15} = 56{,}188.20$	No	$x_{30} = 57{,}309.10$	No

managers, we use the data in Table 7.2 to calculate the corresponding sample statistics: the sample mean $\bar{x}$ and the sample standard deviation s. Using the formulas for a sample mean and a sample standard deviation presented in Chapter 3, the sample mean is

$$\bar{x} = \frac{\Sigma x_i}{n} = \frac{1{,}554{,}420}{30} = \$51{,}814$$

and the sample standard deviation is

$$s = \sqrt{\frac{\Sigma(x_i - \bar{x})^2}{n - 1}} = \sqrt{\frac{325{,}009{,}260}{29}} = \$3348$$

To estimate p, the proportion of managers in the population who completed the management training program, we use the corresponding sample proportion $\bar{p}$. Let x denote the number of managers in the sample who completed the management training program. The data in Table 7.2 show that $x = 19$. Thus, with a sample size of $n = 30$, the sample proportion is

$$\bar{p} = \frac{x}{n} = \frac{19}{30} = .63$$

By making the preceding computations, we perform the statistical procedure called *point estimation*. We refer to the sample mean $\bar{x}$ as the **point estimator** of the population mean μ, the sample standard deviation s as the point estimator of the population standard deviation σ, and the sample proportion $\bar{p}$ as the point estimator of the population proportion p. The numerical value obtained for $\bar{x}$, s, or $\bar{p}$ is called the **point estimate**. Thus, for the simple random sample of 30 EAI managers shown in Table 7.2, \$51,814 is the point estimate of μ, \$3348 is the point estimate of σ, and .63 is the point estimate of p. Table 7.3 summarizes the sample results and compares the point estimates to the actual values of the population parameters.

TABLE 7.3   SUMMARY OF POINT ESTIMATES OBTAINED FROM A SIMPLE RANDOM SAMPLE OF 30 EAI MANAGERS

Population Parameter	Parameter Value	Point Estimator	Point Estimate
μ = Population mean annual salary	$51,800	$\bar{x}$ = Sample mean annual salary	$51,814
σ = Population standard deviation for annual salary	$4000	s = Sample standard deviation for annual salary	$3348
p = Population proportion having completed the management training program	.60	$\bar{p}$ = Sample proportion having completed the management training program	.63

As evident from Table 7.3, the point estimates differ somewhat from the corresponding population parameters. This difference is to be expected because a sample, and not a census of the entire population, is being used to develop the point estimates. In the next chapter, we will show how to construct an interval estimate in order to provide information about how close the point estimate is to the population parameter.

Exercises

Methods

11. The following data are from a simple random sample.

    5   8   10   7   10   14

    a. What is the point estimate of the population mean?
    b. What is the point estimate of the population standard deviation?

12. A survey question for a sample of 150 individuals yielded 75 Yes responses, 55 No responses, and 20 No Opinions.
    a. What is the point estimate of the proportion in the population who respond Yes?
    b. What is the point estimate of the proportion in the population who respond No?

Applications

13. A simple random sample of five months of sales data provided the following information:

Month	1	2	3	4	5
Units Sold	94	100	85	94	92

    a. Develop a point estimate of the population mean number of units sold per month.
    b. Develop a point estimate of the population standard deviation.

14. *Business Week* published information on 283 equity mutual funds (*Business Week*, January 26, 2004). A sample of 40 of those funds is contained in the data set MutualFund. Use the data set to answer the following questions.

    MutualFund
    a. Develop a point estimate of the proportion of the *Business Week* equity funds that are load funds.
    b. Develop a point estimate of the proportion of funds that are classified as high risk.
    c. Develop a point estimate of the proportion of funds that have a below-average risk rating.

15. *Appliance Magazine* provided estimates of the life expectancy of household appliances (*USA Today*, September 5, 2000). A simple random sample of 10 VCRs shows the following useful life in years.

    6.5   8.0   6.2   7.4   7.0   8.4   9.5   4.6   5.0   7.4

      a.   Develop a point estimate of the population mean life expectancy for VCRs.

      b.   Develop a point estimate of the population standard deviation for life expectancy of VCRs.

16.   A sample of 50 *Fortune* 500 companies (*Fortune,* April 14, 2003) showed 5 were based in New York, 6 in California, 2 in Minnesota, and 1 in Wisconsin.

      a.   Develop an estimate of the proportion of *Fortune* 500 companies based in New York.

      b.   Develop an estimate of the number of *Fortune* 500 companies based in Minnesota.

      c.   Develop an estimate of the proportion of *Fortune* 500 companies that are not based in these four states.

17.   A Louis Harris poll used a survey of 1008 adults to learn about how people feel about the economy (*Business Week,* August 7, 2000). Responses were as follows:

          595 adults   The economy is growing.
          332 adults   The economy is staying about the same.
           81 adults   The economy is shrinking.

    Develop a point estimate of the following population parameters.

      a.   The proportion of all adults who feel the economy is growing.

      b.   The proportion of all adults who feel the economy is staying about the same.

      c.   The proportion of all adults who feel the economy is shrinking.

7.4   Introduction to Sampling Distributions

In the preceding section we said that the sample mean $\bar{x}$ is the point estimator of the population mean μ, and the sample proportion $\bar{p}$ is the point estimator of the population proportion p. For the simple random sample of 30 EAI managers shown in Table 7.2, the point estimate of μ is $\bar{x} = \$51,814$ and the point estimate of p is $\bar{p} = .63$. Suppose we select another simple random sample of 30 EAI managers and obtain the following point estimates:

$$\text{Sample mean: } \bar{x} = \$52,670$$
$$\text{Sample proportion: } \bar{p} = .70$$

Note that different values of $\bar{x}$ and $\bar{p}$ were obtained. Indeed, a second simple random sample of 30 EAI managers cannot be expected to provide the same point estimates as the first sample.

    Now, suppose we repeat the process of selecting a simple random sample of 30 EAI managers over and over again, each time computing the values of $\bar{x}$ and $\bar{p}$. Table 7.4 contains a portion of the results obtained for 500 simple random samples, and Table 7.5 shows the frequency and relative frequency distributions for the 500 $\bar{x}$ values. Figure 7.1 shows the relative frequency histogram for the $\bar{x}$ values.

    In Chapter 5 we defined a random variable as a numerical description of the outcome of an experiment. If we consider the process of selecting a simple random sample as an experiment, the sample mean $\bar{x}$ is a numerical description of the outcome of the experiment. Thus, the sample mean $\bar{x}$ is a random variable. As a result, just like other random variables, $\bar{x}$ has a mean or expected value, a standard deviation, and a probability distribution. Because the various possible values of $\bar{x}$ are the result of different simple random samples, the probability distribution of $\bar{x}$ is called the **sampling distribution** of $\bar{x}$. Knowledge of this sampling distribution and its properties will enable us to make probability statements about how close the sample mean $\bar{x}$ is to the population mean μ.

TABLE 7.4   VALUES OF $\bar{x}$ AND $\bar{p}$ FROM 500 SIMPLE RANDOM SAMPLES OF 30 EAI MANAGERS

Sample Number	Sample Mean ($\bar{x}$)	Sample Proportion ($\bar{p}$)
1	51,814	.63
2	52,670	.70
3	51,780	.67
4	51,588	.53
.	.	.
.	.	.
.	.	.
500	51,752	.50

Let us return to Figure 7.1. We would need to enumerate every possible sample of 30 managers and compute each sample mean to completely determine the sampling distribution of $\bar{x}$. However, the histogram of 500 $\bar{x}$ values gives an approximation of this sampling distribution. From the approximation we observe the bell-shaped appearance of the distribution. We note that the largest concentration of the $\bar{x}$ values and the mean of the 500 $\bar{x}$ values are near the population mean $\mu = \$51,800$. We will describe the properties of the sampling distribution of $\bar{x}$ more fully in the next section.

The 500 values of the sample proportion $\bar{p}$ are summarized by the relative frequency histogram in Figure 7.2. As in the case of $\bar{x}$, $\bar{p}$ is a random variable. If every possible sample of size 30 were selected from the population and if a value of $\bar{p}$ were computed for each sample, the resulting probability distribution would be the sampling distribution of $\bar{p}$. The relative frequency histogram of the 500 sample values in Figure 7.2 provides a general idea of the appearance of the sampling distribution of $\bar{p}$.

In practice, we select only one simple random sample from the population. We repeated the sampling process 500 times in this section simply to illustrate that many different samples are possible and that the different samples generate a variety of values for the sample statistics $\bar{x}$ and $\bar{p}$. The probability distribution of any particular sample statistic is called the sampling distribution of the statistic. In Section 7.5 we show the characteristics of the sampling distribution of $\bar{x}$. In Section 7.6 we show the characteristics of the sampling distribution of $\bar{p}$.

TABLE 7.5   FREQUENCY DISTRIBUTION OF $\bar{x}$ FROM 500 SIMPLE RANDOM SAMPLES OF 30 EAI MANAGERS

Mean Annual Salary ($)	Frequency	Relative Frequency
49,500.00–49,999.99	2	.004
50,000.00–50,499.99	16	.032
50,500.00–50,999.99	52	.104
51,000.00–51,499.99	101	.202
51,500.00–51,999.99	133	.266
52,000.00–52,499.99	110	.220
52,500.00–52,999.99	54	.108
53,000.00–53,499.99	26	.052
53,500.00–53,999.99	6	.012
Totals 500		1.000

FIGURE 7.1   RELATIVE FREQUENCY HISTOGRAM OF $\bar{x}$ VALUES FROM 500 SIMPLE RANDOM SAMPLES OF SIZE 30 EACH

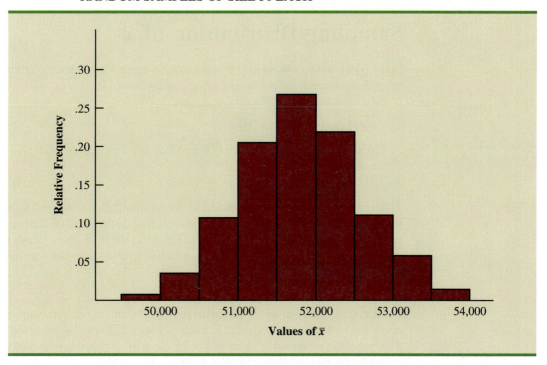

FIGURE 7.2   RELATIVE FREQUENCY HISTOGRAM OF $\bar{p}$ VALUES FROM 500 SIMPLE RANDOM SAMPLES OF SIZE 30 EACH

7.5 Sampling Distribution of $\bar{x}$

In the previous section we said that the sample mean $\bar{x}$ is a random variable and its probability distribution is called the sampling distribution of $\bar{x}$.

> **SAMPLING DISTRIBUTION OF $\bar{x}$**
>
> The sampling distribution of $\bar{x}$ is the probability distribution of all possible values of the sample mean $\bar{x}$.

This section describes the properties of the sampling distribution of $\bar{x}$. Just as with other probability distributions we studied, the sampling distribution of $\bar{x}$ has an expected value or mean, a standard deviation, and a characteristic shape or form. Let us begin by considering the mean of all possible $\bar{x}$ values, which is referred to as the expected value of $\bar{x}$.

Expected Value of $\bar{x}$

In the EAI sampling problem we saw that different simple random samples result in a variety of values for the sample mean $\bar{x}$. Because many different values of the random variable $\bar{x}$ are possible, we are often interested in the mean of all possible values of $\bar{x}$ that can be generated by the various simple random samples. The mean of the $\bar{x}$ random variable is the expected value of $\bar{x}$. Let $E(\bar{x})$ represent the expected value of $\bar{x}$ and μ represent the mean of the population from which we are selecting a simple random sample. It can be shown that with simple random sampling, $E(\bar{x})$ and μ are equal.

The expected value of $\bar{x}$ equals the mean of the population from which the sample is selected.

> **EXPECTED VALUE OF $\bar{x}$**
>
> $$E(\bar{x}) = \mu \qquad (7.1)$$
>
> where
>
> $$E(\bar{x}) = \text{the expected value of } \bar{x}$$
> $$\mu = \text{the population mean}$$

This result shows that with simple random sampling, the expected value or mean of the sampling distribution of $\bar{x}$ is equal to the mean of the population. In Section 7.1 we saw that the mean annual salary for the population of EAI managers is $\mu = \$51,800$. Thus, according to equation (7.1), the mean of all possible sample means for the EAI study is also $\$51,800$.

When the expected value of a point estimator equals the population parameter, we say the point estimator is **unbiased**. Thus, equation (7.1) shows that $\bar{x}$ is an unbiased estimator of the population mean μ.

Standard Deviation of $\bar{x}$

Let us define the standard deviation of the sampling distribution of $\bar{x}$. We will use the following notation.

$$\sigma_{\bar{x}} = \text{the standard deviation of } \bar{x}$$
$$\sigma = \text{the standard deviation of the population}$$
$$n = \text{the sample size}$$
$$N = \text{the population size}$$

It can be shown that with simple random sampling, the standard deviation of $\bar{x}$ depends on whether the population is finite or infinite. The two formulas for the standard deviation of $\bar{x}$ follow.

STANDARD DEVIATION OF $\bar{x}$

Finite Population	Infinite Population

$$\sigma_{\bar{x}} = \sqrt{\frac{N-n}{N-1}}\left(\frac{\sigma}{\sqrt{n}}\right) \qquad\qquad \sigma_{\bar{x}} = \frac{\sigma}{\sqrt{n}} \qquad \textbf{(7.2)}$$

In comparing the two formulas in (7.2), we see that the factor $\sqrt{(N-n)/(N-1)}$ is required for the finite population case but not for the infinite population case. This factor is commonly referred to as the **finite population correction factor**. In many practical sampling situations, we find that the population involved, although finite, is "large," whereas the sample size is relatively "small." In such cases the finite population correction factor $\sqrt{(N-n)/(N-1)}$ is close to 1. As a result, the difference between the values of the standard deviation of $\bar{x}$ for the finite and infinite population cases becomes negligible. Then, $\sigma_{\bar{x}} = \sigma/\sqrt{n}$ becomes a good approximation to the standard deviation of $\bar{x}$ even though the population is finite. This observation leads to the following general guideline, or rule of thumb, for computing the standard deviation of $\bar{x}$.

USE THE FOLLOWING EXPRESSION TO COMPUTE THE STANDARD DEVIATION OF $\bar{x}$

$$\sigma_{\bar{x}} = \frac{\sigma}{\sqrt{n}} \qquad\qquad \textbf{(7.3)}$$

whenever

1. The population is infinite; or
2. The population is finite *and* the sample size is less than or equal to 5% of the population size; that is, $n/N \leq .05$.

Problem 21 shows that when $n/N \leq .05$, the finite population correction factor has little effect on the value of $\sigma_{\bar{x}}$.

The term standard error *is used to refer to the standard deviation of a point estimator.*

In cases where $n/N > .05$, the finite population version of formula (7.2) should be used in the computation of $\sigma_{\bar{x}}$. Unless otherwise noted, throughout the text we will assume that the population size is "large," $n/N \leq .05$, and expression (7.3) can be used to compute $\sigma_{\bar{x}}$.

To compute $\sigma_{\bar{x}}$, we need to know σ, the standard deviation of the population. To further emphasize the difference between $\sigma_{\bar{x}}$ and σ, we refer to the standard deviation of $\bar{x}$, $\sigma_{\bar{x}}$ as the **standard error** of the mean. In general, the term *standard error* refers to the standard deviation of a point estimator. Later we will see that the value of the standard error of the mean is helpful in determining how far the sample mean may be from the population mean. Let us now return to the EAI example and compute the standard error of the mean associated with simple random samples of 30 EAI managers.

In Section 7.1 we saw that the standard deviation of annual salary for the population of 2500 EAI managers is $\sigma = 4000$. In this case, the population is finite, with $N = 2500$. However, with a sample size of 30, we have $n/N = 30/2500 = .012$. Because the sample size is less than 5% of the population size, we can ignore the finite population correction factor and use equation (7.3) to compute the standard error.

$$\sigma_{\bar{x}} = \frac{\sigma}{\sqrt{n}} = \frac{4000}{\sqrt{30}} = 730.3$$

Form of the Sampling Distribution of $\bar{x}$

The preceding results concerning the expected value and standard deviation for the sampling distribution of $\bar{x}$ are applicable for any population. The final step in identifying the characteristics of the sampling distribution of $\bar{x}$ is to determine the form or shape of the sampling distribution. We will consider two cases: (1) the population has a normal distribution; and (2) the population does not have a normal distribution.

Population has a normal distribution In many situations it is reasonable to assume that the population from which we are selecting a simple random sample has a normal, or nearly normal, distribution. When the population has a normal distribution, the sampling distribution of $\bar{x}$ is normally distributed for any sample size.

Population does not have a normal distribution When the population from which we are selecting a simple random sample does not have a normal distribution, the **central limit theorem** is helpful in identifying the shape of the sampling distribution of $\bar{x}$. A statement of the central limit theorem as it applies to the sampling distribution of $\bar{x}$ follows.

> **CENTRAL LIMIT THEOREM**
>
> In selecting simple random samples of size n from a population, the sampling distribution of the sample mean $\bar{x}$ can be approximated by a *normal distribution* as the sample size becomes large.

Figure 7.3 shows how the central limit theorem works for three different populations; each column refers to one of the populations. The top panel of the figure shows that none of the populations are normally distributed. Population I follows a uniform distribution. Population II is often called the rabbit-eared distribution. It is symmetric, but the more likely values fall in the tails of the distribution. Population III is shaped like the exponential distribution; it is skewed to the right.

The bottom three panels of Figure 7.3 show the shape of the sampling distribution for samples of size $n = 2$, $n = 5$, and $n = 30$. When the sample size is 2, we see that the shape of each sampling distribution is different from the shape of the corresponding population distribution. For samples of size 5, we see that the shape of the sampling distributions for populations I and II begin to look similar to the shape of a normal distribution. Even though the shape of the sampling distribution for population III begins to look similar to the shape of a normal distribution, some skewness to the right is still present. Finally, for samples of size 30, the shapes of each of the three sampling distributions are approximately normal.

From a practitioner standpoint, we often want to know how large the sample size needs to be before the central limit theorem applies and we can assume that the shape of the sampling distribution is approximately normal. Statistical researchers have investigated this question by studying the sampling distribution of $\bar{x}$ for a variety of populations and a variety of sample sizes. General statistical practice is to assume that, for most applications, the sampling distribution of $\bar{x}$ can be approximated by a normal distribution whenever the sample is size 30 or more. In cases where the population is highly skewed or outliers are present,

FIGURE 7.3   ILLUSTRATION OF THE CENTRAL LIMIT THEOREM
FOR THREE POPULATIONS

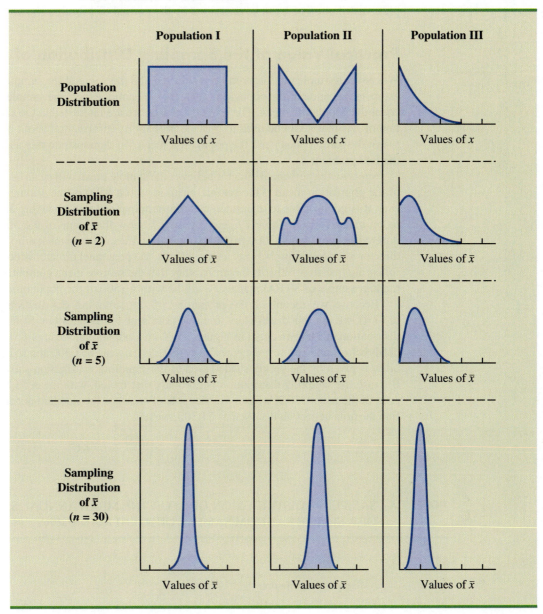

samples of size 50 may be needed. Finally, if the population is discrete, the sample size needed for a normal approximation often depends on the population proportion. We say more about this issue when we discuss the sampling distribution of $\bar{p}$ in Section 7.6.

Sampling Distribution of $\bar{x}$ for the EAI Problem

Let us return to the EAI problem where we previously showed that $E(\bar{x}) = \$51,800$ and $\sigma_{\bar{x}} = 730.3$. At this point, we do not have any information about the population distribution; it may or may not be normally distributed. If the population has a normal distribution, the sampling distribution of $\bar{x}$ is normally distributed. If the population does not have a normal distribution, the simple random sample of 30 managers and the central limit theorem enable us to conclude that the sampling distribution of $\bar{x}$ can be approximated by a normal distribution. In either case, we are comfortable proceeding with the conclusion that the sampling distribution of $\bar{x}$ can be described by the normal distribution shown in Figure 7.4.

Practical Value of the Sampling Distribution of $\bar{x}$

Whenever a simple random sample is selected and the value of the sample mean is used to estimate the value of the population mean μ, we cannot expect the sample mean to exactly equal the population mean. The practical reason we are interested in the sampling distribution of $\bar{x}$ is that it can be used to provide probability information about the difference between the sample mean and the population mean. To demonstrate this use, let us return to the EAI problem.

Suppose the personnel director believes the sample mean will be an acceptable estimate of the population mean if the sample mean is within $500 of the population mean. However, it is not possible to guarantee that the sample mean will be within $500 of the population mean. Indeed, Table 7.5 and Figure 7.1 show that some of the 500 sample means differed by more than $2000 from the population mean. So we must think of the personnel director's request in probability terms. That is, the personnel director is concerned with the following question: What is the probability that the sample mean computed using a simple random sample of 30 EAI managers will be within $500 of the population mean?

Because we identified the properties of the sampling distribution of $\bar{x}$ (see Figure 7.4), we use this distribution to answer the probability question. Refer to the sampling distribution of $\bar{x}$ shown again in Figure 7.5. With a population mean of $51,800, the personnel director wants to know the probability that $\bar{x}$ is between $51,300 and $52,300. This probability is given by the darkly shaded area of the sampling distribution shown in Figure 7.5. Because the sampling distribution is normally distributed, with mean 51,800 and standard error of the mean 730.3, we can use the table of areas for the standard normal distribution to find the area or probability. At $\bar{x} = 51,300$, we have

$$z = \frac{51,300 - 51,800}{730.3} = -.68$$

FIGURE 7.4   SAMPLING DISTRIBUTION OF $\bar{x}$ FOR THE MEAN ANNUAL SALARY OF A SIMPLE RANDOM SAMPLE OF 30 EAI MANAGERS

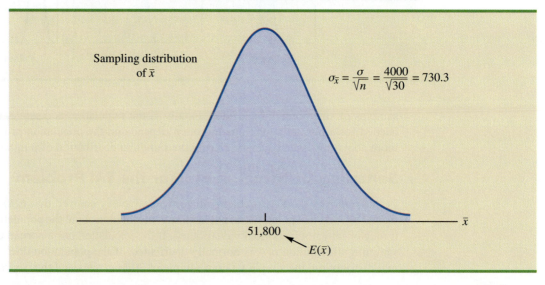

FIGURE 7.5   THE PROBABILITY OF A SAMPLE MEAN BEING WITHIN $500 OF THE POPULATION MEAN

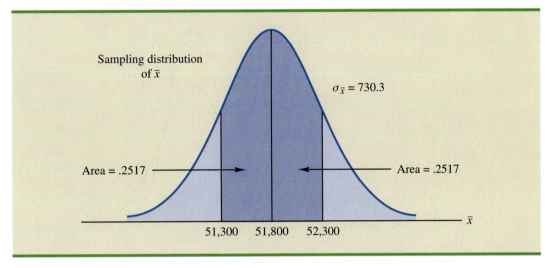

Referring to the standard normal distribution table, we find an area between $z = 0$ and $z = -.68$ of .2517. Similar calculations for $\bar{x} = 52,300$ show an area between $z = 0$ and $z = +.68$ of .2517. Thus, the probability of the value of the sample mean being between 51,300 and 52,300 is .2517 + .2517 = .5034.

The sampling distribution of $\bar{x}$ can be used to provide probability information about how close the sample mean $\bar{x}$ is to the population mean μ.

The preceding computations show that a simple random sample of 30 EAI managers has a .5034 probability of providing a sample mean $\bar{x}$ that is within $500 of the population mean. Thus, there is a $1 - .5034 = .4966$ probability that the difference between $\bar{x}$ and $\mu = \$51,800$ will be more than $500. In other words, a simple random sample of 30 EAI managers has roughly a 50-50 chance of providing a sample mean within the allowable $500. Perhaps a larger sample size should be considered. Let us explore this possibility by considering the relationship between the sample size and the sampling distribution of $\bar{x}$.

Relationship Between the Sample Size and the Sampling Distribution of $\bar{x}$

Suppose that in the EAI sampling problem we select a simple random sample of 100 EAI managers instead of the 30 originally considered. Intuitively, it would seem that with more data provided by the larger sample size, the sample mean based on $n = 100$ should provide a better estimate of the population mean than the sample mean based on $n = 30$. To see how much better, let us consider the relationship between the sample size and the sampling distribution of $\bar{x}$.

First note that $E(\bar{x}) = \mu$ regardless of the sample size. Thus, the mean of all possible values of $\bar{x}$ is equal to the population mean μ regardless of the sample size n. However, note that the standard error of the mean, $\sigma_{\bar{x}} = \sigma/\sqrt{n}$, is related to the square root of the sample size. Whenever the sample size is increased, the standard error of the mean $\sigma_{\bar{x}}$ decreases. With $n = 30$, the standard error of the mean for the EAI problem is 730.3. However, with the increase in the sample size to $n = 100$, the standard error of the mean is decreased to

$$\sigma_{\bar{x}} = \frac{\sigma}{\sqrt{n}} = \frac{4000}{\sqrt{100}} = 400$$

The sampling distributions of $\bar{x}$ with $n = 30$ and $n = 100$ are shown in Figure 7.6. Because the sampling distribution with $n = 100$ has a smaller standard error, the values of $\bar{x}$ have less variation and tend to be closer to the population mean than the values of $\bar{x}$ with $n = 30$.

FIGURE 7.6 A COMPARISON OF THE SAMPLING DISTRIBUTIONS OF $\bar{x}$ FOR SIMPLE RANDOM SAMPLES OF $n = 30$ AND $n = 100$ EAI MANAGERS

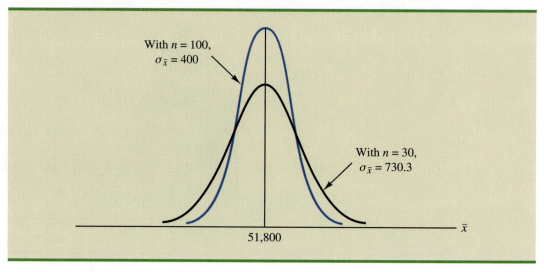

We can use the sampling distribution of $\bar{x}$ for the case with $n = 100$ to compute the probability that a simple random sample of 100 EAI managers will provide a sample mean that is within \$500 of the population mean. Because the sampling distribution is normal, with mean 51,800 and standard error of the mean 400, we can use the standard normal distribution table to find the area or probability. At $\bar{x} = 51,300$ (Figure 7.7), we have

$$z = \frac{51,300 - 51,800}{400} = -1.25$$

FIGURE 7.7 THE PROBABILITY OF A SAMPLE MEAN BEING WITHIN \$500 OF THE POPULATION MEAN WHEN A SIMPLE RANDOM SAMPLE OF 100 EAI MANAGERS IS USED

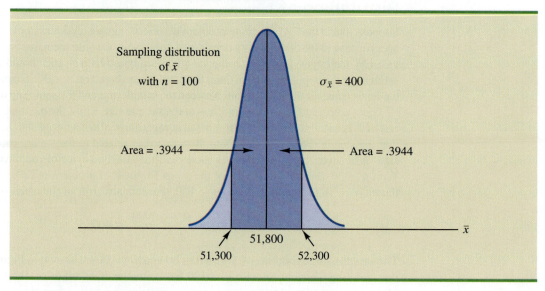

Referring to the standard normal probability distribution table, we find an area between $z = 0$ and $z = -1.25$ of .3944. With a similar calculation for $\bar{x} = 52,300$, we see that the probability of the value of the sample mean being between 51,300 and 52,300 is .3944 + .3944 = .7888. Thus, by increasing the sample size from 30 to 100 EAI managers, we have increased the probability of obtaining a sample mean within $500 of the population mean from .5034 to .7888.

The important point in this discussion is that as the sample size is increased, the standard error of the mean decreases. As a result, the larger sample size provides a higher probability that the sample mean is within a specified distance of the population mean.

NOTES AND COMMENTS

1. In presenting the sampling distribution of $\bar{x}$ for the EAI problem, we took advantage of the fact that the population mean $\mu = 51,800$ and the population standard deviation $\sigma = 4000$ were known. However, usually the values of the population mean μ and the population standard deviation σ that are needed to determine the sampling distribution of $\bar{x}$ will be unknown. In Chapter 8 we show how the sample mean $\bar{x}$ and the sample standard deviation s are used when μ and σ are unknown.

2. The theoretical proof of the central limit theorem requires independent observations in the sample. This condition is met for infinite populations and for finite populations where sampling is done with replacement. Although the central limit theorem does not directly address sampling without replacement from finite populations, general statistical practice applies the findings of the central limit theorem when the population size is large.

Exercises

Methods

18. A population has a mean of 200 and a standard deviation of 50. A simple random sample of size 100 will be taken and the sample mean $\bar{x}$ will be used to estimate the population mean.
    a. What is the expected value of $\bar{x}$?
    b. What is the standard deviation of $\bar{x}$?
    c. Show the sampling distribution of $\bar{x}$.
    d. What does the sampling distribution of $\bar{x}$ show?

19. A population has a mean of 200 and a standard deviation of 50. Suppose a simple random sample of size 100 is selected and $\bar{x}$ is used to estimate μ.
    a. What is the probability that the sample mean will be within ± 5 of the population mean?
    b. What is the probability that the sample mean will be within ± 10 of the population mean?

20. Assume the population standard deviation is $\sigma = 25$. Compute the standard error of the mean, $\sigma_{\bar{x}}$, for sample sizes of 50, 100, 150, and 200. What can you say about the size of the standard error of the mean as the sample size is increased?

21. Suppose a simple random sample of size 50 is selected from a population with $\sigma = 10$. Find the value of the standard error of the mean in each of the following cases (use the finite population correction factor if appropriate).
    a. The population size is infinite.
    b. The population size is $N = 50,000$.
    c. The population size is $N = 5000$.
    d. The population size is $N = 500$.

Applications

22. Refer to the EAI sampling problem. Suppose a simple random sample of 60 managers is used.
    a. Sketch the sampling distribution of $\bar{x}$ when simple random samples of size 60 are used.
    b. What happens to the sampling distribution of $\bar{x}$ if simple random samples of size 120 are used?
    c. What general statement can you make about what happens to the sampling distribution of $\bar{x}$ as the sample size is increased? Does this generalization seem logical? Explain.

23. In the EAI sampling problem (see Figure 7.5), we showed that for $n = 30$, there was .5034 probability of obtaining a sample mean within $\pm\$500$ of the population mean.
    a. What is the probability that $\bar{x}$ is within $500 of the population mean if a sample of size 60 is used?
    b. Answer part (a) for a sample of size 120.

24. The mean tuition cost at state universities throughout the United States is $4260 per year (*St. Petersburg Times,* December 11, 2002). Use this value as the population mean and assume that the population standard deviation is $\sigma = \$900$. Suppose that a random sample of 50 state universities will be selected.
    a. Show the sampling distribution of $\bar{x}$ where $\bar{x}$ is the sample mean tuition cost for the 50 state universities.
    b. What is the probability that the simple random sample will provide a sample mean within $250 of the population mean?
    c. What is the probability that the simple random sample will provide a sample mean within $100 of the population mean?

25. The College Board American College Testing Program reported a population mean SAT score of $\mu = 1020$ (*The World Almanac 2003*). Assume that the population standard deviation is $\sigma = 100$.
    a. What is the probability that a random sample of 75 students will provide a sample mean SAT score within 10 of the population mean?
    b. What is the probability a random sample of 75 students will provide a sample mean SAT score within 20 of the population mean?

26. The mean annual starting salary for marketing majors is $34,000 (*Time,* May 8, 2000). Assume that for the population of graduates with a marketing major, the mean annual starting salary is $\mu = 34{,}000$, and the standard deviation is $\sigma = 2000$.
    a. What is the probability that a simple random sample of marketing majors will have a sample mean within $\pm\$250$ of the population mean for each of the following sample sizes: 30, 50, 100, 200, and 400?
    b. What is the advantage of a larger sample size when attempting to estimate the population mean?

27. *Business Week* conducted a survey of graduates from 30 top MBA programs (*Business Week,* September 22, 2003). The survey found that the average annual salary for male and female graduates 10 years after graduation was $168,000 and $117,000, respectively. Assume the standard deviation for the male graduates is $40,000, and for the female graduates it is $25,000.
    a. What is the probability that a simple random sample of 40 male graduates will provide a sample mean within $10,000 of the population mean, $168,000?
    b. What is the probability that a simple random sample of 40 female graduates will provide a sample mean within $10,000 of the population mean, $117,000?
    c. In which of the preceding two cases, part (a) or part (b), do we have a higher probability of obtaining a sample estimate within $10,000 of the population mean? Why?
    d. What is the probability that a simple random sample of 100 male graduates will provide a sample mean more than $4000 below the population mean?

28. The average annual cost of automobile insurance is $687 (*National Association of Insurance Commissioners,* January 2003). Use this value as the population mean and assume that the population standard deviation is $\sigma = \$230$. Consider a sample of 45 automobile insurance policies.
    a. Show the sampling distribution of $\bar{x}$ where $\bar{x}$ is the sample mean annual cost of automobile insurance.
    b. What is the probability that the sample mean is within $100 of the population mean?
    c. What is the probability that the sample mean is within $25 of the population mean?
    d. What would you recommend if an insurance agency wanted the sample mean to estimate the population mean within $\pm\$25$?

29. *Money* magazine reported that the average price of a gallon of gasoline in the United States during the first quarter of 2001 was $1.46 (*Money,* August 2001). Assume the price reported by *Money* is the population mean, and the population standard deviation is $\sigma = \$.15$.
    a. What is the probability that the mean price for a sample of 30 gas stations is within $.03 of the population mean?
    b. What is the probability that the mean price for a sample of 50 gas stations is within $.03 of the population mean?
    c. What is the probability that the mean price for a sample 100 gas stations is within $.03 of the population mean?
    d. Would you recommend a sample size of 30, 50, or 100 to have at least a .95 probability that the sample mean is within $.03 of the population mean?

30. To estimate the mean age for a population of 4000 employees, a simple random sample of 40 employees is selected.
    a. Would you use the finite population correction factor in calculating the standard error of the mean? Explain.
    b. If the population standard deviation is $\sigma = 8.2$ years, compute the standard error both with and without the finite population correction factor. What is the rationale for ignoring the finite population correction factor whenever $n/N \leq .05$?
    c. What is the probability that the sample mean age of the employees will be within ± 2 years of the population mean age?

7.6 Sampling Distribution of $\bar{p}$

The sample proportion $\bar{p}$ is the point estimator of the population proportion p. The formula for computing the sample proportion is

$$\bar{p} = \frac{x}{n}$$

where

$x =$ the number of elements in the sample that possess the characteristic of interest
$n =$ sample size

As noted in Section 7.4, the sample proportion $\bar{p}$ is a random variable and its probability distribution is called the sampling distribution of $\bar{p}$.

> **SAMPLING DISTRIBUTION OF $\bar{p}$**
>
> The sampling distribution of $\bar{p}$ is the probability distribution of all possible values of the sample proportion $\bar{p}$.

To determine how close the sample proportion $\bar{p}$ is to the population proportion p, we need to understand the properties of the sampling distribution of $\bar{p}$: the expected value of $\bar{p}$, the standard deviation of $\bar{p}$, and the shape or form of the sampling distribution of $\bar{p}$.

Expected Value of $\bar{p}$

The expected value of $\bar{p}$, the mean of all possible values of $\bar{p}$, is equal to the population proportion p.

EXPECTED VALUE OF $\bar{p}$

$$E(\bar{p}) = p \qquad (7.4)$$

where

$$E(\bar{p}) = \text{the expected value of } \bar{p}$$
$$p = \text{the population proportion}$$

Because $E(\bar{p}) = p$, $\bar{p}$ is an unbiased estimator of p. Recall from Section 7.1 we noted that $p = .60$ for the EAI population, where p is the proportion of the population of managers who participated in the company's management training program. Thus, the expected value of $\bar{p}$ for the EAI sampling problem is .60.

Standard Deviation of $\bar{p}$

Just as we found for the standard deviation of $\bar{x}$, the standard deviation of $\bar{p}$ depends on whether the population is finite or infinite. The two formulas for computing the standard deviation of $\bar{p}$ follow.

STANDARD DEVIATION OF $\bar{p}$

Finite Population	Infinite Population
$\sigma_{\bar{p}} = \sqrt{\dfrac{N-n}{N-1}} \sqrt{\dfrac{p(1-p)}{n}}$	$\sigma_{\bar{p}} = \sqrt{\dfrac{p(1-p)}{n}}$ **(7.5)**

Comparing the two formulas in (7.5), we see that the only difference is the use of the finite population correction factor $\sqrt{(N-n)/(N-1)}$.

As was the case with the sample mean $\bar{x}$, the difference between the expressions for the finite population and the infinite population becomes negligible if the size of the finite population is large in comparison to the sample size. We follow the same rule of thumb that we recommended for the sample mean. That is, if the population is finite with $n/N \leq .05$, we will use $\sigma_{\bar{p}} = \sqrt{p(1-p)/n}$. However, if the population is finite with $n/N > .05$, the finite population correction factor should be used. Again, unless specifically noted, throughout the text we will assume that the population size is large in relation to the sample size and thus the finite population correction factor is unnecessary.

In Section 7.5 we used standard error of the mean to refer to the standard deviation of $\bar{x}$. We stated that in general the term *standard error* refers to the standard deviation of a point estimator. Thus, for proportions we use *standard error of the proportion* to refer to the standard deviation of $\bar{p}$. Let us now return to the EAI example and compute the standard error of the proportion associated with simple random samples of 30 EAI managers.

For the EAI study we know that the population proportion of managers who participated in the management training program is $p = .60$. With $n/N = 30/2500 = .012$, we can ignore the finite population correction factor when we compute the standard error of the proportion. For the simple random sample of 30 managers, $\sigma_{\bar{p}}$ is

$$\sigma_{\bar{p}} = \sqrt{\frac{p(1-p)}{n}} = \sqrt{\frac{.60(1-.60)}{30}} = .0894$$

Form of the Sampling Distribution of $\bar{p}$

Now that we know the mean and standard deviation of the sampling distribution of $\bar{p}$, the final step is to determine the form or shape of the sampling distribution. The sample proportion is $\bar{p} = x/n$. For a simple random sample from a large population, the value of x is a binomial random variable indicating the number of elements in the sample with the characteristic of interest. Because n is a constant, the probability of x/n is the same as the binomial probability of x, which means that the sampling distribution of $\bar{p}$ is also a discrete probability distribution and that the probability for each value of x/n is the same as the binomial probability of x.

In Chapter 6 we also showed that a binomial distribution can be approximated by a normal distribution whenever the sample size is large enough to satisfy the following two conditions:

$$np \geq 5 \quad \text{and} \quad n(1-p) \geq 5$$

Assuming these two conditions are satisfied, the probability distribution of x, the number of elements in the sample with the characteristic of interest, can be approximated by a normal distribution. And because n is a constant, the sampling distribution of $\bar{p} = x/n$ can also be approximated by a normal distribution. This approximation is stated as follows:

> The sampling distribution of $\bar{p}$ can be approximated by a normal distribution whenever $np \geq 5$ and $n(1-p) \geq 5$.

In practical applications, when an estimate of a population proportion is desired, we find that sample sizes are almost always large enough to permit the use of a normal approximation for the sampling distribution of $\bar{p}$.

Recall that for the EAI sampling problem we know that the population proportion of managers who participated in the training program is $p = .60$. With a simple random sample of size 30, we have $np = 30(.60) = 18$ and $n(1-p) = 30(.40) = 12$. Thus, the sampling distribution of $\bar{p}$ can be approximated by the normal distribution shown in Figure 7.8.

Practical Value of the Sampling Distribution of $\bar{p}$

The practical value of the sampling distribution of $\bar{p}$ is that it can be used to provide probability information about the difference between the sample proportion and the population proportion. For instance, suppose that in the EAI problem the personnel director wants to know the probability of obtaining a value of $\bar{p}$ that is within .05 of the population proportion of EAI managers who participated in the training program. That is, what is the probability of obtaining a sample with a sample proportion $\bar{p}$ between .55 and .65? The darkly shaded area in Figure 7.9 shows this probability. Using the fact that the sampling distribution of $\bar{p}$ can be approximated by a normal distribution with a mean of .60 and a standard error of the proportion of $\sigma_{\bar{p}} = .0894$, we find that the standard normal random variable corresponding to $\bar{p} = .55$ has a value of $z = (.55 - .60)/.0894 = -.56$. Referring to the

FIGURE 7.8 SAMPLING DISTRIBUTION OF $\bar{p}$ FOR THE PROPORTION OF EAI MANAGERS WHO PARTICIPATED IN THE MANAGEMENT TRAINING PROGRAM

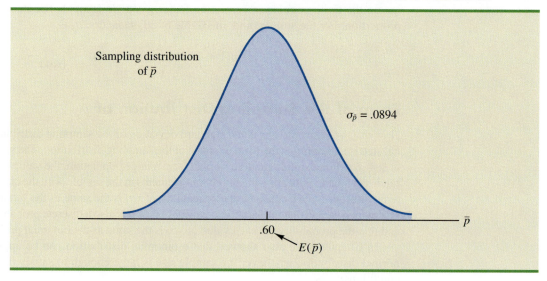

standard normal distribution table, we see that the area between $z = -.56$ and $z = 0$ is .2123. Similarly, at $\bar{p} = .65$ we find an area between $z = 0$ and $z = .56$ of .2123. Thus, the probability of selecting a sample that provides a sample proportion $\bar{p}$ within .05 of the population proportion p is $.2123 + .2123 = .4246$.

If we consider increasing the sample size to $n = 100$, the standard error of the proportion becomes

$$\sigma_{\bar{p}} = \sqrt{\frac{.60(1 - .60)}{100}} = .049$$

With a sample size of 100 EAI managers, the probability of the sample proportion having a value within .05 of the population proportion can now be computed. Because the sam-

FIGURE 7.9 PROBABILITY OF OBTAINING $\bar{p}$ BETWEEN .55 AND .65

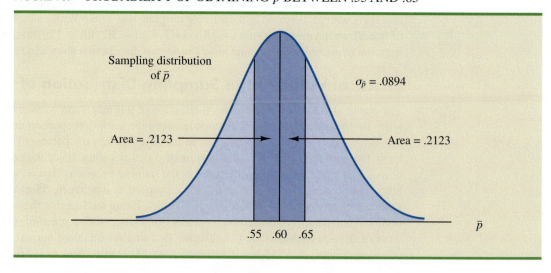

pling distribution is approximately normal, with mean .60 and standard error .049, we can use the standard normal distribution table to find the area or probability. At $\bar{p} = .55$, we have $z = (.55 - .60)/.049 = -1.02$. Referring to the standard normal distribution table, we see that the area between $z = -1.02$ and $z = 0$ is .3461. Similarly, at .65 the area between $z = 0$ and $z = 1.02$ is .3461. Thus, if the sample size is increased from 30 to 100, the probability that the sample proportion $\bar{p}$ is within .05 of the population proportion p will increase to $.3461 + .3461 = .6922$.

Exercises

Methods

31. A simple random sample of size 100 is selected from a population with $p = .40$.
   a. What is the expected value of $\bar{p}$?
   b. What is the standard error of $\bar{p}$?
   c. Show the sampling distribution of $\bar{p}$.
   d. What does the sampling distribution of $\bar{p}$ show?

32. A population proportion is .40. A simple random sample of size 200 will be taken and the sample proportion $\bar{p}$ will be used to estimate the population proportion.
   a. What is the probability that the sample proportion will be within $\pm.03$ of the population proportion?
   b. What is the probability that the sample proportion will be within $\pm.05$ of the population proportion?

33. Assume that the population proportion is .55. Compute the standard error of the proportion, $\sigma_{\bar{p}}$, for sample sizes of 100, 200, 500, and 1000. What can you say about the size of the standard error of the proportion as the sample size is increased?

34. The population proportion is .30. What is the probability that a sample proportion will be within $\pm.04$ of the population proportion for each of the following sample sizes?
   a. $n = 100$
   b. $n = 200$
   c. $n = 500$
   d. $n = 1000$
   e. What is the advantage of a larger sample size?

Applications

35. The president of Doerman Distributors, Inc., believes that 30% of the firm's orders come from first-time customers. A simple random sample of 100 orders will be used to estimate the proportion of first-time customers.
   a. Assume that the president is correct and $p = .30$. What is the sampling distribution of $\bar{p}$ for this study?
   b. What is the probability that the sample proportion $\bar{p}$ will be between .20 and .40?
   c. What is the probability that the sample proportion will be between .25 and .35?

36. *Business Week* reported that 56% of the households in the United States have Internet access (*Business Week,* May 21, 2001). Use a population proportion $p = .56$ and assume that a sample of 300 households will be selected.
   a. Show the sampling distribution of $\bar{p}$ where $\bar{p}$ is the sample proportion of households that have Internet access.
   b. What is the probability that the sample proportion will be within $\pm.03$ of the population proportion?
   c. Answer part (b) for sample sizes of 600 and 1000.

37. *Time*/CNN voter polls monitored public opinion for the presidential candidates during the 2000 presidential election campaign. One *Time*/CNN poll conducted by Yankelovich Partners, Inc., used a sample of 589 likely voters (*Time*, June 26, 2000). Assume the population proportion for a presidential candidate is $p = .50$. Let $\bar{p}$ be the sample proportion of likely voters favoring the presidential candidate.
   a. Show the sampling distribution of $\bar{p}$.
   b. What is the probability the *Time*/CNN poll will provide a sample proportion within $\pm.04$ of the population proportion?
   c. What is the probability the *Time*/CNN poll will provide a sample proportion within $\pm.03$ of the population proportion?
   d. What is the probability the *Time*/CNN poll will provide a sample proportion within $\pm.02$ of the population proportion?

38. Roper ASW conducted a survey to learn about American adults' attitudes toward money and happiness (*Money*, October 2003). Fifty-six percent of the respondents said they balance their checkbook at least once a month.
   a. Suppose a sample of 400 American adults were taken. Show the sampling distribution of the proportion of adults who balance their checkbook at least once a month.
   b. What is the probability that the sample proportion will be within $\pm.02$ of the population proportion?
   c. What is the probability that the sample proportion will be within $\pm.04$ of the population proportion?

39. The *Democrat and Chronicle* reported that 25% of the flights arriving at the San Diego airport during the first five months of 2001 were late (*Democrat and Chronicle*, July 23, 2001). Assume the population proportion is $p = .25$.
   a. Show the sampling distribution of $\bar{p}$, the proportion of late flights in a sample of 1000 flights.
   b. What is the probability that the sample proportion will be within $\pm.03$ of the population proportion if a sample of size 1000 is selected?
   c. Answer part (b) for a sample of 500 flights.

40. The Grocery Manufacturers of America reported that 76% of consumers read the ingredients listed on a product's label. Assume the population proportion is $p = .76$ and a sample of 400 consumers is selected from the population.
   a. Show the sampling distribution of the sample proportion $\bar{p}$ where $\bar{p}$ is the proportion of the sampled consumers who read the ingredients listed on a product's label.
   b. What is the probability that the sample proportion will be within $\pm.03$ of the population proportion?
   c. Answer part (b) for a sample of 750 consumers.

41. The Food Marketing Institute shows that 17% of households spend more than $100 per week on groceries. Assume the population proportion is $p = .17$ and a simple random sample of 800 households will be selected from the population.
   a. Show the sampling distribution of $\bar{p}$, the sample proportion of households spending more than $100 per week on groceries.
   b. What is the probability that the sample proportion will be within $\pm.02$ of the population proportion?
   c. Answer part (b) for a sample of 1600 households.

7.7 Sampling Methods

We described the simple random sampling procedure and discussed the properties of the sampling distributions of $\bar{x}$ and $\bar{p}$ when simple random sampling is used. However, simple random sampling is not the only sampling method available. Such methods as stratified ran-

FIGURE 7.10   DIAGRAM FOR STRATIFIED RANDOM SAMPLING

This section provides a brief introduction to sampling methods other than simple random sampling.

dom sampling, cluster sampling, and systematic sampling provide advantages over simple random sampling in some situations. In this section we briefly introduce these alternative sampling methods.

Stratified Random Sampling

In **stratified random sampling**, the elements in the population are first divided into groups called *strata,* such that each element in the population belongs to one and only one stratum. The basis for forming the strata, such as department, location, age, industry type, and so on, is at the discretion of the designer of the sample. However, the best results are obtained when the elements within each stratum are as much alike as possible. Figure 7.10 is a diagram of a population divided into *H* strata.

Stratified random sampling works best when the variance among elements in each stratum is relatively small.

After the strata are formed, a simple random sample is taken from each stratum. Formulas are available for combining the results for the individual stratum samples into one estimate of the population parameter of interest. The value of stratified random sampling depends on how homogeneous the elements are within the strata. If elements within strata are alike, the strata will have low variances. Thus relatively small sample sizes can be used to obtain good estimates of the strata characteristics. If strata are homogeneous, the stratified random sampling procedure provides results just as precise as those of simple random sampling by using a smaller total sample size.

Cluster Sampling

Cluster sampling works best when each cluster provides a small-scale representation of the population.

In **cluster sampling**, the elements in the population are first divided into separate groups called *clusters.* Each element of the population belongs to one and only one cluster (see Figure 7.11). A simple random sample of the clusters is then taken. All elements within each sampled cluster

FIGURE 7.11   DIAGRAM FOR CLUSTER SAMPLING

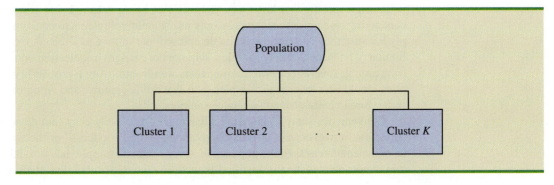

form the sample. Cluster sampling tends to provide the best results when the elements within the clusters are not alike. In the ideal case, each cluster is a representative small-scale version of the entire population. The value of cluster sampling depends on how representative each cluster is of the entire population. If all clusters are alike in this regard, sampling a small number of clusters will provide good estimates of the population parameters.

One of the primary applications of cluster sampling is area sampling, where clusters are city blocks or other well-defined areas. Cluster sampling generally requires a larger total sample size than either simple random sampling or stratified random sampling. However, it can result in cost savings because of the fact that when an interviewer is sent to a sampled cluster (e.g., a city-block location), many sample observations can be obtained in a relatively short time. Hence, a larger sample size may be obtainable with a significantly lower total cost.

Systematic Sampling

In some sampling situations, especially those with large populations, it is time-consuming to select a simple random sample by first finding a random number and then counting or searching through the list of the population until the corresponding element is found. An alternative to simple random sampling is **systematic sampling**. For example, if a sample size of 50 is desired from a population containing 5000 elements, we will sample one element for every 5000/50 = 100 elements in the population. A systematic sample for this case involves selecting randomly one of the first 100 elements from the population list. Other sample elements are identified by starting with the first sampled element and then selecting every 100th element that follows in the population list. In effect, the sample of 50 is identified by moving systematically through the population and identifying every 100th element after the first randomly selected element. The sample of 50 usually will be easier to identify in this way than it would be if simple random sampling were used. Because the first element selected is a random choice, a systematic sample is usually assumed to have the properties of a simple random sample. This assumption is especially applicable when the list of elements in the population is a random ordering of the elements.

Convenience Sampling

The sampling methods discussed thus far are referred to as *probability sampling* techniques. Elements selected from the population have a known probability of being included in the sample. The advantage of probability sampling is that the sampling distribution of the appropriate sample statistic generally can be identified. Formulas such as the ones for simple random sampling presented in this chapter can be used to determine the properties of the sampling distribution. Then the sampling distribution can be used to make probability statements about the error associated with the sample results.

Convenience sampling is a *nonprobability sampling* technique. As the name implies, the sample is identified primarily by convenience. Elements are included in the sample without prespecified or known probabilities of being selected. For example, a professor conducting research at a university may use student volunteers to constitute a sample simply because they are readily available and will participate as subjects for little or no cost. Similarly, an inspector may sample a shipment of oranges by selecting oranges haphazardly from among several crates. Labeling each orange and using a probability method of sampling would be impractical. Samples such as wildlife captures and volunteer panels for consumer research are also convenience samples.

Convenience samples have the advantage of relatively easy sample selection and data collection; however, it is impossible to evaluate the "goodness" of the sample in terms of its representativeness of the population. A convenience sample may provide good results or it may not; no statistically justified procedure allows a probability analysis and inference about the quality of the sample results. Sometimes researchers apply statistical methods designed for probability samples to a convenience sample, arguing that the convenience sample can be treated as though it were a probability sample. However, this argument cannot be supported, and we should be cautious in interpreting the results of convenience samples that are used to make inferences about populations.

Judgment Sampling

One additional nonprobability sampling technique is **judgment sampling**. In this approach, the person most knowledgeable on the subject of the study selects elements of the population that he or she feels are most representative of the population. Often this method is a relatively easy way of selecting a sample. For example, a reporter may sample two or three senators, judging that those senators reflect the general opinion of all senators. However, the quality of the sample results depends on the judgment of the person selecting the sample. Again, great caution is warranted in drawing conclusions based on judgment samples used to make inferences about populations.

NOTES AND COMMENTS

We recommend using probability sampling methods: simple random sampling, stratified random sampling, cluster sampling, or systematic sampling. For these methods, formulas are available for evaluating the "goodness" of the sample results in terms of the closeness of the results to the popula-tion parameters being estimated. An evaluation of the goodness cannot be made with convenience or judgment sampling. Thus, great care should be used in interpreting the results based on nonproba-bility sampling methods.

Summary

In this chapter we presented the concepts of simple random sampling and sampling distributions. We demonstrated how a simple random sample can be selected and how the data collected for the sample can be used to develop point estimates of population parameters. Because different simple random samples provide different values for the point estimators, point estimators such as $\bar{x}$ and $\bar{p}$ are random variables. The probability distribution of such a random variable is called a sampling distribution. In particular, we described the sampling distributions of the sample mean $\bar{x}$ and the sample proportion $\bar{p}$.

In considering the characteristics of the sampling distributions of $\bar{x}$ and $\bar{p}$, we stated that $E(\bar{x}) = \mu$ and $E(\bar{p}) = p$. After developing the standard deviation or standard error formu-las for these estimators, we described the conditions necessary for the sampling distribu-tions of $\bar{x}$ and $\bar{p}$ to follow a normal distribution. Other sampling methods including stratified random sampling, cluster sampling, systematic sampling, convenience sampling, and judg-ment sampling were discussed.

Glossary

Parameter A numerical characteristic of a population, such as a population mean μ, a popu-lation standard deviation σ, a population proportion p, and so on.
Simple random sampling Finite population: a sample selected such that each possible sample of size n has the same probability of being selected. Infinite population: a sample

selected such that each element comes from the same population and the elements are selected independently.

Sampling without replacement Once an element has been included in the sample, it is removed from the population and cannot be selected a second time.

Sampling with replacement Once an element has been included in the sample, it is returned to the population. A previously selected element can be selected again and therefore may appear in the sample more than once.

Sample statistic A sample characteristic, such as a sample mean $\bar{x}$, a sample standard deviation s, a sample proportion $\bar{p}$, and so on. The value of the sample statistic is used to estimate the value of the corresponding population parameter.

Point estimator The sample statistic, such as $\bar{x}$, s, or $\bar{p}$, that provides the point estimate of the population parameter.

Point estimate The value of a point estimator used in a particular instance as an estimate of a population parameter.

Sampling distribution A probability distribution consisting of all possible values of a sample statistic.

Unbiased A property of a point estimator that is present when the expected value of the point estimator is equal to the population parameter it estimates.

Finite population correction factor The term $\sqrt{(N - n)/(N - 1)}$ that is used in the formulas for $\sigma_{\bar{x}}$ and $\sigma_{\bar{p}}$ whenever a finite population, rather than an infinite population, is being sampled. The generally accepted rule of thumb is to ignore the finite population correction factor whenever $n/N \leq .05$.

Standard error The standard deviation of a point estimator.

Central limit theorem A theorem that enables one to use the normal probability distribution to approximate the sampling distribution of $\bar{x}$ whenever the sample size is large.

Stratified random sampling A probability sampling method in which the population is first divided into strata and a simple random sample is then taken from each stratum.

Cluster sampling A probability sampling method in which the population is first divided into clusters and then a simple random sample of the clusters is taken.

Systematic sampling A probability sampling method in which we randomly select one of the first k elements and then select every kth element thereafter.

Convenience sampling A nonprobability method of sampling whereby elements are selected for the sample on the basis of convenience.

Judgment sampling A nonprobability method of sampling whereby elements are selected for the sample based on the judgment of the person doing the study.

Key Formulas

Expected Value of $\bar{x}$

$$E(\bar{x}) = \mu \tag{7.1}$$

Standard Deviation of $\bar{x}$ (Standard Error)

Finite Population *Infinite Population*

$$\sigma_{\bar{x}} = \sqrt{\frac{N - n}{N - 1}} \left(\frac{\sigma}{\sqrt{n}}\right) \qquad \sigma_{\bar{x}} = \frac{\sigma}{\sqrt{n}} \tag{7.2}$$

Expected Value of $\bar{p}$

$$E(\bar{p}) = p \tag{7.4}$$

Standard Deviation of $\bar{p}$ (Standard Error)

Finite Population   *Infinite Population*

$$\sigma_{\bar{p}} = \sqrt{\frac{N-n}{N-1}} \sqrt{\frac{p(1-p)}{n}} \qquad \sigma_{\bar{p}} = \sqrt{\frac{p(1-p)}{n}} \qquad \textbf{(7.5)}$$

Supplementary Exercises

42. *Business Week*'s Corporate Scoreboard provides quarterly data on sales, profits, net income, return on equity, price/earnings ratio, and earnings per share for 899 companies (*Business Week,* August 14, 2000). The companies can be numbered 1 to 899 in the order they appear on the Corporate Scoreboard list. Begin at the bottom of the second column of random digits in Table 7.1. Ignoring the first two digits in each group and using three-digit random numbers beginning with 112, read *up* the column to identify the number (from 1 to 899) of the first eight companies to be included in a simple random sample.

43. Americans have become increasingly concerned about the rising cost of Medicare. In 1990, the average annual Medicare spending per enrollee was $3267; in 2003, the average annual Medicare spending per enrollee was $6883 (*Money,* Fall 2003). Suppose you hired a consulting firm to take a sample of fifty 2003 Medicare enrollees to further investigate the nature of expenditures. Assume the population standard deviation for 2003 was $2000.
    a. Show the sampling distribution of the mean amount of Medicare spending for a sample of fifty 2003 enrollees.
    b. What is the probability the sample mean will be within ±$300 of the population mean?
    c. What is the probability the sample mean will be greater than $7500? If the consulting firm tells you the sample mean for the Medicare enrollees they interviewed was $7500, would you question whether they followed correct simple random sampling procedures? Why or why not?

44. *Business Week* surveyed MBA alumni 10 years after graduation (*Business Week,* September 22, 2003). One finding was that alumni spend an average of $115.50 per week eating out socially. You have been asked to conduct a follow-up study by taking a sample of 40 of these MBA alumni. Assume the population standard deviation is $35.
    a. Show the sampling distribution of $\bar{x}$, the sample mean weekly expenditure for the 40 MBA alumni.
    b. What is the probability the sample mean will be within $10 of the population mean?
    c. Suppose you find a sample mean of $100. What is the probability of finding a sample mean of $100 or less? Would you consider this sample to be an unusually low spending group of alumni? Why or why not?

45. The mean television viewing time for Americans is 15 hours per week (*Money,* November 2003). Suppose a sample of 60 Americans is taken to further investigate viewing habits. Assume the population standard deviation for weekly viewing time is $\sigma = 4$ hours.
    a. What is the probability the sample mean will be within 1 hour of the population mean?
    b. What is the probability the sample mean will be within 45 minutes of the population mean?

46. The average annual salary for federal government employees in Indiana is $41,979 (*The World Almanac 2001*). Use this figure as the population mean and assume the population standard deviation is $\sigma = $5000. Suppose that a random sample of 50 federal government employees will be selected from the population.
    a. What is the value of the standard error of the mean?
    b. What is the probability that the sample mean will be more than $41,979?

c. What is the probability the sample mean will be within $1000 of the population mean?

d. How would the probability in part (c) change if the sample size were increased to 100?

47. Three firms carry inventories that differ in size. Firm A's inventory contains 2000 items, firm B's inventory contains 5000 items, and firm C's inventory contains 10,000 items. The population standard deviation for the cost of the items in each firm's inventory is $\sigma = 144$. A statistical consultant recommends that each firm take a sample of 50 items from its inventory to provide statistically valid estimates of the average cost per item. Managers of the small firm state that because it has the smallest population, it should be able to make the estimate from a much smaller sample than that required by the larger firms. However, the consultant states that to obtain the same standard error and thus the same precision in the sample results, all firms should use the same sample size regardless of population size.

a. Using the finite population correction factor, compute the standard error for each of the three firms given a sample of size 50.

b. What is the probability that for each firm the sample mean $\bar{x}$ will be within ± 25 of the population mean μ?

48. A researcher reports survey results by stating that the standard error of the mean is 20. The population standard deviation is 500.

a. How large was the sample used in this survey?

b. What is the probability that the point estimate was within ± 25 of the population mean?

49. A production process is checked periodically by a quality control inspector. The inspector selects simple random samples of 30 finished products and computes the sample mean product weights $\bar{x}$. If test results over a long period of time show that 5% of the $\bar{x}$ values are over 2.1 pounds and 5% are under 1.9 pounds, what are the mean and the standard deviation for the population of products produced with this process?

50. As of June 13, 2001, 30.5% of individual investors were bullish on the stock market short term (*AAII Journal,* July 2001). Answer the following questions assuming a sample of 200 individual investors is used.

a. Show the sampling distribution of $\bar{p}$, the sample proportion of individual investors who are bullish on the market short term.

b. What is the probability that the sample proportion will be within $\pm .04$ of the population proportion?

c. What is the probability that the sample proportion will be within $\pm .02$ of the population proportion?

51. A market research firm conducts telephone surveys with a 40% historical response rate. What is the probability that in a new sample of 400 telephone numbers, at least 150 individuals will cooperate and respond to the questions? In other words, what is the probability that the sample proportion will be at least $150/400 = .375$?

52. According to ORC International, 71% of Internet users connect their computers to the Internet by normal telephone lines (*USA Today,* January 18, 2000). Assume a population proportion $p = .71$.

a. What is the probability that a sample proportion from a simple random sample of 350 Internet users will be within $\pm .05$ of the population proportion?

b. What is the probability that a sample proportion from a simple random sample of 350 Internet users will be .75 or greater?

53. The proportion of individuals insured by the All-Driver Automobile Insurance Company who received at least one traffic ticket during a five-year period is .15.

a. Show the sampling distribution of $\bar{p}$ if a random sample of 150 insured individuals is used to estimate the proportion having received at least one ticket.

b. What is the probability that the sample proportion will be within $\pm .03$ of the population proportion?

54. Lori Jeffrey is a successful sales representative for a major publisher of college textbooks. Historically, Lori obtains a book adoption on 25% of her sales calls. Viewing her sales calls for one month as a sample of all possible sales calls, assume that a statistical analysis of the data yields a standard error of the proportion of .0625.
   a. How large was the sample used in this analysis? That is, how many sales calls did Lori make during the month?
   b. Let $\bar{p}$ indicate the sample proportion of book adoptions obtained during the month. Show the sampling distribution $\bar{p}$.
   c. Using the sampling distribution of $\bar{p}$, compute the probability that Lori will obtain book adoptions on 30% or more of her sales calls during a one-month period.

Appendix 7.1   Random Sampling with Minitab

If a list of the elements in a population is available in a Minitab file, Minitab can be used to select a simple random sample. For example, a list of the top 100 metropolitan areas in the United States and Canada is provided in column 1 of the data set MetAreas (*Places Rated Almanac—The Millennium Edition 2000*). Column 2 contains the overall rating of each metropolitan area. The first 10 metropolitan areas in the data set and their corresponding ratings are shown in Table 7.6

Suppose that you would like to select a simple random sample of 30 metropolitan areas in order to do an in-depth study of the cost of living in the United States and Canada. The following steps can be used to select the sample.

Step 1. Select the **Calc** menu
Step 2. Choose **Random Data**
Step 3. Choose **Sample From Columns**
Step 4. When the Sample From Columns dialog box appears:
   Enter 30 in the **Sample** box
   Enter C1 C2 in the box below
   Enter C3 C4 in the **Store samples in** box
Step 5. Click **OK**

The random sample of 30 metropolitan areas appears in columns C3 and C4.

Appendix 7.2   Random Sampling with Excel

If a list of the elements in a population is available in an Excel file, Excel can be used to select a simple random sample. For example, a list of the top 100 metropolitan areas in the United States and Canada is provided in column A of the data set MetAreas (*Places Rated*

TABLE 7.6   OVERALL RATING FOR THE FIRST 10 METROPOLITAN AREAS IN THE DATA SET METAREAS

MetAreas

Metropolitan Area	Rating	Metropolitan Area	Rating
Albany, NY	64.18	Baltimore, MD	69.75
Albuquerque, NM	66.16	Birmingham, AL	69.59
Appleton, WI	60.56	Boise City, ID	68.36
Atlanta, GA	69.97	Boston, MA	68.99
Austin, TX	71.48	Buffalo, NY	66.10

Almanac—The Millennium Edition 2000). Column B contains the overall rating of each metropolitan area. The first 10 metropolitan areas in the data set and their corresponding ratings are shown in Table 7.6. Assume that you would like to select a simple random sample of 30 metropolitan areas in order to do an in-depth study of the cost of living in the United States and Canada.

The rows of any Excel data set can be placed in a random order by adding an extra column to the data set and filling the column with random numbers using the =RAND() function. Then using Excel's sort ascending capability on the random number column, the rows of the data set will be reordered randomly. The random sample of size *n* appears in the first *n* rows of the reordered data set.

In the MetAreas data set, labels are in row 1 and the 100 metropolitan areas are in rows 2 to 101. The following steps can be used to select a simple random sample of 30 metropolitan areas.

Step 1. Enter =RAND() in cell C2
Step 2. Copy cell C2 to cells C3:C101
Step 3. Select any cell in column C
Step 4. Click the **Sort Ascending** button on the toolbar

The random sample of 30 metropolitan areas appears in rows 2 to 31 of the reordered data set. The random numbers in column C are no longer necessary and can be deleted if desired.

CHAPTER 8

Interval Estimation

CONTENTS

STATISTICS IN PRACTICE:
FOOD LION

STATISTICS *in* PRACTICE

FOOD LION*
SALISBURY, NORTH CAROLINA

Founded in 1957 as Food Town, Food Lion is one of the largest supermarket chains in the United States with 1200 stores in 11 Southeastern and Mid-Atlantic states. The company sells more than 24,000 different products and offers nationally and regionally advertised brand-name merchandise, as well as a growing number of high-quality private label products manufactured especially for Food Lion. The company maintains its low price leadership and quality assurance through operating efficiencies such as standard store formats, innovative warehouse design, energy-efficient facilities, and data synchronization with suppliers. Food Lion looks to a future of continued innovation, growth, price leadership, and service to its customers.

Being in an inventory-intense business, Food Lion made the decision to adopt the LIFO (last-in, first-out) method of inventory valuation. This method matches current costs against current revenues, which minimizes the effect of radical price changes on profit and loss results. In addition, the LIFO method reduces net income thereby reducing income taxes during periods of inflation.

Food Lion establishes a LIFO index for each of seven inventory pools: Grocery, Paper/Household, Pet Supplies, Health & Beauty Aids, Dairy, Cigarette/Tobacco, and Beer/Wine. For example, a LIFO index of 1.008 for the Grocery pool would indicate that the company's grocery inventory value at current costs reflects a 0.8% increase due to inflation over the most recent one-year period.

A LIFO index for each inventory pool requires that the year-end inventory count for each product be valued at the current year-end cost and at the preceding year-end cost. To avoid ex-

The Food Lion store in the Cambridge Shopping Center, Charlotte, North Carolina. © Courtesy of Food Lion.

cessive time and expense associated with counting the inventory in all 1200 store locations, Food Lion selects a random sample of 50 stores. Year-end physical inventories are taken in each of the sample stores. The current-year and preceding-year costs for each item are then used to construct the required LIFO indexes for each inventory pool.

For a recent year, the sample estimate of the LIFO index for the Health & Beauty Aids inventory pool was 1.015. Using a 95% confidence level, Food Lion computed a margin of error of .006 for the sample estimate. Thus, the interval from 1.009 to 1.021 provided a 95% confidence interval estimate of the population LIFO index. This level of precision was judged to be very good.

In this chapter you will learn how to compute the margin of error associated with sample estimates. You will also learn how to use this information to construct and interpret interval estimates of a population mean and a population proportion.

---

*The authors are indebted to Keith Cunningham, Tax Director, and Bobby Harkey, Staff Tax Accountant, at Food Lion for providing this Statistics in Practice.

In Chapter 7, we stated that a point estimator is a sample statistic used to estimate a population parameter. For instance, the sample mean $\bar{x}$ is a point estimator of the population mean μ and the sample proportion $\bar{p}$ is a point estimator of the population proportion p. Because a point estimator cannot be expected to provide the exact value of the population parameter, an **interval estimate** is often computed by adding and subtracting a value, called the **margin of error**, to the point estimate. The general form of an interval estimate is as follows:

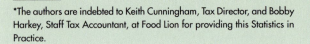

Point estimate $\pm$ Margin of error

The purpose of an interval estimate is to provide information about how close the point estimate, provided by the sample, is to the value of the population parameter.

In this chapter we show how to compute interval estimates of a population mean μ and a population proportion p. The general form of an interval estimate of a population mean is

$$\bar{x} \pm \text{Margin of error}$$

Similarly, the general form of an interval estimate of a population proportion is

$$\bar{p} \pm \text{Margin of error}$$

The sampling distributions of $\bar{x}$ and $\bar{p}$ play key roles in computing these interval estimates.

8.1 Population Mean: σ Known

In order to develop an interval estimate of a population mean, either the population standard deviation σ or the sample standard deviation s must be used to compute the margin of error. In most applications σ is not known, and s is used to compute the margin of error. In some applications, however, large amounts of relevant historical data are available and can be used to estimate the population standard deviation prior to sampling. Also, in quality control applications where a process is assumed to be operating correctly, or "in control," it is appropriate to treat the population standard deviation as known. We refer to such cases as the **σ known** case. In this section we introduce an example in which it is reasonable to treat σ as known and show how to construct an interval estimate for this case.

Each week Lloyd's Department Store selects a simple random sample of 100 customers in order to learn about the amount spent per shopping trip. With x representing the amount spent per shopping trip, the sample mean $\bar{x}$ provides a point estimate of μ, the mean amount spent per shopping trip for the population of all Lloyd's customers. Lloyd's has been using the weekly survey for several years. Based on the historical data, Lloyd's now assumes a known value of $\sigma = \$20$ for the population standard deviation. The historical data also indicate that the population follows a normal distribution.

During the most recent week, Lloyd's surveyed 100 customers ($n = 100$) and obtained a sample mean of $\bar{x} = \$82$. The sample mean amount spent provides a point estimate of the population mean amount spent per shopping trip, μ. In the discussion that follows, we show how to compute the margin of error for this estimate and develop an interval estimate of the population mean.

Margin of Error and the Interval Estimate

In Chapter 7 we showed that the sampling distribution of $\bar{x}$ can be used to compute the probability that $\bar{x}$ will be within a given distance of μ. In the Lloyd's example, the historical data show that the population of amounts spent is normally distributed with a standard deviation of $\sigma = 20$. So, using what we learned in Chapter 7, we can conclude that the sampling distribution of $\bar{x}$ follows a normal distribution with a standard error of $\sigma_{\bar{x}} = \sigma/\sqrt{n} = 20/\sqrt{100} = 2$. This sampling distribution is shown in Figure 8.1.* Because

---

*We use the fact that the population of amounts spent has a normal distribution to conclude that the sampling distribution of $\bar{x}$ has a normal distribution. If the population did not have a normal distribution, we could rely on the central limit theorem and the sample size of $n = 100$ to conclude that the sampling distribution of $\bar{x}$ is approximately normal. In either case, the sampling distribution of $\bar{x}$ would appear as shown in Figure 8.1.

FIGURE 8.1   SAMPLING DISTRIBUTION OF THE SAMPLE MEAN AMOUNT
SPENT FROM SIMPLE RANDOM SAMPLES OF 100 CUSTOMERS

the sampling distribution shows how values of $\bar{x}$ are distributed around the population mean μ, the sampling distribution of $\bar{x}$ provides information about the possible differences between $\bar{x}$ and μ.

Using the table of areas for the standard normal distribution, we find that 95% of the values of any normally distributed random variable are within ± 1.96 standard deviations of the mean. Thus, when the sampling distribution of $\bar{x}$ is normally distributed, 95% of the $\bar{x}$ values must be within $\pm 1.96\sigma_{\bar{x}}$ of the mean μ. In the Lloyd's example we know that the sampling distribution of $\bar{x}$ is normally distributed with a standard error of $\sigma_{\bar{x}} = 2$. Because $\pm 1.96\sigma_{\bar{x}} = 1.96(2) = 3.92$, we can conclude that 95% of all $\bar{x}$ values obtained using a sample size of $n = 100$ will be within ± 3.92 of the population mean μ. See Figure 8.2.

FIGURE 8.2   SAMPLING DISTRIBUTION OF $\bar{x}$ SHOWING THE LOCATION OF SAMPLE
MEANS THAT ARE WITHIN 3.92 OF μ

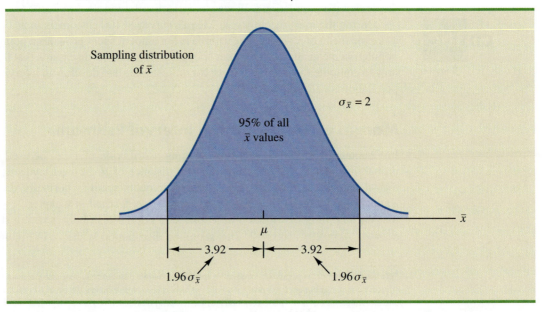

In the introduction to this chapter we said that the general form of an interval estimate of the population mean μ is $\bar{x} \pm$ margin of error. For the Lloyd's example, suppose we set the margin of error equal to 3.92 and compute the interval estimate of μ using $\bar{x} \pm 3.92$. To provide an interpretation for this interval estimate, let us consider the values of $\bar{x}$ that could be obtained if we took three *different* simple random samples, each consisting of 100 Lloyd's customers. The first sample mean might turn out to have the value shown as $\bar{x}_1$ in Figure 8.3. In this case, Figure 8.3 shows that the interval formed by subtracting 3.92 from $\bar{x}_1$ and adding 3.92 to $\bar{x}_1$ includes the population mean μ. Now consider what happens if the second sample mean turns out to have the value shown as $\bar{x}_2$ in Figure 8.3. Although this sample mean differs from the first sample mean, we see that the interval formed by subtracting 3.92 from $\bar{x}_2$ and adding 3.92 to $\bar{x}_2$ also includes the population mean μ. However, consider what happens if the third sample mean turns out to have the value shown as $\bar{x}_3$ in Figure 8.3. In this case, the interval formed by subtracting 3.92 from $\bar{x}_3$ and adding 3.92 to $\bar{x}_3$ does not include the population mean μ. Because $\bar{x}_3$ falls in the upper tail of the sampling distribution and is farther than 3.92 from μ, subtracting and adding 3.92 to $\bar{x}_3$ forms an interval that does not include μ.

Any sample mean $\bar{x}$ that is within the darkly shaded region of Figure 8.3 will provide an interval that contains the population mean μ. Because 95% of all possible sample means are in the darkly shaded region, 95% of all intervals formed by subtracting 3.92 from $\bar{x}$ and adding 3.92 to $\bar{x}$ will include the population mean μ.

Recall that during the most recent week, the quality assurance team at Lloyd's surveyed 100 customers and obtained a sample mean amount spent of $\bar{x} = 82$. Using $\bar{x} \pm 3.92$ to

FIGURE 8.3   INTERVALS FORMED FROM SELECTED SAMPLE MEANS AT LOCATIONS $\bar{x}_1$, $\bar{x}_2$, AND $\bar{x}_3$

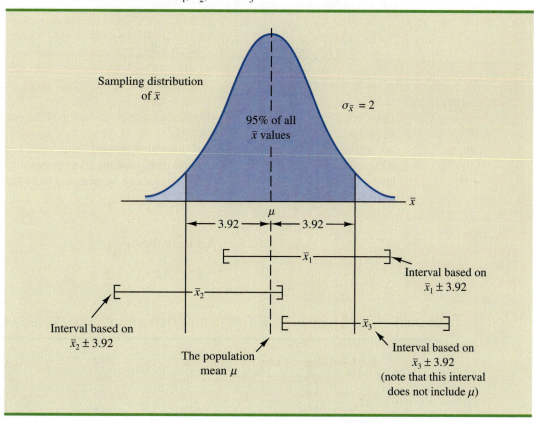

construct the interval estimate, we obtain 82 ± 3.92. Thus, the specific interval estimate of μ based on the data from the most recent week is $82 - 3.92 = 78.08$ to $82 + 3.92 = 85.92$. Because 95% of all the intervals constructed using $\bar{x} \pm 3.92$ will contain the population mean, we say that we are 95% confident that the interval 78.08 to 85.92 includes the population mean μ. We say that this interval has been established at the 95% **confidence level**. The value .95 is referred to as the **confidence coefficient**, and the interval 78.08 to 85.92 is called the 95% **confidence interval**.

This discussion provides insight as to why the interval is called a 95% confidence interval.

With the margin of error given by $z_{\alpha/2}(\sigma/\sqrt{n})$, the general form of an interval estimate of a population mean for the σ known case follows.

INTERVAL ESTIMATE OF A POPULATION MEAN: σ KNOWN

$$\bar{x} \pm z_{\alpha/2} \frac{\sigma}{\sqrt{n}} \qquad\qquad (8.1)$$

where $(1 - \alpha)$ is the confidence coefficient and $z_{\alpha/2}$ is the z value providing an area of $\alpha/2$ in the upper tail of the standard normal probability distribution.

Let us use expression (8.1) to construct a 95% confidence interval for the Lloyd's example. For a 95% confidence interval, the confidence coefficient is $(1 - \alpha) = .95$ and thus, $\alpha = .05$. Using the tables of areas for the standard normal distribution, an area of $\alpha/2 = .05/2 = .025$ in the upper tail provides $z_{.025} = 1.96$. With the Lloyd's sample mean $\bar{x} = 82$, $\sigma = 20$, and a sample size $n = 100$, we obtain

$$82 \pm 1.96 \frac{20}{\sqrt{100}}$$

$$82 \pm 3.92$$

Thus, using expression (8.1), the margin of error is 3.92 and the 95% confidence interval is $82 - 3.92 = 78.08$ to $82 + 3.92 = 85.92$.

Although a 95% confidence level is frequently used, other confidence levels such as 90% and 99% may be considered. Values of $z_{\alpha/2}$ for the most commonly used confidence levels are shown in Table 8.1. Using these values and expression (8.1), the 90% confidence interval for the Lloyd's example is

$$82 \pm 1.645 \frac{20}{\sqrt{100}}$$

$$82 \pm 3.29$$

TABLE 8.1   VALUES OF $z_{\alpha/2}$ FOR THE MOST COMMONLY USED CONFIDENCE LEVELS

Confidence Level	α	$\alpha/2$	$z_{\alpha/2}$
90%	.10	.05	1.645
95%	.05	.025	1.960
99%	.01	.005	2.576

Thus, at 90% confidence, the margin of error is 3.29 and the confidence interval is $82 - 3.29 = 78.71$ to $82 + 3.29 = 85.29$. Similarly, the 99% confidence interval is

$$82 \pm 2.576 \frac{20}{\sqrt{100}}$$

$$82 \pm 5.15$$

Thus, at 99% confidence, the margin of error is 5.15 and the confidence interval is $82 - 5.15 = 76.85$ to $82 + 5.15 = 87.15$.

Comparing the results for the 90%, 95%, and 99% confidence levels, we see that in order to have a higher degree of confidence, the margin of error and thus the width of the confidence interval must be larger.

Practical Advice

If the population follows a normal distribution, the confidence interval provided by expression (8.1) is exact. In other words, if expression (8.1) were used repeatedly to generate 95% confidence intervals, exactly 95% of the intervals generated would contain the population mean. If the population does not follow a normal distribution, the confidence interval provided by expression (8.1) will be approximate. In this case, the quality of the approximation depends on both the distribution of the population and the sample size.

In most applications, a sample size of $n \geq 30$ is adequate when using expression (8.1) to develop an interval estimate of a population mean. If the population is not normally distributed, but is roughly symmetric, sample sizes as small as 15 can be expected to provide good approximate confidence intervals. With smaller sample sizes, expression (8.1) should only be used if the analyst believes, or is willing to assume, that the population distribution is at least approximately normal.

NOTES AND COMMENTS

1. The interval estimation procedure discussed in this section is based on the assumption that the population standard deviation σ is known. By σ known we mean that historical data or other information are available that permit us to obtain a good estimate of the population standard deviation prior to taking the sample that will be used to develop an estimate of the population mean. So technically we don't mean that σ is actually known with certainty. We just mean that we obtained a good estimate of the standard deviation prior to sampling and thus we won't be using the same sample to estimate both the population mean and the population standard deviation.

2. The sample size n appears in the denominator of the interval estimation expression (8.1). Thus, if a particular sample size provides too wide an interval to be of any practical use, we may want to consider increasing the sample size. With n in the denominator, a larger sample size will provide a smaller margin of error, a narrower interval, and greater precision. The procedure for determining the size of a simple random sample necessary to obtain a desired precision is discussed in Section 8.3.

Exercises

Methods

1. A simple random sample of 40 items resulted in a sample mean of 25. The population standard deviation is $\sigma = 5$.
   a. What is the standard error of the mean, $\sigma_{\bar{x}}$?
   b. At 95% confidence, what is the margin of error?

2. A simple random sample of 50 items from a population with $\sigma = 6$ resulted in a sample mean of 32.
   a. Provide a 90% confidence interval for the population mean.
   b. Provide a 95% confidence interval for the population mean.
   c. Provide a 99% confidence interval for the population mean.

3. A simple random sample of 60 items resulted in a sample mean of 80. The population standard deviation is $\sigma = 15$.
   a. Compute the 95% confidence interval for the population mean.
   b. Assume that the same sample mean was obtained from a sample of 120 items. Provide a 95% confidence interval for the population mean.
   c. What is the effect of a larger sample size on the interval estimate?

4. A 95% confidence interval for a population mean was reported to be 152 to 160. If $\sigma = 15$, what sample size was used in this study?

Applications

5. In an effort to estimate the mean amount spent per customer for dinner at a major Atlanta restaurant, data were collected for a sample of 49 customers. Assume a population standard deviation of $5.
   a. At 95% confidence, what is the margin of error?
   b. If the sample mean is $24.80, what is the 95% confidence interval for the population mean?

6. Nielsen Media Research reported that the household mean television viewing time during the 8 P.M. to 11 P.M. time period is 8.5 hours per week (*The World Almanac 2003*). Given a sample size of 300 households and a population standard deviation of $\sigma = 3.5$ hours, what is the 95% confidence interval estimate of the mean television viewing time per week during the 8 P.M. to 11 P.M. time period?

7. A survey of small businesses with Web sites found that the average amount spent on a site was $11,500 per year (*Fortune,* March 5, 2001). Given a sample of 60 businesses and a population standard deviation of $\sigma = 4000, what is the margin of error? Use 95% confidence. What would you recommend if the study required a margin of error of $500?

8. The National Quality Research Center at the University of Michigan provides a quarterly measure of consumer opinions about products and services (*The Wall Street Journal,* February 18, 2003). A survey of 10 restaurants in the Fast Food/Pizza group showed a sample mean customer satisfaction index of 71. Past data indicate that the population standard deviation of the index has been relatively stable with $\sigma = 5$.
   a. What assumption should the researcher be willing to make if a margin of error is desired?
   b. Using 95% confidence, what is the margin of error?
   c. What is the margin of error if 99% confidence is desired?

9. The undergraduate grade point average (GPA) for students admitted to the top graduate business schools was 3.37 (*Best Graduate Schools, U.S. News and World Report,* 2001). Assume this estimate was based on a sample of 120 students admitted to the top schools. Using past years' data, the population standard deviation can be assumed known with $\sigma = .28$. What is the 95% confidence interval estimate of the mean undergraduate GPA for students admitted to the top graduate business schools?

10. *Playbill* magazine reported that the mean annual household income of its readers is $119,155 (*Playbill,* December 2003). Assume this estimate of the mean annual household income is based on a sample of 80 households, and based on past studies, the population standard deviation is known to be $\sigma = $30,000$.

a. Develop a 90% confidence interval estimate of the population mean.
b. Develop a 95% confidence interval estimate of the population mean.
c. Develop a 99% confidence interval estimate of the population mean.
d. Discuss what happens to the width of the confidence interval as the confidence level is increased. Does this result seem reasonable? Explain.

8.2 Population Mean: σ Unknown

When developing an interval estimate of a population mean we usually do not have a good estimate of the population standard deviation either. In these cases, we must use the same sample to estimate μ and σ. This situation represents the **σ unknown** case. When s is used to estimate σ, the margin of error and the interval estimate for the population mean are based on a probability distribution known as the **t distribution**. Although the mathematical development of the t distribution is based on the assumption of a normal distribution for the population we are sampling from, research shows that the t distribution can be successfully applied in many situations where the population deviates significantly from normal. Later in this section we provide guidelines for using the t distribution if the population is not normally distributed.

William Sealy Gosset, writing under the name "Student," is the founder of the t distribution. Gosset, an Oxford graduate in mathematics, worked for the Guinness Brewery in Dublin, Ireland. He developed the t distribution while working on small-scale materials and temperature experiments.

The t distribution is a family of similar probability distributions, with a specific t distribution depending on a parameter known as the **degrees of freedom**. The t distribution with one degree of freedom is unique, as is the t distribution with two degrees of freedom, with three degrees of freedom, and so on. As the number of degrees of freedom increases, the difference between the t distribution and the standard normal distribution becomes smaller and smaller. Figure 8.4 shows t distributions with 10 and 20 degrees of freedom and their relationship to the standard normal probability distribution. Note that a t distribution with more degrees of freedom exhibits less variability and more

FIGURE 8.4   COMPARISON OF THE STANDARD NORMAL DISTRIBUTION WITH t DISTRIBUTIONS HAVING 10 AND 20 DEGREES OF FREEDOM

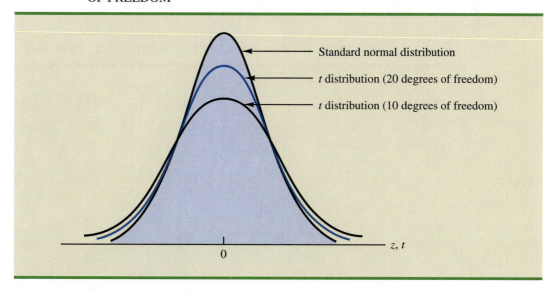

closely resembles the standard normal distribution. Note also that the mean of the t distribution is zero.

We place a subscript on t to indicate the area in the upper tail of the t distribution. For example, just as we used $z_{.025}$ to indicate the z value providing a .025 area in the upper tail of a standard normal distribution, we will use $t_{.025}$ to indicate the t value providing a .025 area in the upper tail of a t distribution. In general, we will use the notation $t_{\alpha/2}$ to represent a t value with an area of $\alpha/2$ in the upper tail of the t distribution. See Figure 8.5.

Table 8.2 contains a table for the t distribution. This table also appears inside the front cover of the text. Each row in the table corresponds to a separate t distribution with the degrees of freedom shown. For example, for a t distribution with 10 degrees of freedom, $t_{.025} = 2.228$. Similarly, for a t distribution with 20 degrees of freedom, $t_{.025} = 2.086$. As the degrees of freedom continue to increase, $t_{.025}$ approaches $z_{.025} = 1.96$. In fact, the standard normal distribution z values can be found in the infinite degrees of freedom row (labeled ∞) of the t distribution table. If the degrees of freedom exceed 100, the infinite degrees of freedom row can be used to approximate the actual t value; in other words, for more than 100 degrees of freedom, the standard normal z value provides a good approximation to the t value. Table 2 in Appendix B provides a more extensive t distribution table, with all the degrees of freedom from 1 to 100 included.

As the degrees of freedom increase, the t distribution approaches the standard normal distribution.

Margin of Error and the Interval Estimate

In Section 8.1 we showed that an interval estimate of a population mean for the σ known case is

$$\bar{x} \pm z_{\alpha/2}\frac{\sigma}{\sqrt{n}}$$

To compute an interval estimate of μ for the σ unknown case, the sample standard deviation s is used to estimate σ, and $z_{\alpha/2}$ is replaced by the t distribution value $t_{\alpha/2}$. The margin

FIGURE 8.5 t DISTRIBUTION WITH $\alpha/2$ AREA OR PROBABILITY IN THE UPPER TAIL

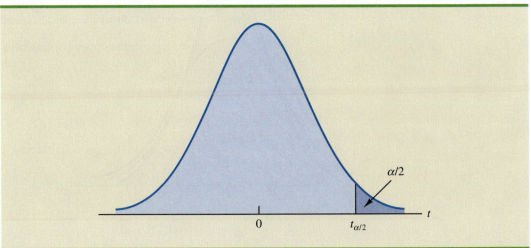

TABLE 8.2 *t* DISTRIBUTION TABLE FOR AN AREA OF $\alpha/2$ IN THE UPPER TAIL. EXAMPLE: WITH 10 DEGREES OF FREEDOM, THE *t* VALUE PROVIDING AN AREA OF .025 IN THE UPPER TAIL IS $t_{.025} = 2.228$

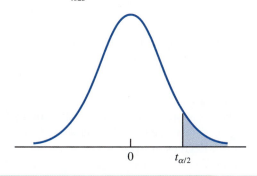

Degrees of Freedom	Area in Upper Tail					
	.20	**.10**	**.05**	**.025**	**.01**	**.005**
1	1.376	3.078	6.314	12.706	31.821	63.656
2	1.061	1.886	2.920	4.303	6.965	9.925
3	.978	1.638	2.353	3.182	4.541	5.841
4	.941	1.533	2.132	2.776	3.747	4.604
5	.920	1.476	2.015	2.571	3.365	4.032
6	.906	1.440	1.943	2.447	3.143	3.707
7	.896	1.415	1.895	2.365	2.998	3.499
8	.889	1.397	1.860	2.306	2.896	3.355
9	.883	1.383	1.833	2.262	2.821	3.250
10	.879	1.372	1.812	2.228	2.764	3.169
11	.876	1.363	1.796	2.201	2.718	3.106
12	.873	1.356	1.782	2.179	2.681	3.055
13	.870	1.350	1.771	2.160	2.650	3.012
14	.868	1.345	1.761	2.145	2.624	2.977
15	.866	1.341	1.753	2.131	2.602	2.947
16	.865	1.337	1.746	2.120	2.583	2.921
17	.863	1.333	1.740	2.110	2.567	2.898
18	.862	1.330	1.734	2.101	2.552	2.878
19	.861	1.328	1.729	2.093	2.539	2.861
20	.860	1.325	1.725	2.086	2.528	2.845
21	.859	1.323	1.721	2.080	2.518	2.831
22	.858	1.321	1.717	2.074	2.508	2.819
23	.858	1.319	1.714	2.069	2.500	2.807
24	.857	1.318	1.711	2.064	2.492	2.797
25	.856	1.316	1.708	2.060	2.485	2.787
26	.856	1.315	1.706	2.056	2.479	2.779
27	.855	1.314	1.703	2.052	2.473	2.771
28	.855	1.313	1.701	2.048	2.467	2.763
29	.854	1.311	1.699	2.045	2.462	2.756
30	.854	1.310	1.697	2.042	2.457	2.750
40	.851	1.303	1.684	2.021	2.423	2.704
50	.849	1.299	1.676	2.009	2.403	2.678
60	.848	1.296	1.671	2.000	2.390	2.660
80	.846	1.292	1.664	1.990	2.374	2.639
100	.845	1.290	1.660	1.984	2.364	2.626
∞	.842	1.282	1.645	1.960	2.326	2.576

Note: A more extensive table is provided as Table 2 of Appendix B.

of error is then given by $t_{\alpha/2} s/\sqrt{n}$. With this margin of error, the general expression for an interval estimate of a population mean when σ is unknown follows.

> **INTERVAL ESTIMATE OF A POPULATION MEAN: σ UNKNOWN**
>
> $$\bar{x} \pm t_{\alpha/2} \frac{s}{\sqrt{n}} \tag{8.2}$$
>
> where s is the sample standard deviation, $(1 - \alpha)$ is the confidence coefficient, and $t_{\alpha/2}$ is the t value providing an area of $\alpha/2$ in the upper tail of the t distribution with $n - 1$ degrees of freedom.

The reason the number of degrees of freedom associated with the t value in expression (8.2) is $n - 1$ concerns the use of s as an estimate of the population standard deviation σ. The expression for the sample standard deviation is

$$s = \sqrt{\frac{\Sigma(x_i - \bar{x})^2}{n - 1}}$$

Degrees of freedom refer to the number of independent pieces of information that go into the computation of $\Sigma(x_i - \bar{x})^2$. The n pieces of information involved in computing $\Sigma(x_i - \bar{x})^2$ are as follows: $x_1 - \bar{x}, x_2 - \bar{x}, \ldots, x_n - \bar{x}$. In Section 3.2 we indicated that $\Sigma(x_i - \bar{x}) = 0$ for any data set. Thus, only $n - 1$ of the $x_i - \bar{x}$ values are independent; that is, if we know $n - 1$ of the values, the remaining value can be determined exactly by using the condition that the sum of the $x_i - \bar{x}$ values must be 0. Thus, $n - 1$ is the number of degrees of freedom associated with $\Sigma(x_i - \bar{x})^2$ and hence the number of degrees of freedom for the t distribution in expression (8.2).

To illustrate the interval estimation procedure for the σ unknown case, we will consider a study designed to estimate the mean credit card debt for the population of U.S. households. A sample of $n = 85$ households provided the credit card balances shown in Table 8.3. For this situation, no previous estimate of the population standard deviation σ is available. Thus,

TABLE 8.3 CREDIT CARD BALANCES FOR A SAMPLE OF 85 HOUSEHOLDS

Balance

9619	5994	3344	7888	7581	9980
5364	4652	13627	3091	12545	8718
8348	5376	968	943	7959	8452
7348	5998	4714	8762	2563	4935
381	7530	4334	1407	6787	5938
2998	3678	4911	6644	5071	5266
1686	3581	1920	7644	9536	10658
1962	5625	3780	11169	4459	3910
4920	5619	3478	7979	8047	7503
5047	9032	6185	3258	8083	1582
6921	13236	1141	8660	2153	
5759	4447	7577	7511	8003	
8047	609	4667	14442	6795	
3924	414	5219	4447	5915	
3470	7636	6416	6550	7164	

the sample data must be used to estimate both the population mean and the population standard deviation. Using the data in Table 8.3, we compute the sample mean $\bar{x} = \$5900$ and the sample standard deviation $s = \$3058$. With 95% confidence and $n - 1 = 84$ degrees of freedom, Table 2 in Appendix B provides $t_{.025} = 1.989$. We can now use expression (8.2) to compute an interval estimate of the population mean.

$$5900 \pm 1.989 \frac{3058}{\sqrt{85}}$$

$$5900 \pm 660$$

The point estimate of the population mean is $5900, the margin of error is $660, and the 95% confidence interval is $5900 - 660 = \$5240$ to $5900 + 660 = \$6560$. Thus, we are 95% confident that the population mean credit card balance for all households is between $5240 and $6560.

The procedures used by Minitab and Excel to develop confidence intervals for a population mean are described in Appendixes 8.1 and 8.2. For the household credit card balances study, the results of the Minitab interval estimation procedure are shown in Figure 8.6. The sample of 85 households provides a sample mean credit card balance of $5900, a sample standard deviation of $3058, and (after rounding) an estimate of the standard error of the mean of $332, and a 95% confidence interval of $5240 to $6560.

Practical Advice

If the population follows a normal distribution, the confidence interval provided by expression (8.2) is exact and can be used for any sample size. If the population does not follow a normal distribution, the confidence interval provided by expression (8.2) will be approximate. In this case, the quality of the approximation depends on both the distribution of the population and the sample size.

Larger sample sizes are needed if the distribution of the population is highly skewed or includes outliers.

In most applications, a sample size of $n \geq 30$ is adequate when using expression (8.2) to develop an interval estimate of a population mean. However, if the population distribution is highly skewed or contains outliers, most statisticians would recommend increasing the sample size to 50 or more. If the population is not normally distributed but is roughly symmetric, sample sizes as small as 15 can be expected to provide good approximate confidence intervals. With smaller sample sizes, expression (8.2) should only be used if the analyst believes, or is willing to assume, that the population distribution is at least approximately normal.

Using a Small Sample

In the following example we develop an interval estimate for a population mean when the sample size is small. As we already noted, an understanding of the distribution of the population becomes a factor in deciding whether the interval estimation procedure provides acceptable results.

Scheer Industries is considering a new computer-assisted program to train maintenance employees to do machine repairs. In order to fully evaluate the program, the director of

FIGURE 8.6   MINITAB CONFIDENCE INTERVAL FOR THE CREDIT CARD BALANCE SURVEY

Variable	N	Mean	StDev	SE Mean	95% CI
Balance	85	5900.00	3058.00	331.69	(5240.40, 6559.60)

TABLE 8.4   TRAINING TIME IN DAYS FOR A SAMPLE OF 20 SCHEER INDUSTRIES EMPLOYEES

Scheer

52	59	54	42
44	50	42	48
55	54	60	55
44	62	62	57
45	46	43	56

manufacturing requested an estimate of the population mean time required for maintenance employees to complete the computer-assisted training.

A sample of 20 employees is selected, with each employee in the sample completing the training program. Data on the training time in days for the 20 employees are shown in Table 8.4. A histogram of the sample data appears in Figure 8.7. What can we say about the distribution of the population based on this histogram? First, the sample data do not support the conclusion that the distribution of the population is normal, yet we do not see any evidence of skewness or outliers. Therefore, using the guidelines in the previous subsection, we conclude that an interval estimate based on the t distribution appears acceptable for the sample of 20 employees.

We continue by computing the sample mean and sample standard deviation as follows.

$$\bar{x} = \frac{\Sigma x_i}{n} = \frac{1030}{20} = 51.5 \text{ days}$$

$$s = \sqrt{\frac{\Sigma(x_i - \bar{x})^2}{n - 1}} = \sqrt{\frac{889}{20 - 1}} = 6.84 \text{ days}$$

FIGURE 8.7   HISTOGRAM OF TRAINING TIMES FOR THE SCHEER INDUSTRIES SAMPLE

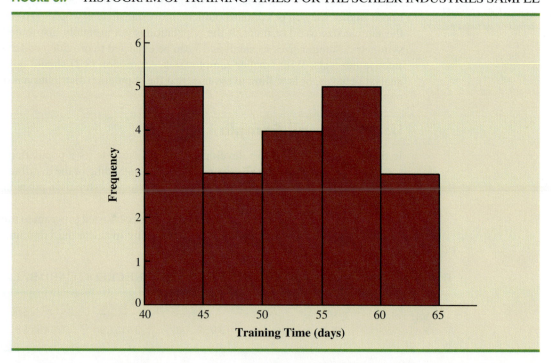

For a 95% confidence interval, we use Table 8.2 and $n - 1 = 19$ degrees of freedom to obtain $t_{.025} = 2.093$. Expression (8.2) provides the interval estimate of the population mean.

$$51.5 \pm 2.093 \left(\frac{6.84}{\sqrt{20}} \right)$$

$$51.5 \pm 3.2$$

The point estimate of the population mean is 51.5 days. The margin of error is 3.2 days and the 95% confidence interval is $51.5 - 3.2 = 48.3$ days to $51.5 + 3.2 = 54.7$ days.

Using a histogram of the sample data to learn about the distribution of a population is not always conclusive, but in many cases it provides the only information available. The histogram, along with judgment on the part of the analyst, can often be used to decide whether expression (8.2) can be used to develop the interval estimate.

Summary of Interval Estimation Procedures

We provided two approaches to developing an interval estimate of a population mean. For the σ known case, σ and the standard normal distribution are used in expression (8.1) to compute the margin of error and to develop the interval estimate. For the σ unknown case, the sample standard deviation s and the t distribution are used in expression (8.2) to compute the margin of error and to develop the interval estimate.

A summary of the interval estimation procedures for the two cases is shown in Figure 8.8. In most applications, a sample size of $n \geq 30$ is adequate. If the population has a normal or approximately normal distribution, however, smaller sample sizes may be used. For the σ unknown case a sample size of $n \geq 50$ is recommended if the population distribution is believed to be highly skewed or has outliers.

FIGURE 8.8   SUMMARY OF INTERVAL ESTIMATION PROCEDURES FOR A POPULATION MEAN

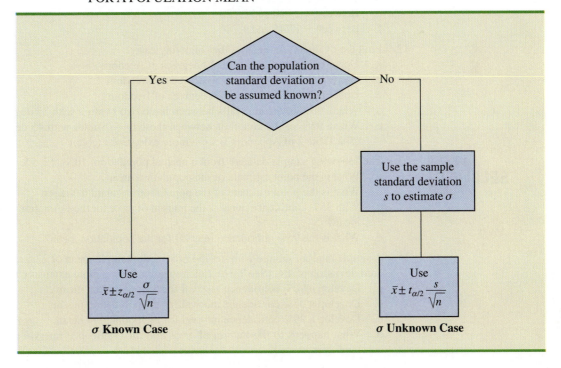

NOTES AND COMMENTS

1. When σ is known, the margin of error, $z_{\alpha/2}(\sigma/\sqrt{n})$, is fixed and is the same for all samples of size n. When σ is unknown, the margin of error, $t_{\alpha/2}(s/\sqrt{n})$, varies from sample to sample. This variation occurs because the sample standard deviation s varies depending upon the sample selected. A large value for s provides a larger margin of error, while a small value for s provides a smaller margin of error.

2. What happens to confidence interval estimates when the population is skewed? Consider a population that is skewed to the right with large data values stretching the distribution to the right. When such skewness exists, the sample mean $\bar{x}$ and the sample standard deviation s are positively correlated. Larger values of s tend to be associated with larger values of $\bar{x}$. Thus, when $\bar{x}$ is larger than the population mean, s tends to be larger than σ. This skewness causes the margin of error, $t_{\alpha/2}(s/\sqrt{n})$, to be larger than it would be with σ known. The confidence interval with the larger margin of error tends to include the population mean μ more often than it would if the true value of σ were used. But when $\bar{x}$ is smaller than the population mean, the correlation between $\bar{x}$ and s causes the margin of error to be small. In this case, the confidence interval with the smaller margin of error tends to miss the population mean more than it would if we knew σ and used it. For this reason, we recommend using larger sample sizes with highly skewed population distributions.

Exercises

Methods

11. For a t distribution with 16 degrees of freedom, find the area, or probability, in each region.
    a. To the right of 2.120
    b. To the left of 1.337
    c. To the left of -1.746
    d. To the right of 2.583
    e. Between -2.120 and 2.120
    f. Between -1.746 and 1.746

12. Find the t value(s) for each of the following cases.
    a. Upper tail area of .025 with 12 degrees of freedom
    b. Lower tail area of .05 with 50 degrees of freedom
    c. Upper tail area of .01 with 30 degrees of freedom
    d. Where 90% of the area falls between these two t values with 25 degrees of freedom
    e. Where 95% of the area falls between these two t values with 45 degrees of freedom
       (See Table 2 of Appendix B for a more extensive t table.)

13. The following sample data are from a normal population: 10, 8, 12, 15, 13, 11, 6, 5.
    a. What is the point estimate of the population mean?
    b. What is the point estimate of the population standard deviation?
    c. With 95% confidence, what is the margin of error for the estimation of the population mean?
    d. What is the 95% confidence interval for the population mean?

14. A simple random sample with $n = 54$ provided a sample mean of 22.5 and a sample standard deviation of 4.4. (See Table 2 of Appendix B for a more extensive t table.)
    a. Develop a 90% confidence interval for the population mean.
    b. Develop a 95% confidence interval for the population mean.
    c. Develop a 99% confidence interval for the population mean.
    d. What happens to the margin of error and the confidence interval as the confidence level is increased?

Applications

15. Sales personnel for Skillings Distributors submit weekly reports listing the customer contacts made during the week. A sample of 65 weekly reports showed a sample mean of 19.5 customer contacts per week. The sample standard deviation was 5.2. Provide 90% and 95% confidence intervals for the population mean number of weekly customer contacts for the sales personnel.

16. The mean number of hours of flying time for pilots at Continental Airlines is 49 hours per month (*The Wall Street Journal,* February 25, 2003). Assume that this mean was based on actual flying times for a sample of 100 Continental pilots and that the sample standard deviation was 8.5 hours.
    a. At 95% confidence, what is the margin of error?
    b. What is the 95% confidence interval estimate of the population mean flying time for the pilots?
    c. The mean number of hours of flying time for pilots at United Airlines is 36 hours per month. Use your results from part (b) to discuss differences between the flying times for the pilots at the two airlines. *The Wall Street Journal* reported United Airlines as having the highest labor cost among all airlines. Does the information in this exercise provide insight as to why United Airlines might expect higher labor costs?

17. The International Air Transport Association surveys business travelers to develop quality ratings for transatlantic gateway airports. The maximum possible rating is 10. Suppose a simple random sample of 50 business travelers is selected and each traveler is asked to provide a rating for the Miami International Airport. The ratings obtained from the sample of 50 business travelers follow.

Miami

6	4	6	8	7	7	6	3	3	8	10	4	8
7	8	7	5	9	5	8	4	3	8	5	5	4
4	4	8	4	5	6	2	5	9	9	8	4	8
9	9	5	9	7	8	3	10	8	9	6		

Develop a 95% confidence interval estimate of the population mean rating for Miami.

FastFood

18. Thirty fast-food restaurants including Wendy's, McDonald's, and Burger King were visited during the summer of 2000 (*The Cincinnati Enquirer,* July 9, 2000). During each visit, the customer went to the drive-through and ordered a basic meal such as a "combo" meal or a sandwich, fries, and shake. The time between pulling up to the menu board and receiving the filled order was recorded. The times in minutes for the 30 visits are as follows:

0.9	1.0	1.2	2.2	1.9	3.6	2.8	5.2	1.8	2.1
6.8	1.3	3.0	4.5	2.8	2.3	2.7	5.7	4.8	3.5
2.6	3.3	5.0	4.0	7.2	9.1	2.8	3.6	7.3	9.0

   a. Provide a point estimate of the population mean drive-through time at fast-food restaurants.
   b. At 95% confidence, what is the margin of error?
   c. What is the 95% confidence interval estimate of the population mean?
   d. Discuss skewness that may be present in this population. What suggestion would you make for a repeat of this study?

19. A National Retail Foundation survey found households intended to spend an average of $649 during the December holiday season (*The Wall Street Journal,* December 2, 2002). Assume that the survey included 600 households and that the sample standard deviation was $175.
   a. With 95% confidence, what is the margin of error?
   b. What is the 95% confidence interval estimate of the population mean?
   c. The prior year, the population mean expenditure per household was $632. Discuss the change in holiday season expenditures over the one-year period.

TVtime

20. The American Association of Advertising Agencies records data on nonprogram minutes on half-hour, prime-time television shows. Representative data in minutes for a sample of 20 prime-time shows on major networks at 8:30 P.M. follow.

6.0	6.6	5.8
7.0	6.3	6.2
7.2	5.7	6.4
7.0	6.5	6.2
6.0	6.5	7.2
7.3	7.6	6.8
6.0	6.2	

Assume a normal population and provide a point estimate and a 95% confidence interval for the mean number of nonprogram minutes on half-hour, prime-time television shows at 8:30 P.M.

21. Complaints about rising prescription drug prices caused the U.S. Congress to consider laws that would force pharmaceutical companies to offer prescription discounts to senior citizens without drug benefits. The House Government Reform Committee provided data on the prescription cost for some of the most widely used drugs (*Newsweek,* May 8, 2000). Assume the following data show a sample of the prescription cost in dollars for Zocor, a drug used to lower cholesterol.

110	112	115	99	100	98	104	126

Given a normal population, what is the 95% confidence interval estimate of the population mean cost for a prescription of Zocor?

22. The first few weeks of 2004 were good for the stock market. A sample of 25 large open-end funds showed the following year-to-date returns through January 16, 2004 (*Barron's,* January 19, 2004).

CD file

OpenEndFunds

7.0	3.2	1.4	5.4	8.5
2.5	2.5	1.9	5.4	1.6
1.0	2.1	8.5	4.3	6.2
1.5	1.2	2.7	3.8	2.0
1.2	2.6	4.0	2.6	0.6

a. What is the point estimate of the population mean year-to-date return for large open-end funds?

b. Given that the population has a normal distribution, develop a 95% confidence interval for the population mean year-to-date return for open-end funds.

8.3 # Determining the Sample Size

In providing practical advice in the two preceding sections, we commented on the role of the sample size in providing good approximate confidence intervals when the population is not normally distributed. In this section, we focus on another aspect of the sample size issue. We describe how to choose a sample size large enough to provide a desired margin of error. To understand how this process is done, we return to the σ known case presented in Section 8.1. Using expression (8.1), the interval estimate is

If a desired margin of error is selected prior to sampling, the procedures in this section can be used to determine the sample size necessary to satisfy the margin of error requirement.

$$\bar{x} \pm z_{\alpha/2} \frac{\sigma}{\sqrt{n}}$$

The quantity $z_{\alpha/2}(\sigma/\sqrt{n})$ is the margin of error. Thus, we see that $z_{\alpha/2}$, the population standard deviation σ, and the sample size n combine to determine the margin of error. Once we select a confidence coefficient $1 - \alpha$, $z_{\alpha/2}$ can be determined. Then, if we have a value for σ, we can determine the sample size n needed to provide any desired margin of error. Development of the formula used to compute the required sample size n follows.

Let E = the desired margin of error:

$$E = z_{\alpha/2} \frac{\sigma}{\sqrt{n}}$$

Solving for $\sqrt{n}$, we have

$$\sqrt{n} = \frac{z_{\alpha/2}\sigma}{E}$$

Squaring both sides of this equation, we obtain the following expression for the sample size.

Equation (8.3) can be used to provide a good sample size recommendation. However, judgment on the part of the analyst should be used to determine whether the final sample size should be adjusted upward.

SAMPLE SIZE FOR AN INTERVAL ESTIMATE OF A POPULATION MEAN

$$n = \frac{(z_{\alpha/2})^2\sigma^2}{E^2} \tag{8.3}$$

This sample size provides the desired margin of error at the chosen confidence level.

In equation (8.3) E is the margin of error that the user is willing to accept, and the value of $z_{\alpha/2}$ follows directly from the confidence level to be used in developing the interval estimate. Although user preference must be considered, 95% confidence is the most frequently chosen value ($z_{.025} = 1.96$).

Finally, use of equation (8.3) requires a value for the population standard deviation σ. However, even if σ is unknown, we can use equation (8.3) provided we have a preliminary or *planning value* for σ. In practice, one of the following procedures can be chosen.

A planning value for the population standard deviation σ must be specified before the sample size can be determined. Three methods of obtaining a planning value for σ are discussed here.

1. Use the estimate of the population standard deviation computed from data of previous studies as the planning value for σ.
2. Use a pilot study to select a preliminary sample. The sample standard deviation from the preliminary sample can be used as the planning value for σ.
3. Use judgment or a "best guess" for the value of σ. For example, we might begin by estimating the largest and smallest data values in the population. The difference between the largest and smallest values provides an estimate of the range for the data. Finally, the range divided by 4 is often suggested as a rough approximation of the standard deviation and thus an acceptable planning value for σ.

Let us demonstrate the use of equation (8.3) to determine the sample size by considering the following example. A previous study that investigated the cost of renting automobiles in the United States found a mean cost of approximately $55 per day for renting a midsize automobile. Suppose that the organization that conducted this study would like to conduct a new study in order to estimate the population mean daily rental cost for a midsize automobile in the United States. In designing the new study, the project director specifies that the population mean daily rental cost be estimated with a margin of error of $2 and a 95% level of confidence.

The project director specified a desired margin of error of $E = 2$, and the 95% level of confidence indicates $z_{.025} = 1.96$. Thus, we only need a planning value for the population standard deviation σ in order to compute the required sample size. At this point, an analyst

Equation (8.3) provides the minimum sample size needed to satisfy the desired margin of error requirement. If the computed sample size is not an integer, rounding up to the next integer value will provide a margin of error slightly smaller than required.

reviewed the sample data from the previous study and found that the sample standard deviation for the daily rental cost was $9.65. Using 9.65 as the planning value for σ, we obtain

$$n = \frac{(z_{\alpha/2})^2 \sigma^2}{E^2} = \frac{(1.96)^2 (9.65)^2}{2^2} = 89.43$$

Thus, the sample size for the new study needs to be at least 89.43 midsize automobile rentals in order to satisfy the project director's $2 margin-of-error requirement. In cases where the computed n is not an integer, we round up to the next integer value; hence, the recommended sample size is 90 midsize automobile rentals.

Exercises

Methods

23. How large a sample should be selected to provide a 95% confidence interval with a margin of error of 10? Assume that the population standard deviation is 40.

24. The range for a set of data is estimated to be 36.
    a. What is the planning value for the population standard deviation?
    b. At 95% confidence, how large a sample would provide a margin of error of 3?
    c. At 95% confidence, how large a sample would provide a margin of error of 2?

Applications

25. Refer to the Scheer Industries example in Section 8.2. Use 6.82 days as a planning value for the population standard deviation.
    a. Assuming 95% confidence, what sample size would be required to obtain a margin of error of 1.5 days?
    b. If the precision statement was made with 90% confidence, what sample size would be required to obtain a margin of error of 2 days?

26. *Bride's* magazine reported that the mean cost of a wedding is $19,000 (*USA Today,* April 17, 2000). Assume that the population standard deviation is $9400. *Bride's* plans to use an annual survey to monitor the cost of a wedding. Use 95% confidence.
    a. What is the recommended sample size if the desired margin of error is $1000?
    b. What is the recommended sample size if the desired margin of error is $500?
    c. What is the recommended sample size if the desired margin of error is $200?

27. Annual starting salaries for college graduates with degrees in business administration are generally expected to be between $30,000 and $45,000. Assume that a 95% confidence interval estimate of the population mean annual starting salary is desired. What is the planning value for the population standard deviation? How large a sample should be taken if the desired margin of error is
    a. $500?
    b. $200?
    c. $100?
    d. Would you recommend trying to obtain the $100 margin of error? Explain.

28. Smith Travel Research provides information on the one-night cost of hotel rooms throughout the United States (*USA Today,* July 8, 2002). Use $2 as the desired margin of error and $22.50 as the planning value for the population standard deviation to find the sample size recommended in (a), (b), and (c).
    a. A 90% confidence interval estimate of the population mean cost of hotel rooms.
    b. A 95% confidence interval estimate of the population mean cost of hotel rooms.

c. A 99% confidence interval estimate of the population mean cost of hotel rooms.
d. When the desired margin of error is fixed, what happens to the sample size as the confidence level is increased? Would you recommend a 99% confidence level be used by Smith Travel Research? Discuss.

29. The travel-to-work time for residents of the 15 largest cities in the United States is reported in the *2003 Information Please Almanac*. Suppose that a preliminary simple random sample of residents of San Francisco is used to develop a planning value of 6.25 minutes for the population standard deviation.
a. If we want to estimate the population mean travel-to-work time for San Francisco residents with a margin of error of 2 minutes, what sample size should be used? Assume 95% confidence.
b. If we want to estimate the population mean travel-to-work time for San Francisco residents with a margin of error of 1 minute, what sample size should be used? Assume 95% confidence.

30. During the first quarter of 2003, the price/earnings (P/E) ratio for stocks listed on the New York Stock Exchange generally ranged from 5 to 60 (*The Wall Street Journal,* March 7, 2003). Assume that we want to estimate the population mean P/E ratio for all stocks listed on the exchange. How many stocks should be included in the sample if we want a margin of error of 3? Use 95% confidence.

8.4 Population Proportion

In the introduction to this chapter we said that the general form of an interval estimate of a population proportion p is

$$\bar{p} \pm \text{Margin of error}$$

The sampling distribution of $\bar{p}$ plays a key role in computing the margin of error for this interval estimate.

In Chapter 7 we said that the sampling distribution of $\bar{p}$ can be approximated by a normal distribution whenever $np \geq 5$ and $n(1 - p) \geq 5$. Figure 8.9 shows the normal approximation

FIGURE 8.9   NORMAL APPROXIMATION OF THE SAMPLING DISTRIBUTION OF $\bar{p}$

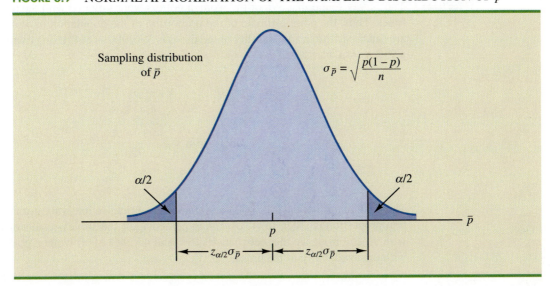

of the sampling distribution of $\bar{p}$. The mean of the sampling distribution of $\bar{p}$ is the population proportion p, and the standard error of $\bar{p}$ is

$$\sigma_{\bar{p}} = \sqrt{\frac{p(1 - p)}{n}} \qquad (8.4)$$

Because the sampling distribution of $\bar{p}$ is normally distributed, if we choose $z_{\alpha/2}\sigma_{\bar{p}}$ as the margin of error in an interval estimate of a population proportion, we know that $100(1 - \alpha)\%$ of the intervals generated will contain the true population proportion. But $\sigma_{\bar{p}}$ cannot be used directly in the computation of the margin of error because p will not be known; p is what we are trying to estimate. So, $\bar{p}$ is substituted for p and the margin of error for an interval estimate of a population proportion is given by

$$\text{Margin of error} = z_{\alpha/2} \sqrt{\frac{\bar{p}(1 - \bar{p})}{n}} \qquad (8.5)$$

With this margin of error, the general expression for an interval estimate of a population proportion is as follows.

When developing confidence intervals for proportions, the quantity $z_{\alpha/2}\sqrt{\bar{p}(1 - \bar{p})/n}$ provides the margin of error.

INTERVAL ESTIMATE OF A POPULATION PROPORTION

$$\bar{p} \pm z_{\alpha/2} \sqrt{\frac{\bar{p}(1 - \bar{p})}{n}} \qquad (8.6)$$

where $1 - \alpha$ is the confidence coefficient and $z_{\alpha/2}$ is the z value providing an area of $\alpha/2$ in the upper tail of the standard normal distribution.

TeeTimes

The following example illustrates the computation of the margin of error and interval estimate for a population proportion. A national survey of 900 women golfers was conducted to learn how women golfers view their treatment at golf courses in the United States. The survey found that 396 of the women golfers were satisfied with the availability of tee times. Thus, the point estimate of the proportion of the population of women golfers who are satisfied with the availability of tee times is 396/900 = .44. Using expression (8.6) and a 95% confidence level,

$$\bar{p} \pm z_{\alpha/2} \sqrt{\frac{\bar{p}(1 - \bar{p})}{n}}$$

$$.44 \pm 1.96 \sqrt{\frac{.44(1 - .44)}{900}}$$

$$.44 \pm .0324$$

Thus, the margin of error is .0324 and the 95% confidence interval estimate of the population proportion is .4076 to .4724. Using percentages, the survey results enable us to state with 95% confidence that between 40.76% and 47.24% of all women golfers are satisfied with the availability of tee times.

Determining the Sample Size

Let us consider the question of how large the sample size should be to obtain an estimate of a population proportion at a specified level of precision. The rationale for the sample size determination in developing interval estimates of p is similar to the rationale used in Section 8.3 to determine the sample size for estimating a population mean.

Previously in this section we said that the margin of error associated with an interval estimate of a population proportion is $z_{\alpha/2}\sqrt{\bar{p}(1-\bar{p})/n}$. The margin of error is based on the value of $z_{\alpha/2}$, the sample proportion $\bar{p}$, and the sample size n. Larger sample sizes provide a smaller margin of error and better precision.

Let E denote the desired margin of error.

$$E = z_{\alpha/2}\sqrt{\frac{\bar{p}(1-\bar{p})}{n}}$$

Solving this equation for n provides a formula for the sample size that will provide a margin of error of size E.

$$n = \frac{(z_{\alpha/2})^2\bar{p}(1-\bar{p})}{E^2}$$

Note, however, that we cannot use this formula to compute the sample size that will provide the desired margin of error because $\bar{p}$ will not be known until after we select the sample. What we need, then, is a planning value for $\bar{p}$ that can be used to make the computation. Using p^* to denote the planning value for $\bar{p}$, the following formula can be used to compute the sample size that will provide a margin of error of size E.

SAMPLE SIZE FOR AN INTERVAL ESTIMATE OF A POPULATION PROPORTION

$$n = \frac{(z_{\alpha/2})^2 p^*(1-p^*)}{E^2} \tag{8.7}$$

In practice, the planning value p^* can be chosen by one of the following procedures.

1. Use the sample proportion from a previous sample of the same or similar units.
2. Use a pilot study to select a preliminary sample. The sample proportion from this sample can be used as the planning value, p^*.
3. Use judgment or a "best guess" for the value of p^*.
4. If none of the preceding alternatives apply, use a planning value of $p^* = .50$.

Let us return to the survey of women golfers and assume that the company is interested in conducting a new survey to estimate the current proportion of the population of women golfers who are satisfied with the availability of tee times. How large should the sample be if the survey director wants to estimate the population proportion with a margin of error of .025 at 95% confidence? With $E = .025$ and $z_{\alpha/2} = 1.96$, we need a planning value p^* to answer the sample size question. Using the previous survey result of $\bar{p} = .44$ as the planning value p^*, equation (8.7) shows that

$$n = \frac{(z_{\alpha/2})^2 p^*(1-p^*)}{E^2} = \frac{(1.96)^2(.44)(1-.44)}{(.025)^2} = 1514.5$$

TABLE 8.5   SOME POSSIBLE VALUES FOR $p^*(1 - p^*)$

p^*	$p^*(1 - p^*)$	
.10	$(.10)(.90) = .09$	
.30	$(.30)(.70) = .21$	
.40	$(.40)(.60) = .24$	
.50	$(.50)(.50) = .25$	← Largest value for $p^*(1 - p^*)$
.60	$(.60)(.40) = .24$	
.70	$(.70)(.30) = .21$	
.90	$(.90)(.10) = .09$	

Thus, the sample size must be at least 1514.5 women golfers to satisfy the margin of error requirement. Rounding up to the next integer value indicates that a sample of 1515 women golfers is recommended to satisfy the margin of error requirement.

The fourth alternative suggested for selecting a planning value p^* is to use $p^* = .50$. This value of p^* is frequently used when no other information is available. To understand why, note that the numerator of equation (8.7) shows that the sample size is proportional to the quantity $p^*(1 - p^*)$. A larger value for the quantity $p^*(1 - p^*)$ will result in a larger sample size. Table 8.5 gives some possible values of $p^*(1 - p^*)$. Note that the largest value of $p^*(1 - p^*)$ occurs when $p^* = .50$. Thus, in case of any uncertainty about an appropriate planning value, we know that $p^* = .50$ will provide the largest sample size recommendation. In effect, we play it safe by recommending the largest possible sample size. If the sample proportion turns out to be different from the .50 planning value, the margin of error will be smaller than anticipated. Thus, in using $p^* = .50$, we guarantee that the sample size will be sufficient to obtain the desired margin of error.

In the survey of women golfers example, a planning value of $p^* = .50$ would have provided the sample size

$$n = \frac{(z_{\alpha/2})^2 p^*(1 - p^*)}{E^2} = \frac{(1.96)^2(.50)(1 - .50)}{(.025)^2} = 1536.6$$

Thus, a slightly larger sample size of 1537 women golfers would be recommended.

NOTES AND COMMENTS

The desired margin of error for estimating a population proportion is almost always .10 or less. In national public opinion polls conducted by organizations such as Gallup and Harris, a .03 or .04 margin of error is common. With such margins of error, equation (8.7) will almost always provide a sample size that is large enough to satisfy the requirements of $np \geq 5$ and $n(1 - p) \geq 5$ for using a normal distribution as an approximation for the sampling distribution of $\bar{x}$.

Exercises

Methods

31.   A simple random sample of 400 individuals provides 100 Yes responses.
   a.   What is the point estimate of the proportion of the population that would provide Yes responses?
   b.   What is your estimate of the standard error of the proportion, $\sigma_{\bar{p}}$?
   c.   Compute the 95% confidence interval for the population proportion.

32. A simple random sample of 800 elements generates a sample proportion $\bar{p} = .70$.
     a. Provide a 90% confidence interval for the population proportion.
     b. Provide a 95% confidence interval for the population proportion.

33. In a survey, the planning value for the population proportion is $p^* = .35$. How large a sample should be taken to provide a 95% confidence interval with a margin of error of .05?

34. At 95% confidence, how large a sample should be taken to obtain a margin of error of .03 for the estimation of a population proportion? Assume that past data are not available for developing a planning value for p^*.

Applications

35. A survey of 611 office workers investigated telephone answering practices, including how often each office worker was able to answer incoming telephone calls and how often incoming telephone calls went directly to voice mail (*USA Today,* April 21, 2002). A total of 281 office workers indicated that they never need voice mail and are able to take every telephone call.
     a. What is the point estimate of the proportion of the population of office workers who are able to take every telephone call?
     b. At 90% confidence, what is the margin of error?
     c. What is the 90% confidence interval for the proportion of the population of office workers who are able to take every telephone call?

36. A survey by the Society for Human Resource Management asked 346 job seekers why employees change jobs so frequently (*The Wall Street Journal,* March 28, 2000). The answer selected most (152 times) was "higher compensation elsewhere."
     a. What is the point estimate of the proportion of job seekers who would select "higher compensation elsewhere" as the reason for changing jobs?
     b. What is the 95% confidence interval estimate of the population proportion?

37. Towers Perrin, a New York human resources consulting firm, conducted a survey of 1100 employees at medium-sized and large companies to determine how dissatisfied employees were with their jobs (*The Wall Street Journal,* January 29, 2003). A total of 473 employees indicated they strongly disliked their current work experience.
     a. What is the point estimate of the proportion of the population of employees who strongly dislike their current work experience?
     b. At 95% confidence, what is the margin of error?
     c. What is the 95% confidence interval for the proportion of the population of employees who strongly dislike their current work experience?
     d. Towers Perrin estimates that it costs employers one-third of an hourly employee's annual salary to find a successor and as much as 1.5 times the annual salary to find a successor for a highly compensated employee. What message did this survey send to employers?

38. Audience profile data collected at the ESPN SportsZone Web site showed that 26% of the users were women (*USA Today,* January 21, 1998). Assume that this percentage was based on a sample of 400 users.
     a. At 95% confidence, what is the margin of error associated with the estimated proportion of users who are women?
     b. What is the 95% confidence interval for the population proportion of ESPN SportsZone Web site users who are women?
     c. How large a sample should be taken if the desired margin of error is .03?

39. An Employee Benefit Research Institute survey explored the reasons small business employers offer a retirement plan to their employees (*USA Today,* April 4, 2000). The reason "competitive advantage in recruitment/retention" was anticipated 33% of the time.
     a. What sample size is recommended if a survey goal is to estimate the proportion of small business employers who offer a retirement plan primarily for "competitive advantage in recruitment/retention" with a margin of error of .03? Use 95% confidence.
     b. Repeat part (a) using 99% confidence.

40. The professional baseball home run record of 61 home runs in a season was held for 37 years by Roger Maris of the New York Yankees. However, between 1998 and 2001, three players—Mark McGwire, Sammy Sosa, and Barry Bonds—broke the standard set by Maris with Bonds holding the current record 73 home runs in a single season. With the long-standing home run record being broken and with many other new offensive records being set, suspicion arose that baseball players might be using illegal muscle-building drugs called steroids. A *USA Today/CNN/Gallup* poll found that 86% of baseball fans think professional baseball players should be tested for steroids (*USA Today*, July 8, 2002). If 650 baseball fans were included in the sample, compute the margin of error and the 95% confidence interval for the population proportion of baseball fans who think professional baseball players should be tested for steroids.

41. An American Express retail survey found that 16% of U.S. consumers used the Internet to buy gifts during the holiday season (*USA Today*, January 18, 2000). If 1285 customers participated in the survey, what is the margin of error and what is the interval estimate of the population proportion of customers using the Internet to buy gifts? Use 95% confidence.

42. A *USA Today/CNN/Gallup* poll for the presidential campaign sampled 491 potential voters in June (*USA Today*, June 9, 2000). A primary purpose of the poll was to obtain an estimate of the proportion of potential voters who favor each candidate. Assume a planning value of $p^* = .50$ and a 95% confidence level.
    a. For $p^* = .50$, what was the planned margin of error for the June poll?
    b. Closer to the November election, better precision and smaller margins of error are desired. Assume the following margins of error are requested for surveys to be conducted during the presidential campaign. Compute the recommended sample size for each survey.

Survey	Margin of Error
September	.04
October	.03
Early November	.02
Pre-Election Day	.01

43. A Phoenix Wealth Management/Harris Interactive survey of 1500 individuals with net worth of $1 million or more provided a variety of statistics on wealthy people (*Business Week*, September 22, 2003). The previous three-year period had been bad for the stock market, which motivated some of the questions asked.
    a. The survey reported that 53% of the respondents lost 25% or more of their portfolio value over the past three years. Develop a 95% confidence interval for the proportion of wealthy people who lost 25% or more of their portfolio value over the past three years.
    b. The survey reported that 31% of the respondents feel they have to save more for retirement to make up for what they lost. Develop a 95% confidence interval for the population proportion.
    c. Five percent of the respondents gave $25,000 or more to charity over the previous year. Develop a 95% confidence interval for the proportion who gave $25,000 or more to charity.
    d. Compare the margin of error for the interval estimates in parts (a), (b), and (c). How is the margin of error related to $\bar{p}$? When the same sample is being used to estimate a variety of proportions, which of the proportions should be used to choose the planning value p^*? Why do you think $p^* = .50$ is often used in these cases?

Summary

In this chapter we presented methods for developing interval estimates of a population mean and a population proportion. A point estimator may or may not provide a good estimate of a population parameter. The use of an interval estimate provides a measure of the precision of an estimate. Both the interval estimate of the population mean and the population proportion are of the form: point estimate ± margin of error.

We presented interval estimates for a population mean for two cases. In the σ known case, historical data or other information is used to develop an estimate of σ prior to taking a sample. Analysis of new sample data then proceeds based on the assumption that σ is known. In the σ unknown case, the sample data are used to estimate both the population mean and the population standard deviation. The final choice of which interval estimation procedure to use depends upon the analyst's understanding of which method provides the best estimate of σ.

In the σ known case, the interval estimation procedure is based on the assumed value of σ and the use of the standard normal distribution. In the σ unknown case, the interval estimation procedure uses the sample standard deviation s and the t distribution. In both cases the quality of the interval estimates obtained depends on the distribution of the population and the sample size. If the population is normally distributed the interval estimates will be exact in both cases, even for small sample sizes. If the population is not normally distributed, the interval estimates obtained will be approximate. Larger sample sizes will provide better approximations, but the more highly skewed the population is, the larger the sample size needs to be to obtain a good approximation. Practical advice about the sample size necessary to obtain good approximations was included in Sections 8.1 and 8.2. In most cases a sample of size 30 or more will provide good approximate confidence intervals.

The general form of the interval estimate for a population proportion is $\bar{p}$ ± margin of error. In practice the sample sizes used for interval estimates of a population proportion are generally large. Thus, the interval estimation procedure is based on the standard normal distribution.

Often a desired margin of error is specified prior to developing a sampling plan. We showed how to choose a sample size large enough to provide the desired precision.

Glossary

Interval estimate An estimate of a population parameter that provides an interval believed to contain the value of the parameter. For the interval estimates in this chapter, it has the form: point estimate ± margin of error.

Margin of error The ± value added to and subtracted from a point estimate in order to develop an interval estimate of a population parameter.

σ known The case when historical data or other information provides a good value for the population standard deviation prior to taking a sample. The interval estimation procedure uses this known value of σ in computing the margin of error.

σ unknown The more common case when no good basis exists for estimating the population standard deviation prior to taking the sample. The interval estimation procedure uses the sample standard deviation s in computing the margin of error.

Confidence level The confidence associated with an interval estimate. For example, if an interval estimation procedure provides intervals such that 95% of the intervals formed using the procedure will include the population parameter, the interval estimate is said to be constructed at the 95% confidence level.

Confidence coefficient The confidence level expressed as a decimal value. For example, .95 is the confidence coefficient for a 95% confidence level.

Confidence interval Another name for an interval estimate.

t distribution A family of probability distributions that can be used to develop an interval estimate of a population mean whenever the population standard deviation σ is unknown and is estimated by the sample standard deviation s.

Degrees of freedom A parameter of the t distribution. When the t distribution is used in the computation of an interval estimate of a population mean, the appropriate t distribution has $n - 1$ degrees of freedom, where n is the size of the simple random sample.

Key Formulas

Interval Estimate of a Population Mean: σ Known

$$\bar{x} \pm z_{\alpha/2} \frac{\sigma}{\sqrt{n}}$$

← margin error

(8.1)

Interval Estimate of a Population Mean: σ Unknown

$$\bar{x} \pm t_{\alpha/2} \frac{s}{\sqrt{n}}$$

(8.2)

Sample Size for an Interval Estimate of a Population Mean

$$n = \frac{(z_{\alpha/2})^2 \sigma^2}{E^2}$$

(8.3)

Interval Estimate of a Population Proportion

$$\bar{p} \pm z_{\alpha/2} \sqrt{\frac{\bar{p}(1 - \bar{p})}{n}}$$

(8.6)

Sample Size for an Interval Estimate of a Population Proportion

$$n = \frac{(z_{\alpha/2})^2 p^*(1 - p^*)}{E^2}$$

(8.7)

Supplementary Exercises

44. A survey of first-time home buyers found that the mean of annual household income was $50,000 (CNBC.com, July 11, 2000). Assume the survey used a sample of 400 first-time home buyers and assume that the population standard deviation is $20,500.
    a. At 95% confidence, what is the margin of error for this study?
    b. What is the 95% confidence interval for the population mean annual household income for first-time home buyers?

45. A survey conducted by the American Automobile Association showed that a family of four spends an average of $215.60 per day while on vacation. Suppose a sample of 64 families of four vacationing at Niagara Falls resulted in a sample mean of $252.45 per day and a sample standard deviation of $74.50.
    a. Develop a 95% confidence interval estimate of the mean amount spent per day by a family of four visiting Niagara Falls.
    b. Based on the confidence interval from part (a), does it appear that the population mean amount spent per day by families visiting Niagara Falls differs from the mean reported by the American Automobile Association? Explain.

46. The motion picture *Harry Potter and the Sorcerer's Stone* shattered the box office debut record previously held by *The Lost World: Jurassic Park* (*The Wall Street Journal,* November 19, 2001). A sample of 100 movie theaters showed that the mean three-day weekend gross was $25,467 per theater. The sample standard deviation was $4980.
    a. What is the margin of error for this study? Use 95% confidence.
    b. What is the 95% confidence interval estimate for the population mean weekend gross per theater?
    c. *The Lost World* took in $72.1 million in its first three-day weekend. *Harry Potter and the Sorcerer's Stone* was shown in 3672 theaters. What is an estimate of the total *Harry Potter and the Sorcerer's Stone* took in during its first three-day weekend?
    d. An Associated Press article claimed *Harry Potter* "shattered" the box office debut record held by *The Lost World*. Do your results agree with this claim?

47. Many stock market observers say that when the P/E ratio for stocks gets over 20 the market is overvalued. The P/E ratio is the stock price divided by the most recent 12 months of earnings. Suppose you are interested in seeing whether the current market is overvalued and would also like to know what proportion of companies pay dividends. A random sample of 30 companies listed on the New York Stock Exchange (NYSE) is provided (*Barron's*, January 19, 2004).

NYSEStocks

Company	Dividend	P/E Ratio	Company	Dividend	P/E Ratio
Albertsons	Yes	14	NY Times A	Yes	25
BRE Prop	Yes	18	Omnicare	Yes	25
CityNtl	Yes	16	PallCp	Yes	23
DelMonte	No	21	PubSvcEnt	Yes	11
EnrgzHldg	No	20	SensientTch	Yes	11
Ford Motor	Yes	22	SmtProp	Yes	12
Gildan A	No	12	TJX Cos	Yes	21
HudsnUtdBcp	Yes	13	Thomson	Yes	30
IBM	Yes	22	USB Hldg	Yes	12
JeffPilot	Yes	16	US Restr	Yes	26
KingswayFin	No	6	Varian Med	No	41
Libbey	Yes	13	Visx	No	72
MasoniteIntl	No	15	Waste Mgt	No	23
Motorola	Yes	68	Wiley A	Yes	21
Ntl City	Yes	10	Yum Brands	No	18

   a. What is a point estimate of the P/E ratio for the population of stocks listed on the New York Stock Exchange? Develop a 95% confidence interval.
   b. Based on your answer to part (a), do you believe that the market is overvalued?
   c. What is a point estimate of the proportion of companies on the NYSE that pay dividends? Is the sample size large enough to justify using the normal distribution to construct a confidence interval for this proportion? Why or why not?

48. US Airways conducted a number of studies that indicated a substantial savings could be obtained by encouraging Dividend Miles frequent flyer customers to redeem miles and schedule award flights online (*US Airways Attaché*, February 2003). One study collected data on the amount of time required to redeem miles and schedule an award flight over the telephone. A sample showing the time in minutes required for each of 150 award flights scheduled by telephone is contained in the data set Flights. Use Minitab or Excel to help answer the following questions.

Flights

   a. What is the sample mean number of minutes required to schedule an award flight by telephone?
   b. What is the 95% confidence interval for the population mean time to schedule an award flight by telephone?
   c. Assume a telephone ticket agent works 7.5 hours per day. How many award flights can one ticket agent be expected to handle a day?
   d. Discuss why this information supported US Airways' plans to use an online system to reduce costs.

49. A survey by Accountemps asked a sample of 200 executives to provide data on the number of minutes per day office workers waste trying to locate mislabeled, misfiled, or misplaced items. Data consistent with this survey are contained in the data set ActTemps.

ActTemps

   a. Use ActTemps to develop a point estimate of the number of minutes per day office workers waste trying to locate mislabeled, misfiled, or misplaced items.
   b. What is the sample standard deviation?
   c. What is the 95% confidence interval for the mean number of minutes wasted per day?

50. Mileage tests are conducted for a particular model of automobile. If a 98% confidence interval with a margin of error of 1 mile per gallon is desired, how many automobiles should be used in the test? Assume that preliminary mileage tests indicate the standard deviation is 2.6 miles per gallon.

51. In developing patient appointment schedules, a medical center wants to estimate the mean time that a staff member spends with each patient. How large a sample should be taken if the desired margin of error is two minutes at a 95% level of confidence? How large a sample should be taken for a 99% level of confidence? Use a planning value for the population standard deviation of eight minutes.

52. Annual salary plus bonus data for chief executive officers are presented in the *Business Week* Annual Pay Survey. A preliminary sample showed that the standard deviation is $675 with data provided in thousands of dollars. How many chief executive officers should be in a sample if we want to estimate the population mean annual salary plus bonus with a margin of error of $100,000? (*Note:* The desired margin of error would be $E = 100$ if the data are in thousands of dollars.) Use 95% confidence.

53. The National Center for Education Statistics reported that 47% of college students work to pay for tuition and living expenses. Assume that a sample of 450 college students was used in the study.
    a. Provide a 95% confidence interval for the population proportion of college students who work to pay for tuition and living expenses.
    b. Provide a 99% confidence interval for the population proportion of college students who work to pay for tuition and living expenses.
    c. What happens to the margin of error as the confidence is increased from 95% to 99%?

54. A *USA Today*/CNN/Gallup survey of 369 working parents found 200 who said they spend too little time with their children because of work commitments.
    a. What is the point estimate of the proportion of the population of working parents who feel they spend too little time with their children because of work commitments?
    b. At 95% confidence, what is the margin of error?
    c. What is the 95% confidence interval estimate of the population proportion of working parents who feel they spend too little time with their children because of work commitments?

55. Which would be hardest for you to give up: Your computer or your television? In a recent survey of 1677 U.S. Internet users, 74% of the young tech elite (average age of 22) say their computer would be very hard to give up (*PC Magazine*, February 3, 2004). Only 48% say their television would be very hard to give up.
    a. Develop a 95% confidence interval for the proportion of the young tech elite that would find it very hard to give up their computer.
    b. Develop a 99% confidence interval for the proportion of the young tech elite that would find it very hard to give up their television.
    c. In which case, part (a) or part (b), is the margin of error larger? Explain why.

56. A Roper Starch survey asked employees ages 18 to 29 whether they would prefer better health insurance or a raise in salary (*USA Today,* September 5, 2000). Answer the following questions assuming 340 of 500 employees said they would prefer better health insurance over a raise.
    a. What is the point estimate of the proportion of employees ages 18 to 29 who would prefer better health insurance?
    b. What is the 95% confidence interval estimate of the population proportion?

57. The *2003 Statistical Abstract of the United States* reported the percentage of people 18 years of age and older who smoke. Suppose that a study designed to collect new data on smokers and nonsmokers uses a preliminary estimate of the proportion who smoke of .30.
    a. How large a sample should be taken to estimate the proportion of smokers in the population with a margin of error of .02? Use 95% confidence.
    b. Assume that the study uses your sample size recommendation in part (a) and finds 520 smokers. What is the point estimate of the proportion of smokers in the population?
    c. What is the 95% confidence interval for the proportion of smokers in the population?

58. A well-known bank credit card firm wishes to estimate the proportion of credit card holders who carry a nonzero balance at the end of the month and incur an interest charge. Assume that the desired margin of error is .03 at 98% confidence.

a. How large a sample should be selected if it is anticipated that roughly 70% of the firm's card holders carry a nonzero balance at the end of the month?

b. How large a sample should be selected if no planning value for the proportion could be specified?

59. In a survey, 200 people were asked to identify their major source of news information; 110 stated that their major source was television news.

a. Construct a 95% confidence interval for the proportion of people in the population who consider television their major source of news information.

b. How large a sample would be necessary to estimate the population proportion with a margin of error of .05 at 95% confidence?

60. Although airline schedules and cost are important factors for business travelers when choosing an airline carrier, a *USA Today* survey found that business travelers list an airline's frequent flyer program as the most important factor. From a sample of $n = 1993$ business travelers who responded to the survey, 618 listed a frequent flyer program as the most important factor.

a. What is the point estimate of the proportion of the population of business travelers who believe a frequent flyer program is the most important factor when choosing an airline carrier?

b. Develop a 95% confidence interval estimate of the population proportion.

c. How large a sample would be required to report the margin of error of .01 at 95% confidence? Would you recommend that *USA Today* attempt to provide this degree of precision? Why or why not?

Case Problem 1 Bock Investment Services

The goal of Bock Investment Services (BIS) is to be the leading money market advisory service in South Carolina. To provide better service for its present clients and to attract new clients, BIS developed a weekly newsletter. BIS is considering adding a new feature to the newsletter that will report the results of a weekly telephone survey of fund managers. To investigate the feasibility of offering this service, and to determine what type of information to include in the newsletter, BIS selected a simple random sample of 45 money market funds. A portion of the data obtained is shown in Table 8.6, which reports fund assets and yields for the past 7 and 30 days. Before calling the money market fund managers to obtain additional data, BIS decided to do some preliminary analysis of the data already collected.

Managerial Report

1. Use appropriate descriptive statistics to summarize the data on assets and yields for the money market funds.
2. Develop a 95% confidence interval estimate of the mean assets, mean 7-day yield, and mean 30-day yield for the population of money market funds. Provide a managerial interpretation of each interval estimate.
3. Discuss the implication of your findings in terms of how BIS could use this type of information in preparing its weekly newsletter.
4. What other information would you recommend that BIS gather to provide the most useful information to its clients?

Case Problem 2 Gulf Real Estate Properties

Gulf Real Estate Properties, Inc., is a real estate firm located in southwest Florida. The company, which advertises itself as "expert in the real estate market," monitors condominium sales by collecting data on location, list price, sale price, and number of days it takes to sell

TABLE 8.6   DATA FOR BOCK INVESTMENT SERVICES

Bock

Money Market Fund	Assets ($ millions)	7-Day Yield (%)	30-Day Yield (%)
Amcore	103.9	4.10	4.08
Alger	156.7	4.79	4.73
Arch MM/Trust	496.5	4.17	4.13
BT Instit Treas	197.8	4.37	4.32
Benchmark Div	2755.4	4.54	4.47
Bradford	707.6	3.88	3.83
Capital Cash	1.7	4.29	4.22
Cash Mgt Trust	2707.8	4.14	4.04
Composite	122.8	4.03	3.91
Cowen Standby	694.7	4.25	4.19
Cortland	217.3	3.57	3.51
Declaration	38.4	2.67	2.61
Dreyfus	4832.8	4.01	3.89
Elfun	81.7	4.51	4.41
FFB Cash	506.2	4.17	4.11
Federated Master	738.7	4.41	4.34
Fidelity Cash	13272.8	4.51	4.42
Flex-fund	172.8	4.60	4.48
Fortis	105.6	3.87	3.85
Franklin Money	996.8	3.97	3.92
Freedom Cash	1079.0	4.07	4.01
Galaxy Money	801.4	4.11	3.96
Government Cash	409.4	3.83	3.82
Hanover Cash	794.3	4.32	4.23
Heritage Cash	1008.3	4.08	4.00
Infinity/Alpha	53.6	3.99	3.91
John Hancock	226.4	3.93	3.87
Landmark Funds	481.3	4.28	4.26
Liquid Cash	388.9	4.61	4.64
MarketWatch	10.6	4.13	4.05
Merrill Lynch Money	27005.6	4.24	4.18
NCC Funds	113.4	4.22	4.20
Nationwide	517.3	4.22	4.14
Overland	291.5	4.26	4.17
Pierpont Money	1991.7	4.50	4.40
Portico Money	161.6	4.28	4.20
Prudential MoneyMart	6835.1	4.20	4.16
Reserve Primary	1408.8	3.91	3.86
Schwab Money	10531.0	4.16	4.07
Smith Barney Cash	2947.6	4.16	4.12
Stagecoach	1502.2	4.18	4.13
Strong Money	470.2	4.37	4.29
Transamerica Cash	175.5	4.20	4.19
United Cash	323.7	3.96	3.89
Woodward Money	1330.0	4.24	4.21

Source: Barron's, October 3, 1994.

TABLE 8.7   SALES DATA FOR GULF REAL ESTATE PROPERTIES

Gulf View Condominiums			No Gulf View Condominiums		
List Price	Sale Price	Days to Sell	List Price	Sale Price	Days to Sell
495.0	475.0	130	217.0	217.0	182
379.0	350.0	71	148.0	135.5	338
529.0	519.0	85	186.5	179.0	122
552.5	534.5	95	239.0	230.0	150
334.9	334.9	119	279.0	267.5	169
550.0	505.0	92	215.0	214.0	58
169.9	165.0	197	279.0	259.0	110
210.0	210.0	56	179.9	176.5	130
975.0	945.0	73	149.9	144.9	149
314.0	314.0	126	235.0	230.0	114
315.0	305.0	88	199.8	192.0	120
885.0	800.0	282	210.0	195.0	61
975.0	975.0	100	226.0	212.0	146
469.0	445.0	56	149.9	146.5	137
329.0	305.0	49	160.0	160.0	281
365.0	330.0	48	322.0	292.5	63
332.0	312.0	88	187.5	179.0	48
520.0	495.0	161	247.0	227.0	52
425.0	405.0	149			
675.0	669.0	142			
409.0	400.0	28			
649.0	649.0	29			
319.0	305.0	140			
425.0	410.0	85			
359.0	340.0	107			
469.0	449.0	72			
895.0	875.0	129			
439.0	430.0	160			
435.0	400.0	206			
235.0	227.0	91			
638.0	618.0	100			
629.0	600.0	97			
329.0	309.0	114			
595.0	555.0	45			
339.0	315.0	150			
215.0	200.0	48			
395.0	375.0	135			
449.0	425.0	53			
499.0	465.0	86			
439.0	428.5	158			

CD file

GulfProp

each unit. Each condominium is classified as *Gulf View* if it is located directly on the Gulf of Mexico or *No Gulf View* if it is located on the bay or a golf course, near but not on the Gulf. Sample data from the Multiple Listing Service in Naples, Florida, provided recent sales data for 40 Gulf View condominiums and 18 No Gulf View condominiums.* Prices are in thousands of dollars. The data are shown in Table 8.7.

---

*Data based on condominium sales reported in the Naples MLS (Coldwell Banker, June 2000).

Managerial Report

1. Use appropriate descriptive statistics to summarize each of the three variables for the 40 Gulf View condominiums.
2. Use appropriate descriptive statistics to summarize each of the three variables for the 18 No Gulf View condominiums.
3. Compare your summary results. Discuss any specific statistical results that would help a real estate agent understand the condominium market.
4. Develop a 95% confidence interval estimate of the population mean sales price and population mean number of days to sell for Gulf View condominiums. Interpret your results.
5. Develop a 95% confidence interval estimate of the population mean sales price and population mean number of days to sell for No Gulf View condominiums. Interpret your results.
6. Assume the branch manager requested estimates of the mean selling price of Gulf View condominiums with a margin of error of $40,000 and the mean selling price of No Gulf View condominiums with a margin of error of $15,000. Using 95% confidence, how large should the sample sizes be?
7. Gulf Real Estate Properties just signed contracts for two new listings: a Gulf View condominium with a list price of $589,000 and a No Gulf View condominium with a list price of $285,000. What is your estimate of the final selling price and number of days required to sell each of these units?

Case Problem 3   Metropolitan Research, Inc.

Metropolitan Research, Inc., a consumer research organization, conducts surveys designed to evaluate a wide variety of products and services available to consumers. In one particular study, Metropolitan looked at consumer satisfaction with the performance of automobiles produced by a major Detroit manufacturer. A questionnaire sent to owners of one of the manufacturer's full-sized cars revealed several complaints about early transmission problems. To learn more about the transmission failures, Metropolitan used a sample of actual transmission repairs provided by a transmission repair firm in the Detroit area. The following data show the actual number of miles driven for 50 vehicles at the time of transmission failure.

85,092	32,609	59,465	77,437	32,534	64,090	32,464	59,902
39,323	89,641	94,219	116,803	92,857	63,436	65,605	85,861
64,342	61,978	67,998	59,817	101,769	95,774	121,352	69,568
74,276	66,998	40,001	72,069	25,066	77,098	69,922	35,662
74,425	67,202	118,444	53,500	79,294	64,544	86,813	116,269
37,831	89,341	73,341	85,288	138,114	53,402	85,586	82,256
77,539	88,798						

Managerial Report

1. Use appropriate descriptive statistics to summarize the transmission failure data.
2. Develop a 95% confidence interval for the mean number of miles driven until transmission failure for the population of automobiles with transmission failure. Provide a managerial interpretation of the interval estimate.
3. Discuss the implication of your statistical finding in terms of the belief that some owners of the automobiles experienced early transmission failures.

4. How many repair records should be sampled if the research firm wants the population mean number of miles driven until transmission failure to be estimated with a margin of error of 5000 miles? Use 95% confidence.

5. What other information would you like to gather to evaluate the transmission failure problem more fully?

Appendix 8.1   Interval Estimation with Minitab

We describe the use of Minitab in constructing confidence intervals for a population mean and a population proportion.

Population Mean: σ Known

Lloyd's

We illustrate interval estimation using the Lloyd's example in Section 8.1. The amounts spent per shopping trip for the sample of 100 customers are in column C1 of a Minitab worksheet. The population standard deviation $\sigma = 20$ is assumed known. The following steps can be used to compute a 95% confidence interval estimate of the population mean.

Step 1. Select the **Stat** menu
Step 2. Choose **Basic Statistics**
Step 3. Choose **1-Sample Z**
Step 4. When the 1-Sample Z dialog box appears:
    Enter C1 in the **Samples in columns** box
    Enter 20 in the **Standard deviation** box
Step 5. Click **OK**

The Minitab default is a 95% confidence level. In order to specify a different confidence level such as 90%, add the following to step 4.

  Select **Options**
  When the 1-Sample Z-Options dialog box appears:
    Enter 90 in the **Confidence level** box
  Click **OK**

Population Mean: σ Unknown

Balance

We illustrate interval estimation using the data in Table 8.3 showing the credit card balances for a sample of 85 households. The data are in column C1 of a Minitab worksheet. In this case the population standard deviation σ will be estimated by the sample standard deviation s. The following steps can be used to compute a 95% confidence interval estimate of the population mean.

Step 1. Select the **Stat** menu
Step 2. Choose **Basic Statistics**
Step 3. Choose **1-Sample t**
Step 4. When the 1-Sample t dialog box appears:
    Enter C1 in the **Samples in columns** box
Step 5. Click **OK**

The Minitab default is a 95% confidence level. In order to specify a different confidence level such as 90%, add the following to step 4.

  Select **Options**
  When the 1-Sample t-Options dialog box appears:
    Enter 90 in the **Confidence level** box
  Click **OK**

Population Proportion

CD file

TeeTimes

We illustrate interval estimation using the survey data for women golfers presented in Section 8.4. The data are in column C1 of a Minitab worksheet. Individual responses are recorded as Yes if the golfer is satisfied with the availability of tee times and No otherwise. The following steps can be used to compute a 95% confidence interval estimate of the proportion of women golfers who are satisfied with the availability of tee times.

Step 1. Select the **Stat** menu
Step 2. Choose **Basic Statistics**
Step 3. Choose **1 Proportion**
Step 4. When the 1 Proportion dialog box appears:
        Enter C1 in the **Samples in columns** box
Step 5. Select **Options**
Step 6. When the 1 Proportion-Options dialog box appears:
        Select **Use test and interval based on normal distribution**
        Click **OK**
Step 7. Click **OK**

The Minitab default is a 95% confidence level. In order to specify a different confidence level such as 90%, enter 90 in the **Confidence Level** box when the 1 Proportion-Options dialog box appears in step 6.

Note: Minitab's 1 Proportion routine uses an alphabetical ordering of the responses and selects the *second response* for the population proportion of interest. In the women golfers example, Minitab used the alphabetical ordering No-Yes and then provided the confidence interval for the proportion of Yes responses. Because Yes was the response of interest, the Minitab output was fine. However, if Minitab's alphabetical ordering does not provide the response of interest, select any cell in the column and use the sequence: Editor > Column > Value Order. It will provide you with the option of entering a user-specified order, but you must list the response of interest second in the define-an-order box.

Appendix 8.2   Interval Estimation Using Excel

We describe the use of Excel in constructing confidence intervals for a population mean and a population proportion.

Population Mean: σ Known

CD file

Lloyd's

We illustrate interval estimation using the Lloyd's example in Section 8.1. The population standard deviation $\sigma = 20$ is assumed known. The amounts spent for the sample of 100 customers are in column A of an Excel worksheet. The following steps can be used to compute the margin of error for an estimate of the population mean. We begin by using Excel's Descriptive Statistics Tool described in Chapter 3.

Step 1. Select the **Tools** menu
Step 2. Choose **Data Analysis**
Step 3. Choose **Descriptive Statistics** from the list of Analysis Tools
Step 4. When the Descriptive Statistics dialog box appears:
        Enter A1:A101 in the **Input Range** box
        Select **Grouped by Columns**
        Select **Labels in First Row**
        Select **Output Range**

Enter C1 in the **Output Range** box
Select **Summary Statistics**
Click **OK**

The summary statistics will appear in columns C and D. Continue by computing the margin of error using Excel's Confidence function as follows:

Step 5. Select cell C16 and enter the label Margin of Error
Step 6. Select cell D16 and enter the Excel formula =CONFIDENCE(.05,20,100)

The three parameters of the Confidence function are

Alpha = 1 − confidence coefficient = 1 − .95 = .05
The population standard deviation = 20
The sample size = 100 (*Note:* This parameter appears as Count in cell D15.)

The point estimate of the population mean is in cell D3 and the margin of error is in cell D16. The point estimate (82) and the margin of error (3.92) allow the confidence interval for the population mean to be easily computed.

Population Mean: σ Unknown

Balance

We illustrate interval estimation using the data in Table 8.3, which show the credit card balances for a sample of 85 households. The data are in column A of an Excel worksheet. The following steps can be used to compute the point estimate and the margin of error for an interval estimate of a population mean. We will use Excel's Descriptive Statistics Tool described in Chapter 3.

Step 1. Select the **Tools** menu
Step 2. Choose **Data Analysis**
Step 3. Choose **Descriptive Statistics** from the list of Analysis Tools
Step 4. When the Descriptive Statistics dialog box appears:
      Enter A1:A86 in the **Input Range** box
      Select **Grouped by Columns**
      Select **Labels in First Row**
      Select **Output Range**
      Enter C1 in the Output Range box
      Select **Summary Statistics**
      Select **Confidence Level for Mean**
         Enter 95 in the Confidence Level for Mean box
      Click **OK**

The summary statistics will appear in columns C and D. The point estimate of the population mean appears in cell D3. The margin of error, labeled "Confidence Level(95.0%)," appears in cell D16. The point estimate ($5900) and the margin of error ($660) allow the confidence interval for the population mean to be easily computed. The output from this Excel procedure is shown in Figure 8.10.

Population Proportion

We illustrate interval estimation using the survey data for women golfers presented in Section 8.4. The data are in column A of an Excel worksheet. Individual responses are recorded as Yes if the golfer is satisfied with the availability of tee times and No otherwise. Excel does not offer a built-in routine to handle the estimation of a population proportion; however, it

FIGURE 8.10   INTERVAL ESTIMATION OF THE POPULATION MEAN CREDIT CARD BALANCE USING EXCEL

	A	B	C	D	E	F
1	**Balance**		*Balance*			
2	9619					
3	5364		Mean	5900	Point Estimate	
4	8348		Standard Error	331.7		
5	7348		Median	5759		
6	381		Mode	8047		
7	2998		Standard Deviation	3058		
8	1686		Sample Variance	9351364		
9	1962		Kurtosis	0.2327		
10	4920		Skewness	0.4076		
11	5047		Range	14061		
12	6921		Minimum	381		
13	5759		Maximum	14442		
14	8047		Sum	501500		
15	3924		Count	85	Margin of Error	
16	3470		Confidence Level(95.0%)	660		
17	5994					
81	5938					
82	5266					
83	10658					
84	3910					
85	7503					
86	1582					
87						

Note: Rows 18 to 80 are hidden.

Interval p

is relatively easy to develop an Excel template that can be used for this purpose. The template shown in Figure 8.11 provides the 95% confidence interval estimate of the proportion of women golfers who are satisfied with the availability of tee times. Note that the background worksheet in Figure 8.11 shows the cell formulas that provide the interval estimation results shown in the foreground worksheet. The following steps are necessary to use the template for this data set.

Step 1. Enter the data range A2:A901 into the =COUNTA cell formula in cell D3
Step 2. Enter Yes as the response of interest in cell D4
Step 3. Enter the data range A2:A901 into the =COUNTIF cell formula in cell D5
Step 4. Enter .95 as the confidence coefficient in cell D8

The template automatically provides the confidence interval in cells D15 and D16.

This template can be used to compute the confidence interval for a population proportion for other applications. For instance, to compute the interval estimate for a new data set, enter the new sample data into column A of the worksheet and then make the changes to the four cells as shown. If the new sample data have already been summarized, the sample data do not have to be entered into the worksheet. In this case, enter the sample size into cell D3 and the sample proportion into cell D6; the worksheet template will then provide the confidence interval for the population proportion. The worksheet in Figure 8.11 is available in the file Interval p on the CD that accompanies this book.

FIGURE 8.11   EXCEL TEMPLATE FOR INTERVAL ESTIMATION OF A POPULATION PROPORTION

	A	B	C	D	E
1	Response		**Interval Estimate of a Population Proportion**		
2	Yes				
3	No		Sample Size	=COUNTA(A2:A901)	
4	Yes		Response of Interest	Yes	
5	Yes		Count for Response	=COUNTIF(A2:A901,D4)	
6	No		Sample Proportion	=D5/D3	
7	No				
8	No		Confidence Coefficient	0.95	
9	Yes		z Value	=NORMSINV(0.5+D8/2)	
10	Yes				
11	Yes		Standard Error	=SQRT(D6*(1-D6)/D3)	
12	No		Margin of Error	=D9*D11	
13	No				
14	Yes		Point Estimate	=D6	
15	No		Lower Limit	=D14-D12	
16	No		Upper Limit	=D14+D12	
17	Yes				
18	No				
901	Yes				
902					

	A	B	C	D	E	F	G
1	Response		**Interval Estimate of a Population Proportion**				
2	Yes						
3	No		Sample Size	900			
4	Yes		Response of Interest	Yes			
5	Yes		Count for Response	396			
6	No		Sample Proportion	0.4400			
7	No						
8	No		Confidence Coefficient	0.95			
9	Yes		z Value	1.960			
10	Yes						
11	Yes		Standard Error	0.0165			
12	No		Margin of Error	0.0324			
13	No						
14	Yes		Point Estimate	0.4400			
15	No		Lower Limit	0.4076			
16	No		Upper Limit	0.4724			
17	Yes						
18	No						
901	Yes						
902							

Enter the response of interest

Enter the confidence coefficient

Note: Rows 19 to 900 are hidden.

CHAPTER 9

Hypothesis Tests

CONTENTS

STATISTICS *in* PRACTICE

JOHN MORRELL & COMPANY*
CINCINNATI, OHIO

John Morrell & Company, which began in England in 1827, is considered the oldest continuously operating meat manufacturer in the United States. It is a wholly owned and independently managed subsidiary of Smithfield Foods, Smithfield, Virginia. John Morrell & Company offers an extensive product line of processed meats and fresh pork to consumers under 13 regional brands including John Morrell, E-Z-Cut, Tobin's First Prize, Dinner Bell, Hunter, Kretschmar, Rath, Rodeo, Shenson, Farmers Hickory Brand, Iowa Quality, and Peyton's. Each regional brand enjoys high brand recognition and loyalty among consumers.

Market research at Morrell provides management with up-to-date information on the company's various products and how the products compare with competing brands of similar products. A recent study investigated consumer preference for Morrell's Convenient Cuisine Beef Pot Roast compared to similar beef products from two major competitors. In the three-product comparison test, a sample of consumers was used to indicate how the products rated in terms of taste, appearance, aroma, and overall preference.

One research question concerned whether Morrell's Convenient Cuisine Beef Pot Roast was the preferred choice of more than 50% of the consumer population. Letting p indicate the population proportion preferring Morrell's product, the hypothesis test for the research question is as follows:

$$H_0: p \leq .50$$
$$H_a: p > .50$$

The null hypothesis H_0 indicates the preference for Morrell's product is less than or equal to 50%. If the sample data sup-

Convenient Cuisine fully-cooked entrees allow consumers to heat and serve in the same microwaveable tray. © Courtesy of John Morrell's Convenient Cuisine products.

port rejecting H_0 in favor of the alternate hypothesis H_a, Morrell will draw the research conclusion that in a three-product comparison, their product is preferred by more than 50% of the consumer population.

In an independent taste test study using a sample of 224 consumers in Cincinnati, Milwaukee, and Los Angeles, 150 consumers selected the Morrell Convenient Cuisine Beef Pot Roast as the preferred product. Using statistical hypothesis testing procedures, the null hypothesis H_0 was rejected. The study provided statistical evidence supporting H_a and the conclusion that the Morrell product is preferred by more than 50% of the consumer population.

The point estimate of the population proportion was $\bar{p} = 150/224 = .67$. Thus, the sample data provided support for a food magazine advertisement showing that in a three-product taste comparison, Morrell's Convenient Cuisine Beef Pot Roast was "preferred 2 to 1 over the competition."

In this chapter we will discuss how to formulate hypotheses and how to conduct tests like the one used by Morrell. Through the analysis of sample data, we will be able to determine whether a hypothesis should or should not be rejected.

*The authors are indebted to Marty Butler, Vice President of Marketing, John Morrell, for providing this Statistics in Practice.

In Chapters 7 and 8 we showed how a sample could be used to develop point and interval estimates of population parameters. In this chapter we continue the discussion of statistical inference by showing how hypothesis testing can be used to determine whether a statement about the value of a population parameter should or should not be rejected.

In hypothesis testing we begin by making a tentative assumption about a population parameter. This tentative assumption is called the **null hypothesis** and is denoted by H_0. We then define another hypothesis, called the **alternative hypothesis**, which is the opposite of what is stated in the null hypothesis. The alternative hypothesis is denoted by H_a.

The hypothesis testing procedure uses data from a sample to test the two competing statements indicated by H_0 and H_a.

This chapter shows how hypothesis tests can be conducted about a population mean and a population proportion. We begin by providing examples that illustrate approaches to developing null and alternative hypotheses.

9.1 Developing Null and Alternative Hypotheses

Learning to formulate hypotheses correctly will take practice. Expect some initial confusion over the proper choice for H_0 and H_a. The examples in this section show a variety of forms for H_0 and H_a depending upon the application.

In some applications it may not be obvious how the null and alternative hypotheses should be formulated. Care must be taken to structure the hypotheses appropriately so that the hypothesis testing conclusion provides the information the researcher or decision maker wants. Guidelines for establishing the null and alternative hypotheses are given for three types of situations in which hypothesis testing procedures are commonly employed.

Testing Research Hypotheses

Consider a particular automobile model that currently attains an average fuel efficiency of 24 miles per gallon. A product research group developed a new fuel injection system specifically designed to increase the miles-per-gallon rating. To evaluate the new system, several will be manufactured, installed in automobiles, and subjected to research-controlled driving tests. Here the product research group is looking for evidence to conclude that the new system *increases* the mean miles-per-gallon rating. In this case, the research hypothesis is that the new fuel injection system will provide a mean miles-per-gallon rating exceeding 24; that is, $\mu > 24$. As a general guideline, a research hypothesis should be stated as the *alternative hypothesis*. Hence, the appropriate null and alternative hypotheses for the study are

$$H_0: \mu \leq 24$$
$$H_a: \mu > 24$$

The conclusion that the research hypothesis is true is made if the sample data contradict the null hypothesis.

If the sample results indicate that H_0 cannot be rejected, researchers cannot conclude that the new fuel injection system is better. Perhaps more research and subsequent testing should be conducted. However, if the sample results indicate that H_0 can be rejected, researchers can make the inference that $H_a: \mu > 24$ is true. With this conclusion, the researchers gain the statistical support necessary to state that the new system increases the mean number of miles per gallon. Production with the new system should be considered.

In research studies such as these, the null and alternative hypotheses should be formulated so that the rejection of H_0 supports the research conclusion. The research hypothesis therefore should be expressed as the alternative hypothesis.

Testing the Validity of a Claim

As an illustration of testing the validity of a claim, consider the situation of a manufacturer of soft drinks who states that two-liter containers of its products contain an average of at least 67.6 fluid ounces. A sample of two-liter containers will be selected, and the contents will be measured to test the manufacturer's claim. In this type of hypothesis testing situation, we generally assume that the manufacturer's claim is true unless the sample evidence is contradictory. Using this approach for the soft drink example, we would state the null and alternative hypotheses as follows.

$$H_0: \mu \geq 67.6$$
$$H_a: \mu < 67.6$$

If the sample results indicate H_0 cannot be rejected, the manufacturer's claim will not be challenged. However, if the sample results indicate H_0 can be rejected, the inference will be made that H_a: $\mu < 67.6$ is true. With this conclusion, statistical evidence indicates that the manufacturer's claim is incorrect and that the soft drink containers are being filled with a mean less than the claimed 67.6 ounces. Appropriate action against the manufacturer may be considered.

A manufacturer's claim is usually given the benefit of the doubt and stated as the null hypothesis. The conclusion that the claim is false can be made if the null hypothesis is rejected.

In situations involving testing the validity of a claim, the null hypothesis is generally based on the assumption that the claim is true. The alternative hypothesis is then formulated so that rejection of H_0 will provide statistical evidence that the stated assumption is incorrect. Action to correct the claim should be considered whenever H_0 is rejected.

Testing in Decision-Making Situations

In testing research hypotheses or testing the validity of a claim, action is taken if H_0 is rejected. In many instances, however, action must be taken both when H_0 cannot be rejected and when H_0 can be rejected. In general, this type of situation occurs when a decision maker must choose between two courses of action, one associated with the null hypothesis and another associated with the alternative hypothesis. For example, on the basis of a sample of parts from a shipment just received, a quality control inspector must decide whether to accept the shipment or to return the shipment to the supplier because it does not meet specifications. Assume that specifications for a particular part require a mean length of 2 inches per part. If the mean length is greater or less than the 2-inch standard, the parts will cause quality problems in the assembly operation. In this case, the null and alternative hypotheses would be formulated as follows.

$$H_0: \mu = 2$$
$$H_a: \mu \neq 2$$

If the sample results indicate H_0 cannot be rejected, the quality control inspector will have no reason to doubt that the shipment meets specifications, and the shipment will be accepted. However, if the sample results indicate H_0 should be rejected, the conclusion will be that the parts do not meet specifications. In this case, the quality control inspector will have sufficient evidence to return the shipment to the supplier. Thus, we see that for these types of situations, action is taken both when H_0 cannot be rejected and when H_0 can be rejected.

Summary of Forms for Null and Alternative Hypotheses

The hypothesis tests in this chapter involve two population parameters: the population mean and the population proportion. Depending on the situation, hypothesis tests about a population parameter may take one of three forms: two use inequalities in the null hypothesis; the third uses an equality in the null hypothesis. For hypothesis tests involving a population mean, we let μ_0 denote the hypothesized value and we must choose one of the following three forms for the hypothesis test.

The three possible forms of hypotheses H_0 and H_a are shown here. Note that the equality always appears in the null hypothesis H_0.

$$H_0: \mu \geq \mu_0 \qquad H_0: \mu \leq \mu_0 \qquad H_0: \mu = \mu_0$$
$$H_a: \mu < \mu_0 \qquad H_a: \mu > \mu_0 \qquad H_a: \mu \neq \mu_0$$

For reasons that will be clear later, the first two forms are called one-tailed tests. The third form is called a two-tailed test.

In many situations, the choice of H_0 and H_a is not obvious and judgment is necessary to select the proper form. However, as the preceding forms show, the equality part of the expression (either $\geq$, $\leq$, or $=$) *always* appears in the null hypothesis. In selecting the proper form of H_0 and H_a, keep in mind that the alternative hypothesis is often what the test is attempting to establish. Hence, asking whether the user is looking for evidence to support $\mu < \mu_0$, $\mu > \mu_0$, or $\mu \neq \mu_0$ will help determine H_a. The following exercises are designed to provide practice in choosing the proper form for a hypothesis test involving a population mean.

Exercises

1. The manager of the Danvers-Hilton Resort Hotel stated that the mean guest bill for a weekend is $600 or less. A member of the hotel's accounting staff noticed that the total charges for guest bills have been increasing in recent months. The accountant will use a sample of weekend guest bills to test the manager's claim.
   a. Which form of the hypotheses should be used to test the manager's claim? Explain.

   $$H_0: \mu \geq 600 \qquad H_0: \mu \leq 600 \qquad H_0: \mu = 600$$
   $$H_a: \mu < 600 \qquad H_a: \mu > 600 \qquad H_a: \mu \neq 600$$

   b. What conclusion is appropriate when H_0 cannot be rejected?
   c. What conclusion is appropriate when H_0 can be rejected?

2. The manager of an automobile dealership is considering a new bonus plan designed to increase sales volume. Currently, the mean sales volume is 14 automobiles per month. The manager wants to conduct a research study to see whether the new bonus plan increases sales volume. To collect data on the plan, a sample of sales personnel will be allowed to sell under the new bonus plan for a one-month period.
   a. Develop the null and alternative hypotheses most appropriate for this research situation.
   b. Comment on the conclusion when H_0 cannot be rejected.
   c. Comment on the conclusion when H_0 can be rejected.

3. A production line operation is designed to fill cartons with laundry detergent to a mean weight of 32 ounces. A sample of cartons is periodically selected and weighed to determine whether underfilling or overfilling is occurring. If the sample data lead to a conclusion of underfilling or overfilling, the production line will be shut down and adjusted to obtain proper filling.
   a. Formulate the null and alternative hypotheses that will help in deciding whether to shut down and adjust the production line.
   b. Comment on the conclusion and the decision when H_0 cannot be rejected.
   c. Comment on the conclusion and the decision when H_0 can be rejected.

4. Because of high production-changeover time and costs, a director of manufacturing must convince management that a proposed manufacturing method reduces costs before the new method can be implemented. The current production method operates with a mean cost of $220 per hour. A research study will measure the cost of the new method over a sample production period.
   a. Develop the null and alternative hypotheses most appropriate for this study.
   b. Comment on the conclusion when H_0 cannot be rejected.
   c. Comment on the conclusion when H_0 can be rejected.

 9.2 ## Type I and Type II Errors

The null and alternative hypotheses are competing statements about the population. Either the null hypothesis H_0 is true or the alternative hypothesis H_a is true, but not both. Ideally the hypothesis testing procedure should lead to the acceptance of H_0 when H_0 is true and the

TABLE 9.1   ERRORS AND CORRECT CONCLUSIONS IN HYPOTHESIS TESTING

		Population Condition	
		H_0 **True**	H_a **True**
Conclusion	**Accept** H_0	Correct Conclusion	Type II Error
	Reject H_0	Type I Error	Correct Conclusion

rejection of H_0 when H_a is true. Unfortunately, the correct conclusions are not always possible. Because hypothesis tests are based on sample information, we must allow for the possibility of errors. Table 9.1 illustrates the two kinds of errors that can be made in hypothesis testing.

The first row of Table 9.1 shows what can happen if the conclusion is to accept H_0. If H_0 is true, this conclusion is correct. However, if H_a is true, we make a **Type II error**; that is, we accept H_0 when it is false. The second row of Table 9.1 shows what can happen if the conclusion is to reject H_0. If H_0 is true, we make a **Type I error**; that is, we reject H_0 when it is true. However, if H_a is true, rejecting H_0 is correct.

Recall the hypothesis testing illustration discussed in Section 9.1 in which an automobile product research group developed a new fuel injection system designed to increase the miles-per-gallon rating of a particular automobile. With the current model obtaining an average of 24 miles per gallon, the hypothesis test was formulated as follows.

$$H_0: \mu \le 24$$
$$H_a: \mu > 24$$

The alternative hypothesis, $H_a: \mu > 24$, indicates that the researchers are looking for sample evidence to support the conclusion that the population mean miles per gallon with the new fuel injection system is greater than 24.

In this application, the Type I error of rejecting H_0 when it is true corresponds to the researchers claiming that the new system improves the miles-per-gallon rating ($\mu > 24$) when in fact the new system is not any better than the current system. In contrast, the Type II error of accepting H_0 when it is false corresponds to the researchers concluding that the new system is not any better than the current system ($\mu \le 24$) when in fact the new system improves miles-per-gallon performance.

For the miles-per-gallon rating hypothesis test, the null hypothesis is $H_0: \mu \le 24$. Suppose the null hypothesis is true as an equality; that is, $\mu = 24$. The probability of making a Type I error when the null hypothesis is true as an equality is called the **level of significance**. Thus, for the miles-per-gallon rating hypothesis test, the level of significance is the probability of rejecting $H_0: \mu \le 24$ when $\mu = 24$. Because of the importance of this concept, we now restate the definition of level of significance.

LEVEL OF SIGNIFICANCE

The level of significance is the probability of making a Type I error when the null hypothesis is true as an equality.

The Greek symbol α (alpha) is used to denote the level of significance, and common choices for α are .05 and .01.

In practice, the person conducting the hypothesis test specifies the level of significance. By selecting α, that person is controlling the probability of making a Type I error. If the cost of making a Type I error is high, small values of α are preferred. If the cost of making a Type I error is not too high, larger values of α are typically used. Applications of hypothesis testing that only control for the Type I error are often called *significance tests*. Most applications of hypothesis testing are of this type.

Although most applications of hypothesis testing control for the probability of making a Type I error, they do not always control for the probability of making a Type II error. Hence, if we decide to accept H_0, we cannot determine how confident we can be with that decision. Because of the uncertainty associated with making a Type II error when conducting significance tests, statisticians often recommend that we use the statement "do not reject H_0" instead of "accept H_0." Using the statement "do not reject H_0" carries the recommendation to withhold both judgment and action. In effect, by not directly accepting H_0, the statistician avoids the risk of making a Type II error. Whenever the probability of making a Type II error has not been determined and controlled, we will not make the statement "accept H_0." In such cases, only two conclusions are possible: *do not reject H_0 or reject H_0*.

Although controlling for a Type II error in hypothesis testing is not common, it can be done. More advanced texts describe procedures for determining and controlling the probability of making a Type II error.* If proper controls have been established for this error, action based on the "accept H_0" conclusion can be appropriate.

> *If the sample data are consistent with the null hypothesis H_0, we will follow the practice of concluding "do not reject H_0." This conclusion is preferred over "accept H_0," because the conclusion to accept H_0 puts us at risk of making a Type II error.*

Exercises

5. Nielsen reported that young men in the United States watch 56.2 minutes of prime-time TV daily (*The Wall Street Journal Europe,* November 18, 2003). A researcher believes that young men in Germany spend more time watching prime-time TV. A sample of German young men will be selected by the researcher and the time they spend watching TV in one day will be recorded. The sample results will be used to test the following null and alternative hypotheses.

$$H_0:\ \mu \le 56.2$$
$$H_a:\ \mu > 56.2$$

   a. What is the Type I error in this situation? What are the consequences of making this error?
   b. What is the Type II error in this situation? What are the consequences of making this error?

6. The label on a 3-quart container of orange juice claims that the orange juice contains an average of 1 gram of fat or less. Answer the following questions for a hypothesis test that could be used to test the claim on the label.
   a. Develop the appropriate null and alternative hypotheses.
   b. What is the Type I error in this situation? What are the consequences of making this error?
   c. What is the Type II error in this situation? What are the consequences of making this error?

7. Carpetland salespersons average $8000 per week in sales. Steve Contois, the firm's vice president, proposes a compensation plan with new selling incentives. Steve hopes that the results of a trial selling period will enable him to conclude that the compensation plan increases the average sales per salesperson.

---

*See, for example, Anderson, D. R., D. J. Sweeney, and T. A. Williams, *Statistics for Business and Economics,* 9th ed. (Cincinnati: South-Western, 2005).

   a.   Develop the appropriate null and alternative hypotheses.
   b.   What is the Type I error in this situation? What are the consequences of making this error?
   c.   What is the Type II error in this situation? What are the consequences of making this error?

8.   Suppose a new production method will be implemented if a hypothesis test supports the conclusion that the new method reduces the mean operating cost per hour.
   a.   State the appropriate null and alternative hypotheses if the mean cost for the current production method is \$220 per hour.
   b.   What is the Type I error in this situation? What are the consequences of making this error?
   c.   What is the Type II error in this situation? What are the consequences of making this error?

Population Mean: σ Known

In Chapter 8 we said that the σ known case corresponds to applications in which historical data or other information is available that enables us to obtain a good estimate of the population standard deviation prior to sampling. In such cases the population standard deviation can, for all practical purposes, be considered known. In this section we show how to conduct a hypothesis test about a population mean for the σ known case.

The methods presented in this section are exact if the sample is selected from a population that is normally distributed. In cases where it is not reasonable to assume the population is normally distributed, these methods are still applicable if the sample size is large enough. We provide some practical advice concerning the population distribution and the sample size at the end of this section.

One-Tailed Test

One-tailed tests about a population mean take one of the following two forms.

Lower Tail Test	**Upper Tail Test**
$H_0: \mu \geq \mu_0$	$H_0: \mu \leq \mu_0$
$H_a: \mu < \mu_0$	$H_a: \mu > \mu_0$

Let us consider an example involving a lower tail test.

The Federal Trade Commission (FTC) periodically conducts statistical studies designed to test the claims that manufacturers make about their products. For example, the label on a large can of Hilltop Coffee states that the can contains 3 pounds of coffee. The FTC knows that Hilltop's production process cannot place exactly 3 pounds of coffee in each can, even if the mean filling weight for the population of all cans filled is 3 pounds per can. However, as long as the population mean filling weight is at least 3 pounds per can, the rights of consumers will be protected. Thus, the FTC interprets the label information on a large can of coffee as a claim by Hilltop that the population mean filling weight is at least 3 pounds per can. We will show how the FTC can check Hilltop's claim by conducting a lower tail hypothesis test.

The first step is to develop the null and alternative hypotheses for the test. If the population mean filling weight is at least 3 pounds per can, Hilltop's claim is correct. This result establishes the null hypothesis for the test. However, if the population mean weight is less than 3 pounds per can, Hilltop's claim is incorrect. This result establishes the alternative hypothesis. With μ denoting the population mean filling weight, the null and alternative hypotheses are as follows:

$$H_0: \mu \geq 3$$
$$H_a: \mu < 3$$

Note that the hypothesized value of the population mean is $\mu_0 = 3$.

If the sample data indicate that H_0 cannot be rejected, the statistical evidence does not support the conclusion that a label violation has occurred. Hence, no action should be taken against Hilltop. However, if the sample data indicate H_0 can be rejected, we will conclude that the alternative hypothesis, H_a: $\mu < 3$, is true. In this case a conclusion of underfilling and a charge of a label violation against Hilltop would be justified.

Suppose a sample of 36 cans of coffee is selected and the sample mean $\bar{x}$ is computed as an estimate of the population mean μ. If the value of the sample mean $\bar{x}$ is less than 3 pounds, the sample results will cast doubt on the null hypothesis. What we want to know is how much less than 3 pounds must $\bar{x}$ be before we would be willing to declare the difference significant and risk making a Type I error by falsely accusing Hilltop of a label violation. A key factor in addressing this issue is the value the decision maker selects for the level of significance.

As noted in the preceding section, the level of significance, denoted by α, is the probability of making a Type I error by rejecting H_0 when the null hypothesis is true as an equality. The decision maker must specify the level of significance. If the cost of making a Type I error is high, a small value should be chosen for the level of significance. If the cost is not high, a larger value is more appropriate. In the Hilltop Coffee study, the director of the FTC's testing program made the following statement: "If the company is meeting its weight specifications at $\mu = 3$, I do not want to take action against them. Even so, I am willing to risk a 1% chance of making such an error." From the director's statement, we set the level of significance for the hypothesis test at $\alpha = .01$. Thus, we must design the hypothesis test so that the probability of making a Type I error when $\mu = 3$ is .01.

For the Hilltop Coffee study, by developing the null and alternative hypotheses and specifying the level of significance for the test, we carry out the first two steps required in conducting every hypothesis test. We are now ready to perform the third step of hypothesis testing: collect the sample data and compute the value of what is called a test statistic.

Test statistic   For the Hilltop Coffee study, previous FTC tests show that the population standard deviation can be assumed known with a value of $\sigma = .18$. In addition, these tests also show that the population of filling weights can be assumed to have a normal distribution. From the study of sampling distributions in Chapter 7 we know that if the population from which we are sampling is normally distributed, the sampling distribution of $\bar{x}$ will also be normally distributed. Thus, for the Hilltop Coffee study, the sampling distribution of $\bar{x}$ is normally distributed. With a known value of $\sigma = .18$ and a sample size of $n = 36$, Figure 9.1 shows the sampling distribution of $\bar{x}$ when the null hypothesis is true

FIGURE 9.1   SAMPLING DISTRIBUTION OF $\bar{x}$ FOR THE HILLTOP COFFEE STUDY WHEN THE NULL HYPOTHESIS IS TRUE AS AN EQUALITY ($\mu = \mu_0 = 3$)

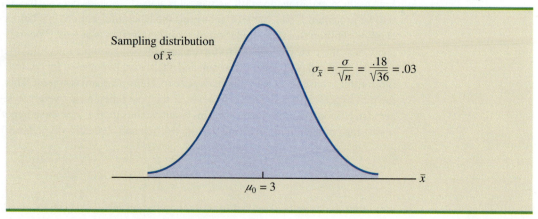

The standard error of $\bar{x}$ is the standard deviation of the sampling distribution of $\bar{x}$.

as an equality; that is, when $\mu = \mu_0 = 3$.* Note that the standard error of $\bar{x}$ is given by $\sigma_{\bar{x}} = \sigma/\sqrt{n} = .18/\sqrt{36} = .03$.

Because the sampling distribution of $\bar{x}$ is normally distributed, the sampling distribution of

$$z = \frac{\bar{x} - \mu_0}{\sigma_{\bar{x}}} = \frac{\bar{x} - 3}{.03}$$

is a standard normal distribution. A value of $z = -1$ means that the value of $\bar{x}$ is one standard error below the hypothesized value of the mean, a value of $z = -2$ means that the value of $\bar{x}$ is two standard errors below the hypothesized value of the mean, and so on. We can use the standard normal distribution table to find the lower tail probability corresponding to any z value. For instance, the standard normal table shows that the area between the mean and $z = -3.00$ is .4987. Hence, the probability of obtaining a value of z that is three or more standard errors below the mean is $.5000 - .4987 = .0013$. As a result, the probability of obtaining a value of $\bar{x}$ that is 3 or more standard errors below the hypothesized population mean $\mu_0 = 3$ is also .0013. Such a result is unlikely if the null hypothesis is true.

For hypothesis tests about a population mean for the σ known case, we use the standard normal random variable z as a **test statistic** to determine whether $\bar{x}$ deviates from the hypothesized value μ enough to justify rejecting the null hypothesis. With $\sigma_{\bar{x}} = \sigma/\sqrt{n}$, the test statistic used in the σ known case is as follows.

TEST STATISTIC FOR HYPOTHESIS TESTS ABOUT A POPULATION MEAN:
σ KNOWN

$$z = \frac{\bar{x} - \mu_0}{\sigma/\sqrt{n}} \tag{9.1}$$

The key question for a lower tail test is: How small must the test statistic z be before we choose to reject the null hypothesis? Two approaches can be used to answer this question.

The first approach uses the value of the test statistic z to compute a probability called a **p-value**. The p-value measures the support (or lack of support) provided by the sample for the null hypothesis and is the basis for determining whether the null hypothesis should be rejected given the level of significance. The second approach requires that we first determine a value for the test statistic called the **critical value**. For a lower tail test, the critical value serves as a benchmark for determining whether the value of the test statistic is small enough to reject the null hypothesis. We begin with the p-value approach.

p-value approach In practice, the p-value approach has become the preferred method of determining whether the null hypothesis can be rejected, especially when using computer software packages such as Minitab and Excel. To begin our discussion of the use of p-values in hypothesis testing, we now provide a formal definition for a p-value.

p-VALUE

The p-value is a probability, computed using the test statistic, that measures the support (or lack of support) provided by the sample for the null hypothesis.

*In constructing sampling distributions for hypothesis tests, it is assumed that H_0 is satisfied as an equality.

Because a *p*-value is a probability, it ranges from 0 to 1. In general, the larger the *p*-value, the more support the test statistic provides for the null hypothesis. On the other hand, a small *p*-value indicates a sample test statistic that is unusual given the assumption that H_0 is true. Small *p*-values lead to rejection of H_0, whereas large *p*-values indicate the null hypothesis should not be rejected.

Two steps are required to use the *p*-value approach. First, we must use the value of the test statistic to compute the *p*-value. The method used to compute a *p*-value depends on whether the test is a lower tail, an upper tail, or a two-tailed test. For a lower tail test, the *p*-value is the probability of obtaining a value for the test statistic as small as or smaller than that provided by the sample. Thus, to compute the *p*-value for the lower tail test in the σ known case, we must find the area under the standard normal curve to the left of the test statistic. After computing the *p*-value, we must then decide whether it is small enough to reject the null hypothesis; as we will show, this decision involves comparing the *p*-value to the level of significance.

Let us now illustrate the *p*-value approach by computing the *p*-value for the Hilltop Coffee lower tail test. Suppose the sample of 36 Hilltop coffee cans provides a sample mean of $\bar{x} = 2.92$ pounds. Is $\bar{x} = 2.92$ small enough to cause us to reject H_0? Because it is a lower tail test, the *p*-value is the area under the standard normal curve to the left of the test statistic. Using $\bar{x} = 2.92$, $\sigma = .18$, and $n = 36$, we compute the value of the test statistic z.

CD file

Coffee

$$z = \frac{\bar{x} - \mu_0}{\sigma/\sqrt{n}} = \frac{2.92 - 3}{.18/\sqrt{36}} = -2.67$$

Thus, the *p*-value is the probability that the test statistic z is less than or equal to -2.67 (the area under the standard normal curve to the left of the test statistic).

Using the standard normal distribution table, we find that the area between the mean and $z = -2.67$ is .4962. Thus, the *p*-value is $.5000 - .4962 = .0038$. Figure 9.2 shows that $\bar{x} = 2.92$ corresponds to $z = -2.67$ and a *p*-value $= .0038$. This *p*-value indicates a small probability of obtaining a sample mean of $\bar{x} = 2.92$ (and a test statistic of -2.67) or smaller when sampling from a population with $\mu = 3$. This *p*-value does not provide much support for the null hypothesis, but is it small enough to cause us to reject H_0? The answer depends upon the level of significance for the test.

As noted previously, the director of the FTC's testing program selected a value of .01 for the level of significance. The selection of $\alpha = .01$ means that the director is willing to accept a probability of .01 of rejecting the null hypothesis when it is true as an equality ($\mu_0 = 3$). The sample of 36 coffee cans in the Hilltop Coffee study resulted in a *p*-value $= .0038$, which means that the probability of obtaining a value of $\bar{x} = 2.92$ or less when the null hypothesis is true as an equality is .0038. Because .0038 is less than or equal to $\alpha = .01$, we reject H_0. Therefore, we find sufficient statistical evidence to reject the null hypothesis at the .01 level of significance.

We can now state the general rule for determining whether the null hypothesis can be rejected when using the *p*-value approach. For a level of significance α, the rejection rule using the *p*-value approach is as follows:

REJECTION RULE USING *p*-VALUE

Reject H_0 if *p*-value $\leq \alpha$

In the Hilltop Coffee test, the *p*-value of .0038 resulted in the rejection of the null hypothesis. Although the basis for making the rejection decision involves a comparison of the *p*-value to the level of significance specified by the FTC director, the observed *p*-value of

FIGURE 9.2   *p*-VALUE FOR THE HILLTOP COFFEE STUDY WHEN $\bar{x} = 2.92$ AND $z = -2.67$

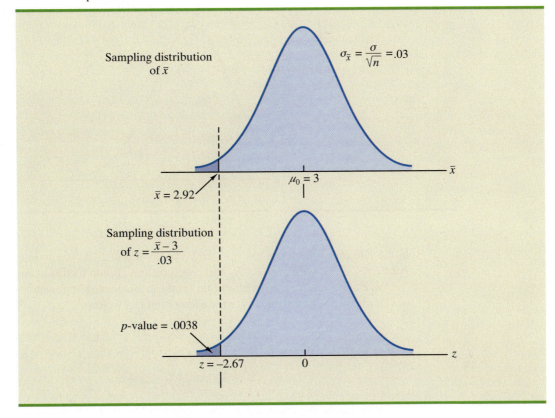

.0038 means that we would reject H_0 for any value $\alpha \geq .0038$. For this reason, the *p*-value is also called the *observed level of significance.*

Different decision makers may express different opinions concerning the cost of making a Type I error and may choose a different level of significance. By providing the *p*-value as part of the hypothesis testing results, another decision maker can compare the reported *p*-value to his or her own level of significance and possibly make a different decision with respect to rejecting H_0.

Critical value approach   For a lower tail test, the critical value is the value of the test statistic that corresponds to an area of α (the level of significance) in the lower tail of the sampling distribution of the test statistic. In other words, the critical value is the largest value of the test statistic that will result in the rejection of the null hypothesis. Let us return to the Hilltop Coffee example and see how this approach works.

In the σ known case, the sampling distribution for the test statistic z is a standard normal distribution. Therefore, the critical value is the value of the test statistic that corresponds to an area of $\alpha = .01$ in the lower tail of a standard normal distribution. Using the standard normal distribution table, we find that $z = -2.33$ provides an area of .01 in the lower tail (see Figure 9.3). Thus, if the sample results in a value of the test statistic that is less than or equal to -2.33, the corresponding *p*-value will be less than or equal to .01; in this case, we should reject the null hypothesis. Hence, for the Hilltop Coffee study the critical value rejection rule for a level of significance of .01 is

$$\text{Reject } H_0 \text{ if } z \leq -2.33$$

FIGURE 9.3   CRITICAL VALUE $= -2.33$ FOR THE HILLTOP COFFEE HYPOTHESIS TEST

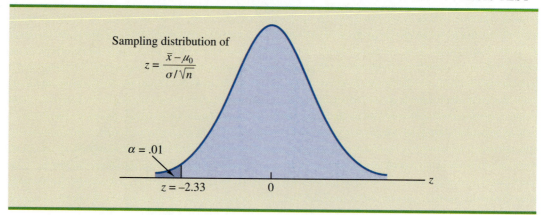

In the Hilltop Coffee example, $\bar{x} = 2.92$ and the test statistic is $z = -2.67$. Because $z = -2.67 < -2.33$, we can reject H_0 and conclude that Hilltop Coffee is underfilling cans.

We can generalize the rejection rule for the critical value approach to handle any level of significance. The rejection rule for a lower tail test follows.

REJECTION RULE FOR A LOWER TAIL TEST: CRITICAL VALUE APPROACH

$$\text{Reject } H_0 \text{ if } z \leq -z_\alpha$$

where $-z_\alpha$ is the critical value; that is, the z value that provides an area of α in the lower tail of the standard normal distribution.

The p-value approach to hypothesis testing and the critical value approach will always lead to the same rejection decision; that is, whenever the p-value is less than or equal to α, the value of the test statistic will be less than or equal to the critical value. The advantage of the p-value approach is that the p-value tells us *how* significant the results are (the observed level of significance). If we use the critical value approach, we only know that the results are significant at the stated level of significance.

Computer procedures for hypothesis testing provide the p-value, so it is rapidly becoming the preferred method of conducting hypothesis tests. If you do not have access to a computer, you may prefer to use the critical value approach. For some probability distributions it is easier to use statistical tables to find a critical value than to use the tables to compute the p-value. This topic is discussed further in the next section.

At the beginning of this section, we said that one-tailed tests about a population mean take one of the following two forms:

Lower Tail Test	**Upper Tail Test**
$H_0: \mu \geq \mu_0$	$H_0: \mu \leq \mu_0$
$H_a: \mu < \mu_0$	$H_a: \mu > \mu_0$

We used the Hilltop Coffee study to illustrate how to conduct a lower tail test. We can use the same general approach to conduct an upper tail test. The test statistic z is still computed using equation (9.1). But, for an upper tail test, the p-value is the probability of obtaining a value for the test statistic as large as or larger than that provided by the sample. Thus, to compute the p-value for the upper tail test in the σ known case, we must find the area under the standard normal curve to the right of the test statistic. Using the critical value approach causes us to reject the null hypothesis if the value of the test statistic is greater than or equal to the critical value z_α; in other words, we reject H_0 if $z \geq z_\alpha$.

Two-Tailed Test

In hypothesis testing, the general form for a **two-tailed test** about a population mean is as follows:

$$H_0: \mu = \mu_0$$
$$H_a: \mu \neq \mu_0$$

In this subsection we show how to conduct a two-tailed test about a population mean for the σ known case. As an illustration, we consider the hypothesis testing situation facing MaxFlight, Inc.

The U.S. Golf Association (USGA) establishes rules that manufacturers of golf equipment must meet if their products are to be acceptable for use in USGA events. MaxFlight uses a high-technology manufacturing process to produce golf balls with a mean driving distance of 295 yards. Sometimes, however, the process gets out of adjustment and produces golf balls with a mean driving distance different from 295 yards. When the mean distance falls below 295 yards, the company worries about losing sales because the golf balls do not provide as much distance as advertised. When the mean distance passes 295 yards, MaxFlight's golf balls may be rejected by the USGA for exceeding the overall distance standard concerning carry and roll.

MaxFlight's quality control program involves taking periodic samples of 50 golf balls to monitor the manufacturing process. For each sample, a hypothesis test is conducted to determine whether the process has fallen out of adjustment. Let us develop the null and alternative hypotheses. We begin by assuming that the process is functioning correctly; that is, the golf balls being produced have a mean distance of 295 yards. This assumption establishes the null hypothesis. The alternative hypothesis is that the mean distance is not equal to 295 yards. With a hypothesized value of $\mu_0 = 295$, the null and alternative hypotheses for the MaxFlight hypothesis test are as follows:

$$H_0: \mu = 295$$
$$H_a: \mu \neq 295$$

If the sample mean $\bar{x}$ is significantly less than 295 yards or significantly greater than 295 yards, we will reject H_0. In this case, corrective action will be taken to adjust the manufacturing process. On the other hand, if $\bar{x}$ does not deviate from the hypothesized mean $\mu_0 = 295$ by a significant amount, H_0 will not be rejected and no action will be taken to adjust the manufacturing process.

The quality control team selected $\alpha = .05$ as the level of significance for the test. Data from previous tests conducted when the process was known to be in adjustment show that the population standard deviation can be assumed known with a value of $\sigma = 12$. Thus, with a sample size of $n = 50$, the standard error of $\bar{x}$ is

$$\sigma_{\bar{x}} = \frac{\sigma}{\sqrt{n}} = \frac{12}{\sqrt{50}} = 1.7$$

Because the sample size is large, the central limit theorem (see Chapter 7) allows us to conclude that the sampling distribution of $\bar{x}$ can be approximated by a normal distribution.

Figure 9.4 shows the sampling distribution of $\bar{x}$ for the MaxFlight hypothesis test with a hypothesized population mean of $\mu_0 = 295$.

Suppose that a sample of 50 golf balls is selected and that the sample mean is $\bar{x} = 297.6$ yards. This sample mean provides support for the conclusion that the population mean is larger than 295 yards. Is this value of $\bar{x}$ enough larger than 295 to cause us to reject H_0 at the .05 level of significance? In the previous section we described two approaches that can be used to answer this question: the p-value approach and the critical value approach.

p-value approach Recall that the p-value is a probability, computed using the test statistic, that measures the support (or lack of support) provided by the sample for the null hypothesis. For a two-tailed test, values of the test statistic in *either* tail show a lack of support for the null hypothesis. For a two-tailed test, the p-value is the probability of obtaining a value for the test statistic *as unlikely as or more unlikely than* that provided by the sample. Let us see how the p-value is computed for the MaxFlight hypothesis test.

First we compute the value of the test statistic. For the σ known case, the test statistic z is a standard normal random variable. Using equation (9.1) with $\bar{x} = 297.6$, the value of the test statistic is

$$z = \frac{\bar{x} - \mu_0}{\sigma/\sqrt{n}} = \frac{297.6 - 295}{12/\sqrt{50}} = 1.53$$

Now to compute the p-value we must find the probability of obtaining a value for the test statistic *at least as unlikely as* $z = 1.53$. Clearly values of $z \geq 1.53$ are *at least as unlikely*. But, because this is a two-tailed test, values of $z \leq -1.53$ are also *at least as unlikely as* the value of the test statistic provided by the sample. Referring to Figure 9.5, we see that the two-tailed p-value in this case is given by $P(z \leq -1.53) + P(z \geq 1.53)$. Because the normal curve is symmetric, we can compute this probability by finding the area under the standard normal curve to the right of $z = 1.53$ and doubling it. The table for the standard normal distribution shows that the area between the mean and $z = 1.53$ is .4370. Thus, the area under the standard normal curve to the right of the test statistic $z = 1.53$ is $.5000 - .4370 = .0630$. Doubling this, we find the p-value for the MaxFlight two-tailed hypothesis test is p-value $= 2(.0630) = .1260$.

Next we compare the p-value to the level of significance to see whether the null hypothesis should be rejected. With a level of significance of $\alpha = .05$, we do not reject H_0 because the p-value $= .1260 > .05$. Because the null hypothesis is not rejected, no action will be taken to adjust the MaxFlight manufacturing process.

FIGURE 9.4   SAMPLING DISTRIBUTION OF $\bar{x}$ FOR THE MAXFLIGHT HYPOTHESIS TEST

FIGURE 9.5 *p*-VALUE FOR THE MAXFLIGHT HYPOTHESIS TEST

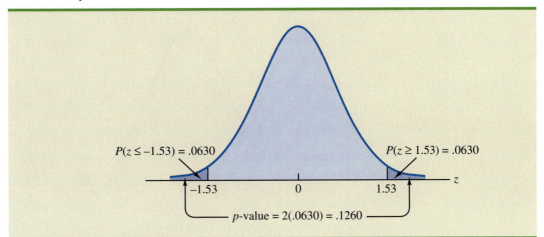

$P(z \leq -1.53) = .0630$

$P(z \geq 1.53) = .0630$

-1.53 0 1.53 z

p-value = 2(.0630) = .1260

The computation of the *p*-value for a two-tailed test may seem a bit confusing as compared to the computation of the *p*-value for a one-tailed test. But, it can be simplified by following these three steps.

1. Compute the value of the test statistic *z*.
2. If the value of the test statistic is in the upper tail ($z > 0$), find the area under the standard normal curve to the right of *z*. If the value of the test statistic is in the lower tail, find the area under the standard normal curve to the left of *z*.
3. Double the tail area, or probability, obtained in step 2 to obtain the *p*-value.

In practice, the computation of the *p*-value is done automatically when using computer software such as Minitab and Excel. For instance, Figure 9.6 shows the Minitab output for the MaxFlight hypothesis test. The sample mean $\bar{x} = 297.6$, the test statistic $z = 1.53$, and the *p*-value $= .126$ are highlighted. The step-by-step procedure used to obtain the Minitab output is described in Appendix 9.1.

Critical value approach Before leaving this section, let us see how the test statistic *z* can be compared to a critical value to make the hypothesis testing decision for a two-tailed test. Figure 9.7 shows that the critical values for the test will occur in both the lower and upper tails of the standard normal distribution. With a level of significance of $\alpha = .05$, the area in each tail beyond the critical values is $\alpha/2 = .05/2 = .025$. Using the table of areas for the standard normal distribution, we find the critical values for the test statistic are

FIGURE 9.6 MINITAB OUTPUT FOR THE MAXFLIGHT HYPOTHESIS TEST

```
Test of mu = 295 vs not = 295
The assumed sigma = 12

Variable       N         Mean        StDev      SE Mean
Yards         50       297.600      11.297        1.697

Variable           95.0% CI            Z            P
Yards         (294.274, 300.926)      1.53        0.126
```

FIGURE 9.7 CRITICAL VALUES FOR THE MAXFLIGHT HYPOTHESIS TEST

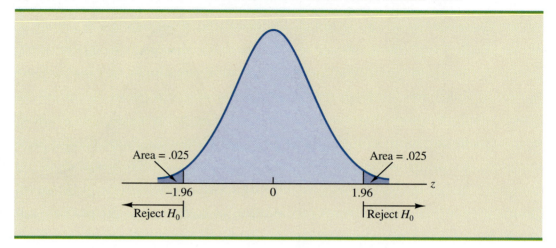

$-z_{.025} = -1.96$ and $z_{.025} = 1.96$. Thus, using the critical value approach, the two-tailed rejection rule is

$$\text{Reject } H_0 \text{ if } z \le -1.96 \text{ or if } z \ge 1.96$$

Because the value of the test statistic for the MaxFlight study is $z = 1.53$, the statistical evidence will not permit us to reject the null hypothesis at the .05 level of significance.

Summary and Practical Advice

We presented examples of a lower tail test and a two-tailed test about a population mean. Based upon these examples, we can now summarize the hypothesis testing procedures about a population mean for the σ known case as shown in Table 9.2. Note that μ_0 is the hypothesized value of the population mean.

The hypothesis testing steps followed in the two examples presented in this section are common to every hypothesis test.

STEPS OF HYPOTHESIS TESTING

Step 1. Develop the null and alternative hypotheses.
Step 2. Specify the level of significance.
Step 3. Collect the sample data and compute the value of the test statistic.

p-Value Approach

Step 4. Use the value of the test statistic to compute the *p*-value.
Step 5. Reject H_0 if the *p*-value $\le \alpha$.

Critical Value Approach

Step 4. Use the level of significance to determine the critical value and the rejection rule.
Step 5. Use the value of the test statistic and the rejection rule to determine whether to reject H_0.

TABLE 9.2   SUMMARY OF HYPOTHESIS TESTS ABOUT A POPULATION MEAN: σ KNOWN CASE

	Lower Tail Test	Upper Tail Test	Two-Tailed Test
Hypotheses	$H_0: \mu \geq \mu_0$ $H_a: \mu < \mu_0$	$H_0: \mu \leq \mu_0$ $H_a: \mu > \mu_0$	$H_0: \mu = \mu_0$ $H_a: \mu \neq \mu_0$
Test Statistic	$z = \dfrac{\bar{x} - \mu_0}{\sigma/\sqrt{n}}$	$z = \dfrac{\bar{x} - \mu_0}{\sigma/\sqrt{n}}$	$z = \dfrac{\bar{x} - \mu_0}{\sigma/\sqrt{n}}$
Rejection Rule: ***p*-Value Approach**	Reject H_0 if p-value $\leq \alpha$	Reject H_0 if p-value $\leq \alpha$	Reject H_0 if p-value $\leq \alpha$
Rejection Rule: **Critical Value** **Approach**	Reject H_0 if $z \leq -z_\alpha$	Reject H_0 if $z \geq z_\alpha$	Reject H_0 if $z \leq -z_{\alpha/2}$ or if $z \geq z_{\alpha/2}$

Practical advice about the sample size for hypothesis tests is similar to the advice we provided about the sample size for interval estimation in Chapter 8. In most applications, a sample size of $n \geq 30$ is adequate when using the hypothesis testing procedure described in this section. In cases where the sample size is less than 30, the distribution of the population from which we are sampling becomes an important consideration. If the population is normally distributed, the hypothesis testing procedure that we described is exact and can be used for any sample size. If the population is not normally distributed but is at least roughly symmetric, sample sizes as small as 15 can be expected to provide acceptable results. With smaller sample sizes, the hypothesis testing procedure presented in this section should only be used if the analyst believes, or is willing to assume, that the population is at least approximately normally distributed.

Relationship Between Interval Estimation and Hypothesis Testing

We close this section by discussing the relationship between interval estimation and hypothesis testing. In Chapter 8 we showed how to develop a confidence interval estimate of a population mean. For the σ known case, the confidence interval estimate of a population mean corresponding to a $1 - \alpha$ confidence coefficient is given by

$$\bar{x} \pm z_{\alpha/2} \frac{\sigma}{\sqrt{n}} \qquad (9.2)$$

Conducting a hypothesis test requires us first to develop the hypotheses about the value of a population parameter. In the case of the population mean, the two-tailed test takes the form

$$H_0: \mu = \mu_0$$
$$H_a: \mu \neq \mu_0$$

where μ_0 is the hypothesized value for the population mean. Using the two-tailed critical value approach, we do not reject H_0 for values of the sample mean $\bar{x}$ that are within $-z_{\alpha/2}$ and $+z_{\alpha/2}$ standard errors of μ_0. Thus, the do-not-reject region for the sample mean $\bar{x}$ in a two-tailed hypothesis test with a level of significance of α is given by

$$\mu_0 \pm z_{\alpha/2} \frac{\sigma}{\sqrt{n}} \qquad (9.3)$$

A close look at expressions (9.2) and (9.3) provides insight about the relationship between the estimation and hypothesis testing approaches to statistical inference. Note in particular that both procedures require the computation of the values $z_{\alpha/2}$ and $\sigma/\sqrt{n}$. Focusing on α, we see that a confidence coefficient of $(1 - \alpha)$ for interval estimation corresponds to a level of significance of α in hypothesis testing. For example, a 95% confidence interval corresponds to a .05 level of significance for hypothesis testing. Furthermore, expressions (9.2) and (9.3) show that, because $z_{\alpha/2}(\sigma/\sqrt{n})$ is the plus or minus value for both expressions, if $\bar{x}$ is in the do-not-reject region defined by expression (9.3), the hypothesized value μ_0 will be in the confidence interval defined by expression (9.2). Conversely, if the hypothesized value μ_0 is in the confidence interval defined by expression (9.2), the sample mean $\bar{x}$ will be in the do-not-reject region for the hypothesis $H_0: \mu = \mu_0$ as defined by expression (9.3). These observations lead to the following procedure for using a confidence interval to conduct a two-tailed hypothesis test.

A CONFIDENCE INTERVAL APPROACH TO TESTING A HYPOTHESIS OF THE FORM

$$H_0: \mu = \mu_0$$
$$H_a: \mu \neq \mu_0$$

1. Select a simple random sample from the population and use the value of the sample mean $\bar{x}$ to develop the confidence interval for the population mean μ.

$$\bar{x} \pm z_{\alpha/2}\frac{\sigma}{\sqrt{n}}$$

For a two-tailed hypothesis test, the null hypothesis can be rejected if the confidence interval does not include μ_0.

2. If the confidence interval contains the hypothesized value μ_0, do not reject H_0. Otherwise, reject H_0.

Let us return to the MaxFlight hypothesis test, which resulted in the following two-tailed test.

$$H_0: \mu = 295$$
$$H_a: \mu \neq 295$$

To test this hypothesis with a level of significance of $\alpha = .05$, we sampled 50 golf balls and found a sample mean distance of $\bar{x} = 297.6$ yards. Recall that the population standard deviation is $\sigma = 12$. Using these results with $z_{.025} = 1.96$, we find that the 95% confidence interval estimate of the population mean is

$$\bar{x} \pm z_{.025}\frac{\sigma}{\sqrt{n}}$$
$$297.6 \pm 1.96\frac{12}{\sqrt{50}}$$
$$297.6 \pm 3.3$$

or

$$294.3 \text{ to } 300.9$$

This finding enables the quality control manager to conclude with 95% confidence that the mean distance for the population of golf balls is between 294.3 and 300.9 yards. Because the hypothesized value for the population mean, $\mu_0 = 295$, is in this interval, the hypothesis testing conclusion is that the null hypothesis, $H_0: \mu = 295$, cannot be rejected.

Note that this discussion and example pertain to two-tailed hypothesis tests about a population mean. However, the same confidence interval and two-tailed hypothesis testing relationship exists for other population parameters. The relationship can also be extended to one-tailed tests about population parameters. Doing so, however, requires the development of one-sided confidence intervals, which are rarely used in practice.

NOTES AND COMMENTS

1. In Appendix 9.2 we show how to compute *p*-values using Excel.
2. The smaller the *p*-value the greater the evidence against H_0 and the more the evidence in favor of H_a. Here are some guidelines statisticians suggest for interpreting small *p*-values.
- Less than .01—Overwhelming evidence to conclude H_a is true.

- Between .01 and .05—Strong evidence to conclude H_a is true.
- Between .05 and .10—Weak evidence to conclude H_a is true.
- Greater than .10—Insufficient evidence to conclude H_a is true.

Exercises

Note to Student: Some of the exercises that follow ask you to use the *p*-value approach and others ask you to use the critical value approach. Both methods will provide the same hypothesis testing conclusion. We provide exercises with both methods to give you practice using both. In later sections and in following chapters, we will generally emphasize the *p*-value approach as the preferred method, but you may select either based on personal preference.

Methods

9. Consider the following hypothesis test:

$$H_0: \mu \geq 20$$
$$H_a: \mu < 20$$

A sample of 50 provided a sample mean of 19.4. The population standard deviation is 2.
a. Compute the value of the test statistic.
b. What is the *p*-value?
c. Using $\alpha = .05$, what is your conclusion?
d. What is the rejection rule using the critical value? What is your conclusion?

10. Consider the following hypothesis test:

$$H_0: \mu \leq 25$$
$$H_a: \mu > 25$$

A sample of 40 provided a sample mean of 26.4. The population standard deviation is 6.
a. Compute the value of the test statistic.
b. What is the *p*-value?
c. At $\alpha = .01$, what is your conclusion?
d. What is the rejection rule using the critical value? What is your conclusion?

11. Consider the following hypothesis test:

$$H_0: \mu = 15$$
$$H_a: \mu \neq 15$$

A sample of 50 provided a sample mean of 14.15. The population standard deviation is 3.

a. Compute the value of the test statistic.
b. What is the *p*-value?
c. At $\alpha = .05$, what is your conclusion?
d. What is the rejection rule using the critical value? What is your conclusion?

12. Consider the following hypothesis test:

$$H_0: \mu \geq 80$$
$$H_a: \mu < 80$$

A sample of 100 is used and the population standard deviation is 12. Compute the *p*-value and state your conclusion for each of the following sample results. Use $\alpha = .01$.
a. $\bar{x} = 78.5$
b. $\bar{x} = 77$
c. $\bar{x} = 75.5$
d. $\bar{x} = 81$

13. Consider the following hypothesis test:

$$H_0: \mu \leq 50$$
$$H_a: \mu > 50$$

A sample of 60 is used and the population standard deviation is 8. Use the critical value approach to state your conclusion for each of the following sample results. Use $\alpha = .05$.
a. $\bar{x} = 52.5$
b. $\bar{x} = 51$
c. $\bar{x} = 51.8$

14. Consider the following hypothesis test:

$$H_0: \mu = 22$$
$$H_a: \mu \neq 22$$

A sample of 75 is used and the population standard deviation is 10. Compute the *p*-value and state your conclusion for each of the following sample results. Use $\alpha = .01$.
a. $\bar{x} = 23$
b. $\bar{x} = 25.1$
c. $\bar{x} = 20$

Applications

15. Individuals filing federal income tax returns prior to March 31 received an average refund of $1056. Consider the population of "last-minute" filers who mail their tax return during the last five days of the income tax period (typically April 10 to April 15).
a. A researcher suggests that a reason individuals wait until the last five days is that on average these individuals receive lower refunds than do early filers. Develop appropriate hypotheses such that rejection of H_0 will support the researcher's contention.
b. For a sample of 400 individuals who filed a tax return between April 10 and 15, the sample mean refund was $910. Based on prior experience a population standard deviation of $\sigma = \$1600$ may be assumed. What is the *p*-value?
c. At $\alpha = .05$, what is your conclusion?
d. Repeat the preceding hypothesis test using the critical value approach.

16. Reis, Inc., a New York real estate research firm, tracks the cost of apartment rentals in the United States. In mid-2002, the nationwide mean apartment rental rate was $895 per month (*The Wall Street Journal,* July 8, 2002). Assume that, based on the historical quarterly surveys, a population standard deviation of $\sigma = \$225$ is reasonable. In a current study of apartment rental rates, a sample of 180 apartments nationwide provided a sample mean of $915 per month. Do the sample data enable Reis to conclude that the population mean apartment rental rate now exceeds the level reported in 2002?
    a. State the null and alternative hypotheses.
    b. What is the *p*-value?
    c. At $\alpha = .01$, what is your conclusion?
    d. What would you recommend Reis consider doing at this time?

17. The mean length of a work week for the population of workers was reported to be 39.2 hours (*Investor's Business Daily,* September 11, 2000). Suppose that we would like to take a current sample of workers to see whether the mean length of a work week has changed from the previously reported 39.2 hours.
    a. State the hypotheses that will help us determine whether a change occurred in the mean length of a work week.
    b. Suppose a current sample of 112 workers provided a sample mean of 38.5 hours. Use a population standard deviation $\sigma = 4.8$ hours. What is the *p*-value?
    c. At $\alpha = .05$, can the null hypothesis be rejected? What is your conclusion?
    d. Repeat the preceding hypothesis test using the critical value approach.

18. The average annual total return for U.S. Diversified Equity mutual funds from 1999 to 2003 was 4.1% (*Business Week,* January 26, 2004). A researcher would like to conduct a hypothesis test to see whether the returns for mid-cap growth funds over the same period are significantly different from the average for U.S. Diversified Equity funds.
    a. Formulate the hypotheses that can be used to determine whether the mean annual return for mid-cap growth funds differ from the mean for U.S. Diversified Equity funds.
    b. A sample of 40 mid-cap growth funds provides a mean return of $\bar{x} = 3.4\%$. Assume the population standard deviation for mid-cap growth funds is known from previous studies to be $\sigma = 2\%$, and use the sample results to compute the test statistic and *p*-value for the hypothesis test.
    c. At $\alpha = .05$, what is your conclusion?

19. In 2001, the U.S. Department of Labor reported the average hourly earnings for U.S. production workers to be $14.32 per hour (*The World Almanac 2003*). A sample of 75 production workers during 2003 showed a sample mean of $14.68 per hour. Assuming the population standard deviation $\sigma = \$1.45$, can we conclude that an increase occurred in the mean hourly earnings since 2001? Use $\alpha = .05$.

20. The national mean sales price for new one-family homes is $181,900 (*The New York Times Almanac 2000*). A sample of 40 one-family home sales in the South showed a sample mean of $166,400. Use a population standard deviation of $33,500.
    a. Formulate the null and alternative hypotheses that can be used to determine whether the sample data support the conclusion that the population mean sales price for new one-family homes in the South is less than the national mean of $181,900.
    b. What is the value of the test statistic?
    c. What is the *p*-value?
    d. At $\alpha = .01$, what is your conclusion?

21. Fowle Marketing Research, Inc., bases charges to a client on the assumption that telephone surveys can be completed in a mean time of 15 minutes or less. If a longer mean survey time is necessary, a premium rate is charged. Suppose a sample of 35 surveys shows a sample mean of 17 minutes. Use $\sigma = 4$ minutes. Is the premium rate justified?
    a. Formulate the null and alternative hypotheses for this application.
    b. Compute the value of the test statistic.

c. What is the *p*-value?

d. At $\alpha = .01$, what is your conclusion?

22. CCN and ActMedia provided a television channel targeted to individuals waiting in super-market checkout lines. The channel showed news, short features, and advertisements. The length of the program was based on the assumption that the population mean time a shopper stands in a supermarket checkout line is 8 minutes. A sample of actual waiting times will be used to test this assumption and determine whether actual mean waiting time differs from this standard.

a. Formulate the hypotheses for this application.

b. A sample of 120 shoppers showed a sample mean waiting time of 8.5 minutes. Assume a population standard deviation $\sigma = 3.2$ minutes. What is the *p*-value?

c. At $\alpha = .05$, what is your conclusion?

d. Compute a 95% confidence interval for the population mean. Does it support your conclusion?

Population Mean: σ Unknown

In this section we describe how to conduct hypothesis tests about a population mean for the σ unknown case. Because the σ unknown case corresponds to situations in which an estimate of the population standard deviation cannot be developed prior to sampling, the sample must be used to develop an estimate of both μ and σ. Thus, to conduct a hypothesis test about a population mean for the σ unknown case, the sample mean $\bar{x}$ is used as an estimate of μ and the sample standard deviation s is used as an estimate of σ.

The steps of the hypothesis testing procedure for the σ unknown case are the same as those for the σ known case described in Section 9.3. But, with σ unknown, the computation of the test statistic and *p*-value is a bit different. Recall that for the σ known case, the sampling distribution of the test statistic has a standard normal distribution. For the σ unknown case, however, the sampling distribution of the test statistic has slightly more variability because the sample is used to develop estimates of both μ and σ.

In Section 8.2 we showed that an interval estimate of a population mean for the σ unknown case is based on a probability distribution known as the *t* distribution. Hypothesis tests about a population mean for the σ unknown case are also based on the *t* distribution. For the σ unknown case, the test statistic has a *t* distribution with $n - 1$ degrees of freedom.

> **TEST STATISTIC FOR HYPOTHESIS TESTS ABOUT A POPULATION MEAN: σ UNKNOWN**
>
> $$t = \frac{\bar{x} - \mu_0}{s/\sqrt{n}} \qquad d.f: n-1 \qquad (9.4)$$

In Chapter 8 we said that the *t* distribution is based on an assumption that the population from which we are sampling has a normal distribution. However, research shows that this assumption can be relaxed considerably when the sample size is large enough. We provide some practical advice concerning the population distribution and sample size at the end of the section.

One-Tailed Test

Let us consider an example of a one-tailed test about a population mean for the σ unknown case. A business travel magazine wants to classify transatlantic gateway airports according to the mean rating for the population of business travelers. A rating scale with a low score

AirRating

of 0 and a high score of 10 will be used, and airports with a population mean rating greater than 7 will be designated as superior service airports. The magazine staff surveyed a sample of 60 business travelers at each airport to obtain the ratings data. The sample for London's Heathrow Airport provided a sample mean rating of $\bar{x} = 7.25$ and a sample standard deviation of $s = 1.052$. Do the data indicate that Heathrow should be designated as a superior service airport?

We want to develop a hypothesis test for which the decision to reject H_0 will lead to the conclusion that the population mean rating for the Heathrow Airport is *greater* than 7. Thus, an upper tail test with $H_a: \mu > 7$ is required. The null and alternative hypotheses for this upper tail test are as follows:

$$H_0: \mu \leq 7$$
$$H_a: \mu > 7$$

We will use $\alpha = .05$ as the level of significance for the test.

Using equation (9.4) with $\bar{x} = 7.25$, $s = 1.052$, and $n = 60$, the value of the test statistic is

$$t = \frac{\bar{x} - \mu_0}{s/\sqrt{n}} = \frac{7.25 - 7}{1.052/\sqrt{60}} = 1.84$$

The sampling distribution of t has $n - 1 = 60 - 1 = 59$ degrees of freedom. Because the test is an upper tail test, the p-value is the area under the curve of the t distribution to the right of $t = 1.84$.

The t distribution table provided in most textbooks will not contain sufficient detail to determine the exact p-value, such as the p-value corresponding to $t = 1.84$. For instance, using Table 2 in Appendix B, the t distribution with 59 degrees of freedom provides the following information.

Area in Upper Tail	.20	.10	.05	.025	.01	.005
t Value (59 df)	0.848	1.296	1.671	2.001	2.391	2.662

$t = 1.84$

We see that $t = 1.84$ is between 1.671 and 2.001. Although the table does not provide the exact p-value, the values in the "Area in Upper Tail" row show that the p-value must be less than .05 and greater than .025. With a level of significance of $\alpha = .05$, this placement is all we need to know to make the decision to reject the null hypothesis and conclude that Heathrow should be classified as a superior service airport.

Appendixes 9.1 and 9.2 explain how to obtain the exact p-value using Minitab and Excel.

Computer packages such as Minitab and Excel can easily determine the exact p-value associated with the test statistic $t = 1.84$. For example, the Minitab output in Figure 9.8 shows the sample mean $\bar{x} = 7.25$, the sample standard deviation $s = 1.052$ (rounded), the test statistic $t = 1.84$, and the exact p-value $= .035$ for the Heathrow rating hypothesis test. A p-value $= .035 < .05$ leads to the rejection of the null hypothesis and to the conclusion Heathrow should be classified as a superior service airport. The step-by-step procedure used to obtain the Minitab output shown in Figure 9.8 is described in Appendix 9.1.

The critical value approach can also be used to make the rejection decision. With $\alpha = .05$ and the t distribution with 59 degrees of freedom, $t_{.05} = 1.671$ is the critical value for the test. The rejection rule is thus

$$\text{Reject } H_0 \text{ if } t \geq 1.671$$

FIGURE 9.8   MINITAB OUTPUT FOR THE HEATHROW RATING HYPOTHESIS TEST

```
Test of mu = 7 vs > 7

                                                 95%
                                               Lower
Variable    N    Mean    StDev    SE Mean     Bound      T        P
Rating     60   7.250   1.05163   0.13577   7.02312    1.84    0.035
```

With the test statistic $t = 1.84 \geq 1.671$, H_0 is rejected and we can conclude that Heathrow can be classified as a superior service airport.

Two-Tailed Test

To illustrate how to conduct a two-tailed test about a population mean for the σ unknown case, let us consider the hypothesis testing situation facing Holiday Toys. The company manufactures and distributes its products through more than 1000 retail outlets. In planning production levels for the coming winter season, Holiday must decide how many units of each product to produce prior to knowing the actual demand at the retail level. For this year's most important new toy, Holiday's marketing director is expecting demand to average 40 units per retail outlet. Prior to making the final production decision based upon this estimate, Holiday decided to survey a sample of 25 retailers in order to develop more information about the demand for the new product. Each retailer was provided with information about the features of the new toy along with the cost and the suggested selling price. Then each retailer was asked to specify an anticipated order quantity.

With μ denoting the population mean order quantity per retail outlet, the sample data will be used to conduct the following two-tailed hypothesis test:

$$H_0: \mu = 40$$
$$H_a: \mu \neq 40$$

If H_0 cannot be rejected, Holiday will continue its production planning based on the marketing director's estimate that the population mean order quantity per retail outlet will be $\mu = 40$ units. However, if H_0 is rejected. Holiday will immediately reevaluate its production plan for the product. A two-tailed hypothesis test is used because Holiday wants to reevaluate the production plan if the population mean quantity per retail outlet is less than anticipated or greater than anticipated. Because no historical data are available (it's a new product), the population mean μ and the population standard deviation must both be estimated using $\bar{x}$ and s from the sample data.

Orders

The sample of 25 retailers provided a mean of $\bar{x} = 37.4$ and a standard deviation of $s = 11.79$ units. Before going ahead with the use of the t distribution, the analyst constructed a histogram of the sample data in order to check on the form of the population distribution. The histogram of the sample data showed no evidence of skewness or any extreme outliers, so the analyst concluded that the use of the t distribution with $n - 1 = 24$ degrees of freedom was appropriate. Using equation (9.4) with $\bar{x} = 37.4$, $\mu_0 = 40$, $s = 11.79$, and $n = 25$, the value of the test statistic is

$$t = \frac{\bar{x} - \mu_0}{s/\sqrt{n}} = \frac{37.4 - 40}{11.79/\sqrt{25}} = -1.10$$

Because we have a two-tailed test, the p-value is two times the area under the curve for the t distribution to the left of $t = -1.10$. Using Table 2 in Appendix B, the t distribution table for 24 degrees of freedom provides the following information.

Area in Upper Tail	.20	.10	.05	.025	.01	.005
t **Value (24 df)**	0.857	1.318	1.711	2.064	2.492	2.797

$$t = 1.10$$

The t distribution table only contains positive t values. Because the t distribution is symmetric, however, we can find the area under the curve to the right of $t = 1.10$ and double it to find the p-value. We see that $t = 1.10$ is between 0.857 and 1.318. From the "Area in Upper Tail" row, we see that the area in the tail to the right of $t = 1.10$ is between .20 and .10. Doubling these amounts, we see that the p-value must be between .40 and .20. With a level of significance of $\alpha = .05$, we now know that the p-value is greater than α. Therefore, H_0 cannot be rejected. Sufficient evidence is not available to conclude that Holiday should change its production plan for the coming season. Using Minitab or Excel, we find that the exact p-value is .282. Figure 9.9 shows the two areas under the curve of the t distribution providing the exact p-value.

The test statistic can also be compared to the critical value to make the two-tailed hypothesis testing decision. With $\alpha = .05$ and the t distribution with 24 degrees of freedom, $-t_{.025} = -2.064$ and $t_{.025} = 2.064$ are the critical values for the two-tailed test. The rejection rule using the test statistic is

$$\text{Reject } H_0 \text{ if } t \leq -2.064 \text{ or if } t \geq 2.064$$

Based on the test statistic $t = -1.10$, H_0 cannot be rejected. This result indicates that Holiday should continue its production planning for the coming season based on the expectation that $\mu = 40$.

Summary and Practical Advice

Table 9.3 provides a summary of the hypothesis testing procedures about a population mean for the σ unknown case. The key difference between these procedures and the ones for the σ known case are that s is used, instead of σ, in the computation of the test statistic. For this reason, the test statistic follows the t distribution.

FIGURE 9.9   AREA UNDER THE CURVE IN BOTH TAILS PROVIDES THE p-VALUE

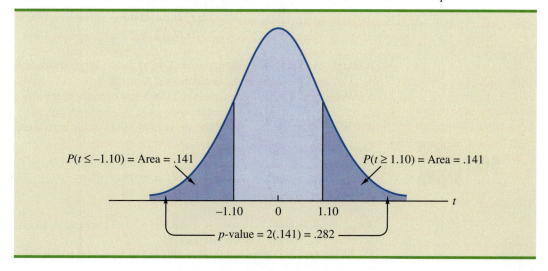

$P(t \leq -1.10) = \text{Area} = .141$ $P(t \geq 1.10) = \text{Area} = .141$

$-1.10 \qquad 0 \qquad 1.10$

$p\text{-value} = 2(.141) = .282$

TABLE 9.3   SUMMARY OF HYPOTHESIS TESTS ABOUT A POPULATION MEAN: σ UNKNOWN CASE

	Lower Tail Test	Upper Tail Test	Two-Tailed Test
Hypotheses	$H_0: \mu \geq \mu_0$ $H_a: \mu < \mu_0$	$H_0: \mu \leq \mu_0$ $H_a: \mu > \mu_0$	$H_0: \mu = \mu_0$ $H_a: \mu \neq \mu_0$
Test Statistic	$t = \dfrac{\bar{x} - \mu_0}{s/\sqrt{n}}$	$t = \dfrac{\bar{x} - \mu_0}{s/\sqrt{n}}$	$t = \dfrac{\bar{x} - \mu_0}{s/\sqrt{n}}$
Rejection Rule: *p*-Value Approach	Reject H_0 if *p*-value $\leq \alpha$	Reject H_0 if *p*-value $\leq \alpha$	Reject H_0 if *p*-value $\leq \alpha$
Rejection Rule: Critical Value Approach	Reject H_0 if $t \leq -t_\alpha$	Reject H_0 if $t \geq t_\alpha$	Reject H_0 if $t \leq -t_{\alpha/2}$ or if $t \geq t_{\alpha/2}$

The applicability of the hypothesis testing procedures of this section is dependent on the distribution of the population being sampled from and the sample size. When the population is normally distributed, the hypothesis tests described in this section provide exact results for any sample size. When the population is not normally distributed, the procedures are approximations. Nonetheless, we find that sample sizes greater than 50 will provide good results in almost all cases. If the population is approximately normal, small sample sizes (e.g., $n < 15$) can provide acceptable results. In situations where the population cannot be approximated by a normal distribution, sample sizes of $n \geq 15$ will provide acceptable results as long as the population is not highly skewed and does not contain outliers. If the population is highly skewed or contains outliers, samples sizes approaching 50 are a good idea.

Exercises

Methods

23. Consider the following hypothesis test:

$$H_0: \mu \leq 12$$
$$H_a: \mu > 12$$

A sample of 25 provided a sample mean $\bar{x} = 14$ and a sample standard deviation $s = 4.32$.
   a.   Compute the value of the test statistic.
   b.   What does the *t* distribution table (Table 2 in Appendix B) tell you about the *p*-value?
   c.   At $\alpha = .05$, what is your conclusion?
   d.   What is the rejection rule using the critical value? What is your conclusion?

24. Consider the following hypothesis test:

$$H_0: \mu = 18$$
$$H_a: \mu \neq 18$$

A sample of 48 provided a sample mean $\bar{x} = 17$ and a sample standard deviation $s = 4.5$.
   a.   Compute the value of the test statistic.
   b.   What does the *t* distribution table (Table 2 in Appendix B) tell you about the *p*-value?

c.   At $\alpha = .05$, what is your conclusion?

d.   What is the rejection rule using the critical value? What is your conclusion?

25.   Consider the following hypothesis test:

$$H_0: \mu \geq 45$$
$$H_a: \mu < 45$$

A sample of 36 is used. Identify the p-value and state your conclusion for each of the following sample results. Use $\alpha = .01$.

a. $\bar{x} = 44$ and $s = 5.2$

b. $\bar{x} = 43$ and $s = 4.6$

c. $\bar{x} = 46$ and $s = 5.0$

26.   Consider the following hypothesis test:

$$H_0: \mu = 100$$
$$H_a: \mu \neq 100$$

A sample of 65 is used. Identify the p-value and state your conclusion for each of the following sample results. Use $\alpha = .05$.

a. $\bar{x} = 103$ and $s = 11.5$

b. $\bar{x} = 96.5$ and $s = 11.0$

c. $\bar{x} = 102$ and $s = 10.5$

Applications

27.   The Employment and Training Administration reported the U.S. mean unemployment insurance benefit of \$238 per week (*The World Almanac 2003*). A researcher in the state of Virginia anticipated that sample data would show evidence that the mean weekly unemployment insurance benefit in Virginia was below the national level.

a.   Develop appropriate hypotheses such that rejection of H_0 will support the researcher's contention.

b.   For a sample of 100 individuals, the sample mean weekly unemployment insurance benefit was \$231 with a sample standard deviation of \$80. What is the p-value?

c.   At $\alpha = .05$, what is your conclusion?

d.   Repeat the preceding hypothesis test using the critical value approach.

28.   The National Association of Professional Baseball Leagues, Inc., reported that attendance for 176 minor league baseball teams reached an all-time high during the 2001 season (*New York Times,* July 28, 2002). On a per-game basis, the mean attendance for minor league baseball was 3530 people per game. Midway through the 2002 season, the president of the association asked for an attendance report that would hopefully show that the mean attendance for 2002 was exceeding the 2001 level.

a.   Formulate hypotheses that could be used determine whether the mean attendance per game in 2002 was greater than the previous year's level.

b.   Assume that a sample of 92 minor league baseball games played during the first half of the 2002 season showed a mean attendance of 3740 people per game with a sample standard deviation of 810. What is the p-value?

c.   At $\alpha = .01$, what is your conclusion?

29.   The cost of a one-carat VS2 clarity, H color diamond from Diamond Source USA is \$5600 (diasource.com, March 2003). A midwestern jeweler makes calls to contacts in the diamond district of New York City to see whether the mean price of diamonds there differs from \$5600.

a.   Formulate hypotheses that can be used to determine whether the mean price in New York City differs from \$5600.

b.   Assume that a sample of 25 New York City contacts provided a sample mean price of \$5835 and a sample standard deviation of \$520. What is the p-value?

    c.   At $\alpha = .05$, can the null hypothesis be rejected? What is your conclusion?

    d.   Repeat the preceding hypothesis test using the critical value approach.

30.   AOL Time Warner Inc.'s CNN has been the longtime ratings leader of cable television news. Nielsen Media Research indicated that the mean CNN viewing audience was 600,000 viewers per day during 2002 (*The Wall Street Journal,* March 10, 2003). Assume that for a sample of 40 days during the first half of 2003, the daily audience was 612,000 viewers with a sample standard deviation of 65,000 viewers.

    a.   What are the hypotheses if CNN management would like information on any change in the CNN viewing audience?

    b.   What is the *p*-value?

    c.   Select your own level of significance. What is your conclusion?

    d.   What recommendation would you make to CNN management in this application?

31.   Raftelis Financial Consulting reported that the mean quarterly water bill in the United States is $47.50 (*U.S. News & World Report,* August 12, 2002). Some water systems are operated by public utilities, whereas other water systems are operated by private companies. An economist pointed out that privatization does not equal competition and that monopoly powers provided to public utilities are now being transferred to private companies. The concern is that consumers end up paying higher-than-average rates for water provided by private companies. The water system for Atlanta, Georgia, is provided by a private company. A sample of 64 Atlanta consumers showed a mean quarterly water bill of $51 with a sample standard deviation of $12. At $\alpha = .05$, does the Atlanta sample support the conclusion that above-average rates exist for this private water system? What is your conclusion?

32.   According to the National Automobile Dealers Association, the mean price for used cars is $10,192. A manager of a Kansas City used car dealership reviewed a sample of 50 recent used car sales at the dealership in an attempt to determine whether the population mean price for used cars at this particular dealership differed from the national mean.

    a.   Formulate the hypotheses that can be used to determine whether a difference exists in the mean price for used cars at the dealership.

    b.   What is the *p*-value based on a sample mean price of $9750 and a sample standard deviation of $1400?

    c.   At $\alpha = .05$, what is your conclusion?

33.   Callaway Golf Company's new forged titanium ERC driver has been described as "illegal" because it promises driving distances that exceed the USGA's standard. *Golf Digest* compared actual driving distances with the ERC driver and a USGA-approved driver with a population mean driving distance of 280 yards. Based on nine test drives, the mean driving distance by the ERC driver was 286.9 yards (*Golf Digest,* May 12, 2000). Answer the following questions assuming a sample standard deviation driving distance of 10 yards.

    a.   Formulate the null and alternative hypotheses that can be used to determine whether the new ERC driver has a population mean driving distance greater than 280 yards.

    b.   On average, how many yards farther did the golf ball travel with the ERC driver?

    c.   At $\alpha = .05$, what is your conclusion?

34.   Joan's Nursery specializes in custom-designed landscaping for residential areas. The estimated labor cost associated with a particular landscaping proposal is based on the number of plantings of trees, shrubs, and so on to be used for the project. For cost-estimating purposes, managers use two hours of labor time for the planting of a medium-sized tree. Actual times from a sample of 10 plantings during the past month follow (times in hours).

1.7	1.5	2.6	2.2	2.4	2.3	2.6	3.0	1.4	2.3

With a .05 level of significance, test to see whether the mean tree-planting time differs from two hours.

a. State the null and alternative hypotheses.
b. Compute the sample mean.
c. Compute the sample standard deviation.
d. What is the *p*-value?
e. What is your conclusion?

9.5 Population Proportion

In this section we show how to conduct a hypothesis test about a population proportion *p*. Using p_0 to denote the hypothesized value for the population proportion, the three forms for a hypothesis test about a population proportion are as follows.

$$H_0: p \geq p_0 \qquad H_0: p \leq p_0 \qquad H_0: p = p_0$$
$$H_a: p < p_0 \qquad H_a: p > p_0 \qquad H_a: p \neq p_0$$

The first form is called a lower tail test, the second form is called an upper tail test, and the third form is called a two-tailed test.

Hypothesis tests about a population proportion are based on the difference between the sample proportion $\bar{p}$ and the hypothesized population proportion p_0. The methods used to conduct the hypothesis test are similar to those used for hypothesis tests about a population mean. The only difference is that we use the sample proportion and its standard error to compute the test statistic. The *p*-value approach or the critical value approach is then used to determine whether the null hypothesis should be rejected.

Let us consider an example involving a situation faced by Pine Creek golf course. Over the past year, 20% of the players at Pine Creek were women. In an effort to increase the proportion of women players, Pine Creek implemented a special promotion designed to attract women golfers. One month after the promotion was implemented, the course manager requested a statistical study to determine whether the proportion of women players at Pine Creek had increased. Because the objective of the study is to determine whether the proportion of women golfers increased, an upper tail test with $H_a: p > .20$ is appropriate. The null and alternative hypotheses for the Pine Creek hypothesis test are as follows:

$$H_0: p \leq .20$$
$$H_a: p > .20$$

If H_0 can be rejected, the test results will give statistical support for the conclusion that the proportion of women golfers increased and the promotion was beneficial. The course manager specified that a level of significance of $\alpha = .05$ be used in carrying out this hypothesis test.

The next step of the hypothesis testing procedure is to select a sample and compute the value of an appropriate test statistic. To show how this step is done for the Pine Creek upper tail test, we begin with a general discussion of how to compute the value of the test statistic for any form of a hypothesis test about a population proportion. The sampling distribution of $\bar{p}$, the point estimator of the population parameter *p*, is the basis for developing the test statistic.

When the null hypothesis is true as an equality, the expected value of $\bar{p}$ equals the hypothesized value p_0; that is, $E(\bar{p}) = p_0$. The standard error of $\bar{p}$ is given by

$$\sigma_{\bar{p}} = \sqrt{\frac{p_0(1 - p_0)}{n}}$$

In Chapter 7 we said that if $np \geq 5$ and $n(1 - p) \geq 5$, the sampling distribution of $\bar{p}$ can be approximated by a normal distribution.* Under these conditions, which usually apply in practice, the quantity

$$z = \frac{\bar{p} - p_0}{\sigma_{\bar{p}}} \tag{9.5}$$

has a standard normal probability distribution. With $\sigma_{\bar{p}} = \sqrt{p_0(1 - p_0)/n}$, the standard normal random variable z is the test statistic used to conduct hypothesis tests about a population proportion.

> **TEST STATISTIC FOR HYPOTHESIS TESTS ABOUT A POPULATION PROPORTION**
>
> $$z = \frac{\bar{p} - p_0}{\sqrt{\dfrac{p_0(1 - p_0)}{n}}} \tag{9.6}$$

WomenGolf

We can now compute the test statistic for the Pine Creek hypothesis test. Suppose a random sample of 400 players was selected, and that 100 of the players were women. The proportion of women golfers in the sample is

$$\bar{p} = \frac{100}{400} = .25$$

Using equation (9.6), the value of the test statistic is

$$z = \frac{\bar{p} - p_0}{\sqrt{\dfrac{p_0(1 - p_0)}{n}}} = \frac{.25 - .20}{\sqrt{\dfrac{.20(1 - .20)}{400}}} = \frac{.05}{.02} = 2.50$$

Because the Pine Creek hypothesis test is an upper tail test, the p-value is the probability that z is greater than or equal to $z = 2.50$; that is, it is the area under the standard normal curve to the right of $z = 2.50$. Using the table of areas for the standard normal distribution, we find that the area between the mean and $z = 2.50$ is .4938. Thus, the p-value for the Pine Creek test is $.5000 - .4938 = .0062$. Figure 9.10 shows this p-value calculation.

Recall that the course manager specified a level of significance of $\alpha = .05$. A p-value $= .0062 < .05$ gives sufficient statistical evidence to reject H_0 at the .05 level of significance. Thus, the test provides statistical support for the conclusion that the special promotion increased the proportion of women players at the Pine Creek golf course.

The decision whether to reject the null hypothesis can also be made using the critical value approach. The critical value corresponding to an area of .05 in the upper tail of a stan-

---

*In most applications involving hypothesis tests of a population proportion, sample sizes are large enough to use the normal approximation. The exact sampling distribution of $\bar{p}$ is discrete with the probability for each value of $\bar{p}$ given by the binomial distribution. So hypothesis testing is a bit more complicated for small samples when the normal approximation cannot be used.

FIGURE 9.10   CALCULATION OF THE *p*-VALUE FOR THE PINE CREEK HYPOTHESIS TEST

Area = .4938

p-value = $P(z \geq 2.50) = .0062$

0   2.5   *z*

dard normal distribution is $z_{.05} = 1.645$. Thus, the rejection rule using the critical value approach is to reject H_0 if $z \geq 1.645$. Because $z = 2.50 > 1.645$, H_0 is rejected.

Again, we see that the *p*-value approach and the critical value approach lead to the same hypothesis testing conclusion, but the *p*-value approach provides more information. With a *p*-value $= .0062$, the null hypothesis would be rejected for any level of significance greater than or equal to .0062.

Summary

The procedure used to conduct a hypothesis test about a population proportion is similar to the procedure used to conduct a hypothesis test about a population mean. Although we only illustrated how to conduct a hypothesis test about a population proportion for an upper tail test, similar procedures can be used for lower tail and two-tailed tests. Table 9.4 provides a summary of the hypothesis tests about a population proportion.

TABLE 9.4   SUMMARY OF HYPOTHESIS TESTS ABOUT A POPULATION PROPORTION

	Lower Tail Test	Upper Tail Test	Two-Tailed Test
Hypotheses	$H_0: p \geq p_0$ $H_a: p < p_0$	$H_0: p \leq p_0$ $H_a: p > p_0$	$H_0: p = p_0$ $H_a: p \neq p_0$
Test Statistic	$z = \dfrac{\bar{p} - p_0}{\sqrt{\dfrac{p_0(1 - p_0)}{n}}}$	$z = \dfrac{\bar{p} - p_0}{\sqrt{\dfrac{p_0(1 - p_0)}{n}}}$	$z = \dfrac{\bar{p} - p_0}{\sqrt{\dfrac{p_0(1 - p_0)}{n}}}$
Rejection Rule: ***p*-Value Approach**	Reject H_0 if *p*-value $\leq \alpha$	Reject H_0 if *p*-value $\leq \alpha$	Reject H_0 if *p*-value $\leq \alpha$
Rejection Rule: **Critical Value** **Approach**	Reject H_0 if $z \leq -z_\alpha$	Reject H_0 if $z \geq z_\alpha$	Reject H_0 if $z \leq -z_{\alpha/2}$ or if $z \geq z_{\alpha/2}$

Exercises

Methods

35. Consider the following hypothesis test:

$$H_0: p = .20$$
$$H_a: p \neq .20$$

A sample of 400 provided a sample proportion $\bar{p} = .175$.
   a. Compute the value of the test statistic.
   b. What is the p-value?
   c. At $\alpha = .05$, what is your conclusion?
   d. What is the rejection rule using the critical value? What is your conclusion?

36. Consider the following hypothesis test:

$$H_0: p \geq .75$$
$$H_a: p < .75$$

A sample of 300 items was selected. Compute the p-value and state your conclusion for each of the following sample results. Use $\alpha = .05$.
   a. $\bar{p} = .68$
   b. $\bar{p} = .72$
   c. $\bar{p} = .70$
   d. $\bar{p} = .77$

Applications

37. The Heldrich Center for Workforce Development found that 40% of Internet users received more than 10 e-mail messages per day (*USA Today,* May 7, 2000). A similar study on the use of e-mail was repeated in 2002.
   a. Formulate the hypotheses that can be used to determine whether the proportion of Internet users receiving more than 10 e-mail messages per day increased.
   b. If a sample of 425 Internet users found 189 receiving more than 10 e-mail messages per day, what is the p-value?
   c. At $\alpha = .05$, what is your conclusion?

38. A study by *Consumer Reports* showed that 64% of supermarket shoppers believe supermarket brands to be as good as national name brands. To investigate whether this result applies to its own product, the manufacturer of a national name-brand ketchup asked a sample of shoppers whether they believed that supermarket ketchup was as good as the national brand ketchup.
   a. Formulate the hypotheses that could be used to determine whether the percentage of supermarket shoppers who believe that the supermarket ketchup was as good as the national brand ketchup differed from 64%.
   b. If a sample of 100 shoppers showed 52 stating that the supermarket brand was as good as the national brand, what is the p-value?
   c. At $\alpha = .05$, what is your conclusion?
   d. Should the national brand ketchup manufacturer be pleased with this conclusion? Explain.

39. The National Center for Health Statistics released a report that stated 70% of adults do not exercise regularly (Associated Press, April 7, 2002). A researcher decided to conduct a study to see whether the National Center for Health Statistics' claim differed on a state-by-state basis.

a.   State the null and alternative hypotheses assuming the intent of the researcher is to identify states that differ from the 70% reported by the National Center for Health Statistics.

b.   At $\alpha = .05$, what is the research conclusion for the following states:

> Wisconsin: 252 of 350 adults did not exercise regularly
> California: 189 of 300 adults did not exercise regularly

40.   Before the 2003 Super Bowl, ABC predicted that 22% of the Super Bowl audience would express an interest in seeing one of its forthcoming new television shows, including "8 Simple Rules," "Are You Hot?," and "Dragnet." ABC ran commercials for these television shows during the Super Bowl. The day after the Super Bowl, Intermediate Advertising Group of New York sampled 1532 viewers who saw the commercials and found that 414 said that they would watch one of the ABC advertised television shows (*The Wall Street Journal,* January 30, 2003).

a.   What is the point estimate of the proportion of the audience that said they would watch the television shows after seeing the television commercials?

b.   At $\alpha = .05$, determine whether the intent to watch the ABC television shows significantly increased after seeing the television commercials. Formulate the appropriate hypotheses, compute the *p*-value, and state your conclusion.

c.   Why are such studies valuable to companies and advertising firms?

41.   Microsoft Outlook is the most widely used e-mail manager. A Microsoft executive claims that Microsoft Outlook is used by at least 75% of Internet users. A sample of Internet users will be used to test this claim.

a.   Formulate the hypotheses that can be used to test the claim.

b.   A Merrill Lynch study reported that Microsoft Outlook is used by 72% of Internet users (CNBC, June 2000). Assume that the report was based on a sample size of 300 Internet users. What is the *p*-value?

c.   At $\alpha = .05$, should the executive's claim of at least 75% be rejected?

42.   According to the Census Bureau's American Housing Survey, the primary reason people who move chose their new neighborhood is because the location is convenient to work (*USA Today,* December 24, 2002). Based on 1990 Census Bureau data, we know that 24% of the population of people who moved selected "location convenient to work" as the reason for selecting their new neighborhood. Assume a sample of 300 people who moved during 2003 found 93 did so to be closer to work. Do the sample data support the research conclusion that in 2003 more people are choosing where to live based on how close they will be to their work? What is the point estimate of the proportion of people who moved during 2003 that chose their new neighborhood because the location is convenient to work? What is your research conclusion? Use $\alpha = .05$.

43.   An article about driving practices in Strathcona County, Alberta, Canada, claimed that 48% of drivers did not stop at stop sign intersections on county roads (*Edmonton Journal,* July 19, 2000). Two months later, a follow-up study collected data in order to see whether this percentage had changed.

a.   Formulate the hypotheses to determine whether the proportion of drivers who did not stop at stop sign intersections had changed.

b.   Assume the study found 360 of 800 drivers did not stop at stop sign intersections. What is the sample proportion? What is the *p*-value?

c.   At $\alpha = .05$, what is your conclusion?

44.   In a cover story, *Business Week* published information about sleep habits of Americans (*Business Week,* January 26, 2004). The article noted that sleep deprivation causes a number of problems. They note that lack of sleep causes highway deaths. Fifty-one percent of adult drivers admit to driving while drowsy. A researcher hypothesized that this issue was an even bigger problem for people working night shifts.

    a.   Formulate the hypotheses that can be used to help determine whether more than 51% of the population of night shift workers admit to driving while drowsy.

    b.   A sample of 500 night shift workers found that 232 admitted to driving while drowsy. What is the sample proportion? What is the p-value?

    c.   At $\alpha = .01$, what is your conclusion?

45.   Drugstore.com was the first e-commerce company to offer Internet drugstore retailing. Drugstore.com customers were provided the opportunity to buy health, beauty, personal care, wellness, and pharmaceutical replenishment products over the Internet. At the end of 10 months of operation, the company reported that 44% of orders were from repeat customers (*Drugstore.com Annual Report,* January 2, 2000). Assume that Drugstore.com will use a sample of customer orders each quarter to determine whether the proportion of orders from repeat customers changed from the initial $p = .44$.

    a.   Formulate the null and alternative hypotheses.

    b.   During the first quarter a sample of 500 orders showed 205 repeat customers. What is the p-value? Use $\alpha = .05$. What is your conclusion?

    c.   During the second quarter a sample of 500 orders showed 245 repeat customers. What is the p-value? Use $\alpha = .05$. What is your conclusion?

Summary

Hypothesis testing is a statistical procedure that uses sample data to determine whether a statement about the value of a population parameter should or should not be rejected. The hypotheses are two competing statements about a population parameter. One statement is called the null hypothesis (H_0) and the other statement is called the alternative hypothesis (H_a). In Section 9.1 we provided guidelines for developing hypotheses for three situations frequently encountered in practice.

Whenever historical data or other information provides a basis for assuming that the population standard deviation is known, the hypothesis testing procedure is based on the standard normal distribution. Whenever σ is unknown, the sample standard deviation s is used to estimate σ and the hypothesis testing procedure is based on the t distribution. In both cases, the quality of results depends on both the form of the population distribution and the sample size. If the population has a normal distribution, both hypothesis testing procedures are applicable, even with small sample sizes. If the population is not normally distributed, larger sample sizes are needed. General guidelines about the sample size were provided in Sections 9.3 and 9.4. In the case of hypothesis tests about a population proportion, the hypothesis testing procedure uses a test statistic based on the standard normal distribution.

In all cases, the value of the test statistic is used to compute a p-value for the test. A p-value is a probability, computed using the test statistic, that measures the support (or lack of support) provided by the sample for the null hypothesis. If the p-value is less than or equal to the level of significance α, the null hypothesis can be rejected.

Hypothesis testing conclusions can also be made by comparing the value of the test statistic to a critical value. For lower tail tests, the null hypothesis is rejected if the value of the test statistic is less than or equal to the critical value. For upper tail tests, the null hypothesis is rejected if the value of the test statistic is greater than or equal to the critical value. Two-tailed tests consist of two critical values: one in the lower tail of the sampling distribution and one in the upper tail. In this case, the null hypothesis is rejected if the value of the test statistic is less than or equal to the critical value in the lower tail or greater than or equal to the critical value in the upper tail.

Glossary

Null hypothesis The hypothesis tentatively assumed true in the hypothesis testing procedure.

Alternative hypothesis The hypothesis concluded to be true if the null hypothesis is rejected.

Type I error The error of rejecting H_0 when it is true.

Type II error The error of accepting H_0 when it is false.

Level of significance The probability of making a Type I error when the null hypothesis is true as an equality.

One-tailed test A hypothesis test in which rejection of the null hypothesis occurs for values of the test statistic in one tail of its sampling distribution.

Test statistic A statistic whose value helps determine whether a null hypothesis can be rejected.

_p_-value A probability, computed using the test statistic, that measures the support (or lack of support) provided by the sample for the null hypothesis. For a lower tail test, the p-value is the probability of obtaining a value for the test statistic as small as or smaller than that provided by the sample. For an upper tail test, the p-value is the probability of obtaining a value for the test statistic as large as or larger than that provided by the sample. For a two-tailed test, the p-value is the probability of obtaining a value for the test statistic as unlikely as or more unlikely than that provided by the sample.

Critical value A value that is compared with the test statistic to determine whether H_0 should be rejected.

Two-tailed test A hypothesis test in which rejection of the null hypothesis occurs for values of the test statistic in either tail of its sampling distribution.

Key Formulas

Test Statistic for Hypothesis Tests About a Population Mean: σ Known

$$z = \frac{\bar{x} - \mu_0}{\sigma/\sqrt{n}} \tag{9.1}$$

Test Statistic for Hypothesis Tests About a Population Mean: σ Unknown

$$t = \frac{\bar{x} - \mu_0}{s/\sqrt{n}} \tag{9.4}$$

Test Statistic for Hypothesis Tests About a Population Proportion

$$z = \frac{\bar{p} - p_0}{\sqrt{\dfrac{p_0(1 - p_0)}{n}}} \tag{9.6}$$

Supplementary Exercises

46. A production line operates with a mean filling weight of 16 ounces per container. Overfilling or underfilling presents a serious problem and when detected requires the operator to shut down the production line to readjust the filling mechanism. From past data, a population standard deviation $\sigma = .8$ ounces is assumed. A quality control inspector selects a

sample of 30 items every hour and at that time makes the decision of whether to shut down the line for readjustment. The level of significance is $\alpha = .05$.

a.   State the hypothesis test for this quality control application.

b.   If a sample mean of $\bar{x} = 16.32$ ounces was found, what is the p-value? What action would you recommend?

c.   If a sample mean of $\bar{x} = 15.82$ ounces was found, what is the p-value? What action would you recommend?

d.   Use the critical value approach. What is the rejection rule for the preceding hypothesis testing procedure? Repeat parts (b) and (c). Do you reach the same conclusion?

47.   At Western University the historical mean of scholarship examination scores for freshman applications is 900. A historical population standard deviation $\sigma = 180$ is assumed known. Each year, the assistant dean uses a sample of applications to determine whether the mean examination score for the new freshman applications has changed.

a.   State the hypotheses.

b.   What is the 95% confidence interval estimate of the population mean examination score if a sample of 200 applications provided a sample mean $\bar{x} = 935$?

c.   Use the confidence interval to conduct a hypothesis test. Using $\alpha = .05$, what is your conclusion?

d.   What is the p-value?

48.   The population mean annual salary for public school teachers in the state of New York is $45,250. A sample mean annual salary of public school teachers in New York City is $47,000 (*Time,* April 3, 2000). Assume the New York City results are based on a sample of 95 teachers. Assume the population standard deviation is $\sigma = \$6300$.

a.   Formulate the null and alternative hypotheses that can be used to determine whether the sample data support the conclusion that public school teachers in New York City have a higher mean salary than the public school teachers in the state of New York.

b.   What is the p-value?

c.   Use $\alpha = .01$. What is your conclusion?

49.   According to the National Association of Colleges and Employers, the 2000 mean annual salary of business degree graduates in accounting was $37,000 (*Time,* May 8, 2000). In a follow-up study in June 2001, a sample of 48 graduating accounting majors provided a sample mean of $38,100 and a sample standard deviation of $5200.

a.   Formulate the null and alternative hypotheses that can be used to determine whether the sample data support the conclusion that June 2001 graduates in accounting have a mean salary greater than the 2000 mean annual salary of $37,000.

b.   What is the p-value?

c.   Use $\alpha = .05$. What is your conclusion?

50.   The College Board reported that the average number of freshman class applications to public colleges and universities is 6000 (*USA Today,* December 26, 2002). During a recent application/ enrollment period, a sample of 32 colleges and universities showed that the sample mean number of freshman class applications was 5812 with a sample standard deviation of 1140. Do the data indicate a change in the mean number of applications? Use $\alpha = .05$.

51.   An extensive study of the cost of health care in the United States presented data showing that the mean spending per Medicare enrollee in 2003 was $6883 (*Money,* Fall 2003). To investigate differences across the country, a researcher took a sample of 40 Medicare enrollees in Indianapolis. For the Indianapolis sample, the mean 2003 Medicare spending was $5980 and the standard deviation was $2518.

a.   State the hypotheses that should be used if we would like to determine whether the mean annual Medicare spending in Indianapolis is lower than the national mean.

b.   Use the preceding sample results to compute the test statistic and the p-value.

c.   Use $\alpha = .05$. What is your conclusion?

d.   Repeat the hypothesis test using the critical value approach.

52. The chamber of commerce of a Florida Gulf Coast community advertises that area residential property is available at a mean cost of $125,000 or less per lot. Suppose a sample of 32 properties provided a sample mean of $130,000 per lot and a sample standard deviation of $12,500. Using a .05 level of significance, test the validity of the advertising claim.

53. The population mean earnings per share for financial services corporations including American Express, E*TRADE Group, Goldman Sachs, and Merrill Lynch was $3 (*Business Week,* August 14, 2000). In 2001, a sample of 10 financial services corporations provided the following earnings per share data:

    1.92   2.16   3.63   3.16   4.02   3.14   2.20   2.34   3.05   2.38

    a. Formulate the null and alternative hypotheses that can be used to determine whether the population mean earnings per share in 2001 differ from the $3 reported in 2000.
    b. Compute the sample mean.
    c. Compute the sample standard deviation.
    d. What is the *p*-value?
    e. Use $\alpha = .05$. What is your conclusion?

54. A study by the Centers for Disease Control (CDC) found that 23.3% of adults are smokers and that roughly 70% of those who do smoke indicate that they want to quit (Associated Press, July 26, 2002). CDC reported that, of people who smoked at some point in their lives, 50% have been able to kick the habit. Part of the study suggested that the success rate for quitting rose by education level. Assume that a sample of 100 college graduates who smoked at some point in their lives showed that 64 had been able to successfully stop smoking.
    a. State the hypotheses that can be used to determine whether the population of college graduates has a success rate higher than the overall population when it comes to breaking the smoking habit.
    b. Given the sample data, what is the proportion of college graduates who, having smoked at some point in their lives, were able to stop smoking?
    c. What is the *p*-value? At $\alpha = .01$, what is your hypothesis testing conclusion?

55. An airline promotion to business travelers is based on the assumption that two-thirds of business travelers use a laptop computer on overnight business trips.
    a. State the hypotheses that can be used to test the assumption.
    b. What is the sample proportion from an American Express–sponsored survey that found 355 of 546 business travelers use a laptop computer on overnight business trips?
    c. What is the *p*-value?
    d. Use $\alpha = .05$. What is your conclusion?

56. Shell Oil office workers were asked which work schedule appealed most: working five 8-hour days a week or working four 10-hour days a week (*USA Today,* September 11, 2000). Let $p =$ the proportion of the office worker population preferring the four-10-hour-days work week.
    a. State the hypotheses if Shell management is interested in statistical support that shows more than 50% of office workers prefer the four-10-hour-days work week.
    b. What is the sample proportion if a sample of 105 office workers showed 67 preferred the four-10-hour-days schedule?
    c. What is the *p*-value? Use $\alpha = .01$. What is your conclusion?

57. During the 2004 election year, new polling results were reported daily. In an IBD/TIPP poll of 910 adults, 503 respondents reported that they were optimistic about the national outlook, and President Bush's leadership index jumped 4.7 points to 55.3 (*Investor's Business Daily,* January 14, 2004).
    a. What is the sample proportion of respondents that are optimistic about the national outlook?
    b. A campaign manager wants to claim that this poll indicates that the majority of adults are optimistic about the national outlook. Construct a hypothesis test so that rejection

of the null hypothesis will permit the conclusion that the proportion optimistic is greater than 50%.

c.   Use the polling data to compute the *p*-value for the hypothesis test in part (b). Explain to the manager what this *p*-value means about the level of significance of the results.

58. A radio station in Myrtle Beach announced that at least 90% of the hotels and motels would be full for the Memorial Day weekend. The station advised listeners to make reservations in advance if they planned to be in the resort over the weekend. On Saturday night a sample of 58 hotels and motels showed 49 with a no-vacancy sign and 9 with vacancies. What is your reaction to the radio station's claim after seeing the sample evidence? Use $\alpha = .05$ in making the statistical test. What is the *p*-value?

59. Environmental health indicators include air quality, water quality, and food quality. Twenty-five years ago, 47% of U.S. food samples contained pesticide residues (*U.S. News & World Report*, April 17, 2000). In a recent study, 44 of 125 food samples contained pesticide residues.
a.   State the hypotheses that can be used to show that the population proportion declined.
b.   What is the sample proportion?
c.   What is the *p*-value?
d.   Use $\alpha = .01$. What is your conclusion?

Case Problem 1   Quality Associates, Inc.

Quality Associates, Inc., a consulting firm, advises its clients about sampling and statistical procedures that can be used to control their manufacturing processes. In one particular application, a client gave Quality Associates a sample of 800 observations taken during a time in which that client's process was operating satisfactorily. The sample standard deviation for these data was .21; hence, with so much data, the population standard deviation was assumed to be .21. Quality Associates then suggested that random samples of size 30 be taken periodically to monitor the process on an ongoing basis. By analyzing the new samples, the client could quickly learn whether the process was operating satisfactorily. When the process was not operating satisfactorily, corrective action could be taken to eliminate the problem. The design specification indicated the mean for the process should be 12. The hypothesis test suggested by Quality Associates follows.

$$H_0: \mu = 12$$
$$H_a: \mu \neq 12$$

Corrective action will be taken any time H_0 is rejected.

The following samples were collected at hourly intervals during the first day of operation of the new statistical process control procedure. These data are available in the data set Quality.

Quality

Sample 1	Sample 2	Sample 3	Sample 4
11.55	11.62	11.91	12.02
11.62	11.69	11.36	12.02
11.52	11.59	11.75	12.05
11.75	11.82	11.95	12.18
11.90	11.97	12.14	12.11
11.64	11.71	11.72	12.07
11.80	11.87	11.61	12.05
12.03	12.10	11.85	11.64

Sample 1	Sample 2	Sample 3	Sample 4
11.94	12.01	12.16	12.39
11.92	11.99	11.91	11.65
12.13	12.20	12.12	12.11
12.09	12.16	11.61	11.90
11.93	12.00	12.21	12.22
12.21	12.28	11.56	11.88
12.32	12.39	11.95	12.03
11.93	12.00	12.01	12.35
11.85	11.92	12.06	12.09
11.76	11.83	11.76	11.77
12.16	12.23	11.82	12.20
11.77	11.84	12.12	11.79
12.00	12.07	11.60	12.30
12.04	12.11	11.95	12.27
11.98	12.05	11.96	12.29
12.30	12.37	12.22	12.47
12.18	12.25	11.75	12.03
11.97	12.04	11.96	12.17
12.17	12.24	11.95	11.94
11.85	11.92	11.89	11.97
12.30	12.37	11.88	12.23
12.15	12.22	11.93	12.25

Managerial Report

1. Conduct a hypothesis test for each sample at the .01 level of significance and determine what action, if any, should be taken. Provide the test statistic and p-value for each test.
2. Compute the standard deviation for each of the four samples. Does the assumption of .21 for the population standard deviation appear reasonable?
3. Compute limits for the sample mean $\bar{x}$ around $\mu = 12$ such that, as long as a new sample mean is within those limits, the process will be considered to be operating satisfactorily. If $\bar{x}$ exceeds the upper limit or if $\bar{x}$ is below the lower limit, corrective action will be taken. These limits are referred to as upper and lower control limits for quality control purposes.
4. Discuss the implications of changing the level of significance to a larger value. What mistake or error could increase if the level of significance is increased?

Case Problem 2   Unemployment Study

Each month the U.S. Bureau of Labor Statistics publishes a variety of unemployment statistics, including the number of individuals who are unemployed and the mean length of time the individuals have been unemployed. For November 1998, the Bureau of Labor Statistics reported that the national mean length of time of unemployment was 14.6 weeks.

The mayor of Philadelphia requested a study on the status of unemployment in the Philadelphia area. A sample of 50 unemployed residents of Philadelphia included data on their age and the number of weeks without a job. A portion of the data collected in November 1998 follows. The complete data set is available in the data file BLS.

BLS

Age	Weeks	Age	Weeks	Age	Weeks
56	22	22	11	25	12
35	19	48	6	25	1
22	7	48	22	59	33
57	37	25	5	49	26
40	18	40	20	33	13

Managerial Report

1. Use descriptive statistics to summarize the data.
2. Develop a 95% confidence interval estimate of the mean age of unemployed individuals in Philadelphia.
3. Conduct a hypothesis test to determine whether the mean duration of unemployment in Philadelphia is greater than the national mean duration of 14.6 weeks. Use a .01 level of significance. What is your conclusion?
4. Is there a relationship between the age of an unemployed individual and the number of weeks of unemployment? Explain.

Appendix 9.1 Hypothesis Tests with Minitab

We describe the use of Minitab to conduct hypothesis tests about a population mean and a population proportion.

Population Mean: σ Known

We illustrate using the MaxFlight golf ball distance example in Section 9.3. The data are in column C1 of a Minitab worksheet. The population standard deviation $\sigma = 12$ is assumed known and the level of significance is $\alpha = .05$. The following steps can be used to test the hypothesis $H_0: \mu = 295$ versus $H_a: \mu \neq 295$.

GolfTest

Step 1. Select the **Stat** menu
Step 2. Choose **Basic Statistics**
Step 3. Choose **1-Sample Z**
Step 4. When the 1-Sample Z dialog box appears:
   Enter C1 in the **Samples in columns** box
   Enter 12 in the **Standard deviation** box
   Enter 295 in the **Test mean** box
   Select **Options**
Step 5. When the 1-Sample Z-Options dialog box appears:
   Enter 95 in the **Confidence level** box*
   Select **not equal** in the **Alternative** box
   Click **OK**
Step 6. Click **OK**

In addition to the hypothesis testing results, Minitab provides a 95% confidence interval for the population mean.

---

*Minitab provides both hypothesis testing and interval estimation results simultaneously. The user may select any confidence level for the interval estimate of the population mean: 95% confidence is suggested here.

The procedure can be easily modified for a one-tailed hypothesis test by selecting the **less than** or **greater than** option in the **Alternative** box in step 5.

Population Mean: σ Unknown

AirRating

The ratings that 60 business travelers gave for Heathrow Airport are entered in column C1 of a Minitab worksheet. The level of significance for the test is $\alpha = .05$, and the population standard deviation σ will be estimated by the sample standard deviation s. The following steps can be used to test the hypothesis $H_0: \mu \leq 7$ against $H_a: \mu > 7$.

Step 1. Select the **Stat** menu
Step 2. Choose **Basic Statistics**
Step 3. Choose **1-Sample t**
Step 4. When the 1-Sample t dialog box appears:
  Enter C1 in the **Samples in columns** box
  Enter 7 in the **Test mean** box
  Select **Options**
Step 5. When the 1-Sample t-options dialog box appears:
  Enter 95 in the **Confidence level** box*
  Select **greater than** in the **Alternative** box
  Click **OK**
Step 6. Click **OK**

The Heathrow Airport rating study involved a greater than alternative hypothesis. The preceding steps can be easily modified for other hypothesis tests by selecting the **less than** or **not equal** options in the **Alternative** box in step 5.

Population Proportion

WomenGolf

We illustrate using the Pine Creek golf course example in Section 9.5. The data with responses Female and Male are in column C1 of a Minitab worksheet. Minitab uses an alphabetical ordering of the responses and selects the *second response* for the population proportion of interest. In this example, Minitab uses the alphabetical ordering Female-Male to provide results for the population proportion of Male responses. Because Female is the response of interest, we change Minitab's ordering as follows: Select any cell in the column and use the sequence: Editor > Column > Value Order. Then choose the option of entering a user-specified order. Make sure that the responses are ordered Male-Female in the **Define-an-order** box. Minitab's 1 Proportion routine will then provide the hypothesis test results for the population proportion of female golfers. We proceed as follows:

Step 1. Select the **Stat** menu
Step 2. Choose **Basic Statistics**
Step 3. Choose **1 Proportion**
Step 4. When the 1 Proportion dialog box appears:
  Enter C1 in the **Samples in Columns** box
  Select **Options**
Step 5. When the 1 Proportion-Options dialog box appears:
  Enter 95 in the **Confidence level** box*
  Enter .20 in the **Test proportion** box
  Select **greater than** in the **Alternative** box
  Select **Use test and interval based on normal distribution**
  Click **OK**
Step 6. Click **OK**

---

*Minitab provides both hypothesis testing and interval estimation results simultaneously. The user may select any confidence level for the interval estimate of the population mean: 95% confidence is suggested here.

Appendix 9.2   # Hypothesis Tests with Excel

Excel does not provide built-in routines for the hypothesis tests presented in this chapter. To handle these situations, we present Excel worksheets that we designed to test hypotheses about a population mean and a population proportion. The worksheets are easy to use and can be modified to handle any sample data. The worksheets are available on the CD that accompanies this book.

Population Mean: σ Known

We illustrate using the MaxFlight golf ball distance example in Section 9.3. The data are in column A of an Excel worksheet. The population standard deviation $\sigma = 12$ is assumed known and the level of significance is $\alpha = .05$. The following steps can be used to test the hypothesis $H_0: \mu = 295$ versus $H_a: \mu \neq 295$.

Hyp Sigma Known

Refer to Figure 9.11 as we describe the procedure. The worksheet in the background shows the cell formulas used to compute the results shown in the foreground worksheet. The data are entered into cells A2:A51. The following steps are necessary to use the template for this data set.

Step 1. Enter the data range A2:A51 into the =COUNT cell formula in cell D4
Step 2. Enter the data range A2:A51 into the =AVERAGE cell formula in cell D5
Step 3. Enter the population standard deviation $\sigma = 12$ in cell D6
Step 4. Enter the hypothesized value for the population mean 295 in cell D8

The remaining cell formulas automatically provide the standard error, the value of the test statistic z, and three p-values. Because the alternative hypothesis ($\mu_0 \neq 295$) indicates a two-tailed test, the p-value (Two Tail) in cell D15 is used to make the rejection decision. With p-value $= .1255 > \alpha = .05$, the null hypothesis cannot be rejected. The p-values in cells D13 or D14 would be used if the hypotheses involved a one-tailed test.

This template can be used to make hypothesis testing computations for other applications. For instance, to conduct a hypothesis test for a new data set, enter the new sample data into column A of the worksheet. Modify the formulas in cells D4 and D5 to correspond to the new data range. Enter the population standard deviation into cell D6 and the hypothesized value for the population mean into cell D8 to obtain the results. If the new sample data have already been summarized, the new sample data do not have to be entered into the worksheet. In this case, enter the sample size into cell D4, the sample mean into cell D5, the population standard deviation into cell D6, and the hypothesized value for the population mean into cell D8 to obtain the results. The worksheet in Figure 9.11 is available in the file Hyp Sigma Known on the CD that accompanies this book.

Population Mean: σ Unknown

We illustrate using the Heathrow Airport rating example in Section 9.4. The data are in column A of an Excel worksheet. The population standard deviation σ is unknown and will be estimated by the sample standard deviation s. The level of significance is $\alpha = .05$. The following steps can be used to test the hypothesis $H_0: \mu \leq 7$ versus $H_a: \mu > 7$.

Hyp Sigma Unknown

Refer to Figure 9.12 as we describe the procedure. The background worksheet shows the cell formulas used to compute the results shown in the foreground version of the worksheet. The data are entered into cells A2:A61. The following steps are necessary to use the template for this data set.

FIGURE 9.11   EXCEL WORKSHEET FOR HYPOTHESIS TESTS ABOUT A POPULATION MEAN WITH σ KNOWN

	A	B	C	D	E
1	Yards		Hypothesis Test About a Population Mean		
2	303		With σ Known		
3	282				
4	289		Sample Size	=COUNT(A2:A51)	
5	298		Sample Mean	=AVERAGE(A2:A51)	
6	283		Population Std. Deviation	12	
7	317				
8	297		Hypothesized Value	295	
9	308				
10	317		Standard Error	=D6/SQRT(D4)	
11	293		Test Statistic z	=(D5-D8)/D10	
12	284				
13	290		p-value (Lower Tail)	=NORMSDIST(D11)	
14	304		p-value (Upper Tail)	=1-D13	
15	290		p-value (Two Tail)	=2*MIN(D13,D14)	
16	311				
17	305				
49	303				
50	301				
51	292				
52					

	A	B	C	D	E
1	Yards		Hypothesis Test About a Population Mean		
2	303		With σ Known		
3	282				
4	289		Sample Size	50	
5	298		Sample Mean	297.6	
6	283		Population Std. Deviation	12	
7	317				
8	297		Hypothesized Value	295	
9	308				
10	317		Standard Error	1.70	
11	293		Test Statistic z	1.53	
12	284				
13	290		p-value (Lower Tail)	0.9372	
14	304		p-value (Upper Tail)	0.0628	
15	290		p-value (Two Tail)	0.1255	
16	311				
17	305				
49	303				
50	301				
51	292				
52					

Note: Rows 18 to 48 are hidden.

Step 1. Enter the data range A2:A61 into the =COUNT cell formula in cell D4
Step 2. Enter the data range A2:A61 into the =AVERAGE cell formula in cell D5
Step 3. Enter the data range A2:A61 into the =STDEV cell formula in cell D6
Step 4. Enter the hypothesized value for the population mean 7 into cell D8

The remaining cell formulas automatically provide the standard error, the value of the test statistic t, the number of degrees of freedom, and three p-values. Because the alternative hypothesis ($\mu > 7$) indicates an upper tail test, the p-value (Upper Tail) in cell D15 is used

FIGURE 9.12   EXCEL WORKSHEET FOR HYPOTHESIS TESTS ABOUT A POPULATION MEAN WITH σ UNKNOWN

	A	B	C	D	E
1	Rating		Hypothesis Test About a Population Mean		
2	5		With σ Unknown		
3	7				
4	8		Sample Size	=COUNT(A2:A61)	
5	7		Sample Mean	=AVERAGE(A2:A61)	
6	8		Sample Std. Deviation	=STDEV(A2:A61)	
7	8				
8	8		Hypothesized Value	7	
9	7				
10	8		Standard Error	=D6/SQRT(D4)	
11	10		Test Statistic t	=(D5-D8)/D10	
12	6		Degrees of Freedom	=D4-1	
13	7				
14	8		p-value (Lower Tail)	=IF(D11<0,TDIST(-D11,D12,1),1-TDIST(D11,D12,1))	
15	8		p-value (Upper Tail)	=1-D14	
16	9		p-value (Two Tail)	=2*MIN(D14,D15)	
17	7				
59	7				
60	7				
61	8				
62					

	A	B	C	D	E
1	Rating		Hypothesis Test About a Population Mean		
2	5		With σ Unknown		
3	7				
4	8		Sample Size	60	
5	7		Sample Mean	7.25	
6	8		Sample Std. Deviation	1.05	
7	8				
8	8		Hypothesized Value	7	
9	7				
10	8		Standard Error	0.136	
11	10		Test Statistic t	1.841	
12	6		Degrees of Freedom	59	
13	7				
14	8		p-value (Lower Tail)	0.9647	
15	8		p-value (Upper Tail)	0.0353	
16	9		p-value (Two Tail)	0.0706	
17	7				
59	7				
60	7				
61	8				
62					

Note: Rows 18 to 58 are hidden.

to make the decision. With p-value $= .0353 < \alpha = .05$, the null hypothesis is rejected. The p-values in cells D14 or D16 would be used if the hypotheses involved a lower tail test or a two-tailed test.

This template can be used to make hypothesis testing computations for other applications. For instance, to conduct a hypothesis test for a new data set, enter the new sample data into column A of the worksheet and modify the formulas in cells D4, D5, and D6 to correspond to the new data range. Enter the hypothesized value for the population mean into cell D8 to obtain the results. If the new sample data have already been summarized, the new sample data do not have to be entered into the worksheet. In this case, enter the sample size into cell D4, the sample mean into cell D5, the sample standard deviation into cell D6, and the hypothesized value for the population mean into cell D8 to obtain the results. The worksheet in Figure 9.12 is available in the file Hyp Sigma Unknown on the CD that accompanies this book.

Population Proportion

CD file

Hypothesis p

We illustrate using the Pine Creek golf course survey data presented in Section 9.5. The data of Male or Female golfer are in column A of an Excel worksheet. Refer to Figure 9.13 as we describe the procedure. The background worksheet shows the cell formulas

FIGURE 9.13   EXCEL WORKSHEET FOR HYPOTHESIS TESTS ABOUT A POPULATION PROPORTION

	A	B	C	D	E
1	Golfer		Interval Estimate of a Population Proportion		
2	Female				
3	Male		Sample Size	=COUNTA(A2:A401)	
4	Female		Response of Interest	Female	
5	Male		Count for Response	=COUNTIF(A2:A401,D4)	
6	Male		Sample Proportion	=D5/D3	
7	Female				
8	Male		Hypothesized Value	0.20	
9	Male				
10	Female		Standard Error	=SQRT(D8*(1-D8)/D3)	
11	Male		Test Statistic z	=(D6-D8)/D10	
12	Male				
13	Male		p-value (Lower Tail)	=NORMSDIST(D11)	
14	Male		p-value (Upper Tail)	=1-D13	
15	Male		p-value (Two Tail)	=2*MIN(D13,D14)	
16	Female				
400	Male				
401	Male				
402					

Note: Rows 17 to 399 are hidden.

	A	B	C	D	E
1	Golfer		Interval Estimate of a Population Proportion		
2	Female				
3	Male		Sample Size	400	
4	Female		Response of Interest	Female	
5	Male		Count for Response	100	
6	Male		Sample Proportion	0.2500	
7	Female				
8	Male		Hypothesized Value	0.20	
9	Male				
10	Female		Standard Error	0.0200	
11	Male		Test Statistic z	2.50	
12	Male				
13	Male		p-value (Lower Tail)	0.9938	
14	Male		p-value (Upper Tail)	0.0062	
15	Male		p-value (Two Tail)	0.0124	
16	Female				
400	Male				
401	Male				
402					

used to compute the results shown in the foreground worksheet. The data are entered into cells A2:A401. The following steps can be used to test the hypothesis H_0: $p \le .20$ versus H_a: $p > .20$.

Step 1. Enter the data range A2:A401 into the =COUNTA cell formula in cell D3
Step 2. Enter Female as the response of interest in cell D4
Step 3. Enter the data range A2:A401 into the =COUNTIF cell formula in cell D5
Step 4. Enter the hypothesized value for the population proportion .20 into cell D8

The remaining cell formulas automatically provide the standard error, the value of the test statistic z, and three p-values. Because the alternative hypothesis ($p_0 > .20$) indicates an upper tail test, the p-value (Upper Tail) in cell D14 is used to make the decision. With p-value $= .0062 < \alpha = .05$, the null hypothesis is rejected. The p-values in cells D13 or D15 would be used if the hypothesis involved a lower tail test or a two-tailed test.

This template can be used to make hypothesis testing computations for other applications. For instance, to conduct a hypothesis test for a new data set, enter the new sample data into column A of the worksheet. Modify the formulas in cells D3 and D5 to correspond to the new data range. Enter the response of interest into cell D4 and the hypothesized value for the population proportion into cell D8 to obtain the results. If the new sample data have already been summarized, the new sample data do not have to be entered into the worksheet. In this case, enter the sample size into cell D3, the sample proportion into cell D6, and the hypothesized value for the population proportion into cell D8 to obtain the results. The worksheet in Figure 9.13 is available in the file Hypothesis p on the CD that accompanies this book.

CHAPTER 10

Comparisons Involving Means

CONTENTS

STATISTICS *in* PRACTICE

FISONS CORPORATION
ROCHESTER, NEW YORK

Fisons Corporation, Rochester, New York, is a unit of Fisons Plc., UK. Fisons opened its U.S. operations in 1966.

Fisons Pharmaceutical Division uses extensive statistical procedures to test and develop new drugs. The testing process in the pharmaceutical industry usually consists of three stages: (1) preclinical testing, (2) testing for long-term usage and safety, and (3) clinical efficacy testing. At each successive stage, the chance that a drug will pass the rigorous tests decreases; however, the cost of further testing increases dramatically. Industry surveys indicate that on average the research and development for one new drug costs $250 million and takes 12 years. Hence, it is important to eliminate unsuccessful new drugs in the early stages of the testing process, as well as identify promising ones for further testing.

Statistics plays a major role in pharmaceutical research, where government regulations are stringent and rigorously enforced. In preclinical testing, a two- or three-population statistical study typically is used to determine whether a new drug should continue to be studied in the long-term usage and safety program. The populations may consist of the new drug, a control, and a standard drug. The preclinical testing process begins when a new drug is sent to the pharmacology group for evaluation of efficacy—the capacity of the drug to produce the desired effects. As part of the process, a statistician is asked to design an experiment that can be used to test the new drug. The design must specify the sample size and the statistical methods of analysis. In a two-population study, one sample is used to obtain data on the efficacy of the new drug (population 1) and a second sample is used to obtain data on the efficacy of a standard drug (population 2). Depending on the intended use, the new and standard drugs are tested in such disciplines as neurology, cardiology, and immunology. In most studies, the statistical method involves hypothesis testing for the difference between the means of the new drug population and the standard drug population. If a new drug

Statistical methods are used to test and develop new drugs. © Mark Richards/PhotoEdit.

lacks efficacy or produces undesirable effects in comparison with the standard drug, the new drug is rejected and withdrawn from further testing. Only new drugs that show promising comparisons with the standard drugs are forwarded to the long-term usage and safety testing program.

Further data collection and multipopulation studies are conducted in the long-term usage and safety testing program and in the clinical testing programs. The Food and Drug Administration (FDA) requires that statistical methods be defined prior to such testing to avoid data-related biases. In addition, to avoid human biases, some of the clinical trials are double or triple blind. That is, neither the subject nor the investigator knows what drug is administered to whom. If the new drug meets all requirements in relation to the standard drug, a new drug application (NDA) is filed with the FDA. The application is rigorously scrutinized by statisticians and scientists at the agency.

In this chapter you will learn how to construct interval estimates and make hypothesis tests about means and proportions with two populations. Techniques will be presented for analyzing independent random samples as well as matched samples.

In Chapters 8 and 9 we showed how to develop interval estimates and conduct hypothesis tests for situations involving one population mean. In this chapter we extend our discussion of statistical inference to applications that compare the means of two or more populations. For example, we may want to develop an interval estimate of the difference between the mean starting salary for a population of men and the mean starting salary for a population of women or test the hypothesis that the mean number of hours between breakdowns is the same for four different machines. We begin by showing how to develop interval estimates and conduct hypothesis tests about the difference between two population means when the two population standard deviations are assumed known.

10.1 Inferences About the Difference Between Two Population Means: σ_1 and σ_2 Known

Letting μ_1 denote the mean of population 1 and μ_2 denote the mean of population 2, we will focus on inferences about the difference between the means: $\mu_1 - \mu_2$. To make an inference about this difference, we select a simple random sample of n_1 units from population 1 and a simple random sample of n_2 units from population 2. The two samples, taken separately and independently, are referred to as **independent simple random samples**. In this section, we assume information is available such that the two population standard deviations, σ_1 and σ_2, can be assumed known prior to collecting the samples. We refer to this situation as the σ_1 and σ_2 known case. In the following example we show how to compute a margin of error and develop an interval estimate of the difference between the two population means.

Interval Estimation of $\mu_1 - \mu_2$

Greystone Department Stores, Inc., operates two stores in Buffalo, New York: one is in the inner city and the other is in a suburban shopping center. The regional manager noticed that products that sell well in one store do not always sell well in the other. The manager believes this situation may be attributable to differences in customer demographics at the two locations. Customers may differ in age, education, income, and so on. Suppose the manager asks us to investigate the difference between the mean ages of the customers who shop at the two stores.

Let us define population 1 as all customers who shop at the inner-city store and population 2 as all customers who shop at the suburban store.

$$\mu_1 = \text{mean of population 1 (i.e., the mean age of all customers who shop at the inner-city store)}$$

$$\mu_2 = \text{mean of population 2 (i.e., the mean age of all customers who shop at the suburban store)}$$

The difference between the two population means is $\mu_1 - \mu_2$.

To estimate $\mu_1 - \mu_2$, we select a simple random sample of n_1 customers from population 1 and a simple random sample of n_2 customers from population 2. We then compute the two sample means.

$$\bar{x}_1 = \text{sample mean age for the simple random sample of } n_1 \text{ inner-city customers}$$

$$\bar{x}_2 = \text{sample mean age for the simple random sample of } n_2 \text{ suburban customers}$$

The point estimator of the difference between the two population means is the difference between the two sample means.

POINT ESTIMATOR OF THE DIFFERENCE BETWEEN TWO POPULATION MEANS

$$\bar{x}_1 - \bar{x}_2 \qquad\qquad \textbf{(10.1)}$$

Figure 10.1 provides an overview of the process used to estimate the difference between two population means based on two independent simple random samples.

FIGURE 10.1   ESTIMATING THE DIFFERENCE BETWEEN TWO POPULATION MEANS

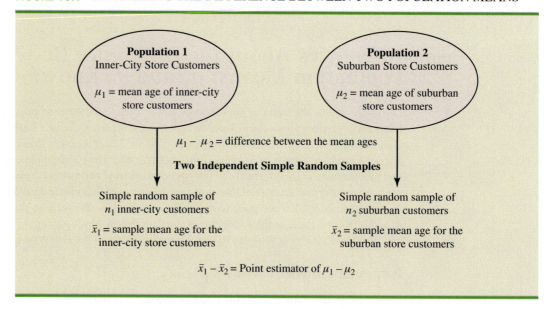

The standard error of $\bar{x}_1 - \bar{x}_2$ is the standard deviation of the sampling distribution of $\bar{x}_1 - \bar{x}_2$.

As with other point estimators, the point estimator $\bar{x}_1 - \bar{x}_2$ has a standard error that describes the variation in the sampling distribution of the estimator. With two independent simple random samples, the standard error of $\bar{x}_1 - \bar{x}_2$ is as follows:

$$\sigma_{\bar{x}_1 - \bar{x}_2} = \sqrt{\frac{\sigma_1^2}{n_1} + \frac{\sigma_2^2}{n_2}} \tag{10.2}$$

If both populations have a normal distribution, or if the sample sizes are large enough that the central limit theorem enables us to conclude that the sampling distributions of $\bar{x}_1$ and $\bar{x}_2$ can be approximated by a normal distribution, the sampling distribution of $\bar{x}_1 - \bar{x}_2$ will have a normal distribution with mean given by $\mu_1 - \mu_2$.

As we showed in Chapter 8, an interval estimate is given by a point estimate $\pm$ a margin of error. In the case of estimation of the difference between two population means, an interval estimate will take the following form:

$$\bar{x}_1 - \bar{x}_2 \pm \text{Margin of error}$$

With the sampling distribution of $\bar{x}_1 - \bar{x}_2$ having a normal distribution, we can write the margin of error as follows:

The margin of error is given by multiplying the standard error by $z_{\alpha/2}$.

$$\text{Margin of error} = z_{\alpha/2}\sigma_{\bar{x}_1 - \bar{x}_2} = z_{\alpha/2}\sqrt{\frac{\sigma_1^2}{n_1} + \frac{\sigma_2^2}{n_2}} \tag{10.3}$$

Thus the interval estimate of the difference between two population means is as follows:

INTERVAL ESTIMATE OF THE DIFFERENCE BETWEEN TWO POPULATION MEANS: σ_1 AND σ_2 KNOWN

$$\bar{x}_1 - \bar{x}_2 \pm z_{\alpha/2}\sqrt{\frac{\sigma_1^2}{n_1} + \frac{\sigma_2^2}{n_2}} \tag{10.4}$$

where $1 - \alpha$ is the confidence coefficient.

Let us return to the Greystone example. Based on data from previous customer demographic studies, the two population standard deviations are known with $\sigma_1 = 9$ years and $\sigma_2 = 10$ years. The data collected from the two independent simple random samples of Greystone customers provided the following results.

	Inner-City Store	Suburban Store
Sample Size	$n_1 = 36$	$n_2 = 49$
Sample Mean	$\bar{x}_1 = 40$ years	$\bar{x}_2 = 35$ years

Using expression (10.1), we find that the point estimate of the difference between the mean ages of the two populations is $\bar{x}_1 - \bar{x}_2 = 40 - 35 = 5$ years. Thus, we estimate that the customers at the inner-city store have a mean age five years greater than the mean age of the suburban store customers. We can now use expression (10.4) to compute the margin of error and provide the interval estimate of $\mu_1 - \mu_2$. Using 95% confidence and $z_{\alpha/2} = z_{.025} = 1.96$, we have

$$\bar{x}_1 - \bar{x}_2 \pm z_{\alpha/2} \sqrt{\frac{\sigma_1^2}{n_1} + \frac{\sigma_2^2}{n_2}}$$

$$40 - 35 \pm 1.96 \sqrt{\frac{9^2}{36} + \frac{10^2}{49}}$$

$$5 \pm 4.06$$

Thus, the margin of error is 4.06 years and the 95% confidence interval estimate of the difference between the two population means is $5 - 4.06 = .94$ years to $5 + 4.06 = 9.06$ years.

Hypothesis Tests About $\mu_1 - \mu_2$

Let us consider hypothesis tests about the difference between two population means. Using D_0 to denote the hypothesized difference between μ_1 and μ_2, the three forms for a hypothesis test are as follows:

$$H_0: \mu_1 - \mu_2 \geq D_0 \qquad H_0: \mu_1 - \mu_2 \leq D_0 \qquad H_0: \mu_1 - \mu_2 = D_0$$
$$H_a: \mu_1 - \mu_2 < D_0 \qquad H_a: \mu_1 - \mu_2 > D_0 \qquad H_a: \mu_1 - \mu_2 \neq D_0$$

In many applications, $D_0 = 0$. Using the two-tailed test as an example, when $D_0 = 0$ the null hypothesis is $H_0: \mu_1 - \mu_2 = 0$. In this case, the null hypothesis is that μ_1 and μ_2 are equal. Rejection of H_0 leads to the conclusion that $H_a: \mu_1 - \mu_2 \neq 0$ is true; that is, μ_1 and μ_2 are not equal.

The steps for conducting hypothesis tests presented in Chapter 9 are applicable here. We must choose a level of significance, compute the value of the test statistic, and find the p-value to determine whether the null hypothesis should be rejected. With two independent simple random samples, we showed that the point estimator $\bar{x}_1 - \bar{x}_2$ has a standard error $\sigma_{\bar{x}_1 - \bar{x}_2}$ given by expression (10.2) and the distribution of $\bar{x}_1 - \bar{x}_2$ can be described by a normal distribution. In this case, the test statistic for the difference between two population means when σ_1 and σ_2 are known is as follows.

> **TEST STATISTIC FOR HYPOTHESIS TESTS ABOUT $\mu_1 - \mu_2$: σ_1 AND σ_2 KNOWN**
>
> $$z = \frac{(\bar{x}_1 - \bar{x}_2) - D_0}{\sqrt{\dfrac{\sigma_1^2}{n_1} + \dfrac{\sigma_2^2}{n_2}}} \qquad\qquad \textbf{(10.5)}$$

Let us demonstrate the use of this test statistic in the following hypothesis testing example.

As part of a study to evaluate differences in education quality between two training centers, a standardized examination is given to individuals who are trained at the centers. The difference between the mean examination scores is used to assess quality differences between the centers. The population means for the two centers are as follows.

μ_1 = the mean examination score for the population
of individuals trained at center A

μ_2 = the mean examination score for the population
of individuals trained at center B

We begin with the tentative assumption that no difference exists between the training quality provided at the two centers. Hence, in terms of the mean examination scores, the null hypothesis is that $\mu_1 - \mu_2 = 0$. If sample evidence leads to the rejection of this hypothesis, we will conclude that the mean examination scores differ for the two populations. This conclusion indicates a quality differential between the two centers and suggests that a follow-up study investigating the reason for the differential may be warranted. The null and alternative hypotheses for this two-tailed test are written as follows.

$$H_0: \mu_1 - \mu_2 = 0$$
$$H_a: \mu_1 - \mu_2 \neq 0$$

The standardized examination given previously in a variety of settings always resulted in an examination score standard deviation near 10 points. Thus, we will use this information to assume that the population standard deviations are known with $\sigma_1 = 10$ and $\sigma_2 = 10$. An $\alpha = .05$ level of significance is specified for the study.

Independent simple random samples of $n_1 = 30$ individuals from training center A and $n_2 = 40$ individuals from training center B are taken. The respective sample means are $\bar{x}_1 = 82$ and $\bar{x}_2 = 78$. Do these data suggest a significant difference between the population means at the two training centers? To help answer this question, we compute the test statistic using equation (10.5).

$$z = \frac{(\bar{x}_1 - \bar{x}_2) - D_0}{\sqrt{\dfrac{\sigma_1^2}{n_1} + \dfrac{\sigma_2^2}{n_2}}} = \frac{(82 - 78) - 0}{\sqrt{\dfrac{10^2}{30} + \dfrac{10^2}{40}}} = 1.66$$

Next let us compute the p-value for this two-tailed test. Because the test statistic z is in the upper tail, we first compute the area under the curve to the right of $z = 1.66$. Using the standard normal distribution table, the area between the mean and $z = 1.66$ is .4515. Thus, the area in the upper tail of the distribution is $.5000 - .4515 = .0485$. Because this test is a two-tailed test, we must double the tail area: p-value $= 2(.0485) = .0970$. Following the usual rule to reject H_0 if p-value $\leq \alpha$, we see that the p-value of .0970 does not allow us to reject H_0 at the .05 level of significance. The sample results do not provide sufficient evidence to conclude the training centers differ in quality.

In this chapter we will use the p-value approach to hypothesis testing as described in Chapter 9. However, if you prefer, the test statistic and the critical value rejection rule may be used. With $\alpha = .05$ and $z_{\alpha/2} = z_{.025} = 1.96$, the rejection rule employing the critical value approach would be to reject H_0 if $z \leq -1.96$ or if $z \geq 1.96$. With $z = 1.66$, we reach the same do-not-reject H_0 conclusion.

In the preceding example, we demonstrated a two-tailed hypothesis test about the difference between two population means. Lower tail and upper tail tests can also be considered. These tests use the same test statistic as given in equation (10.5). The procedure for computing the p-value and the rejection rules for these one-tailed tests are the same as those presented in Chapter 9.

Practical Advice

In most applications of the interval estimation and hypothesis testing procedures presented in this section, random samples with $n_1 \geq 30$ and $n_2 \geq 30$ are adequate. In cases where either or both sample sizes are less than 30, the distributions of the populations become important considerations. In general, with smaller sample sizes, it is more important for the analyst to be satisfied that it is reasonable to assume that the distributions of the two populations are at least approximately normal.

Exercises

Methods

1. Consider the following results for two independent random samples taken from two populations.

Sample 1	Sample 2
$n_1 = 50$	$n_2 = 35$
$\bar{x}_1 = 13.6$	$\bar{x}_2 = 11.6$
$\sigma_1 = 2.2$	$\sigma_2 = 3.0$

   a. What is the point estimate of the difference between the two population means?
   b. Provide a 90% confidence interval for the difference between the two population means.
   c. Provide a 95% confidence interval for the difference between the two population means.

2. Consider the following hypothesis test.

   $$H_0: \mu_1 - \mu_2 \leq 0$$
   $$H_a: \mu_1 - \mu_2 > 0$$

   The following results are for two independent samples taken from the two populations.

Sample 1	Sample 2
$n_1 = 40$	$n_2 = 50$
$\bar{x}_1 = 25.2$	$\bar{x}_2 = 22.8$
$\sigma_1 = 5.2$	$\sigma_2 = 6.0$

   a. What is the value of the test statistic?
   b. What is the p-value?
   c. With $\alpha = .05$, what is your hypothesis testing conclusion?

3. Consider the following hypothesis test.

   $$H_0: \mu_1 - \mu_2 = 0$$
   $$H_a: \mu_1 - \mu_2 \neq 0$$

The following results are for two independent samples taken from the two populations.

Sample 1	Sample 2
$n_1 = 80$	$n_2 = 70$
$\bar{x}_1 = 104$	$\bar{x}_2 = 106$
$\sigma_1 = 8.4$	$\sigma_2 = 7.6$

a. What is the value of the test statistic?
b. What is the p-value?
c. With $\alpha = .05$, what is your hypothesis testing conclusion?

Applications

4. Gasoline prices reached record high levels in 16 states during 2003 (*The Wall Street Journal*, March 7, 2003). Two of the affected states were California and Florida. The American Automobile Association reported a sample mean price of $2.04 per gallon in California and a sample mean price of $1.72 per gallon in Florida. Use a sample size of 40 for the California data and a sample size of 35 for the Florida data. Assume that prior studies indicating a population standard deviation of .10 in California and .08 in Florida are reasonable.
    a. What is a point estimate of the difference between the population mean prices per gallon in California and Florida?
    b. At 95% confidence, what is the margin of error?
    c. What is the 95% confidence interval estimate of the difference between the population mean prices per gallon in the two states?

5. A Cornell University study of wage differentials between men and women reported that one of the reasons wages for men are higher than wages for women is that men tend to have more years of work experience than women (*Business Week*, August 28, 2000). Assume the following sample summaries show the years of experience for each group.

Men	Women
$n_1 = 100$	$n_2 = 85$
$\bar{x}_1 = 14.9$ years	$\bar{x}_2 = 10.3$ years
$\sigma_1 = 5.2$ years	$\sigma_2 = 3.8$ years

    a. What is the point estimate of the difference between the two population means?
    b. At 95% confidence, what is the margin of error?
    c. What is the 95% confidence interval estimate of the difference between the two population means?

6. The nation's 40,000 mortgage brokerages are some of the most profitable small businesses in the United States. These low-profile companies find loans for customers in exchange for commissions. Mortgage Bankers Association of America provides data on the average size of loans handled by mortgage brokerages (*The Wall Street Journal*, February 24, 2003). Using sample data consistent with the Mortgage Bankers Association data, a sample of 270 loans made in 2002 provided a mean loan of $175,000. Data for 2001 showed a sample of 250 loans made with a mean loan of $165,000. Based on historical loan data, the population standard deviations for the loan amounts can be assumed known at $55,000 in 2002 and $50,000 in 2001. Do the sample data indicate an increase in the mean loan amount between 2001 and 2002? Use $\alpha = .05$.

7. During the 2003 season, Major League Baseball took steps to speed up the play of baseball games in order to maintain fan interest (*CNN Headline News*, September 30, 2003). The following results come from a sample of 60 games played during the summer of 2002 and a sample of 50 games played during the summer of 2003. The sample mean shows the mean duration of the games included in each sample.

2002 Season	2003 Season
$n_1 = 60$	$n_2 = 50$
$\bar{x}_1 = 2$ hours, 52 minutes	$\bar{x}_2 = 2$ hours, 46 minutes

a. A research hypothesis was that the steps taken during the 2003 season would reduce the population mean duration of baseball games. Formulate the null and alternative hypotheses.

b. What is the point estimate of the reduction in the mean duration of games during the 2003 season?

c. Historical data indicate a population standard deviation of 12 minutes is a reasonable assumption for both years. Conduct the hypothesis test and report the p-value. At a .05 level of significance, what is your conclusion?

d. Provide a 95% confidence interval estimate of the reduction in the mean duration of games during the 2003 season.

e. What was the percentage reduction in the mean time of baseball games during the 2003 season? Should management be pleased with the results of the statistical analysis? Discuss. Should the length of baseball games continue to be an issue in future years? Explain.

8. Arnold Palmer and Tiger Woods are two of the best golfers to ever play the game. To show how these two golfers would compare if both were playing at the top of their game, the following sample data provide the results of 18-hole scores during a PGA tournament competition. Palmer's scores are from his 1960 season, while Woods' scores are from his 1999 season (*Golf Magazine,* February 2000).

Arnold Palmer	Tiger Woods
$n_1 = 112$	$n_2 = 84$
$\bar{x}_1 = 69.95$	$\bar{x}_2 = 69.56$

Use the sample results to test the hypothesis of no difference between the population mean 18-hole scores for the two golfers.

a. Assume a population standard deviation of 2.5 for both golfers. What is the value of the test statistic?

b. What is the p-value?

c. At $\alpha = .01$, what is your conclusion?

10.2 Inferences About the Difference Between Two Population Means: σ_1 and σ_2 Unknown

In this section we extend the discussion of inferences about the difference between two population means to the case when the two population standard deviations, σ_1 and σ_2, are unknown. In this case, we will use the sample standard deviations, s_1 and s_2, to estimate the unknown population standard deviations. When we use the sample standard deviations, the interval estimation and hypothesis testing procedures will be based on the t distribution rather than the standard normal distribution.

Interval Estimation of $\mu_1 - \mu_2$

In the following example we show how to compute a margin of error and develop an interval estimate of the difference between two population means when σ_1 and σ_2 are unknown. Clearwater National Bank is conducting a study designed to identify differences between checking account practices by customers at two of its branch banks. A simple random sample of 28 checking accounts is selected from the Cherry Grove branch and an independent simple random sample of 22 checking accounts is selected from the Beechmont branch. The current checking account balance is recorded for each of the checking accounts. A summary of the account balances follows:

CheckAcct

	Cherry Grove	**Beechmont**
Sample Size	$n_1 = 28$	$n_2 = 22$
Sample Mean	$\bar{x}_1 = \$1025$	$\bar{x}_2 = \$910$
Sample Standard Deviation	$s_1 = \$150$	$s_2 = \$125$

Clearwater National Bank would like to estimate the difference between the mean checking account balance maintained by the population of Cherry Grove customers and the population of Beechmont customers. Let us develop the margin of error and an interval estimate of the difference between these two population means.

In Section 10.1, we provided the following interval estimate for the case when the population standard deviations, σ_1 and σ_2, are known.

$$\bar{x}_1 - \bar{x}_2 \pm z_{\alpha/2} \sqrt{\frac{\sigma_1^2}{n_1} + \frac{\sigma_2^2}{n_2}}$$

When σ_1 and σ_2 are estimated by s_1 and s_2, the t distribution is used to make inferences about the difference between two population means.

With σ_1 and σ_2 unknown, we will use the sample standard deviations s_1 and s_2 to estimate σ_1 and σ_2 and replace $z_{\alpha/2}$ with $t_{\alpha/2}$. As a result, the interval estimate of the difference between two population means is given by the following expression:

INTERVAL ESTIMATE OF THE DIFFERENCE BETWEEN TWO POPULATION MEANS: σ_1 AND σ_2 UNKNOWN

$$\bar{x}_1 - \bar{x}_2 \pm t_{\alpha/2} \sqrt{\frac{s_1^2}{n_1} + \frac{s_2^2}{n_2}} \tag{10.6}$$

where $1 - \alpha$ is the confidence coefficient.

In this expression, the use of the t distribution is an approximation, but it provides excellent results and is relatively easy to use. The only difficulty that we encounter in using expression (10.6) is determining the appropriate degrees of freedom for $t_{\alpha/2}$. Statistical software packages compute the appropriate degrees of freedom automatically. The formula used is as follows:

$$df = \frac{\left(\dfrac{s_1^2}{n_1} + \dfrac{s_2^2}{n_2}\right)^2}{\dfrac{1}{n_1 - 1}\left(\dfrac{s_1^2}{n_1}\right)^2 + \dfrac{1}{n_2 - 1}\left(\dfrac{s_2^2}{n_2}\right)^2} \tag{10.7}$$

Let us return to the Clearwater National Bank example and show how to use expression (10.6) to provide a 95% confidence interval estimate of the difference between the population mean checking account balances at the two branch banks. The sample data show $n_1 = 28$, $\bar{x}_1 = \$1025$, and $s_1 = \$150$ for the Cherry Grove branch, and $n_2 = 22$, $\bar{x}_2 = \$910$, and $s_2 = \$125$ for the Beechmont branch. The calculation for degrees of freedom for $t_{\alpha/2}$ is as follows:

$$df = \frac{\left(\dfrac{s_1^2}{n_1} + \dfrac{s_2^2}{n_2}\right)^2}{\dfrac{1}{n_1 - 1}\left(\dfrac{s_1^2}{n_1}\right)^2 + \dfrac{1}{n_2 - 1}\left(\dfrac{s_2^2}{n_2}\right)^2} = \frac{\left(\dfrac{150^2}{28} + \dfrac{125^2}{22}\right)^2}{\dfrac{1}{28 - 1}\left(\dfrac{150^2}{28}\right)^2 + \dfrac{1}{22 - 1}\left(\dfrac{125^2}{22}\right)^2} = 47.8$$

We round the noninteger degrees of freedom *down* to 47 to provide a slightly larger value of t and a more conservative interval estimate. Using the t distribution table with 47 degrees of freedom, we find $t_{.025} = 2.012$. Using expression (10.6), we develop the 95% confidence interval estimate of the difference between the two population means as follows.

$$\bar{x}_1 - \bar{x}_2 \pm t_{.025}\sqrt{\frac{s_1^2}{n_1} + \frac{s_2^2}{n_2}}$$

$$1025 - 910 \pm 2.012\sqrt{\frac{150^2}{28} + \frac{125^2}{22}}$$

$$115 \pm 78$$

The point estimate of the difference between the population mean checking account balances at the two branches is $115. The margin of error is $78, and the 95% confidence interval estimate of the difference between the two population means is $115 - 78 = \$37$ to $115 + 78 = \$193$.

This suggestion should help if you are using equation (10.7) to calculate the degrees of freedom by hand.

The computation of the degrees of freedom (equation (10.7)) is cumbersome if you are doing the calculation by hand, but it is easily implemented with a computer software package. However, note that the expressions s_1^2/n_1 and s_2^2/n_2 appear in both expression (10.6) and equation (10.7). These values only need to be computed once in order to evaluate both (10.6) and (10.7).

Hypothesis Tests About $\mu_1 - \mu_2$

Let us now consider hypothesis tests about the difference between the means of two populations when the population standard deviations σ_1 and σ_2 are unknown. Letting D_0 denote the hypothesized difference between μ_1 and μ_2, Section 10.1 showed that the test statistic used for the case where σ_1 and σ_2 are known is as follows.

$$z = \frac{(\bar{x}_1 - \bar{x}_2) - D_0}{\sqrt{\dfrac{\sigma_1^2}{n_1} + \dfrac{\sigma_2^2}{n_2}}}$$

The test statistic, z, follows the standard normal distribution.

When σ_1 and σ_2 are unknown, we use s_1 as an estimator of σ_1 and s_2 as an estimator of σ_2. Substituting these sample standard deviations for σ_1 and σ_2 provides the following test statistic when σ_1 and σ_2 are unknown.

TEST STATISTIC FOR HYPOTHESIS TESTS ABOUT $\mu_1 - \mu_2$: σ_1 AND σ_2 UNKNOWN

$$t = \frac{(\bar{x}_1 - \bar{x}_2) - D_0}{\sqrt{\dfrac{s_1^2}{n_1} + \dfrac{s_2^2}{n_2}}} \tag{10.8}$$

The degrees of freedom for t are given by equation (10.7).

Let us demonstrate the use of this test statistic in the following hypothesis testing example.

Consider a new computer software package developed to help systems analysts reduce the time required to design, develop, and implement an information system. To evaluate the benefits of the new software package, a random sample of 24 systems analysts is selected. Each analyst is given specifications for a hypothetical information system. Then 12 of the analysts are instructed to produce the information system by using current technology. The other 12 analysts are trained in the use of the new software package and then instructed to use it to produce the information system.

This study involves two populations: a population of systems analysts using the current technology and a population of systems analysts using the new software package. In terms of the time required to complete the information system design project, the population means are as follows.

$$\mu_1 = \text{the mean project completion time for systems analysts}$$
$$\text{using the current technology}$$

$$\mu_2 = \text{the mean project completion time for systems analysts}$$
$$\text{using the new software package}$$

The researcher in charge of the new software evaluation project hopes to show that the new software package will provide a shorter mean project completion time. Thus, the researcher is looking for evidence to conclude that μ_2 is less than μ_1; in this case, the difference between the two population means, $\mu_1 - \mu_2$, will be greater than zero. The research hypothesis $\mu_1 - \mu_2 > 0$ is stated as the alternative hypothesis. Thus, the hypothesis test becomes

$$H_0: \mu_1 - \mu_2 \leq 0$$
$$H_a: \mu_1 - \mu_2 > 0$$

We will use $\alpha = .05$ as the level of significance.

Suppose that the 24 analysts complete the study with the results shown in Table 10.1. Using the test statistic in equation (10.8), we have

$$t = \frac{(\bar{x}_1 - \bar{x}_2) - D_0}{\sqrt{\dfrac{s_1^2}{n_1} + \dfrac{s_2^2}{n_2}}} = \frac{(325 - 286) - 0}{\sqrt{\dfrac{40^2}{12} + \dfrac{44^2}{12}}} = 2.27$$

Computing the degrees of freedom using equation (10.7), we have

$$df = \frac{\left(\dfrac{s_1^2}{n_1} + \dfrac{s_2^2}{n_2}\right)^2}{\dfrac{1}{n_1 - 1}\left(\dfrac{s_1^2}{n_1}\right)^2 + \dfrac{1}{n_2 - 1}\left(\dfrac{s_2^2}{n_2}\right)^2} = \frac{\left(\dfrac{40^2}{12} + \dfrac{44^2}{12}\right)^2}{\dfrac{1}{12 - 1}\left(\dfrac{40^2}{12}\right)^2 + \dfrac{1}{12 - 1}\left(\dfrac{44^2}{12}\right)^2} = 21.8$$

Rounding down, we will use a t distribution with 21 degrees of freedom. This row of the t distribution table is as follows:

Area in Upper Tail	.20	.10	.05	.025	.01	.005
t **Value (21 df)**	0.859	1.323	1.721	2.080	2.518	2.831

$$t = 2.27$$

Using the t distribution table, we can only determine a range for the p-value. Use of the computer is required to determine the exact p-value.

With an upper tail test, the p-value is the area in the upper tail to the right of $t = 2.27$. From the preceding results, we see that the p-value is between .025 and .01. Thus, the p-value is less than $\alpha = .05$ and H_0 is rejected. The sample results enable the researcher to conclude

TABLE 10.1 COMPLETION TIME DATA AND SUMMARY STATISTICS FOR THE SOFTWARE TESTING STUDY

CD file

SoftwareTest

	Current Technology	New Software
	300	274
	280	220
	344	308
	385	336
	372	198
	360	300
	288	315
	321	258
	376	318
	290	310
	301	332
	283	263
Summary Statistics		
Sample size	$n_1 = 12$	$n_2 = 12$
Sample mean	$\bar{x}_1 = 325$ hours	$\bar{x}_2 = 286$ hours
Sample standard deviation	$s_1 = 40$	$s_2 = 44$

that $\mu_1 - \mu_2 > 0$, or $\mu_1 > \mu_2$. Thus, the research study supports the conclusion that the new software package provides a smaller population mean completion time.

Minitab can be used to analyze data for testing hypotheses about the difference between two population means. The output comparing the current and new software technology is shown in Figure 10.2. The last line of the output shows $t = 2.27$ and p-value $= .017$. Note that Minitab used equation (10.7) to compute 21 degrees of freedom for this analysis.

Practical Advice

Whenever possible, equal sample sizes, $n_1 = n_2$, are recommended.

The interval estimation and hypothesis testing procedures presented in this section are robust and can be used with relatively small sample sizes. In most applications, equal or nearly equal sample sizes such that the total sample size $n_1 + n_2$ is at least 20 can be expected to provide very good results even if the populations are not normal. Larger sample sizes are recommended if the distributions of the populations are highly skewed or contain outliers. Smaller sample sizes should only be used if the analyst is satisfied that the distributions of the populations are at least approximately normal.

FIGURE 10.2 MINITAB OUTPUT FOR THE HYPOTHESIS TEST OF THE CURRENT AND NEW SOFTWARE TECHNOLOGY

```
Two-sample T for Current vs New
                N      Mean     StDev     SE Mean
Current         12     325.0     40.0          12
New             12     286.0     44.0          13

Difference = mu Current - mu New
Estimate for difference:   39.0000
95% lower bound for difference = 9.4643
T-Test of difference = 0 (vs >):  T-Value = 2.27  P-Value = 0.017  DF = 21
```

NOTES AND COMMENTS

Another approach used to make inferences about the difference between two population means when σ_1 and σ_2 are unknown is based on the assumption that the two population standard deviations are *equal* ($\sigma_1 = \sigma_2 = \sigma$). Under this assumption, the two sample standard deviations are combined to provide the following *pooled sample variance*:

$$s_p^2 = \frac{(n_1 - 1)s_1^2 + (n_2 - 1)s_2^2}{n_1 + n_2 - 2}$$

The *t* test statistic becomes

$$t = \frac{(\bar{x}_1 - \bar{x}_2) - D_0}{s_p\sqrt{\dfrac{1}{n_1} + \dfrac{1}{n_2}}}$$

and has $n_1 + n_2 - 2$ degrees of freedom. At this point, the computation of the *p*-value and the interpretation of the sample results are identical to the procedures discussed earlier in this section.

A difficulty with this procedure is that the assumption that the two population standard deviations are equal is usually difficult to verify. Unequal population standard deviations are frequently encountered. Using the pooled procedure may not provide satisfactory results especially if the sample sizes n_1 and n_2 are quite different.

The *t* procedure that we presented in this section does not require the assumption of equal population standard deviations and can be applied whether the population standard deviations are equal or not. It is a more general procedure and is recommended for most applications.

Exercises

Methods

9. Consider the following results for independent random samples taken from two populations.

Sample 1	Sample 2
$n_1 = 20$	$n_2 = 30$
$\bar{x}_1 = 22.5$	$\bar{x}_2 = 20.1$
$s_1 = 2.5$	$s_2 = 4.8$

   a. What is the point estimate of the difference between the two population means?
   b. What is the degrees of freedom for the *t* distribution?
   c. At 95% confidence, what is the margin of error?
   d. What is the 95% confidence interval for the difference between the two population means?

10. Consider the following hypothesis test.

$$H_0: \mu_1 - \mu_2 = 0$$
$$H_a: \mu_1 - \mu_2 \neq 0$$

The following results are from independent samples taken from two populations.

Sample 1	Sample 2
$n_1 = 35$	$n_2 = 40$
$\bar{x}_1 = 13.6$	$\bar{x}_2 = 10.1$
$s_1 = 5.2$	$s_2 = 8.5$

     a.   What is the value of the test statistic?

     b.   What is the degrees of freedom for the t distribution?

     c.   What is the p-value?

     d.   At $\alpha = .05$, what is your conclusion?

11. Consider the following data for two independent random samples taken from two normal populations.

Sample 1	10	7	13	7	9	8
Sample 2	8	7	8	4	6	9

     a.   Compute the two sample means.

     b.   Compute the two sample standard deviations.

     c.   What is the point estimate of the difference between the two population means?

     d.   What is the 90% confidence interval estimate of the difference between the two population means?

Applications

12. The U.S. Department of Transportation provides the number of miles that residents of the 75 largest metropolitan areas travel per day in a car. Suppose that for a simple random sample of 50 Buffalo residents the mean is 22.5 miles a day and the standard deviation is 8.4 miles a day, and for an independent simple random sample of 40 Boston residents the mean is 18.6 miles a day and the standard deviation is 7.4 miles a day.

     a.   What is the point estimate of the difference between the mean number of miles that Buffalo residents travel per day and the mean number of miles that Boston residents travel per day?

     b.   What is the 95% confidence interval for the difference between the two population means?

Cargo

13. FedEx and United Parcel Service (UPS) are the world's two leading cargo carriers by volume and revenue (*The Wall Street Journal*, January 27, 2004). According to the Airports Council International, the Memphis International Airport (FedEx) and the Louisville International Airport (UPS) are two of the ten largest cargo airports in the world. The following random samples show the tons of cargo per day handled by these airports. Data are in thousands of tons.

Memphis					
9.1	15.1	8.8	10.0	7.5	10.5
8.3	9.1	6.0	5.8	12.1	9.3
Louisville					
4.7	5.0	4.2	3.3	5.5	
2.2	4.1	2.6	3.4	7.0	

     a.   Compute the sample mean and sample standard deviation for each airport.

     b.   What is the point estimate of the difference between the two population means? Interpret this value in terms of the higher-volume airport and a comparison of the volume difference between the two airports.

     c.   Develop a 95% confidence interval of the difference between the daily population means for the two airports.

14. Coastal areas of the United States including Cape Cod, the Outer Banks, the Carolinas, and the Gulf Coast had relatively high population growth rates during the 1990s. Data were collected on residents living in the coastal communities as well as on residents living in noncoastal areas throughout the United States (*USA Today,* July 21, 2000). Assume that the following sample results were obtained on the ages of individuals in the two populations:

Coastal Areas	Noncoastal Areas
$n_1 = 150$	$n_2 = 175$
$\bar{x}_1 = 39.3$ years	$\bar{x}_2 = 35.4$ years
$s_1 = 16.8$ years	$s_2 = 15.2$ years

Test the hypothesis of no difference between the two population means. Use $\alpha = .05$.
a. Formulate the null and alternative hypotheses.
b. What is the value of the test statistic?
c. What is the *p*-value?
d. What is your conclusion?

15. Injuries to Major League Baseball players have been increasing in recent years. For the period 1992 to 2001, league expansion caused Major League Baseball rosters to increase 15%. However, the number of players being put on the disabled list due to injury increased 32% over the same period (*USA Today,* July 8, 2002). A research question addressed whether Major League Baseball players being put on the disabled list are on the list longer in 2001 than players put on the disabled list a decade earlier.
a. Using the population mean number of days a player is on the disabled list, formulate null and alternative hypotheses that can be used to test the research question.
b. Assume that the following data apply:

	2001 Season	1992 Season
Sample Players	$n_1 = 45$	$n_2 = 38$
Sample Mean Days	$\bar{x}_1 = 60$ days	$\bar{x}_2 = 51$ days
Sample Std Deviation	$s_1 = 18$ days	$s_2 = 15$ days

What is the point estimate of the difference between population mean days on the disabled list for 2001 compared to 1992? What is the percentage increase in the number of days on the disabled list?
c. Use $\alpha = .01$. What is your conclusion about number of days on the disabled list? What is the *p*-value?
d. Do these data suggest that Major League Baseball should be concerned about the situation?

16. The College Board provided comparisons of Scholastic Aptitude Test (SAT) scores based on the highest level of education attained by the test taker's parents. A research hypothesis was that students whose parents had attained a higher level of education would on average score higher on the SAT. During 2003, the overall mean SAT verbal score was 507 (*The World Almanac 2004*). SAT verbal scores for independent samples of students follow. The first sample shows the SAT verbal test scores for students whose parents are college graduates with a bachelor's degree. The second sample shows the SAT verbal test scores for students whose parents are high school graduates but do not have a college degree.

Student's Parents

College Grads		High School Grads	
485	487	442	492
534	533	580	478
650	526	479	425
554	410	486	485
550	515	528	390
572	578	524	535
497	448		
592	469		

a. Formulate the hypotheses that can be used to determine whether the sample data support the hypothesis that students show a higher population mean verbal score on the SAT if their parents attained a higher level of education.
b. What is the point estimate of the difference between the means for the two populations?
c. Compute the p-value for the hypothesis test.
d. At $\alpha = .05$, what is your conclusion?

17. Periodically, Merrill Lynch customers are asked to evaluate Merrill Lynch financial consultants and services (2000 Merrill Lynch Client Satisfaction Survey). Higher ratings on the client satisfaction survey indicate better service with 7 the maximum service rating. Independent samples of service ratings for two financial consultants are summarized here. Consultant A has 10 years of experience, whereas consultant B has 1 year of experience. Use $\alpha = .05$ and test to see whether the consultant with more experience has the higher population mean service rating.

Consultant A	Consultant B
$n_1 = 16$	$n_2 = 10$
$\bar{x}_1 = 6.82$	$\bar{x}_2 = 6.25$
$s_1 = .64$	$s_2 = .75$

a. State the null and alternative hypotheses.
b. Compute the value of the test statistic.
c. What is the p-value?
d. What is your conclusion?

18. Educational testing companies provide tutoring, classroom learning, and practice tests in an effort to help students perform better on tests such as the Scholastic Aptitude Test (SAT). The test preparation companies claim that their courses will improve SAT score performances by an average of 120 points (*The Wall Street Journal,* January 23, 2003). A researcher is uncertain of this claim and believes that 120 points may be an overstatement in an effort to encourage students to take the test preparation course. In an evaluation study of one test preparation service, the researcher collects SAT score data for 35 students who took the test preparation course and 48 students who did not take the course.
a. Formulate the hypotheses that can be used to test the researcher's belief that the improvement in SAT scores may be less than the stated average of 120 points.
b. Use $\alpha = .05$ and the following data. What is your conclusion?

	Course	No Course
Sample Mean	1058	983
Sample Standard Deviation	90	105

    c.   What is the point estimate of the improvement in the average SAT scores provided by the test preparation course? Provide a 95% confidence interval estimate of the improvement.

    d.   What advice would you have for the researcher after seeing the confidence interval?

10.3   Inferences About the Difference Between Two Population Means: Matched Samples

Suppose employees at a manufacturing company can use two different methods to perform a production task. To maximize production output, the company wants to identify the method with the smaller population mean completion time. Let μ_1 denote the population mean completion time for production method 1 and μ_2 denote the population mean completion time for production method 2. With no preliminary indication of the preferred production method, we begin by tentatively assuming that the two production methods have the same population mean completion time. Thus, the null hypothesis is $H_0: \mu_1 - \mu_2 = 0$. If this hypothesis is rejected, we can conclude that the population mean completion times differ. In this case, the method providing the smaller mean completion time would be recommended. The null and alternative hypotheses are written as follows.

$$H_0: \mu_1 - \mu_2 = 0$$
$$H_a: \mu_1 - \mu_2 \neq 0$$

In choosing the sampling procedure that will be used to collect production time data and test the hypotheses, we consider two alternative designs. One is based on independent samples and the other is based on **matched samples**.

1. *Independent sample design:* A simple random sample of workers is selected and each worker in the sample uses method 1. A second independent simple random sample of workers is selected and each worker in this sample uses method 2. The test of the difference between population means is based on the procedures in Section 10.2.

2. *Matched sample design:* One simple random sample of workers is selected. Each worker first uses one method and then uses the other method. The order of the two methods is assigned randomly to the workers, with some workers performing method 1 first and others performing method 2 first. Each worker provides a pair of data values, one value for method 1 and another value for method 2.

In the matched sample design the two production methods are tested under similar conditions (i.e., with the same workers); hence this design often leads to a smaller sampling error than the independent sample design. The primary reason is that in a matched sample design, variation between workers is eliminated because the same workers are used for both production methods.

Let us demonstrate the analysis of a matched sample design by assuming it is the method used to test the difference between population means for the two production methods. A random sample of six workers is used. The data on completion times for the six workers are given in Table 10.2. Note that each worker provides a pair of data values, one for each production method. Also note that the last column contains the difference in completion times d_i for each worker in the sample.

The key to the analysis of the matched sample design is to realize that we consider only the column of differences. Therefore, we have six data values (.6, −.2, .5, .3, .0, and .6) that will be used to analyze the difference between population means of the two production methods.

TABLE 10.2   TASK COMPLETION TIMES FOR A MATCHED SAMPLE DESIGN

Worker	Completion Time for Method 1 (minutes)	Completion Time for Method 2 (minutes)	Difference in Completion Times (d_i)
1	6.0	5.4	.6
2	5.0	5.2	−.2
3	7.0	6.5	.5
4	6.2	5.9	.3
5	6.0	6.0	.0
6	6.4	5.8	.6

CD file

Matched

Let μ_d = the mean of the *difference* values for the population of workers. With this notation, the null and alternative hypotheses are rewritten as follows.

$$H_0\text{: } \mu_d = 0$$
$$H_a\text{: } \mu_d \neq 0$$

If H_0 is rejected, we can conclude that the population mean completion times differ.

Other than the use of the d notation, the formulas for the sample mean and sample standard deviation are the same ones used previously in the text.

The d notation is a reminder that the matched sample provides *difference* data. The sample mean and sample standard deviation for the six difference values in Table 10.2 follow.

$$\bar{d} = \frac{\Sigma d_i}{n} = \frac{1.8}{6} = .30$$

$$s_d = \sqrt{\frac{\Sigma(d_i - \bar{d})^2}{n - 1}} = \sqrt{\frac{.56}{5}} = .335$$

It is not necessary to make the assumption that the population has a normal distribution if the sample size is large. Sample size guidelines for using the t distribution were presented in Chapters 8 and 9.

With the small sample of $n = 6$ workers, we need to make the assumption that the population of differences has a normal distribution. This assumption is necessary so that we may use the t distribution for hypothesis testing and interval estimation procedures. Based on this assumption, the following test statistic has a t distribution with $n - 1$ degrees of freedom.

$$t = \frac{\bar{d} - \mu_d}{s_d/\sqrt{n}} \qquad (10.9)$$

Once the difference data are computed, the t distribution procedure for matched samples is the same as the one-population estimation and hypothesis testing procedures described in Chapters 8 and 9.

Let us use equation (10.9) to test the hypotheses $H_0\text{: } \mu_d = 0$ and $H_a\text{: } \mu_d \neq 0$, using $\alpha = .05$. Substituting the sample results $\bar{d} = .30$, $s_d = .335$, and $n = 6$ into equation (10.9), we compute the value of the test statistic.

$$t = \frac{\bar{d} - \mu_d}{s_d/\sqrt{n}} = \frac{.30 - 0}{.335/\sqrt{6}} = 2.20$$

Now let us compute the p-value for this two-tailed test. Because $t = 2.20 > 0$, the test statistic is in the upper tail of the t distribution. With $t = 2.20$, the area in the upper tail to the right of the test statistic can be found by using the t distribution table with degrees of freedom $= n - 1 = 6 - 1 = 5$. Information from the 5 degrees of freedom row of the t distribution table is as follows:

Area in Upper Tail	.20	.10	.05	.025	.01	.005
t Value (5 df)	0.920	1.476	2.015	2.571	3.365	4.032

$$t = 2.20$$

Thus, we see that the area in the upper tail is between .05 and .025. Because this test is a two-tailed test, we double these values to conclude that the p-value is between .10 and .05. This p-value is greater than $\alpha = .05$. Thus, the null hypothesis H_0: $\mu_d = 0$ is not rejected. Using Minitab and the data in Table 10.2, we find the p-value $= .080$.

In addition we can obtain an interval estimate of the difference between the two population means by using the single population methodology of Chapter 8. At 95% confidence, the calculation follows.

$$\bar{d} \pm t_{.025} \frac{s_d}{\sqrt{n}}$$

$$.3 \pm 2.571 \left(\frac{.335}{\sqrt{6}} \right)$$

$$.3 \pm .35$$

Thus, the margin of error is .35 and the 95% confidence interval for the difference between the population means of the two production methods is $-.05$ minutes to .65 minutes.

NOTES AND COMMENTS

1. In the example presented in this section, workers performed the production task with first one method and then the other method. This example illustrates a matched sample design in which each sampled element (worker) provides a pair of data values. It is also possible to use different but "similar" elements to provide the pair of data values. For example, a worker at one location could be matched with a similar worker at another location (similarity based on age, education, gender, experience, etc.). The pairs of workers would provide the difference data that could be used in the matched sample analysis.

2. A matched sample procedure for inferences about two population means generally provides better precision than the independent sample approach, therefore it is the recommended design. However, in some applications the matching cannot be achieved, or perhaps the time and cost associated with matching are excessive. In such cases, the independent sample design should be used.

Exercises

Methods

19. Consider the following hypothesis test.

$$H_0: \mu_d \leq 0$$
$$H_a: \mu_d > 0$$

The following data are from matched samples taken from two populations.

| | Population | |
Element	1	2
1	21	20
2	28	26
3	18	18
4	20	20
5	26	24

a.   Compute the difference value for each element.
b.   Compute $\bar{d}$.
c.   Compute the standard deviation s_d.
d.   Conduct a hypothesis test using $\alpha = .05$. What is your conclusion?

20.   The following data are from matched samples taken from two populations.

| | Population | |
Element	1	2
1	11	8
2	7	8
3	9	6
4	12	7
5	13	10
6	15	15
7	15	14

a.   Compute the difference value for each element.
b.   Compute $\bar{d}$.
c.   Compute the standard deviation s_d.
d.   What is the point estimate of the difference between the two population means?
e.   Provide a 95% confidence interval for the difference between the two population means.

Applications

21.   A market research firm used a sample of individuals to rate the purchase potential of a particular product before and after the individuals saw a new television commercial about the product. The purchase potential ratings were based on a 0 to 10 scale, with higher values indicating a higher purchase potential. The null hypothesis stated that the mean rating "after" would be less than or equal to the mean rating "before." Rejection of this hypothesis would show that the commercial improved the mean purchase potential rating. Use $\alpha = .05$ and the following data to test the hypothesis and comment on the value of the commercial.

Individual	Purchase Rating After	Before	Individual	Purchase Rating After	Before
1	6	5	5	3	5
2	6	4	6	9	8
3	7	7	7	7	5
4	4	3	8	6	6

22. A sample of 10 international telephone calls provided Sprint and WorldCom calling rates per minute for calls from the United States (*World Traveler,* July 2000).

Country	Sprint	WorldCom
Australia	.46	.26
Belgium	.69	.40
Brazil	.92	.53
Colombia	.55	.53
Denmark	.50	.26
France	.46	.26
Germany	.46	.26
Hong Kong	.92	.40
Japan	.69	.40
United Kingdom	.46	.26

Provide a 95% confidence interval estimate of the difference between the two population means.

23. Bank of America's Consumer Spending Survey collected data on annual credit card charges in seven different categories of expenditures: transportation, groceries, dining out, household expenses, home furnishings, apparel, and entertainment (*U.S. Airways Attaché,* December 2003). Using data from a sample of 42 credit card accounts, assume that each account was used to identify the annual credit card charges for groceries (population 1) and the annual credit card charges for dining out (population 2). Using the difference data, the sample mean difference was $\bar{d} = \$850$, and the sample standard deviation was $s_d = \$1123$.
    a. Formulate the null and alternative hypotheses to test for no difference between the population mean credit card charges for groceries and the population mean credit card charges for dining out.
    b. Use a .05 level of significance. Can you conclude that the population means differ? What is the *p*-value?
    c. Which category, groceries or dining out, has a higher population mean annual credit card charge? What is the point estimate of the difference between the population means? What is the 95% confidence interval estimate of the difference between the population means?

24. Rental car gasoline prices per gallon were sampled at eight major airports. Data for Hertz and National car rental companies follow (*USA Today,* April 4, 2000).

Airport	Hertz	National
Boston Logan	1.55	1.56
Chicago O'Hare	1.62	1.59
Los Angeles	1.72	1.78
Miami	1.65	1.49
New York (JFK)	1.72	1.51
New York (LaGuardia)	1.67	1.50
Orange County, CA	1.68	1.77
Washington (Dulles)	1.52	1.41

Use $\alpha = .05$ to test the hypothesis of no difference between the population mean prices per gallon for the two companies.

25. In recent years, a growing array of entertainment options competes for consumer time. By 2004, cable television and radio surpassed broadcast television, recorded music, and the daily newspaper to become the two entertainment media with the greatest usage (*The Wall Street Journal,* January 26, 2004). Researchers used a sample of 15 individuals and collected data on the hours per week spent watching cable television and hours per week spent listening to the radio.

TVRadio

Individual	Television	Radio	Individual	Television	Radio
1	22	25	9	21	21
2	8	10	10	23	23
3	25	29	11	14	15
4	22	19	12	14	18
5	12	13	13	14	17
6	26	28	14	16	15
7	22	23	15	24	23
8	19	21			

a. Use a .05 level of significance and test for a difference between the population mean usage for cable television and radio. What is the *p*-value?

b. What is the sample mean number of hours per week spent watching cable television? What is the sample mean number of hours per week spent listening to radio? Which medium has the greater usage?

26. StreetInsider.com reported 2002 earnings per share data for a sample of major companies (February 12, 2003). Prior to 2002, financial analysts predicted the 2002 earnings per share for these same companies (*Barron's,* September 10, 2001). Use the following data to comment on differences between actual and estimated earnings per share.

Earnings

Company	Actual	Predicted
AT&T	1.29	0.38
American Express	2.01	2.31
Citigroup	2.59	3.43
Coca-Cola	1.60	1.78
DuPont	1.84	2.18
Exxon-Mobil	2.72	2.19
General Electric	1.51	1.71
Johnson & Johnson	2.28	2.18
McDonald's	0.77	1.55
Wal-Mart	1.81	1.74

a. Use $\alpha = .05$ and test for any difference between the population mean actual and population mean estimated earnings per share. What is the *p*-value? What is your conclusion?

b. What is the point estimate of the difference between the two means? Did the analysts tend to underestimate or overestimate the earnings?

c. At 95% confidence, what is the margin of error for the estimate in part (b)? What would you recommend based on this information?

10.4   Introduction to Analysis of Variance

Thus far we focused on statistical procedures used to compare two population means. In this section, we introduce **analysis of variance (ANOVA)** and show how it can be used to test the hypothesis that three or more population means are equal. We begin the discussion by considering a problem faced by National Computer Products, Inc.

National Computer Products, Inc. (NCP), manufactures printers and fax machines at plants located in Atlanta, Dallas, and Seattle. To measure how much employees at these plants know about total quality management, a random sample of six employees was selected from each plant and given a quality awareness examination. The examination scores obtained for these 18 employees are listed in Table 10.3. The sample means, sample variances, and sample standard deviations for each group are also provided. Managers want to use these data to test the hypothesis that the mean examination score is the same for all three plants.

We will define population 1 as all employees at the Atlanta plant, population 2 as all employees at the Dallas plant, and population 3 as all employees at the Seattle plant. Let

$$\mu_1 = \text{mean examination score for population 1}$$
$$\mu_2 = \text{mean examination score for population 2}$$
$$\mu_3 = \text{mean examination score for population 3}$$

Although we will never know the actual values of μ_1, μ_2, and μ_3, we want to use the sample results to test the following hypotheses.

If H_0 is rejected, we cannot conclude that all population means are different. Rejecting H_0 means that at least two population means have different values.

$$H_0: \mu_1 = \mu_2 = \mu_3$$
$$H_a: \text{Not all population means are equal}$$

As we will demonstrate shortly, analysis of variance is a statistical procedure that can be used to determine whether the observed differences in the three sample means are large enough to reject H_0.

In the introduction to this chapter we stated that analysis of variance can be used to analyze data obtained from both an observational study and an experimental study. In order to provide a common set of terminology for discussing the use of analysis of variance in both types of studies, we need to introduce the concepts of a response variable, a factor, and a treatment.

The two variables in the NCP example are plant location and score on the quality awareness examination. Because the objective is to determine whether the mean examination score is the same for plants located in Atlanta, Dallas, and Seattle, examination score is referred to as the dependent or *response variable* and plant location as the independent variable or *factor.* In general, the values of a factor selected for investigation are referred to as levels of the factor or *treatments.* Thus, in the NCP example the three treatments are Atlanta, Dallas, and Seattle. These three treatments define the populations of interest in the NCP example. For each treatment or population, the response variable is the examination score.

TABLE 10.3   EXAMINATION SCORES FOR 18 EMPLOYEES

Observation	Plant 1 Atlanta	Plant 2 Dallas	Plant 3 Seattle
1	85	71	59
2	75	75	64
3	82	73	62
4	76	74	69
5	71	69	75
6	85	82	67
Sample mean	79	74	66
Sample variance	34	20	32
Sample standard deviation	5.83	4.47	5.66

Assumptions for Analysis of Variance

Three assumptions are required to use analysis of variance.

If the sample sizes are equal, analysis of variance is not sensitive to departures from the assumption of normally distributed populations.

1. **For each population, the response variable is normally distributed.** Implication: In the NCP example, the examination scores (response variable) must be normally distributed at each plant.
2. **The variance of the response variable, denoted σ^2, is the same for all of the populations.** Implication: In the NCP example, the variance of examination scores must be the same for all three plants.
3. **The observations must be independent.** Implication: In the NCP example, the examination score for each employee must be independent of the examination score for any other employee.

A Conceptual Overview

If the means for the three populations are equal, we would expect the three sample means to be close together. In fact, the closer the three sample means are to one another, the more evidence we have for the conclusion that the population means are equal. Alternatively, the more the sample means differ, the more evidence we have for the conclusion that the population means are not equal. In other words, if the variability among the sample means is "small," it supports H_0; if the variability among the sample means is "large," it supports H_a.

If the null hypothesis, H_0: $\mu_1 = \mu_2 = \mu_3$, is true, we can use the variability among the sample means to develop an estimate of σ^2. First, note that if the assumptions for analysis of variance are satisfied, each sample will have come from the same normal distribution with mean μ and variance σ^2. Recall from Chapter 7 that the sampling distribution of the sample mean $\bar{x}$ for a simple random sample of size n from a normal population will be normally distributed with mean μ and variance σ^2/n. Figure 10.3 illustrates such a sampling distribution.

Thus, if the null hypothesis is true, we can think of each of the three sample means, $\bar{x}_1 = 79$, $\bar{x}_2 = 74$, and $\bar{x}_3 = 66$, from Table 10.3 as values drawn at random from the sampling distribution shown in Figure 10.3. In this case, the mean and variance of the three $\bar{x}$ values can be used to estimate the mean and variance of the sampling distribution. When the sample sizes are equal, as in the NCP example, the best estimate of the mean of the

FIGURE 10.3   SAMPLING DISTRIBUTION OF $\bar{x}$ GIVEN H_0 IS TRUE sampling distribution of $\bar{x}$ is the mean or average of the sample means. Thus, in the NCP example, an estimate of the mean of the sampling distribution of $\bar{x}$ is $(79 + 74 + 66)/3 = 73$. We refer to this estimate as the *overall sample mean*. An estimate of the variance of the sampling distribution of $\bar{x}$, $\sigma_{\bar{x}}^2$, is provided by the variance of the three sample means.

$$s_{\bar{x}}^2 = \frac{(79 - 73)^2 + (74 - 73)^2 + (66 - 73)^2}{3 - 1} = \frac{86}{2} = 43$$

Because $\sigma_{\bar{x}}^2 = \sigma^2/n$, solving for σ^2 gives

$$\sigma^2 = n\sigma_{\bar{x}}^2$$

Hence,

$$\text{Estimate of } \sigma^2 = n \text{ (Estimate of } \sigma_{\bar{x}}^2) = ns_{\bar{x}}^2 = 6(43) = 258$$

The result, $ns_{\bar{x}}^2 = 258$, is referred to as the *between-treatments* estimate of σ^2.

The between-treatments estimate of σ^2 is based on the assumption that the null hypothesis is true. In this case, each sample comes from the same population, and there is only one sampling distribution of $\bar{x}$. To illustrate what happens when H_0 is false, suppose the population means all differ. Note that because the three samples are from normal populations with different means, they will result in three different sampling distributions. Figure 10.4 shows that in this case, the sample means are not as close together as they were when H_0 was true. Thus, $s_{\bar{x}}^2$ will be larger, causing the between-treatments estimate of σ^2 to be larger. In general, when the population means are not equal, the between-treatments estimate will overestimate the population variance σ^2.

The variation within each of the samples also has an effect on the conclusion we reach in analysis of variance. When a simple random sample is selected from each population, each of the sample variances provides an unbiased estimate of σ^2. Hence, we can combine or pool the individual estimates of σ^2 into one overall estimate. The estimate of σ^2 obtained in this way is called the *pooled* or *within-treatments* estimate of σ^2. Because each sample variance provides an estimate of σ^2 based only on the variation within each sample, the within-treatments estimate of σ^2 is not affected by whether the population means are equal.

FIGURE 10.4   SAMPLING DISTRIBUTIONS OF $\bar{x}$ GIVEN H_0 IS FALSE

Sample means come from
different sampling distributions
and are not as close together when
H_0 is false

When the sample sizes are equal, the within-treatments estimate of σ^2 can be obtained by computing the average of the individual sample variances. For the NCP example we obtain

$$\text{Within-treatments estimate of } \sigma^2 = \frac{34 + 20 + 32}{3} = \frac{86}{3} = 28.67$$

In the NCP example, the between-treatments estimate of σ^2 (258) is much larger than the within-treatments estimate of σ^2 (28.67). In fact, the ratio of these two estimates is $258/28.67 = 9.00$. Recall, however, that the between-treatments approach provides a good estimate of σ^2 only if the null hypothesis is true; if the null hypothesis is false, the between-treatments approach overestimates σ^2. The within-treatments approach provides a good estimate of σ^2 in either case. Thus, if the null hypothesis is true, the two estimates will be similar and their ratio will be close to 1. If the null hypothesis is false, the between-treatments estimate will be larger than the within-treatments estimate, and their ratio will be large. In the next section we will show how large this ratio must be to reject H_0.

In summary, the logic behind ANOVA is based on the development of two independent estimates of the common population variance σ^2. One estimate of σ^2 is based on the variability among the sample means themselves, and the other estimate of σ^2 is based on the variability of the data within each sample. By comparing these two estimates of σ^2, we will be able to determine whether the population means are equal.

NOTES AND COMMENTS

In Sections 10.1 and 10.2 we presented statistical methods for testing the hypothesis that two population means are equal. ANOVA can also be used to test the hypothesis that two population means are equal. In practice, however, analysis of variance is usually not used until dealing with three or more population means.

10.5 Analysis of Variance: Testing for the Equality of k Population Means

Analysis of variance can be used to test for the equality of k population means. The general form of the hypotheses tested is

$$H_0: \mu_1 = \mu_2 = \cdots = \mu_k$$
$$H_a: \text{Not all population means are equal}$$

where

$$\mu_j = \text{mean of the } j\text{th population}$$

We assume that a simple random sample of size n_j has been selected from each of the k populations or treatments. For the resulting sample data, let

$$x_{ij} = \text{value of observation } i \text{ for treatment } j$$
$$n_j = \text{number of observations for treatment } j$$
$$\bar{x}_j = \text{sample mean for treatment } j$$
$$s_j^2 = \text{sample variance for treatment } j$$
$$s_j = \text{sample standard deviation for treatment } j$$

The formulas for the sample mean and sample variance for treatment j are as follows.

$$\bar{x}_j = \frac{\sum_{i=1}^{n_j} x_{ij}}{n_j} \tag{10.10}$$

$$s_j^2 = \frac{\sum_{i=1}^{n_j} (x_{ij} - \bar{x}_j)^2}{n_j - 1} \tag{10.11}$$

The overall sample mean, denoted $\bar{\bar{x}}$, is the sum of all the observations divided by the total number of observations. That is,

$$\bar{\bar{x}} = \frac{\sum_{j=1}^{k} \sum_{i=1}^{n_j} x_{ij}}{n_T} \tag{10.12}$$

where

$$n_T = n_1 + n_2 + \cdots + n_k \tag{10.13}$$

If the size of each sample is n, $n_T = kn$; in this case equation (10.12) reduces to

$$\bar{\bar{x}} = \frac{\sum_{j=1}^{k} \sum_{i=1}^{n_j} x_{ij}}{kn} = \frac{\sum_{j=1}^{k} \sum_{i=1}^{n_j} x_{ij}/n}{k} = \frac{\sum_{j=1}^{k} \bar{x}_j}{k} \tag{10.14}$$

In other words, whenever the sample sizes are the same, the overall sample mean is just the average of the k sample means.

Because each sample in the NCP example consists of $n = 6$ observations, the overall sample mean can be computed by using equation (10.14). For the data in Table 10.3 we obtained the following result.

$$\bar{\bar{x}} = \frac{79 + 74 + 66}{3} = 73$$

If the null hypothesis is true ($\mu_1 = \mu_2 = \mu_3 = \mu$), the overall sample mean of 73 is the best estimate of the population mean μ.

Between-Treatments Estimate of Population Variance

In the preceding section, we introduced the concept of a between-treatments estimate of σ^2 and showed how to compute it when the sample sizes were equal. This estimate of σ^2 is called the *mean square due to treatments* and is denoted MSTR. The general formula for computing MSTR is

$$\text{MSTR} = \frac{\sum_{j=1}^{k} n_j (\bar{x}_j - \bar{\bar{x}})^2}{k - 1} \tag{10.15}$$

The numerator in equation (10.15) is called the *sum of squares due to treatments* and is denoted SSTR. The denominator, $k - 1$, represents the degrees of freedom associated with SSTR. Hence, the mean square due to treatments can be computed by the following formula.

MEAN SQUARE DUE TO TREATMENTS

$$MSTR = \frac{SSTR}{k - 1} \qquad (10.16)$$

where

$$SSTR = \sum_{j=1}^{k} n_j (\bar{x}_j - \bar{\bar{x}})^2 \qquad (10.17)$$

If H_0 is true, MSTR provides an unbiased estimate of σ^2. However, if the means of the k populations are not equal, MSTR is not an unbiased estimate of σ^2; in fact, in that case, MSTR should overestimate σ^2.

For the NCP data in Table 10.3, we obtain the following results.

$$SSTR = \sum_{j=1}^{k} n_j (\bar{x}_j - \bar{\bar{x}})^2 = 6(79 - 73)^2 + 6(74 - 73)^2 + 6(66 - 73)^2 = 516$$

$$MSTR = \frac{SSTR}{k - 1} = \frac{516}{2} = 258$$

Within-Treatments Estimate of Population Variance

Earlier, we introduced the concept of a within-treatments estimate of σ^2 and showed how to compute it when the sample sizes were equal. This estimate of σ^2 is called the *mean square due to error* and is denoted MSE. The general formula for computing MSE is

$$MSE = \frac{\sum_{j=1}^{k}(n_j - 1)s_j^2}{n_T - k} \qquad (10.18)$$

The numerator in equation (10.18) is called the *sum of squares due to error* and is denoted SSE. The denominator of MSE, $n_T - k$, is the degrees of freedom associated with SSE. Hence, the formula for MSE can also be stated as follows.

MEAN SQUARE DUE TO ERROR

$$MSE = \frac{SSE}{n_T - k} \qquad (10.19)$$

where

$$SSE = \sum_{j=1}^{k}(n_j - 1)s_j^2 \qquad (10.20)$$

Note that MSE is based on the variation within each of the treatments; it is not influenced by whether the null hypothesis is true. Thus, MSE always provides an unbiased estimate of σ^2.

For the NCP data in Table 10.3 we obtain the following results

$$\text{SSE} = \sum_{j=1}^{k}(n_j - 1)s_j^2 = (6 - 1)34 + (6 - 1)20 + (6 - 1)32 = 430$$

$$\text{MSE} = \frac{\text{SSE}}{n_T - k} = \frac{430}{18 - 3} = \frac{430}{15} = 28.67$$

Comparing the Variance Estimates: The F Test

If the null hypothesis is true, MSTR and MSE provide two independent estimates of the population variance σ^2. When the null hypothesis is true and the ANOVA assumptions are valid, the sampling distribution of the ratio MSTR/MSE has an **F distribution** with $k - 1$ degrees of freedom in the numerator and $n_T - 1$ degrees of freedom in the denominator. The general shape of this F distribution is shown in Figure 10.5. If the null hypothesis is true, the value of MSTR/MSE should appear to be from this distribution. However, if the null hypothesis is false, the value of MSTR/MSE will be inflated because a large MSTR provides an overestimate of σ^2. The values of MSTR/MSE that lead to the rejection of the null hypothesis will be in the upper tail of the distribution shown in Figure 10.5.

With the decision to reject the null hypothesis H_0 based on the ratio MSTR/MSE, this ratio becomes the test statistic for the hypothesis test about the equality of k population means. The test statistic is as follows.

TEST STATISTIC FOR THE EQUALITY OF k POPULATION MEANS

$$F = \frac{\text{MSTR}}{\text{MSE}} \qquad\qquad \textbf{(10.21)}$$

The F distribution has $k - 1$ degrees of freedom in the numerator and $n_T - k$ degrees of freedom in the denominator.

Let us return to the National Computer Products example and use a level of significance $\alpha = .05$ to conduct the hypothesis test. The null and alternative hypotheses are restated as follows:

$$H_0: \mu_1 = \mu_2 = \mu_3$$
$$H_a: \text{Not all population means are equal}$$

FIGURE 10.5 *F DISTRIBUTION: THE SAMPLING DISTRIBUTION OF MSTR/MSE*

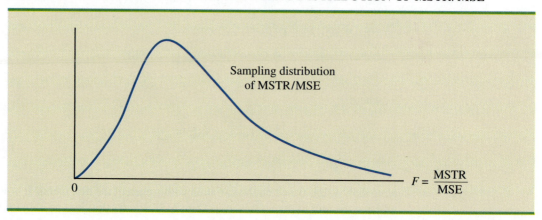

With the previously computed MSTR = 258 and MSE = 28.67, the value of the test statistic is

$$F = \frac{MSTR}{MSE} = \frac{258}{28.67} = 9$$

The numerator degrees of freedom is $k - 1 = 3 - 1 = 2$, and the denominator degrees of freedom is $n_T - k = 18 - 3 = 15$. Because we reject the null hypothesis for large values of the test statistic, we will compute the p-value as the upper tail area of the F distribution to the right of the test statistic $F = 9$. The usual hypothesis testing rule to reject H_0 if p-value $\leq \alpha$ applies.

Table 10.4 shows a portion of the F distribution table that will be helpful in this example. Using 2 numerator degrees of freedom and 15 denominator degrees of freedom, this table shows the following areas in the upper tail.

Area in Upper Tail	.10	.05	.025	.01
F Value ($df_1 = 2$, $df_2 = 15$)	2.70	3.68	4.77	6.36

$F = 9$

Because $F = 9$ is greater than 6.36, the area in the upper tail at $F = 9$ is less than .01. Thus, the p-value is less than .01. With p-value $\leq \alpha = .05$, H_0 is rejected. The test provides sufficient evidence to conclude that the means of the three populations are not equal. In other words, analysis of variance supports the conclusion that the population mean examination scores at the three NCP plants are not equal.

Because the F table only provides values for upper tail areas of .10, .05, .025, and .01, we cannot determine the exact p-value directly from the table. Minitab or Excel provides the p-value as part of the standard ANOVA output. Appendixes 10.3 and 10.4 show the procedures that can be used. For the NCP example, the exact p-value corresponding to the test statistic $F = 9$ is .003.

As with other hypothesis testing procedures, the critical value approach may also be used. With $\alpha = .05$, the critical F value occurs with an area of .05 in the upper tail of an F distribution with 2 and 15 degrees of freedom. From the F distribution table, we find $F_{.05} = 3.68$. Hence, the appropriate upper tail rejection rule for the NCP example is

$$\text{Reject } H_0 \text{ if } F \geq 3.68$$

With $F = 9$, we reject H_0 and conclude that the means of the three populations are not equal. A summary of the overall procedure for testing for the equality of k population means follows.

TEST FOR THE EQUALITY OF k POPULATION MEANS

$$H_0: \mu_1 = \mu_2 = \cdots = \mu_k$$
$$H_a: \text{Not all population means are equal}$$

TEST STATISTIC

$$F = \frac{MSTR}{MSE}$$

REJECTION RULE

p-value approach: Reject H_0 if p-value $\leq \alpha$
Critical value approach: Reject H_0 if $F \geq F_\alpha$

where the value of F_α is based on an F distribution with $k - 1$ numerator degrees of freedom and $n_T - k$ denominator degrees of freedom.

TABLE 10.4   SELECTED VALUES FROM THE *F* DISTRIBUTION TABLE

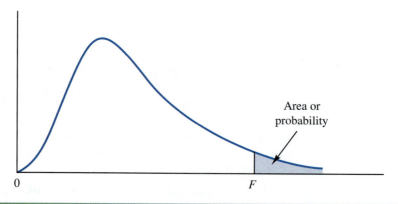

Denominator Degrees of Freedom	Area in Upper Tail	Numerator Degrees of Freedom				
		1	2	3	4	5
10	.10	3.29	2.92	2.73	2.61	2.52
	.05	4.96	4.10	3.71	3.48	3.33
	.025	6.94	5.46	4.83	4.47	4.24
	.01	10.04	7.56	6.55	5.99	5.64
15	.10	3.07	2.70	2.49	2.36	2.27
	.05	4.54	3.68	3.29	3.06	2.90
	.025	6.20	4.77	4.15	3.80	3.58
	.01	8.68	6.36	5.42	4.89	4.56
20	.10	2.97	2.59	2.38	2.25	2.16
	.05	4.35	3.49	3.10	2.87	2.71
	.025	5.87	4.46	3.86	3.51	3.29
	.01	8.10	5.85	4.94	4.43	4.10
25	.10	2.92	2.53	2.32	2.18	2.09
	.05	4.24	3.39	2.99	2.76	2.60
	.025	5.69	4.29	3.69	3.35	3.13
	.01	7.77	5.57	4.68	4.18	3.85
30	.10	2.88	2.49	2.28	2.14	2.05
	.05	4.17	3.32	2.92	2.69	2.53
	.025	5.57	4.18	3.59	3.25	3.03
	.01	7.56	5.39	4.51	4.02	3.70

Note: A more extensive table is provided as Table 4 of Appendix B.

ANOVA Table

The results of the preceding calculations can be displayed conveniently in a table referred to as the analysis of variance table, or **ANOVA table**. Table 10.5 is the analysis of variance table for the National Computer Products example. The sum of squares associated with the source of variation referred to as "Total" is called the *total sum of squares* (SST). Note that the results for the NCP example show SST = SSTR + SSE, and that the degrees of freedom associated with this total sum of squares is the sum of the degrees of freedom associated with the between-treatments estimate of σ^2 and the within-treatments estimate of σ^2.

TABLE 10.5   ANALYSIS OF VARIANCE TABLE FOR THE NCP EXAMPLE

Source of Variation	Sum of Squares	Degrees of Freedom	Mean Square	F
Treatments	516	2	258.00	9.00
Error	430	15	28.67	
Total	946	17		

We point out that SST divided by its degrees of freedom $n_T - 1$ is the overall sample variance that would be obtained if we treated the entire set of 18 observations as one data set. With the entire data set as one sample, the formula for computing the total sum of squares, SST, is

$$\text{SST} = \sum_{j=1}^{k} \sum_{i=1}^{n_j} (x_{ij} - \bar{\bar{x}})^2 \qquad (10.22)$$

It can be shown that the results we observed for the analysis of variance table for the NCP example also apply to other problems. That is,

$$\text{SST} = \text{SSTR} + \text{SSE} \qquad (10.23)$$

Analysis of variance can be thought of as a statistical procedure for partitioning the total sum of squares into separate components.

In other words, SST can be partitioned into two sums of squares: the sum of squares due to treatments and the sum of squares due to error. Note also that the degrees of freedom corresponding to SST, $n_T - 1$, can be partitioned into the degrees of freedom corresponding to SSTR, $k - 1$, and the degrees of freedom corresponding to SSE, $n_T - k$. The analysis of variance can be viewed as the process of **partitioning** the total sum of squares and the degrees of freedom into their corresponding sources: treatments and error. Dividing the sum of squares by the appropriate degrees of freedom provides the variance estimates and the F value used to test the hypothesis of equal population means.

Computer Results for Analysis of Variance

Because of the widespread availability of statistical computer packages, analysis of variance computations with large sample sizes or a large number of populations can be performed easily. In Figure 10.6 we show output for the NCP example obtained from the Minitab computer package. The first part of the computer output contains the familiar ANOVA table format. Comparing Figure 10.6 with Table 10.5, we see that the same information is available, although some of the headings are slightly different. The heading Source is used for the Source of Variation column, and Factor identifies the Treatments row. The Sum of Squares and Degrees of Freedom columns are interchanged, and a p-value is provided for the F test. Thus, at the $\alpha = .05$ level of significance, we reject H_0 because the p-value $= 0.003 \leq \alpha = .05$.

Note that following the ANOVA table the computer output contains the respective sample sizes, the sample means, and the standard deviations. In addition, Minitab provides a figure that shows individual 95% confidence interval estimates of each population mean. In developing these confidence interval estimates, Minitab uses MSE as the estimate of σ^2. Thus, the square root of MSE provides the best estimate of the population standard deviation σ. This estimate of σ on the computer output is Pooled StDev; it is equal to 5.354. To provide an illustration of how these interval estimates are developed, we will compute a 95% confidence interval estimate of the population mean for the Atlanta plant.

FIGURE 10.6   MINITAB OUTPUT FOR THE NCP ANALYSIS OF VARIANCE

```
Analysis of Variance
Source      DF        SS        MS        F        p
Factor       2     516.0     258.0     9.00    0.003
Error       15     430.0      28.7
Total       17     946.0
                                    Individual 95% Cis For Mean
                                    Based on Pooled StDev
Level       N      Mean     StDev   ---+---------+---------+---------+---
Atlanta      6    79.000     5.831                         (-----*-----)
Dallas       6    74.000     4.472                 (-----*-----)
Seattle      6    66.000     5.657   (-----*-----)
                                    ---+---------+---------+---------+---
Pooled StDev =     5.354              63.0      70.0      77.0      84.0
```

From the study of interval estimation in Chapter 8, we know that the general form of an interval estimate of a population mean is

$$\bar{x} \pm t_{\alpha/2}\frac{s}{\sqrt{n}} \tag{10.24}$$

where s is the estimate of the population standard deviation σ. In the analysis of variance the best estimate of σ is provided by the square root of MSE or the Pooled StDev; therefore, we use a value of 5.354 for s in expression (10.24). The degrees of freedom for $t_{\alpha/2}$ is 15, the degrees of freedom associated with the within-treatments estimate of σ^2. Hence, at 95% confidence we have $t_{.025} = 2.131$ and

$$79 \pm 2.131\frac{5.354}{\sqrt{6}} = 79 \pm 4.66$$

Thus, the individual 95% confidence interval for the Atlanta plant is from $79 - 4.66 = 74.34$ to $79 + 4.66 = 83.66$. Because the sample sizes are equal for the NCP example, the individual confidence intervals for the Dallas and Seattle plants are also constructed by adding and subtracting 4.66 from each sample mean. Thus, in the figure provided by Minitab we see that the widths of the confidence intervals are the same.

Exercises

Methods

27. Five observations were selected from each of three populations. The data obtained follow.

Observation	Sample 1	Sample 2	Sample 3
1	32	44	33
2	30	43	36
3	30	44	35

Observation	Sample 1	Sample 2	Sample 3
4	26	46	36
5	32	48	40
Sample mean	30	45	36
Sample variance	6.00	4.00	6.50

a. Compute the between-treatments estimate of σ^2.
b. Compute the within-treatments estimate of σ^2.
c. At the $\alpha = .05$ level of significance, can we reject the null hypothesis that the means of the three populations are equal?
d. Set up the ANOVA table for this problem.

28. Four observations were selected from each of three populations. The data obtained follow.

Observation	Sample 1	Sample 2	Sample 3
1	165	174	169
2	149	164	154
3	156	180	161
4	142	158	148
Sample mean	153	169	158
Sample variance	96.67	97.33	82.00

a. Compute the between-treatments estimate of σ^2.
b. Compute the within-treatments estimate of σ^2.
c. At the $\alpha = .05$ level of significance, can we reject the null hypothesis that the three population means are equal? Explain.
d. Set up the ANOVA table for this problem.

29. Samples were selected from three populations. The data obtained follow.

	Sample 1	Sample 2	Sample 3
	93	77	88
	98	87	75
	107	84	73
	102	95	84
		85	75
		82	
$\bar{x}_j$	100	85	79
s_j^2	35.33	35.60	43.50

a. Compute the between-treatments estimate of σ^2.
b. Compute the within-treatments estimate of σ^2.
c. At the $\alpha = .05$ level of significance, can we reject the null hypothesis that the three population means are equal? Explain.
d. Set up the ANOVA table for this problem.

30. A random sample of 16 observations was selected from each of four populations. A portion of the ANOVA table follows.

Source of Variation	Sum of Squares	Degrees of Freedom	Mean Square	F
Treatments			400	
Error				
Total	1500			

a. Provide the missing entries for the ANOVA table.
b. At the $\alpha = .05$ level of significance, can we reject the null hypothesis that the means of the four populations are equal?

31. Random samples of 25 observations were selected from each of three populations. For these data, SSTR = 120 and SSE = 216.
a. Set up the ANOVA table for this problem.
b. At the $\alpha = .05$ level of significance, can we reject the null hypothesis that the three population means are equal?

Applications

32. To test whether the mean time needed to mix a batch of material is the same for machines produced by three manufacturers, the Jacobs Chemical Company obtained the following data on the time (in minutes) needed to mix the material. Use these data to test whether the population mean times for mixing a batch of material differ for the three manufacturers. Use $\alpha = .05$.

	Manufacturer		
	1	2	3
	20	28	20
	26	26	19
	24	31	23
	22	27	22

33. The Texas Transportation Institute at Texas A&M University conducted a survey to determine the number of hours per year drivers waste sitting in traffic. Of 75 urban areas studied, the most jammed urban area was Los Angeles where drivers wasted an average of 90 hours per year (*U.S. News & World Report,* October 13, 2003). Other jammed urban areas included Denver, Miami, and San Francisco. Assume sample data for six drivers in each of these cities show the following number of hours wasted per year sitting in traffic.

Denver	Miami	San Francisco
70	66	65
62	70	62
71	55	74
58	65	69
57	56	63
66	66	75

a.   Compute the sample mean hours wasted per year for each of these urban areas.

b.   Using $\alpha = .05$, test for significance differences among the population mean wasted time for these three urban areas. What is the p-value? What is your conclusion?

34. New York City, Boston, and the Silicon Valley of California are among the areas with the highest technology salaries in the United States (*USA Today,* February 28, 2002). The following sample data show individual annual salaries reported in thousands of dollars.

Technology

New York City	Boston	Silicon Valley
82	85	82
79	80	91
72	74	94
89	78	88
79	75	85
85	80	
	86	
	74	

Use $\alpha = .05$ and test for a significance difference among the population mean annual technology salaries for these three locations. What is the p-value? What is your conclusion? If a difference exists, which location appears to have the highest mean technology salary?

35. A study reported in the *Journal of Small Business Management* concluded that self-employed individuals experience higher job stress than individuals who are not self-employed. In this study job stress was assessed with a 15-item scale designed to measure various aspects of ambiguity and role conflict. Ratings for each of the 15 items were made using a scale of 1–5 indicating response options ranging from strong agreement to strong disagreement. The sum of the ratings for the 15 items for each individual surveyed is between 15 and 75, with higher values indicating a higher degree of job stress. Suppose that a similar approach, using a 20-item scale with 1–5 response options, was used to measure the job stress of individuals for 15 randomly selected real estate agents, 15 architects, and 15 stockbrokers. The results obtained follow.

Stress

Real Estate Agent	Architect	Stockbroker
81	43	65
48	63	48
68	60	57
69	52	91
54	54	70
62	77	67
76	68	83
56	57	75
61	61	53
65	80	71
64	50	54
69	37	72
83	73	65
85	84	58
75	58	58

Use $\alpha = .05$ to test for any significant difference in job stress among the three professions.

36. *Condé Nast Traveler* conducts an annual survey in which readers rate their favorite cruise ships. Ratings are provided for small ships (carrying up to 500 passengers), medium ships (carrying 500 to 1500 passengers), and large ships (carrying a minimum of 1500 passengers). The following data show the service ratings for eight randomly selected small ships, eight randomly selected medium ships, and eight randomly selected large ships. All ships are rated on a 100-point scale, with higher values indicating better service (*Condé Nast Traveler,* February 2003).

Ships

Small Ships		Medium Ships		Large Ships	
Name	**Rating**	**Name**	**Rating**	**Name**	**Rating**
Hanseactic	90.5	Amsterdam	91.1	Century	89.2
Mississippi Queen	78.2	Crystal Symphony	98.9	Disney Wonder	90.2
Philae	92.3	Maasdam	94.2	Enchantment of the Seas	85.9
Royal Clipper	95.7	Noordam	84.3	Grand Princess	84.2
Seabourn Pride	94.1	Royal Princess	84.8	Infinity	90.2
Seabourn Spirit	100	Ryndam	89.2	Legend of the Seas	80.6
Silver Cloud	91.8	Statendam	86.4	Paradise	75.8
Silver Wind	95	Veendam	88.3	Sun Princess	82.3

Use $\alpha = .05$ to test for any significant difference in the mean service ratings among the three sizes of cruise ships.

Summary

In this chapter we presented procedures for comparing two or more population means. First, we showed how to make inferences about the difference between two population means when independent simple random samples are selected. We considered the case where the population standard deviations, σ_1 and σ_2, could be assumed known. The standard normal distribution z was used to develop the interval estimate and served as the test statistic for hypothesis tests. We then considered the case where the population standard deviations were unknown and estimated by the sample standard deviations s_1 and s_2. In this case, the t distribution was used to develop the interval estimate and served as the test statistic for hypothesis tests.

Inferences about the difference between two population means were then discussed for the matched sample design. In the matched sample design each element provides a pair of data values, one from each population. The difference between the paired data values is then used in the statistical analysis. The matched sample design is generally preferred to the independent sample design because the matched-sample procedure often improves the precision of the estimate.

Finally, we showed how analysis of variance can be used to test for differences among three or more population means. The analysis of variance procedure uses two estimates of the population variance, σ^2. The ratio of these two estimates (the F statistic) can be used to provide the p-value and determine whether to reject the null hypothesis that the population means are equal.

Glossary

Independent simple random samples Samples selected from two populations in such a way that the elements making up one sample are chosen independently of the elements making up the other sample.

Matched samples Samples in which each data value of one sample is matched with a corresponding data value of the other sample.

Analysis of variance (ANOVA) A statistical technique that can be used to test the hypothesis that three or more population means are equal.

***F* distribution** A distribution based on the ratio of two independent estimates of the variance of a normal population. The distribution is used in hypothesis tests about the equality of *k* population means.

ANOVA table A table used to summarize the analysis of variance computations and results. It contains columns showing the source of variation, the sum of squares, the degrees of freedom, the mean square, and the *F* value.

Partitioning The process of allocating the total sum of squares and degrees of freedom to the various components.

Key Formulas

Point Estimator of the Difference Between Two Population Means

$$\bar{x}_1 - \bar{x}_2 \tag{10.1}$$

Standard Error of $\bar{x}_1 - \bar{x}_2$

$$\sigma_{\bar{x}_1 - \bar{x}_2} = \sqrt{\frac{\sigma_1^2}{n_1} + \frac{\sigma_2^2}{n_2}} \tag{10.2}$$

Interval Estimate of the Difference Between Two Population Means:
σ_1 and σ_2 Known

$$\bar{x}_1 - \bar{x}_2 \pm z_{\alpha/2} \sqrt{\frac{\sigma_1^2}{n_1} + \frac{\sigma_2^2}{n_2}} \tag{10.4}$$

Test Statistic for Hypothesis Tests About $\mu_1 - \mu_2$: σ_1 and σ_2 Known

$$z = \frac{(\bar{x}_1 - \bar{x}_2) - D_0}{\sqrt{\frac{\sigma_1^2}{n_1} + \frac{\sigma_2^2}{n_2}}} \tag{10.5}$$

Interval Estimate of the Difference Between Two Population Means:
σ_1 and σ_2 Unknown

$$\bar{x}_1 - \bar{x}_2 \pm t_{\alpha/2} \sqrt{\frac{s_1^2}{n_1} + \frac{s_2^2}{n_2}} \tag{10.6}$$

Degrees of Freedom for the *t* Distribution Using Two Independent Random Samples

$$df = \frac{\left(\frac{s_1^2}{n_1} + \frac{s_2^2}{n_2}\right)^2}{\frac{1}{n_1 - 1}\left(\frac{s_1^2}{n_1}\right)^2 + \frac{1}{n_2 - 1}\left(\frac{s_2^2}{n_2}\right)^2} \tag{10.7}$$

Test Statistic for Hypothesis Tests About $\mu_1 - \mu_2$: σ_1 and σ_2 Unknown

$$t = \frac{(\bar{x}_1 - \bar{x}_2) - D_0}{\sqrt{\frac{s_1^2}{n_1} + \frac{s_2^2}{n_2}}} \tag{10.8}$$

Test Statistic for Hypothesis Tests Involving Matched Samples

$$t = \frac{\bar{d} - \mu_d}{s_d/\sqrt{n}} \qquad (10.9)$$

Sample Mean for Treatment j

$$\bar{x}_j = \frac{\sum_{i=1}^{n_j} x_{ij}}{n_j} \qquad (10.10)$$

Sample Variance for Treatment j

$$s_j^2 = \frac{\sum_{i=1}^{n_j}(x_{ij} - \bar{x}_j)^2}{n_j - 1} \qquad (10.11)$$

Overall Sample Mean

$$\bar{\bar{x}} = \frac{\sum_{j=1}^{k}\sum_{i=1}^{n_j} x_{ij}}{n_T} \qquad (10.12)$$

$$n_T = n_1 + n_2 + \cdots + n_k \qquad (10.13)$$

Mean Square Due to Treatments

$$MSTR = \frac{SSTR}{k - 1} \qquad (10.16)$$

Sum of Squares Due to Treatments

$$SSTR = \sum_{j=1}^{k} n_j(\bar{x}_j - \bar{\bar{x}})^2 \qquad (10.17)$$

Mean Square Due to Error

$$MSE = \frac{SSE}{n_T - k} \qquad (10.19)$$

Sum of Squares Due to Error

$$SSE = \sum_{j=1}^{k}(n_j - 1)s_j^2 \qquad (10.20)$$

Test Statistic for the Equality of k Population Means

$$F = \frac{MSTR}{MSE} \qquad (10.21)$$

Total Sum of Squares

$$SST = \sum_{j=1}^{k}\sum_{i=1}^{n_j}(x_{ij} - \bar{\bar{x}})^2 \qquad (10.22)$$

Partitioning of Sum of Squares

$$SST = SSTR + SSE \qquad (10.23)$$

Supplementary Exercises

37. Safegate Foods, Inc., is redesigning the checkout lanes in its supermarkets throughout the country and is considering two designs. Tests on customer checkout times conducted at two stores where the two new systems have been installed result in the following summary of the data.

System A	System B
$n_1 = 120$	$n_2 = 100$
$\bar{x}_1 = 4.1$ minutes	$\bar{x}_2 = 3.4$ minutes
$\sigma_1 = 2.2$ minutes	$\sigma_2 = 1.5$ minutes

Test at the .05 level of significance to determine whether the population mean checkout times of the two systems differ. Which system is preferred?

38. Starting annual salaries for individuals with master's and bachelor's degrees in business were collected in two independent random samples. Use the following data to develop a 90% confidence interval estimate of the increase in starting salary that can be expected upon completion of a master's program.

Master's Degree	Bachelor's Degree
$n_1 = 60$	$n_2 = 80$
$\bar{x}_1 = \$45,000$	$\bar{x}_2 = \$35,000$
$\sigma_1 = \$4000$	$\sigma_2 = \$3500$

39. Three-megapixel digital cameras are typically the lightest, most compact, and easiest to use. However, if you plan to enlarge or crop images, you will probably want to spend more for a higher-resolution model. The following shows sample prices of five-megapixel and three-megapixel digital cameras (*Consumer Reports Buying Guide*, 2004).

Five-Megapixel		Three-Megapixel	
Model	**Price**	**Model**	**Price**
Nikon 5700	890	Kodak DX4330	280
Olympus C-5050	620	Canon A70	290
Sony DCS-F717	730	Sony DSC P8	370
Olympus C-5050	480	Minolta XI	400
Minolta 7Hi	1060	Sony DSC P72	310
HP 935	450	Nikon 3100	340
Pentax 550	540	Panasonic DMC-LC33	270
Canon S50	500	Pentax S	380
Kyocera TVS	890		
Minolta F300	440		

CD file

Digital

a. Provide a point estimate of the difference between population mean prices for the two types of digital cameras. What observation can you make about the price of the higher-quality five-megapixel model?

b. Develop a 95% confidence interval estimate of the difference between the two population mean prices.

40. Mutual funds are classified as *load* or *no-load* funds. Load funds require an investor to pay an initial fee based on a percentage of the amount invested in the fund. The no-load funds do not require this initial fee. Some financial advisors argue that the load mutual funds may be worth the extra fee because these funds provide a higher mean rate of return than the no-load mutual funds. A sample of 30 load mutual funds and a sample of 30 no-load mutual funds were selected. Data were collected on the annual return for the funds over a five-year period. The data are contained in the data set Mutual. The data for the first five load and first five no-load mutual funds are as follows.

CD file

Mutual

Mutual Funds—Load	Return	Mutual Funds—No Load	Return
American National Growth	15.51	Amana Income Fund	13.24
Arch Small Cap Equity	14.57	Berger One Hundred	12.13
Bartlett Cap Basic	17.73	Columbia International Stock	12.17
Calvert World International	10.31	Dodge & Cox Balanced	16.06
Colonial Fund A	16.23	Evergreen Fund	17.61

a. Formulate H_0 and H_a such that rejection of H_0 leads to the conclusion that the load mutual funds have a higher mean annual return over the five-year period.
b. Use the 60 mutual funds in the data set Mutual to conduct the hypothesis test. What is the p-value? At $\alpha = .05$, what is your conclusion?

41. The National Association of Home Builders provided data on the cost of the most popular home remodeling projects. Sample data on cost in thousands of dollars for two types of remodeling projects are as follows.

Kitchen	Master Bedroom	Kitchen	Master Bedroom
25.2	18.0	23.0	17.8
17.4	22.9	19.7	24.6
22.8	26.4	16.9	21.0
21.9	24.8	21.8	
19.7	26.9	23.6	

a. Develop a point estimate of the difference between the population mean remodeling costs for the two types of projects.
b. Develop a 90% confidence interval for the difference between the two population means.

42. Typical prices of single-family homes in the state of Florida are shown for a sample of 15 metropolitan areas (*Naples Daily News*, February 23, 2003). Data are in thousands of dollars.

CD file

Florida

Metropolitan Area	January 2003	January 2002
Daytona Beach	117	96
Fort Lauderdale	207	169
Fort Myers	143	129
Fort Walton Beach	139	134
Gainesville	131	119
Jacksonville	128	119
Lakeland	91	85
Miami	193	165
Naples	263	233
Ocala	86	90

Metropolitan Area	January 2003	January 2002
Orlando	134	121
Pensacola	111	105
Sarasota-Bradenton	168	141
Tallahassee	140	130
Tampa-St. Petersburg	139	129

a. Use a matched-sample analysis to develop a point estimate of the population mean one-year increase in the price of single-family homes in Florida.

b. Develop a 90% confidence interval estimate of the population mean one-year increase in the price of single-family homes in Florida.

c. What was the percentage increase over the one-year period?

43. *Money* magazine reports percentage returns and expense ratios for stock and bond funds. The following data are the expense ratios for 10 midcap stock funds, 10 small-cap stock funds, 10 hybrid stock funds, and 10 specialty stock funds (*Money,* March 2003).

Funds

Midcap	Small-Cap	Hybrid	Specialty
1.2	2.0	2.0	1.6
1.1	1.2	2.7	2.7
1.0	1.7	1.8	2.6
1.2	1.8	1.5	2.5
1.3	1.5	2.5	1.9
1.8	2.3	1.0	1.5
1.4	1.9	0.9	1.6
1.4	1.3	1.9	2.7
1.0	1.2	1.4	2.2
1.4	1.3	0.3	0.7

Use $\alpha = .05$ to test for any significant difference in the mean expense ratio among the four types of stock funds.

44. Buyers of sport utility vehicles (SUVs) and pickup trucks find a wide choice in today's marketplace. One of the factors important to many buyers is the resale value of the vehicle. The following table shows the resale value (%) after two years for 10 SUVs, 10 small pickup trucks, and 10 large pickup trucks (*Kiplinger's New Cars & Trucks 2000 Buyer's Guide*).

Trucks

Sport Utility	Resale Value	Small Pickup	Resale Value
Chevrolet Blazer LS	55	Chevrolet S-10 Extended Cab	46
Ford Explorer Sport	57	Dodge Dakota Club Cab Sport	53
GMC Yukon XL 1500	67	Ford Ranger XLT Regular Cab	48
Honda CR-V	65	Ford Ranger XLT Supercab	55
Isuzu VehiCross	62	GMC Sonoma Regular Cab	44
Jeep Cherokee Limited	57	Isuzu Hombre Spacecab	41
Mercury Mountaineer	59	Mazda B4000 SE Cab Plus	51
Nissan Pathfinder XE	54	Nissan Frontier XE Regular Cab	51
Toyota 4Runner	55	Toyota Tacoma Xtracab	49
Toyota RAV4	55	Toyota Tacoma Xtracab V6	50

(*continued*)

Full-Size Pickup	Resale Value
Chevrolet K2500	60
Chevrolet Silverado 2500 Ext	64
Dodge Ram 1500	54
Dodge Ram Quad Cab 2500	63
Dodge Ram Regular Cab 2500	59
Ford F150 XL	58
Ford F350 Super Duty Crew Cab XL	64
GMC New Sierra 1500 Ext Cab	68
Toyota Tundra Access Cab Limited	53
Toyota Tundra Regular Cab	58

At the $\alpha = .05$ level of significance, test for any significant difference in the mean resale value for the three types of vehicles.

45. Crown Plaza Hotels and Resorts offered special weekend rates at hotels at resorts nationwide. A sample of 30 properties from three regions of the country provided the following room rates (*USA Today*, April 14, 2000).

CD file

Resorts

West	Rate ($)	South	Rate ($)	Northeast	Rate ($)
Albuquerque	89	Atlanta	105	Albany	89
Irvine	79	Dallas	80	Boston	139
Las Vegas	119	Greenville	79	Hartford	85
Los Angeles	99	Houston	79	New York	159
Palo Alto	109	Jackson	69	Philadelphia	99
Phoenix	149	Macon	69	Pittsfield	99
Portland	79	Miami	89	Providence	149
San Francisco	139	Orlando	119	Washington	159
San Jose	99	Richmond	109	White Plains	109
Seattle	119	Tampa	119	Worchester	124

At the $\alpha = .05$ level of significance, test whether the mean rates are the same for the three regions.

46. The National Football League rates prospects by position on a scale that ranges from 5 to 9. The ratings are interpreted as follows: 8–9 should start the first year; 7.0–7.9 should start; 6.0–6.9 will make the team as backup; and 5.0–5.9 can make the club and contribute. The following table shows the ratings for three positions for 40 NFL prospects (*USA Today*, April 14, 2000). Does there appear to be any significant effect on the rating due to the player's position?

CD file

NFL

Wide Receiver		Guard		Offensive Tackle	
Name	Rating	Name	Rating	Name	Rating
Peter Warrick	9.0	Cosey Coleman	7.4	Chris Samuels	8.5
Plaxico Burress	8.8	Travis Claridge	7.0	Stockar McDougle	8.0
Sylvester Morris	8.3	Kaulana Noa	6.8	Chris McIngosh	7.8
Travis Taylor	8.1	Leander Jordan	6.7	Adrian Klemm	7.6
Laveranues Coles	8.0	Chad Clifton	6.3	Todd Wade	7.3
Dez White	7.9	Manula Savea	6.1	Marvel Smith	7.1
Jerry Porter	7.4	Ryan Johanningmeir	6.0	Michael Thompson	6.8
Ron Dugans	7.1	Mark Tauscher	6.0	Bobby Williams	6.8
Todd Pinkston	7.0	Blaine Saipaia	6.0	Darnell Alford	6.4

Wide Receiver		Guard		Offensive Tackle	
Name	**Rating**	**Name**	**Rating**	**Name**	**Rating**
Dennis Northcutt	7.0	Richard Mercier	5.8	Terrance Beadles	6.3
Anthony Lucas	6.9	Damion McIntosh	5.3	Tutan Reyes	6.1
Darrell Jackson	6.6	Jeno James	5.5	Greg Robinson-Ran	6.0
Danny Farmer	6.5	Al Jackson	5.5		
Sherrod Gideon	6.4				
Trevor Gaylor	6.2				

Case Problem 1   Par, Inc.

Par, Inc., is a major manufacturer of golf equipment. Management believes that Par's market share could be increased with the introduction of a cut-resistant, longer-lasting golf ball. Therefore, the research group at Par has been investigating a new golf ball coating designed to resist cuts and provide a more durable ball. The tests with the coating have been promising.

One of the researchers voiced concern about the effect of the new coating on driving distances. Par would like the new cut-resistant ball to offer driving distances comparable to those of the current-model golf ball. To compare the driving distances for the two balls, 40 balls of both the new and current models were subjected to distance tests. The testing was performed with a mechanical hitting machine so that any difference between the mean distances for the two models could be attributed to a difference in the two models. The results of the tests, with distances measured to the nearest yard, follow. These data are available on the CD that accompanies the text.

CD **file**

Golf

Model		Model		Model		Model	
Current	**New**	**Current**	**New**	**Current**	**New**	**Current**	**New**
264	277	270	272	263	274	281	283
261	269	287	259	264	266	274	250
267	263	289	264	284	262	273	253
272	266	280	280	263	271	263	260
258	262	272	274	260	260	275	270
283	251	275	281	283	281	267	263
258	262	265	276	255	250	279	261
266	289	260	269	272	263	274	255
259	286	278	268	266	278	276	263
270	264	275	262	268	264	262	279

Managerial Report

1. Formulate and present the rationale for a hypothesis test that Par could use to compare the driving distances of the current and new golf balls.
2. Analyze the data to provide the hypothesis testing conclusion. What is the p-value for your test? What is your recommendation for Par, Inc.?
3. Provide descriptive statistical summaries of the data for each model.
4. What is the 95% confidence interval for the population mean of each model, and what is the 95% confidence interval for the difference between the means of the two populations?
5. Do you see a need for larger sample sizes and more testing with the golf balls? Discuss.

Case Problem 2 Wentworth Medical Center

As part of a long-term study of individuals 65 years of age or older, sociologists and physicians at the Wentworth Medical Center in upstate New York investigated the relationship between geographic location and depression. A sample of 60 individuals, all in reasonably good health, was selected; 20 individuals were residents of Florida, 20 were residents of New York, and 20 were residents of North Carolina. Each of the individuals sampled was given a standardized test to measure depression. The data collected follow; higher test scores indicate higher levels of depression. These data are available on the data disk in the file Medical1.

A second part of the study considered the relationship between geographic location and depression for individuals 65 years of age or older who had a chronic health condition such as arthritis, hypertension, and/or heart ailment. A sample of 60 individuals with such conditions was identified. Again, 20 were residents of Florida, 20 were residents of New York, and 20 were residents of North Carolina. The levels of depression recorded for this study follow. These data are available on the CD accompanying the text in the file named Medical2.

Medical1

Medical2

Data from Medical1			Data from Medical2		
Florida	New York	North Carolina	Florida	New York	North Carolina
3	8	10	13	14	10
7	11	7	12	9	12
7	9	3	17	15	15
3	7	5	17	12	18
8	8	11	20	16	12
8	7	8	21	24	14
8	8	4	16	18	17
5	4	3	14	14	8
5	13	7	13	15	14
2	10	8	17	17	16
6	6	8	12	20	18
2	8	7	9	11	17
6	12	3	12	23	19
6	8	9	15	19	15
9	6	8	16	17	13
7	8	12	15	14	14
5	5	6	13	9	11
4	7	3	10	14	12
7	7	8	11	13	13
3	8	11	17	11	11

Managerial Report

1. Use descriptive statistics to summarize the data from the two studies. What are your preliminary observations about the depression scores?
2. Use analysis of variance on both data sets. State the hypotheses being tested in each case. What are your conclusions?
3. Use inferences about individual treatment means where appropriate. What are your conclusions?
4. Discuss extensions of this study or other analyses that you feel might be helpful.

Case Problem 3 Compensation for ID Professionals

For the preceding 10 years *Industrial Distribution* tracked compensation of industrial distribution (ID) professionals. Results for the 358 respondents in the 1997 Annual Salary Survey showed that 27% of the respondents work for companies with sales over $40 million, with the typical ID professional working for a $12 million firm. Those who work for small to mid-sized companies (between $6 million and $20 million) report higher earnings than those in larger firms. The lowest paid employees work for firms with sales of less than $1 million. The typical outside salesperson made $50,000 in 1996, and the typical inside salesperson earned just $30,000 (*Industrial Distribution*, November 1997). Suppose that a local chapter of ID professionals in the greater San Francisco area conducted a survey of its membership to study the relationship, if any, between the years of experience and salary for individuals employed in outside and inside sales positions. On the survey, respondents were asked to specify one of three levels of years of experience: low (1–10 years), medium (11–20 years), and high (21 or more years). A portion of the data obtained follows. The complete data set, consisting of 120 observations, is available on the CD accompanying the text in the file named IDSalary.

IDSalary

Observation	Salary $	Position	Experience
1	28938	Inside	Medium
2	27694	Inside	Medium
3	45515	Outside	Low
4	27031	Inside	Medium
5	37283	Outside	Low
6	32718	Inside	Low
7	54081	Outside	High
8	23621	Inside	Low
9	47835	Outside	High
10	29768	Inside	Medium
.	.	.	.
.	.	.	.
.	.	.	.
115	33080	Inside	High
116	53702	Outside	Medium
117	58131	Outside	Medium
118	32788	Inside	High
119	28070	Inside	Medium
120	35259	Outside	Low

Managerial Report

1. Use descriptive statistics to summarize the data.
2. Develop a 95% confidence interval estimate of the mean annual salary for all salespersons, regardless of years of experience and type of position.
3. Develop a 95% confidence interval estimate of the mean salary for outside salespersons. Compare your results with the national value reported by *Industrial Distribution*.
4. Develop a 95% confidence interval estimate of the mean salary for inside salespersons. Compare your results with the national value reported by *Industrial Distribution*.
5. Ignoring the years of experience, develop a 95% confidence interval estimate of the mean difference between the annual salary for outside salespersons and the mean annual salary for inside salespersons. What is your conclusion?

6. Use analysis of variance to test for any significant differences due to position. Use a .05 level of significance, and for now, ignore the effect of years of experience.

7. Use analysis of variance to test for any significant differences due to years of experience. Use a .05 level of significance, and for now, ignore the effect of position.

8. At the .05 level of significance test for any significant differences due to position, years of experience, and interaction. Use inferences about individual treatment means where appropriate.

Appendix 10.1 Inferences About Two Populations Using Minitab

We describe the use of Minitab to develop interval estimates and conduct hypothesis tests about the difference between two population means and the difference between two population proportions. Minitab provides both interval estimation and hypothesis testing results within the same module. Thus, the Minitab procedure is the same for both types of inferences. In the examples that follow, we will demonstrate interval estimation and hypothesis testing for the same two samples. We note that Minitab does not provide a routine for inferences about the difference between two population means when the population standard deviations σ_1 and σ_2 are known.

Difference Between Two Population Means: σ_1 and σ_2 Unknown

CheckAcct

We will use the data for the checking account balances example presented in Section 10.2. The checking account balances at the Cherry Grove branch are in column C1, and the checking account balances at the Beechmont branch are in column C2. In this example, we will use the Minitab 2-Sample *t* procedure to provide a 95% confidence interval estimate of the difference between population means for the checking account balances at the two branch banks. The output of the procedure also provides the *p*-value for the hypothesis test: $H_0: \mu_1 - \mu_2 = 0$ versus $H_a: \mu_1 - \mu_2 \neq 0$. The following steps are necessary to execute the procedure:

Step 1. Select the **Stat** menu
Step 2. Choose **Basic Statistics**
Step 3. Choose **2-Sample t**
Step 4. When the 2-Sample t (Test and Confidence Interval) dialog box appears:
    Select **Samples in different columns**
    Enter C1 in the **First** box
    Enter C2 in the **Second** box
    Select **Options**
Step 5. When the 2-Sample t - Options dialog box appears:
    Enter 95 in the **Confidence level** box
    Enter 0 in the **Test difference** box
    Enter not equal in the **Alternative** box
    Click **OK**
Step 6. Click **OK**

The 95% confidence interval estimate is $37 to $193 as described in Section 10.2. The *p*-value = .005 shows the null hypothesis of equal population means can be rejected at the $\alpha = .01$ level of significance. In other applications, step 5 may be modified to provide different confidence levels, different hypothesized values, and different forms of the hypotheses.

Difference Between Two Population Means with Matched Samples

Matched

We use the data on production times in Table 10.2 to illustrate the matched sample procedure. The completion times for method 1 are entered into column C1 and the completion times for method 2 are entered into column C2. The Minitab steps for a matched sample are as follows:

> **Step 1.** Select the **Stat** menu
> **Step 2.** Choose **Basic Statistics**
> **Step 3.** Choose **Paired t**
> **Step 4.** When the Paired t (Test and Confidence Interval) dialog box appears:
> > Select **Samples in columns**
> > Enter C1 in the **First sample** box
> > Enter C2 in the **Second sample** box
> > Select **Options**
> **Step 5.** When the Paired t - Options dialog box appears:
> > Enter 95 in the **Confidence level**
> > Enter 0 in the **Test mean** box
> > Enter not equal in the **Alternative** box
> > Click **OK**
> **Step 6.** Click **OK**

Step 5 may be modified to provide different confidence levels, different hypothesized values, and different forms of the hypotheses.

Appendix 10.2   # Inferences About Two Populations Using Excel

We describe the use of Excel to conduct hypothesis tests about the difference between two population means.* We begin with inferences about the difference between the means of two populations when the population standard deviations σ_1 and σ_2 are known.

Difference Between Two Population Means: σ_1 and σ_2 Known

ExamScores

We will use the examination scores for the two training centers discussed in Section 10.1. The label Center A is in cell A1 and the label Center B is in cell B1. The examination scores for center A are in cells A2:A31, and examination scores for center B are in cells B2:B41. The population standard deviations are assumed known with $\sigma_1 = 10$ and $\sigma_2 = 10$. The Excel routine will request the input of variances, which are $\sigma_1^2 = 100$ and $\sigma_2^2 = 100$. The following steps can be used to conduct a hypothesis test about the difference between the two population means.

> **Step 1.** Select the **Tools** menu
> **Step 2.** Choose **Data Analysis**
> **Step 3.** When the Data Analysis dialog box appears:
> > Choose **z-Test: Two Sample for Means**
> > Click **OK**

---

*Excel's data analysis tools provide hypothesis testing procedures for the difference between two population means. However, there is no Excel routine for interval estimation of the difference between two population means.

Step 4. When the z-Test: Two Sample for Means dialog box appears:
Enter A1:A31 in the **Variable 1 Range** box
Enter B1:B41 in the **Variable 2 Range** box
Enter 0 in the **Hypothesized Mean Difference** box
Enter 100 in the **Variable 1 Variance** box
Enter 100 in the **Variable 2 Variance** box
Select **Labels**
Enter .05 in the **Alpha** box
Select **Output Range** and enter C1 in the box
Click **OK**

Difference Between Two Population Means: σ_1 and σ_2 Unknown

CD file

SoftwareTest

We use the data for the software testing study in Table 10.1. The data are already entered into an Excel worksheet with the label Current in cell A1 and the label New in cell B1. The completion times for the current technology are in cells A2:A13, and the completion times for the new software are in cells B2:B13. The following steps can be used to conduct a hypothesis test about the difference between two population means with σ_1 and σ_2 unknown.

Step 1. Select the **Tools** menu
Step 2. Choose **Data Analysis**
Step 3. When the Data Analysis dialog box appears:
Choose **t-Test: Two Sample Assuming Unequal Variances**
Click **OK**
Step 4. When the t-Test: Two Sample Assuming Unequal Variances dialog box appears:
Enter A1:A13 in the **Variable 1 Range** box
Enter B1:B13 in the **Variable 2 Range** box
Enter 0 in the **Hypothesized Mean Difference** box
Select **Labels**
Enter .05 in the **Alpha** box
Select **Output Range** and enter C1 in the box
Click **OK**

Difference Between Two Population Means with Matched Samples

CD file

Matched

We use the matched sample completion times in Table 10.2 to illustrate. The data are entered into a worksheet with the label Method 1 in cell A1 and the label Method 2 in cell B1. The completion times for method 1 are in cells A2:A7 and the completion times for method 2 are in cells B2:B7. The Excel procedure uses the steps previously described for the *t*-Test except the user chooses the **t-Test: Paired Two Sample for Means** data analysis tool in step 3. The variable 1 range is A1:A7 and the variable 2 range is B1:B7.

Appendix 10.3   Analysis of Variance with Minitab

CD file

NCP

To illustrate how Minitab can be used to test for the equality of k population means, we show how to test whether the mean examination score is the same at each plant in the National Computer Products example introduced in Section 10.4. The examination score data are entered into the first three columns of a Minitab worksheet; column 1 is labeled Atlanta, column 2 is labeled Dallas, and column 3 is labeled Seattle. The following steps produce the Minitab output in Figure 10.6.

Step 1. Select the **Stat** menu
Step 2. Choose **ANOVA**
Step 3. Choose **One-way (Unstacked)**
Step 4. When the One-way Analysis of Variance dialog box appears:
Enter C1-C3 in the **Responses (in separate columns)** box
Click **OK**

Appendix 10.4   Analysis of Variance with Excel

NCP

To illustrate how Excel can be used to test for the equality of k population means for both of these cases, we show how to test whether the mean examination score is the same at each plant in the National Computer Products example introduced in Section 10.4. The examination score data are entered into worksheet rows 2 to 7 of columns B, C, and D as shown in Figure 10.7; note that the cells in row 1 are labeled Atlanta, Dallas, and Seattle. The following steps are used to obtain the output shown in cells A9:G23; the ANOVA portion of this output corresponds to the ANOVA table shown in Table 10.5.

Step 1. Select the **Tools** menu
Step 2. Choose **Data Analysis**

FIGURE 10.7   EXCEL SOLUTION FOR THE NCP ANALYSIS OF VARIANCE EXAMPLE

	A	B	C	D	E	F	G	H
1	Observation	Atlanta	Dallas	Seattle				
2	1	85	71	59				
3	2	75	75	64				
4	3	82	73	62				
5	4	76	74	69				
6	5	71	69	75				
7	6	85	82	67				
8								
9	Anova: Single Factor							
10								
11	SUMMARY							
12	*Groups*	*Count*	*Sum*	*Average*	*Variance*			
13	Atlanta	6	474	79	34			
14	Dallas	6	444	74	20			
15	Seattle	6	396	66	32			
16								
17								
18	ANOVA							
19	*Source of Variation*	*SS*	*df*	*MS*	*F*	*P-value*	*F crit*	
20	Between Groups	516	2	258	9	0.0027	3.68	
21	Within Groups	430	15	28.6667				
22								
23	Total	946	17					
24								

Step 3. When the Data Analysis dialog box appears:

Choose **Anova: Single-Factor** from the list of Analysis Tools

Click **OK**

Step 4. When the Anova: Single-Factor dialog box appears:

Enter B1:D7 in the **Input Range** box

Select **Columns**

Select **Labels in First Row**

Select **Output Range** and enter A9 in the box

Click **OK**

CHAPTER 11

Comparisons Involving Proportions and a Test of Independence

STATISTICS *in* PRACTICE

UNITED WAY*
ROCHESTER, NEW YORK

United Way of Greater Rochester is a nonprofit organization dedicated to improving the quality of life for all people in the seven counties it serves by meeting the community's most important human care needs.

The annual United Way/Red Cross fund-raising campaign, conducted each spring, funds hundreds of programs offered by more than 200 service providers. These providers meet a wide variety of human needs—physical, mental, and social—and serve people of all ages, backgrounds, and economic means.

Because of enormous volunteer involvement, United Way of Greater Rochester is able to hold its operating costs at just eight cents of every dollar raised.

The United Way of Greater Rochester decided to conduct a survey to learn more about community perceptions of charities. Focus-group interviews were held with professional, service, and general worker groups to get preliminary information on perceptions. The information obtained was then used to help develop the questionnaire for the survey. The questionnaire was pretested, modified, and distributed to 440 individuals; 323 completed questionnaires were obtained.

A variety of descriptive statistics, including frequency distributions and crosstabulations, were provided from the data collected. An important part of the analysis involved the use of contingency tables and chi-square tests of independence. One use of such statistical tests was to determine whether perceptions of administrative expenses were independent of occupation.

The hypotheses for the test of independence were:

> H_0: Perception of United Way administrative expenses is independent of the occupation of the respondent.
>
> H_a: Perception of United Way administrative expenses is not independent of the occupation of the respondent.

Statistical surveys help United Way adjust its program to better meet the needs of the people it serves. © Tony Freeman/PhotoEdit.

Two questions in the survey provided the data for the statistical test. One question obtained data on perceptions of the percentage of funds going to administrative expenses (up to 10%, 11–20%, and 21% or more). The other question asked for the occupation of the respondent.

The chi-square test at a .05 level of significance led to rejection of the null hypothesis of independence and to the conclusion that perceptions of United Way's administrative expenses did vary by occupation. Actual administrative expenses were less than 9%, but 35% of the respondents perceived that administrative expenses were 21% or more. Hence, many had inaccurate perceptions of administrative costs. In this group, production-line, clerical, sales, and professional-technical employees had more inaccurate perceptions than other groups.

The community perceptions study helped United Way of Greater Rochester to develop adjustments to its program and fund-raising activities. In this chapter, you will learn how a statistical test of independence, such as that described here, is conducted.

*The authors are indebted to Dr. Philip R. Tyler, marketing consultant to the United Way, for providing this Statistics in Practice.

Many statistical applications call for a comparison of population proportions. In Section 11.1, we describe statistical inferences concerning differences in the proportions for two populations. Two samples are required, one from each population, and the statistical inference is based on the two sample proportions. The second section looks at a hypothesis test comparing the proportions of a single multinomial population with the proportions stated in a null hypothesis. One sample from the multinomial population is used, and the hypothesis test is based on comparing the sample proportions with those stated in the null hypothesis. In the last section of the chapter, we show how contingency tables can be used to test for the independence of two variables. One sample is used for the test of independence, but measures on two variables are required for each sampled element. Both Sections 11.2 and 11.3 rely on the use of a chi-square statistical test.

 # Inferences About the Difference Between Two Population Proportions

Letting p_1 denote the proportion for population 1 and p_2 denote the proportion for population 2, we consider inferences about the difference between the two population proportions: $p_1 - p_2$. To make an inference about this difference, we will select two independent random samples consisting of n_1 units from population 1 and n_2 units from population 2.

Interval Estimation of $p_1 - p_2$

In the following example, we show how to compute a margin of error and develop an interval estimate of the difference between two population proportions.

A tax preparation firm is interested in comparing the quality of work at two of its regional offices. By randomly selecting samples of tax returns prepared at each office and verifying the sample returns' accuracy, the firm will be able to estimate the proportion of erroneous returns prepared at each office. Of particular interest is the difference between these proportions.

p_1 = proportion of erroneous returns for population 1 (office 1)
p_2 = proportion of erroneous returns for population 2 (office 2)
$\bar{p}_1$ = sample proportion for a simple random sample from population 1
$\bar{p}_2$ = sample proportion for a simple random sample from population 2

The difference between the two population proportions is given by $p_1 - p_2$. The point estimator of $p_1 - p_2$ is as follows.

> **POINT ESTIMATOR OF THE DIFFERENCE BETWEEN TWO POPULATION PROPORTIONS**
>
> $$\bar{p}_1 - \bar{p}_2 \tag{11.1}$$

Thus, the point estimator of the difference between two population proportions is the difference between the sample proportions of two independent simple random samples.

As with other point estimators, the point estimator $\bar{p}_1 - \bar{p}_2$ has a sampling distribution that reflects the possible values of $\bar{p}_1 - \bar{p}_2$ if we repeatedly took two independent random samples. The mean of this sampling distribution is $p_1 - p_2$ and the standard error of $\bar{p}_1 - \bar{p}_2$ is as follows:

$$\sigma_{\bar{p}_1 - \bar{p}_2} = \sqrt{\frac{p_1(1 - p_1)}{n_1} + \frac{p_2(1 - p_2)}{n_2}} \tag{11.2}$$

If the sample sizes are large enough that n_1p_1, $n_1(1 - p_1)$, n_2p_2, and $n_2(1 - p_2)$ are all greater than or equal to 5, the sampling distribution of $\bar{p}_1 - \bar{p}_2$ can be approximated by a normal distribution.

As we showed previously, an interval estimate is given by a point estimate ± a margin of error. In the estimation of the difference between two population proportions, an interval estimate will take the following form:

$$\bar{p}_1 - \bar{p}_2 \pm \text{Margin of error}$$

With the sampling distribution of $\bar{p}_1 - \bar{p}_2$ approximated by a normal distribution, we would like to use $z_{\alpha/2}\sigma_{\bar{p}_1 - \bar{p}_2}$ as the margin of error. However, $\sigma_{\bar{p}_1 - \bar{p}_2}$ given by equation (11.2) cannot be used directly because the two population proportions, p_1 and p_2, are unknown. Using the sample proportion $\bar{p}_1$ to estimate p_1 and the sample proportion $\bar{p}_2$ to estimate p_2, the margin of error is as follows.

$$\text{Margin of error} = z_{\alpha/2}\sqrt{\frac{\bar{p}_1(1 - \bar{p}_1)}{n_1} + \frac{\bar{p}_2(1 - \bar{p}_2)}{n_2}} \tag{11.3}$$

The general form of an interval estimate of the difference between two population proportions is as follows.

INTERVAL ESTIMATE OF THE DIFFERENCE BETWEEN TWO POPULATION PROPORTIONS

$$\bar{p}_1 - \bar{p}_2 \pm z_{\alpha/2}\sqrt{\frac{\bar{p}_1(1 - \bar{p}_1)}{n_1} + \frac{\bar{p}_2(1 - \bar{p}_2)}{n_2}} \tag{11.4}$$

where $1 - \alpha$ is the confidence coefficient.

Returning to the tax preparation example, we find that independent simple random samples from the two offices provide the following information.

Office 1	Office 2
$n_1 = 250$	$n_2 = 300$
Number of returns with errors = 35	Number of returns with errors = 27

TaxPrep

The sample proportions for the two offices follow.

$$\bar{p}_1 = \frac{35}{250} = .14$$

$$\bar{p}_2 = \frac{27}{300} = .09$$

The point estimate of the difference between the proportions of erroneous tax returns for the two populations is $\bar{p}_1 - \bar{p}_2 = .14 - .09 = .05$. Thus, we estimate that office 1 has a .05, or 5%, greater error rate than office 2.

Expression (11.4) can now be used to provide a margin of error and interval estimate of the difference between the two population proportions. Using a 90% confidence interval with $z_{\alpha/2} = z_{.05} = 1.645$, we have

$$\bar{p}_1 - \bar{p}_2 \pm z_{\alpha/2} \sqrt{\frac{\bar{p}_1(1 - \bar{p}_1)}{n_1} + \frac{\bar{p}_2(1 - \bar{p}_2)}{n_2}}$$

$$.14 - .09 \pm 1.645 \sqrt{\frac{.14(1 - .14)}{250} + \frac{.09(1 - .09)}{300}}$$

$$.05 \pm .045$$

Thus, the margin of error is .045, and the 90% confidence interval is .005 to .095.

Hypothesis Tests About $p_1 - p_2$

Let us now consider hypothesis tests about the difference between the proportions of two populations. We focus on tests involving no difference between the two population proportions. In this case, the three forms for a hypothesis test are as follows:

All hypotheses considered use 0 as the difference of interest.

$$\begin{array}{lll} H_0: p_1 - p_2 \geq 0 & H_0: p_1 - p_2 \leq 0 & H_0: p_1 - p_2 = 0 \\ H_a: p_1 - p_2 < 0 & H_a: p_1 - p_2 > 0 & H_a: p_1 - p_2 \neq 0 \end{array}$$

When we assume H_0 is true as an equality, we have $p_1 - p_2 = 0$, which is the same as saying that the population proportions are equal, $p_1 = p_2$.

We will base the test statistic on the sampling distribution of the point estimator $\bar{p}_1 - \bar{p}_2$. In equation (11.2), we showed that the standard error of $\bar{p}_1 - \bar{p}_2$ is given by

$$\sigma_{\bar{p}_1 - \bar{p}_2} = \sqrt{\frac{p_1(1 - p_1)}{n_1} + \frac{p_2(1 - p_2)}{n_2}}$$

Under the assumption H_0 is true as an equality, the population proportions are equal and $p_1 = p_2 = p$. In this case, $\sigma_{\bar{p}_1 - \bar{p}_2}$ becomes

$$\sigma_{\bar{p}_1 - \bar{p}_2} = \sqrt{\frac{p(1 - p)}{n_1} + \frac{p(1 - p)}{n_2}} = \sqrt{p(1 - p)\left(\frac{1}{n_1} + \frac{1}{n_2}\right)} \qquad \textbf{(11.5)}$$

With p unknown, we pool, or combine, the point estimators from the two samples ($\bar{p}_1$ and $\bar{p}_2$) to obtain a single point estimator of p as follows:

$$\bar{p} = \frac{n_1\bar{p}_1 + n_2\bar{p}_2}{n_1 + n_2} \qquad \textbf{(11.6)}$$

This **pooled estimator** of p is a weighted average of $\bar{p}_1$ and $\bar{p}_2$.

Substituting $\bar{p}$ for p in equation (11.5), we obtain an estimate of the standard error of $\bar{p}_1 - \bar{p}_2$. This estimate of the standard error is used in the test statistic. The general form of the test statistic for hypothesis tests about the difference between two population proportions is the point estimator divided by the estimate of $\sigma_{\bar{p}_1 - \bar{p}_2}$.

TEST STATISTIC FOR HYPOTHESIS TESTS ABOUT $p_1 - p_2$

$$z = \frac{(\bar{p}_1 - \bar{p}_2)}{\sqrt{\bar{p}(1 - \bar{p})\left(\frac{1}{n_1} + \frac{1}{n_2}\right)}} \qquad \textbf{(11.7)}$$

This test statistic applies to large sample situations where n_1p_1, $n_1(1 - p_1)$, n_2p_2, and $n_2(1 - p_2)$ are all greater than or equal to 5.

Let us return to the tax preparation firm example and assume that the firm wants to use a hypothesis test to determine whether the error proportions differ between the two offices. A two-tailed test is required. The null and alternative hypotheses are as follows:

$$H_0: p_1 - p_2 = 0$$
$$H_a: p_1 - p_2 \neq 0$$

If H_0 is rejected, the firm can conclude that the error rates at the two offices differ. We will use $\alpha = .10$ as the level of significance.

The sample data previously collected showed $\bar{p}_1 = .14$ for the $n_1 = 250$ returns sampled at office 1 and $\bar{p}_2 = .09$ for the $n_2 = 300$ returns sampled at office 2. We continue by computing the pooled estimate of p.

$$\bar{p} = \frac{n_1\bar{p}_1 + n_2\bar{p}_2}{n_1 + n_2} = \frac{250(.14) + 300(.09)}{250 + 300} = .1127$$

Using this pooled estimate and the difference between the sample proportions, the value of the test statistic is as follows.

$$z = \frac{(\bar{p}_1 - \bar{p}_2)}{\sqrt{\bar{p}(1 - \bar{p})\left(\dfrac{1}{n_1} + \dfrac{1}{n_2}\right)}} = \frac{(.14 - .09)}{\sqrt{.1127(1 - .1127)\left(\dfrac{1}{250} + \dfrac{1}{300}\right)}} = 1.85$$

In computing the p-value for this two-tailed test, we first note that $z = 1.85$ is in the upper tail of the standard normal distribution. Using $z = 1.85$ and the standard normal distribution table, we find the area in the upper tail is $.5000 - .4678 = .0322$. Doubling this area for a two-tailed test, we find the p-value $= 2(.0322) = .0644$. With the p-value less than $\alpha = .10$, H_0 is rejected at the .10 level of significance. The firm can conclude that the error rates differ between the two offices. This hypothesis testing conclusion is consistent with the earlier interval estimation results that showed the interval estimate of the difference between the population error rates at the two offices to be .005 to .095, with office 1 having the higher error rate.

Exercises

Methods

1. Consider the following results for independent samples taken from two populations.

Sample 1	Sample 2
$n_1 = 400$	$n_2 = 300$
$\bar{p}_1 = .48$	$\bar{p}_2 = .36$

a. What is the point estimate of the difference between the two population proportions?
b. Develop a 90% confidence interval for the difference between the two population proportions.
c. Develop a 95% confidence interval for the difference between the two population proportions.

2. Consider the hypothesis test

$$H_0: p_1 - p_2 \leq 0$$
$$H_a: p_1 - p_2 > 0$$

The following results are for independent samples taken from the two populations.

Sample 1	Sample 2
$n_1 = 200$	$n_2 = 300$
$\bar{p}_1 = .22$	$\bar{p}_2 = .16$

a. What is the *p*-value?
b. With $\alpha = .05$, what is your hypothesis testing conclusion?

Applications

3. A *Business Week*/Harris survey asked senior executives at large corporations their opinions about the economic outlook for the future. One question was "Do you think that there will be an increase in the number of full-time employees at your company over the next 12 months?" In the current survey, 220 of 400 executives answered yes, while in a previous year survey, 192 of 400 executives had answered yes. Provide a 95% confidence interval estimate for the difference between the proportions at the two points in time. What is your interpretation of the interval estimate?

4. In recent years, the number of people who use the Internet to obtain political news has grown. Often the political Web sites ask Internet users to register their opinions by participating in online surveys. Pew Research Center conducted a survey of its own to learn about the participation of Republicans and Democrats in online surveys (Associated Press, January 6, 2003). The following sample data apply.

Political Party	Sample Size	Participate in Online Surveys
Republican	250	115
Democrat	350	98

a. Compute the point estimate of the proportion of Republicans who indicate they would participate in online surveys. Compute the point estimate for the Democrats.
b. What is the point estimate of the difference between the two population proportions?
c. At 95% confidence, what is the margin of error?
d. Representatives of the scientific polling industry claim that the profusion of online surveys can confuse people about actual public opinion. Do you agree with this statement? Use the 95% confidence interval estimate of the difference between the Republican and Democrat population proportions to help justify your answer.

5. Slot machines are the favorite game at casinos throughout the United States (*Harrah's Survey 2002: Profile of the American Gamble*). The following sample data show the number of women and number of men who selected slot machines as their favorite game.

	Women	Men
Sample Size	320	250
Favorite Game–Slots	256	165

    a.   What is the point estimate of the proportion of women who say slots is their favorite game?

    b.   What is the point estimate of the proportion of men who say slots is their favorite game?

    c.   Provide a 95% confidence interval estimate of the difference between the proportion of women and proportion of men who say slots is their favorite game.

6. The Bureau of Transportation tracks the flight arrival performances of the 10 biggest airlines in the United States (*The Wall Street Journal,* March 4, 2003). Flights that arrive within 15 minutes of schedule are considered on time. Using sample data consistent with Bureau of Transportation statistics reported in January 2001 and January 2002, consider the following:

> January 2001   A sample of 924 flights showed 742 on time.
> January 2002   A sample of 841 flights showed 714 on time.

    a.   What is the point estimate of on-time flights in January 2001?

    b.   What is the point estimate of on-time flights in January 2002?

    c.   Let p_1 denote the population proportion of on-time flights in January 2001 and p_2 denote the population proportion of on-time flights in January 2002. State the hypotheses that could be tested to determine whether the major airlines improved on-time flight performance during the one-year period.

    d.   What is the p-value? At $\alpha = .05$, what is your conclusion?

7. In a test of the quality of two television commercials, each commercial was shown in a separate test area six times over a one-week period. The following week a telephone survey was conducted to identify individuals who had seen the commercials. Those individuals were asked to state the primary message in the commercials. The following results were recorded.

	Commercial A	Commercial B
Number Who Saw Commercial	150	200
Number Who Recalled Message	63	60

    a.   Use $\alpha = .05$ and test the hypothesis that there is no difference in the recall proportions for the two commercials.

    b.   Compute a 95% confidence interval for the difference between the recall proportions for the two populations.

8. During the 2003 Super Bowl, Miller Lite Beer's commercial referred to as "The Miller Lite Girls" ranked among the top three most effective advertisements aired during the Super Bowl (*USA Today,* December 29, 2003). The survey of advertising effectiveness, conducted by *USA Today*'s Ad Track poll, reported separate samples by respondent age group to learn about how the Super Bowl advertisement appealed to different age groups. The following sample data apply to the "The Miller Lite Girls" commercial.

Age Group	Sample Size	Liked the Ad a Lot
Under 30	100	49
30 to 49	150	54

    a.   Formulate a hypothesis test that can be used to determine whether there is a difference between the population proportions for the two age groups.

    b.   What is the point estimate of the difference between the two population proportions?

    c. Conduct the hypothesis test and report the *p*-value. At $\alpha = .05$, what is your conclusion?

    d. Discuss the appeal of the advertisements to the younger and the older age groups. Would the Miller Lite organization find the results of the *USA Today* Ad Track poll encouraging? Explain.

9. A 2003 *New York Times*/CBS News poll sampled 523 adults who were planning a vacation during the next six months and found that 141 were expecting to travel by airplane (*New York Times News Service,* March 2, 2003). A similar survey question in a May 1993 *New York Times*/CBS News poll found that of 477 adults who were planning a vacation in the next six months, 81 were expecting to travel by airplane.

    a. State the hypotheses that can be used to determine whether a significant change occurred in the population proportion planning to travel by airplane over the 10-year period.

    b. What is the sample proportion expecting to travel by airplane in 2003? In 1993?

    c. Use $\alpha = .01$ and test for a significant difference. What is your conclusion?

    d. Discuss reasons that might provide an explanation for this conclusion.

10. *Yahoo! Internet Life* sponsored surveys in several metropolitan areas to estimate the proportion of adults using the Internet at work (*USA Today,* May 7, 2000). Results showed 40% of Washington, D.C., adults use the Internet at work, while 32% of San Francisco adults use the Internet at work. If the sample sizes are 240 and 250, respectively, do the sample results indicate that the population proportion of adults using the Internet at work in Washington, D.C., is greater than the population proportion in San Francisco? What is the *p*-value? Using $\alpha = .05$, what is the conclusion?

11.2 Hypothesis Test for Proportions of a Multinomial Population

In this section, we consider hypothesis tests concerning the proportion of elements in a population belonging to each of several classes or categories. In contrast to the preceding section, we deal with a single population: a **multinomial population.** The parameters of the multinomial population are the proportion of elements belonging to each category; the hypothesis tests we describe concern the value of those parameters. The multinomial probability distribution can be thought of as an extension of the binomial distribution to the case of three or more categories of outcomes. On each trial of a multinomial experiment, one and only one of the outcomes occurs. Each trial of the experiment is assumed independent, and the probabilities of the outcomes stay the same for each trial.

The assumptions for the multinomial experiment parallel those for the binomial experiment with the exception that the multinomial experiment has three or more outcomes per trial.

    As an example, consider the market share study being conducted by Scott Marketing Research. Over the past year market shares stabilized at 30% for company A, 50% for company B, and 20% for company C. Recently company C developed a "new and improved" product to replace its current entry in the market. Company C retained Scott Marketing Research to determine whether the new product will alter market shares.

    In this case, the population of interest is a multinomial population; each customer is classified as buying from company A, company B, or company C. Thus, we have a multinomial population with three outcomes. Let us use the following notation for the proportions.

$$p_A = \text{market share for company A}$$
$$p_B = \text{market share for company B}$$
$$p_C = \text{market share for company C}$$

    Scott Marketing Research will conduct a sample survey and compute the proportion preferring each company's product. A hypothesis test will then be conducted to see whether the new product caused a change in market shares. Assuming that company C's new product will not alter the market shares, the null and alternative hypotheses are stated as follows.

$$H_0: p_A = .30, p_B = .50, \text{ and } p_C = .20$$

H_a: The population proportions are not
$$p_A = .30, p_B = .50, \text{ and } p_C = .20$$

If the sample results lead to the rejection of H_0, Scott Marketing Research will have evidence that the introduction of the new product affects market shares.

Let us assume that the market research firm has used a consumer panel of 200 customers for the study. Each individual was asked to specify a purchase preference among the three alternatives: company A's product, company B's product, and company C's new product. The 200 responses are summarized here.

The consumer panel of 200 customers in which each individual is asked to select one of three alternatives is equivalent to a multinomial experiment consisting of 200 trials.

	Observed Frequency	
Company A's Product	**Company B's Product**	**Company C's New Product**
48	98	54

We now can perform a **goodness of fit test** that will determine whether the sample of 200 customer purchase preferences is consistent with the null hypothesis. The goodness of fit test is based on a comparison of the sample of *observed* results with the *expected* results under the assumption that the null hypothesis is true. Hence, the next step is to compute expected purchase preferences for the 200 customers under the assumption that $p_A = .30$, $p_B = .50$, and $p_C = .20$. Doing so provides the expected results.

	Expected Frequency	
Company A's Product	**Company B's Product**	**Company C's New Product**
$200(.30) = 60$	$200(.50) = 100$	$200(.20) = 40$

Thus, we see that the expected frequency for each category is found by multiplying the sample size of 200 by the hypothesized proportion for the category.

The goodness of fit test now focuses on the differences between the observed frequencies and the expected frequencies. Large differences between observed and expected frequencies cast doubt on the assumption that the hypothesized proportions or market shares are correct. Whether the differences between the observed and expected frequencies are "large" or "small" is a question answered with the aid of the following test statistic.

TEST STATISTIC FOR GOODNESS OF FIT

$$\chi^2 = \sum_{i=1}^{k} \frac{(f_i - e_i)^2}{e_i} \tag{11.8}$$

where

f_i = observed frequency for category i

e_i = expected frequency for category i

k = the number of categories

Note: The test statistic has a chi-square distribution with $k - 1$ degrees of freedom provided that the expected frequencies are 5 *or more* for all categories.

Let us continue with the Scott Market Research example and use the sample data to test the hypothesis that the multinomial population retains the proportions $p_A = .30$, $p_B = .50$, and $p_C = .20$. We will use an $\alpha = .05$ level of significance. We proceed by using the observed and expected frequencies to compute the value of the test statistic. With the expected frequencies all 5 or more, the computation of the chi-square test statistic is shown in Table 11.1. Thus, we have $\chi^2 = 7.34$.

The test for goodness of fit is always a one-tailed test with the rejection occurring in the upper tail of the chi-square distribution.

We will reject the null hypothesis if the differences between the observed and expected frequencies are *large*. Large differences between the observed and expected frequencies will result in a large value for the test statistic. Thus the test of goodness of fit will always be an upper tail test. We use the upper tail area of a chi-square distribution and the *p*-value approach to determine whether the null hypothesis can be rejected. With $k - 1 = 3 - 1 = 2$ degrees of freedom, Table 11.2 shows the following areas in the upper tail and their corresponding chi-square (χ^2) values:

Area in Upper Tail	.10	.05	.025	.01
χ^2 **Value (2 df)**	4.605	5.991	7.378	9.210

$\chi^2 = 7.34$

The test statistic $\chi^2 = 7.34$ is between 5.991 and 7.378. Thus, the corresponding upper tail area or *p*-value must be between .05 and .025. With *p*-value $\leq \alpha = .05$, we reject H_0 and conclude that the introduction of the new product by company C will alter the current market share structure. Minitab or Excel can be used to show $\chi^2 = 7.34$ provides a *p*-value $= .0255$.

TABLE 11.1   COMPUTATION OF THE CHI-SQUARE TEST STATISTIC FOR THE SCOTT MARKETING RESEARCH MARKET SHARE STUDY

Category	Hypothesized Proportion	Observed Frequency (f_i)	Expected Frequency (e_i)	Difference $(f_i - e_i)$	Squared Difference $(f_i - e_i)^2$	Squared Difference Divided by Expected Frequency $(f_i - e_i)^2/e_i$
Company A	.30	48	60	−12	144	2.40
Company B	.50	98	100	−2	4	0.04
Company C	.20	54	40	14	196	4.90
Total		200				$\chi^2 = 7.34$

TABLE 11.2   SELECTED VALUES FROM THE CHI-SQUARE DISTRIBUTION TABLE*

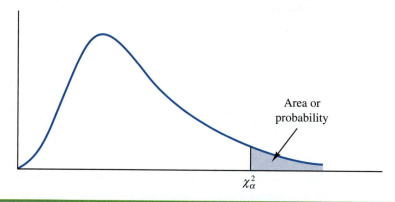

Degrees of Freedom	.99	.975	.95	.90	.10	.05	.025	.01
				Area in Upper Tail				
1	.000	.001	.004	.016	2.706	3.841	5.024	6.635
2	.020	.051	.103	.211	4.605	5.991	7.378	9.210
3	.115	.216	.352	.584	6.251	7.815	9.348	11.345
4	.297	.484	.711	1.064	7.779	9.488	11.143	13.277
5	.554	.831	1.145	1.610	9.236	11.070	12.832	15.086
6	.872	1.237	1.635	2.204	10.645	12.592	14.449	16.812
7	1.239	1.690	2.167	2.833	12.017	14.067	16.013	18.475
8	1.647	2.180	2.733	3.490	13.362	15.507	17.535	20.090
9	2.088	2.700	3.325	4.168	14.684	16.919	19.023	21.666
10	2.558	3.247	3.940	4.865	15.987	18.307	20.483	23.209
11	3.053	3.816	4.575	5.578	17.275	19.675	21.920	24.725
12	3.571	4.404	5.226	6.304	18.549	21.026	23.337	26.217
13	4.107	5.009	5.892	7.041	19.812	22.362	24.736	27.688
14	4.660	5.629	6.571	7.790	21.064	23.685	26.119	29.141
15	5.229	6.262	7.261	8.547	22.307	24.996	27.488	30.578
16	5.812	6.908	7.962	9.312	23.542	26.296	28.845	32.000
17	6.408	7.564	8.672	10.085	24.769	27.587	30.191	33.409
18	7.015	8.231	9.390	10.865	25.989	28.869	31.526	34.805
19	7.633	8.907	10.117	11.651	27.204	30.144	32.852	36.191
20	8.260	9.591	10.851	12.443	28.412	31.410	34.170	37.566
21	8.897	10.283	11.591	13.240	29.615	32.671	35.479	38.932
22	9.542	10.982	12.338	14.041	30.813	33.924	36.781	40.289
23	10.196	11.689	13.091	14.848	32.007	35.172	38.076	41.638
24	10.856	12.401	13.848	15.659	33.196	36.415	39.364	42.980
25	11.524	13.120	14.611	16.473	34.382	37.652	40.646	44.314
26	12.198	13.844	15.379	17.292	35.563	38.885	41.923	45.642
27	12.878	14.573	16.151	18.114	36.741	40.113	43.195	46.963
28	13.565	15.308	16.928	18.939	37.916	41.337	44.461	48.278
29	14.256	16.047	17.708	19.768	39.087	42.557	45.722	49.588
30	14.953	16.791	18.493	20.599	40.256	43.773	46.979	50.892
40	22.164	24.433	26.509	29.051	51.805	55.758	59.342	63.691
60	37.485	40.482	43.188	46.459	74.397	79.082	83.298	88.379
80	53.540	57.153	60.391	64.278	96.578	101.879	106.629	112.329
100	70.065	74.222	77.929	82.358	118.498	124.342	129.561	135.807

*Note: A more extensive table is provided as Table 3 of Appendix B.

Instead of using the *p*-value, we could use the critical value approach to draw the same conclusion. With $\alpha = .05$ and 2 degrees of freedom, the critical value for the test statistic is $\chi^2_{.05} = 5.991$. The upper tail rejection rule becomes

$$\text{Reject } H_0 \text{ if } \chi^2 \geq 5.991$$

With $7.34 > 5.991$, we reject H_0. The *p*-value approach and critical value approach provide the same hypothesis testing conclusion.

Although no further conclusions can be made as a result of the test, we can compare the observed and expected frequencies informally to obtain an idea of how the market share structure may change. Considering company C, we find that the observed frequency of 54 is larger than the expected frequency of 40. Because the expected frequency was based on current market shares, the larger observed frequency suggests that the new product will have a positive effect on company C's market share. Comparisons of the observed and expected frequencies for the other two companies indicate that company C's gain in market share will hurt company A more than company B.

Let us summarize the general steps that can be used to conduct a goodness of fit test for a hypothesized multinomial population distribution.

MULTINOMIAL DISTRIBUTION GOODNESS OF FIT TEST: A SUMMARY

1. State the null and alternative hypotheses.

   H_0: The population follows a multinomial distribution with specified probabilities for each of the *k* categories

   H_a: The population does not follow a multinomial distribution with the specified probabilities for each of the *k* categories

2. Select a random sample and record the observed frequencies f_i for each category.
3. Assume the null hypothesis is true and determine the expected frequency e_i in each category by multiplying the category probability by the sample size.
4. Compute the value of the test statistic.

$$\chi^2 = \sum_{i=1}^{k} \frac{(f_i - e_i)^2}{e_i}$$

5. Rejection rule:

p-value approach:	Reject H_0 if *p*-value $\leq \alpha$
Critical value approach:	Reject H_0 if $\chi^2 \geq \chi^2_\alpha$

   where α is the level of significance for the test and there are $k - 1$ degrees of freedom.

Exercises

Methods

11. Test the following hypotheses by using the χ^2 goodness of fit test.

$$H_0: p_A = .40, p_B = .40, \text{ and } p_C = .20$$
$$H_a: \text{The population proportions are not}$$
$$p_A = .40, p_B = .40, \text{ and } p_C = .20$$

A sample of size 200 yielded 60 in category A, 120 in category B, and 20 in category C. Use $\alpha = .01$ and test to see whether the proportions are as stated in H_0.

  a.   Use the p-value approach.

  b.   Repeat the test using the critical value approach.

12.   Suppose we have a multinomial population with four categories: A, B, C, and D. The null hypothesis is that the proportion of items is the same in every category. The null hypothesis is

$$H_0: p_A = p_B = p_C = p_D = .25$$

A sample of size 300 yielded the following results.

A: 85   B: 95   C: 50   D: 70

Use $\alpha = .05$ to determine whether H_0 should be rejected. What is the p-value?

Applications

13.   During the first 13 weeks of the television season, the Saturday evening 8:00 P.M. to 9:00 P.M. audience proportions were recorded as ABC 29%, CBS 28%, NBC 25%, and independents 18%. A sample of 300 homes two weeks after a Saturday night schedule revision yielded the following viewing audience data: ABC 95 homes, CBS 70 homes, NBC 89 homes, and independents 46 homes. Test with $\alpha = .05$ to determine whether the viewing audience proportions changed.

14.   M&M/MARS, makers of M&M® Chocolate Candies, conducted a national poll in which consumers indicated their preference for colors. In the brochure "Colors," made available by M&M/MARS Consumer Affairs, the traditional distribution of colors for the plain candies is as follows:

Brown	Yellow	Red	Orange	Green	Blue
30%	20%	20%	10%	10%	10%

In a follow-up study, 1-pound bags were used to determine whether the reported percentages were valid. The following results were obtained for a sample of 506 plain candies.

Brown	Yellow	Red	Orange	Green	Blue
177	135	79	41	36	38

Use $\alpha = .05$ to determine whether these data support the percentages reported by the company.

15.   Where do women most often buy casual clothing? Data from the U.S. Shopper Database provided the following percentages for women shopping at each of the various outlets (*The Wall Street Journal*, January 28, 2004).

Outlet	Percentage	Outlet	Percentage
Wal-Mart	24%	Kohl's	8%
Traditional department stores	11%	Mail order	12%
J.C. Penney	8%	Other	37%

The other category included outlets such as Target, Kmart, and Sears as well as numerous smaller specialty outlets. No individual outlet in this group accounted for more than 5% of the women shoppers. A recent survey using a sample of 140 women shoppers in Atlanta, Georgia, found 42 Wal-Mart, 20 traditional department store, 8 J.C. Penney, 10 Kohl's, 21 mail order, and 39 other outlet shoppers. Does this sample suggest that women shoppers in Atlanta differ from the shopping preferences expressed in the U.S. Shopper Database? What is the p-value? Use $\alpha = .05$. What is your conclusion?

16. The American Bankers Association collects data on the use of credit cards, debit cards, personal checks, and cash when consumers pay for in-store purchases (*The Wall Street Journal,* December 16, 2003). In 1999, the following usages were reported.

In-Store Purchase	Percentage
Credit card	22%
Debit card	21%
Personal check	18%
Cash	39%

A sample taken in 2003 found that for 220 in-stores purchases, 46 used credit card, 67 used debit card, 33 used personal check, and 74 used cash.

a. At $\alpha = .01$, can we conclude that a change occurred in how customers paid for in-store purchases over the four-year period from 1999 to 2003? What is the p-value?

b. Compute the percentage of use for each method of payment using the 2003 sample data. What appears to have been the major change or changes over the four-year period?

c. In 2003, what percentage of payments was made using plastic (credit card or debit card)?

17. *The Wall Street Journal's* Shareholder Scoreboard tracks the performance of 1000 major U.S. companies (*The Wall Street Journal,* March 10, 2003). The performance of each company is rated based on the annual total return, including stock price changes and the reinvestment of dividends. Ratings are assigned by dividing all 1000 companies into five groups from A (top 20%), B (next 20%), to E (bottom 20%). Shown here are the one-year ratings for a sample of 60 of the largest companies. Do the largest companies differ in performance from the performance of the 1000 companies in the Shareholder Scoreboard? Use $\alpha = .05$.

A	B	C	D	E
5	8	15	20	12

18. How well do airline companies serve their customers? A study showed the following customer ratings: 3% excellent, 28% good, 45% fair, and 24% poor (*Business Week,* September 11, 2000). In a follow-up study of service by telephone companies, assume that a sample of 400 adults found the following customer ratings: 24 excellent, 124 good, 172 fair, and 80 poor. Is the distribution of the customer ratings for telephone companies different from the distribution of customer ratings for airline companies? Test with $\alpha = .01$. What is your conclusion?

11.3 Test of Independence

Another important application of the chi-square distribution involves using sample data to test for the independence of two variables. Let us illustrate the test of independence by considering the study conducted by the Alber's Brewery of Tucson, Arizona. Alber's

TABLE 11.3 CONTINGENCY TABLE FOR BEER PREFERENCE AND GENDER OF BEER DRINKER

		Beer Preference		
		Light	**Regular**	**Dark**
Gender	**Male**	cell(1,1)	cell(1,2)	cell(1,3)
	Female	cell(2,1)	cell(2,2)	cell(2,3)

manufactures and distributes three types of beer: light, regular, and dark. In an analysis of the market segments for the three beers, the firm's market research group raised the question of whether preferences for the three beers differ among male and female beer drinkers. If beer preference is independent of the gender of the beer drinker, one advertising campaign will be initiated for all of Alber's beers. However, if beer preference depends on the gender of the beer drinker, the firm will tailor its promotions to different target markets.

A test of independence addresses the question of whether the beer preference (light, regular, or dark) is independent of the gender of the beer drinker (male, female). The hypotheses for this test of independence are:

H_0: Beer preference is independent of the gender of the beer drinker

H_a: Beer preference is not independent of the gender of the beer drinker

Table 11.3 can be used to describe the situation being studied. After identification of the population as all male and female beer drinkers, a sample can be selected and each individual asked to state his or her preference for the three Alber's beers. Every individual in the sample will be classified in one of the six cells in the table. For example, an individual may be a male preferring regular beer (cell (1,2)), a female preferring light beer (cell (2,1)), a female preferring dark beer (cell (2,3)), and so on. Because we have listed all possible combinations of beer preference and gender or, in other words, listed all possible contingencies, Table 11.3 is called a **contingency table**. The test of independence uses the contingency table format and for that reason is sometimes referred to as a *contingency table test*.

To test whether two variables are independent, one sample is selected and crosstabulation is used to summarize the data for the two variables simultaneously.

Suppose a simple random sample of 150 beer drinkers is selected. After tasting each beer, the individuals in the sample are asked to state their preference or first choice. The crosstabulation in Table 11.4 summarizes the responses for the study. As we see, the data for the test of independence are collected in terms of counts or frequencies for each cell or category. Of the 150 individuals in the sample, 20 were men who favored light beer, 40 were men who favored regular beer, 20 were men who favored dark beer, and so on.

The data in Table 11.4 are the observed frequencies for the six classes or categories. If we can determine the expected frequencies under the assumption of independence between

TABLE 11.4 SAMPLE RESULTS FOR BEER PREFERENCES OF MALE AND FEMALE BEER DRINKERS (OBSERVED FREQUENCIES)

		Beer Preference			
		Light	**Regular**	**Dark**	**Total**
Gender	**Male**	20	40	20	80
	Female	30	30	10	70
	Total	50	70	30	150

TABLE 11.5   EXPECTED FREQUENCIES IF BEER PREFERENCE IS INDEPENDENT
OF THE GENDER OF THE BEER DRINKER

		Beer Preference			
		Light	**Regular**	**Dark**	**Total**
Gender	**Male**	26.67	37.33	16.00	80
	Female	23.33	32.67	14.00	70
	Total	50.00	70.00	30.00	150

beer preference and gender of the beer drinker, we can use the chi-square distribution to determine whether there is a significant difference between observed and expected frequencies.

Expected frequencies for the cells of the contingency table are based on the following rationale. First we assume that the null hypothesis of independence between beer preference and gender of the beer drinker is true. Then we note that in the entire sample of 150 beer drinkers, a total of 50 prefer light beer, 70 prefer regular beer, and 30 prefer dark beer. In terms of fractions we conclude that $^{50}/_{150} = \frac{1}{3}$ of the beer drinkers prefer light beer, $^{70}/_{150} = ^{7}/_{15}$ prefer regular beer, and $^{30}/_{150} = \frac{1}{5}$ prefer dark beer. If the *independence* assumption is valid, we argue that these fractions must be applicable to both male and female beer drinkers. Thus, under the assumption of independence, we would expect the sample of 80 male beer drinkers to show that $(\frac{1}{3})80 = 26.67$ prefer light beer, $(^{7}/_{15})80 = 37.33$ prefer regular beer, and $(\frac{1}{5})80 = 16$ prefer dark beer. Application of the same fractions to the 70 female beer drinkers provides the expected frequencies shown in Table 11.5.

Let e_{ij} denote the expected frequency for the contingency table category in row i and column j. With this notation, let us reconsider the expected frequency calculation for males (row $i = 1$) who prefer regular beer (column $j = 2$); that is, expected frequency e_{12}. Following the preceding argument for the computation of expected frequencies, we can show that

$$e_{12} = (^{7}/_{15})80 = 37.33$$

This expression can be written slightly differently as

$$e_{12} = (^{7}/_{15})80 = (^{70}/_{150})80 = \frac{(80)(70)}{150} = 37.33$$

Note that 80 in the expression is the total number of males (row 1 total), 70 is the total number of individuals preferring regular beer (column 2 total), and 150 is the total sample size. Hence, we see that

$$e_{12} = \frac{(\text{Row 1 Total})(\text{Column 2 Total})}{\text{Sample Size}}$$

Generalization of the expression shows that the following formula provides the expected frequencies for a contingency table in the test of independence.

EXPECTED FREQUENCIES FOR CONTINGENCY TABLES UNDER THE
ASSUMPTION OF INDEPENDENCE

$$e_{ij} = \frac{(\text{Row } i \text{ Total})(\text{Column } j \text{ Total})}{\text{Sample Size}} \tag{11.9}$$

Using the formula for male beer drinkers who prefer dark beer, we find an expected frequency of $e_{13} = (80)(30)/150 = 16.00$, as shown in Table 11.5. Use equation (11.9) to verify the other expected frequencies shown in Table 11.5.

The test procedure for comparing the observed frequencies of Table 11.4 with the expected frequencies of Table 11.5 is similar to the goodness of fit calculations made in Section 11.2. Specifically, the χ^2 value based on the observed and expected frequencies is computed as follows.

TEST STATISTIC FOR INDEPENDENCE

$$\chi^2 = \sum_i \sum_j \frac{(f_{ij} - e_{ij})^2}{e_{ij}}$$

(11.10)

where

f_{ij} = observed frequency for contingency table category in row i and column j

e_{ij} = expected frequency for contingency table category in row i and column j based on the assumption of independence

Note: With n rows and m columns in the contingency table, the test statistic has a chi-square distribution with $(n - 1)(m - 1)$ degrees of freedom provided that the expected frequencies are five or more for all categories.

The double summation in equation (11.10) is used to indicate that the calculation must be made for all the cells in the contingency table.

By reviewing the expected frequencies in Table 11.5, we see that the expected frequencies are five or more for each category. We therefore proceed with the computation of the chi-square test statistic. The calculations necessary to compute the chi-square test statistic for determining whether beer preference is independent of the gender of the beer drinker are shown in Table 11.6. We see that the value of the test statistic is $\chi^2 = 6.12$.

The number of degrees of freedom for the appropriate chi-square distribution is computed by multiplying the number of rows minus 1 by the number of columns minus 1. With two rows and three columns, we have $(2 - 1)(3 - 1) = 2$ degrees of freedom. Just like the test for goodness of fit, the test for independence rejects H_0 if the differences between ob-

TABLE 11.6 COMPUTATION OF THE CHI-SQUARE TEST STATISTIC FOR DETERMINING WHETHER BEER PREFERENCE IS INDEPENDENT OF THE GENDER OF THE BEER DRINKER

Gender	Beer Preference	Observed Frequency (f_{ij})	Expected Frequency (e_{ij})	Difference ($f_{ij} - e_{ij}$)	Squared Difference ($f_{ij} - e_{ij}$)^2	Squared Difference Divided by Expected Frequency ($f_{ij} - e_{ij}$)$^2/e_{ij}$
Male	Light	20	26.67	−6.67	44.44	1.67
Male	Regular	40	37.33	2.67	7.11	0.19
Male	Dark	20	16.00	4.00	16.00	1.00
Female	Light	30	23.33	6.67	44.44	1.90
Female	Regular	30	32.67	−2.67	7.11	0.22
Female	Dark	10	14.00	−4.00	16.00	1.14
	Total	150				$\chi^2 = 6.12$

FIGURE 11.1   MINITAB OUTPUT FOR THE ALBER'S BREWERY TEST OF INDEPENDENCE

```
      Expected counts are printed below observed counts

                Light      Regular      Dark      Total
          1        20           40         20         80
                 26.67        37.33      16.00

          2        30           30         10         70
                 23.33        32.67      14.00

      Total        50           70         30        150

      DF = 2,  P-Value = 0.047
```

The test for independence is always a one-tailed test with the rejection region in the upper tail of the chi-square distribution.

served and expected frequencies provide a large value for the test statistic. Thus the test for independence is also an upper tail test. Using the chi-square table (Table 3 of Appendix B), we conclude that the upper tail area or *p*-value at $\chi^2 = 6.12$ is between .025 and .05. Excel shows *p*-value = .0468. At the .05 level of significance, *p*-value $\leq \alpha = .05$. We reject the null hypothesis of independence and conclude that beer preference is not independent of the gender of the beer drinker.

Computer software packages such as Minitab and Excel can simplify the computations for a test of independence and provide the *p*-value for the test. The steps used to obtain computer results for a test of independence are presented in Appendixes 11.2 and 11.3. The Minitab output for the Alber's Brewery test of independence is shown in Figure 11.1.

Although no further conclusions can be made as a result of the test, we can compare the observed and expected frequencies informally to obtain an idea about the dependence between beer preference and gender. Refer to Tables 11.4 and 11.5. We see that male beer drinkers have higher observed than expected frequencies for both regular and dark beers, whereas female beer drinkers have a higher observed than expected frequency only for light beer. These observations give us insight about the beer preference differences between male and female beer drinkers.

Let us summarize the steps in a contingency table test of independence.

TEST OF INDEPENDENCE: A SUMMARY

1. State the null and alternative hypotheses.

   H_0: The column variable is independent of the row variable
   H_a: The column variable is not independent of the row variable

2. Select a random sample and record the observed frequencies for each cell of the contingency table.
3. Use equation (11.9) to compute the expected frequency for each cell.
4. Use equation (11.10) to compute the value of the test statistic.
5. Rejection rule:

   p-value approach: Reject H_0 if *p*-value $\leq \alpha$
   Critical value approach: Reject H_0 if $\chi^2 \geq \chi_\alpha^2$

   where α is the level of significance, with *n* rows and *m* columns providing $(n - 1)(m - 1)$ degrees of freedom.

NOTES AND COMMENTS

The test statistic for the chi-square tests in this chapter requires an expected frequency of five for each category. When a category has fewer than five, it is often appropriate to combine two adjacent categories to obtain an expected frequency of five or more in each category.

Exercises

Methods

19. The following 2×3 contingency table contains observed frequencies for a sample of 200. Test for independence of the row and column variables using the χ^2 test with $\alpha = .05$.

	Column Variable		
Row Variable	**A**	**B**	**C**
P	20	44	50
Q	30	26	30

20. The following 3×3 contingency table contains observed frequencies for a sample of 240. Test for independence of the row and column variables using the χ^2 test with $\alpha = .05$.

	Column Variable		
Row Variable	**A**	**B**	**C**
P	20	30	20
Q	30	60	25
R	10	15	30

Applications

21. One of the questions on the *Business Week* Subscriber Study was, "In the past 12 months, when traveling for business, what type of airline ticket did you purchase most often?" The data obtained are shown in the following contingency table.

	Type of Flight	
Type of Ticket	**Domestic Flights**	**International Flights**
First class	29	22
Business/executive class	95	121
Full fare economy/coach class	518	135

Use $\alpha = .05$ and test for the independence of type of flight and type of ticket. What is your conclusion?

22. In a study of brand loyalty in the automotive industry, new-car customers were asked whether the make of their new car was the same as the make of their previous car (*Business Week,* May 8, 2000). The breakdown of 600 responses shows the brand loyalty for domestic, European, and Asian cars.

| | Manufacturer | | |
Purchased	Domestic	European	Asian
Same Make	125	55	68
Different Make	140	105	107

    a.   Test a hypothesis to determine whether brand loyalty is independent of the manufacturer. Use $\alpha = .05$. What is your conclusion?

    b.   If a significant difference is found, which manufacturer appears to have the greatest brand loyalty?

23.   With double-digit annual percentage increases in the cost of health insurance, more and more workers are likely to lack health insurance coverage (*USA Today,* January 23, 2004). The following sample data provide a comparison of workers with and without health insurance coverage for small, medium, and large companies. For the purposes of this study, small companies are companies that have fewer than 100 employees. Medium companies have 100 to 999 employees, and large companies have 1000 or more employees. Sample data are reported for 50 employees of small companies, 75 employees of medium companies, and 100 employees of large companies.

| | Health Insurance | | |
Size of Company	Yes	No	Total
Small	36	14	50
Medium	65	10	75
Large	88	12	100

    a.   Conduct a test of independence to determine whether employee health insurance coverage is independent of the size of the company. Use $\alpha = .05$. What is the *p*-value, and what is your conclusion?

    b.   The *USA Today* article indicated employees of small companies are more likely to lack health insurance coverage. Use percentages based on the preceding data to support this conclusion.

24.   A State of Washington's Public Interest Research Group (PIRG) study showed that 46% of full-time college students work 25 or more hours per week. The PIRG study provided data on the effects of working on grades (*USA Today,* April 17, 2002). A sample of 200 students included 90 who worked 1–15 hours per week, 60 who worked 16–24 hours per week, and 50 who worked 25–34 hours per week. The sample number of students indicating their work had a positive effect, no effect, or a negative effect on grades is as follows.

| | Effect on Grades | | | |
Hours Worked per Week	Positive	None	Negative	Total
1–15 hours	26	50	14	90
16–24 hours	16	27	17	60
25–34 hours	11	19	20	50

    a.   Conduct a test of independence to determine whether the effect on grades is independent of the hours worked per week. Use $\alpha = .05$. What is the *p*-value, and what is your conclusion?

    b.   Use row percentages to learn more about how working affects grades. What is your conclusion?

25. Negative appeal is recognized as an effective method of persuasion in advertising. A study in *The Journal of Advertising* reported the results of a content analysis of guilt and fear advertisements in 24 magazines. The number of ads with guilt and fear appeals that appeared in selected magazine types follows.

| | Type of Appeal | |
Magazine Type	Number of Ads with Guilt Appeals	Number of Ads with Fear Appeals
News and opinion	20	10
General editorial	15	11
Family-oriented	30	19
Business/financial	22	17
Female-oriented	16	14
African-American	12	15

Use the chi-square test of independence with a .01 level of significance to analyze the data. What is your conclusion?

26. Businesses are increasingly placing orders online. The Performance Measurement Group collected data on the rates of correctly filled electronic orders by industry (*Investor's Business Daily,* May 8, 2000). Assume a sample of 700 electronic orders provided the following results.

| | Industry | | | |
Order	Pharmaceutical	Consumer	Computers	Telecommunications
Correct	207	136	151	178
Incorrect	3	4	9	12

a. Test a hypothesis to determine whether correctness of order fulfillment is independent of industry. Use $\alpha = .05$. What is your conclusion?
b. Which industry has the highest percentage of correctly filled orders?

27. The National Sleep Foundation used a survey to determine whether hours of sleeping per night are independent of age (*Newsweek,* January 19, 2004). The following show the hours of sleep on weeknights for a sample of individuals age 49 and younger and for a sample of individuals age 50 and older.

| | Hours of Sleep | | | | |
Age	Fewer than 6	6 to 6.9	7 to 7.9	8 or more	Total
49 or younger	38	60	77	65	240
50 or older	36	57	75	92	260

a. Conduct a test of independence to determine whether the hours of sleep on weeknights are independent of age. Use $\alpha = .05$. What is the *p*-value, and what is your conclusion?
b. What is your estimate of the percentage of people who sleep fewer than 6 hours, 6 to 6.9 hours, 7 to 7.9 hours, and 8 or more hours on weeknights?

Summary

In this chapter, we described statistical procedures for comparisons involving proportions and the contingency table test for independence of two variables. In the first section, we compared a proportion for one population with the same proportion from another population. We described how to construct an interval estimate for the difference between the proportions and how to conduct a hypothesis test to learn whether the difference between the proportions was statistically significant.

In the second section, we focused on a single multinomial population. There we saw how to conduct hypothesis tests to determine whether the sample proportions for the categories of the multinomial population were significantly different from the hypothesized values. The chi-square goodness of fit test was used to make the comparison.

The final section was concerned with tests of independence for two variables. A test of independence for two variables is an extension of the methodology employed in the goodness of fit test for a multinomial population. A contingency table is used to determine the observed and expected frequencies. Then a chi-square value is computed. Large chi-square values, caused by large differences between observed and expected frequencies, lead to the rejection of the null hypothesis of independence.

Glossary

Pooled estimator of p An estimator of a population proportion obtained by computing a weighted average of the sample proportions obtained from two independent samples.

Multinomial population A population in which each element is assigned to one and only one of several categories. The multinomial distribution extends the binomial distribution from two to three or more outcomes.

Goodness of fit test A statistical test conducted to determine whether to reject a hypothesized probability distribution for a population.

Contingency table A table used to summarize observed and expected frequencies for a test of independence.

Key Formulas

Point Estimator of the Difference Between Two Population Proportions

$$\bar{p}_1 - \bar{p}_2 \tag{11.1}$$

Standard Error of $\bar{p}_1 - \bar{p}_2$

$$\sigma_{\bar{p}_1 - \bar{p}_2} = \sqrt{\frac{p_1(1 - p_1)}{n_1} + \frac{p_2(1 - p_2)}{n_2}} \tag{11.2}$$

Interval Estimate of the Difference Between Two Population Proportions

$$\bar{p}_1 - \bar{p}_2 \pm z_{\alpha/2}\sqrt{\frac{\bar{p}_1(1 - \bar{p}_1)}{n_1} + \frac{\bar{p}_2(1 - \bar{p}_2)}{n_2}} \tag{11.4}$$

Standard Error of $\bar{p}_1 - \bar{p}_2$ When $p_1 = p_2 = p$

$$\sigma_{\bar{p}_1 - \bar{p}_2} = \sqrt{p(1 - p)\left(\frac{1}{n_1} + \frac{1}{n_2}\right)} \tag{11.5}$$

Pooled Estimator of p When $p_1 = p_2 = p$

$$\bar{p} = \frac{n_1\bar{p}_1 + n_2\bar{p}_2}{n_1 + n_2} \tag{11.6}$$

Test Statistic for Hypothesis Tests About $p_1 - p_2$

$$z = \frac{(\bar{p}_1 - \bar{p}_2)}{\sqrt{\bar{p}(1-\bar{p})\left(\frac{1}{n_1} + \frac{1}{n_2}\right)}} \tag{11.7}$$

Test Statistic for Goodness of Fit

$$\chi^2 = \sum_{i=1}^{k} \frac{(f_i - e_i)^2}{e_i} \tag{11.8}$$

Expected Frequencies for Contingency Tables Under the Assumption of Independence

$$e_{ij} = \frac{(\text{Row } i \text{ Total})(\text{Column } j \text{ Total})}{\text{Sample Size}} \tag{11.9}$$

Test Statistic for Independence

$$\chi^2 = \sum_i \sum_j \frac{(f_{ij} - e_{ij})^2}{e_{ij}} \tag{11.10}$$

Supplementary Exercises

28. Jupiter Media used a survey to determine how people use their free time. Watching television was the most popular activity selected by both men and women (*The Wall Street Journal,* January 26, 2004). The proportion of men and the proportion of women who selected watching television as their most popular leisure time activity can be estimated from the following sample data.

Gender	Sample Size	Watching Television
Men	800	248
Women	600	156

   a. State the hypotheses that can be used to test for a difference between the proportion for the population of men and the proportion for the population of women who selected watching television as their most popular leisure time activity.
   b. What is the sample proportion of men who selected watching television as their most popular leisure time activity? What is the sample proportion of women?
   c. Conduct the hypothesis test and compute the p-value. At a .05 level of significance, what is your conclusion?
   d. What is the margin of error and 95% confidence interval estimate of the difference between the population proportions?

29. A large automobile insurance company selected samples of single and married male policy-holders and recorded the number who made an insurance claim over the preceding three-year period.

Single Policyholders	Married Policyholders
$n_1 = 400$	$n_2 = 900$
Number making claims = 76	Number making claims = 90

   a. Use $\alpha = .05$. Test to determine whether the claim rates differ between single and married male policyholders.
   b. Provide a 95% confidence interval for the difference between the proportions for the two populations.

30. Medical tests were conducted to learn about drug-resistant tuberculosis. Of 142 cases tested in New Jersey, nine were found to be drug-resistant. Of 268 cases tested in Texas, five were found to be drug-resistant. Do these data suggest a statistically significant difference between the proportions of drug-resistant cases in the two states? Use a .02 level of significance. What is the p-value, and what is your conclusion?

31. In July 2001, the Harris Ad Track Research Service conducted a survey to evaluate the effectiveness of a major advertising campaign for Kodak cameras (*USA Today*, August 27, 2001). In a sample of 430 respondents, 38% thought the ads were very effective. In another sample of 285 respondents to other ad campaigns, 23% thought the ads were very effective.
   a. Estimate the number of respondents who thought the Kodak ads were very effective and the number of respondents who felt the other ads were very effective.
   b. Provide a 95% confidence interval for the difference in proportions.
   c. On the basis of your results in part (b), do you believe the Kodak advertising campaign is more effective than most advertising campaigns?

32. In June 2001, 38% of fund managers surveyed believed that the core inflation rate would be higher in one year. One month later a similar survey revealed that 22% of fund managers expected the core inflation rate to be higher in one year (*Global Research Highlights,* Merrill Lynch, July 20, 2001). Assume that the sample size was 200 in both the June and July surveys.
   a. Develop a point estimate of the difference between the June and July proportions of fund managers who felt the core inflation rate would be higher in one year.
   b. Develop hypotheses such that rejection of the null hypothesis allows us to conclude that inflation expectations diminished between June and July.
   c. Conduct a test of the hypotheses in part (b) using $\alpha = .01$. What is your conclusion?

33. Seven percent of mutual fund investors rate corporate stocks "very safe," 58% rate them "somewhat safe," 24% rate them "not very safe," 4% rate them "not at all safe," and 7% are "not sure." A *Business Week*/Harris poll asked 529 mutual fund investors how they would rate corporate bonds on safety. The responses are as follows.

Safety Rating	Frequency
Very safe	48
Somewhat safe	323
Not very safe	79
Not at all safe	16
Not sure	63
Total	529

Do mutual fund investors' attitudes toward corporate bonds differ from their attitudes toward corporate stocks? Support your conclusion with a statistical test. Use $\alpha = .01$.

34. Since 2000, the Toyota Camry, Honda Accord, and Ford Taurus have been the three best-selling passenger cars in the United States. Based on the 2003 sales data, the market shares among the top three are as follows: Toyota Camry 37%, Honda Accord 34%, and Ford Taurus 29% (*The World Almanac,* 2004). Assume a sample of 1200 sales of passenger cars during the first quarter of 2004 shows the following.

Passenger Car	Units Sold
Toyota Camry	480
Honda Accord	390
Ford Taurus	330

Can these data be used to conclude that the market shares among the top three passenger cars have changed during the first quarter of 2004? What is the *p*-value? Use a .05 level of significance. What is your conclusion?

35. A regional transit authority is concerned about the number of riders on one of its bus routes. In setting up the route, the assumption is that the number of riders is the same on every day from Monday through Friday. Using the following data, test with $\alpha = .05$ to determine whether the transit authority's assumption is correct.

Day	Number of Riders
Monday	13
Tuesday	16
Wednesday	28
Thursday	17
Friday	16

36. The results of *Computerworld*'s Annual Job Satisfaction Survey showed that 28% of Information Systems (IS) managers are very satisfied with their job, 46% are somewhat satisfied, 12% are neither satisfied nor dissatisfied, 10% are somewhat dissatisfied, and 4% are very dissatisfied. Suppose that a sample of 500 computer programmers yielded the following results.

Category	Number of Respondents
Very satisfied	105
Somewhat satisfied	235
Neither	55
Somewhat dissatisfied	90
Very dissatisfied	15

Use $\alpha = .05$ and test to determine whether the job satisfaction for computer programmers is different from the job satisfaction for IS managers.

37.   A sample of parts provided the following contingency table data on part quality by production shift.

Shift	Number Good	Number Defective
First	368	32
Second	285	15
Third	176	24

Use $\alpha = .05$ and test the hypothesis that part quality is independent of the production shift. What is your conclusion?

38.   *The Wall Street Journal* Subscriber Study showed data on the employment status of subscribers. Sample results corresponding to subscribers of the eastern and western editions are shown here.

	Region	
Employment Status	Eastern Edition	Western Edition
Full-time	1105	574
Part-time	31	15
Self-employed/consultant	229	186
Not employed	485	344

Use $\alpha = .05$ and test the hypothesis that employment status is independent of the region. What is your conclusion?

39.   A lending institution supplied the following data on loan approvals by four loan officers. Use $\alpha = .05$ and test to determine whether the loan approval decision is independent of the loan officer reviewing the loan application.

	Loan Approval Decision	
Loan Officer	Approved	Rejected
Miller	24	16
McMahon	17	13
Games	35	15
Runk	11	9

40.   Data on the marital status of men and women ages 20 to 29 were obtained as part of a national survey. The results from a sample of 350 men and 400 women follow.

	Marital Status		
Gender	Never Married	Married	Divorced
Men	234	106	10
Women	216	168	16

a. Use $\alpha = .01$ and test for independence between marital status and gender. What is your conclusion?

b. Summarize the percentage in each marital status category for men and for women.

41. Barna Research Group collected data showing church attendance by age group (*USA Today*, November 20, 2003). Use the sample data to determine whether attending church is independent of age. Use a .05 level of significance. What is your conclusion? What conclusion can you draw about church attendance as individuals grow older?

	Church Attendance		
Age	**Yes**	**No**	**Total**
20 to 29	31	69	100
30 to 39	63	87	150
40 to 49	94	106	200
50 to 59	72	78	150

42. A salesperson makes four calls per day. A sample of 100 days gives the following frequencies of sales volumes.

Number of Sales	**Observed Frequency (days)**
0	30
1	32
2	25
3	10
4	3
Total	100

Records show sales are made to 30% of all sales calls. Assuming independent sales calls, the number of sales per day should follow a binomial distribution. The binomial probability function presented in Chapter 5 is

$$f(x) = \frac{n!}{x!(n-x)!} p^x (1-p)^{n-x}$$

For this exercise, assume that the population has a binomial distribution with $n = 4$, $p = .30$, and $x = 0, 1, 2, 3$, and 4.

a. Compute the expected frequencies for $x = 0, 1, 2, 3$, and 4 by using the binomial probability function. Combine categories if necessary to satisfy the requirement that the expected frequency is five or more for all categories.

b. Use the goodness of fit test to determine whether the assumption of a binomial distribution should be rejected. Use $\alpha = .05$. Because no parameters of the binomial distribution were estimated from the sample data, the degrees of freedom is $k - 1$ when k is the number of categories.

Case Problem A Bipartisan Agenda for Change

In a study conducted by Zogby International for the *Democrat and Chronicle*, more than 700 New Yorkers were polled to determine whether the New York state government works. Respondents surveyed were asked questions involving pay cuts for state legislators, restrictions on lobbyists, term limits for legislators, and whether state citizens should be able to put matters directly on the state ballot for a vote. The results regarding several proposed reforms had broad support, crossing all demographic and political lines.

Suppose that a follow-up survey of 100 individuals who live in the western region of New York was conducted. The party affiliation (Democrat, Independent, Republican) of each individual surveyed was recorded, as well as individual responses to the following three questions.

1. Should legislative pay be cut for every day the state budget is late?
    Yes _____   No _____
2. Should there be more restrictions on lobbyists?
    Yes _____   No _____
3. Should there be term limits requiring that legislators serve a fixed number of years?
    Yes _____   No _____

NYReform

The responses were coded using 1 for a *yes* response and 2 for a *no* response. The complete data set is available on the CD in the data set named NYReform.

Managerial Report

1. Use descriptive statistics to summarize the data from this study. What are your preliminary conclusions about the independence of the response (Yes or No) and party affiliation for each of the three questions in the survey?
2. With regard to question 1, test for the independence of the response (Yes and No) and party affiliation. Use $\alpha = .05$.
3. With regard to question 2, test for the independence of the response (Yes and No) and party affiliation. Use $\alpha = .05$.
4. With regard to question 3, test for the independence of the response (Yes and No) and party affiliation. Use $\alpha = .05$.
5. Does it appear that there is broad support for change across all political lines? Explain.

Appendix 11.1   Inferences About Two Population Proportions Using Minitab

TaxPrep

We describe the use of Minitab to develop interval estimates and conduct hypothesis tests about the difference between two population proportions. We will use the data on tax preparation errors presented in Section 11.1. The sample results for 250 tax returns prepared at office 1 are in column C1 and the sample results for 300 tax returns prepared at office 2 are in column C2. Yes denotes an error was found in the tax return and No indicates no error was found. The procedure we describe provides both a 90% confidence interval estimate of the difference between the two population proportions and hypothesis testing results for $H_0: p_1 - p_2 = 0$ vs. $H_a: p_1 - p_2 \neq 0$.

Step 1. Select the **Stat** menu
Step 2. Choose **Basic Statistics**
Step 3. Choose **2 Proportions**
Step 4. When the 2 Proportions (Test and Confidence Interval) dialog box appears:
    Select **Samples in different columns**
    Enter C1 in the **First** box
    Enter C2 in the **Second** box
    Select **Options**

Step 5. When the 2 Proportions-Options dialog box appears:

> Enter 90 in the **Confidence level** box
> Enter 0 in the **Test difference** box
> Enter not equal in the **Alternative** box
> Select **Use pooled estimate of p for test**
> Click **OK**

Step 6. Click **OK**

Step 5 may be modified to provide different confidence levels, different hypothesized values, and different forms of the hypotheses.

In the tax preparation example, the data are qualitative. Yes and No are used to indicate whether an error is present. In modules involving proportions, Minitab calculates proportions for the response coming second in alphabetic order. Thus, in the tax preparation example, Minitab computes the proportion of Yes responses, which is the proportion we wanted.

If Minitab's alphabetical ordering does not compute the proportion for the response of interest, we can fix it. Select any cell in the data column, go to the Minitab menu bar, and select Editor > Column > Value Order. This sequence will provide the option of entering a user-specified order. Simply make sure that the response of interest is listed second in the define-an-order box. Minitab's 2 Proportion routine will then provide the confidence interval and hypothesis testing results for the population proportion of interest.

Finally, we note that Minitab's 2 Proportion routine uses a computational procedure different from the procedure described in the text. Thus, the Minitab output can be expected to provide slightly different interval estimates and slightly different p-values. However, results from the two methods should be close and are expected to provide the same interpretation and conclusion.

Appendix 11.2   Tests of Goodness of Fit and Independence Using Minitab

Goodness of Fit Test

This Minitab procedure can be used for a goodness of fit test for a multinomial distribution. The user must obtain the observed frequencies, calculate the expected frequencies, and enter both the observed and expected frequencies in a Minitab worksheet. Column C1 is labeled Observed and contains the observed frequencies. Column C2 is labeled Expected and contains the expected frequencies. Use the Scott Marketing Research example presented in Section 11.2, open a Minitab worksheet, and enter the observed frequencies 48, 98, and 54 in column C1 and enter the expected frequencies 60, 100, and 40 in column C2. The Minitab steps for the goodness of fit test follow.

Step 1. Select the **Calc** menu
Step 2. Choose **Calculator**
Step 3. When the Calculator dialog box appears:

> Enter ChiSquare in the **Store result in variable** box
> Enter Sum((C1-C2)**2/C2) in the **Expression** box
> Click **OK**

Step 4. Select the **Calc** menu
Step 5. Choose **Probability Distributions**
Step 6. Choose **Chi-Square**

Step 7. When the Chi-Square Distribution dialog box appears:
Select **Cumulative probability**
Enter 2 in the **Degrees of freedom** box
Select **Input column** and enter ChiSquare in the box
Click **OK**

The Minitab output provides the cumulative probability .9745, which is the area under the curve to the left of $\chi^2 = 7.34$. The area remaining in the upper tail is the *p*-value. Thus, we have *p*-value $= 1 - .9745 = .0255$.

Test of Independence

We begin with a new Minitab worksheet and enter the observed frequency data for the Alber's Brewery example from Section 11.3 into columns 1, 2, and 3, respectively. Thus, we entered the observed frequencies corresponding to a light beer preference (20 and 30) in C1, the observed frequencies corresponding to a regular beer preference (40 and 30) in C2, and the observed frequencies corresponding to a dark beer preference (20 and 10) in C3. The Minitab steps for the test of independence are as follows.

Step 1. Select the **Stat** menu
Step 2. Select **Tables**
Step 3. Choose **Chi-Square Test (Table in Worksheet)**
Step 4. When the Chi-Square Test dialog box appears:
Enter C1-C3 in the **Columns containing the table** box
Click **OK**

Appendix 11.3   Tests of Goodness of Fit and Independence Using Excel*

Goodness of Fit Test

FitTest

This Excel procedure uses a goodness of fit test for a multinomial distribution. The user must obtain the observed frequencies, calculate the expected frequencies, and enter both the observed and expected frequencies in an Excel worksheet.

The observed frequencies and expected frequencies for the Scott Market Research example presented in Section 11.2 are entered in columns A and B as shown in Figure 11.2. The test statistic $\chi^2 = 7.34$ is calculated in column D. With $k = 3$ categories, the user enters the degrees of freedom $k - 1 = 3 - 1 = 2$ in cell D11. The CHIDIST function provides the *p*-value in cell D13. The background worksheet shows the cell formulas.

Test of Independence

Independence

The Excel procedure for the test of independence requires the user to obtain the observed frequencies and enter them in the worksheet. The Alber's Brewery example from Section 11.3 provides the observed frequencies, which are entered in cells B7 to D8 as shown in the worksheet in Figure 11.3. The cell formulas in the background worksheet show the procedure used to compute the expected frequencies. With two rows and three columns, the user enters the degrees of freedom $(2 - 1)(3 - 1) = 2$ in cell E22. The CHITEST function provides the *p*-value in cell E24.

---

*No routines are available for inferences about the difference between two population proportions.

FIGURE 11.2   EXCEL WORKSHEET FOR THE SCOTT MARKETING RESEARCH
GOODNESS OF FIT TEST

	A	B	C	D	E
1	**Goodness of Fit Test**				
2					
3	Observed	Expected			
4	Frequency	Frequency		Calculations	
5	48	60		=(A5-B5)^2/B5	
6	98	100		=(A6-B6)^2/B6	
7	54	40		=(A7-B7)^2/B7	
8					
9			Test Statistic	=SUM(D5:D7)	
10					
11			Degrees of Freedom	2	
12					
13			p-Value	=CHIDIST(D9,D11)	
14					

	A	B	C	D	E
1	**Goodness of Fit Test**				
2					
3	Observed	Expected			
4	Frequency	Frequency		Calculations	
5	48	60		2.40	
6	98	100		0.04	
7	54	40		4.90	
8					
9			Test Statistic	7.34	
10					
11			Degrees of Freedom	2	
12					
13			p-Value	0.0255	
14					

FIGURE 11.3   EXCEL WORKSHEET FOR THE ALBER'S BREWERY TEST OF INDEPENDENCE

	A	B	C	D	E	F
1	Test of Independence					
2						
3	Observed Frequencies					
4						
5			Beer Preference			
6	Gender	Light	Regular	Dark	Total	
7	Male	20	40	20	=SUM(B7:D7)	
8	Female	30	30	10	=SUM(B8:D8)	
9	Total	=SUM(B7:B8)	=SUM(C7:C8)	=SUM(D7:D8)	=SUM(E7:E8)	
10						
11						
12	Expected Frequencies					
13						
14			Beer Preference			
15	Gender	Light	Regular	Dark	Total	
16	Male	=E7*B$9/$E$9	=E7*C$9/$E$9	=E7*D$9/$E$9	=SUM(B16:D16)	
17	Female	=E8*B$9/$E$9	=E8*C$9/$E$9	=E8*D$9/$E$9	=SUM(B17:D17)	
18	Total	=SUM(B16:B17)	=SUM(C16:C17)	=SUM(D16:D17)	=SUM(E16:E17)	
19						
20				Test Statistic	=CHIINV(E24,E22)	
21						
22				Degrees of Freedom	2	
23						
24				p-value	=CHITEST(C7:E8,C16:E17)	
25						

	A	B	C	D	E	F
1	Test of Independence					
2						
3	Observed Frequencies					
4						
5			Beer Preference			
6	Gender	Light	Regular	Dark	Total	
7	Male	20	40	20	80	
8	Female	30	30	10	70	
9	Total	50	70	30	150	
10						
11						
12	Expected Frequencies					
13						
14			Beer Preference			
15	Gender	Light	Regular	Dark	Total	
16	Male	26.67	37.33	16	80	
17	Female	23.33	32.67	14	70	
18	Total	50	70	30	150	
19						
20				Test Statistic	6.12	
21						
22				Degrees of Freedom	2	
23						
24				p-value	0.0468	
25						

CHAPTER 12

Simple Linear Regression

CONTENTS

STATISTICS *in* PRACTICE

ALLIANCE DATA SYSTEMS*
DALLAS, TEXAS

Alliance Data Systems (ADS) provides transaction processing, credit services, and marketing services for clients in the rapidly growing customer relationship management (CRM) industry. ADS clients are concentrated in four industries: retail, petroleum/convenience stores, utilities, and transportation. In 1983, Alliance began offering end-to-end credit processing services to the retail, petroleum, and casual dining industries; today they employ more than 6500 employees who provide services to clients around the world. Operating more than 140,000 point-of-sale terminals in the United States alone, ADS processes in excess of 2.5 billion transactions annually. The company ranks second in the United States in private label credit services by representing 49 private label programs with nearly 72 million cardholders. In 2001, ADS made an initial public offering and is now listed on the New York Stock Exchange.

As one of its marketing services, ADS designs direct mail campaigns and promotions. With its database containing information on the spending habits of more than 100 million consumers, ADS can target those consumers most likely to benefit from a direct mail promotion. The Analytical Development Group uses regression analysis to build models that measure and predict the responsiveness of consumers to direct market campaigns. Some regression models predict the probability of purchase for individuals receiving a promotion, and others predict the amount spent by those consumers making a purchase.

For one particular campaign, a retail store chain wanted to attract new customers. To predict the effect of the campaign, ADS analysts selected a sample from the consumer database, sent the sampled individuals promotional materials, and then collected transaction data on the consumers' response. Sample data were collected on the amount of purchase made by the consumers responding to the campaign, as well as a variety of consumer-specific variables thought to be useful in predicting sales. The consumer-specific variable that contributed most to predicting the amount purchased was the total amount of credit purchases at related stores over the past 39 months. ADS analysts

Alliance Data analysts discuss use of a regression model to predict sales for a direct marketing campaign. © Courtesy of Alliance Data Systems.

developed an estimated regression equation relating the amount of purchase to the amount spent at related stores:

$$\hat{y} = 26.7 + 0.00205x$$

where

$$\hat{y} = \text{amount of purchase}$$
$$x = \text{amount spent at related stores}$$

Using this equation, we could predict that someone spending $10,000 over the past 39 months at related stores would spend $47.20 when responding to the direct mail promotion. In this chapter, you will learn how to develop this type of estimated regression equation.

The final model developed by ADS analysts also included several other variables that increased the predictive power of the preceding equation. Some of these variables included the absence/presence of a bank credit card, estimated income, and the average amount spent per trip at a selected store. In the following chapter, we will learn how such additional variables can be incorporated into a multiple regression model.

*The authors are indebted to Philip Clemance, director of analytical development at Alliance Data Systems, for providing this Statistics in Practice.

Managerial decisions often are based on the relationship between two or more variables. For example, after considering the relationship between advertising expenditures and sales, a marketing manager might attempt to predict sales for a given level of advertising expenditures. In another case, a public utility might use the relationship between the daily high temperature and the demand for electricity to predict electricity usage on the basis of next month's anticipated daily high temperatures. Sometimes a manager will rely on intuition to judge how two variables are related. However, if data can be obtained, a statistical procedure called *regression analysis* can be used to develop an equation showing how the variables are related.

The statistical methods used in studying the relationship between two variables were first employed by Sir Francis Galton (1822–1911). Galton was interested in studying the relationship between a father's height and the son's height. Galton's disciple, Karl Pearson (1857–1936), analyzed the relationship between the father's height and the son's height for 1078 pairs of subjects.

In regression terminology, the variable being predicted is called the **dependent variable**. The variable or variables being used to predict the value of the dependent variable are called the **independent variables**. For example, in analyzing the effect of advertising expenditures on sales, a marketing manager's desire to predict sales would suggest making sales the dependent variable. Advertising expenditure would be the independent variable used to help predict sales. In statistical notation, y denotes the dependent variable and x denotes the independent variable.

In this chapter we consider the simplest type of regression analysis involving one independent variable and one dependent variable in which the relationship between the variables is approximated by a straight line. It is called **simple linear regression**. Regression analysis involving two or more independent variables is called multiple regression analysis; multiple regression is covered in Chapter 13.

12.1 Simple Linear Regression Model

Armand's Pizza Parlors is a chain of Italian-food restaurants located in a five-state area. Armand's most successful locations are near college campuses. The managers believe that quarterly sales for these restaurants (denoted by y) are related positively to the size of the student population (denoted by x); that is, restaurants near campuses with a large student population tend to generate more sales than those located near campuses with a small student population. Using regression analysis, we can develop an equation showing how the dependent variable y is related to the independent variable x.

Regression Model and Regression Equation

In the Armand's Pizza Parlors example, the population consists of all the Armand's restaurants. For every restaurant in the population, a value of x (student population) corresponds to a value of y (quarterly sales). The equation that describes how y is related to x and an error term is called the **regression model**. The regression model used in simple linear regression follows.

SIMPLE LINEAR REGRESSION MODEL

$$y = \beta_0 + \beta_1 x + \epsilon \tag{12.1}$$

β_0 and β_1 are referred to as the parameters of the model, and ϵ (the Greek letter epsilon) is a random variable referred to as the error term. The error term accounts for the variability in y that cannot be explained by the linear relationship between x and y.

The population of all Armand's restaurants can also be viewed as a collection of subpopulations, one for each distinct value of x. For example, one subpopulation consists of all Armand's restaurants located near college campuses with 8000 students; another subpopulation consists of all Armand's restaurants located near college campuses with 9000 students; and so on. Each subpopulation has a corresponding distribution of y values. Thus, a distribution of y values is associated with restaurants located near campuses with 8000 students; a distribution of y values is associated with restaurants located near campuses with 9000 students; and so on. Each distribution of y values has its own mean or expected value. The equation that describes how the expected value of y, denoted $E(y)$, is related to x is called the **regression equation**. The regression equation for simple linear regression follows.

SIMPLE LINEAR REGRESSION EQUATION

$$E(y) = \beta_0 + \beta_1 x \qquad\qquad \textbf{(12.2)}$$

The graph of the simple linear regression equation is a straight line; β_0 is the y-intercept of the regression line, β_1 is the slope, and $E(y)$ is the mean or expected value of y for a given value of x.

Examples of possible regression lines are shown in Figure 12.1. The regression line in Panel A shows that the mean value of y is related positively to x, with larger values of $E(y)$ associated with larger values of x. The regression line in Panel B shows the mean value of y is related negatively to x, with smaller values of $E(y)$ associated with larger values of x. The regression line in Panel C shows the case in which the mean value of y is not related to x; that is, the mean value of y is the same for every value of x.

Estimated Regression Equation

If the values of the population parameters β_0 and β_1 were known, we could use equation (12.2) to compute the mean value of y for a given value of x. In practice, the parameter values are not known, and must be estimated using sample data. Sample statistics (denoted b_0 and b_1) are computed as estimates of the population parameters β_0 and β_1. Substituting the values of the sample statistics b_0 and b_1 for β_0 and β_1 in the regression equation, we

FIGURE 12.1 POSSIBLE REGRESSION LINES IN SIMPLE LINEAR REGRESSION

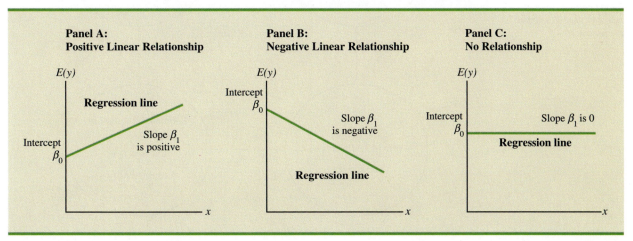

obtain the **estimated regression equation**. The estimated regression equation for simple linear regression follows.

ESTIMATED SIMPLE LINEAR REGRESSION EQUATION

$$\hat{y} = b_0 + b_1 x \qquad (12.3)$$

The graph of the estimated simple linear regression equation is called the *estimated regression line*; b_0 is the *y*-intercept, and b_1 is the slope. In the next section, we show how the least squares method can be used to compute the values of b_0 and b_1 in the estimated regression equation.

In general, $\hat{y}$ is the point estimator of $E(y)$, the mean value of *y* for a given value of *x*. Thus, to estimate the mean or expected value of quarterly sales for all restaurants located near campuses with 10,000 students, Armand's would substitute the value of 10,000 for *x* in equation (12.3). In some cases, however, Armand's may be more interested in predicting sales for one particular restaurant. For example, suppose Armand's would like to predict quarterly sales for the restaurant located near Talbot College, a school with 10,000 students. As it turns out, the best estimate of *y* for a given value of *x* is also provided by $\hat{y}$. Thus, to predict quarterly sales for the restaurant located near Talbot College, Armand's would also substitute the value of 10,000 for *x* in equation (12.3).

Because the value of $\hat{y}$ provides both a point estimate of $E(y)$ for a given value of *x* and a point estimate of an individual value of *y* for a given value of *x*, we will refer to $\hat{y}$ simply as the *estimated value of y*. Figure 12.2 provides a summary of the estimation process for simple linear regression.

FIGURE 12.2   THE ESTIMATION PROCESS IN SIMPLE LINEAR REGRESSION

The estimation of β_0 and β_1 is a statistical process much like the estimation of μ discussed in Chapter 7. β_0 and β_1 are the unknown parameters of interest, and b_0 and b_1 are the sample statistics used to estimate the parameters.

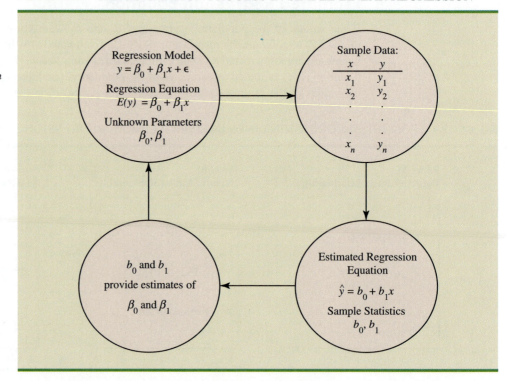

NOTES AND COMMENTS

1. Regression analysis cannot be interpreted as a procedure for establishing a cause-and-effect relationship between variables. It can only indicate how or to what extent variables are associated with each other. Any conclusions about cause and effect must be based upon the judgment of those individuals most knowledgeable about the application.

2. The regression equation in simple linear regression is $E(y) = \beta_0 + \beta_1 x$. More advanced texts in regression analysis often write the regression equation as $E(y|x) = \beta_0 + \beta_1 x$ to emphasize that the regression equation provides the mean value of y for a given value of x.

12.2 Least Squares Method

In simple linear regression, each observation consists of two values: one for the independent variable and one for the dependent variable.

The **least squares method** is a procedure for using sample data to find the estimated regression equation. To illustrate the least squares method, suppose data were collected from a sample of 10 Armand's Pizza Parlors restaurants located near college campuses. For the ith observation or restaurant in the sample, x_i is the size of the student population (in thousands) and y_i is the quarterly sales (in thousands of dollars). The values of x_i and y_i for the 10 restaurants in the sample are summarized in Table 12.1. We see that restaurant 1, with $x_1 = 2$ and $y_1 = 58$, is near a campus with 2000 students and has quarterly sales of $58,000. Restaurant 2, with $x_2 = 6$ and $y_2 = 105$, is near a campus with 6000 students and has quarterly sales of $105,000. The largest sales value is for restaurant 10, which is near a campus with 26,000 students and has quarterly sales of $202,000.

Figure 12.3 is a scatter diagram of the data in Table 12.1. Student population is shown on the horizontal axis and quarterly sales is shown on the vertical axis. **Scatter diagrams** for regression analysis are constructed with the independent variable x on the horizontal axis and the dependent variable y on the vertical axis. The scatter diagram enables us to observe the data graphically and to draw preliminary conclusions about the possible relationship between the variables.

What preliminary conclusions can be drawn from Figure 12.3? Quarterly sales appear to be higher at campuses with larger student populations. In addition, for these data the relationship between the size of the student population and quarterly sales appears to be approximated by a straight line; indeed, a positive linear relationship is indicated between x

TABLE 12.1   STUDENT POPULATION AND QUARTERLY SALES DATA
FOR 10 ARMAND'S PIZZA PARLORS

Armand's

Restaurant i	Student Population (1000s) x_i	Quarterly Sales ($1000s) y_i
1	2	58
2	6	105
3	8	88
4	8	118
5	12	117
6	16	137
7	20	157
8	20	169
9	22	149
10	26	202

FIGURE 12.3 SCATTER DIAGRAM OF STUDENT POPULATION AND QUARTERLY SALES FOR ARMAND'S PIZZA PARLORS

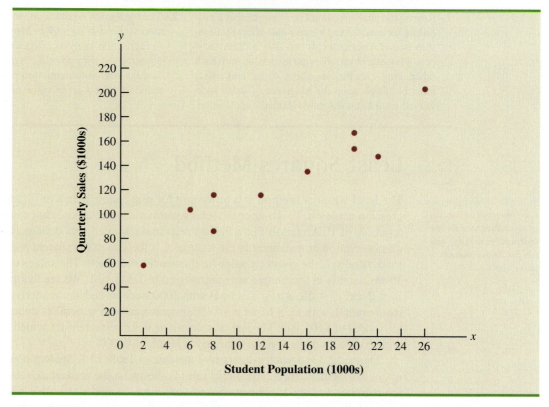

and y. We therefore choose the simple linear regression model to represent the relationship between quarterly sales and student population. Given that choice, our next task is to use the sample data in Table 12.1 to determine the values of b_0 and b_1 in the estimated simple linear regression equation. For the ith restaurant, the estimated regression equation provides

$$\hat{y}_i = b_0 + b_1 x_i \tag{12.4}$$

where

$\hat{y}_i$ = estimated value of quarterly sales ($1000s) for the ith restaurant

b_0 = the y-intercept of the estimated regression line

b_1 = the slope of the estimated regression line

x_i = size of the student population (1000s) for the ith restaurant

With y_i denoting the observed (actual) sales for restaurant i and $\hat{y}_i$ in equation (12.4) representing the estimated value of sales for restaurant i, every restaurant in the sample will have an observed value of sales y_i and an estimated value of sales $\hat{y}_i$. For the estimated regression line to provide a good fit to the data, we want the differences between the observed sales values and the estimated sales values to be small.

The least squares method uses the sample data to provide the values of b_0 and b_1 that minimize the *sum of the squares of the deviations* between the observed values of the dependent variable y_i and the estimated values of the dependent variable. The criterion for the least squares method is given by expression (12.5).

Carl Friedrich Gauss (1777–1855) proposed the least squares method.

LEAST SQUARES CRITERION

$$\min \Sigma(y_i - \hat{y}_i)^2 \qquad \qquad \textbf{(12.5)}$$

where

y_i = observed value of the dependent variable for the ith observation

$\hat{y}_i$ = estimated value of the dependent variable for the ith observation

Differential calculus can be used to show that the values of b_0 and b_1 that minimize expression (12.5) can be found by using equations (12.6) and (12.7).

SLOPE AND y-INTERCEPT FOR THE ESTIMATED REGRESSION EQUATION*

In computing b_1 with a calculator, carry as many significant digits as possible in the intermediate calculations. We recommend carrying at least four significant digits.

$$b_1 = \frac{\Sigma(x_i - \bar{x})(y_i - \bar{y})}{\Sigma(x_i - \bar{x})^2} \qquad \qquad \textbf{(12.6)}$$

$$b_0 = \bar{y} - b_1\bar{x} \qquad \qquad \textbf{(12.7)}$$

where

x_i = value of the independent variable for the ith observation

y_i = value of the dependent variable for the ith observation

$\bar{x}$ = mean value for the independent variable

$\bar{y}$ = mean value for the dependent variable

n = total number of observations

Some of the calculations necessary to develop the least squares estimated regression equation for Armand's Pizza Parlors are shown in Table 12.2. With the sample of 10 restaurants, we have $n = 10$ observations. Because equations (12.6) and (12.7) require $\bar{x}$ and $\bar{y}$ we begin the calculations by computing $\bar{x}$ and $\bar{y}$.

$$\bar{x} = \frac{\Sigma x_i}{n} = \frac{140}{10} = 14$$

$$\bar{y} = \frac{\Sigma y_i}{n} = \frac{1300}{10} = 130$$

Using equations (12.6) and (12.7) and the information in Table 12.2, we can compute the slope and intercept of the estimated regression equation for Armand's Pizza Parlors. The calculation of the slope (b_1) proceeds as follows.

---

*An alternate formula for b_1 is

$$b_1 = \frac{\Sigma x_i y_i - (\Sigma x_i \Sigma y_i)/n}{\Sigma x_i^2 - (\Sigma x_i)^2/n}$$

This form of equation (12.6) is often recommended when using a calculator to compute b_1.

TABLE 12.2   CALCULATIONS FOR THE LEAST SQUARES ESTIMATED REGRESSION EQUATION FOR ARMAND'S PIZZA PARLORS

Restaurant i	x_i	y_i	$x_i - \bar{x}$	$y_i - \bar{y}$	$(x_i - \bar{x})(y_i - \bar{y})$	$(x_i - \bar{x})^2$
1	2	58	−12	−72	864	144
2	6	105	−8	−25	200	64
3	8	88	−6	−42	252	36
4	8	118	−6	−12	72	36
5	12	117	−2	−13	26	4
6	16	137	2	7	14	4
7	20	157	6	27	162	36
8	20	169	6	39	234	36
9	22	149	8	19	152	64
10	26	202	12	72	864	144
Totals	140	1300			2840	568
	Σx_i	Σy_i			$\Sigma(x_i - \bar{x})(y_i - \bar{y})$	$\Sigma(x_i - \bar{x})^2$

$$b_1 = \frac{\Sigma(x_i - \bar{x})(y_i - \bar{y})}{\Sigma(x_i - \bar{x})^2}$$

$$= \frac{2840}{568}$$

$$= 5$$

The calculation of the y-intercept (b_0) follows.

$$b_0 = \bar{y} - b_1\bar{x}$$

$$= 130 - 5(14)$$

$$= 60$$

Appendixes 12.1 and 12.2 show how Minitab and Excel can be used to obtain the estimated regression equation.

Thus, the estimated regression equation is

$$\hat{y} = 60 + 5x$$

Figure 12.4 shows the graph of this equation on the scatter diagram.

The slope of the estimated regression equation ($b_1 = 5$) is positive, implying that as student population increases, sales increase. In fact, we can conclude (based on sales measured in $1000s and student population in 1000s) that an increase in the student population of 1000 is associated with an increase of $5000 in expected sales; that is, quarterly sales are expected to increase by $5 per student.

Using the estimated regression equation to make predictions outside the range of the values of the independent variable should be done with caution because outside that range we cannot be sure that the same relationship is valid.

If we believe the least squares estimated regression equation adequately describes the relationship between x and y, it would seem reasonable to use the estimated regression equation to predict the value of y for a given value of x. For example, if we wanted to predict quarterly sales for a restaurant to be located near a campus with 16,000 students, we would compute

$$\hat{y} = 60 + 5(16) = 140$$

Hence, we would predict quarterly sales of $140,000 for this restaurant. In the following sections we will discuss methods for assessing the appropriateness of using the estimated regression equation for estimation and prediction.

FIGURE 12.4   GRAPH OF THE ESTIMATED REGRESSION EQUATION FOR ARMAND'S
PIZZA PARLORS: $\hat{y} = 60 + 5x$

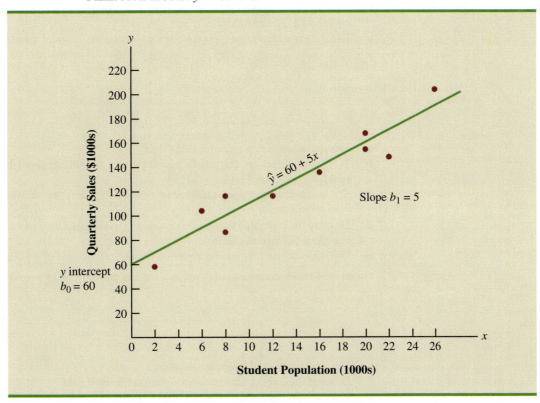

NOTES AND COMMENTS

The least squares method provides an estimated regression equation that minimizes the sum of squared deviations between the observed values of the dependent variable y_i and the estimated values of the dependent variable $\hat{y}_i$. This least squares criterion is used to choose the equation that provides the best fit. If some other criterion were used, such as minimizing the sum of the absolute deviations between y_i and $\hat{y}_i$, a different equation would be obtained. In practice, the least squares method is the most widely used.

Exercises

Methods

1.   Given are five observations for two variables, x and y.

x_i	1	2	3	4	5
y_i	3	7	5	11	14

a.   Develop a scatter diagram for these data.
b.   What does the scatter diagram developed in part (a) indicate about the relationship between the two variables?

   c. Try to approximate the relationship between x and y by drawing a straight line through the data.

   d. Develop the estimated regression equation by computing the values of b_0 and b_1 using equations (12.6) and (12.7).

   e. Use the estimated regression equation to predict the value of y when $x = 4$.

2. Given are five observations for two variables, x and y.

x_i	2	3	5	1	8
y_i	25	25	20	30	16

   a. Develop a scatter diagram for these data.

   b. What does the scatter diagram developed in part (a) indicate about the relationship between the two variables?

   c. Try to approximate the relationship between x and y by drawing a straight line through the data.

   d. Develop the estimated regression equation by computing the values of b_0 and b_1 using equations (12.6) and (12.7).

   e. Use the estimated regression equation to predict the value of y when $x = 6$.

3. Given are five observations collected in a regression study on two variables.

x_i	2	4	5	7	8
y_i	2	3	2	6	4

   a. Develop a scatter diagram for these data.

   b. Develop the estimated regression equation for these data.

   c. Use the estimated regression equation to predict the value of y when $x = 4$.

Applications

4. The following data were collected on the height (inches) and weight (pounds) of women swimmers.

Height	68	64	62	65	66
Weight	132	108	102	115	128

   a. Develop a scatter diagram for these data with height as the independent variable.

   b. What does the scatter diagram developed in part (a) indicate about the relationship between the two variables?

   c. Try to approximate the relationship between height and weight by drawing a straight line through the data.

   d. Develop the estimated regression equation by computing the values of b_0 and b_1.

   e. If a swimmer's height is 63 inches, what would you estimate her weight to be?

5. Technological advances helped make inflatable paddlecraft suitable for backcountry use. These blow-up rubber boats, which can be rolled into a bundle not much bigger than a golf bag, are large enough to accommodate one or two paddlers and their camping gear. *Canoe & Kayak* magazine tested boats from nine manufacturers to determine how they would perform on a three-day wilderness paddling trip. One of the criteria in their evaluation was the baggage capacity of the boat, evaluated using a 4-point rating scale from 1 (lowest rating) to 4 (highest rating). The following data show the baggage capacity rating and the price of the boat (*Canoe & Kayak*, March 2003).

Boat	Baggage Capacity	Price ($)
S14	4	1595
Orinoco	4	1399
Outside Pro	4	1890
Explorer 380X	3	795
River XK2	2.5	600
Sea Tiger	4	1995
Maverik II	3	1205
Starlite 100	2	583
Fat Pack Cat	3	1048

   a.   Develop a scatter diagram for these data with baggage capacity rating as the independent variable.

   b.   What does the scatter diagram developed in part (a) indicate about the relationship between baggage capacity and price?

   c.   Draw a straight line through the data to approximate a linear relationship between baggage capacity and price.

   d.   Use the least squares method to develop the estimated regression equation.

   e.   Provide an interpretation for the slope of the estimated regression equation.

   f.   Predict the price for a boat with a baggage capacity rating of 3.

6.   Wageweb conducts surveys of salary data and presents summaries on its Web site. Based on salary data as of October 1, 2002, Wageweb reported that the average annual salary for sales vice presidents was $142,111, with an average annual bonus of $15,432 (Wageweb.com, March 13, 2003). Assume the following data are a sample of the annual salary and bonus for 10 sales vice presidents. Data are in thousands of dollars.

Vice President	Salary	Bonus
1	135	12
2	115	14
3	146	16
4	167	19
5	165	22
6	176	24
7	98	7
8	136	17
9	163	18
10	119	11

   a.   Develop a scatter diagram for these data with salary as the independent variable.

   b.   What does the scatter diagram developed in part (a) indicate about the relationship between salary and bonus?

   c.   Use the least squares method to develop the estimated regression equation.

   d.   Provide an interpretation for the slope of the estimated regression equation.

   e.   Predict the bonus for a vice president with an annual salary of $120,000.

7.   Would you expect more reliable cars to cost more? *Consumer Reports* rated 15 upscale sedans. Reliability was rated on a 5-point scale: poor (1), fair (2), good (3), very good (4), and excellent (5). The price and reliability rating for each of the 15 cars are shown (*Consumer Reports,* February 2004).

Make and Model	Reliability	Price ($)
Acura TL	4	33,150
BMW 330i	3	40,570
Lexus IS300	5	35,105
Lexus ES330	5	35,174
Mercedes-Benz C320	1	42,230
Lincoln LS Premium (V6)	3	38,225
Audi A4 3.0 Quattro	2	37,605
Cadillac CTS	1	37,695
Nissan Maxima 3.5 SE	4	34,390
Infiniti I35	5	33,845
Saab 9-3 Aero	3	36,910
Infiniti G35	4	34,695
Jaguar X-Type 3.0	1	37,995
Saab 9-5 Arc	3	36,955
Volvo S60 2.5T	3	33,890

CD file

Cars

a. Develop a scatter diagram for these data with the reliability rating as the independent variable.
b. Develop the least squares estimated regression equation.
c. Based upon your analysis, do you think more reliable cars cost more? Explain.
d. Estimate the price for an upscale sedan that has an average reliability rating.

8. Mountain bikes that cost less than $1000 now contain many of the high-quality components that until recently were only available on high-priced models. Today, even sub-$1000 models often offer supple suspensions, clipless pedals, and highly engineered frames. An interesting question is whether higher price still buys a higher level of handling, as measured by the bike's sidetrack capability. To measure sidetrack capability, *Outside Magazine* used a rating scale from 1 to 5, with 1 representing an average rating and 5 representing an excellent rating. The sidetrack capability and the price for 10 mountain bikes tested by *Outside Magazine* follow (*Outside Magazine Buyer's Guide,* 2001).

Manufacturer and Model	Sidetrack Capability	Price ($)
Raleigh M80	1	600
Marin Bear Valley Feminina	1	649
GT Avalanche 2.0	2	799
Kona Jake the Snake	1	899
Schwinn Moab 2	3	950
Giant XTC NRS 3	4	1100
Fisher Paragon Genesisters	4	1149
Jamis Dakota XC	3	1300
Trek Fuel 90	5	1550
Specialized Stumpjumper M4	4	1625

CD file

MtnBikes

a. Develop a scatter diagram for these data with sidetrack capability as the independent variable.
b. Does it appear that higher-priced models have a higher level of handling? Explain.
c. Develop the least squares estimated regression equation.
d. What is the estimated price for a mountain bike if it has a sidetrack capability rating of 4?

9. A sales manager collected the following data on annual sales and years of experience.

Salesperson	Years of Experience	Annual Sales ($1000s)
1	1	80
2	3	97
3	4	92
4	4	102
5	6	103
6	8	111
7	10	119
8	10	123
9	11	117
10	13	136

a. Develop a scatter diagram for these data with years of experience as the independent variable.
b. Develop an estimated regression equation that can be used to predict annual sales given the years of experience.
c. Use the estimated regression equation to predict annual sales for a salesperson with 9 years of experience.

10. *PC World* provided ratings for the top 15 notebook PCs (*PC World,* February 2000). The performance score is a measure of how fast a PC can run a mix of common business applications as compared to how fast a baseline machine can run them. For example, a PC with a performance score of 200 is twice as fast as the baseline machine. A 100-point scale was used to provide an overall rating for each notebook tested in the study. A score in the 90s is exceptional, while one in the 70s is above average. The performance scores and the overall ratings for the 15 notebooks follow.

PCs

Make and Model	Performance Score	Overall Rating
AMS Tech Roadster 15CTA380	115	67
Compaq Armada M700	191	78
Compaq Prosignia Notebook 150	153	79
Dell Inspiron 3700 C466GT	194	80
Dell Inspiron 7500 R500VT	236	84
Dell Latitude Cpi A366XT	184	76
Enpower ENP-313 Pro	184	77
Gateway Solo 9300LS	216	92
HP Pavilion Notebook PC	185	83
IBM ThinkPad I Series 1480	183	78
Micro Express NP7400	189	77
Micron TransPort NX PII-400	202	78
NEC Versa SX	192	78
Sceptre Soundx 5200	141	73
Sony VAIO PCG-F340	187	77

a. Develop a scatter diagram for these data with performance score as the independent variable.
b. Develop the least squares estimated regression equation.
c. Estimate the overall rating for a new PC that has a performance score of 225.

11. Although delays at major airports are now less frequent, it helps to know which airports are likely to throw off your schedule. In addition, if your plane is late arriving at a particular airport where you must make a connection, how likely is it that the departure will be

late and thus increase your chances of making the connection? The following data show the percentage of late arrivals and departures during August for 13 airports (*Business 2.0,* February 2002).

Airport

Airport	Late Arrivals (%)	Late Departures (%)
Atlanta	24	22
Charlotte	20	20
Chicago	30	29
Cincinnati	20	19
Dallas	20	22
Denver	23	23
Detroit	18	19
Houston	20	16
Minneapolis	18	18
Phoenix	21	22
Pittsburgh	25	22
Salt Lake City	18	17
St. Louis	16	16

a. Develop a scatter diagram for these data with the percentage of late arrivals as the independent variable.
b. What does the scatter diagram developed in part (a) indicate about the relationship between late arrivals and late departures?
c. Use the least squares method to develop the estimated regression equation.
d. Provide an interpretation for the slope of the estimated regression equation.
e. Suppose the percentage of late arrivals at the Philadelphia airport for August was 22%. What is an estimate of the percentage of late departures?

12. The following table gives the number of employees and the revenue (in millions of dollars) for 20 companies (*Fortune,* April 17, 2000).

EmpRev

Company	Employees	Revenue ($millions)
Sprint	77,600	19,930
Chase Manhattan	74,801	33,710
Computer Sciences	50,000	7,660
Wells Fargo	89,355	21,795
Sunbeam	12,200	2,398
CBS	29,000	7,510
Time Warner	69,722	27,333
Steelcase	16,200	2,743
Georgia-Pacific	57,000	17,796
Toro	1,275	4,673
American Financial	9,400	3,334
Fluor	53,561	12,417
Phillips Petroleum	15,900	13,852
Cardinal Health	36,000	25,034
Borders Group	23,500	2,999
MCI Worldcom	77,000	37,120
Consolidated Edison	14,269	7,491
IBP	45,000	14,075
Super Value	50,000	17,421
H&R Block	4,200	1,669

a. Develop a scatter diagram for these data with number of employees as the independent variable.
b. What does the scatter diagram developed in part (a) indicate about the relationship between number of employees and revenue?
c. Develop the estimated regression equation for these data.
d. Use the estimated regression equation to predict the revenue for a firm with 75,000 employees.

13. To the Internal Revenue Service, the reasonableness of total itemized deductions depends on the taxpayer's adjusted gross income. Large deductions, which include charity and medical deductions, are more reasonable for taxpayers with large adjusted gross incomes. If a taxpayer claims larger than average itemized deductions for a given level of income, the chances of an IRS audit are increased. Data (in thousands of dollars) on adjusted gross income and the average or reasonable amount of itemized deductions follow.

Adjusted Gross Income ($1000s)	Reasonable Amount of Itemized Deductions ($1000s)
22	9.6
27	9.6
32	10.1
48	11.1
65	13.5
85	17.7
120	25.5

a. Develop a scatter diagram for these data with adjusted gross income as the independent variable.
b. Use the least squares method to develop the estimated regression equation.
c. Estimate a reasonable level of total itemized deductions for a taxpayer with an adjusted gross income of $52,500. If this taxpayer claimed itemized deductions of $20,400, would the IRS agent's request for an audit appear justified? Explain.

14. Starting salaries for accountants and auditors in Rochester, New York, trail those of many U.S. cities. The following data show the starting salary (in thousands of dollars) and the cost of living index for Rochester and nine other metropolitan areas (*Democrat and Chronicle,* September 1, 2002). The cost of living index, based on a city's food, housing, taxes, and other costs, ranges from 0 (most expensive) to 100 (least expensive).

CD file

Salaries

Metropolitan Area	Index	Salary ($1000s)
Oklahoma City	82.44	23.9
Tampa/St. Petersburg/Clearwater	79.89	24.5
Indianapolis	55.53	27.4
Buffalo/Niagara Falls	41.36	27.7
Atlanta	39.38	27.1
Rochester	28.05	25.6
Sacramento	25.50	28.7
Raleigh/Durham/Chapel Hill	13.32	26.7
San Diego	3.12	27.8
Honolulu	0.57	28.3

a. Develop a scatter diagram for these data with the cost of living index as the independent variable.
b. Develop the estimated regression equation relating the cost of living index to the starting salary.
c. Estimate the starting salary for a metropolitan area with a cost of living index of 50.

12.3 Coefficient of Determination

For the Armand's Pizza Parlors example, we developed the estimated regression equation $\hat{y} = 60 + 5x$ to approximate the linear relationship between the size of the student population x and quarterly sales y. A question now is: How well does the estimated regression equation fit the data? In this section, we show that the **coefficient of determination** provides a measure of the goodness of fit for the estimated regression equation.

For the ith observation, the difference between the observed value of the dependent variable, y_i, and the estimated value of the dependent variable, $\hat{y}_i$, is called the **ith residual**. The ith residual represents the error in using $\hat{y}_i$ to estimate y_i. Thus, for the ith observation, the residual is $y_i - \hat{y}_i$. The sum of squares of these residuals or errors is the quantity that is minimized by the least squares method. This quantity, also known as the *sum of squares due to error,* is denoted by SSE.

> **SUM OF SQUARES DUE TO ERROR**
>
> $$SSE = \Sigma(y_i - \hat{y}_i)^2 \tag{12.8}$$

The value of SSE is a measure of the error in using the estimated regression equation to estimate the values of the dependent variable in the sample.

In Table 12.3 we show the calculations required to compute the sum of squares due to error for the Armand's Pizza Parlors example. For instance, for restaurant 1 the values of the independent and dependent variables are $x_1 = 2$ and $y_1 = 58$. Using the estimated regression equation, we find that the estimated value of quarterly sales for restaurant 1 is $\hat{y}_1 = 60 + 5(2) = 70$. Thus, the error in using $\hat{y}_1$ to estimate y_1 for restaurant 1 is $y_1 - \hat{y}_1 = 58 - 70 = -12$. The squared error, $(-12)^2 = 144$, is shown in the last column of Table 12.3. After computing and squaring the residuals for each restaurant in the sample, we sum them to obtain SSE = 1530. Thus, SSE = 1530 measures the error in using the estimated regression equation $\hat{y} = 60 + 5x$ to predict sales.

Now suppose we are asked to develop an estimate of quarterly sales without knowledge of the size of the student population. Without knowledge of any related variables, we would

TABLE 12.3   CALCULATION OF SSE FOR ARMAND'S PIZZA PARLORS

Restaurant i	x_i = Student Population (1000s)	y_i = Quarterly Sales ($1000s)	Predicted Sales $\hat{y}_i = 60 + 5x_i$	Error $y_i - \hat{y}_i$	Squared Error $(y_i - \hat{y}_i)^2$
1	2	58	70	−12	144
2	6	105	90	15	225
3	8	88	100	−12	144
4	8	118	100	18	324
5	12	117	120	−3	9
6	16	137	140	−3	9
7	20	157	160	−3	9
8	20	169	160	9	81
9	22	149	170	−21	441
10	26	202	190	12	144
					SSE = 1530

TABLE 12.4   COMPUTATION OF THE TOTAL SUM OF SQUARES FOR ARMAND'S PIZZA PARLORS

Restaurant i	x_i = Student Population (1000s)	y_i = Quarterly Sales ($1000s)	Deviation $y_i - \bar{y}$	Squared Deviation $(y_i - \bar{y})^2$
1	2	58	-72	5,184
2	6	105	-25	625
3	8	88	-42	1,764
4	8	118	-12	144
5	12	117	-13	169
6	16	137	7	49
7	20	157	27	729
8	20	169	39	1,521
9	22	149	19	361
10	26	202	72	5,184
				SST = 15,730

use the sample mean as an estimate of quarterly sales at any given restaurant. Table 12.2 shows that for the sales data, $\Sigma y_i = 1300$. Hence, the mean value of quarterly sales for the sample of 10 Armand's restaurants is $\bar{y} = \Sigma y_i/n = 1300/10 = 130$. In Table 12.4 we show the sum of squared deviations obtained by using the sample mean $\bar{y} = 130$ to estimate the value of quarterly sales for each restaurant in the sample. For the ith restaurant in the sample, the difference $y_i - \bar{y}$ provides a measure of the error involved in using $\bar{y}$ to estimate sales. The corresponding sum of squares, called the *total sum of squares,* is denoted SST.

TOTAL SUM OF SQUARES

$$SST = \Sigma(y_i - \bar{y})^2 \tag{12.9}$$

The sum at the bottom of the last column in Table 12.4 is the total sum of squares for Armand's Pizza Parlors; it is SST = 15,730.

In Figure 12.5 we show the estimated regression line $\hat{y} = 60 + 5x$ and the line corresponding to $\bar{y} = 130$. Note that the points cluster more closely around the estimated regression line than they do about the line $\bar{y} = 130$. For example, for the 10th restaurant in the sample we see that the error is much larger when $\bar{y} = 130$ is used as an estimate of y_{10} than when $\hat{y}_{10} = 60 + 5(26) = 190$ is used. We can think of SST as a measure of how well the observations cluster about the $\bar{y}$ line and SSE as a measure of how well the observations cluster about the $\hat{y}$ line.

To measure how much the $\hat{y}$ values on the estimated regression line deviate from $\bar{y}$, another sum of squares is computed. This sum of squares, called the *sum of squares due to regression,* is denoted SSR.

SUM OF SQUARES DUE TO REGRESSION

$$SSR = \Sigma(\hat{y}_i - \bar{y})^2 \tag{12.10}$$

FIGURE 12.5   DEVIATIONS ABOUT THE ESTIMATED REGRESSION LINE AND THE LINE
$y = \bar{y}$ FOR ARMAND'S PIZZA PARLORS

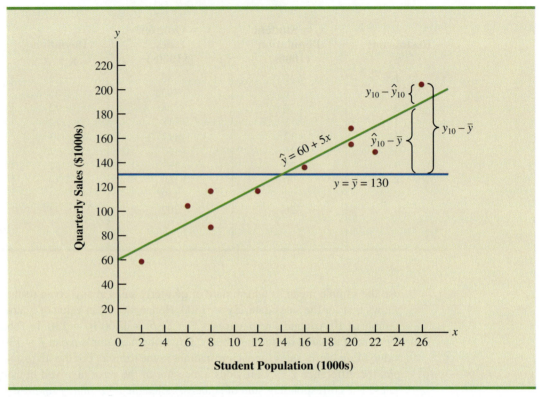

From the preceding discussion, we should expect that SST, SSR, and SSE are related.
Indeed, the relationship among these three sums of squares provides one of the most important results in statistics.

*SSR can be thought of as
the explained portion of
SST, and SSE can be
thought of as the
unexplained portion of SST.*

RELATIONSHIP AMONG SST, SSR, AND SSE

$$SST = SSR + SSE \qquad (12.11)$$

where

      SST = total sum of squares
      SSR = sum of squares due to regression
      SSE = sum of squares due to error

Equation (12.11) shows that the total sum of squares can be partitioned into two components, the regression sum of squares and the sum of squares due to error. Hence, if the values of any two of these sums of squares are known, the third sum of squares can be computed easily. For instance, in the Armand's Pizza Parlors example, we already know that SSE = 1530 and SST = 15,730; therefore, solving for SSR in equation (12.11), we find that the sum of squares due to regression is

$$SSR = SST - SSE = 15,730 - 1530 = 14,200$$

Now let us see how the three sums of squares, SST, SSR, and SSE, can be used to provide a measure of the goodness of fit for the estimated regression equation. The estimated regression equation would provide a perfect fit if every value of the dependent variable y_i happened to lie on the estimated regression line. In this case, $y_i - \hat{y}_i$ would be zero for each observation, resulting in SSE $= 0$. Because SST $=$ SSR $+$ SSE, we see that for a perfect fit SSR must equal SST, and the ratio (SSR/SST) must equal one. Poorer fits will result in larger values for SSE. Solving for SSE in equation (12.11), we see that SSE $=$ SST $-$ SSR. Hence, the largest value for SSE (and hence the poorest fit) occurs when SSR $= 0$ and SSE $=$ SST.

The ratio SSR/SST, which will take values between zero and one, is used to evaluate the goodness of fit for the estimated regression equation. This ratio is called the *coefficient of determination* and is denoted by r^2.

COEFFICIENT OF DETERMINATION

$$r^2 = \frac{\text{SSR}}{\text{SST}}$$

(12.12)

For the Armand's Pizza Parlors example, the value of the coefficient of determination is

$$r^2 = \frac{\text{SSR}}{\text{SST}} = \frac{14{,}200}{15{,}730} = .9027$$

When we express the coefficient of determination as a percentage, r^2 can be interpreted as the percentage of the total sum of squares that can be explained by using the estimated regression equation. For Armand's Pizza Parlors, we can conclude that 90.27% of the total sum of squares can be explained by using the estimated regression equation $\hat{y} = 60 + 5x$ to predict quarterly sales. In other words, 90.27% of the variability in sales can be explained by the linear relationship between the size of the student population and sales. We should be pleased to find such a good fit for the estimated regression equation.

Correlation Coefficient

In Chapter 3 we introduced the **correlation coefficient** as a descriptive measure of the strength of linear association between two variables, x and y. Values of the correlation coefficient are always between -1 and $+1$. A value of $+1$ indicates that the two variables x and y are perfectly related in a positive linear sense. That is, all data points are on a straight line that has a positive slope. A value of -1 indicates that x and y are perfectly related in a negative linear sense, with all data points on a straight line that has a negative slope. Values of the correlation coefficient close to zero indicate that x and y are not linearly related.

In Section 3.5 we presented the equation for computing the sample correlation coefficient. If a regression analysis has already been performed and the coefficient of determination r^2 computed, the sample correlation coefficient can be computed as follows.

SAMPLE CORRELATION COEFFICIENT

$$r_{xy} = (\text{sign of } b_1)\sqrt{\text{Coefficient of determination}}$$
$$= (\text{sign of } b_1)\sqrt{r^2}$$

(12.13)

---

where

b_1 = the slope of the estimated regression equation $\hat{y} = b_0 + b_1x$

The sign for the sample correlation coefficient is positive if the estimated regression equation has a positive slope ($b_1 > 0$) and negative if the estimated regression equation has a negative slope ($b_1 < 0$).

For the Armand's Pizza Parlors example, the value of the coefficient of determination corresponding to the estimated regression equation $\hat{y} = 60 + 5x$ is .9027. Because the slope of the estimated regression equation is positive, equation (12.13) shows that the sample correlation coefficient is $+\sqrt{.9027} = +.9501$. With a sample correlation coefficient of $r_{xy} = +.9501$, we would conclude that a strong positive linear association exists between x and y.

In the case of a linear relationship between two variables, both the coefficient of determination and the sample correlation coefficient provide measures of the strength of the relationship. The coefficient of determination provides a measure between zero and one, whereas the sample correlation coefficient provides a measure between -1 and $+1$. Although the sample correlation coefficient is restricted to a linear relationship between two variables, the coefficient of determination can be used for nonlinear relationships and for relationships that have two or more independent variables. Thus, the coefficient of determination provides a wider range of applicability.

NOTES AND COMMENTS

1. In developing the least squares estimated regression equation and computing the coefficient of determination, we made no probabilistic assumptions about the error term ϵ, and no statistical tests for significance of the relationship between x and y were conducted. Larger values of r^2 imply that the least squares line provides a better fit to the data; that is, the observations are more closely grouped about the least squares line. But, using only r^2, we can draw no conclusion about whether the relationship between x and y is statistically significant. Such a conclusion must be based on considerations that involve the sample size and the properties of the appropriate sampling distributions of the least squares estimators.

2. As a practical matter, for typical data found in the social sciences, values of r^2 as low as .25 are often considered useful. For data in the physical and life sciences, r^2 values of .60 or greater are often found; in fact, in some cases, r^2 values greater than .90 can be found. In business applications, r^2 values vary greatly, depending on the unique characteristics of each application.

Exercises

Methods

15. The data from exercise 1 follow.

x_i	1	2	3	4	5
y_i	3	7	5	11	14

The estimated regression equation for these data is $\hat{y} = .20 + 2.60x$.
   a. Compute SSE, SST, and SSR using equations (12.8), (12.9), and (12.10).
   b. Compute the coefficient of determination r^2. Comment on the goodness of fit.
   c. Compute the sample correlation coefficient.

16. The data from exercise 2 follow.

x_i	2	3	5	1	8
y_i	25	25	20	30	16

The estimated regression equation for these data is $\hat{y} = 30.33 - 1.88x$.
a. Compute SSE, SST, and SSR.
b. Compute the coefficient of determination r^2. Comment on the goodness of fit.
c. Compute the sample correlation coefficient.

17. The data from exercise 3 follow.

x_i	2	4	5	7	8
y_i	2	3	2	6	4

The estimated regression equation for these data is $\hat{y} = .75 + .51x$. What percentage of the total sum of squares can be accounted for by the estimated regression equation? What is the value of the sample correlation coefficient?

Applications

18. The following data are the monthly salaries y and the grade point averages x for students who obtained a bachelor's degree in business administration with a major in information systems. The estimated regression equation for these data is $\hat{y} = 1790.5 + 581.1x$.

GPA	Monthly Salary ($)	GPA	Monthly Salary ($)
2.6	3300	3.2	3500
3.4	3600	3.5	3900
3.6	4000	2.9	3600

a. Compute SST, SSR, and SSE.
b. Compute the coefficient of determination r^2. Comment on the goodness of fit.
c. What is the value of the sample correlation coefficient?

19. The data from exercise 7 follow:

Cars

Make and Model	x = Reliability	y = Price ($)
Acura TL	4	33,150
BMW 330i	3	40,570
Lexus IS300	5	35,105
Lexus ES330	5	35,174
Mercedes-Benz C320	1	42,230
Lincoln LS Premium (V6)	3	38,225
Audi A4 3.0 Quattro	2	37,605
Cadillac CTS	1	37,695
Nissan Maxima 3.5 SE	4	34,390
Infiniti I35	5	33,845
Saab 9-3 Aero	3	36,910
Infiniti G35	4	34,695
Jaguar X-Type 3.0	1	37,995
Saab 9-5 Arc	3	36,955
Volvo S60 2.5T	3	33,890

The estimated regression equation for these data is $\hat{y} = 40,639 - 1301x$. What percentage of the total sum of squares can be accounted for by the estimated regression equation? Comment on the goodness of fit. What is the sample correlation coefficient?

20. The typical household income and typical home price for a sample of 18 cities follow (*Places Rated Almanac,* 2000). Data are in thousands of dollars.

Cities

City	Income	Home Price
Akron, OH	74.1	114.9
Atlanta, GA	82.4	126.9
Birmingham, AL	71.2	130.9
Bismarck, ND	62.8	92.8
Cleveland, OH	79.2	135.8
Columbia, SC	66.8	116.7
Denver, CO	82.6	161.9
Detroit, MI	85.3	145.0
Fort Lauderdale, FL	75.8	145.3
Hartford, CT	89.1	162.1
Lancaster, PA	75.2	125.9
Madison, WI	78.8	145.2
Naples, FL	100.0	173.6
Nashville, TN	77.3	125.9
Philadelphia, PA	87.0	151.5
Savannah, GA	67.8	108.1
Toledo, OH	71.2	101.1
Washington, DC	97.4	191.9

a. With these data, develop an estimated regression equation that could be used to estimate the typical home price for a city given the typical household income.

b. Compute r^2. Would you feel comfortable using this estimated regression equation to estimate the typical home price for a city?

c. Estimate the typical home price for a city with a typical household income of $95,000.

21. An important application of regression analysis in accounting is in the estimation of cost. By collecting data on volume and cost and using the least squares method to develop an estimated regression equation relating volume and cost, an accountant can estimate the cost associated with a particular manufacturing volume. Consider the following sample of production volumes and total cost data for a manufacturing operation.

Production Volume (units)	Total Cost ($)
400	4000
450	5000
550	5400
600	5900
700	6400
750	7000

a. With these data, develop an estimated regression equation that could be used to predict the total cost for a given production volume.

b. What is the variable cost per unit produced?

c. Compute the coefficient of determination. What percentage of the variation in total cost can be explained by production volume?

d. The company's production schedule shows 500 units must be produced next month. What is the estimated total cost for this operation?

22. *PC World* provided ratings for the top five small-office laser printers and five corporate laser printers (*PC World,* February 2003). The highest-rated small-office laser printer was the Minolta-QMS PagePro 1250W, with an overall rating of 91. The highest-rated corporate

laser printer, the Xerox Phaser 4400/N, had an overall rating of 83. The following data show the speed for plain text printing in pages per minute (ppm) and the price for each printer.

Printers

Name	Type	Speed (ppm)	Price ($)
Minolta-QMS PagePro 1250W	Small Office	12	199
Brother HL-1850	Small Office	10	499
Lexmark E320	Small Office	12.2	299
Minolta-QMS PagePro 1250E	Small Office	10.3	299
HP Laserjet 1200	Small Office	11.7	399
Xerox Phaser 4400/N	Corporate	17.8	1850
Brother HL-2460N	Corporate	16.1	1000
IBM Infoprint 1120n	Corporate	11.8	1387
Lexmark W812	Corporate	19.8	2089
Oki Data B8300n	Corporate	28.2	2200

a. Develop the estimated regression equation with speed as the independent variable.
b. Compute r^2. What percentage of the variation in cost can be explained by the printing speed?
c. What is the sample correlation coefficient between speed and price? Does it reflect a strong or weak relationship between printing speed and cost?

12.4 Model Assumptions

In conducting a regression analysis, we begin by making an assumption about the appropriate model for the relationship between the dependent and independent variable(s). For the case of simple linear regression, the assumed regression model is

$$y = \beta_0 + \beta_1 x + \epsilon$$

Then, the least squares method is used to develop values for b_0 and b_1, the estimates of the model parameters β_0 and β_1, respectively. The resulting estimated regression equation is

$$\hat{y} = b_0 + b_1 x$$

We saw that the value of the coefficient of determination (r^2) is a measure of the goodness of fit of the estimated regression equation. However, even with a large value of r^2, the estimated regression equation should not be used until further analysis of the appropriateness of the assumed model has been conducted. An important step in determining whether the assumed model is appropriate involves testing for the significance of the relationship. The tests of significance in regression analysis are based on the following assumptions about the error term ϵ.

ASSUMPTIONS ABOUT THE ERROR TERM ϵ IN THE REGRESSION MODEL

$$y = \beta_0 + \beta_1 x + \epsilon$$

1. The error term ϵ is a random variable with a mean or expected value of zero; that is, $E(\epsilon) = 0$.
Implication: β_0 and β_1 are constants, therefore $E(\beta_0) = \beta_0$ and $E(\beta_1) = \beta_1$; thus, for a given value of x, the expected value of y is

$$E(y) = \beta_0 + \beta_1 x \qquad \text{(12.14)}$$

As we indicated previously, equation (12.14) is referred to as the regression equation.

2. The variance of ϵ, denoted by σ^2, is the same for all values of x.
   Implication: The variance of y about the regression line equals σ^2 and is the same for all values of x.

3. The values of ϵ are independent.
   Implication: The value of ϵ for a particular value of x is not related to the value of ϵ for any other value of x; thus, the value of y for a particular value of x is not related to the value of y for any other value of x.

4. The error term ϵ is a normally distributed random variable.
   Implication: Because y is a linear function of ϵ, y is also a normally distributed random variable.

Figure 12.6 illustrates the model assumptions and their implications; note that in this graphical interpretation, the value of $E(y)$ changes according to the specific value of x considered. However, regardless of the x value, the probability distribution of ϵ and hence the probability distributions of y are normally distributed, each with the same variance. The specific value of the error ϵ at any particular point depends on whether the actual value of y is greater than or less than $E(y)$.

At this point, we must keep in mind that we are also making an assumption or hypothesis about the form of the relationship between x and y. That is, we assume that a straight

FIGURE 12.6   ASSUMPTIONS FOR THE REGRESSION MODEL

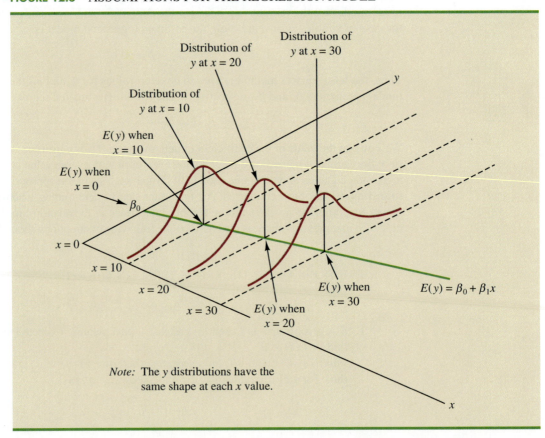

Note: The y distributions have the same shape at each x value.

line represented by $\beta_0 + \beta_1 x$ is the basis for the relationship between the variables. We must not lose sight of the fact that some other model, for instance $y = \beta_0 + \beta_1 x^2 + \epsilon$, may turn out to be a better model for the underlying relationship.

12.5   Testing for Significance

In a simple linear regression equation, the mean or expected value of y is a linear function of x: $E(y) = \beta_0 + \beta_1 x$. If the value of β_1 is zero, $E(y) = \beta_0 + (0)x = \beta_0$. In this case, the mean value of y does not depend on the value of x and hence we would conclude that x and y are not linearly related. Alternatively, if the value of β_1 is not equal to zero, we would conclude that the two variables are related. Thus, to test for a significant regression relationship, we must conduct a hypothesis test to determine whether the value of β_1 is zero. Two tests are commonly used. Both require an estimate of σ^2, the variance of ϵ in the regression model.

Estimate of σ^2

From the regression model and its assumptions we can conclude that σ^2, the variance of ϵ, also represents the variance of the y values about the regression line. Recall that the deviations of the y values about the estimated regression line are called residuals. Thus, SSE, the sum of squared residuals, is a measure of the variability of the actual observations about the estimated regression line. The **mean square error** (MSE) provides the estimate of σ^2; it is SSE divided by its degrees of freedom.

With $\hat{y}_i = b_0 + b_1 x_i$, SSE can be written as

$$\text{SSE} = \Sigma(y_i - \hat{y}_i)^2 = \Sigma(y_i - b_0 - b_1 x_i)^2$$

Every sum of squares is associated with a number called its degrees of freedom. Statisticians have shown that SSE has $n - 2$ degrees of freedom because two parameters (β_0 and β_1) must be estimated to compute SSE. Thus, the mean square is computed by dividing SSE by $n - 2$. MSE provides an unbiased estimator of σ^2. Because the value of MSE provides an estimate of σ^2, the notation s^2 is also used.

> **MEAN SQUARE ERROR (ESTIMATE OF σ^2)**
>
> $$s^2 = \text{MSE} = \frac{\text{SSE}}{n - 2} \qquad (12.15)$$

In Section 12.3 we showed that for the Armand's Pizza Parlors example, SSE = 1530; hence,

$$s^2 = \text{MSE} = \frac{1530}{8} = 191.25$$

provides an unbiased estimate of σ^2.

To estimate σ we take the square root of s^2. The resulting value, s, is referred to as the **standard error of the estimate**.

> **STANDARD ERROR OF THE ESTIMATE**
>
> $$s = \sqrt{\text{MSE}} = \sqrt{\frac{\text{SSE}}{n - 2}} \qquad (12.16)$$

For the Armand's Pizza Parlors example, $s = \sqrt{\text{MSE}} = \sqrt{191.25} = 13.829$. In the following discussion, we use the standard error of the estimate in the tests for a significant relationship between x and y.

t Test

The simple linear regression model is $y = \beta_0 + \beta_1 x + \epsilon$. If x and y are linearly related, we must have $\beta_1 \neq 0$. The purpose of the t test is to see whether we can conclude that $\beta_1 \neq 0$. We will use the sample data to test the following hypotheses about the parameter β_1.

$$H_0: \beta_1 = 0$$
$$H_a: \beta_1 \neq 0$$

If H_0 is rejected, we will conclude that $\beta_1 \neq 0$ and that a statistically significant relationship exists between the two variables. However, if H_0 cannot be rejected, we will have insufficient evidence to conclude that a significant relationship exists. The properties of the sampling distribution of b_1, the least squares estimator of β_1, provide the basis for the hypothesis test.

First, let us consider what would happen if we used a different random sample for the same regression study. For example, suppose that Armand's Pizza Parlors used the sales records of a different sample of 10 restaurants. A regression analysis of this new sample might result in an estimated regression equation similar to our previous estimated regression equation $\hat{y} = 60 + 5x$. However, it is doubtful that we would obtain exactly the same equation (with an intercept of exactly 60 and a slope of exactly 5). Indeed, b_0 and b_1, the least squares estimators, are sample statistics with their own sampling distributions. The properties of the sampling distribution of b_1 follow.

SAMPLING DISTRIBUTION OF b_1

Expected Value
$$E(b_1) = \beta_1$$

Standard Deviation
$$\sigma_{b_1} = \frac{\sigma}{\sqrt{\Sigma(x_i - \bar{x})^2}} \qquad \textbf{(12.17)}$$

Distribution Form
Normal

Note that the expected value of b_1 is equal to β_1, so b_1 is an unbiased estimator of β_1.

Because we do not know the value of σ, we develop an estimate of σ_{b_1}, denoted s_{b_1}, by estimating σ with s in equation (12.17). Thus, we obtain the following estimate of σ_{b_1}.

The standard deviation of b_1 is also referred to as the standard error of b_1. Thus, s_{b_1} provides an estimate of the standard error of b_1.

ESTIMATED STANDARD DEVIATION OF b_1

$$s_{b_1} = \frac{s}{\sqrt{\Sigma(x_i - \bar{x})^2}} \qquad \textbf{(12.18)}$$

For Armand's Pizza Parlors, $s = 13.829$. Hence, using $\Sigma(x_i - \bar{x})^2 = 568$ as shown in Table 12.2, we have

$$s_{b_1} = \frac{13.829}{\sqrt{568}} = .5803$$

as the estimated standard deviation of b_1.

The t test for a significant relationship is based on the fact that the test statistic

$$\frac{b_1 - \beta_1}{s_{b_1}}$$

follows a t distribution with $n - 2$ degrees of freedom. If the null hypothesis is true, then $\beta_1 = 0$ and $t = b_1/s_{b_1}$.

Let us conduct this test of significance for Armand's Pizza Parlors at the $\alpha = .01$ level of significance. The test statistic is

$$t = \frac{b_1}{s_{b_1}} = \frac{5}{.5803} = 8.62$$

Appendixes 12.1 and 12.2 show how Minitab and Excel can be used to compute the p-value.

The t distribution table shows that with $n - 2 = 10 - 2 = 8$ degrees of freedom, $t = 3.355$ provides an area of .005 in the upper tail. Thus, the area in the upper tail of the t distribution corresponding to the test statistic $t = 8.62$ must be less than .005. Because this test is a two-tailed test, we double this value to conclude that the p-value associated with $t = 8.62$ must be less than $2(.005) = .01$. Minitab or Excel shows the p-value $= .000$. Because the p-value is less than $\alpha = .01$, we reject H_0 and conclude that β_1 is not equal to zero. This evidence is sufficient to conclude that a significant relationship exists between student population and quarterly sales. A summary of the t test for significance in simple linear regression follows.

t TEST FOR SIGNIFICANCE IN SIMPLE LINEAR REGRESSION

$$H_0: \beta_1 = 0$$
$$H_a: \beta_1 \neq 0$$

TEST STATISTIC

$$t = \frac{b_1}{s_{b_1}} \qquad\qquad \textbf{(12.19)}$$

REJECTION RULE

p-value approach: Reject H_0 if p-value $\leq \alpha$

Critical value approach: Reject H_0 if $t \leq -t_{\alpha/2}$ or if $t \geq t_{\alpha/2}$

where $t_{\alpha/2}$ is based on a t distribution with $n - 2$ degrees of freedom.

Confidence Interval for β_1

The form of a confidence interval for β_1 is as follows:

$$b_1 \pm t_{\alpha/2} s_{b_1}$$

The point estimator is b_1 and the margin of error is $t_{\alpha/2}s_{b_1}$. The confidence coefficient associated with this interval is $1 - \alpha$, and $t_{\alpha/2}$ is the t value providing an area of $\alpha/2$ in the upper tail of a t distribution with $n - 2$ degrees of freedom. For example, suppose that we wanted to develop a 99% confidence interval estimate of β_1 for Armand's Pizza Parlors. From Table 2 of Appendix B we find that the t value corresponding to $\alpha = .01$ and $n - 2 = 10 - 2 = 8$ degrees of freedom is $t_{.005} = 3.355$. Thus, the 99% confidence interval estimate of β_1 is

$$b_1 \pm t_{\alpha/2}s_{b_1} = 5 \pm 3.355(.5803) = 5 \pm 1.95$$

or 3.05 to 6.95.

In using the t test for significance, the hypotheses tested were

$$H_0\!: \beta_1 = 0$$
$$H_a\!: \beta_1 \neq 0$$

At the $\alpha = .01$ level of significance, we can use the 99% confidence interval as an alternative for drawing the hypothesis testing conclusion for the Armand's data. Because 0, the hypothesized value of β_1, is not included in the confidence interval (3.05 to 6.95), we can reject H_0 and conclude that a significant statistical relationship exists between the size of the student population and quarterly sales. In general, a confidence interval can be used to test any two-sided hypothesis about β_1. If the hypothesized value of β_1 is contained in the confidence interval, do not reject H_0. Otherwise, reject H_0.

F Test

An F test, based on the F probability distribution, can also be used to test for significance in regression. With only one independent variable, the F test will provide the same conclusion as the t test; that is, if the t test indicates $\beta_1 \neq 0$ and hence a significant relationship, the F test will also indicate a significant relationship. But with more than one independent variable, only the F test can be used to test for an overall significant relationship.

The logic behind the use of the F test for determining whether the regression relationship is statistically significant is based on the development of two independent estimates of σ^2. We explained how MSE provides an estimate of σ^2. If the null hypothesis $H_0\!: \beta_1 = 0$ is true, the sum of squares due to regression, SSR, divided by its degrees of freedom provides another independent estimate of σ^2. This estimate is called the *mean square due to regression,* or simply the *mean square regression,* and is denoted MSR. In general,

$$\text{MSR} = \frac{\text{SSR}}{\text{Regression degrees of freedom}}$$

For the models we consider in this text, the regression degrees of freedom is always equal to the number of independent variables in the model:

$$\text{MSR} = \frac{\text{SSR}}{\text{Number of independent variables}} \qquad (12.20)$$

Because we consider only regression models with one independent variable in this chapter, we have MSR = SSR/1 = SSR. Hence, for Armand's Pizza Parlors, MSR = SSR = 14,200.

If the null hypothesis ($H_0\!: \beta_1 = 0$) is true, MSR and MSE are two independent estimates of σ^2 and the sampling distribution of MSR/MSE follows an F distribution with numerator degrees of freedom equal to 1 and denominator degrees of freedom equal to $n - 2$. Therefore, when $\beta_1 = 0$, the value of MSR/MSE should be close to one. However, if the null hypothesis is false ($\beta_1 \neq 0$), MSR will overestimate σ^2 and the value of MSR/MSE will be inflated; thus, large values of MSR/MSE lead to the rejection of H_0 and the conclusion that the relationship between x and y is statistically significant.

Let us conduct the F test for the Armand's Pizza Parlors example. The test statistic is

In Section 10.4 we showed how to determine a p-value using the F distribution table.

$$F = \frac{\text{MSR}}{\text{MSE}} = \frac{14,200}{191.25} = 74.25$$

The F distribution table (Table 4 of Appendix B) shows that with one degree of freedom in the numerator and $n - 2 = 10 - 2 = 8$ degrees of freedom in the denominator, $F = 11.26$ provides an area of .01 in the upper tail. Thus, the area in the upper tail of the F distribution corresponding to the test statistic $F = 74.25$ must be less than .01. Thus, we conclude that the p-value must be less than .01. Minitab or Excel shows the p-value $= .000$. Because the p-value is less than $\alpha = .01$, we reject H_0 and conclude that a significant relationship exists between the size of the student population and quarterly sales. A summary of the F test for significance in simple linear regression follows.

The F test and the t test provide identical results for simple linear regression.

If H_0 is false, MSE still provides an unbiased estimate of σ^2 and MSR overestimates σ^2. If H_0 is true, both MSE and MSR provide unbiased estimates of σ^2; in this case the value of MSR/MSE should be close to 1.

F TEST FOR SIGNIFICANCE IN SIMPLE LINEAR REGRESSION

$$H_0: \beta_1 = 0$$
$$H_a: \beta_1 \neq 0$$

TEST STATISTIC

$$F = \frac{\text{MSR}}{\text{MSE}} \qquad\qquad \textbf{(12.21)}$$

REJECTION RULE

p-value approach:	Reject H_0 if p-value $\leq \alpha$
Critical value approach:	Reject H_0 if $F \geq F_\alpha$

where F_α is based on an F distribution with 1 degree of freedom in the numerator and $n - 2$ degrees of freedom in the denominator.

In Chapter 10 we covered analysis of variance (ANOVA) and showed how an **ANOVA table** could be used to provide a convenient summary of the computational aspects of analysis of variance. A similar ANOVA table can be used to summarize the results of the F test for significance in regression. Table 12.5 is the general form of the ANOVA table for simple linear regression. Table 12.6 is the ANOVA table with the F test computations performed for Armand's Pizza Parlors. Regression, Error, and Total are the labels for the three sources of variation, with SSR, SSE, and SST appearing as the corresponding sum of squares in column 2. The degrees of freedom, 1 for SSR, $n - 2$ for SSE, and $n - 1$ for SST, are shown in column 3. Column 4 contains the values of MSR and MSE and column 5 contains the value of $F = \text{MSR}/\text{MSE}$. Almost all computer printouts of regression analysis include an ANOVA table summary of the F test for significance.

TABLE 12.5   GENERAL FORM OF THE ANOVA TABLE FOR SIMPLE LINEAR REGRESSION

In every analysis of variance table the total sum of squares is the sum of the regression sum of squares and the error sum of squares; in addition, the total degrees of freedom is the sum of the regression degrees of freedom and the error degrees of freedom.

Source of Variation	Sum of Squares	Degrees of Freedom	Mean Square	F
Regression	SSR	1	$MSR = \dfrac{SSR}{1}$	$F = \dfrac{MSR}{MSE}$
Error	SSE	$n - 2$	$MSE = \dfrac{SSE}{n - 2}$	
Total	SST	$n - 1$		

Some Cautions About the Interpretation of Significance Tests

Rejecting the null hypothesis $H_0: \beta_1 = 0$ and concluding that the relationship between x and y is significant do not enable us to conclude that a cause-and-effect relationship is present between x and y. Concluding a cause-and-effect relationship is warranted only if the analyst can provide some type of theoretical justification that the relationship is in fact causal. In the Armand's Pizza Parlors example, we can conclude that there is a significant relationship between the size of the student population x and quarterly sales y; moreover, the estimated regression equation $\hat{y} = 60 + 5x$ provides the least squares estimate of the relationship. We cannot, however, conclude that changes in student population x *cause* changes in quarterly sales y just because we identified a statistically significant relationship. The appropriateness of such a cause-and-effect conclusion is left to supporting theoretical justification and to good judgment on the part of the analyst. Armand's managers felt that increases in the student population were a likely cause of increased quarterly sales. Thus, the result of the significance test enabled them to conclude that a cause-and-effect relationship was present.

Regression analysis, which can be used to identify how variables are associated with one another, cannot be used as evidence of a cause-and-effect relationship.

In addition, just because we are able to reject $H_0: \beta_1 = 0$ and demonstrate statistical significance does not enable us to conclude that the relationship between x and y is linear. We can state only that x and y are related and that a linear relationship explains a significant portion of the variability in y over the range of values for x observed in the sample. Figure 12.7 illustrates this situation. The test for significance calls for the rejection of the null hypothesis $H_0: \beta_1 = 0$ and leads to the conclusion that x and y are significantly related, but the figure shows that the actual relationship between x and y is not linear. Although the

TABLE 12.6   ANOVA TABLE FOR THE ARMAND'S PIZZA PARLORS PROBLEM

Source of Variation	Sum of Squares	Degrees of Freedom	Mean Square	F
Regression	14,200	1	$\dfrac{14,200}{1} = 14,200$	$\dfrac{14,200}{191.25} = 74.25$
Error	1,530	8	$\dfrac{1530}{8} = 191.25$	
Total	15,730	9		

FIGURE 12.7   EXAMPLE OF A LINEAR APPROXIMATION OF A NONLINEAR
RELATIONSHIP

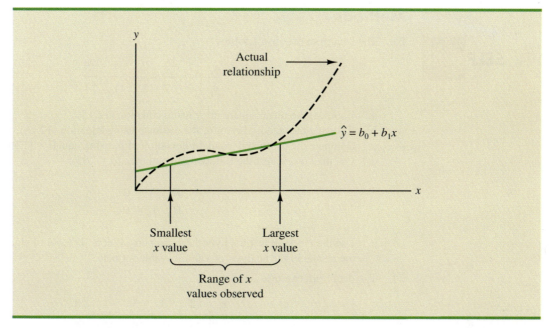

linear approximation provided by $\hat{y} = b_0 + b_1 x$ is good over the range of x values observed in the sample, it becomes poor for x values outside that range.

Given a significant relationship, we should feel confident in using the estimated regression equation for predictions corresponding to x values within the range of the x values observed in the sample. For Armand's Pizza Parlors, this range corresponds to values of x between 2 and 26. Unless other reasons indicate that the model is valid beyond this range, predictions outside the range of the independent variable should be made with caution. For Armand's Pizza Parlors, because the regression relationship has been found significant at the .01 level, we should feel confident using it to predict sales for restaurants where the associated student population is between 2000 and 26,000.

NOTES AND COMMENTS

1. The assumptions made about the error term (Section 12.4) are what allow the tests of statistical significance in this section. The properties of the sampling distribution of b_1 and the subsequent t and F tests follow directly from these assumptions.

2. Do not confuse statistical significance with practical significance. With very large sample sizes, statistically significant results can be obtained for small values of b_1; in such cases, one must exercise care in concluding that the relationship has practical significance.

3. A test of significance for a linear relationship between x and y can also be performed by using the sample correlation coefficient r_{xy}. With ρ_{xy}

denoting the population correlation coefficient, the hypotheses are as follows.

$$H_0\colon \rho_{xy} = 0$$
$$H_a\colon \rho_{xy} \neq 0$$

A significant relationship can be concluded if H_0 is rejected. The details of this test are provided in more advanced texts. However, the t and F tests presented previously in this section give the same result as the test for significance using the correlation coefficient. Conducting a test for significance using the correlation coefficient therefore is not necessary if a t or F test has already been conducted.

Exercises

Methods

23. The data from exercise 1 follow.

x_i	1	2	3	4	5
y_i	3	7	5	11	14

a. Compute the mean square error using equation (12.15).
b. Compute the standard error of the estimate using equation (12.16).
c. Compute the estimated standard deviation of b_1 using equation (12.18).
d. Use the t test to test the following hypotheses ($\alpha = .05$):

$$H_0: \beta_1 = 0$$
$$H_a: \beta_1 \neq 0$$

e. Use the F test to test the hypotheses in part (d) at a .05 level of significance. Present the results in the analysis of variance table format.

24. The data from exercise 2 follow.

x_i	2	3	5	1	8
y_i	25	25	20	30	16

a. Compute the mean square error using equation (12.15).
b. Compute the standard error of the estimate using equation (12.16).
c. Compute the estimated standard deviation of b_1 using equation (12.18).
d. Use the t test to test the following hypotheses ($\alpha = .05$):

$$H_0: \beta_1 = 0$$
$$H_a: \beta_1 \neq 0$$

e. Use the F test to test the hypotheses in part (d) at a .05 level of significance. Present the results in the analysis of variance table format.

25. The data from exercise 3 follow.

x_i	2	4	5	7	8
y_i	2	3	2	6	4

a. What is the value of the standard error of the estimate?
b. Test for a significant relationship by using the t test. Use $\alpha = .05$.
c. Use the F test to test for a significant relationship. Use $\alpha = .05$. What is your conclusion?

Applications

26. In exercise 18 the data on grade point average and monthly salary were as follows.

GPA	Monthly Salary ($)	GPA	Monthly Salary ($)
2.6	3300	3.2	3500
3.4	3600	3.5	3900
3.6	4000	2.9	3600

a. Does the *t* test indicate a significant relationship between grade point average and monthly salary? What is your conclusion? Use $\alpha = .05$.
b. Test for a significant relationship using the *F* test. What is your conclusion? Use $\alpha = .05$.
c. Show the ANOVA table.

27. *Outside Magazine* tested 10 different models of day hikers and backpacking boots. The following data show the upper support and price for each model tested. Upper support was measured using a rating from 1 to 5, with a rating of 1 denoting average upper support and a rating of 5 denoting excellent upper support (*Outside Magazine Buyer's Guide,* 2001).

Boots

Manufacturer and Model	Upper Support	Price ($)
Salomon Super Raid	2	120
Merrell Chameleon Prime	3	125
Teva Challenger	3	130
Vasque Fusion GTX	3	135
Boreal Maigmo	3	150
L.L. Bean GTX Super Guide	5	189
Lowa Kibo	5	190
Asolo AFX 520 GTX	4	195
Raichle Mt. Trail GTX	4	200
Scarpa Delta SL M3	5	220

a. Use these data to develop an estimated regression equation to estimate the price of a day hiker and backpacking boot given the upper support rating.
b. At the .05 level of significance, determine whether upper support and price are related.
c. Would you feel comfortable using the estimated regression equation developed in part (a) to estimate the price for a day hiker or backpacking boot given the upper support rating?
d. Estimate the price for a day hiker with an upper support rating of 4.

28. Refer to exercise 10, where an estimated regression equation relating the performance score and the overall rating for notebook PCs was developed. At the .05 level of significance, test whether performance score and overall rating are related. Show the ANOVA table. What is your conclusion?

PCs

29. Refer to exercise 21, where data on production volume and cost were used to develop an estimated regression equation relating production volume and cost for a particular manufacturing operation. Use $\alpha = .05$ to test whether the production volume is significantly related to the total cost. Show the ANOVA table. What is your conclusion?

30. Refer to exercise 22 where the following data were used to determine whether the price of a printer is related to the speed for plain text printing (*PC World,* February 2003).

Printers

Name	Type	Speed (ppm)	Price ($)
Minolta-QMS PagePro 1250W	Small Office	12	199
Brother HL-1850	Small Office	10	499
Lexmark E320	Small Office	12.2	299
Minolta-QMS PagePro 1250E	Small Office	10.3	299
HP Laserjet 1200	Small Office	11.7	399
Xerox Phaser 4400/N	Corporate	17.8	1850
Brother HL-2460N	Corporate	16.1	1000

(continued)

Name	Type	Speed (ppm)	Price ($)
IBM Infoprint 1120n	Corporate	11.8	1387
Lexmark W812	Corporate	19.8	2089
Oki Data B8300n	Corporate	28.2	2200

Does the evidence indicate a significant relationship between printing speed and price? Conduct the appropriate statistical test and state your conclusion. Use $\alpha = .05$.

31. Refer to exercise 20, where an estimated regression equation was developed relating typical household income and typical home price. Test whether the typical household income for a city and the typical home price are related at the .01 level of significance.

12.6 Using the Estimated Regression Equation for Estimation and Prediction

When using the simple linear regression model we are making an assumption about the relationship between x and y. We then use the least squares method to obtain the estimated simple linear regression equation. If a significant relationship exists between x and y, and the coefficient of determination shows that the fit is good, the estimated regression equation should be useful for estimation and prediction.

Point Estimation

In the Armand's Pizza Parlors example, the estimated regression equation $\hat{y} = 60 + 5x$ provides an estimate of the relationship between the size of the student population x and quarterly sales y. We can use the estimated regression equation to develop a point estimate of the mean value of y for a particular value of x or to predict an individual value of y corresponding to a given value of x. For instance, suppose Armand's managers want a point estimate of the mean quarterly sales for all restaurants located near college campuses with 10,000 students. Using the estimated regression equation $\hat{y} = 60 + 5x$, we see that for $x = 10$ (or 10,000 students), $\hat{y} = 60 + 5(10) = 110$. Thus, a point estimate of the mean quarterly sales for all restaurants located near campuses with 10,000 students is $110,000.

Now suppose Armand's managers want to predict sales for an individual restaurant located near Talbot College, a school with 10,000 students. In this case we are not interested in the mean value for all restaurants located near campuses with 10,000 students; we are just interested in predicting quarterly sales for one individual restaurant. As it turns out, the point estimate for an individual value of y is the same as the point estimate for the mean value of y. Hence, we would predict quarterly sales of $\hat{y} = 60 + 5(10) = 110$ or $110,000 for this one restaurant.

Interval Estimation

Confidence intervals and prediction intervals show the precision of the regression results. Narrower intervals provide a higher degree of precision.

Point estimates do not provide any information about the precision associated with an estimate. For that we must develop interval estimates much like those in Chapters 8, 10, and 11. The first type of interval estimate, a **confidence interval**, is an interval estimate of the *mean value of y* for a given value of x. The second type of interval estimate, a **prediction interval**, is used whenever we want an interval estimate of an *individual value of y* for a given value of x. The point estimate of the mean value of y is the same as the point estimate of an individual value of y. But, the interval estimates we obtain for the two cases are different. The margin of error is larger for a prediction interval.

Confidence Interval for the Mean Value of y

The estimated regression equation provides a point estimate of the mean value of y for a given value of x. In developing the confidence interval, we will use the following notation.

x_p = the particular or given value of the independent variable x

y_p = the value of the dependent variable y corresponding to the given x_p

$E(y_p)$ = the mean or expected value of the dependent variable y corresponding to the given x_p

$\hat{y}_p = b_0 + b_1 x_p$ = the point estimate of $E(y_p)$ when $x = x_p$

Using this notation to estimate the mean sales for all Armand's restaurants located near a campus with 10,000 students, we have $x_p = 10$, and $E(y_p)$ denotes the unknown mean value of sales for all restaurants where $x_p = 10$. The point estimate of $E(y_p)$ is provided by $\hat{y}_p = 60 + 5(10) = 110$.

In general, we cannot expect $\hat{y}_p$ to equal $E(y_p)$ exactly. If we want to make an inference about how close $\hat{y}_p$ is to the true mean value $E(y_p)$, we will have to estimate the variance of $\hat{y}_p$. The formula for estimating the variance of $\hat{y}_p$ given x_p, denoted by $s_{\hat{y}_p}^2$, is

$$s_{\hat{y}_p}^2 = s^2\left[\frac{1}{n} + \frac{(x_p - \bar{x})^2}{\Sigma(x_i - \bar{x})^2}\right] \tag{12.22}$$

The estimate of the standard deviation of $\hat{y}_p$ is given by the square root of equation (12.22).

$$s_{\hat{y}_p} = s\sqrt{\frac{1}{n} + \frac{(x_p - \bar{x})^2}{\Sigma(x_i - \bar{x})^2}} \tag{12.23}$$

The computational results for Armand's Pizza Parlors in Section 12.5 provided $s = 13.829$. With $x_p = 10$, $\bar{x} = 14$, and $\Sigma(x_i - \bar{x})^2 = 568$, we can use equation (12.23) to obtain

$$s_{\hat{y}_p} = 13.829\sqrt{\frac{1}{10} + \frac{(10 - 14)^2}{568}}$$

$$= 13.829\sqrt{.1282} = 4.95$$

The general expression for a confidence interval follows.

CONFIDENCE INTERVAL FOR $E(y_p)$

$$\hat{y}_p \pm t_{\alpha/2}s_{\hat{y}_p} \tag{12.24}$$

The margin of error associated with this interval estimate is $t_{\alpha/2}s_{\hat{y}_p}$.

where the confidence coefficient is $1 - \alpha$ and $t_{\alpha/2}$ is based on a t distribution with $n - 2$ degrees of freedom.

Using expression (12.24) to develop a 95% confidence interval of the mean quarterly sales for all Armand's restaurants located near campuses with 10,000 students, we need the value of t for $\alpha/2 = .025$ and $n - 2 = 10 - 2 = 8$ degrees of freedom. Using Table 2 of Appendix B, we have $t_{.025} = 2.306$. Thus, with $\hat{y}_p = 110$ and a margin of error of $t_{\alpha/2}s_{\hat{y}_p} = 2.306(4.95) = 11.415$, the 95% confidence interval estimate is

$$110 \pm 11.415$$

In dollars, the 95% confidence interval for the mean quarterly sales of all restaurants near campuses with 10,000 students is $110,000 \pm $11,415. Therefore, the 95% confidence interval for the mean quarterly sales when the student population is 10,000 is $98,585 to $121,415.

Note that the estimated standard deviation of $\hat{y}_p$ given by equation (12.23) is smallest when $x_p = \bar{x}$ and the quantity $x_p - \bar{x} = 0$. In this case, the estimated standard deviation of $\hat{y}_p$ becomes

$$s_{\hat{y}_p} = s\sqrt{\frac{1}{n} + \frac{(\bar{x} - \bar{x})^2}{\Sigma(x_i - \bar{x})^2}} = s\sqrt{\frac{1}{n}}$$

This result implies that we can make the best or most precise estimate of the mean value of y whenever $x_p = \bar{x}$. In fact, the further x_p is from $\bar{x}$ the larger $x_p - \bar{x}$ becomes. As a result, confidence intervals for the mean value of y will become wider as x_p deviates more from $\bar{x}$. This pattern is shown graphically in Figure 12.8.

Prediction Interval for an Individual Value of y

Suppose that instead of estimating the mean value of sales for all Armand's restaurants located near campuses with 10,000 students, we want to estimate the sales for an individual restaurant located near Talbot College, a school with 10,000 students. As noted previously,

FIGURE 12.8   CONFIDENCE INTERVALS FOR THE MEAN SALES y AT GIVEN VALUES OF STUDENT POPULATION x

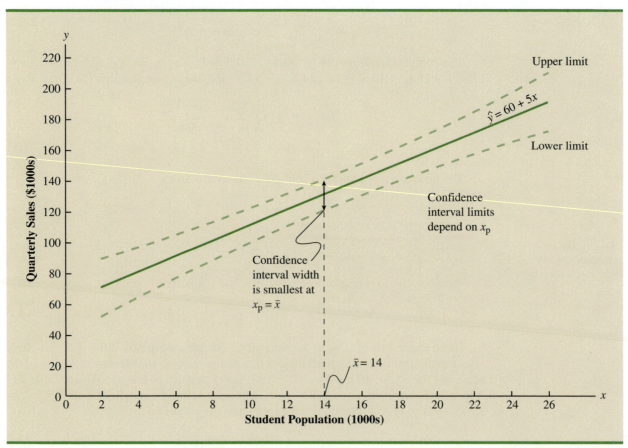

the point estimate of y_p, the value of y corresponding to the given x_p, is provided by the estimated regression equation $\hat{y}_p = b_0 + b_1 x_p$. For the restaurant at Talbot College, we have $x_p = 10$ and a corresponding predicted quarterly sales of $\hat{y}_p = 60 + 5(10) = 110$, or \$110,000. Note that this value is the same as the point estimate of the mean sales for all restaurants located near campuses with 10,000 students.

To develop a prediction interval, we must first determine the variance associated with using $\hat{y}_p$ as an estimate of an individual value of y when $x = x_p$. This variance is made up of the sum of the following two components.

1. The variance of individual y values about the mean $E(y_p)$, an estimate of which is given by s^2

2. The variance associated with using $\hat{y}_p$ to estimate $E(y_p)$, an estimate of which is given by $s_{\hat{y}_p}^2$

The formula for estimating the variance of an individual value of y_p, denoted by s_{ind}^2, is

$$
\begin{aligned}
s_{ind}^2 &= s^2 + s_{\hat{y}_p}^2 \\
&= s^2 + s^2\left[\frac{1}{n} + \frac{(x_p - \bar{x})^2}{\Sigma(x_i - \bar{x})^2}\right] \\
&= s^2\left[1 + \frac{1}{n} + \frac{(x_p - \bar{x})^2}{\Sigma(x_i - \bar{x})^2}\right]
\end{aligned}
\tag{12.25}
$$

Hence, an estimate of the standard deviation of an individual value of y_p is given by

$$
s_{ind} = s\sqrt{1 + \frac{1}{n} + \frac{(x_p - \bar{x})^2}{\Sigma(x_i - \bar{x})^2}}
\tag{12.26}
$$

For Armand's Pizza Parlors, the estimated standard deviation corresponding to the prediction of sales for one specific restaurant located near a campus with 10,000 students is computed as follows.

$$
\begin{aligned}
s_{ind} &= 13.829\sqrt{1 + \frac{1}{10} + \frac{(10 - 14)^2}{568}} \\
&= 13.829\sqrt{1.1282} \\
&= 14.69
\end{aligned}
$$

The general expression for a prediction interval follows.

PREDICTION INTERVAL FOR y_p

The margin of error associated with this interval estimate is $t_{\alpha/2} s_{ind}$.

$$
\hat{y}_p \pm t_{\alpha/2} s_{ind}
\tag{12.27}
$$

where the confidence coefficient is $1 - \alpha$ and $t_{\alpha/2}$ is based on a t distribution with $n - 2$ degrees of freedom.

The 95% prediction interval for quarterly sales at Armand's Talbot College restaurant can be found by using $t_{.025} = 2.306$ and $s_{ind} = 14.69$. Thus, with $\hat{y}_p = 110$ and a margin of error of $t_{\alpha/2} s_{ind} = 2.306(14.69) = 33.875$, the 95% prediction interval is

$$
110 \pm 33.875
$$

FIGURE 12.9 CONFIDENCE AND PREDICTION INTERVALS FOR SALES *y* AT GIVEN VALUES OF STUDENT POPULATION *x*

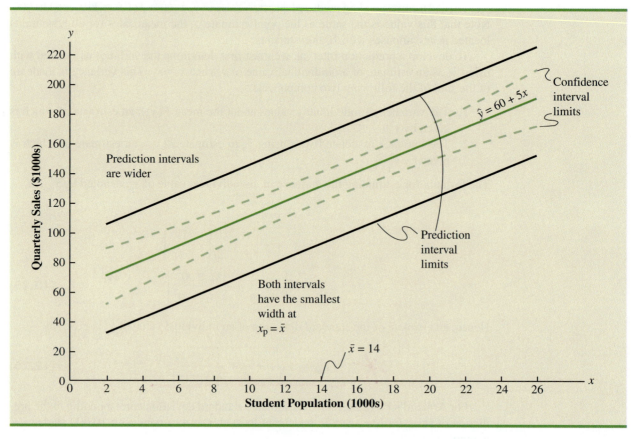

In dollars, this prediction interval is $110,000 \pm $33,875 or $76,125 to $143,875. Note that the prediction interval for an individual restaurant located near a campus with 10,000 students is wider than the confidence interval for the mean sales of all restaurants located near campuses with 10,000 students. The difference reflects the fact that we are able to estimate the mean value of y more precisely than we can an individual value of y.

Both confidence interval estimates and prediction interval estimates are most precise when the value of the independent variable is $x_p = \bar{x}$. The general shapes of confidence intervals and the wider prediction intervals are shown together in Figure 12.9.

Exercises

Methods

32. The data from exercise 1 follow.

x_i	1	2	3	4	5
y_i	3	7	5	11	14

a. Use equation (12.23) to estimate the standard deviation of $\hat{y}_p$ when $x = 4$.
b. Use expression (12.24) to develop a 95% confidence interval for the expected value of y when $x = 4$.

    c. Use equation (12.26) to estimate the standard deviation of an individual value of y when $x = 4$.

    d. Use expression (12.27) to develop a 95% prediction interval for y when $x = 4$.

33. The data from exercise 2 follow.

x_i	2	3	5	1	8
y_i	25	25	20	30	16

    a. Estimate the standard deviation of $\hat{y}_p$ when $x = 3$.

    b. Develop a 95% confidence interval for the expected value of y when $x = 3$.

    c. Estimate the standard deviation of an individual value of y when $x = 3$.

    d. Develop a 95% prediction interval for y when $x = 3$.

34. The data from exercise 3 follow.

x_i	2	4	5	7	8
y_i	2	3	2	6	4

Develop the 95% confidence and prediction intervals when $x = 3$. Explain why these two intervals are different.

Applications

35. In exercise 18, the data on grade point average x and monthly salary y provided the estimated regression equation $\hat{y} = 1790.5 + 581.1x$.

    a. Develop a 95% confidence interval for the mean starting salary for all students with a 3.0 GPA.

    b. Develop a 95% prediction interval for the starting salary for Joe Heller, a student with a GPA of 3.0.

36. In exercise 10, data on the performance score (x) and the overall rating (y) for notebook PCs provided the estimated regression equation $\hat{y} = 51.819 + .1452x$ (*PC World*, February 2000).

    a. Develop a point estimate of the overall rating for a PC with a performance score of 200.

    b. Develop a 95% confidence interval for the mean overall score for all PCs with a performance score of 200.

    c. Suppose that a new PC developed by Dell has a performance score of 200. Develop a 95% prediction interval for the overall score for this new PC.

    d. Discuss the differences in your answers to parts (b) and (c).

37. In exercise 13, data were given on the adjusted gross income x and the amount of itemized deductions taken by taxpayers. Data were reported in thousands of dollars. With the estimated regression equation $\hat{y} = 4.68 + .16x$, the point estimate of a reasonable level of total itemized deductions for a taxpayer with an adjusted gross income of $52,500 is $13,080.

    a. Develop a 95% confidence interval for the mean amount of total itemized deductions for all taxpayers with an adjusted gross income of $52,500.

    b. Develop a 95% prediction interval estimate for the amount of total itemized deductions for a particular taxpayer with an adjusted gross income of $52,500.

    c. If the particular taxpayer referred to in part (b) claimed total itemized deductions of $20,400, would the IRS agent's request for an audit appear to be justified?

    d. Use your answer to part (b) to give the IRS agent a guideline as to the amount of total itemized deductions a taxpayer with an adjusted gross income of $52,500 should claim before an audit is recommended.

38. Refer to Exercise 21, where data on the production volume x and total cost y for a particular manufacturing operation were used to develop the estimated regression equation $\hat{y} = 1246.67 + 7.6x$.

    a. The company's production schedule shows that 500 units must be produced next month. What is the point estimate of the total cost for next month?

b.   Develop a 99% prediction interval for the total cost for next month.
c.   If an accounting cost report at the end of next month shows that the actual production cost during the month was $6000, should managers be concerned about incurring such a high total cost for the month? Discuss.

39. Almost all U.S. light-rail systems use electric cars that run on tracks built at street level. The Federal Transit Administration claims light-rail is one of the safest modes of travel, with an accident rate of .99 accidents per million passenger miles as compared to 2.29 for buses. The following data show the miles of track and the weekday ridership in thousands of passengers for six light-rail systems (*USA Today*, January 7, 2003).

City	Miles of Track	Ridership (1000s)
Cleveland	15	15
Denver	17	35
Portland	38	81
Sacramento	21	31
San Diego	47	75
San Jose	31	30
St. Louis	34	42

a.   Use these data to develop an estimated regression equation that could be used to predict the ridership given the miles of track.
b.   Did the estimated regression equation provide a good fit? Explain.
c.   Develop a 95% confidence interval for the mean weekday ridership for all light-rail systems with 30 miles of track.
d.   Suppose that Charlotte is considering construction of a light-rail system with 30 miles of track. Develop a 95% prediction interval for the weekday ridership for the Charlotte system. Do you think that the prediction interval you developed would be of value to Charlotte planners in anticipating the number of weekday riders for their new light-rail system? Explain.

 12.7 Computer Solution

Performing the regression analysis computations without the help of a computer can be quite time consuming. In this section we discuss how the computational burden can be minimized by using a computer software package such as Minitab.

We entered Armand's student population and sales data into a Minitab worksheet. The independent variable was named Pop and the dependent variable was named Sales to assist with interpretation of the computer output. Using Minitab, we obtained the printout for Armand's Pizza Parlors shown in Figure 12.10.* The interpretation of this printout follows.

1. Minitab prints the estimated regression equation as Sales = 60.0 + 5.00 Pop.
2. A table is printed that shows the values of the coefficients b_0 and b_1, the standard deviation of each coefficient, the t value obtained by dividing each coefficient value by its standard deviation, and the p-value associated with the t test. Because the p-value corresponding to $b_1 = 5.0000$ is zero (to three decimal places), the sample results indicate that the null hypothesis (H_0: $\beta_1 = 0$) should be rejected.

*The Minitab steps necessary to generate the output are given in Appendix 12.1.

FIGURE 12.10   MINITAB OUTPUT FOR THE ARMAND'S PIZZA PARLORS PROBLEM

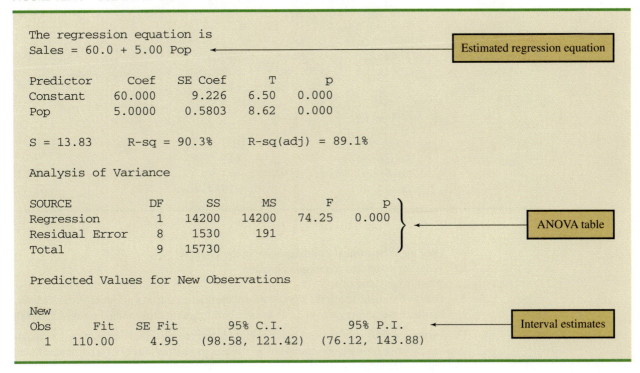

```
The regression equation is
Sales = 60.0 + 5.00 Pop      ◄──────────────────    Estimated regression equation

Predictor       Coef    SE Coef        T        p
Constant      60.000      9.226     6.50    0.000
Pop           5.0000     0.5803     8.62    0.000

S = 13.83      R-sq = 90.3%      R-sq(adj) = 89.1%

Analysis of Variance

SOURCE            DF       SS       MS        F        p
Regression         1    14200    14200    74.25    0.000
Residual Error     8     1530      191                         ◄──────    ANOVA table
Total              9    15730

Predicted Values for New Observations

New
Obs       Fit   SE Fit        95% C.I.            95% P.I.     ◄──────    Interval estimates
  1    110.00     4.95    (98.58, 121.42)    (76.12, 143.88)
```

Alternatively, we could compare 8.62 (located in the *t*-ratio column) to the appropriate critical value. This procedure for the *t* test was described in Section 12.5.

3. Minitab prints the standard error of the estimate, $s = 13.83$, as well as information about the goodness of fit. Note that "R-sq = 90.3%" is the coefficient of determination expressed as a percentage.

4. The ANOVA table is printed below the heading Analysis of Variance. Minitab uses the label Residual Error for the error source of variation. Note that DF is an abbreviation for degrees of freedom and that MSR is given as 14,200 and MSE as 191. The ratio of these two values provides the *F* value of 74.25 and the corresponding *p*-value of 0.000. Because the *p*-value is zero (to three decimal places), the relationship between Sales and Pop is judged statistically significant.

5. The 95% confidence interval estimate of the expected sales and the 95% prediction interval estimate of sales for an individual restaurant located near a campus with 10,000 students are printed below the ANOVA table. The confidence interval is (98.58, 121.42) and the prediction interval is (76.12, 143.88) as we showed in Section 12.6.

Exercises

Applications

SELF test

40. The commercial division of a real estate firm is conducting a regression analysis of the relationship between *x*, annual gross rents (in thousands of dollars), and *y*, selling price (in thousands of dollars), for apartment buildings. Data were collected on several properties recently sold and the following computer output was obtained.

```
The regression equation is
Y = 20.0 + 7.21 X

Predictor        Coef      SE Coef        T
Constant       20.000       3.2213      6.21
X               7.210       1.3626      5.29

Analysis of Variance

SOURCE                DF           SS
Regression             1      41587.3
Residual Error         7
Total                  8      51984.1
```

a. How many apartment buildings were in the sample?
b. Write the estimated regression equation.
c. What is the value of s_{b_1}?
d. Use the F statistic to test the significance of the relationship at a .05 level of significance.
e. Estimate the selling price of an apartment building with gross annual rents of $50,000.

41. Following is a portion of the computer output for a regression analysis relating y = maintenance expense (dollars per month) to x = usage (hours per week) of a particular brand of computer terminal.

```
The regression equation is
Y = 6.1092 + .8951 X

Predictor        Coef      SE Coef
Constant       6.1092       0.9361
X              0.8951       0.1490

Analysis of Variance

SOURCE                DF          SS          MS
Regression             1     1575.76     1575.76
Residual Error         8      349.14       43.64
Total                  9     1924.90
```

a. Write the estimated regression equation.
b. Use a t test to determine whether monthly maintenance expense is related to usage at the .05 level of significance.
c. Use the estimated regression equation to predict monthly maintenance expense for any terminal that is used 25 hours per week.

42. A regression model relating x, number of salespersons at a branch office, to y, annual sales at the office (in thousands of dollars), provided the following computer output from a regression analysis of the data.

```
The regression equation is
Y = 80.0 + 50.00 X

Predictor        Coef      SE Coef          T
Constant         80.0       11.333       7.06
X                50.0        5.482       9.12


Analysis of Variance

SOURCE                DF           SS           MS
Regression             1       6828.6       6828.6
Residual Error        28       2298.8         82.1
Total                 29       9127.4
```

a.   Write the estimated regression equation.

b.   How many branch offices were involved in the study?

c.   Compute the F statistic and test the significance of the relationship at a .05 level of significance.

d.   Predict the annual sales at the Memphis branch office. This branch employs 12 salespersons.

43.   Health experts recommend that runners drink 4 ounces of water every 15 minutes they run. Although handheld bottles work well for many types of runs, all-day cross-country runs require hip-mounted or over-the-shoulder hydration systems. In addition to carrying more water, hip-mounted or over-the-shoulder hydration systems offer more storage space for food and extra clothing. As the capacity increases, however, the weight and cost of these larger-capacity systems also increase. The following data show the weight (ounces) and the price for 26 hip-mounted or over-the-shoulder hydration systems (*Trail Runner Gear Guide,* 2003).

Hydration1

Model	Weight (oz.)	Price ($)
Fastdraw	3	10
Fastdraw Plus	4	12
Fitness	5	12
Access	7	20
Access Plus	8	25
Solo	9	25
Serenade	9	35
Solitaire	11	35
Gemini	21	45
Shadow	15	40
SipStream	18	60
Express	9	30
Lightning	12	40
Elite	14	60
Extender	16	65
Stinger	16	65
GelFlask Belt	3	20
GelDraw	1	7
GelFlask Clip-on Holster	2	10

(continued)

Model	Weight (oz.)	Price ($)
GelFlask Holster SS	1	10
Strider (W)	8	30
Walkabout (W)	14	40
Solitude I.C.E.	9	35
Getaway I.C.E.	19	55
Profile I.C.E.	14	50
Traverse I.C.E.	13	60

a. Use these data to develop an estimated regression equation that could be used to predict the price of a hydration system given its weight.
b. Test the significance of the relationship at the .05 level of significance.
c. Did the estimated regression equation provide a good fit? Explain.
d. Assume that the estimated regression equation developed in part (a) will also apply to hydration systems produced by other companies. Develop a 95% confidence interval estimate of the price for all hydration systems that weigh 10 ounces.
e. Assume that the estimated regression equation developed in part (a) will also apply to hydration systems produced by other companies. Develop a 95% prediction interval estimate of the price for the Back Draft system produced by Eastern Mountain Sports. The Back Draft system weighs 10 ounces.

44. Cushman & Wakefield, Inc., collects data showing the office building vacancy rates and rental rates for markets in the United States. The following data show the overall vacancy rates (%) and the average rental rates (per square foot) for the central business district for 18 selected markets.

CD file

OffRates

Market	Vacancy Rate (%)	Average Rate ($)
Atlanta	21.9	18.54
Boston	6.0	33.70
Hartford	22.8	19.67
Baltimore	18.1	21.01
Washington	12.7	35.09
Philadelphia	14.5	19.41
Miami	20.0	25.28
Tampa	19.2	17.02
Chicago	16.0	24.04
San Francisco	6.6	31.42
Phoenix	15.9	18.74
San Jose	9.2	26.76
West Palm Beach	19.7	27.72
Detroit	20.0	18.20
Brooklyn	8.3	25.00
Downtown, NY	17.1	29.78
Midtown, NY	10.8	37.03
Midtown South, NY	11.1	28.64

a. Develop a scatter diagram for these data; plot the vacancy rate on the horizontal axis.
b. Does there appear to be any relationship between vacancy rates and rental rates?
c. Develop the estimated regression equation that could be used to predict the average rental rate given the overall vacancy rate.
d. Test the significance of the relationship at the .05 level of significance.

e. Did the estimated regression equation provide a good fit? Explain.
f. Predict the expected rental rate for markets with a 25% vacancy rate in the central business district.
g. The overall vacancy rate in the central business district in Ft. Lauderdale is 11.3%. Predict the expected rental rate for Ft. Lauderdale.

12.8 Residual Analysis: Validating Model Assumptions

Residual analysis *is the primary tool for determining whether the assumed regression model is appropriate.*

As we noted previously, the *residual* for observation i is the difference between the observed value of the dependent variable (y_i) and the estimated value of the dependent variable ($\hat{y}_i$).

RESIDUAL FOR OBSERVATION i

$$y_i - \hat{y}_i \qquad \qquad \textbf{(12.28)}$$

where

$$y_i = \text{the observed value of the dependent variable}$$
$$\hat{y}_i = \text{the estimated value of the dependent variable}$$

In other words, the ith residual is the error resulting from using the estimated regression equation to predict the value of the dependent variable. The residuals for the Armand's Pizza Parlors example are computed in Table 12.7. The observed values of the dependent variable are in the second column and the estimated values of the dependent variable, obtained using the estimated regression equation $\hat{y} = 60 + 5x$, are in the third column. An analysis of the corresponding residuals in the fourth column will help determine whether the assumptions made about the regression model are appropriate.

Let us now review the regression assumptions for the Armand's Pizza Parlors example. A simple linear regression model was assumed.

$$y = \beta_0 + \beta_1 x + \epsilon \qquad \qquad \textbf{(12.29)}$$

This model indicates that we assumed quarterly sales (y) to be a linear function of the size of the student population (x) plus an error term ϵ. In Section 12.4 we made the following assumptions about the error term ϵ.

1. $E(\epsilon) = 0$.
2. The variance of ϵ, denoted by σ^2, is the same for all values of x.
3. The values of ϵ are independent.
4. The error term ϵ has a normal distribution.

These assumptions provide the theoretical basis for the t test and the F test used to determine whether the relationship between x and y is significant, and for the confidence and prediction interval estimates presented in Section 12.6. If the assumptions about the error term ϵ appear questionable, the hypothesis tests about the significance of the regression relationship and the interval estimation results may not be valid.

The residuals provide the best information about ϵ; hence an analysis of the residuals is an important step in determining whether the assumptions for ϵ are appropriate. Much of

TABLE 12.7   RESIDUALS FOR ARMAND'S PIZZA PARLORS

Student Population x_i	Sales y_i	Estimated Sales $\hat{y}_i = 60 + 5x_i$	Residuals $y_i - \hat{y}_i$
2	58	70	-12
6	105	90	15
8	88	100	-12
8	118	100	18
12	117	120	-3
16	137	140	-3
20	157	160	-3
20	169	160	9
22	149	170	-21
26	202	190	12

residual analysis is based on an examination of graphical plots. In this section, we discuss the following residual plots.

1. A plot of the residuals against values of the independent variable x
2. A plot of residuals against the predicted values of the dependent variable $\hat{y}$

Residual Plot Against x

A **residual plot** against the independent variable x is a graph in which the values of the independent variable are represented by the horizontal axis and the corresponding residual values are represented by the vertical axis. A point is plotted for each residual. The first coordinate for each point is given by the value of x_i and the second coordinate is given by the corresponding value of the residual $y_i - \hat{y}_i$. For a residual plot against x with the Armand's Pizza Parlors data from Table 12.7, the coordinates of the first point are $(2, -12)$, corresponding to $x_1 = 2$ and $y_1 - \hat{y}_1 = -12$; the coordinates of the second point are $(6, 15)$, corresponding to $x_2 = 6$ and $y_2 - \hat{y}_2 = 15$, and so on. Figure 12.11 shows the resulting residual plot.

Before interpreting the results for this residual plot, let us consider some general patterns that might be observed in any residual plot. Three examples appear in Figure 12.12. If the assumption that the variance of ϵ is the same for all values of x and the assumed regression model is an adequate representation of the relationship between the variables, the residual plot should give an overall impression of a horizontal band of points such as the one in Panel A of Figure 12.12. However, if the variance of ϵ is not the same for all values of x—for example, if variability about the regression line is greater for larger values of x—a pattern such as the one in Panel B of Figure 12.12 could be observed. In this case, the assumption of a constant variance of ϵ is violated. Another possible residual plot is shown in Panel C. In this case, we would conclude that the assumed regression model is not an adequate representation of the relationship between the variables. A curvilinear regression model or multiple regression model should be considered.

Now let us return to the residual plot for Armand's Pizza Parlors shown in Figure 12.11. The residuals appear to approximate the horizontal pattern in Panel A of Figure 12.12. Hence, we conclude that the residual plot does not provide evidence that the assumptions

FIGURE 12.11   PLOT OF THE RESIDUALS AGAINST THE INDEPENDENT VARIABLE x FOR ARMAND'S PIZZA PARLORS

made for Armand's regression model should be challenged. At this point, we are confident in the conclusion that Armand's simple linear regression model is valid.

Experience and good judgment are always factors in the effective interpretation of residual plots. Seldom does a residual plot conform precisely to one of the patterns in Figure 12.12. Yet analysts who frequently conduct regression studies and frequently review residual plots become adept at understanding the differences between patterns that are reasonable and patterns that indicate the assumptions of the model should be questioned. A residual plot provides one technique to assess the validity of the assumptions for a regression model.

Residual Plot Against $\hat{y}$

Another residual plot represents the predicted value of the dependent variable $\hat{y}$ on the horizontal axis and the residual values on the vertical axis. A point is plotted for each residual. The first coordinate for each point is given by $\hat{y}_i$ and the second coordinate is given by the corresponding value of the ith residual $y_i - \hat{y}_i$. With the Armand's data from Table 12.7, the coordinates of the first point are $(70, -12)$, corresponding to $\hat{y}_1 = 70$ and $y_1 - \hat{y}_1 = -12$; the coordinates of the second point are $(90, 15)$, and so on. Figure 12.13 provides the residual plot. Note that the pattern of this residual plot is the same as the pattern of the residual plot against the independent variable x. It is not a pattern that would lead us to question the model assumptions. For simple linear regression, both the residual plot against x and the residual plot against $\hat{y}$ provide the same pattern. For multiple regression analysis, the residual plot against $\hat{y}$ is more widely used because of the presence of more than one independent variable.

FIGURE 12.12 RESIDUAL PLOTS FROM THREE REGRESSION STUDIES

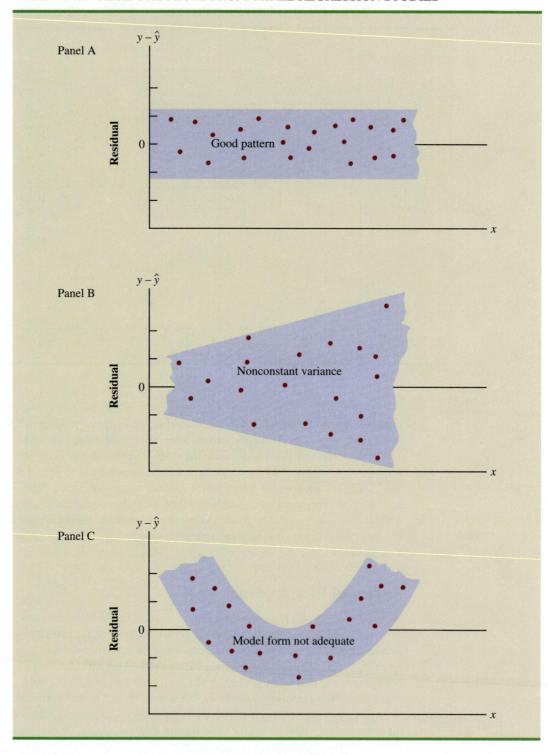

FIGURE 12.13   PLOT OF THE RESIDUALS AGAINST THE PREDICTED VALUES $\hat{y}$
FOR ARMAND'S PIZZA PARLORS

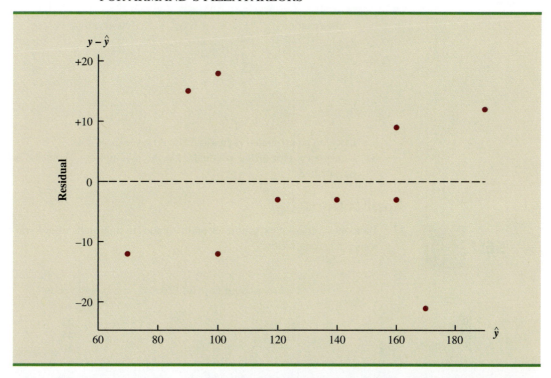

NOTES AND COMMENTS

1. We use residual plots to validate the assumptions of a regression model. If our review indicates that one or more assumptions are questionable, a different regression model or a transformation of the data should be considered. The appropriate corrective action when the assumptions are violated must be based on good judgment; recommendations from an experienced statistician can be valuable.

2. Analysis of residuals is the primary method statisticians use to verify that the assumptions associated with a regression model are valid. Even if no violations are found, it does not necessarily follow that the model will yield good predictions. However, if additional statistical tests support the conclusion of significance and the coefficient of determination is large, we should be able to develop good estimates and predictions using the estimated regression equation.

Exercises

Methods

45. Given are data for two variables, x and y.

x_i	6	11	15	18	20
y_i	6	8	12	20	30

a. Develop an estimated regression equation for these data.
b. Compute the residuals.
c. Develop a plot of the residuals against the independent variable x. Do the assumptions about the error terms seem to be satisfied?

46.   The following data were used in a regression study.

Observation	x_i	y_i	Observation	x_i	y_i
1	2	4	6	7	6
2	3	5	7	7	9
3	4	4	8	8	5
4	5	6	9	9	11
5	7	4			

a.   Develop an estimated regression equation for these data.
b.   Construct a plot of the residuals. Do the assumptions about the error term seem to be satisfied?

Applications

47.   Data on advertising expenditures and revenue (in thousands of dollars) for the Four Seasons Restaurant follow.

Advertising Expenditures	Revenue
1	19
2	32
4	44
6	40
10	52
14	53
20	54

a.   Let x equal advertising expenditures and y equal revenue. Use the method of least squares to develop a straight line approximation of the relationship between the two variables.
b.   Test whether revenue and advertising expenditures are related at a .05 level of significance.
c.   Construct a residual plot against the independent variable.
d.   What conclusions can you draw from residual analysis? Should this model be used, or should we look for a better one?

48.   Refer to exercise 9, where an estimated regression equation relating years of experience and annual sales was developed.
a.   Compute the residuals and construct a residual plot for this problem.
b.   Do the assumptions about the error terms seem reasonable in light of the residual plot?

49.   American Depository Receipts (ADRs) are certificates traded on the NYSE representing shares of a foreign company held on deposit in a bank in its home country. The following table shows the price/earnings (P/E) ratio and the percentage return on investment (ROE) for 10 Indian companies that are likely new ADRs (*Bloomberg Personal Finance*, April 2000).

Company	ROE	P/E
Bharti Televentures	6.43	36.88
Gujarat Ambuja Cements	13.49	27.03
Hindalco Industries	14.04	10.83

Company	ROE	P/E
ICICI	20.67	5.15
Mahanagar Telephone Nigam	22.74	13.35
NIIT	46.23	95.59
Pentamedia Graphics	28.90	54.85
Satyam Computer Services	54.01	189.21
Silverline Technologies	28.02	75.86
Videsh Sanchar Nigam	27.04	13.17

    a.   Use a computer package to develop an estimated regression equation relating y = P/E and x = ROE.

    b.   Construct a residual plot against the independent variable.

    c.   Do the assumptions about the error terms and model form seem reasonable in light of the residual plot?

Summary

In this chapter we showed how regression analysis can be used to determine how a dependent variable y is related to an independent variable x. In simple linear regression, the regression model is $y = \beta_0 + \beta_1 x + \epsilon$. The simple linear regression equation $E(y) = \beta_0 + \beta_1 x$ describes how the mean or expected value of y is related to x. We used sample data and the least squares method to develop the estimated regression equation $\hat{y} = b_0 + b_1 x$. In effect, b_0 and b_1 are the sample statistics used to estimate the unknown model parameters β_0 and β_1.

The coefficient of determination was presented as a measure of the goodness of fit for the estimated regression equation; it can be interpreted as the proportion of the variation in the dependent variable y that can be explained by the estimated regression equation. We reviewed correlation as a descriptive measure of the strength of a linear relationship between two variables.

The assumptions about the regression model and its associated error term ϵ were discussed, and t and F tests, based on those assumptions, were presented as a means for determining whether the relationship between two variables is statistically significant. We showed how to use the estimated regression equation to develop confidence interval estimates of the mean value of y and prediction interval estimates of individual values of y.

The chapter concluded with a section on the computer solution of regression problems and a section on the use of residual analysis to validate the model assumptions.

Glossary

Dependent variable The variable that is being predicted. It is denoted by y.

Independent variable The variable that is used to predict the value of the dependent variable. It is denoted by x.

Simple linear regression Regression analysis involving one independent variable and one dependent variable in which the relationship between the variables is approximated by a straight line.

Regression model The equation that describes how y is related to x and an error term; in simple linear regression, the regression model is $y = \beta_0 + \beta_1 x + \epsilon$.

Regression equation The equation that describes how the mean or expected value of the dependent variable is related to the independent variable; in simple linear regression, $E(y) = \beta_0 + \beta_1 x$.

Estimated regression equation The estimate of the regression equation developed from sample data by using the least squares method. For simple linear regression, the estimated regression equation is $\hat{y} = b_0 + b_1 x$.

Least squares method A procedure for using sample data to find the estimated regression equation. The objective is to minimize $\Sigma(y_i - \hat{y}_i)^2$.

Scatter diagram A graph of bivariate data in which the independent variable is on the horizontal axis and the dependent variable is on the vertical axis.

Coefficient of determination A measure of the goodness of fit of the estimated regression equation. It can be interpreted as the proportion of the variability in the dependent variable y that is explained by the estimated regression equation.

ith residual The difference between the observed value of the dependent variable and the value predicted using the estimated regression equation; for the ith observation the ith residual is $y_i - \hat{y}_i$.

Correlation coefficient A measure of the strength of the linear relationship between two variables (previously discussed in Chapter 3).

Mean square error The unbiased estimate of the variance of the error term σ^2. It is denoted by MSE or s^2.

Standard error of the estimate The square root of the mean square error, denoted by s. It is the estimate of σ, the standard deviation of the error term ϵ.

ANOVA table The analysis of variance table used to summarize the computations associated with the F test for significance.

Confidence interval The interval estimate of the mean value of y for a given value of x.

Prediction interval The interval estimate of an individual value of y for a given value of x.

Residual analysis The primary tool for determining whether the assumed regression model is appropriate.

Residual plot Graphical representation of the residuals that can be used to determine whether the assumptions made about the regression model appear to be valid.

Key Formulas

Simple Linear Regression Model

$$y = \beta_0 + \beta_1 x + \epsilon \qquad (12.1)$$

Simple Linear Regression Equation

$$E(y) = \beta_0 + \beta_1 x \qquad (12.2)$$

Estimated Simple Linear Regression Equation

$$\hat{y} = b_0 + b_1 x \qquad (12.3)$$

Least Squares Criterion

$$\min \Sigma(y_i - \hat{y}_i)^2 \qquad (12.5)$$

Slope and y-Intercept for the Estimated Regression Equation

$$b_1 = \frac{\Sigma(x_i - \bar{x})(y_i - \bar{y})}{\Sigma(x_i - \bar{x})^2} \qquad (12.6)$$

$$b_0 = \bar{y} - b_1 \bar{x} \qquad (12.7)$$

Sum of Squares Due to Error

$$SSE = \Sigma(y_i - \hat{y}_i)^2 \tag{12.8}$$

Total Sum of Squares

$$SST = \Sigma(y_i - \bar{y})^2 \tag{12.9}$$

Sum of Squares Due to Regression

$$SSR = \Sigma(\hat{y}_i - \bar{y})^2 \tag{12.10}$$

Relationship Among SST, SSR, and SSE

$$SST = SSR + SSE \tag{12.11}$$

Coefficient of Determination

$$r^2 = \frac{SSR}{SST} \tag{12.12}$$

Sample Correlation Coefficient

$$r_{xy} = (\text{sign of } b_1)\sqrt{\text{Coefficient of determination}}$$
$$= (\text{sign of } b_1)\sqrt{r^2} \tag{12.13}$$

Mean Square Error (Estimate of σ^2)

$$s^2 = MSE = \frac{SSE}{n-2} \tag{12.15}$$

Standard Error of the Estimate

$$s = \sqrt{MSE} = \sqrt{\frac{SSE}{n-2}} \tag{12.16}$$

Standard Deviation of b_1

$$\sigma_{b_1} = \frac{\sigma}{\sqrt{\Sigma(x_i - \bar{x})^2}} \tag{12.17}$$

Estimated Standard Deviation of b_1

$$s_{b_1} = \frac{s}{\sqrt{\Sigma(x_i - \bar{x})^2}} \tag{12.18}$$

t **Test Statistic**

$$t = \frac{b_1}{s_{b_1}} \tag{12.19}$$

Mean Square Regression

$$MSR = \frac{SSR}{\text{Number of independent variables}} \tag{12.20}$$

F **Test Statistic**

$$F = \frac{MSR}{MSE} \tag{12.21}$$

Estimated Standard Deviation of $\hat{y}_p$

$$s_{\hat{y}_p} = s\sqrt{\frac{1}{n} + \frac{(x_p - \bar{x})^2}{\Sigma(x_i - \bar{x})^2}}$$ (12.23)

Confidence Interval for $E(y_p)$

$$\hat{y}_p \pm t_{\alpha/2}s_{\hat{y}_p}$$ (12.24)

Estimated Standard Deviation of an Individual Value

$$s_{\text{ind}} = s\sqrt{1 + \frac{1}{n} + \frac{(x_p - \bar{x})^2}{\Sigma(x_i - \bar{x})^2}}$$ (12.26)

Prediction Interval for y_p

$$\hat{y}_p \pm t_{\alpha/2}s_{\text{ind}}$$ (12.27)

Residual for Observation i

$$y_i - \hat{y}_i$$ (12.28)

Supplementary Exercises

50. The data in the following table show the number of shares selling (millions) and the expected price (average of projected low price and projected high price) for 10 selected initial public stock offerings.

CD file

IPO

Company	Shares Selling	Expected Price ($)
American Physician	5.0	15
Apex Silver Mines	9.0	14
Dan River	6.7	15
Franchise Mortgage	8.75	17
Gene Logic	3.0	11
International Home Foods	13.6	19
PRT Group	4.6	13
Rayovac	6.7	14
RealNetworks	3.0	10
Software AG Systems	7.7	13

a. Develop an estimated regression equation with the number of shares selling as the independent variable and the expected price as the dependent variable.
b. At the .05 level of significance, is there a significant relationship between the two variables?
c. Did the estimated regression equation provide a good fit? Explain.
d. Use the estimated regression equation to estimate the expected price for a firm considering an initial public offering of 6 million shares.

51. Corporate share repurchase programs are often touted as a benefit for shareholders. But Robert Gabele, director of insider research for First Call/Thomson Financial, noted that many of these programs are undertaken solely to acquire stock for a company's incentive options for top managers. Across all companies, existing stock options in 1998 represented 6.2 percent of all common shares outstanding. The following data show the number of shares covered by option grants and the number of shares outstanding for 13 companies (*Bloomberg Personal Finance,* January/February 2000).

Options

Company	Shares of Option Grants Outstanding (millions)	Common Shares Outstanding (millions)
Adobe Systems	20.3	61.8
Apple Computer	52.7	160.9
Applied Materials	109.1	375.4
Autodesk	15.7	58.9
Best Buy	44.2	203.8
Fruit of the Loom	14.2	66.9
ITT Industries	18.0	87.9
Merrill Lynch	89.9	365.5
Novell	120.2	335.0
Parametric Technology	78.3	269.3
Reebok International	12.8	56.1
Silicon Graphics	52.6	188.8
Toys R Us	54.8	247.6

a.   Develop the estimated regression equation that could be used to estimate the number of shares of option grants outstanding given the number of common shares outstanding.

b.   Use the estimated regression equation to estimate the number of shares of option grants outstanding for a company that has 150 million shares of common stock outstanding.

c.   Do you believe the estimated regression equation would provide a good prediction of the number of shares of option grants outstanding? Use r^2 to support your answer.

52.   *Bloomberg Personal Finance* (July/August 2001) reported the market beta for Texas Instruments was 1.46. Market betas for individual stocks are determined by simple linear regression. For each stock, the dependent variable is its quarterly percentage return (capital appreciation plus dividends) minus the percentage return that could be obtained from a risk-free investment (the Treasury Bill rate is used as the risk-free rate). The independent variable is the quarterly percentage return (capital appreciation plus dividends) for the stock market (S&P 500) minus the percentage return from a risk-free investment. An estimated regression equation is developed with quarterly data; the market beta for the stock is the slope of the estimated regression equation (b_1). The value of the market beta is often interpreted as a measure of the risk associated with the stock. Market betas greater than 1 indicate that the stock is more volatile than the market average; market betas less than 1 indicate that the stock is less volatile than the market average. Suppose that the following figures are the differences between the percentage return and the risk-free return for 10 quarters for the S&P 500 and Horizon Technology.

S&P 500	Horizon
1.2	−0.7
−2.5	−2.0
−3.0	−5.5
2.0	4.7
5.0	1.8
1.2	4.1
3.0	2.6
−1.0	2.0
.5	−1.3
2.5	5.5

a. Develop an estimated regression equation that can be used to determine the market beta for Horizon Technology. What is Horizon Technology's market beta?
b. Test for a significant relationship at the .05 level of significance.
c. Did the estimated regression equation provide a good fit? Explain.
d. Use the market betas of Texas Instruments and Horizon Technology to compare the risk associated with the two stocks.

53. The Australian Public Service Commission's State of the Service Report 2002–2003 reported job satisfaction ratings for employees. One of the survey questions asked employees to choose the five most important workplace factors (from a list of factors) that most affected how satisfied they were with their job. Respondents were then asked to indicate their level of satisfaction with their top five factors. The following data show the percentage of employees who nominated the factor in their top five, and a corresponding satisfaction rating measured using the percentage of employees who nominated the factor in the top five and who were "very satisfied" or "satisfied" with the factor in their current workplace (http://www.apsc.gov.au/stateoftheservice).

JobSat

Workplace Factor	Top Five (%)	Satisfaction Rating (%)
Appropriate workload	30	49
Chance to be creative/innovative	38	64
Chance to make a useful contribution to society	40	67
Duties/expectations made clear	40	69
Flexible working arrangements	55	86
Good working relationships	60	85
Interesting work provided	48	74
Opportunities for career development	33	43
Opportunities to develop my skills	46	66
Opportunities to utilize my skills	50	70
Regular feedback/recognition for effort	42	53
Salary	47	62
Seeing tangible results from my work	42	69

a. Develop a scatter diagram with Top Five (%) on the horizontal axis and Satisfaction Rating (%) on the vertical axis.
b. What does the scatter diagram developed in part (a) indicate about the relationship between the two variables?
c. Develop the estimated regression equation that could be used to predict the Satisfaction Rating (%) given the Top Five (%).
d. Test for a significant relationship at the .05 level of significance.
e. Did the estimated regression equation provide a good fit? Explain.
f. What is the value of the sample correlation coefficient?

54. Jensen Tire & Auto is in the process of deciding whether to purchase a maintenance contract for its new computer wheel alignment and balancing machine. Managers feel that maintenance expense should be related to usage, and they collected the following information on weekly usage (hours) and annual maintenance expense (in hundreds of dollars).

Weekly Usage (hours)	Annual Maintenance Expense
13	17.0
10	22.0
20	30.0

Weekly Usage (hours)	Annual Maintenance Expense
28	37.0
32	47.0
17	30.5
24	32.5
31	39.0
40	51.5
38	40.0

    a.   Develop the estimated regression equation that relates annual maintenance expense to weekly usage.

    b.   Test the significance of the relationship in part (a) at a .05 level of significance.

    c.   Jensen expects to use the new machine 30 hours per week. Develop a 95% prediction interval for the company's annual maintenance expense.

    d.   If the maintenance contract costs $3000 per year, would you recommend purchasing it? Why or why not?

55. In a manufacturing process the assembly line speed (feet per minute) was thought to affect the number of defective parts found during the inspection process. To test this theory, managers devised a situation in which the same batch of parts was inspected visually at a variety of line speeds. They collected the following data.

Line Speed	Number of Defective Parts Found
20	21
20	19
40	15
30	16
60	14
40	17

    a.   Develop the estimated regression equation that relates line speed to the number of defective parts found.

    b.   At a .05 level of significance, determine whether line speed and number of defective parts found are related.

    c.   Did the estimated regression equation provide a good fit to the data?

    d.   Develop a 95% confidence interval to predict the mean number of defective parts for a line speed of 50 feet per minute.

56. A sociologist was hired by a large city hospital to investigate the relationship between the number of unauthorized days that employees are absent per year and the distance (miles) between home and work for the employees. A sample of 10 employees was chosen, and the following data were collected.

Distance to Work	Number of Days Absent
1	8
3	5
4	8
6	7
8	6

(continued)

Distance to Work	Number of Days Absent
10	3
12	5
14	2
14	4
18	2

a. Develop a scatter diagram for these data. Does a linear relationship appear reasonable? Explain.
b. Develop the least squares estimated regression equation.
c. Is there a significant relationship between the two variables? Use $\alpha = .05$.
d. Did the estimated regression equation provide a good fit? Explain.
e. Use the estimated regression equation developed in part (b) to develop a 95% confidence interval for the expected number of days absent for employees living 5 miles from the company.

57. The regional transit authority for a major metropolitan area wants to determine whether there is any relationship between the age of a bus and the annual maintenance cost. A sample of 10 buses resulted in the following data.

Age of Bus (years)	Maintenance Cost ($)
1	350
2	370
2	480
2	520
2	590
3	550
4	750
4	800
5	790
5	950

a. Develop the least squares estimated regression equation.
b. Test to see whether the two variables are significantly related with $\alpha = .05$.
c. Did the least squares line provide a good fit to the observed data? Explain.
d. Develop a 95% prediction interval for the maintenance cost for a specific bus that is 4 years old.

58. A marketing professor at Givens College is interested in the relationship between hours spent studying and total points earned in a course. Data collected on 10 students who took the course last quarter follow.

Hours Spent Studying	Total Points Earned
45	40
30	35
90	75
60	65
105	90
65	50
90	90
80	80
55	45
75	65

a. Develop an estimated regression equation showing how total points earned is related to hours spent studying.
b. Test the significance of the model with $\alpha = .05$.
c. Predict the total points earned by Mark Sweeney. He spent 95 hours studying.
d. Develop a 95% prediction interval for the total points earned by Mark Sweeney.

59. The Transactional Records Access Clearinghouse at Syracuse University reported data showing the odds of an Internal Revenue Service audit. The following table shows the average adjusted gross income reported and the percentage of the returns that were audited for 20 selected IRS districts.

IRSAudit

District	Adjusted Gross Income ($)	Percentage Audited
Los Angeles	36,664	1.3
Sacramento	38,845	1.1
Atlanta	34,886	1.1
Boise	32,512	1.1
Dallas	34,531	1.0
Providence	35,995	1.0
San Jose	37,799	0.9
Cheyenne	33,876	0.9
Fargo	30,513	0.9
New Orleans	30,174	0.9
Oklahoma City	30,060	0.8
Houston	37,153	0.8
Portland	34,918	0.7
Phoenix	33,291	0.7
Augusta	31,504	0.7
Albuquerque	29,199	0.6
Greensboro	33,072	0.6
Columbia	30,859	0.5
Nashville	32,566	0.5
Buffalo	34,296	0.5

a. Develop the estimated regression equation that could be used to predict the percentage audited given the average adjusted gross income reported.
b. At the .05 level of significance, determine whether the adjusted gross income and the percentage audited are related.
c. Did the estimated regression equation provide a good fit? Explain.
d. Use the estimated regression equation developed in part (a) to calculate a 95% confidence interval for the expected percentage audited for districts with an average adjusted gross income of $35,000.

Case Problem 1   Spending and Student Achievement

Is the educational achievement level of students related to how much the state in which they reside spends on education? In many communities taxpayers are asking this important question as school districts request tax revenue increases for education. In this case, you will be asked to analyze data on spending and achievement scores in order to determine whether there is any relationship between spending and student achievement in the public schools.

The federal government's National Assessment of Educational Progress (NAEP) program is frequently used to measure the educational achievement of students. Table 12.8 shows the total current spending per pupil per year, and the composite NAEP test score for 35 states that participated in the NAEP program. These data are available on the CD

TABLE 12.8   SPENDING PER PUPIL AND COMPOSITE TEST SCORES FOR STATES THAT PARTICIPATED IN THE NAEP PROGRAM

State	Spending per Pupil ($)	Composite Test Score
Louisiana	4049	581
Mississippi	3423	582
California	4917	580
Hawaii	5532	580
South Carolina	4304	603
Alabama	3777	604
Georgia	4663	611
Florida	4934	611
New Mexico	4097	614
Arkansas	4060	615
Delaware	6208	615
Tennessee	3800	618
Arizona	4041	618
West Virginia	5247	625
Maryland	6100	625
Kentucky	5020	626
Texas	4520	627
New York	8162	628
North Carolina	4521	629
Rhode Island	6554	638
Washington	5338	639
Missouri	4483	641
Colorado	4772	644
Indiana	5128	649
Utah	3280	650
Wyoming	5515	657
Connecticut	7629	657
Massachusetts	6413	658
Nebraska	5410	660
Minnesota	5477	661
Iowa	5060	665
Montana	4985	667
Wisconsin	6055	667
North Dakota	4374	671
Maine	5561	675

accompanying the text in the file named NAEP. The composite test score is the sum of the math, science, and reading scores on the 1996 (1994 for reading) NAEP test. Pupils tested are in grade 8, except for reading, which is given to fourth-graders only. The maximum possible score is 1300. Table 12.9 shows the spending per pupil for 13 states that did not participate in relevant NAEP surveys. These data were reported in an article on spending and achievement level appearing in *Forbes* (November 3, 1997).

Managerial Report

1. Develop numerical and graphical summaries of the data.
2. Use regression analysis to investigate the relationship between the amount spent per pupil and the composite score on the NAEP test. Discuss your findings.

TABLE 12.9 SPENDING PER PUPIL FOR STATES THAT DID NOT PARTICIPATE
IN THE NAEP PROGRAM

State	Spending per Pupil ($)
Idaho	3602
South Dakota	4067
Oklahoma	4265
Nevada	4658
Kansas	5164
Illinois	5297
New Hampshire	5387
Ohio	5438
Oregon	5588
Vermont	6269
Michigan	6391
Pennsylvania	6579
Alaska	7890

3. Do you think that the estimated regression equation developed for these data could be used to estimate the composite test scores for the states that did not participate in the NAEP program?
4. Suppose that you only considered states that spend at least $4000 per pupil but not more than $6000 per pupil. For these states, does the relationship between the two variables appear to be any different than for the complete data set? Discuss the results of your findings and whether you think deleting states with spending less than $4000 per year and more than $6000 per pupil is appropriate.
5. Develop estimates of the composite test scores for the states that did not participate in the NAEP program.
6. Based upon your analyses, do you think that the educational achievement level of students is related to how much the state spends on education?

Case Problem 2 U.S. Department of Transportation

As part of a study on transportation safety, the U.S. Department of Transportation collected data on the number of fatal accidents per 1000 licenses and the percentage of licensed drivers under the age of 21 in a sample of 42 cities. Data collected over a one-year period follow. These data are available on the CD accompanying the text in the file named Safety.

Safety

Percentage Under 21	Fatal Accidents per 1000 Licenses	Percentage Under 21	Fatal Accidents per 1000 Licenses
13	2.962	17	4.100
12	0.708	8	2.190
8	0.885	16	3.623
12	1.652	15	2.623
11	2.091	9	0.835
17	2.627	8	0.820
18	3.830	14	2.890
8	0.368	8	1.267

(continued)

Percentage Under 21	Fatal Accidents per 1000 Licenses	Percentage Under 21	Fatal Accidents per 1000 Licenses
13	1.142	15	3.224
8	0.645	10	1.014
9	1.028	10	0.493
16	2.801	14	1.443
12	1.405	18	3.614
9	1.433	10	1.926
10	0.039	14	1.643
9	0.338	16	2.943
11	1.849	12	1.913
12	2.246	15	2.814
14	2.855	13	2.634
14	2.352	9	0.926
11	1.294	17	3.256

Managerial Report

1. Develop numerical and graphical summaries of the data.
2. Use regression analysis to investigate the relationship between the number of fatal accidents and the percentage of drivers under the age of 21. Discuss your findings.
3. What conclusion and recommendations can you derive from your analysis?

Case Problem 3   Alumni Giving

Alumni donations are an important source of revenue for colleges and universities. If administrators could determine the factors that influence increases in the percentage of alumni who make a donation, they might be able to implement policies that could lead to increased revenues. Research shows that students who are more satisfied with their contact with teachers are more likely to graduate. As a result, one might suspect that smaller class sizes and lower student-faculty ratios might lead to a higher percentage of satisfied graduates, which in turn might lead to increases in the percentage of alumni who make a donation. Table 12.10 shows data for 48 national universities (*America's Best Colleges*, Year 2000 Edition). The column labeled % of Classes Under 20 shows the percentage of classes offered with fewer than 20 students. The column labeled Student/Faculty Ratio is the number of students enrolled divided by the total number of faculty. Finally, the column labeled Alumni Giving Rate is the percentage of alumni that made a donation to the university.

Managerial Report

1. Develop numerical and graphical summaries of the data.
2. Use regression analysis to develop an estimated regression equation that could be used to predict the alumni giving rate given the percentage of classes with fewer than 20 students.
3. Use regression analysis to develop an estimated regression equation that could be used to predict the alumni giving rate given the student-faculty ratio.
4. Which of the two estimated regression equations provides the best fit? For this estimated regression equation, perform an analysis of the residuals and discuss your findings and conclusions.
5. What conclusions and recommendations can you derive from your analysis?

TABLE 12.10   DATA FOR 48 NATIONAL UNIVERSITIES

Alumni

	% of Classes Under 20	Student/Faculty Ratio	Alumni Giving Rate
Boston College	39	13	25
Brandeis University	68	8	33
Brown University	60	8	40
California Institute of Technology	65	3	46
Carnegie Mellon University	67	10	28
Case Western Reserve Univ.	52	8	31
College of William and Mary	45	12	27
Columbia University	69	7	31
Cornell University	72	13	35
Dartmouth College	61	10	53
Duke University	68	8	45
Emory University	65	7	37
Georgetown University	54	10	29
Harvard University	73	8	46
Johns Hopkins University	64	9	27
Lehigh University	55	11	40
Massachusetts Inst. of Technology	65	6	44
New York University	63	13	13
Northwestern University	66	8	30
Pennsylvania State Univ.	32	19	21
Princeton University	68	5	67
Rice University	62	8	40
Stanford University	69	7	34
Tufts University	67	9	29
Tulane University	56	12	17
U. of California–Berkeley	58	17	18
U. of California–Davis	32	19	7
U. of California–Irvine	42	20	9
U. of California–Los Angeles	41	18	13
U. of California–San Diego	48	19	8
U. of California–Santa Barbara	45	20	12
U. of Chicago	65	4	36
U. of Florida	31	23	19
U. of Illinois–Urbana Champaign	29	15	23
U. of Michigan–Ann Arbor	51	15	13
U. of North Carolina–Chapel Hill	40	16	26
U. of Notre Dame	53	13	49
U. of Pennsylvania	65	7	41
U. of Rochester	63	10	23
U. of Southern California	53	13	22
U. of Texas–Austin	39	21	13
U. of Virginia	44	13	28
U. of Washington	37	12	12
U. of Wisconsin–Madison	37	13	13
Vanderbilt University	68	9	31
Wake Forest University	59	11	38
Washington University–St. Louis	73	7	33
Yale University	77	7	50

Case Problem 4 **Major League Baseball Team Values**

A group led by John Henry paid $700 million to purchase the Boston Red Sox, even though the Red Sox have not won the World Series since 1918 and posted an operating loss of $11.4 million for 2001. Moreover, *Forbes* magazine estimates that the current value of the team is actually $426 million. *Forbes* attributes the difference between the current value for a team and the price investors are willing to pay to the fact that the purchase of a team often includes the acquisition of a grossly undervalued cable network. For instance, in purchasing the Boston Red Sox, the new owners also got an 80% interest in the New England Sports Network. Table 12.11 shows data for the 30 major league teams (*Forbes,* April 15, 2002). The column labeled Value contains the values of the teams based on current stadium deals, without deduction for debt. The column labeled Income indicates the earnings before interest, taxes, and depreciation.

Managerial Report

1. Develop numerical and graphical summaries of the data.
2. Use regression analysis to investigate the relationship between value and income. Discuss your findings.

MLB

TABLE 12.11   DATA FOR MAJOR LEAGUE BASEBALL TEAMS

Team	Value	Revenue	Income
New York Yankees	730	215	18.7
New York Mets	482	169	14.3
Los Angeles Dodgers	435	143	−29.6
Boston Red Sox	426	152	−11.4
Atlanta Braves	424	160	9.5
Seattle Mariners	373	166	14.1
Cleveland Indians	360	150	−3.6
Texas Rangers	356	134	−6.5
San Francisco Giants	355	142	16.8
Colorado Rockies	347	129	6.7
Houston Astros	337	125	4.1
Baltimore Orioles	319	133	3.2
Chicago Cubs	287	131	7.9
Arizona Diamondbacks	280	127	−3.9
St. Louis Cardinals	271	123	−5.1
Detroit Tigers	262	114	12.3
Pittsburgh Pirates	242	108	9.5
Milwaukee Brewers	238	108	18.8
Philadelphia Phillies	231	94	2.6
Chicago White Sox	223	101	−3.8
San Diego Padres	207	92	5.7
Cincinnati Reds	204	87	4.3
Anaheim Angels	195	103	5.7
Toronto Blue Jays	182	91	−20.6
Oakland Athletics	157	90	6.8
Kansas City Royals	152	85	2.2
Tampa Bay Devil Rays	142	92	−6.1
Florida Marlins	137	81	1.4
Minnesota Twins	127	75	3.6
Montreal Expos	108	63	−3.4

3. Use regression analysis to investigate the relationship between value and revenue. Discuss your findings.
4. What conclusions and recommendations can you derive from your analysis?

Appendix 12.1   Regression Analysis with Minitab

CD file

Armand's

In Section 12.7 we discussed the computer solution of regression problems by showing Minitab's output for the Armand's Pizza Parlors problem. In this appendix, we describe the steps required to generate the Minitab computer solution. First, the data must be entered in a Minitab worksheet. Student population data are entered in column C1 and quarterly sales data are entered in column C2. The variable names Pop and Sales are entered as the column headings on the worksheet. In subsequent steps, we refer to the data by using the variable names Pop and Sales or the column indicators C1 and C2. The following steps describe how to use Minitab to produce the regression results shown in Figure 12.10.

Step 1. Select the **Stat** menu
Step 2. Select the **Regression** menu
Step 3. Choose **Regression**
Step 4. When the Regression dialog box appears:
  Enter Sales in the **Response** box
  Enter Pop in the **Predictors** box
  Click the **Options** button
When the Regression-Options dialog box appears:
  Enter 10 in the **Prediction intervals for new observations** box
  Click **OK**
When the Regression dialog box reappears:
  Click **OK**

The Minitab regression dialog box provides additional capabilities that can be obtained by selecting the desired options. For instance, to obtain a residual plot that shows the predicted value of the dependent variable $\hat{y}$ on the horizontal axis and the residual values on the vertical axis, step 4 would be as follows:

Step 4. When the Regression dialog box appears:
  Enter Sales in the **Response** box
  Enter Pop in the **Predictors** box
  Click the **Graphs** button
When the Regression-Graphs dialog box appears:
  Select **Regular** under Residuals for Plots
  Select **Residuals versus fits** under Residual Plots
  Click **OK**
When the Regression dialog box reappears:
  Click **OK**

Appendix 12.2   Regression Analysis with Excel

CD file

Armand's

In this appendix we will illustrate how Excel's Regression tool can be used to perform the regression analysis computations for the Armand's Pizza Parlors problem. Refer to Figure 12.14 as we describe the steps involved. The labels Restaurant, Population, and Sales are entered into cells A1:C1 of the worksheet. To identify each of the 10 observations, we entered the

FIGURE 12.14 EXCEL SOLUTION TO THE ARMAND'S PIZZA PARLORS PROBLEM

	A	B	C	D	E	F	G	H	I	J
1	Restaurant	Population	Sales							
2	1	2	58							
3	2	6	105							
4	3	8	88							
5	4	8	118							
6	5	12	117							
7	6	16	137							
8	7	20	157							
9	8	20	169							
10	9	22	149							
11	10	26	202							
12										
13	SUMMARY OUTPUT									
14										
15	*Regression Statistics*									
16	Multiple R	0.9501								
17	R Square	0.9027								
18	Adjusted R Square	0.8906								
19	Standard Error	13.8293								
20	Observations	10								
21										
22	ANOVA									
23		*df*	*SS*	*MS*	*F*	*Significance F*				
24	Regression	1	14200	14200	74.2484	2.55E-05				
25	Residual	8	1530	191.25						
26	Total	9	15730							
27										
28		*Coefficients*	*Standard Error*	*t Stat*	*P-value*	*Lower 95%*	*Upper 95%*	*Lower 99.0%*	*Upper 99.0%*	
29	Intercept	60	9.2260	6.5033	0.0002	38.7247	81.2753	29.0431	90.9569	
30	Population	5	0.5803	8.6167	2.55E-05	3.6619	6.3381	3.0530	6.9470	
31										

numbers 1 through 10 into cells A2:A11. The sample data are entered into cells B2:C11. The following steps describe how to use Excel to produce the regression results.

Step 1. Select the **Tools** menu
Step 2. Choose **Data Analysis**
Step 3. Choose **Regression** from the list of Analysis Tools
Step 4. Click **OK**
Step 5. When the Regression dialog box appears:
  Enter C1:C11 in the **Input Y Range** box
  Enter B1:B11 in the **Input X Range** box
  Select **Labels**
  Select **Confidence Level**
  Enter 99 in the **Confidence Level** box
  Select **Output Range**

Enter A13 in the **Output Range** box

(Any upper-left-hand corner cell indicating where the output is to begin may be entered here.)

Click **OK**

The first section of the output, titled *Regression Statistics,* contains summary statistics such as the coefficient of determination (R Square). The second section of the output, titled ANOVA, contains the analysis of variance table. The last section of the output, which is not titled, contains the estimated regression coefficients and related information. We will begin our discussion of the interpretation of the regression output with the information contained in cells A28:I30.

Interpretation of Estimated Regression Equation Output

The y-intercept of the estimated regression line, $b_0 = 60$, is shown in cell B29, and the slope of the estimated regression line, $b_1 = 5$, is shown in cell B30. The label Intercept in cell A29 and the label Population in cell A30 are used to identify these two values.

In Section 12.5 we showed that the estimated standard deviation of b_1 is $s_{b_1} = .5803$. Note that the value in cell C30 is .5803. The label Standard Error in cell C28 is Excel's way of indicating that the value in cell C30 is the standard error, or standard deviation, of b_1. Recall that the t test for a significant relationship required the computation of the t statistic, $t = b_1/s_{b_1}$. For the Armand's data, the value of t that we computed was $t = 5/.5803 = 8.62$. The label in cell D28, t Stat, reminds us that cell D30 contains the value of the t test statistic.

The value in cell E30 is the p-value associated with the t test for significance. Excel has displayed the p-value in cell E30 using scientific notation. To obtain the decimal value, we move the decimal point 5 places to the left, obtaining a value of .0000255. Because the p-value $= .0000255 < \alpha = .01$, we can reject H_0 and conclude that we have a significant relationship between student population and quarterly sales.

The information in cells F28:I30 can be used to develop confidence interval estimates of the y-intercept and slope of the estimated regression equation. Excel always provides the lower and upper limits for a 95% confidence interval. Recall that in step 4 we selected Confidence Level and entered 99 in the Confidence Level box. As a result, Excel's Regression tool also provides the lower and upper limits for a 99% confidence interval. The value in cell H30 is the lower limit for the 99% confidence interval estimate of β_1 and the value in cell I30 is the upper limit. Thus, after rounding, the 99% confidence interval estimate of β_1 is 3.05 to 6.95. The values in cells F30 and G30 provide the lower and upper limits for the 95% confidence interval. Thus, the 95% confidence interval is 3.66 to 6.34.

Interpretation of ANOVA Output

The information in cells A22:F26 is a summary of the analysis of variance computations. The three sources of variation are labeled Regression, Residual, and Total. The label df in cell B23 stands for degrees of freedom, the label SS in cell C23 stands for sum of squares, and the label MS in cell D23 stands for mean square.

In Section 12.5 we stated that the mean square error, obtained by dividing the error or residual sum of squares by its degrees of freedom, provides an estimate of σ^2. The value in cell D25, 191.25, is the mean square error for the Armand's regression output. In Section 12.5 we showed that an F test could also be used to test for significance in regression. The value in cell F24, .0000255, is the p-value associated with the F test for significance. Because the p-value $= .0000255 < \alpha = .01$, we can reject H_0 and conclude that we have a

The label Significance F may be more meaningful if you think of the value in cell F24 as the observed level of significance for the F test.

significant relationship between student population and quarterly sales. The label Excel uses to identify the p-value for the F test for significance, shown in cell F23, is *Significance F.*

Interpretation of Regression Statistics Output

The coefficient of determination, .9027, appears in cell B17; the corresponding label, R Square, is shown in cell A17. The square root of the coefficient of determination provides the sample correlation coefficient of .9501 shown in cell B16. Note that Excel uses the label Multiple R (cell A16) to identify this value. In cell A19, the label Standard Error is used to identify the value of the standard error of the estimate shown in cell B19. Thus, the standard error of the estimate is 13.8293. We caution the reader to keep in mind that in the Excel output, the label Standard Error appears in two different places. In the Regression Statistics section of the output, the label Standard Error refers to the estimate of σ. In the Estimated Regression Equation section of the output the label *Standard Error* refers to s_{b_1}, the standard deviation of the sampling distribution of b_1.

Multiple Regression

STATISTICS *in* PRACTICE

INTERNATIONAL PAPER*
PURCHASE, NEW YORK

International Paper is the world's largest paper and forest products company. The company employs more than 117,000 people in its operations in nearly 50 countries, and exports its products to more than 130 nations. International Paper produces building materials such as lumber and plywood; consumer packaging materials such as disposable cups and containers; industrial packaging materials such as corrugated boxes and shipping containers; and a variety of papers for use in photocopiers, printers, books, and advertising materials.

To make paper products, pulp mills process wood chips and chemicals to produce wood pulp. The wood pulp is then used at a paper mill to produce paper products. In the production of white paper products, the pulp must be bleached to remove any discoloration. A key bleaching agent used in the process is chlorine dioxide, which, because of its combustible nature, is usually produced at a pulp mill facility and then piped in solution form into the bleaching tower of the pulp mill. To improve one of the processes used to produce chlorine dioxide, researchers studied the process's control and efficiency. One aspect of the study looked at the chemical-feed rate for chlorine dioxide production.

To produce the chlorine dioxide, four chemicals flow at metered rates into the chlorine dioxide generator. The chlorine dioxide produced in the generator flows to an absorber where chilled water absorbs the chlorine dioxide gas to form a chlorine dioxide solution. The solution is then piped into the paper mill. A key part of controlling the process involves the chemical-feed rates. Historically, experienced operators set the chemical-feed rates, but this approach led to overcontrol by the operators. Consequently, chemical engineers at the mill requested that a set of control equations, one for each chemical feed, be developed to aid the operators in setting the rates.

*The authors are indebted to Marian Williams and Bill Griggs for providing this Statistics in Practice. This application was originally developed at Champion International Corporation, which became part of International Paper in 2000.

Multiple regression analysis assisted in the development of a better bleaching process for making white paper products. © Lester Lefkowitz/Corbis.

Using multiple regression analysis, statistical analysts developed an estimated multiple regression equation for each of the four chemicals used in the process. Each equation related the production of chlorine dioxide to the amount of chemical used and the concentration level of the chlorine dioxide solution. The resulting set of four equations was programmed into a microcomputer at each mill. In the new system, operators enter the concentration of the chlorine dioxide solution and the desired production rate; the computer software then calculates the chemical feed needed to achieve the desired production rate. After the operators began using the control equations, the chlorine dioxide generator efficiency increased, and the number of times the concentrations fell within acceptable ranges increased significantly.

This example shows how multiple regression analysis can be used to develop a better bleaching process for producing white paper products. In this chapter we will discuss how computer software packages are used for such purposes. Most of the concepts introduced in Chapter 12 for simple linear regression can be directly extended to the multiple regression case.

In Chapter 12 we presented simple linear regression and demonstrated its use in developing an estimated regression equation that describes the relationship between two variables. Recall that the variable being predicted or explained is called the dependent variable and the variable being used to predict or explain the dependent variable is called the independent variable. In this chapter we continue our study of regression analysis by considering situations involving two or more independent variables. This subject area, called **multiple regression analysis**, enables us to consider more factors and thus obtain better estimates than are possible with simple linear regression.

13.1   Multiple Regression Model

Multiple regression analysis is the study of how a dependent variable y is related to two or more independent variables. In the general case, we will use p to denote the number of independent variables.

Regression Model and Regression Equation

The concepts of a regression model and a regression equation introduced in the preceding chapter are applicable in the multiple regression case. The equation that describes how the dependent variable y is related to the independent variables $x_1, x_2, \ldots x_p$ and an error term is called the **multiple regression model**. We begin with the assumption that the multiple regression model takes the following form.

MULTIPLE REGRESSION MODEL

$$y = \beta_0 + \beta_1 x_1 + \beta_2 x_2 + \cdots + \beta_p x_p + \epsilon \qquad \textbf{(13.1)}$$

In the multiple regression model, $\beta_0, \beta_1, \beta_2, \ldots, \beta_p$ are the parameters and ϵ (the Greek letter epsilon) is a random variable. A close examination of this model reveals that y is a linear function of $x_1, x_2, \ldots, x_p$ (the $\beta_0 + \beta_1 x_1 + \beta_2 x_2 + \cdots + \beta_p x_p$ part) plus an error term ϵ. The error term accounts for the variability in y that cannot be explained by the linear effect of the p independent variables.

In Section 13.4 we will discuss the assumptions for the multiple regression model and ϵ. One of the assumptions is that the mean or expected value of ϵ is zero. A consequence of this assumption is that the mean or expected value of y, denoted $E(y)$, is equal to $\beta_0 + \beta_1 x_1 + \beta_2 x_2 + \cdots + \beta_p x_p$. The equation that describes how the mean value of y is related to $x_1, x_2, \ldots, x_p$ is called the **multiple regression equation**.

MULTIPLE REGRESSION EQUATION

$$E(y) = \beta_0 + \beta_1 x_1 + \beta_2 x_2 + \cdots + \beta_p x_p \qquad \textbf{(13.2)}$$

Estimated Multiple Regression Equation

If the values of $\beta_0, \beta_1, \beta_2, \ldots, \beta_p$ were known, equation (13.2) could be used to compute the mean value of y at given values of $x_1, x_2, \ldots, x_p$. Unfortunately, these parameter values will not, in general, be known and must be estimated from sample data. A simple random sample is used to compute sample statistics $b_0, b_1, b_2, \ldots, b_p$ that are used as the point estimators of the parameters $\beta_0, \beta_1, \beta_2, \ldots, \beta_p$. These sample statistics provide the following **estimated multiple regression equation**.

ESTIMATED MULTIPLE REGRESSION EQUATION

$$\hat{y} = b_0 + b_1 x_1 + b_2 x_2 + \cdots + b_p x_p \tag{13.3}$$

where

$b_0, b_1, b_2, \ldots, b_p$ are the estimates of $\beta_0, \beta_1, \beta_2, \ldots, \beta_p$

$\hat{y}$ = estimated value of the dependent variable

The estimation process for multiple regression is shown in Figure 13.1.

 ## Least Squares Method

In Chapter 12, we used the **least squares method** to develop the estimated regression equation that best approximated the straight-line relationship between the dependent and independent variables. This same approach is used to develop the estimated multiple regression equation. The least squares criterion is restated as follows.

LEAST SQUARES CRITERION

$$\min \Sigma (y_i - \hat{y}_i)^2 \tag{13.4}$$

FIGURE 13.1   THE ESTIMATION PROCESS FOR MULTIPLE REGRESSION

In simple linear regression, b_0 and b_1 were the sample statistics used to estimate the parameters β_0 and β_1. Multiple regression analysis parallels this statistical inference process, with $b_0, b_1, b_2, \ldots b_p$ denoting the sample statistics used to estimate the parameters $\beta_0, \beta_1, \beta_2, \ldots, \beta_p$.

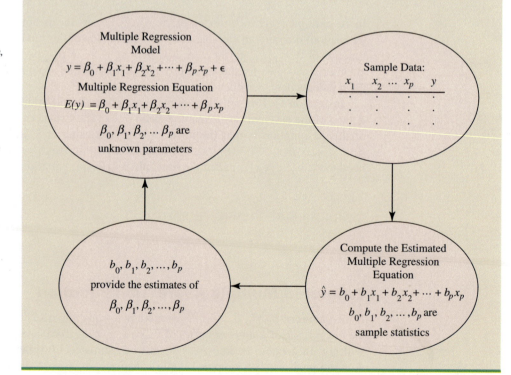

where

$$y_i = \text{observed value of the dependent variable for the } i\text{th observation}$$
$$\hat{y}_i = \text{estimated value of the dependent variable for the } i\text{th observation}$$

The estimated values of the dependent variable are computed by using the estimated multiple regression equation,

$$\hat{y} = b_0 + b_1 x_1 + b_2 x_2 + \cdots + b_p x_p$$

As expression (13.4) shows, the least squares method uses sample data to provide the values of $b_0, b_1, b_2, \ldots, b_p$ that make the sum of squared residuals [the deviations between the observed values of the dependent variable (y_i) and the estimated values of the dependent variable ($\hat{y}_i$)] a minimum.

In Chapter 12 we presented formulas for computing the least squares estimators b_0 and b_1 for the estimated simple linear regression equation $\hat{y} = b_0 + b_1 x$. With relatively small data sets, we were able to use those formulas to compute b_0 and b_1 by manual calculations. In multiple regression, however, the presentation of the formulas for the regression coefficients $b_0, b_1, b_2, \ldots, b_p$ involves the use of matrix algebra and is beyond the scope of this text. Therefore, in presenting multiple regression, we focus on how computer software packages can be used to obtain the estimated regression equation and other information. The emphasis will be on how to interpret the computer output rather than on how to make the multiple regression computations.

An Example: Butler Trucking Company

As an illustration of multiple regression analysis, we will consider a problem faced by the Butler Trucking Company, an independent trucking company in southern California. A major portion of Butler's business involves deliveries throughout its local area. To develop better work schedules, the managers want to estimate the total daily travel time for their drivers.

Initially the managers believed that the total daily travel time would be closely related to the number of miles traveled in making the daily deliveries. A simple random sample of 10 driving assignments provided the data shown in Table 13.1 and the scatter diagram shown in Figure 13.2. After reviewing this scatter diagram, the managers hypothesized that the simple linear regression model $y = \beta_0 + \beta_1 x_1 + \epsilon$ could be used to describe the relationship between the total travel time (y) and the number of miles traveled (x_1). To estimate

TABLE 13.1   PRELIMINARY DATA FOR BUTLER TRUCKING

Butler

Driving Assignment	$x_1 = $ Miles Traveled	$y = $ Travel Time (hours)
1	100	9.3
2	50	4.8
3	100	8.9
4	100	6.5
5	50	4.2
6	80	6.2
7	75	7.4
8	65	6.0
9	90	7.6
10	90	6.1

FIGURE 13.2 SCATTER DIAGRAM OF PRELIMINARY DATA FOR BUTLER TRUCKING

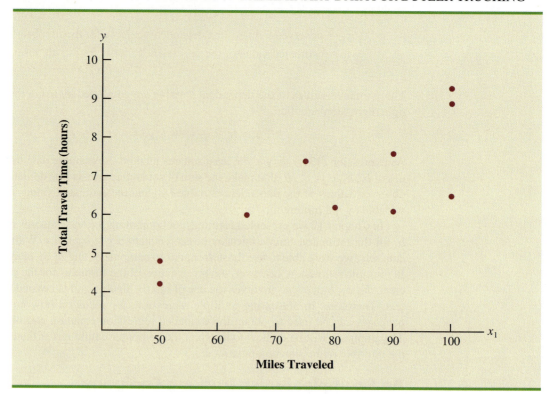

the parameters β_0 and β_1, the least squares method was used to develop the estimated regression equation.

$$\hat{y} = b_0 + b_1 x_1 \qquad (13.5)$$

In Figure 13.3, we show the Minitab computer output from applying simple linear regression to the data in Table 13.1. The estimated regression equation is

$$\hat{y} = 1.27 + .0678 x_1$$

At the .05 level of significance, the F value of 15.81 and its corresponding p-value of .004 indicate that the relationship is significant; that is, we can reject H_0: $\beta_1 = 0$ because the p-value is less than $\alpha = .05$. Note that the same conclusion is obtained from the t value of 3.98 and its associated p-value of .004. Thus, we can conclude that the relationship between the total travel time and the number of miles traveled is significant; longer travel times are associated with more miles traveled. With a coefficient of determination (expressed as a percentage) of R-sq = 66.4%, we see that 66.4% of the variability in travel time can be explained by the linear effect of the number of miles traveled. This finding is fairly good, but the managers might want to consider adding a second independent variable to explain some of the remaining variability in the dependent variable.

In attempting to identify another independent variable, the managers felt that the number of deliveries could also contribute to the total travel time. The Butler Trucking data, with the number of deliveries added, are shown in Table 13.2. The Minitab computer solution with both miles traveled (x_1) and number of deliveries (x_2) as independent variables is shown in Figure 13.4. The estimated regression equation is

$$\hat{y} = -.869 + .0611 x_1 + .923 x_2 \qquad (13.6)$$

FIGURE 13.3 MINITAB OUTPUT FOR BUTLER TRUCKING WITH ONE
INDEPENDENT VARIABLE

*In the Minitab output the
variable names* Miles *and*
Time *were entered as the
column headings on the
worksheet; thus,* $x_1 = $ Miles
and $y = $ Time.

```
The regression equation is
Time = 1.27 + 0.0678 Miles

Predictor       Coef   SE Coef      T      p
Constant       1.274     1.401   0.91  0.390
Miles        0.06783   0.01706   3.98  0.004

S = 1.002    R-sq = 66.4%    R-sq(adj) = 62.2%

Analysis of Variance

SOURCE             DF       SS       MS       F      p
Regression          1   15.871   15.871   15.81  0.004
Residual Error      8    8.029    1.004
Total               9   23.900
```

In the next section we will discuss the use of the coefficient of multiple determination in measuring how good a fit is provided by this estimated regression equation. Before doing so, let us examine more carefully the values of $b_1 = .0611$ and $b_2 = .923$ in equation (13.6).

Note on Interpretation of Coefficients

One observation can be made at this point about the relationship between the estimated regression equation with only the miles traveled as an independent variable and the equation that includes the number of deliveries as a second independent variable. The value of b_1 is not the same in both cases. In simple linear regression, we interpret b_1 as an estimate of the change in y for a one-unit change in the independent variable. In multiple regression analysis, this interpretation must be modified somewhat. That is, in multiple regression analysis, we interpret each regression coefficient as follows: b_i represents an estimate of the change in y corresponding to a one-unit change in x_i when all other independent variables are held constant. In the Butler Trucking example involving two independent variables, $b_1 = .0611$. Thus,

TABLE 13.2 DATA FOR BUTLER TRUCKING WITH MILES TRAVELED (x_1) AND
NUMBER OF DELIVERIES (x_2) AS THE INDEPENDENT VARIABLES

CD file

Butler

Driving Assignment	$x_1 = $ Miles Traveled	$x_2 = $ Number of Deliveries	$y = $ Travel Time (hours)
1	100	4	9.3
2	50	3	4.8
3	100	4	8.9
4	100	2	6.5
5	50	2	4.2
6	80	2	6.2
7	75	3	7.4
8	65	4	6.0
9	90	3	7.6
10	90	2	6.1

FIGURE 13.4   MINITAB OUTPUT FOR BUTLER TRUCKING WITH TWO INDEPENDENT VARIABLES

In the Minitab output the variable names Miles, Deliv, and Time were entered as the column headings on the worksheet; thus, x_1 = Miles, x_2 = Deliv, and y = Time.

```
The regression equation is
Time = - 0.869 + 0.0611 Miles + 0.923 Deliveries

Predictor        Coef     SE Coef       T       p
Constant      -0.8687      0.9515   -0.91   0.392
Miles        0.061135    0.009888    6.18   0.000
Deliveries     0.9234      0.2211    4.18   0.004

S = 0.5731    R-sq = 90.4%    R-sq(adj) = 87.6%

Analysis of Variance

SOURCE             DF       SS       MS       F       p
Regression          2   21.601   10.800   32.88   0.000
Residual Error      7    2.299    0.328
Total               9   23.900
```

.0611 hours is an estimate of the expected increase in travel time corresponding to an increase of 1 mile in the distance traveled when the number of deliveries is held constant. Similarly, because b_2 = .923, an estimate of the expected increase in travel time corresponding to an increase of one delivery when the number of miles traveled is held constant is .923 hours.

Exercises

Note to student: The exercises involving data in this and subsequent sections were designed to be solved using a computer software package.

Methods

1. The estimated regression equation for a model involving two independent variables and 10 observations follows.

    $$\hat{y} = 29.1270 + .5906x_1 + .4980x_2$$

    a. Interpret b_1 and b_2 in this estimated regression equation.
    b. Estimate y when x_1 = 180 and x_2 = 310.

2. Consider the following data for a dependent variable y and two independent variables, x_1 and x_2.

SELF test

Exer2

x_1	x_2	y
30	12	94
47	10	108
25	17	112
51	16	178
40	5	94
51	19	175
74	7	170
36	12	117
59	13	142
76	16	211

a. Develop an estimated regression equation relating y to x_1. Estimate y if $x_1 = 45$.
b. Develop an estimated regression equation relating y to x_2. Estimate y if $x_2 = 15$.
c. Develop an estimated regression equation relating y to x_1 and x_2. Estimate y if $x_1 = 45$ and $x_2 = 15$.

3. In a regression analysis involving 30 observations, the following estimated regression equation was obtained.

$$\hat{y} = 17.6 + 3.8x_1 - 2.3x_2 + 7.6x_3 + 2.7x_4$$

a. Interpret b_1, b_2, b_3, and b_4 in this estimated regression equation.
b. Estimate y when $x_1 = 10$, $x_2 = 5$, $x_3 = 1$, and $x_4 = 2$.

Applications

4. A shoe store developed the following estimated regression equation relating sales to inventory investment and advertising expenditures.

$$\hat{y} = 25 + 10x_1 + 8x_2$$

where

$$x_1 = \text{inventory investment (\$1000s)}$$
$$x_2 = \text{advertising expenditures (\$1000s)}$$
$$y = \text{sales (\$1000s)}$$

a. Estimate sales resulting from a $15,000 investment in inventory and an advertising budget of $10,000.
b. Interpret b_1 and b_2 in this estimated regression equation.

5. The owner of Showtime Movie Theaters, Inc., would like to estimate weekly gross revenue as a function of advertising expenditures. Historical data for a sample of eight weeks follow.

Showtime

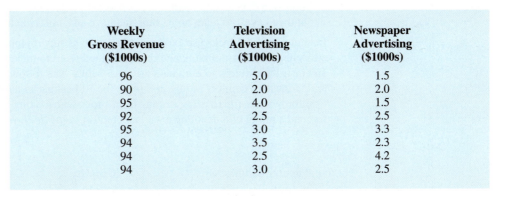

Weekly Gross Revenue ($1000s)	Television Advertising ($1000s)	Newspaper Advertising ($1000s)
96	5.0	1.5
90	2.0	2.0
95	4.0	1.5
92	2.5	2.5
95	3.0	3.3
94	3.5	2.3
94	2.5	4.2
94	3.0	2.5

a. Develop an estimated regression equation with the amount of television advertising as the independent variable.
b. Develop an estimated regression equation with both television advertising and newspaper advertising as the independent variables.
c. Is the estimated regression equation coefficient for television advertising expenditures the same in part (a) and in part (b)? Interpret the coefficient in each case.
d. What is the estimate of the weekly gross revenue for a week when $3500 is spent on television advertising and $1800 is spent on newspaper advertising?

6. In baseball, a team's success is often thought to be a function of the team's hitting performance and pitching performance. One measure of hitting performance is the number of home runs the team has, and one measure of pitching performance is the earned run average for the team's pitching staff. It is generally believed that teams that hit more home runs and have a lower earned run average will win a higher percentage of the games played. The following data show the percentage of games won (PCT), the number of team home runs (HR), and the earned run average (ERA) for the 16 teams in the National League for the 2003 Major League Baseball season (http://www.usatoday, January 7, 2004).

MLB

Team	PCT	HR	ERA	Team	PCT	HR	ERA
Arizona	0.519	152	3.857	Milwaukee	0.420	196	5.058
Atlanta	0.623	235	4.106	Montreal	0.512	144	4.027
Chicago	0.543	172	3.842	New York	0.410	124	4.517
Cincinnati	0.426	182	5.127	Philadelphia	0.531	166	4.072
Colorado	0.457	198	5.269	Pittsburgh	0.463	163	4.664
Florida	0.562	157	4.059	San Diego	0.395	128	4.904
Houston	0.537	191	3.880	San Francisco	0.621	180	3.734
Los Angeles	0.525	124	3.162	St. Louis	0.525	196	4.642

a. Determine the estimated regression equation that could be used to predict the percentage of games won given the number of team home runs.

b. Determine the estimated regression equation that could be used to predict the percentage of games won given the earned run average for the team's pitching staff.

c. Determine the estimated regression equation that could be used to predict the percentage of games won given the number of team home runs and the earned run average for the team's pitching staff.

d. For the 2003 season San Diego won only 39.5% of the games they played, the lowest in the National League. To improve next year's record, the team is trying to acquire new players who will increase the number of team home runs to 180 and decrease the earned run average for the team's pitching staff to 4.0. Use the estimated regression equation developed in part (c) to estimate the percentage of games San Diego will win if they have 180 team home runs and have an earned run average of 4.0.

7. Designers of backpacks use exotic material such as supernylon Delrin, high-density polyethylene, aircraft aluminum, and thermomolded foam to make packs that fit comfortably and distribute weight to eliminate pressure points. The following data show the capacity (cubic inches), comfort rating, and price for 10 backpacks tested by *Outside Magazine*. Comfort was measured using a rating from 1 to 5, with a rating of 1 denoting average comfort and a rating of 5 denoting excellent comfort (*Outside Buyer's Guide,* 2001).

Backpack

Manufacturer and Model	Capacity	Comfort	Price ($)
Camp Trails Paragon II	4330	2	190
EMS 5500	5500	3	219
Lowe Alpomayo 90+20	5500	4	249
Marmot Muir	4700	3	249
Kelly Bigfoot 5200	5200	4	250
Gregory Whitney	5500	4	340
Osprey 75	4700	4	389
Arc'Teryx Bora 95	5500	5	395
Dana Design Terraplane LTW	5800	5	439
The Works @ Mystery Ranch Jazz	5000	5	525

     a.   Determine the estimated regression equation that can be used to predict the price of a backpack given the capacity and the comfort rating.

     b.   Interpret b_1 and b_2.

     c.   Predict the price for a backpack with a capacity of 4500 cubic inches and a comfort rating of 4.

8.   The following table gives the annual return, the safety rating (0 = riskiest, 10 = safest), and the annual expense ratio for 20 foreign funds (*Mutual Funds,* March 2000).

Fund	Safety Rating	Annual Expense Ratio (%)	Annual Return (%)
Accessor Int'l Equity "Adv"	7.1	1.59	49
Aetna "I" International	7.2	1.35	52
Amer Century Int'l Discovery "Inv"	6.8	1.68	89
Columbia International Stock	7.1	1.56	58
Concert Inv "A" Int'l Equity	6.2	2.16	131
Dreyfus Founders Int'l Equity "F"	7.4	1.80	59
Driehaus International Growth	6.5	1.88	99
Excelsior "Inst" Int'l Equity	7.0	0.90	53
Julius Baer International Equity	6.9	1.79	77
Marshall International Stock "Y"	7.2	1.49	54
MassMutual Int'l Equity "S"	7.1	1.05	57
Morgan Grenfell Int'l Sm Cap "Inst"	7.7	1.25	61
New England "A" Int'l Equity	7.0	1.83	88
Pilgrim Int'l Small Cap "A"	7.0	1.94	122
Republic International Equity	7.2	1.09	71
Sit International Growth	6.9	1.50	51
Smith Barney "A" Int'l Equity	7.0	1.28	60
State St Research "S" Int'l Equity	7.1	1.65	50
Strong International Stock	6.5	1.61	93
Vontobel International Equity	7.0	1.50	47

     a.   Develop an estimated regression equation relating the annual return to the safety rating and the annual expense ratio.

     b.   Estimate the annual return for a firm that has a safety rating of 7.5 and annual expense ratio of 2.

9.   Two experts provided subjective lists of school districts that they think are among the best in the country. For each school district the average class size, the combined SAT score, and the percentage of students who attended a four-year college were provided.

District	Average Class Size	Combined SAT Score	% Attend Four-Year College
Blue Springs, MO	25	1083	74
Garden City, NY	18	997	77
Indianapolis, IN	30	716	40
Newport Beach, CA	26	977	51
Novi, MI	20	980	53
Piedmont, CA	28	1042	75
Pittsburg, PA	21	983	66
Scarsdale, NY	20	1110	87
Wayne, PA	22	1040	85
Weston, MA	21	1031	89
Farmingdale, NY	22	947	81

(*continued*)

District	Average Class Size	Combined SAT Score	% Attend Four-Year College
Mamaroneck, NY	20	1000	69
Mayfield, OH	24	1003	48
Morristown, NJ	22	972	64
New Rochelle, NY	23	1039	55
Newtown Square, PA	17	963	79
Omaha, NE	23	1059	81
Shaker Heights, OH	23	940	82

    a. Using these data, develop an estimated regression equation relating the percentage of students who attend a four-year college to the average class size and the combined SAT score.

    b. Estimate the percentage of students who attend a four-year college if the average class size is 20 and the combined SAT score is 1000.

10. The National Basketball Association (NBA) records a variety of statistics for each team. Four of these statistics are the percentage of games won (PCT), the percentage of field goals made by the team (FG%), the percentage of three-point shots made by the team's opponent (Opp 3 Pct%), and the number of turnovers committed by the team's opponent (Opp TO). The following data show the values of these statistics for the 29 teams in the NBA for a portion of the 2004 season (http://www.nba.com, January 3, 2004).

CD file

NBA

Team	PCT	FG%	Opp 3 Pt%	Opp TO	Team	PCT	FG%	Opp 3 Pt%	Opp TO
Atlanta	0.265	0.435	0.346	13.206	Minnesota	0.677	0.473	0.348	13.839
Boston	0.471	0.449	0.369	16.176	New Jersey	0.563	0.435	0.338	17.063
Chicago	0.313	0.417	0.372	15.031	New Orleans	0.636	0.421	0.330	16.909
Cleveland	0.303	0.438	0.345	12.515	New York	0.412	0.442	0.330	13.588
Dallas	0.581	0.439	0.332	15.000	Orlando	0.242	0.417	0.360	14.242
Denver	0.606	0.431	0.366	17.818	Philadelphia	0.438	0.428	0.364	16.938
Detroit	0.606	0.423	0.262	15.788	Phoenix	0.364	0.438	0.326	16.515
Golden State	0.452	0.445	0.384	14.290	Portland	0.484	0.447	0.367	12.548
Houston	0.548	0.426	0.324	13.161	Sacramento	0.724	0.466	0.327	15.207
Indiana	0.706	0.428	0.317	15.647	San Antonio	0.688	0.429	0.293	15.344
L.A. Clippers	0.464	0.424	0.326	14.357	Seattle	0.533	0.436	0.350	16.767
L.A. Lakers	0.724	0.465	0.323	16.000	Toronto	0.516	0.424	0.314	14.129
Memphis	0.485	0.432	0.358	17.848	Utah	0.531	0.456	0.368	15.469
Miami	0.424	0.410	0.369	14.970	Washington	0.300	0.411	0.341	16.133
Milwaukee	0.500	0.438	0.349	14.750					

    a. Determine the estimated regression equation that can be used to predict the percentage of games won given the percentage of field goals made by the team.

    b. Provide an interpretation for the slope of the estimated regression equation developed in part (a).

    c. Determine the estimated regression equation that can be used to predict the percentage of games won given the percentage of field goals made by the team, the percentage of three-point shots made by the team's opponent, and the number of turnovers committed by the team's opponent.

    d. Discuss the practical implications of the estimated regression equation developed in part (c).

    e. Estimate the percentage of games won for a team with the following values for the three independent variables: FG% = .45, Opp 3 Pt% = .34, and Opp TO = 17.

Multiple Coefficient of Determination

In simple linear regression we showed that the total sum of squares can be partitioned into two components: the sum of squares due to regression and the sum of squares due to error. The same procedure applies to the sum of squares in multiple regression.

RELATIONSHIP AMONG SST, SSR, AND SSE

$$SST = SSR + SSE \qquad \text{(13.7)}$$

where

$$SST = \text{total sum of squares} = \Sigma(y_i - \bar{y})^2$$
$$SSR = \text{sum of squares due to regression} = \Sigma(\hat{y}_i - \bar{y})^2$$
$$SSE = \text{sum of squares due to error} = \Sigma(y_i - \hat{y}_i)^2$$

Because of the computational difficulty in computing the three sums of squares, we rely on computer packages to determine those values. The analysis of variance part of the Minitab output in Figure 13.4 shows the three values for the Butler Trucking problem with two independent variables: SST = 23.900, SSR = 21.601, and SSE = 2.299. With only one independent variable (number of miles traveled), the Minitab output in Figure 13.3 shows that SST = 23.900, SSR = 15.871, and SSE = 8.029. The value of SST is the same in both cases because it does not depend on $\hat{y}$, but SSR increases and SSE decreases when a second independent variable (number of deliveries) is added. The implication is that the estimated multiple regression equation provides a better fit for the observed data.

In Chapter 14, we used the coefficient of determination, $r^2 = SSR/SST$, to measure the goodness of fit for the estimated regression equation. The same concept applies to multiple regression. The term **multiple coefficient of determination** indicates that we are measuring the goodness of fit for the estimated multiple regression equation. The multiple coefficient of determination, denoted R^2, is computed as follows.

MULTIPLE COEFFICIENT OF DETERMINATION

$$R^2 = \frac{SSR}{SST} \qquad \text{(13.8)}$$

The multiple coefficient of determination can be interpreted as the proportion of the variability in the dependent variable that can be explained by the estimated multiple regression equation. Hence, when multiplied by 100, it can be interpreted as the percentage of the variability in y that can be explained by the estimated regression equation.

In the two-independent-variable Butler Trucking example, with SSR = 21.601 and SST = 23.900, we have

$$R^2 = \frac{21.601}{23.900} = .904$$

Therefore, 90.4% of the variability in travel time y is explained by the estimated multiple regression equation with miles traveled and number of deliveries as the independent variables. In Figure 13.4, we see that the multiple coefficient of determination is also provided by the Minitab output; it is denoted by R-sq = 90.4%.

Adding independent variables causes the prediction errors to become smaller, thus reducing the sum of squares due to error, SSE. Because SSR = SST − SSE, when SSE becomes smaller, SSR becomes larger, causing R^2 = SSR/SST to increase.

Figure 13.3 shows that the R-sq value for the estimated regression equation with only one independent variable, number of miles traveled (x_1), is 66.4%. Thus, the percentage of the variability in travel times that is explained by the estimated regression equation increases from 66.4% to 90.4% when number of deliveries is added as a second independent variable. In general, R^2 always increases as independent variables are added to the model.

Many analysts prefer adjusting R^2 for the number of independent variables to avoid overestimating the impact of adding an independent variable on the amount of variability explained by the estimated regression equation. With n denoting the number of observations and p denoting the number of independent variables, the **adjusted multiple coefficient of determination** is computed as follows.

If a variable is added to the model, R^2 becomes larger even if the variable added is not statistically significant. The adjusted multiple coefficient of determination compensates for the number of independent variables in the model.

ADJUSTED MULTIPLE COEFFICIENT OF DETERMINATION

$$R_a^2 = 1 - (1 - R^2)\frac{n - 1}{n - p - 1} \qquad (13.9)$$

For the Butler Trucking example with $n = 10$ and $p = 2$, we have

$$R_a^2 = 1 - (1 - .904)\frac{10 - 1}{10 - 2 - 1} = .88$$

Thus, after adjusting for the two independent variables, we have an adjusted multiple coefficient of determination of .88. This value is provided by the Minitab output in Figure 13.4 as R-sq(adj) = 87.6%; the value we calculated differs because we used a rounded value of R^2 in the calculation.

NOTES AND COMMENTS

If the value of R^2 is small and the model contains a large number of independent variables, the adjusted coefficient of determination can take a negative value; in such cases, Minitab sets the adjusted coefficient of determination to zero.

Exercises

Methods

11. In exercise 1, the following estimated regression equation based on 10 observations was presented.

$$\hat{y} = 29.1270 + .5906x_1 + .4980x_2$$

The values of SST and SSR are 6724.125 and 6216.375, respectively.
a. Find SSE.
b. Compute R^2.
c. Compute R_a^2.
d. Comment on the goodness of fit.

12. In exercise 2, 10 observations were provided for a dependent variable y and two independent variables x_1 and x_2; for these data SST = 15,182.9, and SSR = 14,052.2.
    a. Compute R^2.
    b. Compute R_a^2.
    c. Does the estimated regression equation explain a large amount of the variability in the data? Explain.

13. In exercise 3, the following estimated regression equation based on 30 observations was presented.

$$\hat{y} = 17.6 + 3.8x_1 - 2.3x_2 + 7.6x_3 + 2.7x_4$$

The values of SST and SSR are 1805 and 1760, respectively.
    a. Compute R^2.
    b. Compute R_a^2.
    c. Comment on the goodness of fit.

Applications

14. In exercise 4, the following estimated regression equation relating sales to inventory investment and advertising expenditures was given.

$$\hat{y} = 25 + 10x_1 + 8x_2$$

The data used to develop the model came from a survey of 10 stores; for those data, SST = 16,000 and SSR = 12,000.
    a. For the estimated regression equation given, compute R^2.
    b. Compute R_a^2.
    c. Does the model appear to explain a large amount of variability in the data? Explain.

15. In exercise 5, the owner of Showtime Movie Theaters, Inc., used multiple regression analysis to predict gross revenue (y) as a function of television advertising (x_1) and newspaper advertising (x_2). The estimated regression equation was

$$\hat{y} = 83.2 + 2.29x_1 + 1.30x_2$$

Showtime

The computer solution provided SST = 25.5 and SSR = 23.435.
    a. Compute and interpret R^2 and R_a^2.
    b. When television advertising was the only independent variable, $R^2 = .653$ and $R_a^2 = .595$. Do you prefer the multiple regression results? Explain.

MLB

16. In exercise 6, data were given on the percentage of games won, the number of team home runs, and the earned run average for the team's pitching staff for the 16 teams in the National League for the 2003 Major League Baseball season (http://www.usatoday, January 7, 2004).
    a. Did the estimated regression equation that uses only the number of home runs as the independent variable to predict the percentage of games won provide a good fit? Explain.
    b. Discuss the benefits of using both the number of home runs and the earned run average to predict the percentage of games won.

17. In exercise 9, an estimated regression equation was developed relating the percentage of students who attend a four-year college to the average class size and the combined SAT score.
    a. Compute and interpret R^2 and R_a^2.
    b. Does the estimated regression equation provide a good fit to the data? Explain.

Schools

NBA

18. Refer to exercise 10, where data were reported on a variety of statistics for the 29 teams in the National Basketball Association for a portion of the 2004 season (http://www.nba.com, January 3, 2004).
    a. In part (c) of exercise 10, an estimated regression equation was developed relating the percentage of games won given the percentage of field goals made by the team, the percentage of three-point shots made by the team's opponent, and the number of turnovers committed by the team's opponent. What are the values of R^2 and R_a^2?
    b. Does the estimated regression equation provide a good fit to the data? Explain.

13.4 Model Assumptions

In Section 13.1 we introduced the following multiple regression model.

MULTIPLE REGRESSION MODEL

$$y = \beta_0 + \beta_1 x_1 + \beta_2 x_2 + \cdots + \beta_p x_p + \epsilon \qquad \textbf{(13.10)}$$

The assumptions about the error term ϵ in the multiple regression model parallel those for the simple linear regression model.

ASSUMPTIONS ABOUT THE ERROR TERM ϵ IN THE MULTIPLE REGRESSION MODEL $y = \beta_0 + \beta_1 x_1 + \cdots + \beta_p x_p + \epsilon$

1. The error ϵ is a random variable with mean or expected value of zero; that is, $E(\epsilon) = 0$.
   Implication: For given values of $x_1, x_2, \ldots, x_p$, the expected, or average, value of y is given by

$$E(y) = \beta_0 + \beta_1 x_1 + \beta_2 x_2 + \cdots + \beta_p x_p \qquad \textbf{(13.11)}$$

   Equation (13.11) is the multiple regression equation we introduced in Section 13.1. In this equation, $E(y)$ represents the average of all possible values of y that might occur for the given values of $x_1, x_2, \ldots, x_p$.
2. The variance of ϵ is denoted by σ^2 and is the same for all values of the independent variables $x_1, x_2, \ldots, x_p$.
   Implication: The variance of y about the regression line equals σ^2 and is the same for all values of $x_1, x_2, \ldots, x_p$.
3. The values of ϵ are independent.
   Implication: The size of the error for a particular set of values for the independent variables is not related to the size of the error for any other set of values.
4. The error ϵ is a normally distributed random variable reflecting the deviation between the y value and the expected value of y given by $\beta_0 + \beta_1 x_1 + \beta_2 x_2 + \cdots + \beta_p x_p$.
   Implication: Because $\beta_0, \beta_1, \ldots, \beta_p$ are constants for the given values of $x_1, x_2, \ldots, x_p$, the dependent variable y is also a normally distributed random variable.

To obtain more insight about the form of the relationship given by equation (13.11), consider the following two-independent-variable multiple regression equation.

$$E(y) = \beta_0 + \beta_1 x_1 + \beta_2 x_2$$

The graph of this equation is a plane in three-dimensional space. Figure 13.5 provides an example of such a graph. Note that the value of ϵ shown is the difference between the actual y value and the expected value of y, $E(y)$, when $x_1 = x_1^*$ and $x_2 = x_2^*$.

In regression analysis, the term *response variable* is often used in place of the term *dependent variable*. Furthermore, since the multiple regression equation generates a plane or surface, its graph is called a *response surface*.

FIGURE 13.5   GRAPH OF THE REGRESSION EQUATION FOR MULTIPLE REGRESSION ANALYSIS WITH TWO INDEPENDENT VARIABLES

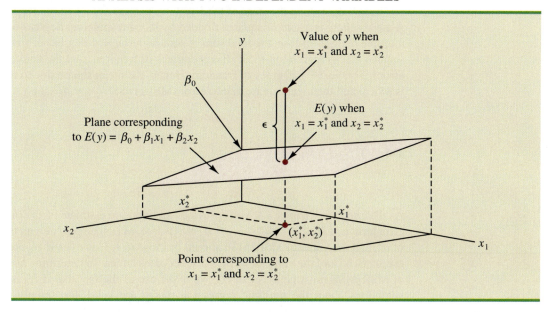

(13.5) Testing for Significance

In this section we show how to conduct significance tests for a multiple regression relationship. The significance tests we used in simple linear regression were a t test and an F test. In simple linear regression, both tests provide the same conclusion; that is, if the null hypothesis is rejected, we conclude that $\beta_1 \neq 0$. In multiple regression, the t test and the F test have different purposes.

  1. The F test is used to determine whether a significant relationship exists between the dependent variable and the set of all the independent variables; we will refer to the F test as the test for *overall significance.*

  2. If the F test shows an overall significance, the t test is used to determine whether each of the individual independent variables is significant. A separate t test is conducted for each of the independent variables in the model; we refer to each of these t tests as a test for *individual significance.*

In the material that follows, we will explain the F test and the t test and apply each to the Butler Trucking Company example.

F Test

The multiple regression model as defined in Section 13.4 is

$$y = \beta_0 + \beta_1 x_1 + \beta_2 x_2 + \cdots + \beta_p x_p + \epsilon$$

The hypotheses for the F test involve the parameters of the multiple regression model.

$$H_0: \beta_1 = \beta_2 = \cdots = \beta_p = 0$$
$$H_a:\ \text{One or more of the parameters is not equal to zero}$$

If H_0 is rejected, the test gives us sufficient statistical evidence to conclude that one or more of the parameters is not equal to zero and that the overall relationship between y and the set of independent variables $x_1, x_2, \ldots, x_p$ is significant. However, if H_0 cannot be rejected, we do not have sufficient evidence to conclude that a significant relationship is present.

Before describing the steps of the F test, we need to review the concept of *mean square*. A mean square is a sum of squares divided by its corresponding degrees of freedom. In the multiple regression case, the total sum of squares has $n - 1$ degrees of freedom, the sum of squares due to regression (SSR) has p degrees of freedom, and the sum of squares due to error has $n - p - 1$ degrees of freedom. Hence, the mean square due to regression (MSR) is SSR/p and the mean square due to error (MSE) is SSE/$(n - p - 1)$.

$$MSR = \frac{SSR}{p} \tag{13.12}$$

and

$$MSE = \frac{SSE}{n - p - 1} \tag{13.13}$$

As discussed in Chapter 12, MSE provides an unbiased estimate of σ^2, the variance of the error term ϵ. If $H_0: \beta_1 = \beta_2 = \cdots = \beta_p = 0$ is true, MSR also provides an unbiased estimate of σ^2, and the value of MSR/MSE should be close to 1. However, if H_0 is false, MSR overestimates σ^2 and the value of MSR/MSE becomes larger. To determine how large the value of MSR/MSE must be to reject H_0, we make use of the fact that if H_0 is true and the assumptions about the multiple regression model are valid, the sampling distribution of MSR/MSE is an F distribution with p degrees of freedom in the numerator and $n - p - 1$ in the denominator. A summary of the F test for significance in multiple regression follows.

F TEST FOR OVERALL SIGNIFICANCE

$H_0: \beta_1 = \beta_2 = \cdots = \beta_p = 0$
H_a: One or more of the parameters is not equal to zero

TEST STATISTIC

$$F = \frac{MSR}{MSE} \tag{13.14}$$

REJECTION RULE

p-value approach:	Reject H_0 if *p*-value $\leq \alpha$
Critical value approach:	Reject H_0 if $F \geq F_\alpha$

where F_α is based on an F distribution with p degrees of freedom in the numerator and $n - p - 1$ degrees of freedom in the denominator.

Let us apply the F test to the Butler Trucking Company multiple regression problem. With two independent variables, the hypotheses are written as follows.

$H_0: \beta_1 = \beta_2 = 0$
$H_a: \beta_1$ and/or β_2 is not equal to zero

Figure 13.6 is the Minitab output for the multiple regression model with miles traveled (x_1) and number of deliveries (x_2) as the two independent variables. In the analysis of variance part of the output, we see that MSR = 10.8 and MSE = .328. Using equation (13.14), we obtain the test statistic.

$$F = \frac{10.8}{.328} = 32.9$$

FIGURE 13.6   MINITAB OUTPUT FOR BUTLER TRUCKING WITH TWO INDEPENDENT
VARIABLES, MILES TRAVELED (x_1) AND NUMBER OF DELIVERIES (x_2)

```
The regression equation is
Time = - 0.869 + 0.0611 Miles + 0.923 Deliveries

Predictor          Coef    SE Coef        T       p
Constant        -0.8687     0.9515    -0.91   0.392
Miles          0.061135   0.009888     6.18   0.000
Deliveries       0.9234     0.2211     4.18   0.004

S = 0.5731    R-sq = 90.4%    R-sq(adj) = 87.6%

Analysis of Variance

SOURCE            DF      SS       MS       F       p
Regression         2  21.601   10.800   32.88   0.000
Residual Error     7   2.299    0.328
Total              9  23.900
```

Note that the F value on the Minitab output is $F = 32.88$; the value we calculated differs because we used rounded values for MSR and MSE in the calculation. Using $\alpha = .01$, the p-value $= 0.000$ in the last column of the analysis of variance table (Figure 13.6) indicates that we can reject $H_0: \beta_1 = \beta_2 = 0$ because the p-value is less than $\alpha = .01$. Alternatively, Table 4 of Appendix B shows that with two degrees of freedom in the numerator and seven degrees of freedom in the denominator, $F_{.01} = 9.55$. With $32.9 > 9.55$, we reject $H_0: \beta_1 = \beta_2 = 0$ and conclude that a significant relationship is present between travel time y and the two independent variables, miles traveled and number of deliveries.

As noted previously, the mean square error provides an unbiased estimate of σ^2, the variance of the error term ϵ. Referring to Figure 13.6, we see that the estimate of σ^2 is MSE $= .328$. The square root of MSE is the estimate of the standard deviation of the error term. As defined in Section 12.5, this standard deviation is called the standard error of the estimate and is denoted s. Hence, we have $s = \sqrt{\text{MSE}} = \sqrt{.328} = .573$. Note that the value of the standard error of the estimate appears in the Minitab output in Figure 13.6.

Table 13.3 is the general analysis of variance (ANOVA) table that provides the F test results for a multiple regression model. The value of the F test statistic appears in the last column and can be compared to F_α with p degrees of freedom in the numerator and $n - p - 1$ degrees of freedom in the denominator to make the hypothesis test conclusion. By reviewing the Minitab output for Butler Trucking Company in Figure 13.6, we see that

TABLE 13.3   ANOVA TABLE FOR A MULTIPLE REGRESSION MODEL
WITH p INDEPENDENT VARIABLES

Source	Sum of Squares	Degrees of Freedom	Mean Square	F
Regression	SSR	p	$\text{MSR} = \dfrac{\text{SSR}}{p}$	$F = \dfrac{\text{MSR}}{\text{MSE}}$
Error	SSE	$n - p - 1$	$\text{MSE} = \dfrac{\text{SSE}}{n - p - 1}$	
Total	SST	$n - 1$		

Minitab's analysis of variance table contains this information. Moreover, Minitab also provides the *p*-value corresponding to the *F* test statistic.

t Test

If the *F* test shows that the multiple regression relationship is significant, a *t* test can be conducted to determine the significance of each of the individual parameters. The *t* test for individual significance follows.

---

t TEST FOR INDIVIDUAL SIGNIFICANCE

For any parameter β_i

$$H_0: \beta_i = 0$$
$$H_a: \beta_i \neq 0$$

TEST STATISTIC

$$t = \frac{b_i}{s_{b_i}} \qquad \text{(13.15)}$$

REJECTION RULE

p-value approach: Reject H_0 if *p*-value $\leq \alpha$

Critical value approach: Reject H_0 if $t \leq -t_{\alpha/2}$ or if $t \geq t_{\alpha/2}$

where $t_{\alpha/2}$ is based on a *t* distribution with $n - p - 1$ degrees of freedom.

In the test statistic, s_{b_i} is the estimate of the standard deviation of b_i. The value of s_{b_i} will be provided by the computer software package.

Let us conduct the *t* test for the Butler Trucking regression problem. Refer to the section of Figure 13.6 that shows the Minitab output for the *t*-ratio calculations. Values of b_1, b_2, s_{b_1}, and s_{b_2} are as follows.

$$b_1 = .061135 \qquad s_{b_1} = .009888$$
$$b_2 = .9234 \qquad s_{b_2} = .2211$$

Using equation (13.15), we obtain the test statistic for the hypotheses involving parameters β_1 and β_2.

$$t = .061135/.009888 = 6.18$$
$$t = .9234/.2211 = 4.18$$

Note that both of these *t*-ratio values and the corresponding *p*-values are provided by the Minitab output in Figure 13.6. Using $\alpha = .01$, the *p*-values of .000 and .004 on the Minitab output indicate that we can reject $H_0: \beta_1 = 0$ and $H_0: \beta_2 = 0$. Hence, both parameters are statistically significant. Alternatively, Table 2 of Appendix B shows that with $n - p - 1 = 10 - 2 - 1 = 7$ degrees of freedom, $t_{.005} = 3.499$. With $6.18 > 3.499$, we reject $H_0: \beta_1 = 0$. Similarly, with $4.18 > 3.499$, we reject $H_0: \beta_2 = 0$.

Multicollinearity

We used the term *independent variable* in regression analysis to refer to any variable being used to predict or explain the value of the dependent variable. The term does not mean, however, that the independent variables themselves are independent in any statistical sense. On the contrary, most independent variables in a multiple regression problem are correlated to some degree with one another. For example, in the Butler Trucking example involving the two independent variables x_1 (miles traveled) and x_2 (number of deliveries), we could treat the miles traveled as the dependent variable and the number of deliveries as the independent variable to determine whether those two variables are themselves related. We could then compute the sample correlation coefficient $r_{x_1 x_2}$ to determine the extent to which the variables are related. Doing so yields $r_{x_1 x_2} = .16$. Thus, we find some degree of linear association between the two independent variables. In multiple regression analysis, **multicollinearity** refers to the correlation among the independent variables.

To provide a better perspective of the potential problems of multicollinearity, let us consider a modification of the Butler Trucking example. Instead of x_2 being the number of deliveries, let x_2 denote the number of gallons of gasoline consumed. Clearly, x_1 (the miles traveled) and x_2 are related; that is, we know that the number of gallons of gasoline used depends on the number of miles traveled. Hence, we would conclude logically that x_1 and x_2 are highly correlated independent variables.

When the independent variables are highly correlated, it is not possible to determine the separate effect of any particular independent variable on the dependent variable.

Assume that we obtain the equation $\hat{y} = b_0 + b_1 x_1 + b_2 x_2$ and find that the F test shows the relationship to be significant. Then suppose we conduct a t test on β_1 to determine whether $\beta_1 \neq 0$, and we cannot reject H_0: $\beta_1 = 0$. Does this result mean that travel time is not related to miles traveled? Not necessarily. What it probably means is that with x_2 already in the model, x_1 does not make a significant contribution to determining the value of y. This interpretation makes sense in our example; if we know the amount of gasoline consumed, we do not gain much additional information useful in predicting y by knowing the miles traveled. Similarly, a t test might lead us to conclude $\beta_2 = 0$ on the grounds that, with x_1 in the model, knowledge of the amount of gasoline consumed does not add much.

To summarize, in t tests for the significance of individual parameters, the difficulty caused by multicollinearity is that it is possible to conclude that none of the individual parameters are significantly different from zero when an F test on the overall multiple regression equation indicates a significant relationship. This problem is avoided when there is little correlation among the independent variables.

A sample correlation coefficient greater than $+0.70$ or less than -0.70 for two independent variables is a rule of thumb warning of potential problems with multicollinearity.

Statisticians have developed several tests for determining whether multicollinearity is high enough to cause problems. According to the rule of thumb test, multicollinearity is a potential problem if the absolute value of the sample correlation coefficient exceeds .7 for any two of the independent variables. The other types of tests are more advanced and beyond the scope of this text.

If possible, every attempt should be made to avoid including independent variables that are highly correlated. In practice, however, strict adherence to this policy is rarely possible. When decision makers have reason to believe substantial multicollinearity is present, they must realize that separating the effects of the individual independent variables on the dependent variable is difficult.

NOTES AND COMMENTS

Ordinarily, multicollinearity does not affect the way in which we perform our regression analysis or interpret the output from a study. However, when multicollinearity is severe—that is, when two or more of the independent variables are highly correlated with one another—we can have difficulty interpreting the results of t tests on the individual parameters. In addition to the type of problem illustrated in this section, severe cases of multicollinearity have been shown to result in least squares estimates that have the wrong sign. That is,

in simulated studies where researchers created the underlying regression model and then applied the least squares technique to develop estimates of β_0, β_1, β_2, and so on, it has been shown that under conditions of high multicollinearity the least squares estimates can have a sign opposite that of the parameter being estimated. For example, β_2 might actually be $+10$ and b_2, its estimate, might turn out to be -2. Thus, little faith can be placed in the individual coefficients if multicollinearity is present to a high degree.

Exercises

Methods

19. In exercise 1, the following estimated regression equation based on 10 observations was presented.

$$\hat{y} = 29.1270 + .5906x_1 + .4980x_2$$

Here SST = 6724.125, SSR = 6216.375, s_{b_1} = .0813, and s_{b_2} = .0567.

a.   Compute MSR and MSE.
b.   Compute F and perform the appropriate F test. Use $\alpha = .05$.
c.   Perform a t test for the significance of β_1. Use $\alpha = .05$.
d.   Perform a t test for the significance of β_2. Use $\alpha = .05$.

20. Refer to the data presented in exercise 2. The estimated regression equation for these data is

$$\hat{y} = -18.4 + 2.01x_1 + 4.74x_2$$

Here SST = 15,182.9, SSR = 14,052.2, s_{b_1} = .2471, and s_{b_2} = .9484.

a.   Test for a significant relationship among x_1, x_2, and y. Use $\alpha = .05$.
b.   Is β_1 significant? Use $\alpha = .05$.
c.   Is β_2 significant? Use $\alpha = .05$.

21. The following estimated regression equation was developed for a model involving two independent variables.

$$\hat{y} = 40.7 + 8.63x_1 + 2.71x_2$$

After x_2 was dropped from the model, the least squares method was used to obtain an estimated regression equation involving only x_1 as an independent variable.

$$\hat{y} = 42.0 + 9.01x_1$$

a.   Give an interpretation of the coefficient of x_1 in both models.
b.   Could multicollinearity explain why the coefficient of x_1 differs in the two models? If so, how?

Applications

22. In exercise 4 the following estimated regression equation relating sales to inventory investment and advertising expenditures was given.

$$\hat{y} = 25 + 10x_1 + 8x_2$$

The data used to develop the model came from a survey of 10 stores; for these data SST = 16,000 and SSR = 12,000.

a.   Compute SSE, MSE, and MSR.
b.   Use an F test and a .05 level of significance to determine whether there is a relationship among the variables.

23. Refer to exercise 5.

a.   Use $\alpha = .01$ to test the hypotheses

$$H_0: \beta_1 = \beta_2 = 0$$
$$H_a: \beta_1 \text{ and/or } \beta_2 \text{ is not equal to zero}$$

CD file

Showtime

for the model $y = \beta_0 + \beta_1 x_1 + \beta_2 x_2 + \epsilon$, where

$$x_1 = \text{television advertising (\$1000s)}$$
$$x_2 = \text{newspaper advertising (\$1000s)}$$

b. Use $\alpha = .05$ to test the significance of β_1. Should x_1 be dropped from the model?

c. Use $\alpha = .05$ to test the significance of β_2. Should x_2 be dropped from the model?

CD file

MLB

24. Refer to the data in exercise 6. Use the number of team home runs and the earned run average for the team's pitching staff to predict the percentage of games won.

    a. Use the F test to determine the overall significance of the relationship. What is your conclusion at the .05 level of significance?

    b. Use the t test to determine the significance of each independent variable. What is your conclusion at the .05 level of significance?

25. *Barron's* conducts an annual review of online brokers, including both brokers that can be accessed via a Web browser, as well as direct-access brokers that connect customers directly with the broker's network server. Each broker's offerings and performance are evaluated in six areas, using a point value of 0–5 in each category. The results are weighted to obtain an overall score, and a final star rating, ranging from zero to five stars, is assigned to each broker. Trade execution, ease of use, and range of offerings are three of the areas evaluated. A point value of 5 in the trade execution area means the order entry and execution process flowed easily from one step to the next. A value of 5 in the ease of use area means that the site was easy to use and can be tailored to show what the user wants to see. A value of 5 in the range offerings area means that all of the investment transactions can be executed online. The following data show the point values for trade execution, ease of use, range of offerings, and the star rating for a sample of 10 of the online brokers that *Barron's* evaluated (*Barron's,* March 10, 2003).

CD file

Brokers

Broker	Trade Execution	Use	Range	Rating
Wall St. Access	3.7	4.5	4.8	4.0
E*TRADE (Power)	3.4	3.0	4.2	3.5
E*TRADE (Standard)	2.5	4.0	4.0	3.5
Preferred Trade	4.8	3.7	3.4	3.5
my Track	4.0	3.5	3.2	3.5
TD Waterhouse	3.0	3.0	4.6	3.5
Brown & Co.	2.7	2.5	3.3	3.0
Brokerage America	1.7	3.5	3.1	3.0
Merrill Lynch Direct	2.2	2.7	3.0	2.5
Strong Funds	1.4	3.6	2.5	2.0

    a. Determine the estimated regression equation that can be used to predict the star rating given the point values for execution, ease of use, and range of offerings.

    b. Use the F test to determine the overall significance of the relationship. What is the conclusion at the .05 level of significance?

    c. Use the t test to determine the significance of each independent variable. What is your conclusion at the .05 level of significance?

    d. Remove any independent variable that is not significant from the estimated regression equation. What is your recommended estimated regression equation? Compare the R^2 with the value of R^2 from part (a). Discuss the differences.

CD file

NBA

26. In exercise 10 an estimated regression equation was developed relating the percentage of games won given the percentage of field goals made by the team, the percentage of three-point shots made by the team's opponent, and the number of turnovers committed by the team's opponent.

    a. Use the F test to determine the overall significance of the relationship. What is your conclusion at the .05 level of significance?

    b. Use the t test to determine the significance of each independent variable. What is your conclusion at the .05 level of significance?

13.6 Using the Estimated Regression Equation for Estimation and Prediction

The procedures for estimating the mean value of y and predicting an individual value of y in multiple regression are similar to those in regression analysis involving one independent variable. First, recall that in Chapter 12 we showed that the point estimate of the expected value of y for a given value of x was the same as the point estimate of an individual value of y. In both cases, we used $\hat{y} = b_0 + b_1 x$ as the point estimate.

In multiple regression we use the same procedure. That is, we substitute the given values of $x_1, x_2, \ldots, x_p$ into the estimated regression equation and use the corresponding value of $\hat{y}$ as the point estimate. Suppose that for the Butler Trucking example we want to use the estimated regression equation involving x_1 (miles traveled) and x_2 (number of deliveries) to develop two interval estimates:

1. A *confidence interval* of the mean travel time for all trucks that travel 100 miles and make two deliveries
2. A *prediction interval* of the travel time for *one specific* truck that travels 100 miles and makes two deliveries

Using the estimated regression equation $\hat{y} = -.869 + .0611x_1 + .923x_2$ with $x_1 = 100$ and $x_2 = 2$, we obtain the following value of $\hat{y}$.

$$\hat{y} = -.869 + .0611(100) + .923(2) = 7.09$$

Hence, the point estimate of travel time in both cases is approximately seven hours.

To develop interval estimates for the mean value of y and for an individual value of y, we use a procedure similar to that for regression analysis involving one independent variable. The formulas required are beyond the scope of the text, but computer packages for multiple regression analysis will often provide confidence intervals once the values of $x_1, x_2, \ldots, x_p$ are specified by the user. In Table 13.4 we show the 95% confidence and prediction intervals for the Butler Trucking example for selected values of x_1 and x_2; these values were obtained using Minitab. Note that the interval estimate for an individual value of y is wider than the interval estimate for the expected value of y. This difference simply reflects the fact that for given values of x_1 and x_2 we can estimate the mean travel time for all trucks with more precision than we can predict the travel time for one specific truck.

TABLE 13.4 THE 95% CONFIDENCE AND PREDICTION INTERVALS FOR BUTLER TRUCKING

Value of x_1	Value of x_2	Confidence Interval		Prediction Interval	
		Lower Limit	Upper Limit	Lower Limit	Upper Limit
50	2	3.146	4.924	2.414	5.656
50	3	4.127	5.789	3.368	6.548
50	4	4.815	6.948	4.157	7.607
100	2	6.258	7.926	5.500	8.683
100	3	7.385	8.645	6.520	9.510
100	4	8.135	9.742	7.362	10.515

Exercises

Methods

27. In exercise 1, the following estimated regression equation based on 10 observations was presented.

$$\hat{y} = 29.1270 + .5906x_1 + .4980x_2$$

   a. Develop a point estimate of the mean value of y when $x_1 = 180$ and $x_2 = 310$.
   b. Develop a point estimate for an individual value of y when $x_1 = 180$ and $x_2 = 310$.

28. Refer to the data in exercise 2. The estimated regression equation for those data is

$$\hat{y} = -18.4 + 2.01x_1 + 4.74x_2$$

   a. Develop a 95% confidence interval for the mean value of y when $x_1 = 45$ and $x_2 = 15$.
   b. Develop a 95% prediction interval for y when $x_1 = 45$ and $x_2 = 15$.

Applications

29. In exercise 5, the owner of Showtime Movie Theaters, Inc., used multiple regression analysis to predict gross revenue (y) as a function of television advertising (x_1) and newspaper advertising (x_2). The estimated regression equation was

Showtime

$$\hat{y} = 83.2 + 2.29x_1 + 1.30x_2$$

   a. What is the gross revenue expected for a week when $3500 is spent on television advertising ($x_1 = 3.5$) and $1800 is spent on newspaper advertising ($x_2 = 1.8$)?
   b. Provide a 95% confidence interval for the mean revenue of all weeks with the expenditures listed in part (a).
   c. Provide a 95% prediction interval for next week's revenue, assuming that the advertising expenditures will be allocated as in part (a).

30. In exercise 9, an estimated regression equation was developed relating the percentage of students who attend a four-year college to the average class size and the combined SAT score.
   a. Develop a 95% confidence interval for the mean percentage of students who attend a four-year college for a school district that has an average class size of 25 and whose students have a combined SAT score of 1000.

Schools

   b. Suppose that a school district in Conway, South Carolina, has an average class size of 25 and a combined SAT score of 950. Develop a 95% prediction interval for the percentage of students who attend a four-year college.

31. The Buyer's Guide section of the Web site for *Car and Driver* magazine provides reviews and road tests for cars, trucks, SUVs, and vans. The average ratings of overall quality, vehicle styling, braking, handling, fuel economy, interior comfort, acceleration, dependability, fit and finish, transmission, and ride are summarized for each vehicle using a scale ranging from 1 (worst) to 10 (best). A portion of the data for 14 Sports/GT cars is shown here (http://www.caranddriver, January 7, 2004).

SportsCar

Sports/GT	Overall	Handling	Dependability	Fit and Finish
Acura 3.2CL	7.80	7.83	8.17	7.67
Acura RSX	9.02	9.46	9.35	8.97
Audi TT	9.00	9.58	8.74	9.38
BMW 3-Series/M3	8.39	9.52	8.39	8.55
Chevrolet Corvette	8.82	9.64	8.54	7.87

(continued)

Sports/GT	Overall	Handling	Dependability	Fit and Finish
Ford Mustang	8.34	8.85	8.70	7.34
Honda Civic Si	8.92	9.31	9.50	7.93
Infinity G35	8.70	9.34	8.96	8.07
Mazda RX-8	8.58	9.79	8.96	8.12
Mini Cooper	8.76	10.00	8.69	8.33
Mitsubishi Eclipse	8.17	8.95	8.25	7.36
Nissan 350Z	8.07	9.35	7.56	8.21
Porsche 911	9.55	9.91	8.86	9.55
Toyota Celica	8.77	9.29	9.04	7.97

a. Develop an estimated regression equation using handling, dependability, and fit and finish to predict overall quality.
b. Another Sports/GT car rated by *Car and Driver* is the Honda Accord. The ratings for handling, dependability, and fit and finish for the Honda Accord were 8.28, 9.06, and 8.07, respectively. Estimate the overall rating for this car.
c. Provide a 95% confidence interval for overall quality for all sports and GT cars with the characteristics listed in part (b).
d. Provide a 95% prediction interval for overall quality for the Honda Accord described in part (b).
e. The overall rating reported by *Car and Driver* for the Honda Accord was 8.65. How does this rating compare to the estimates you developed in parts (b) and (d)?

13.7 Qualitative Independent Variables

The independent variables may be qualitative or quantitative.

Thus far, the examples we considered involved quantitative independent variables such as student population, distance traveled, and number of deliveries. In many situations, however, we must work with **qualitative independent variables** such as gender (male, female), method of payment (cash, credit card, check), and so on. The purpose of this section is to show how qualitative variables are handled in regression analysis. To illustrate the use and interpretation of a qualitative independent variable, we will consider a problem facing the managers of Johnson Filtration, Inc.

An Example: Johnson Filtration, Inc.

Johnson Filtration, Inc., provides maintenance service for water-filtration systems throughout southern Florida. Customers contact Johnson with requests for maintenance service on their water-filtration systems. To estimate the service time and the service cost, Johnson's managers want to predict the repair time necessary for each maintenance request. Hence, repair time in hours is the dependent variable. Repair time is believed to be related to two factors, the number of months since the last maintenance service and the type of repair problem (mechanical or electrical). Data for a sample of 10 service calls are reported in Table 13.5.

Let y denote the repair time in hours and x_1 denote the number of months since the last maintenance service. The regression model that uses only x_1 to predict y is

$$y = \beta_0 + \beta_1 x_1 + \epsilon$$

Using Minitab to develop the estimated regression equation, we obtained the output shown in Figure 13.7. The estimated regression equation is

$$\hat{y} = 2.15 + .304 x_1 \qquad \textbf{(13.16)}$$

TABLE 13.5   DATA FOR THE JOHNSON FILTRATION EXAMPLE

Service Call	Months Since Last Service	Type of Repair	Repair Time in Hours
1	2	Electrical	2.9
2	6	Mechanical	3.0
3	8	Electrical	4.8
4	3	Mechanical	1.8
5	2	Electrical	2.9
6	7	Electrical	4.9
7	9	Mechanical	4.2
8	8	Mechanical	4.8
9	4	Electrical	4.4
10	6	Electrical	4.5

At the .05 level of significance, the p-value of .016 for the t (or F) test indicates that the number of months since the last service is significantly related to repair time. R-sq = 53.4% indicates that x_1 alone explains 53.4% of the variability in repair time.

To incorporate the type of repair into the regression model, we define the following variable.

$$x_2 = \begin{cases} 0 \text{ if the type of repair is mechanical} \\ 1 \text{ if the type of repair is electrical} \end{cases}$$

In regression analysis x_2 is called a **dummy** or *indicator* **variable**. Using this dummy variable, we can write the multiple regression model as

$$y = \beta_0 + \beta_1 x_1 + \beta_2 x_2 + \epsilon$$

Table 13.6 is the revised data set that includes the values of the dummy variable. Using Minitab and the data in Table 13.6, we can develop estimates of the model parameters. The Minitab output in Figure 13.8 shows that the estimated multiple regression equation is

$$\hat{y} = .93 + .388x_1 + 1.26x_2 \tag{13.17}$$

FIGURE 13.7   MINITAB OUTPUT FOR JOHNSON FILTRATION WITH MONTHS SINCE LAST SERVICE (x_1) AS THE INDEPENDENT VARIABLE

In the Minitab output the variable names Months and Time were entered as the column headings on the worksheet; thus, x_1 = Months and y = Time.

```
The regression equation is
Time = 2.15 + 0.304 Months

Predictor    Coef    SE Coef     T       p
Constant    2.1473   0.6050    3.55   0.008
Months      0.3041   0.1004    3.03   0.016

S = 0.7810    R-sq = 53.4%    R-sq(adj) = 47.6%

Analysis of Variance

SOURCE           DF      SS       MS      F       p
Regression        1    5.5960   5.5960  9.17   0.016
Residual Error    8    4.8800   0.6100
Total             9   10.4760
```

TABLE 13.6   DATA FOR THE JOHNSON FILTRATION EXAMPLE WITH TYPE OF REPAIR INDICATED BY A DUMMY VARIABLE ($x_2 = 0$ FOR MECHANICAL; $x_2 = 1$ FOR ELECTRICAL)

Customer	Months Since Last Service (x_1)	Type of Repair (x_2)	Repair Time in Hours (y)
1	2	1	2.9
2	6	0	3.0
3	8	1	4.8
4	3	0	1.8
5	2	1	2.9
6	7	1	4.9
7	9	0	4.2
8	8	0	4.8
9	4	1	4.4
10	6	1	4.5

CD file

Johnson

At the .05 level of significance, the p-value of .001 associated with the F test ($F = 21.36$) indicates that the regression relationship is significant. The t test part of the printout in Figure 13.8 shows that both months since last service (p-value $= .000$) and type of repair (p-value $= .005$) are statistically significant. In addition, R-sq $= 85.9\%$ and R-sq(adj) $= 81.9\%$ indicate that the estimated regression equation does a good job of explaining the variability in repair times. Thus, equation (13.17) should prove helpful in estimating the repair time necessary for the various service calls.

Interpreting the Parameters

The multiple regression equation for the Johnson Filtration example is

$$E(y) = \beta_0 + \beta_1 x_1 + \beta_2 x_2 \qquad \text{(13.18)}$$

FIGURE 13.8   MINITAB OUTPUT FOR JOHNSON FILTRATION WITH MONTHS SINCE LAST SERVICE (x_1) AND TYPE OF REPAIR (x_2) AS THE INDEPENDENT VARIABLES

In the Minitab output the variable names Months, Type, *and* Time *were entered as the column headings on the worksheet; thus, x_1 =* Months, *x_2 =* Type, *and y =* Time.

```
The regression equation is
Time = 0.930 + 0.388 Months + 1.26 Type

Predictor      Coef    SE Coef      T       p
Constant     0.9305    0.4670    1.99    0.087
Months      0.38762   0.06257    6.20    0.000
Type         1.2627    0.3141    4.02    0.005


S = 0.4590    R-sq = 85.9%    R-sq(adj) = 81.9%


Analysis of Variance

SOURCE           DF        SS        MS       F      p
Regression        2    9.0009    4.5005   21.36  0.001
Residual Error    7    1.4751    0.2107
Total             9   10.4760
```

To understand how to interpret the parameters β_0, β_1, and β_2 when a qualitative variable is present, consider the case when $x_2 = 0$ (mechanical repair). Using $E(y \mid \text{mechanical})$ to denote the mean or expected value of repair time *given* a mechanical repair, we have

$$E(y \mid \text{mechanical}) = \beta_0 + \beta_1 x_1 + \beta_2(0) = \beta_0 + \beta_1 x_1 \qquad \textbf{(13.19)}$$

Similarly, for an electrical repair ($x_2 = 1$), we have

$$E(y \mid \text{electrical}) = \beta_0 + \beta_1 x_1 + \beta_2(1) = \beta_0 + \beta_1 x_1 + \beta_2 \qquad \textbf{(13.20)}$$
$$= (\beta_0 + \beta_2) + \beta_1 x_1$$

Comparing equations (13.19) and (13.20), we see that the mean repair time is a linear function of x_1 for both mechanical and electrical repairs. The slope of both equations is β_1, but the y-intercept differs. The y-intercept is β_0 in equation (13.19) for mechanical repairs and ($\beta_0 + \beta_2$) in equation (13.20) for electrical repairs. The interpretation of β_2 is that it indicates the difference between the mean repair time for an electrical repair and the mean repair time for a mechanical repair.

If β_2 is positive, the mean repair time for an electrical repair will be greater than that for a mechanical repair; if β_2 is negative, the mean repair time for an electrical repair will be less than that for a mechanical repair. Finally, if $\beta_2 = 0$, there is no difference in the mean repair time between electrical and mechanical repairs and the type of repair is not related to the repair time.

Using the estimated multiple regression equation $\hat{y} = .93 + .388x_1 + 1.26x_2$, we see that .93 is the estimate of β_0 and 1.26 is the estimate of β_2. Thus, when $x_2 = 0$ (mechanical repair)

$$\hat{y} = .93 + .388x_1 \qquad \textbf{(13.21)}$$

and when $x_2 = 1$ (electrical repair)

$$\hat{y} = .93 + .388x_1 + 1.26(1) \qquad \textbf{(13.22)}$$
$$= 2.19 + .388x_1$$

In effect, the use of a dummy variable for type of repair provides two equations that can be used to predict the repair time, one corresponding to mechanical repairs and one corresponding to electrical repairs. In addition, with $b_2 = 1.26$, we learn that, on average, electrical repairs require 1.26 hours longer than mechanical repairs.

Figure 13.9 is the plot of the Johnson data from Table 13.6. Repair time in hours (y) is represented by the vertical axis and months since last service (x_1) is represented by the horizontal axis. A data point for a mechanical repair is indicated by an M and a data point for an electrical repair is indicated by an E. Equations (13.21) and (13.22) are plotted on the graph to show graphically the two equations that can be used to predict the repair time, one corresponding to mechanical repairs and one corresponding to electrical repairs.

More Complex Qualitative Variables

A qualitative variable with k levels must be modeled using k − 1 dummy variables. Care must be taken in defining and interpreting the dummy variables.

Because the qualitative variable for the Johnson Filtration example had two levels (mechanical and electrical), defining a dummy variable with zero indicating a mechanical repair and one indicating an electrical repair was easy. However, when a qualitative variable has more than two levels, care must be taken in both defining and interpreting the dummy variables. As we will show, if a qualitative variable has k levels, $k - 1$ dummy variables are required, with each dummy variable being coded as 0 or 1.

For example, suppose a manufacturer of copy machines organized the sales territories for a particular state into three regions: A, B, and C. The managers want to use regression analysis to help predict the number of copiers sold per week. With the number of units sold as the dependent variable, they are considering several independent variables (the number of sales personnel, advertising expenditures, and so on). Suppose the managers believe sales region is also an important factor in predicting the number of copiers sold. Because sales

FIGURE 13.9   SCATTER DIAGRAM FOR THE JOHNSON FILTRATION REPAIR DATA
FROM TABLE 13.6

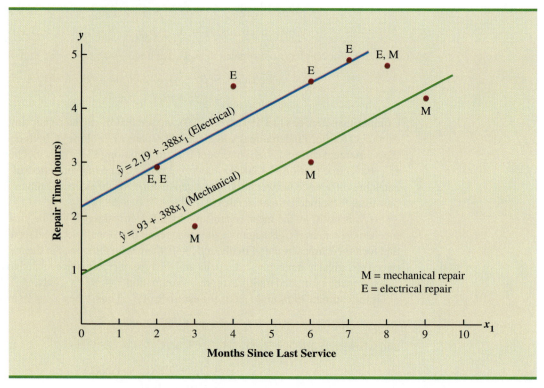

region is a qualitative variable with three levels, A, B, and C, we will need $3 - 1 = 2$ dummy variables to represent the sales region. Each variable can be coded 0 or 1 as follows.

$$x_1 = \begin{cases} 1 \text{ if sales region B} \\ 0 \text{ otherwise} \end{cases}$$

$$x_2 = \begin{cases} 1 \text{ if sales region C} \\ 0 \text{ otherwise} \end{cases}$$

With this definition, we have the following values of x_1 and x_2.

Region	x_1	x_2
A	0	0
B	1	0
C	0	1

Observations corresponding to region A would be coded $x_1 = 0$, $x_2 = 0$; observations corresponding to region B would be coded $x_1 = 1$, $x_2 = 0$; and observations corresponding to region C would be coded $x_1 = 0$, $x_2 = 1$.

The regression equation relating the expected value of the number of units sold, $E(y)$, to the dummy variables would be written as

$$E(y) = \beta_0 + \beta_1 x_1 + \beta_2 x_2$$

To help us interpret the parameters β_0, β_1, and β_2, consider the following three variations of the regression equation.

$$E(y \mid \text{region A}) = \beta_0 + \beta_1(0) + \beta_2(0) = \beta_0$$
$$E(y \mid \text{region B}) = \beta_0 + \beta_1(1) + \beta_2(0) = \beta_0 + \beta_1$$
$$E(y \mid \text{region C}) = \beta_0 + \beta_1(0) + \beta_2(1) = \beta_0 + \beta_2$$

Thus, β_0 is the mean or expected value of sales for region A; β_1 is the difference between the mean number of units sold in region B and the mean number of units sold in region A; and β_2 is the difference between the mean number of units sold in region C and the mean number of units sold in region A.

Two dummy variables were required because sales region is a qualitative variable with three levels. But the assignment of $x_1 = 0, x_2 = 0$ to indicate region A, $x_1 = 1, x_2 = 0$ to indicate region B, and $x_1 = 0, x_2 = 1$ to indicate region C was arbitrary. For example, we could have chosen $x_1 = 1$, $x_2 = 0$ to indicate region A, $x_1 = 0$, $x_2 = 0$ to indicate region B, and $x_1 = 0, x_2 = 1$ to indicate region C. In that case, β_1 would have been interpreted as the mean difference between regions A and B and β_2 as the mean difference between regions C and B.

The important point to remember is that when a qualitative variable has k levels, $k - 1$ dummy variables are required in the multiple regression analysis. Thus, if the sales region example had a fourth region, labeled D, three dummy variables would be necessary. For example, the three dummy variables can be coded as follows.

$$x_1 = \begin{cases} 1 \text{ if sales region B} \\ 0 \text{ otherwise} \end{cases} \quad x_2 = \begin{cases} 1 \text{ if sales region C} \\ 0 \text{ otherwise} \end{cases} \quad x_3 = \begin{cases} 1 \text{ if sales region D} \\ 0 \text{ otherwise} \end{cases}$$

Exercises

Methods

32. Consider a regression study involving a dependent variable y, a quantitative independent variable x_1, and a qualitative variable with two levels (level 1 and level 2).
    a. Write a multiple regression equation relating x_1 and the qualitative variable to y.
    b. What is the expected value of y corresponding to level 1 of the qualitative variable?
    c. What is the expected value of y corresponding to level 2 of the qualitative variable?
    d. Interpret the parameters in your regression equation.

33. Consider a regression study involving a dependent variable y, a quantitative independent variable x_1, and a qualitative independent variable with three possible levels (level 1, level 2, and level 3).
    a. How many dummy variables are required to represent the qualitative variable?
    b. Write a multiple regression equation relating x_1 and the qualitative variable to y.
    c. Interpret the parameters in your regression equation.

Applications

34. Management proposed the following regression model to predict sales at a fast-food outlet.

$$y = \beta_0 + \beta_1 x_1 + \beta_2 x_2 + \beta_3 x_3 + \epsilon$$

where

$$x_1 = \text{number of competitors within one mile}$$
$$x_2 = \text{population within 1 mile (1000s)}$$
$$x_3 = \begin{cases} 1 \text{ if drive-up window present} \\ 0 \text{ otherwise} \end{cases}$$
$$y = \text{sales (\$1000s)}$$

The following estimated regression equation was developed after 20 outlets were surveyed.

$$\hat{y} = 10.1 - 4.2x_1 + 6.8x_2 + 15.3x_3$$

a. What is the expected amount of sales attributable to the drive-up window?
b. Predict sales for a store with two competitors, a population of 8000 within 1 mile, and no drive-up window.
c. Predict sales for a store with one competitor, a population of 3000 within 1 mile, and a drive-up window.

35. Refer to the Johnson Filtration problem introduced in this section. Suppose that in addition to information on the number of months since the machine was serviced and whether a mechanical or an electrical failure had occurred, the managers obtained a list showing which repairperson performed the service. The revised data follow.

Repair Time in Hours	Months Since Last Service	Type of Repair	Repairperson
2.9	2	Electrical	Dave Newton
3.0	6	Mechanical	Dave Newton
4.8	8	Electrical	Bob Jones
1.8	3	Mechanical	Dave Newton
2.9	2	Electrical	Dave Newton
4.9	7	Electrical	Bob Jones
4.2	9	Mechanical	Bob Jones
4.8	8	Mechanical	Bob Jones
4.4	4	Electrical	Bob Jones
4.5	6	Electrical	Dave Newton

a. Ignore for now the months since the last maintenance service (x_1) and the repairperson who performed the service. Develop the estimated simple linear regression equation to predict the repair time (y) given the type of repair (x_2). Recall that $x_2 = 0$ if the type of repair is mechanical and 1 if the type of repair is electrical.
b. Does the equation that you developed in part (a) provide a good fit for the observed data? Explain.
c. Ignore for now the months since the last maintenance service and the type of repair associated with the machine. Develop the estimated simple linear regression equation to predict the repair time given the repairperson who performed the service. Let $x_3 = 0$ if Bob Jones performed the service and $x_3 = 1$ if Dave Newton performed the service.
d. Does the equation that you developed in part (c) provide a good fit for the observed data? Explain.

36. This problem is an extension of the situation described in exercise 35.

a. Develop the estimated regression equation to predict the repair time given the number of months since the last maintenance service, the type of repair, and the repairperson who performed the service.
b. At the .05 level of significance, test whether the estimated regression equation developed in part (a) represents a significant relationship between the independent variables and the dependent variable.
c. Is the addition of the independent variable x_3, the repairperson who performed the service, statistically significant? Use $\alpha = .05$. What explanation can you give for the results observed?

37. The National Football League rates prospects by position on a scale that ranges from 5 to 9. The ratings are interpreted as follows: 8–9 should start the first year; 7.0–7.9 should start; 6.0–6.9 will make the team as backup; and 5.0–5.9 can make the club and contribute. The following table shows the position, weight, speed (for 40 yards), and ratings for 25 NFL prospects (*USA Today,* April 14, 2000).

Name	Position	Weight (pounds)	Speed (seconds)	Rating
Cosey Coleman	Guard	322	5.38	7.4
Travis Claridge	Guard	303	5.18	7.0
Kaulana Noa	Guard	317	5.34	6.8
Leander Jordan	Guard	330	5.46	6.7
Chad Clifton	Guard	334	5.18	6.3
Manula Savea	Guard	308	5.32	6.1
Ryan Johanningmeir	Guard	310	5.28	6.0
Mark Tauscher	Guard	318	5.37	6.0
Blaine Saipaia	Guard	321	5.25	6.0
Richard Mercier	Guard	295	5.34	5.8
Damion McIntosh	Guard	328	5.31	5.3
Jeno James	Guard	320	5.64	5.0
Al Jackson	Guard	304	5.20	5.0
Chris Samuels	Offensive tackle	325	4.95	8.5
Stockar McDougle	Offensive tackle	361	5.50	8.0
Chris McIngosh	Offensive tackle	315	5.39	7.8
Adrian Klemm	Offensive tackle	307	4.98	7.6
Todd Wade	Offensive tackle	326	5.20	7.3
Marvel Smith	Offensive tackle	320	5.36	7.1
Michael Thompson	Offensive tackle	287	5.05	6.8
Bobby Williams	Offensive tackle	332	5.26	6.8
Darnell Alford	Offensive tackle	334	5.55	6.4
Terrance Beadles	Offensive tackle	312	5.15	6.3
Tutan Reyes	Offensive tackle	299	5.35	6.1
Greg Robinson-Ran	Offensive tackle	333	5.59	6.0

Football

a. Develop a dummy variable that will account for the player's position.
b. Develop an estimated regression equation to show how rating is related to position, weight, and speed.
c. At the .05 level of significance, test whether the estimated regression equation developed in part (b) indicates a significant relationship between the independent variables and the dependent variable.
d. Does the estimated regression equation provide a good fit for the observed data? Explain.
e. Is position a significant factor in the player's rating? Use $\alpha = .05$. Explain.
f. Suppose a new offensive tackle prospect who weighs 300 pounds ran the 40 yards in 5.1 seconds. Use the estimated regression equation developed in part (b) to estimate the rating for this player.

38. A 10-year study conducted by the American Heart Association provided data on how age, blood pressure, and smoking relate to the risk of strokes. Assume that the following data are from a portion of this study. Risk is interpreted as the probability (times 100) that the patient will have a stroke over the next 10-year period. For the smoking variable, define a dummy variable with 1 indicating a smoker and 0 indicating a nonsmoker.

Stroke

Risk	Age	Pressure	Smoker
12	57	152	No
24	67	163	No
13	58	155	No
56	86	177	Yes
28	59	196	No
51	76	189	Yes

(*continued*)

Risk	Age	Pressure	Smoker
18	56	155	Yes
31	78	120	No
37	80	135	Yes
15	78	98	No
22	71	152	No
36	70	173	Yes
15	67	135	Yes
48	77	209	Yes
15	60	199	No
36	82	119	Yes
8	66	166	No
34	80	125	Yes
3	62	117	No
37	59	207	Yes

a. Develop an estimated regression equation that relates risk of a stroke to the person's age, blood pressure, and whether the person is a smoker.

b. Is smoking a significant factor in the risk of a stroke? Explain. Use $\alpha = .05$.

c. What is the probability of a stroke over the next 10 years for Art Speen, a 68-year-old smoker who has blood pressure of 175? What action might the physician recommend for this patient?

Summary

In this chapter, we introduced multiple regression analysis as an extension of simple linear regression analysis presented in Chapter 12. Multiple regression analysis enables us to understand how a dependent variable is related to two or more independent variables. The multiple regression equation $E(y) = \beta_0 + \beta_1 x_1 + \beta_2 x_2 + \cdots + \beta_p x_p$ shows that the expected value or mean value of the dependent variable y is related to the values of the independent variables $x_1, x_2, \ldots, x_p$. Sample data and the least squares method are used to develop the estimated multiple regression equation $\hat{y} = b_0 + b_1 x_1 + b_2 x_2 + \ldots + b_p x_p$. In effect $b_0, b_1, b_2, \ldots, b_p$ are sample statistics used to estimate the unknown model parameters $\beta_0, \beta_1, \beta_2, \ldots, \beta_p$. Computer printouts were used throughout the chapter to emphasize the fact that statistical software packages are the only realistic means of performing the numerous computations required in multiple regression analysis.

The multiple coefficient of determination was presented as a measure of the goodness of fit of the estimated regression equation. It determines the proportion of the variation of y that can be explained by the estimated regression equation. The adjusted multiple coefficient of determination is a similar measure of goodness of fit that adjusts for the number of independent variables and thus avoids overestimating the impact of adding more independent variables.

An F test and a t test were presented as ways to determine statistically whether the relationship among the variables is significant. The F test is used to determine whether there is a significant overall relationship between the dependent variable and the set of all independent variables. The t test is used to determine whether there is a significant relationship between the dependent variable and an individual independent variable given the other independent variables in the regression model. Correlation among the independent variables, known as multicollinearity, was discussed.

The chapter concluded with a section on how dummy variables can be used to incorporate qualitative independent variables into multiple regression analysis.

Glossary

Multiple regression analysis Regression analysis involving two or more independent variables.

Multiple regression model The mathematical equation that describes how the dependent variable y is related to the independent variables $x_1, x_2, \ldots, x_p$ and an error term ϵ.

Multiple regression equation The mathematical equation that describes how the mean or expected value of the dependent variable y is related to the values of the independent variables; that is, $E(y) = \beta_0 + \beta_1 x_1 + \beta_2 x_2 + \ldots + \beta_p x_p$.

Estimated multiple regression equation The estimate of the multiple regression equation based on sample data and the least squares method; it is $\hat{y} = b_0 + b_1 x_1 + b_2 x_2 + \ldots + b_p x_p$.

Least squares method The method used to develop the estimated regression equation. It minimizes the sum of squared residuals (the deviations between the observed values of the dependent variable, y_i, and the estimated values of the dependent variable, $\hat{y}_i$).

Multiple coefficient of determination A measure of the goodness of fit of the estimated multiple regression equation. It can be interpreted as the proportion of the variability in the dependent variable that is explained by the estimated regression equation.

Adjusted multiple coefficient of determination A measure of the goodness of fit of the estimated multiple regression equation that adjusts for the number of independent variables in the model and thus avoids overestimating the impact of adding more independent variables.

Multicollinearity The term used to describe the correlation among the independent variables.

Qualitative independent variable An independent variable with qualitative data.

Dummy variable A variable used to model the effect of qualitative independent variables. A dummy variable may take only the value zero or one.

Key Formulas

Multiple Regression Model

$$y = \beta_0 + \beta_1 x_1 + \beta_2 x_2 + \cdots + \beta_p x_p + \epsilon \tag{13.1}$$

Multiple Regression Equation

$$E(y) = \beta_0 + \beta_1 x_1 + \beta_2 x_2 + \cdots + \beta_p x_p \tag{13.2}$$

Estimated Multiple Regression Equation

$$\hat{y} = b_0 + b_1 x_1 + b_2 x_2 + \cdots + b_p x_p \tag{13.3}$$

Least Squares Criterion

$$\min \Sigma(y_i - \hat{y}_i)^2 \tag{13.4}$$

Relationship Among SST, SSR, and SSE

$$\text{SST} = \text{SSR} + \text{SSE} \tag{13.7}$$

Multiple Coefficient of Determination

$$R^2 = \frac{\text{SSR}}{\text{SST}} \tag{13.8}$$

Adjusted Multiple Coefficient of Determination

$$R_a^2 = 1 - (1 - R^2)\frac{n - 1}{n - p - 1} \tag{13.9}$$

Mean Square Regression

$$\text{MSR} = \frac{\text{SSR}}{p} \qquad \textbf{(13.12)}$$

Mean Square Error

$$\text{MSE} = \frac{\text{SSE}}{n - p - 1} \qquad \textbf{(13.13)}$$

F Test Statistic

$$F = \frac{\text{MSR}}{\text{MSE}} \qquad \textbf{(13.14)}$$

t Test Statistic

$$t = \frac{b_i}{s_{b_i}} \qquad \textbf{(13.15)}$$

Supplementary Exercises

39. The admissions officer for Clearwater College developed the following estimated regression equation relating the final college GPA to the student's SAT mathematics score and high-school GPA.

$$\hat{y} = -1.41 + .0235x_1 + .00486x_2$$

where

$$x_1 = \text{high-school grade point average}$$
$$x_2 = \text{SAT mathematics score}$$
$$y = \text{final college grade point average}$$

a. Interpret the coefficients in this estimated regression equation.
b. Estimate the final college GPA for a student who has a high-school average of 84 and a score of 540 on the SAT mathematics test.

40. The personnel director for Electronics Associates developed the following estimated regression equation relating an employee's score on a job satisfaction test to his or her length of service and wage rate.

$$\hat{y} = 14.4 - 8.69x_1 + 13.5x_2$$

where

$$x_1 = \text{length of service (years)}$$
$$x_2 = \text{wage rate (dollars)}$$
$$y = \text{job satisfaction test score (higher scores}$$
$$\text{indicate greater job satisfaction)}$$

a. Interpret the coefficients in this estimated regression equation.
b. Develop an estimate of the job satisfaction test score for an employee who has four years of service and makes $6.50 per hour.

41. A partial computer output from a regression analysis follows.

```
The regression equation is
Y = 8.103 + 7.602 X1 + 3.111 X2

Predictor            Coef          SE Coef             T
Constant          _____         2.667           _____
X1                _____         2.105           _____
X2                _____         0.613           _____

S = 3.335        R-sq = 92.3%      R-sq(adj) = _____%

Analysis of Variance

SOURCE               DF            SS            MS            F
Regression        _____        1612       _____     _____
Residual Error       12         _____     _____
Total             _____     _____
```

   a. Compute the appropriate t-ratios.
   b. Test for the significance of β_1 and β_2 at $\alpha = .05$.
   c. Compute the entries in the DF, SS, and MS columns.
   d. Compute R_a^2.

42. Recall that in exercise 39, the admissions officer for Clearwater College developed the following estimated regression equation relating final college GPA to the student's SAT mathematics score and high-school GPA.

$$\hat{y} = -1.41 + .0235x_1 + .00486x_2$$

   where

$$x_1 = \text{high-school grade point average}$$
$$x_2 = \text{SAT mathematics score}$$
$$y = \text{final college grade point average}$$

A portion of the Minitab computer output follows.

```
The regression equation is
Y = -1.41 + .0235 X1 + .00486 X2

Predictor            Coef          SE Coef             T
Constant          -1.4053         0.4848          _____
X1               0.023467        0.008666         _____
X2               _____        0.001077         _____

S = 0.1298      R-sq = _____    R-sq(adj) = _____

Analysis of Variance

SOURCE               DF            SS            MS            F
Regression        _____       1.76209       _____       _____
Residual Error    _____      _____      _____
Total                9         1.88000
```

a. Complete the missing entries in this output.
b. Compute F and test at a .05 level of significance to see whether a significant relationship is present.
c. Did the estimated regression equation provide a good fit to the data? Explain.
d. Use the t test and $\alpha = .05$ to test $H_0: \beta_1 = 0$ and $H_0: \beta_2 = 0$.

43. Recall that in exercise 40 the personnel director for Electronics Associates developed the following estimated regression equation relating an employee's score on a job satisfaction test to length of service and wage rate.

$$\hat{y} = 14.4 - 8.69x_1 + 13.5x_2$$

where

$$x_1 = \text{length of service (years)}$$
$$x_2 = \text{wage rate (dollars)}$$
$$y = \text{job satisfaction test score (higher scores}$$
$$\text{indicate greater job satisfaction)}$$

A portion of the Minitab computer output follows.

```
The regression equation is
Y = 14.4 - 8.69 X1 + 13.52 X2

Predictor            Coef           SE Coef             T
Constant           14.448            8.191            1.76
X1                 _____           1.555           _____
X2                 13.517           2.085           _____

S = 3.773      R-sq = _____ %   R-sq(adj) = _____ %

Analysis of Variance

SOURCE               DF             SS           MS          F
Regression            2          _____       _____     _____
Residual Error     _____        71.17        _____
Total                 7          720.0
```

a. Complete the missing entries in this output.
b. Compute F and test using $\alpha = .05$ to see whether a significant relationship is present.
c. Did the estimated regression equation provide a good fit to the data? Explain.
d. Use the t test and $\alpha = .05$ to test $H_0: \beta_1 = 0$ and $H_0: \beta_2 = 0$.

44. *SmartMoney* magazine evaluated 65 metropolitan areas to determine where home values are headed. An ideal city would get a score of 100 if all factors measured were as favorable as possible. Areas with a score of 60 or greater are considered to be primed for price appreciation, and areas with a score of below 50 may see housing values erode. Two of the factors evaluated were the recession resistance of the area and its affordability. Both of these factors were rated using a scale ranging from 0 (low score) to 10 (high score). The data obtained for a sample of 20 cities evaluated by *SmartMoney* follow (*SmartMoney,* February 2002).

HomeValue

Metro Area	Recession Resistance	Affordability	Score
Tucson	10	7	70.7
Fort Worth	10	7	68.5
San Antonio	6	8	65.5
Richmond	8	6	63.6
Indianapolis	4	8	62.5
Philadelphia	0	10	61.9
Atlanta	2	6	60.7
Phoenix	4	5	60.3
Cincinnati	2	7	57.0
Miami	6	5	56.5
Hartford	0	7	56.2
Birmingham	0	8	55.7
San Diego	8	2	54.6
Raleigh	2	7	50.9
Oklahoma City	1	6	49.6
Orange County	4	2	49.1
Denver	4	4	48.6
Los Angeles	0	7	45.7
Detroit	0	5	44.3
New Orleans	0	5	41.2

a. Develop an estimated regression equation that can be used to predict the score given the recession resistance rating. At the .05 level of significance, test for a significant relationship.

b. Did the estimated regression equation developed in part (a) provide a good fit to the data? Explain.

c. Develop an estimated regression equation that can be used to predict the score given the recession resistance rating and the affordability rating. At the .05 level of significance, test for overall significance.

45. Today's marketplace offers a wide choice to buyers of sport utility vehicles (SUVs) and pickup trucks. An important factor to many buyers is the resale value of the vehicle. The following table shows the resale value (%) after two years and the suggested retail price for 10 SUVs, 10 small pickup trucks, and 10 large pickup trucks (*Kiplinger's New Cars & Trucks 2000 Buyer's Guide*).

Trucks

Make and Model	Type of Vehicle	Suggested Retail Price ($)	Resale Value (%)
Chevrolet Blazer LS	Sport utility	19,495	55
Ford Explorer Sport	Sport utility	20,495	57
GMC Yukon XL 1500	Sport utility	26,789	67
Honda CR-V	Sport utility	18,965	65
Isuzu VehiCross	Sport utility	30,186	62
Jeep Cherokee Limited	Sport utility	25,745	57
Mercury Mountaineer Monterrey	Sport utility	29,895	59
Nissan Pathfinder XE	Sport utility	26,919	54
Toyota 4Runner	Sport utility	22,418	55
Toyota RAV4	Sport utility	17,148	55
Chevrolet S-10 Extended Cab	Small pickup	18,847	46
Dodge Dakota Club Cab Sport	Small pickup	16,870	53
Ford Ranger XLT Regular Cab	Small pickup	18,510	48

(continued)

Make and Model	Type of Vehicle	Suggested Retail Price ($)	Resale Value (%)
Ford Ranger XLT Supercab	Small pickup	20,225	55
GMC Sonoma Regular Cab	Small pickup	16,938	44
Isuzu Hombre Spacecab	Small pickup	18,820	41
Mazda B4000 SE Cab Plus	Small pickup	23,050	51
Nissan Frontier XE Regular Cab	Small pickup	12,110	51
Toyota Tacoma Xtracab	Small pickup	18,228	49
Toyota Tacoma Xtracab V6	Small pickup	19,318	50
Chevrolet K2500	Full-size pickup	24,417	60
Chevrolet Silverado 2500 Ext	Full-size pickup	24,140	64
Dodge Ram 1500	Full-size pickup	17,460	54
Dodge Ram Quad Cab 2500	Full-size pickup	32,770	63
Dodge Ram Regular Cab 2500	Full-size pickup	23,140	59
Ford F150 XL	Full-size pickup	22,875	58
Ford F350 Super Duty Crew Cab XL	Full-size pickup	34,295	64
GMC New Sierra 1500 Ext Cab	Full-size pickup	27,089	68
Toyota Tundra Access Cab Limited	Full-size pickup	25,605	53
Toyota Tundra Regular Cab	Full-size pickup	15,835	58

a. Develop an estimated regression equation that can be used to predict the resale value given the suggested retail price. At the .05 level of significance, test for a significant relationship.

b. Did the estimated regression equation developed in part (a) provide a good fit to the data? Explain.

c. Develop an estimated regression equation that can be used to predict the resale value given the suggested retail price and the type of vehicle.

d. Use the F test to determine the significance of the regression results. At a .05 level of significance, what is your conclusion?

46. The U.S. Department of Energy's *Fuel Economy Guide* provides fuel efficiency data for cars and trucks. A portion of the data for 35 standard pickup trucks produced by Chevrolet and General Motors follows (http://www.fueleconomy.gov, March 21, 2003). The column labeled Drive identifies whether the vehicle has two-wheel drive (2WD) or four-wheel drive (4WD). The column labeled Displacement shows the engine's displacement in liters, the column labeled Cylinders specifies the number of cylinders the engine has, and the column labeled Transmission shows whether the truck has an automatic transmission or a manual transmission. The column labeled City MPG shows the fuel efficiency rating for the truck for city driving in terms of miles per gallon (mpg).

CD file

FuelEcon

Truck	Name	Drive	Displacement	Cylinders	Transmission	City MPG
1	C1500 Silverado	2WD	4.3	6	Auto	15
2	C1500 Silverado	2WD	4.3	6	Manual	15
3	C1500 Silverado	2WD	4.8	8	Auto	15
4	C1500 Silverado	2WD	4.8	8	Manual	16
5	C1500 Silverado	2WD	5.3	8	Auto	11
.	.	.	.	.	.	.
.	.	.	.	.	.	.
.	.	.	.	.	.	.
32	K1500 Sierra	4WD	5.3	8	Auto	15
33	K1500 Sierra	4WD	5.3	8	Auto	15
34	Sonoma	4WD	4.3	6	Auto	17
35	Sonoma	4WD	4.3	6	Manual	15

a. Develop an estimated regression equation that can be used to predict the fuel efficiency for city driving given the engine's displacement. Test for significance using $\alpha = .05$.
b. Consider the addition of the dummy variable Drive4, where the value of Drive4 is 0 if the truck has two-wheel drive and 1 if the truck has four-wheel drive. Develop the estimated regression equation that can be used to predict the fuel efficiency for city driving given the engine's displacement and the dummy variable Drive4.
c. Use $\alpha = .05$ to determine whether the dummy variable added in part (b) is significant.
d. Consider the addition of the dummy variable EightCyl, where the value of EightCyl is 0 if the truck's engine has six cylinders and 1 if the truck's engine has eight cylinders. Develop the estimated regression equation that can be used to predict the fuel efficiency for city driving given the engine's displacement and the dummy variables Drive4 and EightCyl.
e. For the estimated regression equation developed in part (d), test for overall significance and individual significance using $\alpha = .05$.

Case Problem 1   Consumer Research, Inc.

Consumer Research, Inc., is an independent agency that conducts research on consumer attitudes and behaviors for a variety of firms. In one study, a client asked for an investigation of consumer characteristics that can be used to predict the amount charged by credit card users. Data were collected on annual income, household size, and annual credit card charges for a sample of 50 consumers. The following data are on the CD accompanying the text in the data set named Consumer.

CD file

Consumer

Income ($1000s)	Household Size	Amount Charged ($)	Income ($1000s)	Household Size	Amount Charged ($)
54	3	4016	54	6	5573
30	2	3159	30	1	2583
32	4	5100	48	2	3866
50	5	4742	34	5	3586
31	2	1864	67	4	5037
55	2	4070	50	2	3605
37	1	2731	67	5	5345
40	2	3348	55	6	5370
66	4	4764	52	2	3890
51	3	4110	62	3	4705
25	3	4208	64	2	4157
48	4	4219	22	3	3579
27	1	2477	29	4	3890
33	2	2514	39	2	2972
65	3	4214	35	1	3121
63	4	4965	39	4	4183
42	6	4412	54	3	3730
21	2	2448	23	6	4127
44	1	2995	27	2	2921
37	5	4171	26	7	4603
62	6	5678	61	2	4273
21	3	3623	30	2	3067
55	7	5301	22	4	3074
42	2	3020	46	5	4820
41	7	4828	66	4	5149

Managerial Report

1. Use methods of descriptive statistics to summarize the data. Comment on the findings.
2. Develop estimated regression equations, first using annual income as the independent variable and then using household size as the independent variable. Which variable is the better predictor of annual credit card charges? Discuss your findings.
3. Develop an estimated regression equation with annual income and household size as the independent variables. Discuss your findings.
4. What is the predicted annual credit card charge for a three-person household with an annual income of $40,000?
5. Discuss the need for other independent variables that could be added to the model. What additional variables might be helpful?

Case Problem 2   Predicting Student Proficiency Test Scores

In order to predict how a school district would have scored when accounting for poverty and other income measures, *The Cincinnati Enquirer* gathered data from the Ohio Department of Education's Education Management Services and the Ohio Department of Taxation (*The Cincinnati Enquirer,* November 30, 1997). First, the newspaper obtained passage-rate data on the math, reading, science, writing, and citizenship proficiency exams given to fourth-, sixth-, ninth-, and 12th-graders in early 1996. By combining these data, they computed an overall percentage of students that passed the tests for each district.

The percentage of a school district's students on Aid for Dependent Children (ADC), the percentage who qualify for free or reduced-price lunches, and the district's median family income were also recorded. A portion of the data collected for the 608 school districts follows. The complete data set is available on the CD accompanying the text in the data set named Enquirer.

CD file

Enquirer

Rank	School District	County	% Passed	% on ADC	% Free Lunch	Median Income ($)
1	Ottawa Hills Local	Lucas	93.85	0.11	0.00	48231
2	Wyoming City	Hamilton	93.08	2.95	4.59	42672
3	Oakwood City	Montgomery	92.92	0.20	0.38	42403
4	Madeira City	Hamilton	92.37	1.50	4.83	32889
5	Indian Hill Ex Vill	Hamilton	91.77	1.23	2.70	44135
6	Solon City	Cuyahoga	90.77	0.68	2.24	34993
7	Chagrin Falls Ex Vill	Cuyahoga	89.89	0.47	0.44	38921
8	Mariemont City	Hamilton	89.80	3.00	2.97	31823
9	Upper Arlington City	Franklin	89.77	0.24	0.92	38358
10	Granville Ex Vill	Licking	89.22	1.14	0.00	36235
⋮	⋮	⋮	⋮	⋮	⋮	⋮

The data have been ranked based on the values in the column labeled % Passed; these data are the overall percentage of students passing the tests. Data in the column labeled % on ADC are the percentage of each school district's students on ADC, and the data in the column labeled % Free Lunch are the percentage of students who qualify for free or reduced-price lunches. The column labeled Median Income shows each district's median family income. Also shown for each school district is the county in which the school district is located. Note that in some cases the value in the % Free Lunch column is 0, indicating that the district did not participate in the free lunch program.

Managerial Report

Use the methods presented in this and previous chapters to analyze this data set. Present a summary of your analysis, including key statistical results, conclusions, and recommendations, in a managerial report. Include any technical material you feel is appropriate in an appendix.

Case Problem 3   Alumni Giving

Alumni donations are an important source of revenue for colleges and universities. If administrators could determine the factors that could lead to increases in the percentage of alumni who make a donation, they might be able to implement policies that could lead to increased revenues. Research shows that students who are more satisfied with their contact with teachers are more likely to graduate. As a result, one might suspect that smaller class sizes and lower student-faculty ratios might lead to a higher percentage of satisfied graduates, which in turn might lead to increases in the percentage of alumni who make a donation. Table 13.7 shows data for 48 national universities (*America's Best Colleges,* Year 2000 Edition). The column labeled Graduation Rate is the percentage of students who initially enrolled at the university and graduated. The column labeled % of Classes Under 20 shows the percentage of classes offered with fewer than 20 students. The column labeled Student-Faculty Ratio is the number of students enrolled divided by the total number of faculty. Finally, the column labeled Alumni Giving Rate is the percentage of alumni who made a donation to the university.

Managerial Report

1. Use methods of descriptive statistics to summarize the data.
2. Develop an estimated regression equation that can be used to predict the alumni giving rate given the number of students who graduate. Discuss your findings.
3. Develop an estimated regression equation that could be used to predict the alumni giving rate using the data provided.
4. What conclusions and recommendations can you derive from your analysis?

Appendix 13.1   Multiple Regression with Minitab

Butler

In Section 13.2 we discussed the computer solution of multiple regression problems by showing Minitab's output for the Butler Trucking Company problem. In this appendix we describe the steps required to generate the Minitab computer solution. First, the data must be entered in a Minitab worksheet. The miles traveled are entered in column C1, the number of deliveries are entered in column C2, and the travel times (hours) are entered in column C3. The variable names Miles, Deliv, and Time were entered as the column headings on the worksheet. In subsequent steps, we refer to the data by using the variable names Miles, Deliv, and Time or the column indicators C1, C2, and C3. The following steps describe how to use Minitab to produce the regression results shown in Figure 13.4.

      Step 1. Select the **Stat** menu
      Step 2. Select the **Regression** menu
      Step 3. Choose **Regression**
      Step 4. When the **Regression** dialog box appears
                Enter Time in the **Response** box
                Enter Miles and Deliv in the **Predictors** box
                Click **OK**

TABLE 13.7   DATA FOR 48 NATIONAL UNIVERSITIES

Alumni

University	State	Graduation Rate	% of Classes Under 20	Student-Faculty Ratio	Alumni Giving Rate
Boston College	MA	85	39	13	25
Brandeis University	MA	79	68	8	33
Brown University	RI	93	60	8	40
California Institute of Technology	CA	85	65	3	46
Carnegie Mellon University	PA	75	67	10	28
Case Western Reserve Univ.	OH	72	52	8	31
College of William and Mary	VA	89	45	12	27
Columbia University	NY	90	69	7	31
Cornell University	NY	91	72	13	35
Dartmouth College	NH	94	61	10	53
Duke University	NC	92	68	8	45
Emory University	GA	84	65	7	37
Georgetown University	PA	91	54	10	29
Harvard University	MA	97	73	8	46
Johns Hopkins University	MD	89	64	9	27
Lehigh University	PA	81	55	11	40
Massachusetts Inst. of Technology	MA	92	65	6	44
New York University	NY	72	63	13	13
Northwestern University	IL	90	66	8	30
Pennsylvania State Univ.	PA	80	32	19	21
Princeton University	NJ	95	68	5	67
Rice University	TX	92	62	8	40
Stanford University	CA	92	69	7	34
Tufts University	MA	87	67	9	29
Tulane University	LA	72	56	12	17
U. of California–Berkeley	CA	83	58	17	18
U. of California–Davis	CA	74	32	19	7
U. of California–Irvine	CA	74	42	20	9
U. of California–Los Angeles	CA	78	41	18	13
U. of California–San Diego	CA	80	48	19	8
U. of California–Santa Barbara	CA	70	45	20	12
U. of Chicago	IL	84	65	4	36
U. of Florida	FL	67	31	23	19
U. of Illinois–Urbana Champaign	IL	77	29	15	23
U. of Michigan–Ann Arbor	MI	83	51	15	13
U. of North Carolina–Chapel Hill	NC	82	40	16	26
U. of Notre Dame	IN	94	53	13	49
U. of Pennsylvania	PA	90	65	7	41
U. of Rochester	NY	76	63	10	23
U. of Southern California	CA	70	53	13	22
U. of Texas–Austin	TX	66	39	21	13
U. of Virginia	VA	92	44	13	28
U. of Washington	WA	70	37	12	12
U. of Wisconsin–Madison	WI	73	37	13	13
Vanderbilt University	TN	82	68	9	31
Wake Forest University	NC	82	59	11	38
Washington University–St. Louis	MO	86	73	7	33
Yale University	CT	94	77	7	50

Appendix 13.2 Multiple Regression with Excel

Butler

In Section 13.2 we discussed the computer solution of multiple regression problems by showing Minitab's output for the Butler Trucking Company problem. In this appendix we describe how to use Excel's Regression tool to develop the estimated multiple regression equation for the Butler Trucking problem. Refer to Figure 13.10 as we describe the tasks involved. First, the labels Assignment, Miles, Deliveries, and Time are entered into cells A1:D1 of the worksheet, and the sample data into cells B2:D11. The numbers 1–10 in cells A2:A11 identify each observation.

The following steps describe how to use the Regression tool for the multiple regression analysis.

Step 1. Select the **Tools** menu
Step 2. Choose **Data Analysis**
Step 3. Choose **Regression** from the list of Analysis Tools

FIGURE 13.10 EXCEL OUTPUT FOR BUTLER TRUCKING WITH TWO INDEPENDENT VARIABLES

	A	B	C	D	E	F	G	H	I
1	**Assignment**	**Miles**	**Deliveries**	**Time**					
2	1	100	4	9.3					
3	2	50	3	4.8					
4	3	100	4	8.9					
5	4	100	2	6.5					
6	5	50	2	4.2					
7	6	80	2	6.2					
8	7	75	3	7.4					
9	8	65	4	6					
10	9	90	3	7.6					
11	10	90	2	6.1					
12									
13	SUMMARY OUTPUT								
14									
15	*Regression Statistics*								
16	Multiple R	0.9507							
17	R Square	0.9038							
18	Adjusted R Square	0.8763							
19	Standard Error	0.5731							
20	Observations	10							
21									
22	ANOVA								
23		*df*	*SS*	*MS*	*F*	*Significance F*			
24	Regression	2	21.6006	10.8003	32.8784	0.0003			
25	Residual	7	2.2994	0.3285					
26	Total	9	23.9						
27									
28		*Coefficients*	*Standard Error*	*t Stat*	*P-value*	*Lower 95%*	*Upper 95%*	*Lower 99.0%*	*Upper 99.0%*
29	Intercept	-0.8687	0.9515	-0.9129	0.3916	-3.1188	1.3813	-4.1986	2.4612
30	Miles	0.0611	0.0099	6.1824	0.0005	0.0378	0.0845	0.0265	0.0957
31	Deliveries	0.9234	0.2211	4.1763	0.0042	0.4006	1.4463	0.1496	1.6972

Step 4. When the Regression dialog box appears

Enter D1:D11 in the **Input Y Range** box

Enter B1:C11 in the **Input X Range** box

Select **Labels**

Select **Confidence Level**

Enter 99 in the **Confidence Level** box

Select **Output Range**

Enter A13 in the **Output Range** box (to identify the upper left corner of the section of the worksheet where the output will appear)

Click **OK**

In the Excel output shown in Figure 13.10 the label for the independent variable x_1 is Miles (see cell A30), and the label for the independent variable x_2 is Deliveries (see cell A31). The estimated regression equation is

$$\hat{y} = -.8687 + .0611x_1 + .9234x_2$$

Note that using Excel's Regression tool for multiple regression is almost the same as using it for simple linear regression. The major difference is that in the multiple regression case a larger range of cells is required in order to identify the independent variables.

APPENDIXES

Appendix A: References and Bibliography

General

Bowerman, B. L., and R. T. O'Connell. *Applied Statistics: Improving Business Processes.* Irwin, 1996.

Freedman, D., R. Pisani, and R. Purves. *Statistics,* 3rd ed. W. W. Norton, 1997.

Hogg, R. V., and A. T. Craig. *Introduction to Mathematical Statistics,* 5th ed. Prentice Hall, 1994.

Hogg, R. V., and E. A. Tanis. *Probability and Statistical Inference,* 6th ed. Prentice Hall, 2001.

Joiner, B. L., and B. F. Ryan. *Minitab Handbook.* Brooks/Cole, 2000.

Miller, I., and M. Miller. *John E. Freund's Mathematical Statistics.* Prentice Hall, 1998.

Moore, D. S., and G. P. McCabe. *Introduction to the Practice of Statistics,* 4th ed. Freeman, 2003.

Roberts, H. *Data Analysis for Managers with Minitab.* Scientific Press, 1991.

Tanur, J. M. *Statistics: A Guide to the Unknown,* 4th ed. Brooks/Cole, 2002.

Tukey, J. W. *Exploratory Data Analysis.* Addison-Wesley, 1977.

Probability

Hogg, R. V., and E. A. Tanis. *Probability and Statistical Inference,* 6th ed. Prentice Hall, 2001.

Ross, S. M. *Introduction to Probability Models,* 7th ed. Academic Press, 2000.

Wackerly, D. D., W. Mendenhall, and R. L. Scheaffer. *Mathematical Statistics with Applications,* 6th ed. Duxbury Press, 2002.

Regression Analysis

Belsley, D. A. *Conditioning Diagnostics: Collinearity and Weak Data in Regression.* Wiley, 1991.

Chatterjee, S., and B. Price. *Regression Analysis by Example,* 3rd ed. Wiley, 1999.

Draper, N. R., and H. Smith. *Applied Regression Analysis,* 3rd ed. Wiley, 1998.

Graybill, F. A., and H. Iyer. *Regression Analysis: Concepts and Applications.* Duxbury Press, 1994.

Hosmer, D. W., and S. Lemeshow. *Applied Logistic Regression,* 2nd ed. Wiley, 2000.

Kleinbaum, D. G., L. L. Kupper, and K. E. Muller. *Applied Regression Analysis and Other Multivariate Methods,* 3rd ed. Duxbury Press, 1997.

Kutner, M. H., C. J. Nachtschiem, W. Wasserman, and J. Neter. *Applied Linear Statistical Models,* 4th ed. Irwin, 1996.

Mendenhall, M., and T. Sincich. *A Second Course in Statistics: Regression Analysis,* 5th ed. Prentice Hall, 1996.

Myers, R. H. *Classical and Modern Regression with Applications,* 2nd ed. PWS, 1990.

TABLE 1   STANDARD NORMAL DISTRIBUTION

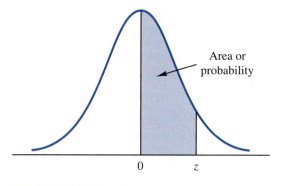

Area or probability

Entries in the table give the area under the curve between the mean and z standard deviations above the mean. For example, for $z = 1.25$ the area under the curve between the mean and z is .3944.

z	.00	.01	.02	.03	.04	.05	.06	.07	.08	.09
.0	.0000	.0040	.0080	.0120	.0160	.0199	.0239	.0279	.0319	.0359
.1	.0398	.0438	.0478	.0517	.0557	.0596	.0636	.0675	.0714	.0753
.2	.0793	.0832	.0871	.0910	.0948	.0987	.1026	.1064	.1103	.1141
.3	.1179	.1217	.1255	.1293	.1331	.1368	.1406	.1443	.1480	.1517
.4	.1554	.1591	.1628	.1664	.1700	.1736	.1772	.1808	.1844	.1879
.5	.1915	.1950	.1985	.2019	.2054	.2088	.2123	.2157	.2190	.2224
.6	.2257	.2291	.2324	.2357	.2389	.2422	.2454	.2486	.2517	.2549
.7	.2580	.2611	.2642	.2673	.2704	.2734	.2764	.2794	.2823	.2852
.8	.2881	.2910	.2939	.2967	.2995	.3023	.3051	.3078	.3106	.3133
.9	.3159	.3186	.3212	.3238	.3264	.3289	.3315	.3340	.3365	.3389
1.0	.3413	.3438	.3461	.3485	.3508	.3531	.3554	.3577	.3599	.3621
1.1	.3643	.3665	.3686	.3708	.3729	.3749	.3770	.3790	.3810	.3830
1.2	.3849	.3869	.3888	.3907	.3925	.3944	.3962	.3980	.3997	.4015
1.3	.4032	.4049	.4066	.4082	.4099	.4115	.4131	.4147	.4162	.4177
1.4	.4192	.4207	.4222	.4236	.4251	.4265	.4279	.4292	.4306	.4319
1.5	.4332	.4345	.4357	.4370	.4382	.4394	.4406	.4418	.4429	.4441
1.6	.4452	.4463	.4474	.4484	.4495	.4505	.4515	.4525	.4535	.4545
1.7	.4554	.4564	.4573	.4582	.4591	.4599	.4608	.4616	.4625	.4633
1.8	.4641	.4649	.4656	.4664	.4671	.4678	.4686	.4693	.4699	.4706
1.9	.4713	.4719	.4726	.4732	.4738	.4744	.4750	.4756	.4761	.4767
2.0	.4772	.4778	.4783	.4788	.4793	.4798	.4803	.4808	.4812	.4817
2.1	.4821	.4826	.4830	.4834	.4838	.4842	.4846	.4850	.4854	.4857
2.2	.4861	.4864	.4868	.4871	.4875	.4878	.4881	.4884	.4887	.4890
2.3	.4893	.4896	.4898	.4901	.4904	.4906	.4909	.4911	.4913	.4916
2.4	.4918	.4920	.4922	.4925	.4927	.4929	.4931	.4932	.4934	.4936
2.5	.4938	.4940	.4941	.4943	.4945	.4946	.4948	.4949	.4951	.4952
2.6	.4953	.4955	.4956	.4957	.4959	.4960	.4961	.4962	.4963	.4964
2.7	.4965	.4966	.4967	.4968	.4969	.4970	.4971	.4972	.4973	.4974
2.8	.4974	.4975	.4976	.4977	.4977	.4978	.4979	.4979	.4980	.4981
2.9	.4981	.4982	.4982	.4983	.4984	.4984	.4985	.4985	.4986	.4986
3.0	.4987	.4987	.4987	.4988	.4988	.4989	.4989	.4989	.4990	.4990

TABLE 2 *t* DISTRIBUTION

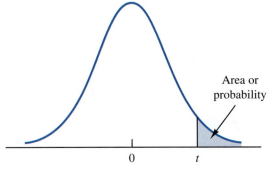

Area or probability

Entries in the table give *t* values for an area or probability in the upper tail of the *t* distribution. For example, with 10 degrees of freedom and a .05 area in the upper tail, $t_{.05} = 1.812$.

Degrees of Freedom	Area in Upper Tail					
	.20	.10	.05	.025	.01	.005
1	1.376	3.078	6.314	12.706	31.821	63.656
2	1.061	1.886	2.920	4.303	6.965	9.925
3	.978	1.638	2.353	3.182	4.541	5.841
4	.941	1.533	2.132	2.776	3.747	4.604
5	.920	1.476	2.015	2.571	3.365	4.032
6	.906	1.440	1.943	2.447	3.143	3.707
7	.896	1.415	1.895	2.365	2.998	3.499
8	.889	1.397	1.860	2.306	2.896	3.355
9	.883	1.383	1.833	2.262	2.821	3.250
10	.879	1.372	1.812	2.228	2.764	3.169
11	.876	1.363	1.796	2.201	2.718	3.106
12	.873	1.356	1.782	2.179	2.681	3.055
13	.870	1.350	1.771	2.160	2.650	3.012
14	.868	1.345	1.761	2.145	2.624	2.977
15	.866	1.341	1.753	2.131	2.602	2.947
16	.865	1.337	1.746	2.120	2.583	2.921
17	.863	1.333	1.740	2.110	2.567	2.898
18	.862	1.330	1.734	2.101	2.552	2.878
19	.861	1.328	1.729	2.093	2.539	2.861
20	.860	1.325	1.725	2.086	2.528	2.845
21	.859	1.323	1.721	2.080	2.518	2.831
22	.858	1.321	1.717	2.074	2.508	2.819
23	.858	1.319	1.714	2.069	2.500	2.807
24	.857	1.318	1.711	2.064	2.492	2.797
25	.856	1.316	1.708	2.060	2.485	2.787
26	.856	1.315	1.706	2.056	2.479	2.779
27	.855	1.314	1.703	2.052	2.473	2.771
28	.855	1.313	1.701	2.048	2.467	2.763
29	.854	1.311	1.699	2.045	2.462	2.756
30	.854	1.310	1.697	2.042	2.457	2.750
31	.853	1.309	1.696	2.040	2.453	2.744
32	.853	1.309	1.694	2.037	2.449	2.738
33	.853	1.308	1.692	2.035	2.445	2.733
34	.852	1.307	1.691	2.032	2.441	2.728

TABLE 2   *t* DISTRIBUTION (*Continued*)

Degrees of Freedom	Area in Upper Tail					
	.20	**.10**	**.05**	**.025**	**.01**	**.005**
35	.852	1.306	1.690	2.030	2.438	2.724
36	.852	1.306	1.688	2.028	2.434	2.719
37	.851	1.305	1.687	2.026	2.431	2.715
38	.851	1.304	1.686	2.024	2.429	2.712
39	.851	1.304	1.685	2.023	2.426	2.708
40	.851	1.303	1.684	2.021	2.423	2.704
41	.850	1.303	1.683	2.020	2.421	2.701
42	.850	1.302	1.682	2.018	2.418	2.698
43	.850	1.302	1.681	2.017	2.416	2.695
44	.850	1.301	1.680	2.015	2.414	2.692
45	.850	1.301	1.679	2.014	2.412	2.690
46	.850	1.300	1.679	2.013	2.410	2.687
47	.849	1.300	1.678	2.012	2.408	2.685
48	.849	1.299	1.677	2.011	2.407	2.682
49	.849	1.299	1.677	2.010	2.405	2.680
50	.849	1.299	1.676	2.009	2.403	2.678
51	.849	1.298	1.675	2.008	2.402	2.676
52	.849	1.298	1.675	2.007	2.400	2.674
53	.848	1.298	1.674	2.006	2.399	2.672
54	.848	1.297	1.674	2.005	2.397	2.670
55	.848	1.297	1.673	2.004	2.396	2.668
56	.848	1.297	1.673	2.003	2.395	2.667
57	.848	1.297	1.672	2.002	2.394	2.665
58	.848	1.296	1.672	2.002	2.392	2.663
59	.848	1.296	1.671	2.001	2.391	2.662
60	.848	1.296	1.671	2.000	2.390	2.660
61	.848	1.296	1.670	2.000	2.389	2.659
62	.847	1.295	1.670	1.999	2.388	2.657
63	.847	1.295	1.669	1.998	2.387	2.656
64	.847	1.295	1.669	1.998	2.386	2.655
65	.847	1.295	1.669	1.997	2.385	2.654
66	.847	1.295	1.668	1.997	2.384	2.652
67	.847	1.294	1.668	1.996	2.383	2.651
68	.847	1.294	1.668	1.995	2.382	2.650
69	.847	1.294	1.667	1.995	2.382	2.649
70	.847	1.294	1.667	1.994	2.381	2.648
71	.847	1.294	1.667	1.994	2.380	2.647
72	.847	1.293	1.666	1.993	2.379	2.646
73	.847	1.293	1.666	1.993	2.379	2.645
74	.847	1.293	1.666	1.993	2.378	2.644
75	.846	1.293	1.665	1.992	2.377	2.643
76	.846	1.293	1.665	1.992	2.376	2.642
77	.846	1.293	1.665	1.991	2.376	2.641
78	.846	1.292	1.665	1.991	2.375	2.640
79	.846	1.292	1.664	1.990	2.374	2.639

TABLE 2 *t* DISTRIBUTION (*Continued*)

Degrees of Freedom	Area in Upper Tail					
	.20	.10	.05	.025	.01	.005
80	.846	1.292	1.664	1.990	2.374	2.639
81	.846	1.292	1.664	1.990	2.373	2.638
82	.846	1.292	1.664	1.989	2.373	2.637
83	.846	1.292	1.663	1.989	2.372	2.636
84	.846	1.292	1.663	1.989	2.372	2.636
85	.846	1.292	1.663	1.988	2.371	2.635
86	.846	1.291	1.663	1.988	2.370	2.634
87	.846	1.291	1.663	1.988	2.370	2.634
88	.846	1.291	1.662	1.987	2.369	2.633
89	.846	1.291	1.662	1.987	2.369	2.632
90	.846	1.291	1.662	1.987	2.368	2.632
91	.846	1.291	1.662	1.986	2.368	2.631
92	.846	1.291	1.662	1.986	2.368	2.630
93	.846	1.291	1.661	1.986	2.367	2.630
94	.845	1.291	1.661	1.986	2.367	2.629
95	.845	1.291	1.661	1.985	2.366	2.629
96	.845	1.290	1.661	1.985	2.366	2.628
97	.845	1.290	1.661	1.985	2.365	2.627
98	.845	1.290	1.661	1.984	2.365	2.627
99	.845	1.290	1.660	1.984	2.364	2.626
100	.845	1.290	1.660	1.984	2.364	2.626
∞	.842	1.282	1.645	1.960	2.326	2.576

TABLE 3   CHI-SQUARE DISTRIBUTION

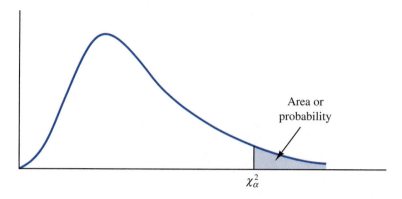

χ_α^2

Entries in the table give χ_α^2 values, where α is the area or probability in the upper tail of the chi-square distribution. For example, with 10 degrees of freedom and a .01 area in the upper tail, $\chi_{.01}^2 = 23.209$.

Degrees of Freedom	Area in Upper Tail									
	.995	.99	.975	.95	.90	.10	.05	.025	.01	.005
1	.000	.000	.001	.004	.016	2.706	3.841	5.024	6.635	7.879
2	.010	.020	.051	.103	.211	4.605	5.991	7.378	9.210	10.597
3	.072	.115	.216	.352	.584	6.251	7.815	9.348	11.345	12.838
4	.207	.297	.484	.711	1.064	7.779	9.488	11.143	13.277	14.860
5	.412	.554	.831	1.145	1.610	9.236	11.070	12.832	15.086	16.750
6	.676	.872	1.237	1.635	2.204	10.645	12.592	14.449	16.812	18.548
7	.989	1.239	1.690	2.167	2.833	12.017	14.067	16.013	18.475	20.278
8	1.344	1.647	2.180	2.733	3.490	13.362	15.507	17.535	20.090	21.955
9	1.735	2.088	2.700	3.325	4.168	14.684	16.919	19.023	21.666	23.589
10	2.156	2.558	3.247	3.940	4.865	15.987	18.307	20.483	23.209	25.188
11	2.603	3.053	3.816	4.575	5.578	17.275	19.675	21.920	24.725	26.757
12	3.074	3.571	4.404	5.226	6.304	18.549	21.026	23.337	26.217	28.300
13	3.565	4.107	5.009	5.892	7.041	19.812	22.362	24.736	27.688	29.819
14	4.075	4.660	5.629	6.571	7.790	21.064	23.685	26.119	29.141	31.319
15	4.601	5.229	6.262	7.261	8.547	22.307	24.996	27.488	30.578	32.801
16	5.142	5.812	6.908	7.962	9.312	23.542	26.296	28.845	32.000	34.267
17	5.697	6.408	7.564	8.672	10.085	24.769	27.587	30.191	33.409	35.718
18	6.265	7.015	8.231	9.390	10.865	25.989	28.869	31.526	34.805	37.156
19	6.844	7.633	8.907	10.117	11.651	27.204	30.144	32.852	36.191	38.582
20	7.434	8.260	9.591	10.851	12.443	28.412	31.410	34.170	37.566	39.997
21	8.034	8.897	10.283	11.591	13.240	29.615	32.671	35.479	38.932	41.401
22	8.643	9.542	10.982	12.338	14.041	30.813	33.924	36.781	40.289	42.796
23	9.260	10.196	11.689	13.091	14.848	32.007	35.172	38.076	41.638	44.181
24	9.886	10.856	12.401	13.848	15.659	33.196	36.415	39.364	42.980	45.558
25	10.520	11.524	13.120	14.611	16.473	34.382	37.652	40.646	44.314	46.928
26	11.160	12.198	13.844	15.379	17.292	35.563	38.885	41.923	45.642	48.290
27	11.808	12.878	14.573	16.151	18.114	36.741	40.113	43.195	46.963	49.645
28	12.461	13.565	15.308	16.928	18.939	37.916	41.337	44.461	48.278	50.994
29	13.121	14.256	16.047	17.708	19.768	39.087	42.557	45.722	49.588	52.335

TABLE 3 CHI-SQUARE DISTRIBUTION (*Continued*)

Degrees of Freedom	Area in Upper Tail									
	.995	.99	.975	.95	.90	.10	.05	.025	.01	.005
30	13.787	14.953	16.791	18.493	20.599	40.256	43.773	46.979	50.892	53.672
35	17.192	18.509	20.569	22.465	24.797	46.059	49.802	53.203	57.342	60.275
40	20.707	22.164	24.433	26.509	29.051	51.805	55.758	59.342	63.691	66.766
45	24.311	25.901	28.366	30.612	33.350	57.505	61.656	65.410	69.957	73.166
50	27.991	29.707	32.357	34.764	37.689	63.167	67.505	71.420	76.154	79.490
55	31.735	33.571	36.398	38.958	42.060	68.796	73.311	77.380	82.292	85.749
60	35.534	37.485	40.482	43.188	46.459	74.397	79.082	83.298	88.379	91.952
65	39.383	41.444	44.603	47.450	50.883	79.973	84.821	89.177	94.422	98.105
70	43.275	45.442	48.758	51.739	55.329	85.527	90.531	95.023	100.425	104.215
75	47.206	49.475	52.942	56.054	59.795	91.061	96.217	100.839	106.393	110.285
80	51.172	53.540	57.153	60.391	64.278	96.578	101.879	106.629	112.329	116.321
85	55.170	57.634	61.389	64.749	68.777	102.079	107.522	112.393	118.236	122.324
90	59.196	61.754	65.647	69.126	73.291	107.565	113.145	118.136	124.116	128.299
95	63.250	65.898	69.925	73.520	77.818	113.038	118.752	123.858	129.973	134.247
100	67.328	70.065	74.222	77.929	82.358	118.498	124.342	129.561	135.807	140.170

TABLE 4 *F* DISTRIBUTION

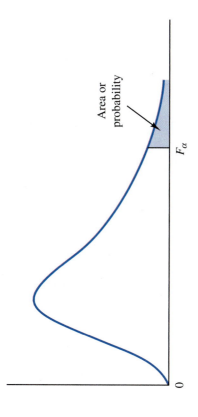

Area or probability

F_α

Entries in the table give F_α values, where α is the area or probability in the upper tail of the F distribution. For example, with 4 numerator degrees of freedom, 8 denominator degrees of freedom, and a .05 area in the upper tail, $F_{.05} = 3.84$.

Denominator Degrees of Freedom	Area in Upper Tail	\multicolumn{18}{c}{Numerator Degrees of Freedom}
		1	2	3	4	5	6	7	8	9	10	15	20	25	30	40	60	100	1000
1	.10	39.86	49.50	53.59	55.83	57.24	58.20	58.91	59.44	59.86	60.19	61.22	61.74	62.05	62.26	62.53	62.79	63.01	63.30
	.05	161.45	199.50	215.71	224.58	230.16	233.99	236.77	238.88	240.54	241.88	245.95	248.02	249.26	250.10	251.14	252.20	253.04	254.19
	.025	647.79	799.48	864.15	899.60	921.83	937.11	948.20	956.64	963.28	968.63	984.87	993.08	998.09	1001.40	1005.60	1009.79	1013.16	1017.76
	.01	4052.18	4999.34	5403.53	5624.26	5763.96	5858.95	5928.33	5980.95	6022.40	6055.93	6156.97	6208.66	6239.86	6260.35	6286.43	6312.97	6333.92	6362.80
2	.10	8.53	9.00	9.16	9.24	9.29	9.33	9.35	9.37	9.38	9.39	9.42	9.44	9.45	9.46	9.47	9.47	9.48	9.49
	.05	18.51	19.00	19.16	19.25	19.30	19.33	19.35	19.37	19.38	19.40	19.43	19.45	19.46	19.46	19.47	19.48	19.49	19.49
	.025	38.51	39.00	39.17	39.25	39.30	39.33	39.36	39.37	39.39	39.40	39.43	39.45	39.46	39.46	39.47	39.48	39.49	39.50
	.01	98.50	99.00	99.16	99.25	99.30	99.33	99.36	99.38	99.39	99.40	99.43	99.45	99.46	99.47	99.48	99.48	99.49	99.50
3	.10	5.54	5.46	5.39	5.34	5.31	5.28	5.27	5.25	5.24	5.23	5.20	5.18	5.17	5.17	5.16	5.15	5.14	5.13
	.05	10.13	9.55	9.28	9.12	9.01	8.94	8.89	8.85	8.81	8.79	8.70	8.66	8.63	8.62	8.59	8.57	8.55	8.53
	.025	17.44	16.04	15.44	15.10	14.88	14.73	14.62	14.54	14.47	14.42	14.25	14.17	14.12	14.08	14.04	13.99	13.96	13.91
	.01	34.12	30.82	29.46	28.71	28.24	27.91	27.67	27.49	27.34	27.23	26.87	26.69	26.58	26.50	26.41	26.32	26.24	26.14
4	.10	4.54	4.32	4.19	4.11	4.05	4.01	3.98	3.95	3.94	3.92	3.87	3.84	3.83	3.82	3.80	3.79	3.78	3.76
	.05	7.71	6.94	6.59	6.39	6.26	6.16	6.09	6.04	6.00	5.96	5.86	5.80	5.77	5.75	5.72	5.69	5.66	5.63
	.025	12.22	10.65	9.98	9.60	9.36	9.20	9.07	8.98	8.90	8.84	8.66	8.56	8.50	8.46	8.41	8.36	8.32	8.26
	.01	21.20	18.00	16.69	15.98	15.52	15.21	14.98	14.80	14.66	14.55	14.20	14.02	13.91	13.84	13.75	13.65	13.58	13.47
5	.10	4.06	3.78	3.62	3.52	3.45	3.40	3.37	3.34	3.32	3.30	3.324	3.21	3.19	3.17	3.16	3.14	3.13	3.11
	.05	6.61.	5.79	5.41	5.19	5.05	4.95	4.88	4.82	4.77	4.74	4.62	4.56	4.52	4.50	4.46	4.43	4.41	4.37
	.025	10.01	8.43	7.76	7.39	7.15	6.98	6.85	6.76	6.68	6.62	6.43	6.33	6.27	6.23	6.18	6.12	6.08	6.02
	.01	16.26	13.27	12.06	11.39	10.97	10.67	10.46	10.29	10.16	10.05	9.72	9.55	9.45	9.38	9.29	9.20	9.13	9.03

TABLE 4 *F* DISTRIBUTION (*Continued*)

Denominator Degrees of Freedom	Area in Upper Tail	Numerator Degrees of Freedom																	
		1	2	3	4	5	6	7	8	9	10	15	20	25	30	40	60	100	1000
6	.10	3.78	3.46	3.29	3.18	3.11	3.05	3.01	2.98	2.96	2.94	2.87	2.84	2.81	2.80	2.78	2.76	2.75	2.72
	.05	5.99	5.14	4.76	4.53	4.39	4.28	4.21	4.15	4.10	4.06	3.94	3.87	3.83	3.81	3.77	3.74	3.71	3.67
	.025	8.81	7.26	6.60	6.23	5.99	5.82	5.70	5.60	5.52	5.46	5.27	5.17	5.11	5.07	5.01	4.96	4.92	4.86
	.01	13.75	10.92	9.78	9.15	8.75	8.47	8.26	8.10	7.98	7.87	7.56	7.40	7.30	7.23	7.14	7.06	6.99	6.89
7	.10	3.59	3.26	3.07	2.96	2.88	2.83	2.78	2.75	2.72	2.70	2.63	2.59	2.57	2.56	2.54	2.51	2.50	2.47
	.05	5.59	4.74	4.35	4.12	3.97	3.87	3.79	3.73	3.68	3.64	3.51	3.44	3.40	3.38	3.34	3.30	3.27	3.23
	.025	8.07	6.54	5.89	5.52	5.29	5.12	4.99	4.90	4.82	4.76	4.57	4.47	4.40	4.36	4.31	4.25	4.21	4.15
	.01	12.25	9.55	8.45	7.85	7.46	7.19	6.99	6.84	6.72	6.62	6.31	6.16	6.06	5.99	5.91	5.82	5.75	5.66
8	.10	3.46	3.11	2.92	2.81	2.73	2.67	2.62	2.59	2.56	2.54	2.46	2.42	2.40	2.38	2.36	2.34	2.32	2.30
	.05	5.32	4.46	4.07	3.84	3.69	3.58	3.50	3.44	3.39	3.35	3.22	3.15	3.11	3.08	3.04	3.01	2.97	2.93
	.025	7.57	6.06	5.42	5.05	4.82	4.65	4.53	4.43	4.36	4.30	4.10	4.00	3.94	3.89	3.84	3.78	3.74	3.68
	.01	11.26	8.65	7.59	7.01	6.63	6.37	6.18	6.03	5.91	5.81	5.52	5.36	5.26	5.20	5.12	5.03	4.96	4.87
9	.10	3.36	3.01	2.81	2.69	2.61	2.55	2.51	2.47	2.44	2.42	2.34	2.30	2.27	2.25	2.23	2.21	2.19	2.16
	.05	5.12	4.26	3.86	3.63	3.48	3.37	3.29	3.23	3.18	3.14	3.01	2.94	2.89	2.86	2.83	2.79	2.76	2.71
	.025	7.21	5.71	5.08	4.72	4.48	4.32	4.20	4.10	4.03	3.96	3.77	3.67	3.60	3.56	3.51	3.45	3.40	3.34
	.01	10.56	8.02	6.99	6.42	6.06	5.80	5.61	5.47	5.35	5.26	4.96	4.81	4.71	4.65	4.57	4.48	4.41	4.32
10	.10	3.29	2.92	2.73	2.61	2.52	2.46	2.41	2.38	2.35	2.32	2.24	2.20	2.17	2.16	2.13	2.11	2.09	2.06
	.05	4.96	4.10	3.71	3.48	3.33	3.22	3.14	3.07	3.02	2.98	2.85	2.77	2.73	2.70	2.66	2.62	2.59	2.54
	.025	6.94	5.46	4.83	4.47	4.24	4.07	3.95	3.85	3.78	3.72	3.52	3.42	3.35	3.31	3.26	3.20	3.15	3.09
	.01	10.04	7.56	6.55	5.99	5.64	5.39	5.20	5.06	4.94	4.85	4.56	4.41	4.31	4.25	4.17	4.08	4.01	3.92
11	.10	3.23	2.86	2.66	2.54	2.45	2.39	2.34	2.30	2.27	2.25	2.17	2.12	2.10	2.08	2.05	2.03	2.01	1.98
	.05	4.84	3.98	3.59	3.36	3.20	3.09	3.01	2.95	2.90	2.85	2.72	2.65	2.60	2.57	2.53	2.49	2.46	2.41
	.025	6.72	5.26	4.63	4.28	4.04	3.88	3.76	3.66	3.59	3.53	3.33	3.23	3.16	3.12	3.06	3.00	2.96	2.89
	.01	9.65	7.21	6.22	5.67	5.32	5.07	4.89	4.74	4.63	4.54	4.25	4.10	4.01	3.94	3.86	3.78	3.71	3.61
12	.10	3.18	2.81	2.61	2.48	2.39	2.33	2.28	2.24	2.21	2.19	2.10	2.06	2.03	2.01	1.99	1.96	1.94	1.91
	.05	4.75	3.89	3.49	3.26	3.11	3.00	2.91	2.85	2.80	2.75	2.62	2.54	2.50	2.47	2.43	2.38	2.35	2.30
	.025	6.55	5.10	4.47	4.12	3.89	3.73	3.61	3.51	3.44	3.37	3.18	3.07	3.01	2.96	2.91	2.85	2.80	2.73
	.01	9.33	6.93	5.95	5.41	5.06	4.82	4.64	4.50	4.39	4.30	4.01	3.86	3.76	3.70	3.62	3.54	3.47	3.37
13	.10	3.14	2.76	2.56	2.43	2.35	2.28	2.23	2.20	2.16	2.14	2.05	2.01	1.98	1.96	1.93	1.90	1.88	1.85
	.05	4.67	3.81	3.41	3.18	3.03	2.92	2.83	2.77	2.71	2.67	2.53	2.46	2.41	2.38	2.34	2.30	2.26	2.21
	.025	6.41	4.97	4.35	4.00	3.77	3.60	3.48	3.39	3.31	3.25	3.05	2.95	2.88	2.84	2.78	2.72	2.67	2.60
	.01	9.07	6.70	5.74	5.21	4.86	4.62	4.44	4.30	4.19	4.10	3.82	3.66	3.57	3.51	3.43	3.34	3.27	3.18
14	.10	3.10	2.73	2.52	2.39	2.31	2.24	2.19	2.15	2.12	2.10	2.01	1.96	1.93	1.91	1.89	1.86	1.83	1.80
	.05	4.60	3.74	3.34	3.11	2.96	2.85	2.76	2.70	2.65	2.60	2.46	2.39	2.34	2.31	2.27	2.22	2.19	2.14
	.025	6.30	4.86	4.24	3.89	3.66	3.50	3.38	3.29	3.21	3.15	2.95	2.84	2.78	2.73	2.67	2.61	2.56	2.50
	.01	8.86	6.51	5.56	5.04	4.69	4.46	4.28	4.14	4.03	3.94	3.66	3.51	3.41	3.35	3.27	3.18	3.11	3.02
15	.10	3.07	2.70	2.49	2.36	2.27	2.21	2.16	2.12	2.09	2.06	1.97	1.92	1.89	1.87	1.85	1.82	1.79	1.76
	.05	4.54	3.68	3.29	3.06	2.90	2.79	2.71	2.64	2.59	2.54	2.40	2.33	2.28	2.25	2.20	2.16	2.12	2.07
	.025	6.20	4.77	4.15	3.80	3.58	3.41	3.29	3.20	3.12	3.06	2.86	2.76	2.69	2.64	2.59	2.52	2.47	2.40
	.01	8.68	6.36	5.42	4.89	4.56	4.32	4.14	4.00	3.89	3.80	3.52	3.37	3.28	3.21	3.13	3.05	2.98	2.88

Numerator Degrees of Freedom

Denominator Degrees of Freedom	Area in Upper Tail	1	2	3	4	5	6	7	8	9	10	15	20	25	30	40	60	100	1000
16	.10	3.05	2.67	2.46	2.33	2.24	2.18	2.13	2.09	2.06	2.03	1.94	1.89	1.86	1.84	1.81	1.78	1.76	1.72
	.05	4.49	3.63	3.24	3.01	2.85	2.74	2.66	2.59	2.54	2.49	2.35	2.28	2.23	2.19	2.15	2.11	2.07	2.02
	.025	6.12	4.69	4.08	3.73	3.50	3.34	3.22	3.12	3.05	2.99	2.79	2.68	2.61	2.57	2.51	2.45	2.40	2.32
	.01	8.53	6.23	5.29	4.77	4.44	4.20	4.03	3.89	3.78	3.69	3.41	3.26	3.16	3.10	3.02	2.93	2.86	2.76
17	.10	3.03	2.64	2.44	2.31	2.22	2.15	2.10	2.06	2.03	2.00	1.91	1.86	1.83	1.81	1.78	1.75	1.73	1.69
	.05	4.45	3.59	3.20	2.96	2.81	2.70	2.61	2.55	2.49	2.45	2.31	2.23	2.18	2.15	2.10	2.06	2.02	1.97
	.025	6.04	4.62	4.01	3.66	3.44	3.28	3.16	3.06	2.98	2.92	2.72	2.62	2.55	2.50	2.44	2.38	2.33	2.26
	.01	8.40	6.11	5.19	4.67	4.34	4.10	3.93	3.79	3.68	3.59	3.31	3.16	3.07	3.00	2.92	2.83	2.76	2.66
18	.10	3.01	2.62	2.42	2.29	2.20	2.13	2.08	2.04	2.00	1.98	1.89	1.84	1.80	1.78	1.75	1.72	1.70	1.66
	.05	4.41	3.55	3.16	2.93	2.77	2.66	2.58	2.51	2.46	2.41	2.27	2.19	2.14	2.11	2.06	2.02	1.98	1.92
	.025	5.98	4.56	3.95	3.61	3.38	3.22	3.10	3.01	2.93	2.87	2.67	2.56	2.49	2.44	2.38	2.32	2.27	2.20
	.01	8.29	6.01	5.09	4.58	4.25	4.01	3.84	3.71	3.60	3.51	3.23	3.08	2.98	2.92	2.84	2.75	2.68	2.58
19	.10	2.99	2.61	2.40	2.27	2.18	2.11	2.06	2.02	1.98	1.96	1.86	1.81	1.78	1.76	1.73	1.70	1.67	1.64
	.05	4.38	3.52	3.13	2.90	2.74	2.63	2.54	2.48	2.42	2.38	2.23	2.16	2.11	2.07	2.03	1.98	1.94	1.88
	.025	5.92	4.51	3.90	3.56	3.33	3.17	3.05	2.96	2.88	2.82	2.62	2.51	2.44	2.39	2.33	2.27	2.22	2.14
	.01	8.18	5.93	5.01	4.50	4.17	3.94	3.77	3.63	3.52	3.43	3.15	3.00	2.91	2.84	2.76	2.67	2.60	2.50
20	.10	2.97	2.59	2.38	2.25	2.16	2.09	2.04	2.00	1.96	1.94	1.84	1.79	1.76	1.74	1.71	1.68	1.65	1.61
	.05	4.35	3.49	3.10	2.87	2.71	2.60	2.51	2.45	2.39	2.35	2.20	2.12	2.07	2.04	1.99	1.95	1.91	1.85
	.025	5.87	4.46	3.86	3.51	3.29	3.13	3.01	2.91	2.84	2.77	2.57	2.46	2.40	2.35	2.29	2.22	2.17	2.09
	.01	8.10	5.85	4.94	4.43	4.10	3.87	3.70	3.56	3.46	3.37	3.09	2.94	2.84	2.78	2.69	2.61	2.54	2.43
21	.10	2.96	2.57	2.36	2.23	2.14	2.08	2.02	1.98	1.95	1.92	1.83	1.78	1.74	1.72	1.69	1.66	1.63	1.59
	.05	4.32	3.47	3.07	2.84	2.68	2.57	2.49	2.42	2.37	2.32	2.18	2.10	2.05	2.01	1.96	1.92	1.88	1.82
	.025	5.83	4.42	3.82	3.48	3.25	3.09	2.97	2.87	2.80	2.73	2.53	2.42	2.36	2.31	2.25	2.18	2.13	2.05
	.01	8.02	5.78	4.87	4.37	4.04	3.81	3.64	3.51	3.40	3.31	3.03	2.88	2.79	2.72	2.64	2.55	2.48	2.37
22	.10	2.95	2.56	2.35	2.22	2.13	2.06	2.01	1.97	1.93	1.90	1.81	1.76	1.73	1.70	1.67	1.64	1.61	1.57
	.05	4.30	3.44	3.05	2.82	2.66	2.55	2.46	2.40	2.34	2.30	2.15	2.07	2.02	1.98	1.94	1.89	1.85	1.79
	.025	5.79	4.38	3.78	3.44	3.22	3.05	2.93	2.84	2.76	2.70	2.50	2.39	2.32	2.27	2.21	2.14	2.09	2.01
	.01	7.95	5.72	4.82	4.31	3.99	3.76	3.59	3.45	3.35	3.26	2.98	2.83	2.73	2.67	2.58	2.50	2.42	2.32
23	.10	2.94	2.55	2.34	2.21	2.11	2.05	1.99	1.95	1.92	1.89	1.80	1.74	1.71	1.69	1.66	1.62	1.59	1.55
	.05	4.28	3.42	3.03	2.80	2.64	2.53	2.44	2.37	2.32	2.27	2.13	2.05	2.00	1.96	1.91	1.86	1.82	1.76
	.025	5.75	4.35	3.75	3.41	3.18	3.02	2.90	2.81	2.73	2.67	2.47	2.36	2.29	2.24	2.18	2.11	2.06	1.98
	.01	7.88	5.66	4.76	4.26	3.94	3.71	3.54	3.41	3.30	3.21	2.93	2.78	2.69	2.62	2.54	2.45	2.37	2.27
24	.10	2.93	2.54	2.33	2.19	2.10	2.04	1.98	1.94	1.91	1.88	1.78	1.73	1.70	1.67	1.64	1.61	1.58	1.54
	.05	4.26	3.40	3.01	2.78	2.62	2.51	2.42	2.36	2.30	2.25	2.11	2.03	1.97	1.94	1.89	1.84	1.80	1.74
	.025	5.72	4.32	3.72	3.38	3.15	2.99	2.87	2.78	2.70	2.64	2.44	2.33	2.26	2.21	2.15	2.08	2.02	1.94
	.01	7.82	5.61	4.72	4.22	3.90	3.67	3.50	3.36	3.26	3.17	2.89	2.74	2.64	2.58	2.49	2.40	2.33	2.22

TABLE 4 *F* DISTRIBUTION (*Continued*)

Denominator Degrees of Freedom	Area in Upper Tail	Numerator Degrees of Freedom																	
		1	2	3	4	5	6	7	8	9	10	15	20	25	30	40	60	100	1000
25	.10	2.92	2.53	2.32	2.18	2.09	2.02	1.97	1.93	1.89	1.87	1.77	1.72	1.68	1.66	1.63	1.59	1.56	1.52
	.05	4.24	3.39	2.99	2.76	2.60	2.49	2.40	2.34	2.28	2.24	2.09	2.01	1.96	1.92	1.87	1.82	1.78	1.72
	.025	5.69	4.29	3.69	3.35	3.13	2.97	2.85	2.75	2.68	2.61	2.41	2.30	2.23	2.18	2.12	2.05	2.00	1.91
	.01	7.77	5.57	4.68	4.18	3.85	3.63	3.46	3.32	3.22	3.13	2.85	2.70	2.60	2.54	2.45	2.36	2.29	2.18
26	.10	2.91	2.52	2.31	2.17	2.08	2.01	1.96	1.92	1.88	1.86	1.76	1.71	1.67	1.65	1.61	1.58	1.55	1.51
	.05	4.23	3.37	2.98	2.74	2.59	2.47	2.39	2.32	2.27	2.22	2.07	1.99	1.94	1.90	1.85	1.80	1.76	1.70
	.025	5.66	4.27	3.67	3.33	3.10	2.94	2.82	2.73	2.65	2.59	2.39	2.28	2.21	2.16	2.09	2.03	1.97	1.89
	.01	7.72	5.53	4.64	4.14	3.82	3.59	3.42	3.29	3.18	3.09	2.81	2.66	2.57	2.50	2.42	2.33	2.25	2.14
27	.10	2.90	2.51	2.30	2.17	2.07	2.00	1.95	1.91	1.87	1.85	1.75	1.70	1.66	1.64	1.60	1.57	1.54	1.50
	.05	4.21	3.35	2.96	2.73	2.57	2.46	2.37	2.31	2.25	2.20	2.06	1.97	1.92	1.88	1.84	1.79	1.74	1.68
	.025	5.63	4.24	3.65	3.31	3.08	2.92	2.80	2.71	2.63	2.57	2.36	2.25	2.18	2.13	2.07	2.00	1.94	1.86
	.01	7.68	5.49	4.60	4.11	3.78	3.56	3.39	3.26	3.15	3.06	2.78	2.63	2.54	2.47	2.38	2.29	2.22	2.11
28	.10	2.89	2.50	2.29	2.16	2.06	2.00	1.94	1.90	1.87	1.84	1.74	1.69	1.65	1.63	1.59	1.56	1.53	1.48
	.05	4.20	3.34	2.95	2.71	2.56	2.45	2.36	2.29	2.24	2.19	2.04	1.96	1.91	1.87	1.82	1.77	1.73	1.66
	.025	5.61	4.22	3.63	3.29	3.06	2.90	2.78	2.69	2.61	2.55	2.34	2.23	2.16	2.11	2.05	1.98	1.92	1.84
	.01	7.64	5.45	4.57	4.07	3.75	3.53	3.36	3.23	3.12	3.03	2.75	2.60	2.51	2.44	2.35	2.26	2.19	2.08
29	.10	2.89	2.50	2.28	2.15	2.06	1.99	1.93	1.89	1.86	1.83	1.73	1.68	1.64	1.62	1.58	1.55	1.52	1.47
	.05	4.18	3.33	2.93	2.70	2.55	2.43	2.35	2.28	2.22	2.18	2.03	1.94	1.89	1.85	1.81	1.75	1.71	1.65
	.025	5.59	4.20	3.61	3.27	3.04	2.88	2.76	2.67	2.59	2.53	2.32	2.21	2.14	2.09	2.03	1.96	1.90	1.82
	.01	7.60	5.42	4.54	4.04	3.73	3.50	3.33	3.20	3.09	3.00	2.73	2.57	2.48	2.41	2.33	2.23	2.16	2.05
30	.10	2.88	2.49	2.28	2.14	2.05	1.98	1.93	1.88	1.85	1.82	1.72	1.67	1.63	1.61	1.57	1.54	1.51	1.46
	.05	4.17	3.32	2.92	2.69	2.53	2.42	2.33	2.27	2.21	2.16	2.01	1.93	1.88	1.84	1.79	1.74	1.70	1.63
	.025	5.57	4.18	3.59	3.25	3.03	2.87	2.75	2.65	2.57	2.51	2.31	2.20	2.12	2.07	2.01	1.94	1.88	1.80
	.01	7.56	5.39	4.51	4.02	3.70	3.47	3.30	3.17	3.07	2.98	2.70	2.55	2.45	2.39	2.30	2.21	2.13	2.02
40	.10	2.84	2.44	2.23	2.09	2.00	1.93	1.87	1.83	1.79	1.76	1.66	1.61	1.57	1.54	1.51	1.47	1.43	1.38
	.05	4.08	3.23	2.84	2.61	2.45	2.34	2.25	2.18	2.12	2.08	1.92	1.84	1.78	1.74	1.69	1.64	1.59	1.52
	.025	5.42	4.05	3.46	3.13	2.90	2.74	2.62	2.53	2.45	2.39	2.18	2.07	1.99	1.94	1.88	1.80	1.74	1.65
	.01	7.31	5.18	4.31	3.83	3.51	3.29	3.12	2.99	2.89	2.80	2.52	2.37	2.27	2.20	2.11	2.02	1.94	1.82
60	.10	2.79	2.39	2.18	2.04	1.95	1.87	1.82	1.77	1.74	1.71	1.60	1.54	1.50	1.48	1.44	1.40	1.36	1.30
	.05	4.00	3.15	2.76	2.53	2.37	2.25	2.17	2.10	2.04	1.99	1.84	1.75	1.69	1.65	1.59	1.53	1.48	1.40
	.025	5.29	3.93	3.34	3.01	2.79	2.63	2.51	2.41	2.33	2.27	2.06	1.94	1.87	1.82	1.74	1.67	1.60	1.49
	.01	7.08	4.98	4.13	3.65	3.34	3.12	2.95	2.82	2.72	2.63	2.35	2.20	2.10	2.03	1.94	1.84	1.75	1.62
100	.10	2.76	2.36	2.14	2.00	1.91	1.83	1.78	1.73	1.69	1.66	1.56	1.49	1.45	1.42	1.38	1.34	1.29	1.22
	.05	3.94	3.09	2.70	2.46	2.31	2.19	2.10	2.03	1.97	1.93	1.77	1.68	1.62	1.57	1.52	1.45	1.39	1.30
	.025	5.18	3.83	3.25	2.92	2.70	2.54	2.42	2.32	2.24	2.18	1.97	1.85	1.77	1.71	1.64	1.56	1.48	1.36
	.01	6.90	4.82	3.98	3.51	3.21	2.99	2.82	2.69	2.59	2.50	2.22	2.07	1.97	1.89	1.80	1.69	1.60	1.45
1000	.10	2.71	2.31	2.09	1.95	1.85	1.78	1.72	1.68	1.64	1.61	1.49	1.43	1.38	1.35	1.30	1.25	1.20	1.08
	.05	3.85	3.00	2.61	2.38	2.22	2.11	2.02	1.95	1.89	1.84	1.68	1.58	1.52	1.47	1.41	1.33	1.26	1.11
	.025	5.04	3.70	3.13	2.80	2.58	2.42	2.30	2.20	2.13	2.06	1.85	1.72	1.64	1.58	1.50	1.41	1.32	1.13
	.01	6.66	4.63	3.80	3.34	3.04	2.82	2.66	2.53	2.43	2.34	2.06	1.90	1.79	1.72	1.61	1.50	1.38	1.16

TABLE 5   BINOMIAL PROBABILITIES

Entries in the table give the probability of x successes in n trials of a binomial experiment, where p is the probability of a success on one trial. For example, with six trials and $p = .05$, the probability of two successes is .0305.

						p				
n	x	.01	.02	.03	.04	.05	.06	.07	.08	.09
2	0	.9801	.9604	.9409	.9216	.9025	.8836	.8649	.8464	.8281
	1	.0198	.0392	.0582	.0768	.0950	.1128	.1302	.1472	.1638
	2	.0001	.0004	.0009	.0016	.0025	.0036	.0049	.0064	.0081
3	0	.9703	.9412	.9127	.8847	.8574	.8306	.8044	.7787	.7536
	1	.0294	.0576	.0847	.1106	.1354	.1590	.1816	.2031	.2236
	2	.0003	.0012	.0026	.0046	.0071	.0102	.0137	.0177	.0221
	3	.0000	.0000	.0000	.0001	.0001	.0002	.0003	.0005	.0007
4	0	.9606	.9224	.8853	.8493	.8145	.7807	.7481	.7164	.6857
	1	.0388	.0753	.1095	.1416	.1715	.1993	.2252	.2492	.2713
	2	.0006	.0023	.0051	.0088	.0135	.0191	.0254	.0325	.0402
	3	.0000	.0000	.0001	.0002	.0005	.0008	.0013	.0019	.0027
	4	.0000	.0000	.0000	.0000	.0000	.0000	.0000	.0000	.0001
5	0	.9510	.9039	.8587	.8154	.7738	.7339	.6957	.6591	.6240
	1	.0480	.0922	.1328	.1699	.2036	.2342	.2618	.2866	.3086
	2	.0010	.0038	.0082	.0142	.0214	.0299	.0394	.0498	.0610
	3	.0000	.0001	.0003	.0006	.0011	.0019	.0030	.0043	.0060
	4	.0000	.0000	.0000	.0000	.0000	.0001	.0001	.0002	.0003
	5	.0000	.0000	.0000	.0000	.0000	.0000	.0000	.0000	.0000
6	0	.9415	.8858	.8330	.7828	.7351	.6899	.6470	.6064	.5679
	1	.0571	.1085	.1546	.1957	.2321	.2642	.2922	.3164	.3370
	2	.0014	.0055	.0120	.0204	.0305	.0422	.0550	.0688	.0833
	3	.0000	.0002	.0005	.0011	.0021	.0036	.0055	.0080	.0110
	4	.0000	.0000	.0000	.0000	.0001	.0002	.0003	.0005	.0008
	5	.0000	.0000	.0000	.0000	.0000	.0000	.0000	.0000	.0000
	6	.0000	.0000	.0000	.0000	.0000	.0000	.0000	.0000	.0000
7	0	.9321	.8681	.8080	.7514	.6983	.6485	.6017	.5578	.5168
	1	.0659	.1240	.1749	.2192	.2573	.2897	.3170	.3396	.3578
	2	.0020	.0076	.0162	.0274	.0406	.0555	.0716	.0886	.1061
	3	.0000	.0003	.0008	.0019	.0036	.0059	.0090	.0128	.0175
	4	.0000	.0000	.0000	.0001	.0002	.0004	.0007	.0011	.0017
	5	.0000	.0000	.0000	.0000	.0000	.0000	.0000	.0001	.0001
	6	.0000	.0000	.0000	.0000	.0000	.0000	.0000	.0000	.0000
	7	.0000	.0000	.0000	.0000	.0000	.0000	.0000	.0000	.0000
8	0	.9227	.8508	.7837	.7214	.6634	.6096	.5596	.5132	.4703
	1	.0746	.1389	.1939	.2405	.2793	.3113	.3370	.3570	.3721
	2	.0026	.0099	.0210	.0351	.0515	.0695	.0888	.1087	.1288
	3	.0001	.0004	.0013	.0029	.0054	.0089	.0134	.0189	.0255
	4	.0000	.0000	.0001	.0002	.0004	.0007	.0013	.0021	.0031
	5	.0000	.0000	.0000	.0000	.0000	.0000	.0001	.0001	.0002
	6	.0000	.0000	.0000	.0000	.0000	.0000	.0000	.0000	.0000
	7	.0000	.0000	.0000	.0000	.0000	.0000	.0000	.0000	.0000
	8	.0000	.0000	.0000	.0000	.0000	.0000	.0000	.0000	.0000

TABLE 5 BINOMIAL PROBABILITIES (*Continued*)

						p				
n	*x*	.01	.02	.03	.04	.05	.06	.07	.08	.09
9	0	.9135	.8337	.7602	.6925	.6302	.5730	.5204	.4722	.4279
	1	.0830	.1531	.2116	.2597	.2985	.3292	.3525	.3695	.3809
	2	.0034	.0125	.0262	.0433	.0629	.0840	.1061	.1285	.1507
	3	.0001	.0006	.0019	.0042	.0077	.0125	.0186	.0261	.0348
	4	.0000	.0000	.0001	.0003	.0006	.0012	.0021	.0034	.0052
	5	.0000	.0000	.0000	.0000	.0000	.0001	.0002	.0003	.0005
	6	.0000	.0000	.0000	.0000	.0000	.0000	.0000	.0000	.0000
	7	.0000	.0000	.0000	.0000	.0000	.0000	.0000	.0000	.0000
	8	.0000	.0000	.0000	.0000	.0000	.0000	.0000	.0000	.0000
	9	.0000	.0000	.0000	.0000	.0000	.0000	.0000	.0000	.0000
10	0	.9044	.8171	.7374	.6648	.5987	.5386	.4840	.4344	.3894
	1	.0914	.1667	.2281	.2770	.3151	.3438	.3643	.3777	.3851
	2	.0042	.0153	.0317	.0519	.0746	.0988	.1234	.1478	.1714
	3	.0001	.0008	.0026	.0058	.0105	.0168	.0248	.0343	.0452
	4	.0000	.0000	.0001	.0004	.0010	.0019	.0033	.0052	.0078
	5	.0000	.0000	.0000	.0000	.0001	.0001	.0003	.0005	.0009
	6	.0000	.0000	.0000	.0000	.0000	.0000	.0000	.0000	.0001
	7	.0000	.0000	.0000	.0000	.0000	.0000	.0000	.0000	.0000
	8	.0000	.0000	.0000	.0000	.0000	.0000	.0000	.0000	.0000
	9	.0000	.0000	.0000	.0000	.0000	.0000	.0000	.0000	.0000
	10	.0000	.0000	.0000	.0000	.0000	.0000	.0000	.0000	.0000
12	0	.8864	.7847	.6938	.6127	.5404	.4759	.4186	.3677	.3225
	1	.1074	.1922	.2575	.3064	.3413	.3645	.3781	.3837	.3827
	2	.0060	.0216	.0438	.0702	.0988	.1280	.1565	.1835	.2082
	3	.0002	.0015	.0045	.0098	.0173	.0272	.0393	.0532	.0686
	4	.0000	.0001	.0003	.0009	.0021	.0039	.0067	.0104	.0153
	5	.0000	.0000	.0000	.0001	.0002	.0004	.0008	.0014	.0024
	6	.0000	.0000	.0000	.0000	.0000	.0000	.0001	.0001	.0003
	7	.0000	.0000	.0000	.0000	.0000	.0000	.0000	.0000	.0000
	8	.0000	.0000	.0000	.0000	.0000	.0000	.0000	.0000	.0000
	9	.0000	.0000	.0000	.0000	.0000	.0000	.0000	.0000	.0000
	10	.0000	.0000	.0000	.0000	.0000	.0000	.0000	.0000	.0000
	11	.0000	.0000	.0000	.0000	.0000	.0000	.0000	.0000	.0000
	12	.0000	.0000	.0000	.0000	.0000	.0000	.0000	.0000	.0000
15	0	.8601	.7386	.6333	.5421	.4633	.3953	.3367	.2863	.2430
	1	.1303	.2261	.2938	.3388	.3658	.3785	.3801	.3734	.3605
	2	.0092	.0323	.0636	.0988	.1348	.1691	.2003	.2273	.2496
	3	.0004	.0029	.0085	.0178	.0307	.0468	.0653	.0857	.1070
	4	.0000	.0002	.0008	.0022	.0049	.0090	.0148	.0223	.0317
	5	.0000	.0000	.0001	.0002	.0006	.0013	.0024	.0043	.0069
	6	.0000	.0000	.0000	.0000	.0000	.0001	.0003	.0006	.0011
	7	.0000	.0000	.0000	.0000	.0000	.0000	.0000	.0001	.0001
	8	.0000	.0000	.0000	.0000	.0000	.0000	.0000	.0000	.0000
	9	.0000	.0000	.0000	.0000	.0000	.0000	.0000	.0000	.0000
	10	.0000	.0000	.0000	.0000	.0000	.0000	.0000	.0000	.0000
	11	.0000	.0000	.0000	.0000	.0000	.0000	.0000	.0000	.0000
	12	.0000	.0000	.0000	.0000	.0000	.0000	.0000	.0000	.0000
	13	.0000	.0000	.0000	.0000	.0000	.0000	.0000	.0000	.0000
	14	.0000	.0000	.0000	.0000	.0000	.0000	.0000	.0000	.0000
	15	.0000	.0000	.0000	.0000	.0000	.0000	.0000	.0000	.0000

TABLE 5   BINOMIAL PROBABILITIES (*Continued*)

n	x	.01	.02	.03	.04	.05	.06	.07	.08	.09
						p				
18	0	.8345	.6951	.5780	.4796	.3972	.3283	.2708	.2229	.1831
	1	.1517	.2554	.3217	.3597	.3763	.3772	.3669	.3489	.3260
	2	.0130	.0443	.0846	.1274	.1683	.2047	.2348	.2579	.2741
	3	.0007	.0048	.0140	.0283	.0473	.0697	.0942	.1196	.1446
	4	.0000	.0004	.0016	.0044	.0093	.0167	.0266	.0390	.0536
	5	.0000	.0000	.0001	.0005	.0014	.0030	.0056	.0095	.0148
	6	.0000	.0000	.0000	.0000	.0002	.0004	.0009	.0018	.0032
	7	.0000	.0000	.0000	.0000	.0000	.0000	.0001	.0003	.0005
	8	.0000	.0000	.0000	.0000	.0000	.0000	.0000	.0000	.0001
	9	.0000	.0000	.0000	.0000	.0000	.0000	.0000	.0000	.0000
	10	.0000	.0000	.0000	.0000	.0000	.0000	.0000	.0000	.0000
	11	.0000	.0000	.0000	.0000	.0000	.0000	.0000	.0000	.0000
	12	.0000	.0000	.0000	.0000	.0000	.0000	.0000	.0000	.0000
	13	.0000	.0000	.0000	.0000	.0000	.0000	.0000	.0000	.0000
	14	.0000	.0000	.0000	.0000	.0000	.0000	.0000	.0000	.0000
	15	.0000	.0000	.0000	.0000	.0000	.0000	.0000	.0000	.0000
	16	.0000	.0000	.0000	.0000	.0000	.0000	.0000	.0000	.0000
	17	.0000	.0000	.0000	.0000	.0000	.0000	.0000	.0000	.0000
	18	.0000	.0000	.0000	.0000	.0000	.0000	.0000	.0000	.0000
20	0	.8179	.6676	.5438	.4420	.3585	.2901	.2342	.1887	.1516
	1	.1652	.2725	.3364	.3683	.3774	.3703	.3526	.3282	.3000
	2	.0159	.0528	.0988	.1458	.1887	.2246	.2521	.2711	.2818
	3	.0010	.0065	.0183	.0364	.0596	.0860	.1139	.1414	.1672
	4	.0000	.0006	.0024	.0065	.0133	.0233	.0364	.0523	.0703
	5	.0000	.0000	.0002	.0009	.0022	.0048	.0088	.0145	.0222
	6	.0000	.0000	.0000	.0001	.0003	.0008	.0017	.0032	.0055
	7	.0000	.0000	.0000	.0000	.0000	.0001	.0002	.0005	.0011
	8	.0000	.0000	.0000	.0000	.0000	.0000	.0000	.0001	.0002
	9	.0000	.0000	.0000	.0000	.0000	.0000	.0000	.0000	.0000
	10	.0000	.0000	.0000	.0000	.0000	.0000	.0000	.0000	.0000
	11	.0000	.0000	.0000	.0000	.0000	.0000	.0000	.0000	.0000
	12	.0000	.0000	.0000	.0000	.0000	.0000	.0000	.0000	.0000
	13	.0000	.0000	.0000	.0000	.0000	.0000	.0000	.0000	.0000
	14	.0000	.0000	.0000	.0000	.0000	.0000	.0000	.0000	.0000
	15	.0000	.0000	.0000	.0000	.0000	.0000	.0000	.0000	.0000
	16	.0000	.0000	.0000	.0000	.0000	.0000	.0000	.0000	.0000
	17	.0000	.0000	.0000	.0000	.0000	.0000	.0000	.0000	.0000
	18	.0000	.0000	.0000	.0000	.0000	.0000	.0000	.0000	.0000
	19	.0000	.0000	.0000	.0000	.0000	.0000	.0000	.0000	.0000
	20	.0000	.0000	.0000	.0000	.0000	.0000	.0000	.0000	.0000

TABLE 5 BINOMIAL PROBABILITIES (*Continued*)

						p				
n	*x*	.10	.15	.20	.25	.30	.35	.40	.45	.50
2	0	.8100	.7225	.6400	.5625	.4900	.4225	.3600	.3025	.2500
	1	.1800	.2550	.3200	.3750	.4200	.4550	.4800	.4950	.5000
	2	.0100	.0225	.0400	.0625	.0900	.1225	.1600	.2025	.2500
3	0	.7290	.6141	.5120	.4219	.3430	.2746	.2160	.1664	.1250
	1	.2430	.3251	.3840	.4219	.4410	.4436	.4320	.4084	.3750
	2	.0270	.0574	.0960	.1406	.1890	.2389	.2880	.3341	.3750
	3	.0010	.0034	.0080	.0156	.0270	.0429	.0640	.0911	.1250
4	0	.6561	.5220	.4096	.3164	.2401	.1785	.1296	.0915	.0625
	1	.2916	.3685	.4096	.4219	.4116	.3845	.3456	.2995	.2500
	2	.0486	.0975	.1536	.2109	.2646	.3105	.3456	.3675	.3750
	3	.0036	.0115	.0256	.0469	.0756	.1115	.1536	.2005	.2500
	4	.0001	.0005	.0016	.0039	.0081	.0150	.0256	.0410	.0625
5	0	.5905	.4437	.3277	.2373	.1681	.1160	.0778	.0503	.0312
	1	.3280	.3915	.4096	.3955	.3602	.3124	.2592	.2059	.1562
	2	.0729	.1382	.2048	.2637	.3087	.3364	.3456	.3369	.3125
	3	.0081	.0244	.0512	.0879	.1323	.1811	.2304	.2757	.3125
	4	.0004	.0022	.0064	.0146	.0284	.0488	.0768	.1128	.1562
	5	.0000	.0001	.0003	.0010	.0024	.0053	.0102	.0185	.0312
6	0	.5314	.3771	.2621	.1780	.1176	.0754	.0467	.0277	.0156
	1	.3543	.3993	.3932	.3560	.3025	.2437	.1866	.1359	.0938
	2	.0984	.1762	.2458	.2966	.3241	.3280	.3110	.2780	.2344
	3	.0146	.0415	.0819	.1318	.1852	.2355	.2765	.3032	.3125
	4	.0012	.0055	.0154	.0330	.0595	.0951	.1382	.1861	.2344
	5	.0001	.0004	.0015	.0044	.0102	.0205	.0369	.0609	.0938
	6	.0000	.0000	.0001	.0002	.0007	.0018	.0041	.0083	.0156
7	0	.4783	.3206	.2097	.1335	.0824	.0490	.0280	.0152	.0078
	1	.3720	.3960	.3670	.3115	.2471	.1848	.1306	.0872	.0547
	2	.1240	.2097	.2753	.3115	.3177	.2985	.2613	.2140	.1641
	3	.0230	.0617	.1147	.1730	.2269	.2679	.2903	.2918	.2734
	4	.0026	.0109	.0287	.0577	.0972	.1442	.1935	.2388	.2734
	5	.0002	.0012	.0043	.0115	.0250	.0466	.0774	.1172	.1641
	6	.0000	.0001	.0004	.0013	.0036	.0084	.0172	.0320	.0547
	7	.0000	.0000	.0000	.0001	.0002	.0006	.0016	.0037	.0078
8	0	.4305	.2725	.1678	.1001	.0576	.0319	.0168	.0084	.0039
	1	.3826	.3847	.3355	.2670	.1977	.1373	.0896	.0548	.0312
	2	.1488	.2376	.2936	.3115	.2965	.2587	.2090	.1569	.1094
	3	.0331	.0839	.1468	.2076	.2541	.2786	.2787	.2568	.2188
	4	.0046	.0185	.0459	.0865	.1361	.1875	.2322	.2627	.2734
	5	.0004	.0026	.0092	.0231	.0467	.0808	.1239	.1719	.2188
	6	.0000	.0002	.0011	.0038	.0100	.0217	.0413	.0703	.1094
	7	.0000	.0000	.0001	.0004	.0012	.0033	.0079	.0164	.0313
	8	.0000	.0000	.0000	.0000	.0001	.0002	.0007	.0017	.0039

TABLE 5   BINOMIAL PROBABILITIES (*Continued*)

n	x	.10	.15	.20	.25	.30	.35	.40	.45	.50
						p				
9	0	.3874	.2316	.1342	.0751	.0404	.0207	.0101	.0046	.0020
	1	.3874	.3679	.3020	.2253	.1556	.1004	.0605	.0339	.0176
	2	.1722	.2597	.3020	.3003	.2668	.2162	.1612	.1110	.0703
	3	.0446	.1069	.1762	.2336	.2668	.2716	.2508	.2119	.1641
	4	.0074	.0283	.0661	.1168	.1715	.2194	.2508	.2600	.2461
	5	.0008	.0050	.0165	.0389	.0735	.1181	.1672	.2128	.2461
	6	.0001	.0006	.0028	.0087	.0210	.0424	.0743	.1160	.1641
	7	.0000	.0000	.0003	.0012	.0039	.0098	.0212	.0407	.0703
	8	.0000	.0000	.0000	.0001	.0004	.0013	.0035	.0083	.0176
	9	.0000	.0000	.0000	.0000	.0000	.0001	.0003	.0008	.0020
10	0	.3487	.1969	.1074	.0563	.0282	.0135	.0060	.0025	.0010
	1	.3874	.3474	.2684	.1877	.1211	.0725	.0403	.0207	.0098
	2	.1937	.2759	.3020	.2816	.2335	.1757	.1209	.0763	.0439
	3	.0574	.1298	.2013	.2503	.2668	.2522	.2150	.1665	.1172
	4	.0112	.0401	.0881	.1460	.2001	.2377	.2508	.2384	.2051
	5	.0015	.0085	.0264	.0584	.1029	.1536	.2007	.2340	.2461
	6	.0001	.0012	.0055	.0162	.0368	.0689	.1115	.1596	.2051
	7	.0000	.0001	.0008	.0031	.0090	.0212	.0425	.0746	.1172
	8	.0000	.0000	.0001	.0004	.0014	.0043	.0106	.0229	.0439
	9	.0000	.0000	.0000	.0000	.0001	.0005	.0016	.0042	.0098
	10	.0000	.0000	.0000	.0000	.0000	.0000	.0001	.0003	.0010
12	0	.2824	.1422	.0687	.0317	.0138	.0057	.0022	.0008	.0002
	1	.3766	.3012	.2062	.1267	.0712	.0368	.0174	.0075	.0029
	2	.2301	.2924	.2835	.2323	.1678	.1088	.0639	.0339	.0161
	3	.0853	.1720	.2362	.2581	.2397	.1954	.1419	.0923	.0537
	4	.0213	.0683	.1329	.1936	.2311	.2367	.2128	.1700	.1208
	5	.0038	.0193	.0532	.1032	.1585	.2039	.2270	.2225	.1934
	6	.0005	.0040	.0155	.0401	.0792	.1281	.1766	.2124	.2256
	7	.0000	.0006	.0033	.0115	.0291	.0591	.1009	.1489	.1934
	8	.0000	.0001	.0005	.0024	.0078	.0199	.0420	.0762	.1208
	9	.0000	.0000	.0001	.0004	.0015	.0048	.0125	.0277	.0537
	10	.0000	.0000	.0000	.0000	.0002	.0008	.0025	.0068	.0161
	11	.0000	.0000	.0000	.0000	.0000	.0001	.0003	.0010	.0029
	12	.0000	.0000	.0000	.0000	.0000	.0000	.0000	.0001	.0002
15	0	.2059	.0874	.0352	.0134	.0047	.0016	.0005	.0001	.0000
	1	.3432	.2312	.1319	.0668	.0305	.0126	.0047	.0016	.0005
	2	.2669	.2856	.2309	.1559	.0916	.0476	.0219	.0090	.0032
	3	.1285	.2184	.2501	.2252	.1700	.1110	.0634	.0318	.0139
	4	.0428	.1156	.1876	.2252	.2186	.1792	.1268	.0780	.0417
	5	.0105	.0449	.1032	.1651	.2061	.2123	.1859	.1404	.0916
	6	.0019	.0132	.0430	.0917	.1472	.1906	.2066	.1914	.1527
	7	.0003	.0030	.0138	.0393	.0811	.1319	.1771	.2013	.1964
	8	.0000	.0005	.0035	.0131	.0348	.0710	.1181	.1647	.1964
	9	.0000	.0001	.0007	.0034	.0016	.0298	.0612	.1048	.1527
	10	.0000	.0000	.0001	.0007	.0030	.0096	.0245	.0515	.0916
	11	.0000	.0000	.0000	.0001	.0006	.0024	.0074	.0191	.0417
	12	.0000	.0000	.0000	.0000	.0001	.0004	.0016	.0052	.0139
	13	.0000	.0000	.0000	.0000	.0000	.0001	.0003	.0010	.0032
	14	.0000	.0000	.0000	.0000	.0000	.0000	.0000	.0001	.0005
	15	.0000	.0000	.0000	.0000	.0000	.0000	.0000	.0000	.0000

TABLE 5   BINOMIAL PROBABILITIES (*Continued*)

						p				
n	x	.10	.15	.20	.25	.30	.35	.40	.45	.50
18	0	.1501	.0536	.0180	.0056	.0016	.0004	.0001	.0000	.0000
	1	.3002	.1704	.0811	.0338	.0126	.0042	.0012	.0003	.0001
	2	.2835	.2556	.1723	.0958	.0458	.0190	.0069	.0022	.0006
	3	.1680	.2406	.2297	.1704	.1046	.0547	.0246	.0095	.0031
	4	.0700	.1592	.2153	.2130	.1681	.1104	.0614	.0291	.0117
	5	.0218	.0787	.1507	.1988	.2017	.1664	.1146	.0666	.0327
	6	.0052	.0301	.0816	.1436	.1873	.1941	.1655	.1181	.0708
	7	.0010	.0091	.0350	.0820	.1376	.1792	.1892	.1657	.1214
	8	.0002	.0022	.0120	.0376	.0811	.1327	.1734	.1864	.1669
	9	.0000	.0004	.0033	.0139	.0386	.0794	.1284	.1694	.1855
	10	.0000	.0001	.0008	.0042	.0149	.0385	.0771	.1248	.1669
	11	.0000	.0000	.0001	.0010	.0046	.0151	.0374	.0742	.1214
	12	.0000	.0000	.0000	.0002	.0012	.0047	.0145	.0354	.0708
	13	.0000	.0000	.0000	.0000	.0002	.0012	.0045	.0134	.0327
	14	.0000	.0000	.0000	.0000	.0000	.0002	.0011	.0039	.0117
	15	.0000	.0000	.0000	.0000	.0000	.0000	.0002	.0009	.0031
	16	.0000	.0000	.0000	.0000	.0000	.0000	.0000	.0001	.0006
	17	.0000	.0000	.0000	.0000	.0000	.0000	.0000	.0000	.0001
	18	.0000	.0000	.0000	.0000	.0000	.0000	.0000	.0000	.0000
20	0	.1216	.0388	.0115	.0032	.0008	.0002	.0000	.0000	.0000
	1	.2702	.1368	.0576	.0211	.0068	.0020	.0005	.0001	.0000
	2	.2852	.2293	.1369	.0669	.0278	.0100	.0031	.0008	.0002
	3	.1901	.2428	.2054	.1339	.0716	.0323	.0123	.0040	.0011
	4	.0898	.1821	.2182	.1897	.1304	.0738	.0350	.0139	.0046
	5	.0319	.1028	.1746	.2023	.1789	.1272	.0746	.0365	.0148
	6	.0089	.0454	.1091	.1686	.1916	.1712	.1244	.0746	.0370
	7	.0020	.0160	.0545	.1124	.1643	.1844	.1659	.1221	.0739
	8	.0004	.0046	.0222	.0609	.1144	.1614	.1797	.1623	.1201
	9	.0001	.0011	.0074	.0271	.0654	.1158	.1597	.1771	.1602
	10	.0000	.0002	.0020	.0099	.0308	.0686	.1171	.1593	.1762
	11	.0000	.0000	.0005	.0030	.0120	.0336	.0710	.1185	.1602
	12	.0000	.0000	.0001	.0008	.0039	.0136	.0355	.0727	.1201
	13	.0000	.0000	.0000	.0002	.0010	.0045	.0146	.0366	.0739
	14	.0000	.0000	.0000	.0000	.0002	.0012	.0049	.0150	.0370
	15	.0000	.0000	.0000	.0000	.0000	.0003	.0013	.0049	.0148
	16	.0000	.0000	.0000	.0000	.0000	.0000	.0003	.0013	.0046
	17	.0000	.0000	.0000	.0000	.0000	.0000	.0000	.0002	.0011
	18	.0000	.0000	.0000	.0000	.0000	.0000	.0000	.0000	.0002
	19	.0000	.0000	.0000	.0000	.0000	.0000	.0000	.0000	.0000
	20	.0000	.0000	.0000	.0000	.0000	.0000	.0000	.0000	.0000

TABLE 6   VALUES OF $e^{-\mu}$

μ	$e^{-\mu}$	μ	$e^{-\mu}$	μ	$e^{-\mu}$
.00	1.0000	2.00	.1353	4.00	.0183
.05	.9512	2.05	.1287	4.05	.0174
.10	.9048	2.10	.1225	4.10	.0166
.15	.8607	2.15	.1165	4.15	.0158
.20	.8187	2.20	.1108	4.20	.0150
.25	.7788	2.25	.1054	4.25	.0143
.30	.7408	2.30	.1003	4.30	.0136
.35	.7047	2.35	.0954	4.35	.0129
.40	.6703	2.40	.0907	4.40	.0123
.45	.6376	2.45	.0863	4.45	.0117
.50	.6065	2.50	.0821	4.50	.0111
.55	.5769	2.55	.0781	4.55	.0106
.60	.5488	2.60	.0743	4.60	.0101
.65	.5220	2.65	.0707	4.65	.0096
.70	.4966	2.70	.0672	4.70	.0091
.75	.4724	2.75	.0639	4.75	.0087
.80	.4493	2.80	.0608	4.80	.0082
.85	.4274	2.85	.0578	4.85	.0078
.90	.4066	2.90	.0550	4.90	.0074
.95	.3867	2.95	.0523	4.95	.0071
1.00	.3679	3.00	.0498	5.00	.0067
1.05	.3499	3.05	.0474	6.00	.0025
1.10	.3329	3.10	.0450	7.00	.0009
1.15	.3166	3.15	.0429	8.00	.000335
1.20	.3012	3.20	.0408	9.00	.000123
				10.00	.000045
1.25	.2865	3.25	.0388		
1.30	.2725	3.30	.0369		
1.35	.2592	3.35	.0351		
1.40	.2466	3.40	.0334		
1.45	.2346	3.45	.0317		
1.50	.2231	3.50	.0302		
1.55	.2122	3.55	.0287		
1.60	.2019	3.60	.0273		
1.65	.1920	3.65	.0260		
1.70	.1827	3.70	.0247		
1.75	.1738	3.75	.0235		
1.80	.1653	3.80	.0224		
1.85	.1572	3.85	.0213		
1.90	.1496	3.90	.0202		
1.95	.1423	3.95	.0193		

TABLE 7   POISSON PROBABILITIES

Entries in the table give the probability of x occurrences for a Poisson process with a mean μ. For example, when $\mu = 2.5$, the probability of four occurrences is .1336.

					μ					
x	0.1	0.2	0.3	0.4	0.5	0.6	0.7	0.8	0.9	1.0
0	.9048	.8187	.7408	.6703	.6065	.5488	.4966	.4493	.4066	.3679
1	.0905	.1637	.2222	.2681	.3033	.3293	.3476	.3595	.3659	.3679
2	.0045	.0164	.0333	.0536	.0758	.0988	.1217	.1438	.1647	.1839
3	.0002	.0011	.0033	.0072	.0126	.0198	.0284	.0383	.0494	.0613
4	.0000	.0001	.0002	.0007	.0016	.0030	.0050	.0077	.0111	.0153
5	.0000	.0000	.0000	.0001	.0002	.0004	.0007	.0012	.0020	.0031
6	.0000	.0000	.0000	.0000	.0000	.0000	.0001	.0002	.0003	.0005
7	.0000	.0000	.0000	.0000	.0000	.0000	.0000	.0000	.0000	.0001

					μ					
x	1.1	1.2	1.3	1.4	1.5	1.6	1.7	1.8	1.9	2.0
0	.3329	.3012	.2725	.2466	.2231	.2019	.1827	.1653	.1496	.1353
1	.3662	.3614	.3543	.3452	.3347	.3230	.3106	.2975	.2842	.2707
2	.2014	.2169	.2303	.2417	.2510	.2584	.2640	.2678	.2700	.2707
3	.0738	.0867	.0998	.1128	.1255	.1378	.1496	.1607	.1710	.1804
4	.0203	.0260	.0324	.0395	.0471	.0551	.0636	.0723	.0812	.0902
5	.0045	.0062	.0084	.0111	.0141	.0176	.0216	.0260	.0309	.0361
6	.0008	.0012	.0018	.0026	.0035	.0047	.0061	.0078	.0098	.0120
7	.0001	.0002	.0003	.0005	.0008	.0011	.0015	.0020	.0027	.0034
8	.0000	.0000	.0001	.0001	.0001	.0002	.0003	.0005	.0006	.0009
9	.0000	.0000	.0000	.0000	.0000	.0000	.0001	.0001	.0001	.0002

					μ					
x	2.1	2.2	2.3	2.4	2.5	2.6	2.7	2.8	2.9	3.0
0	.1225	.1108	.1003	.0907	.0821	.0743	.0672	.0608	.0550	.0498
1	.2572	.2438	.2306	.2177	.2052	.1931	.1815	.1703	.1596	.1494
2	.2700	.2681	.2652	.2613	.2565	.2510	.2450	.2384	.2314	.2240
3	.1890	.1966	.2033	.2090	.2138	.2176	.2205	.2225	.2237	.2240
4	.0992	.1082	.1169	.1254	.1336	.1414	.1488	.1557	.1622	.1680
5	.0417	.0476	.0538	.0602	.0668	.0735	.0804	.0872	.0940	.1008
6	.0146	.0174	.0206	.0241	.0278	.0319	.0362	.0407	.0455	.0504
7	.0044	.0055	.0068	.0083	.0099	.0118	.0139	.0163	.0188	.0216
8	.0011	.0015	.0019	.0025	.0031	.0038	.0047	.0057	.0068	.0081
9	.0003	.0004	.0005	.0007	.0009	.0011	.0014	.0018	.0022	.0027
10	.0001	.0001	.0001	.0002	.0002	.0003	.0004	.0005	.0006	.0008
11	.0000	.0000	.0000	.0000	.0000	.0001	.0001	.0001	.0002	.0002
12	.0000	.0000	.0000	.0000	.0000	.0000	.0000	.0000	.0000	.0001

TABLE 7   POISSON PROBABILITIES (*Continued*)

x	3.1	3.2	3.3	3.4	3.5	3.6	3.7	3.8	3.9	4.0
0	.0450	.0408	.0369	.0344	.0302	.0273	.0247	.0224	.0202	.0183
1	.1397	.1304	.1217	.1135	.1057	.0984	.0915	.0850	.0789	.0733
2	.2165	.2087	.2008	.1929	.1850	.1771	.1692	.1615	.1539	.1465
3	.2237	.2226	.2209	.2186	.2158	.2125	.2087	.2046	.2001	.1954
4	.1734	.1781	.1823	.1858	.1888	.1912	.1931	.1944	.1951	.1954
5	.1075	.1140	.1203	.1264	.1322	.1377	.1429	.1477	.1522	.1563
6	.0555	.0608	.0662	.0716	.0771	.0826	.0881	.0936	.0989	.1042
7	.0246	.0278	.0312	.0348	.0385	.0425	.0466	.0508	.0551	.0595
8	.0095	.0111	.0129	.0148	.0169	.0191	.0215	.0241	.0269	.0298
9	.0033	.0040	.0047	.0056	.0066	.0076	.0089	.0102	.0116	.0132
10	.0010	.0013	.0016	.0019	.0023	.0028	.0033	.0039	.0045	.0053
11	.0003	.0004	.0005	.0006	.0007	.0009	.0011	.0013	.0016	.0019
12	.0001	.0001	.0001	.0002	.0002	.0003	.0003	.0004	.0005	.0006
13	.0000	.0000	.0000	.0000	.0001	.0001	.0001	.0001	.0002	.0002
14	.0000	.0000	.0000	.0000	.0000	.0000	.0000	.0000	.0000	.0001

x	4.1	4.2	4.3	4.4	4.5	4.6	4.7	4.8	4.9	5.0
0	.0166	.0150	.0136	.0123	.0111	.0101	.0091	.0082	.0074	.0067
1	.0679	.0630	.0583	.0540	.0500	.0462	.0427	.0395	.0365	.0337
2	.1393	.1323	.1254	.1188	.1125	.1063	.1005	.0948	.0894	.0842
3	.1904	.1852	.1798	.1743	.1687	.1631	.1574	.1517	.1460	.1404
4	.1951	.1944	.1933	.1917	.1898	.1875	.1849	.1820	.1789	.1755
5	.1600	.1633	.1662	.1687	.1708	.1725	.1738	.1747	.1753	.1755
6	.1093	.1143	.1191	.1237	.1281	.1323	.1362	.1398	.1432	.1462
7	.0640	.0686	.0732	.0778	.0824	.0869	.0914	.0959	.1002	.1044
8	.0328	.0360	.0393	.0428	.0463	.0500	.0537	.0575	.0614	.0653
9	.0150	.0168	.0188	.0209	.0232	.0255	.0280	.0307	.0334	.0363
10	.0061	.0071	.0081	.0092	.0104	.0118	.0132	.0147	.0164	.0181
11	.0023	.0027	.0032	.0037	.0043	.0049	.0056	.0064	.0073	.0082
12	.0008	.0009	.0011	.0014	.0016	.0019	.0022	.0026	.0030	.0034
13	.0002	.0003	.0004	.0005	.0006	.0007	.0008	.0009	.0011	.0013
14	.0001	.0001	.0001	.0001	.0002	.0002	.0003	.0003	.0004	.0005
15	.0000	.0000	.0000	.0000	.0001	.0001	.0001	.0001	.0001	.0002

x	5.1	5.2	5.3	5.4	5.5	5.6	5.7	5.8	5.9	6.0
0	.0061	.0055	.0050	.0045	.0041	.0037	.0033	.0030	.0027	.0025
1	.0311	.0287	.0265	.0244	.0225	.0207	.0191	.0176	.0162	.0149
2	.0793	.0746	.0701	.0659	.0618	.0580	.0544	.0509	.0477	.0446
3	.1348	.1293	.1239	.1185	.1133	.1082	.1033	.0985	.0938	.0892
4	.1719	.1681	.1641	.1600	.1558	.1515	.1472	.1428	.1383	.1339

TABLE 7   POISSON PROBABILITIES (*Continued*)

x										
5	.1753	.1748	.1740	.1728	.1714	.1697	.1678	.1656	.1632	.1606
6	.1490	.1515	.1537	.1555	.1571	.1587	.1594	.1601	.1605	.1606
7	.1086	.1125	.1163	.1200	.1234	.1267	.1298	.1326	.1353	.1377
8	.0692	.0731	.0771	.0810	.0849	.0887	.0925	.0962	.0998	.1033
9	.0392	.0423	.0454	.0486	.0519	.0552	.0586	.0620	.0654	.0688
10	.0200	.0220	.0241	.0262	.0285	.0309	.0334	.0359	.0386	.0413
11	.0093	.0104	.0116	.0129	.0143	.0157	.0173	.0190	.0207	.0225
12	.0039	.0045	.0051	.0058	.0065	.0073	.0082	.0092	.0102	.0113
13	.0015	.0018	.0021	.0024	.0028	.0032	.0036	.0041	.0046	.0052
14	.0006	.0007	.0008	.0009	.0011	.0013	.0015	.0017	.0019	.0022
15	.0002	.0002	.0003	.0003	.0004	.0005	.0006	.0007	.0008	.0009
16	.0001	.0001	.0001	.0001	.0001	.0002	.0002	.0002	.0003	.0003
17	.0000	.0000	.0000	.0000	.0000	.0001	.0001	.0001	.0001	.0001

					μ					
x	6.1	6.2	6.3	6.4	6.5	6.6	6.7	6.8	6.9	7.0
0	.0022	.0020	.0018	.0017	.0015	.0014	.0012	.0011	.0010	.0009
1	.0137	.0126	.0116	.0106	.0098	.0090	.0082	.0076	.0070	.0064
2	.0417	.0390	.0364	.0340	.0318	.0296	.0276	.0258	.0240	.0223
3	.0848	.0806	.0765	.0726	.0688	.0652	.0617	.0584	.0552	.0521
4	.1294	.1249	.1205	.1162	.1118	.1076	.1034	.0992	.0952	.0912
5	.1579	.1549	.1519	.1487	.1454	.1420	.1385	.1349	.1314	.1277
6	.1605	.1601	.1595	.1586	.1575	.1562	.1546	.1529	.1511	.1490
7	.1399	.1418	.1435	.1450	.1462	.1472	.1480	.1486	.1489	.1490
8	.1066	.1099	.1130	.1160	.1188	.1215	.1240	.1263	.1284	.1304
9	.0723	.0757	.0791	.0825	.0858	.0891	.0923	.0954	.0985	.1014
10	.0441	.0469	.0498	.0528	.0558	.0588	.0618	.0649	.0679	.0710
11	.0245	.0265	.0285	.0307	.0330	.0353	.0377	.0401	.0426	.0452
12	.0124	.0137	.0150	.0164	.0179	.0194	.0210	.0227	.0245	.0264
13	.0058	.0065	.0073	.0081	.0089	.0098	.0108	.0119	.0130	.0142
14	.0025	.0029	.0033	.0037	.0041	.0046	.0052	.0058	.0064	.0071
15	.0010	.0012	.0014	.0016	.0018	.0020	.0023	.0026	.0029	.0033
16	.0004	.0005	.0005	.0006	.0007	.0008	.0010	.0011	.0013	.0014
17	.0001	.0002	.0002	.0002	.0003	.0003	.0004	.0004	.0005	.0006
18	.0000	.0001	.0001	.0001	.0001	.0001	.0001	.0002	.0002	.0002
19	.0000	.0000	.0000	.0000	.0000	.0000	.0000	.0001	.0001	.0001

					μ					
x	7.1	7.2	7.3	7.4	7.5	7.6	7.7	7.8	7.9	8.0
0	.0008	.0007	.0007	.0006	.0006	.0005	.0005	.0004	.0004	.0003
1	.0059	.0054	.0049	.0045	.0041	.0038	.0035	.0032	.0029	.0027
2	.0208	.0194	.0180	.0167	.0156	.0145	.0134	.0125	.0116	.0107
3	.0492	.0464	.0438	.0413	.0389	.0366	.0345	.0324	.0305	.0286
4	.0874	.0836	.0799	.0764	.0729	.0696	.0663	.0632	.0602	.0573

TABLE 7   POISSON PROBABILITIES (*Continued*)

					μ					
x	7.1	7.2	7.3	7.4	7.5	7.6	7.7	7.8	7.9	8.0
5	.1241	.1204	.1167	.1130	.1094	.1057	.1021	.0986	.0951	.0916
6	.1468	.1445	.1420	.1394	.1367	.1339	.1311	.1282	.1252	.1221
7	.1489	.1486	.1481	.1474	.1465	.1454	.1442	.1428	.1413	.1396
8	.1321	.1337	.1351	.1363	.1373	.1382	.1388	.1392	.1395	.1396
9	.1042	.1070	.1096	.1121	.1144	.1167	.1187	.1207	.1224	.1241
10	.0740	.0770	.0800	.0829	.0858	.0887	.0914	.0941	.0967	.0993
11	.0478	.0504	.0531	.0558	.0585	.0613	.0640	.0667	.0695	.0722
12	.0283	.0303	.0323	.0344	.0366	.0388	.0411	.0434	.0457	.0481
13	.0154	.0168	.0181	.0196	.0211	.0227	.0243	.0260	.0278	.0296
14	.0078	.0086	.0095	.0104	.0113	.0123	.0134	.0145	.0157	.0169
15	.0037	.0041	.0046	.0051	.0057	.0062	.0069	.0075	.0083	.0090
16	.0016	.0019	.0021	.0024	.0026	.0030	.0033	.0037	.0041	.0045
17	.0007	.0008	.0009	.0010	.0012	.0013	.0015	.0017	.0019	.0021
18	.0003	.0003	.0004	.0004	.0005	.0006	.0006	.0007	.0008	.0009
19	.0001	.0001	.0001	.0002	.0002	.0002	.0003	.0003	.0003	.0004
20	.0000	.0000	.0001	.0001	.0001	.0001	.0001	.0001	.0001	.0002
21	.0000	.0000	.0000	.0000	.0000	.0000	.0000	.0000	.0001	.0001

					μ					
x	8.1	8.2	8.3	8.4	8.5	8.6	8.7	8.8	8.9	9.0
0	.0003	.0003	.0002	.0002	.0002	.0002	.0002	.0002	.0001	.0001
1	.0025	.0023	.0021	.0019	.0017	.0016	.0014	.0013	.0012	.0011
2	.0100	.0092	.0086	.0079	.0074	.0068	.0063	.0058	.0054	.0050
3	.0269	.0252	.0237	.0222	.0208	.0195	.0183	.0171	.0160	.0150
4	.0544	.0517	.0491	.0466	.0443	.0420	.0398	.0377	.0357	.0337
5	.0882	.0849	.0816	.0784	.0752	.0722	.0692	.0663	.0635	.0607
6	.1191	.1160	.1128	.1097	.1066	.1034	.1003	.0972	.0941	.0911
7	.1378	.1358	.1338	.1317	.1294	.1271	.1247	.1222	.1197	.1171
8	.1395	.1392	.1388	.1382	.1375	.1366	.1356	.1344	.1332	.1318
9	.1256	.1269	.1280	.1290	.1299	.1306	.1311	.1315	.1317	.1318
10	.1017	.1040	.1063	.1084	.1104	.1123	.1140	.1157	.1172	.1186
11	.0749	.0776	.0802	.0828	.0853	.0878	.0902	.0925	.0948	.0970
12	.0505	.0530	.0555	.0579	.0604	.0629	.0654	.0679	.0703	.0728
13	.0315	.0334	.0354	.0374	.0395	.0416	.0438	.0459	.0481	.0504
14	.0182	.0196	.0210	.0225	.0240	.0256	.0272	.0289	.0306	.0324
15	.0098	.0107	.0116	.0126	.0136	.0147	.0158	.0169	.0182	.1094
16	.0050	.0055	.0060	.0066	.0072	.0079	.0086	.0093	.0101	.0109
17	.0024	.0026	.0029	.0033	.0036	.0040	.0044	.0048	.0053	.0058
18	.0011	.0012	.0014	.0015	.0017	.0019	.0021	.0024	.0026	.0029
19	.0005	.0005	.0006	.0007	.0008	.0009	.0010	.0011	.0012	.0014
20	.0002	.0002	.0002	.0003	.0003	.0004	.0004	.0005	.0005	.0006
21	.0001	.0001	.0001	.0001	.0001	.0002	.0002	.0002	.0002	.0003
22	.0000	.0000	.0000	.0000	.0001	.0001	.0001	.0001	.0001	.0001

TABLE 7 POISSON PROBABILITIES (*Continued*)

	μ									
x	9.1	9.2	9.3	9.4	9.5	9.6	9.7	9.8	9.9	10
0	.0001	.0001	.0001	.0001	.0001	.0001	.0001	.0001	.0001	.0000
1	.0010	.0009	.0009	.0008	.0007	.0007	.0006	.0005	.0005	.0005
2	.0046	.0043	.0040	.0037	.0034	.0031	.0029	.0027	.0025	.0023
3	.0140	.0131	.0123	.0115	.0107	.0100	.0093	.0087	.0081	.0076
4	.0319	.0302	.0285	.0269	.0254	.0240	.0226	.0213	.0201	.0189
5	.0581	.0555	.0530	.0506	.0483	.0460	.0439	.0418	.0398	.0378
6	.0881	.0851	.0822	.0793	.0764	.0736	.0709	.0682	.0656	.0631
7	.1145	.1118	.1091	.1064	.1037	.1010	.0982	.0955	.0928	.0901
8	.1302	.1286	.1269	.1251	.1232	.1212	.1191	.1170	.1148	.1126
9	.1317	.1315	.1311	.1306	.1300	.1293	.1284	.1274	.1263	.1251
10	.1198	.1210	.1219	.1228	.1235	.1241	.1245	.1249	.1250	.1251
11	.0991	.1012	.1031	.1049	.1067	.1083	.1098	.1112	.1125	.1137
12	.0752	.0776	.0799	.0822	.0844	.0866	.0888	.0908	.0928	.0948
13	.0526	.0549	.0572	.0594	.0617	.0640	.0662	.0685	.0707	.0729
14	.0342	.0361	.0380	.0399	.0419	.0439	.0459	.0479	.0500	.0521
15	.0208	.0221	.0235	.0250	.0265	.0281	.0297	.0313	.0330	.0347
16	.0118	.0127	.0137	.0147	.0157	.0168	.0180	.0192	.0204	.0217
17	.0063	.0069	.0075	.0081	.0088	.0095	.0103	.0111	.0119	.0128
18	.0032	.0035	.0039	.0042	.0046	.0051	.0055	.0060	.0065	.0071
19	.0015	.0017	.0019	.0021	.0023	.0026	.0028	.0031	.0034	.0037
20	.0007	.0008	.0009	.0010	.0011	.0012	.0014	.0015	.0017	.0019
21	.0003	.0003	.0004	.0004	.0005	.0006	.0006	.0007	.0008	.0009
22	.0001	.0001	.0002	.0002	.0002	.0002	.0003	.0003	.0004	.0004
23	.0000	.0001	.0001	.0001	.0001	.0001	.0001	.0001	.0002	.0002
24	.0000	.0000	.0000	.0000	.0000	.0000	.0000	.0001	.0001	.0001

	μ									
x	11	12	13	14	15	16	17	18	19	20
0	.0000	.0000	.0000	.0000	.0000	.0000	.0000	.0000	.0000	.0000
1	.0002	.0001	.0000	.0000	.0000	.0000	.0000	.0000	.0000	.0000
2	.0010	.0004	.0002	.0001	.0000	.0000	.0000	.0000	.0000	.0000
3	.0037	.0018	.0008	.0004	.0002	.0001	.0000	.0000	.0000	.0000
4	.0102	.0053	.0027	.0013	.0006	.0003	.0001	.0001	.0000	.0000
5	.0224	.0127	.0070	.0037	.0019	.0010	.0005	.0002	.0001	.0001
6	.0411	.0255	.0152	.0087	.0048	.0026	.0014	.0007	.0004	.0002
7	.0646	.0437	.0281	.0174	.0104	.0060	.0034	.0018	.0010	.0005
8	.0888	.0655	.0457	.0304	.0194	.0120	.0072	.0042	.0024	.0013
9	.1085	.0874	.0661	.0473	.0324	.0213	.0135	.0083	.0050	.0029
10	.1194	.1048	.0859	.0663	.0486	.0341	.0230	.0150	.0095	.0058
11	.1194	.1144	.1015	.0844	.0663	.0496	.0355	.0245	.0164	.0106
12	.1094	.1144	.1099	.0984	.0829	.0661	.0504	.0368	.0259	.0176
13	.0926	.1056	.1099	.1060	.0956	.0814	.0658	.0509	.0378	.0271
14	.0728	.0905	.1021	.1060	.1024	.0930	.0800	.0655	.0514	.0387

TABLE 7   POISSON PROBABILITIES (*Continued*)

					μ					
x	11	12	13	14	15	16	17	18	19	20
15	.0534	.0724	.0885	.0989	.1024	.0992	.0906	.0786	.0650	.0516
16	.0367	.0543	.0719	.0866	.0960	.0992	.0963	.0884	.0772	.0646
17	.0237	.0383	.0550	.0713	.0847	.0934	.0963	.0936	.0863	.0760
18	.0145	.0256	.0397	.0554	.0706	.0830	.0909	.0936	.0911	.0844
19	.0084	.0161	.0272	.0409	.0557	.0699	.0814	.0887	.0911	.0888
20	.0046	.0097	.0177	.0286	.0418	.0559	.0692	.0798	.0866	.0888
21	.0024	.0055	.0109	.0191	.0299	.0426	.0560	.0684	.0783	.0846
22	.0012	.0030	.0065	.0121	.0204	.0310	.0433	.0560	.0676	.0769
23	.0006	.0016	.0037	.0074	.0133	.0216	.0320	.0438	.0559	.0669
24	.0003	.0008	.0020	.0043	.0083	.0144	.0226	.0328	.0442	.0557
25	.0001	.0004	.0010	.0024	.0050	.0092	.0154	.0237	.0336	.0446
26	.0000	.0002	.0005	.0013	.0029	.0057	.0101	.0164	.0246	.0343
27	.0000	.0001	.0002	.0007	.0016	.0034	.0063	.0109	.0173	.0254
28	.0000	.0000	.0001	.0003	.0009	.0019	.0038	.0070	.0117	.0181
29	.0000	.0000	.0001	.0002	.0004	.0011	.0023	.0044	.0077	.0125
30	.0000	.0000	.0000	.0001	.0002	.0006	.0013	.0026	.0049	.0083
31	.0000	.0000	.0000	.0000	.0001	.0003	.0007	.0015	.0030	.0054
32	.0000	.0000	.0000	.0000	.0001	.0001	.0004	.0009	.0018	.0034
33	.0000	.0000	.0000	.0000	.0000	.0001	.0002	.0005	.0010	.0020
34	.0000	.0000	.0000	.0000	.0000	.0000	.0001	.0002	.0006	.0012
35	.0000	.0000	.0000	.0000	.0000	.0000	.0000	.0001	.0003	.0007
36	.0000	.0000	.0000	.0000	.0000	.0000	.0000	.0001	.0002	.0004
37	.0000	.0000	.0000	.0000	.0000	.0000	.0000	.0000	.0001	.0002
38	.0000	.0000	.0000	.0000	.0000	.0000	.0000	.0000	.0000	.0001
39	.0000	.0000	.0000	.0000	.0000	.0000	.0000	.0000	.0000	.0001

Summations

Definition

$$\sum_{i=1}^{n} x_i = x_1 + x_2 + \cdots + x_n \tag{C.1}$$

Example for $x_1 = 5, x_2 = 8, x_3 = 14$:

$$\sum_{i=1}^{3} x_i = x_1 + x_2 + x_3$$
$$= 5 + 8 + 14$$
$$= 27$$

Result 1

For a constant c:

$$\sum_{i=1}^{n} c = \underbrace{(c + c + \cdots + c)}_{n \text{ times}} = nc \tag{C.2}$$

Example for $c = 5, n = 10$:

$$\sum_{i=1}^{10} 5 = 10(5) = 50$$

Example for $c = \bar{x}$:

$$\sum_{i=1}^{n} \bar{x} = n\bar{x}$$

Result 2

$$\sum_{i=1}^{n} cx_i = cx_1 + cx_2 + \cdots + cx_n$$
$$= c(x_1 + x_2 + \cdots + x_n) = c\sum_{i=1}^{n} x_i \tag{C.3}$$

Example for $x_1 = 5, x_2 = 8, x_3 = 14, c = 2$:

$$\sum_{i=1}^{3} 2x_i = 2\sum_{i=1}^{3} x_i = 2(27) = 54$$

Result 3

$$\sum_{i=1}^{n} (ax_i + by_i) = a\sum_{i=1}^{n} x_i + b\sum_{i=1}^{n} y_i \tag{C.4}$$

Example for $x_1 = 5$, $x_2 = 8$, $x_3 = 14$, $a = 2$, $y_1 = 7$, $y_2 = 3$, $y_3 = 8$, $b = 4$:

$$\sum_{i=1}^{3}(2x_i + 4y_i) = 2\sum_{i=1}^{3}x_i + 4\sum_{i=1}^{3}y_i$$
$$= 2(27) + 4(18)$$
$$= 54 + 72$$
$$= 126$$

Double Summations

Consider the following data involving the variable x_{ij}, where i is the subscript denoting the row position and j is the subscript denoting the column position:

		Column		
		1	**2**	**3**
Row	**1**	$x_{11} = 10$	$x_{12} = 8$	$x_{13} = 6$
	2	$x_{21} = 7$	$x_{22} = 4$	$x_{23} = 12$

Definition

$$\sum_{i=1}^{n}\sum_{j=1}^{m}x_{ij} = (x_{11} + x_{12} + \cdots + x_{1m}) + (x_{21} + x_{22} + \cdots + x_{2m})$$
$$+ (x_{31} + x_{32} + \cdots + x_{3m}) + \cdots + (x_{n1} + x_{n2} + \cdots + x_{nm}) \qquad \textbf{(C.5)}$$

Example:

$$\sum_{i=1}^{2}\sum_{j=1}^{3}x_{ij} = x_{11} + x_{12} + x_{13} + x_{21} + x_{22} + x_{23}$$
$$= 10 + 8 + 6 + 7 + 4 + 12$$
$$= 47$$

Definition

$$\sum_{i=1}^{n}x_{ij} = x_{1j} + x_{2j} + \cdots + x_{nj} \qquad \textbf{(C.6)}$$

Example:

$$\sum_{i=1}^{2}x_{i2} = x_{12} + x_{22}$$
$$= 8 + 4$$
$$= 12$$

Shorthand Notation

Sometimes when a summation is for all values of the subscript, we use the following shorthand notations:

$$\sum_{i=1}^{n}x_i = \sum_i x_i \qquad \textbf{(C.7)}$$

$$\sum_{i=1}^{n}\sum_{j=1}^{m}x_{ij} = \sum\sum x_{ij} \qquad \textbf{(C.8)}$$

$$\sum_{i=1}^{n}x_{ij} = \sum_i x_{ij} \qquad \textbf{(C.9)}$$

Chapter 1

2. a. 9

  b. 4

  c. Qualitative: country and room rate
    Quantitative: number of rooms and overall score

  d. Country is nominal; room rate is ordinal; number of rooms is ratio; overall score is interval

3. a. Average number of rooms = 808/9 = 89.78, or approximately 90 rooms

  b. Average overall score = 732.1/9 = 81.3

  c. 2 of 9 are located in England; approximately 22%

  d. 4 of 9 have a room rate of $$; approximately 44%

4. a. 10

  b. All brands of minisystems manufactured

  c. $314

  d. $314

6. Questions a, c, and d provide quantitative data
Questions b and e provide qualitative data

8. a. 1005

  b. Qualitative

  c. Percentages

  d. Approximately 291

10. a. Quantitative; ratio

  b. Qualitative; nominal

  c. Qualitative; ordinal

  d. Quantitative; ratio

  e. Qualitative; nominal

12. a. All visitors to Hawaii

  b. Yes

  c. First and fourth questions provide quantitative data
Second and third questions provide qualitative data

13. a. Quantitative

  b. Time series with 6 observations

  c. Earnings for Volkswagen

  d. An increase would be expected in 2003, but it appears that the rate of increase is slowing

14. a. Qualitative

16. a. Product taste tests and test marketing

  b. Specially designed statistical studies

18. a. 36%

  b. 189

  c. Qualitative

20. a. 43% of managers were bullish or very bullish, and 21% of managers expected health care to be the leading industry over the next 12 months.

  b. The average 12-month return estimate is 11.2% for the population of investment managers.

  c. The sample average of 2.5 years is an estimate of how long the population of investment managers think it will take to resume sustainable growth.

22. a. All registered voters in California

  b. Registered voters contacted by the Policy Institute

  c. Too time consuming and costly to reach the entire population

24. a. Correct

  b. Incorrect

  c. Correct

  d. Incorrect

  e. Incorrect

Chapter 2

2. a. .20

  b. 40

  c/d.

Class	Frequency	Percent Frequency
A	44	22
B	36	18
C	80	40
D	40	20
Total	200	100

3. a. $360° \times 58/120 = 174°$

  b. $360° \times 42/120 = 126°$

  c.

  d.

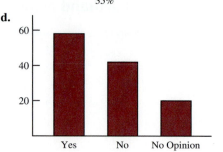

4. a. Qualitative

b.

TV Show	Frequency	Percent Frequency
CSI	18	36
ER	11	22
Friends	15	30
Raymond	6	12
Total	50	100

d. CSI had the largest; Friends was second

6. a.

Book	Frequency	Percent Frequency
7 Habits	10	16.66
Millionaire	16	26.67
Motley	9	15.00
Dad	13	21.67
WSJ Guide	6	10.00
Other	6	10.00
Total	60	100.00

b. First 5: *Millionaire, Dad, 7 Habits, Motley, WSJ Guide*
c. 48.33%

7.

Rating	Frequency	Relative Frequency
Outstanding	19	.38
Very good	13	.26
Good	10	.20
Average	6	.12
Poor	2	.04

Management should be pleased with these results: 64% of the ratings are very good to outstanding, and 84% of the ratings are good or better; comparing these ratings to previous results will show whether the restaurant is making improvements in its customers' ratings of food quality

8. a.

Position	Frequency	Relative Frequency
P	17	.309
H	4	.073
1	5	.091
2	4	.073
3	2	.036
S	5	.091
L	6	.109
C	5	.091
R	7	.127
Totals	55	1.000

b. Pitcher
c. 3rd base

d. Right field
e. Infielders 16 to outfielders 18

10. a. The data are ordinal; they simply provide quality classifications.

b.

Response	Frequency	Relative Frequency
3	2	.03
4	4	.07
5	12	.20
6	24	.40
7	18	.30
Totals	60	1.00

12.

Class	Cumulative Frequency	Cumulative Relative Frequency
≤19	10	.20
≤29	24	.48
≤39	41	.82
≤49	48	.96
≤59	50	1.00

14. b/c.

Class	Frequency	Percent Frequency
6.0–7.9	4	20
8.0–9.9	2	10
10.0–11.9	8	40
12.0–13.9	3	15
14.0–15.9	3	15
Totals	20	100

15. a/b.

Waiting Time	Frequency	Relative Frequency
0–4	4	.20
5–9	8	.40
10–14	5	.25
15–19	2	.10
20–24	1	.05
Totals	20	1.00

c/d.

Waiting Time	Cumulative Frequency	Cumulative Relative Frequency
≤4	4	.20
≤9	12	.60
≤14	17	.85
≤19	19	.95
≤24	20	1.00

e. 12/20 = .60

16. a. Adjusted Gross Income

Histogram is skewed to the right

b. Exam Scores

Histogram is skewed to the left

c.

Histogram skewed slightly to the left, but roughly symmetric

18. a. Lowest salary: $93,000
     Highest salary: $178,000

b.

Salary ($1000s)	Frequency	Relative Frequency	Percent Frequency
91–105	4	0.08	8
106–120	5	0.10	10
121–135	11	0.22	22
136–150	18	0.36	36
151–165	9	0.18	18
166–180	3	0.06	6
Total	50	1.00	100

c. 20/50
d. 24%

20. a.

Price	Frequency	Percent Frequency
30–39.99	7	35
40–49.99	5	25
50–59.99	2	10
60–69.99	3	15
70–79.99	3	15
Total	20	100

c. Fleetwood Mac, Harper/Johnson

22.
```
5 | 7  8
6 | 4  5  8
7 | 0  2  2  5  5  6  8
8 | 0  2  3  5
```

23. Leaf unit = .1
```
 6 | 3
 7 | 5  5  7
 8 | 1  3  4  8
 9 | 3  6
10 | 0  4  5
11 | 3
```

24. Leaf unit = 10
```
11 | 6
12 | 0  2
13 | 0  6  7
14 | 2  2  7
15 | 5
16 | 0  2  8
17 | 0  2  3
```

25.

```
 9 | 8  9
10 | 2  4  6  6
11 | 4  5  7  8  8  9
12 | 2  4  5  7
13 | 1  2
14 | 4
15 | 1
```

26. a.

```
1 | 0  3  7  7
2 | 4  5  5
3 | 0  0  5  5  9
4 | 0  0  0  5  5  8
5 | 0  0  0  4  5  5
```

b.

```
0 | 5  7
1 | 0  1  1  3  4
1 | 5  5  5  8
2 | 0  0  0  0  0  0
2 | 5  5
3 | 0  0  0
3 | 6
4 |
4 |
5 |
5 |
6 | 3
```

28. a.

```
2 | 14
2 | 67
3 | 011123
3 | 5677
4 | 003333344
4 | 6679
5 | 00022
5 | 5679
6 | 14
6 | 6
7 | 2
```

b. 40–44 with 9

c. 43 with 5

d. 10%; relative small participation in the race

29. a.

	y		
	1	**2**	**Total**
A	5	0	5
B	11	2	13
C	2	10	12
Total	18	12	30

x labels rows A, B, C.

b.

	y		
	1	**2**	**Total**
A	100.0	0.0	100.0
B	84.6	15.4	100.0
C	16.7	83.3	100.0

x labels rows A, B, C.

c.

	y	
	1	**2**
A	27.8	0.0
B	61.1	16.7
C	11.1	83.3
Total	100.0	100.0

x labels rows A, B, C.

d. *A* values are always in $y = 1$
   B values are most often in $y = 1$
   C values are most often in $y = 2$

30. a.

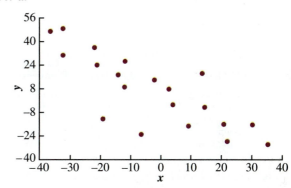

b. A negative relationship between *x* and *y*; *y* decreases as *x* increases

32. a.

Education Level	Household Income ($1000s)					
	Under 25	**25.0– 49.9**	**50.0– 74.9**	**75.0– 99.9**	**100 or more**	**Total**
Not H.S. Graduate	32.70	14.82	8.27	5.02	2.53	15.86
H.S. Graduate	35.74	35.56	31.48	25.39	14.47	30.78
Some College	21.17	29.77	30.25	29.82	22.26	26.37
Bachelor's Degree	7.53	14.43	20.56	25.03	33.88	17.52
Beyond Bach. Deg.	2.86	5.42	9.44	14.74	26.86	9.48
Total	100.00	100.00	100.00	100.00	100.00	100.00

15.86% of the heads of households did not graduate from high school

b. 26.86%, 39.72%

34. a.

Sales/ Margins/ ROE	EPS Rating					
	0– 19	**20– 39**	**40– 59**	**60– 79**	**80– 100**	**Total**
A				1	8	9
B		1	4	5	2	12
C	1		1	2	3	7
D	3	1		1		5
E		2	1			3
Total	4	4	6	9	13	36

b.

Sales/ Margins/ ROE	EPS Rating 0– 19	20– 39	40– 59	60– 79	80– 100	Total
A				11.11	88.89	100
B		8.33	33.33	41.67	16.67	100
C	14.29		14.29	28.57	42.86	100
D	60.00	20.00		20.00		100
E		66.67	33.33			100

Higher EPS ratings seem to be associated with higher ratings on Sales/Margins/ROE

36. b. No apparent relationship

38. a.

Vehicle	Frequency	Percent Frequency
Accord	6	12
Camry	7	14
F-Series	14	28
Ram	10	20
Silverado	13	26

b. Ford F-Series and the Toyota Camry

40. a.

Response	Frequency	Percent Frequency
Accuracy	16	16
Approach shots	3	3
Mental approach	17	17
Power	8	8
Practice	15	15
Putting	10	10
Short game	24	24
Strategic decisions	7	7
Total	100	100

b. Poor short game, poor mental approach, lack of accuracy, and limited practice

42. a/b.

Closing Price	Freq.	Rel. Freq.	Cum. Freq.	Cum. Rel. Freq.
0–9.99	9	.225	9	.225
10–19.99	10	.250	19	.475
20–29.99	5	.125	24	.600
30–39.99	11	.275	35	.875
40–49.99	2	.050	37	.925
50–59.99	2	.050	39	.975
60–69.99	0	.000	39	.975
70–79.99	1	.025	40	1.000
Total	40	1.000		

44.

Income ($)	Frequency	Relative Frequency
18,000–21,999	13	0.255
22,000–25,999	20	0.392
26,000–29,999	12	0.235
30,000–33,999	4	0.078
34,000–37,999	2	0.039
Total	51	1.000

46. a. High Temperature

```
3 |
4 |
5 | 7
6 | 1  4  4  4  4  6  8
7 | 3  5  7  9
8 | 0  1  1  4  6
9 | 0  2  3
```

b. Low Temperature

```
3 | 9
4 | 3  6  8
5 | 0  0  0  2  4  4  5  5  7  9
6 | 1  8
7 | 2  4  5  5
8 |
9 |
```

c. The range of low temperatures is below the range of high temperatures

d. 8 cities

e.

Temperature	Frequency High Temp.	Low Temp.
30–39	0	1
40–49	0	3
50–59	1	10
60–69	7	2
70–79	4	4
80–89	5	0
90–99	3	0
Total	20	20

48. a.

Occupation	Satisfaction Score 30– 39	40– 49	50– 59	60– 69	70– 79	80– 89	Total
Cabinetmaker			2	4	3	1	10
Lawyer	1	5	2	1	1		10
Physical Therapist			5	2	1	2	10
Systems Analyst		2	1	4	3		10
Total	1	7	10	11	8	3	40

b.

Occupation	Satisfaction Score 30–39	40–49	50–59	60–69	70–79	80–89	Total
Cabinetmaker			20	40	30	10	100
Lawyer	10	50	20	10	10		100
Physical Therapist				50	20	10	20	100
Systems Analyst			20	10	40	30	100

c. Cabinetmakers seem to have the highest job satisfaction scores; lawyers seem to have the lowest

50. a. Row totals: 247; 54; 82; 121
Column totals: 149; 317; 17; 7; 14

b.

Year	Freq.	Fuel	Freq.
1973 or before	247	Elect.	149
1974–79	54	Nat. Gas	317
1980–86	82	Oil	17
1987–91	121	Propane	7
Total	504	Other	14
		Total	504

c. Crosstabulation of column percentages

Year Constructed	Fuel Type Elect.	Nat. Gas	Oil	Propane	Other
1973 or before	26.9	57.7	70.5	71.4	50.0
1974–1979	16.1	8.2	11.8	28.6	0.0
1980–1986	24.8	12.0	5.9	0.0	42.9
1987–1991	32.2	22.1	11.8	0.0	7.1
Total	100.0	100.0	100.0	100.0	100.0

d. Crosstabulation of row percentages.

Year Constructed	Fuel Type Elect.	Nat. Gas	Oil	Propane	Other	Total
1973 or before	16.2	74.1	4.9	2.0	2.8	100.0
1974–1979	44.5	48.1	3.7	3.7	0.0	100.0
1980–1986	45.1	46.4	1.2	0.0	7.3	100.0
1987–1991	39.7	57.8	1.7	0.0	0.8	100.0

52. a. Crosstabulation of market value and profit

Market Value ($1000s)	Profit ($1000s) 0–300	300–600	600–900	900–1200	Total
0–8000	23	4			27
8000–16,000	4	4	2	2	12
16,000–24,000		2	1	1	4
24,000–32,000		1	2	1	4
32,000–40,000		2	1		3
Total	27	13	6	4	50

b. Crosstabulation of row percentages

Market Value ($1000s)	Profit ($1000s) 0–300	300–600	600–900	900–1200	Total
0–8000	85.19	14.81	0.00	0.00	100
8000–16,000	33.33	33.33	16.67	16.67	100
16,000–24,000	0.00	50.00	25.00	25.00	100
24,000–32,000	0.00	25.00	50.00	25.00	100
32,000–40,000	0.00	66.67	33.33	0.00	100

c. A positive relationship is indicated between profit and market value; as profit goes up, market value goes up

54. b. A positive relationship is demonstrated between market value and stockholders' equity

Chapter 3

2. 16, 16.5

3. Arrange data in order: 15, 20, 25, 25, 27, 28, 30, 34

$i = \dfrac{20}{100}(8) = 1.6$; round up to position 2

20th percentile $= 20$

$i = \dfrac{25}{100}(8) = 2$; use positions 2 and 3

25th percentile $= \dfrac{20 + 25}{2} = 22.5$

$i = \dfrac{65}{100}(8) = 5.2$; round up to position 6

65th percentile $= 28$

$i = \dfrac{75}{100}(8) = 6$; use positions 6 and 7

75th percentile $= \dfrac{28 + 30}{2} = 29$

4. 59.727, 57, 53

6. a. 422
b. 380
c. 690
d. Not using capacity

8. a. $\bar{x} = \dfrac{\Sigma x_i}{n} = \dfrac{695}{20} = 34.75$

Mode $= 25$ (appears three times)

b. Data in order: 18, 20, 25, 25, 25, 26, 27, 27, 28, 33, 36, 37, 40, 40, 42, 45, 46, 48, 53, 54

Median (10th and 11th positions)

$\dfrac{33 + 36}{2} = 34.5$

At-home workers are slightly younger

c. $i = \dfrac{25}{100}(20) = 5$; use positions 5 and 6

$Q_1 = \dfrac{25 + 26}{2} = 25.5$

$i = \dfrac{75}{100}(20) = 15$; use positions 15 and 16

$Q_3 = \dfrac{42 + 45}{2} = 43.5$

d. $i = \dfrac{32}{100}(20) = 6.4$; round up to position 7

32nd percentile $= 27$

At least 32% of the people are 27 or younger

10. a. 76, 76

   b. 39, 37.5

   c. Yes; emergency wait too long

12. a. $639

   b. 98.8 pictures

   c. 110.2 minutes

14. 16, 4

15. Range $= 34 - 15 = 19$

Arrange data in order: 15, 20, 25, 25, 27, 28, 30, 34

$i = \dfrac{25}{100}(8) = 2; \; Q_1 = \dfrac{20 + 25}{2} = 22.5$

$i = \dfrac{75}{100}(8) = 6; \; Q_3 = \dfrac{28 + 30}{2} = 29$

$\text{IQR} = Q_3 - Q_1 = 29 - 22.5 = 6.5$

$\bar{x} = \dfrac{\Sigma x_i}{n} = \dfrac{204}{8} = 25.5$

x_i	$(x_i - \bar{x})$	$(x_i - \bar{x})^2$
27	1.5	2.25
25	−.5	.25
20	−5.5	30.25
15	−10.5	110.25
30	4.5	20.25
34	8.5	72.25
28	2.5	6.25
25	−.5	.25
		242.00

$s^2 = \dfrac{\Sigma(x_i - \bar{x})^2}{n - 1} = \dfrac{242}{8 - 1} = 34.57$

$s = \sqrt{34.57} = 5.88$

16. a. Range $= 190 - 168 = 22$

   b. $\bar{x} = \dfrac{\Sigma x_i}{n} = \dfrac{1068}{6} = 178$

$s^2 = \dfrac{\Sigma(x_i - \bar{x})^2}{n - 1}$

$= \dfrac{4^2 + (-10)^2 + 6^2 + 12^2 + (-8)^2 + (-4)^2}{6 - 1}$

$= \dfrac{376}{5} = 75.2$

   c. $s = \sqrt{75.2} = 8.67$

   d. $\dfrac{s}{\bar{x}}(100) = \dfrac{8.67}{178}(100\%) = 4.87\%$

18. a. 38, 97, 9.85

   b. Eastern shows more variation

20. *Dawson:* range $= 2$, $s = .67$

   Clark: range $= 8$, $s = 2.58$

22. a. 45.05, 23.98; 57.50, 11.475

   b. 190.67, 13.81; 140.63, 11.86

   c. 38.02%; 57.97%

   d. Greater for broker-assisted trades

24. *Quarter-milers:* $s = .0564$, Coef. of Var. $= 5.8\%$

   Milers: $s = .1295$, Coef. of Var. $= 2.9\%$

26. .20, 1.50, 0, $-.50$, -2.20

27. Chebyshev's theorem: *at least* $(1 - 1/z^2)$

   a. $z = \dfrac{40 - 30}{5} = 2; \; 1 - \dfrac{1}{(2)^2} = .75$

   b. $z = \dfrac{45 - 30}{5} = 3; \; 1 - \dfrac{1}{(3)^2} = .89$

   c. $z = \dfrac{38 - 30}{5} = 1.6; \; 1 - \dfrac{1}{(1.6)^2} = .61$

   d. $z = \dfrac{42 - 30}{5} = 2.4; \; 1 - \dfrac{1}{(2.4)^2} = .83$

   e. $z = \dfrac{48 - 30}{5} = 3.6; \; 1 - \dfrac{1}{(3.6)^2} = .92$

28. a. 95%

   b. Almost all

   c. 68%

29. a. $z = 2$ standard deviations

$1 - \dfrac{1}{z^2} = 1 - \dfrac{1}{2^2} = \dfrac{3}{4}$; at least 75%

   b. $z = 2.5$ standard deviations

$1 - \dfrac{1}{z^2} = 1 - \dfrac{1}{2.5^2} = .84$; at least 84%

   c. $z = 2$ standard deviations

Empirical rule: 95%

30. a. 68%

   b. 81.5%

   c. 2.5%

32. a. $-.67$

   b. 1.50

   c. Neither an outlier

   d. Yes; $z = 8.25$

34. a. 76.5, 7

   b. 16%, 2.5%

   c. 12.2, 7.89; no

36. 15, 22.5, 26, 29, 34

38. Arrange data in order: 5, 6, 8, 10, 10, 12, 15, 16, 18

$i = \dfrac{25}{100}(9) = 2.25$; round up to position 3

$Q_1 = 8$

Median (5th position) $= 10$

$i = \dfrac{75}{100}(9) = 6.75$; round up to position 7

$Q_3 = 15$

5-number summary: 5, 8, 10, 15, 18

40. a. 619, 725, 1016, 1699, 4450
   b. Limits: 0, 3160
   c. Yes
   d. No

41. a. Arrange data in order low to high

$i = \dfrac{25}{100}(21) = 5.25$; round up to 6th position

$Q_1 = 1872$
Median (11th position) = 4019

$i = \dfrac{75}{100}(21) = 15.75$; round up to 16th position

$Q_3 = 8305$
5-number summary: 608, 1872, 4019, 8305, 14138
   b. IQR $= Q_3 - Q_1 = 8305 - 1872 = 6433$
Lower limit: $1872 - 1.5(6433) = -7777$
Upper limit: $8305 + 1.5(6433) = 17{,}955$
   c. No; data are within limits
   d. $41{,}138 > 27{,}604$; 41,138 would be an outlier; data value would be reviewed and corrected
   e.

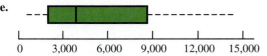

42. a. 61
   b. 34, 45, 61, 90, 126
   c. No; upper limit = 157.5

44. a. 18.2, 15.35
   b. 11.7, 23.5
   c. 3.4, 11.7, 15.35, 23.5, 41.3
   d. Yes; Alger Small Cap 41.3

45. b. There appears to be a negative linear relationship between x and y
   c.

x_i	y_i	$x_i - \bar{x}$	$y_i - \bar{y}$	$(x_i - \bar{x})(y_i - \bar{y})$
4	50	−4	4	−16
6	50	−2	4	−8
11	40	3	−6	−18
3	60	−5	14	−70
16	30	8	−16	−128
40	230	0	0	−240

$\bar{x} = 8$; $\bar{y} = 46$

$s_{xy} = \dfrac{\Sigma(x_i - \bar{x})(y_i - \bar{y})}{n - 1} = \dfrac{-240}{4} = -60$

The sample covariance indicates a negative linear association between x and y

d. $r_{xy} = \dfrac{s_{xy}}{s_x s_y} = \dfrac{-60}{(5.43)(11.40)} = -.969$
The sample correlation coefficient of $-.969$ is indicative of a strong negative linear relationship

46. b. There appears to be a positive linear relationship between x and y
   c. $s_{xy} = 26.5$
   d. $r_{xy} = .693$

48. $-.91$; negative relationship

50. a. .92
   b. Strong positive linear relationship

52. a. 3.69
   b. 3.175

53. a.

f_i	M_i	$f_i M_i$
4	5	20
7	10	70
9	15	135
5	20	100
25		325

$\bar{x} = \dfrac{\Sigma f_i M_i}{n} = \dfrac{325}{25} = 13$

b.

f_i	M_i	$(M_i - \bar{x})$	$(M_i - \bar{x})^2$	$f_i(M_i - \bar{x})^2$
4	5	−8	64	256
7	10	−3	9	63
9	15	2	4	36
5	20	7	49	245
25				600

$s^2 = \dfrac{\Sigma f_i(M_i - \bar{x})^2}{n - 1} = \dfrac{600}{25 - 1} = 25$

$s = \sqrt{25} = 5$

54. a.

Grade x_i	Weight w_i
4 (A)	9
3 (B)	15
2 (C)	33
1 (D)	3
0 (F)	0
	60 credit hours

$\bar{x} = \dfrac{\Sigma w_i x_i}{\Sigma w_i} = \dfrac{9(4) + 15(3) + 33(2) + 3(1)}{9 + 15 + 33 + 3}$

$= \dfrac{150}{60} = 2.5$

b. Yes

56. 10.74, 25.63, 5.06; Estimate = 1288.8

58. a. 1800, 1351
  b. 387, 1710
  c. 7280, 1323
  d. 3,675,303, 1917
  e. 9271.01, 96.29
  f. High positive
  g. Using a box plot: 4135 and 7450

60. a. 2.3, 1.85
  b. 1.90, 1.38
  c. Altria Group 5%
  d. $-.51$, below mean
  e. 1.02, above mean
  f. No

62. a. $\bar{x} = 83.135$, $s = 16.173$
  b. \$50,789 to \$115,481
  c. Same range as in part (b); higher probability
  d. Danbury, CT, is an outlier

64. a. 502.67; positive linear relationship
  b. .933

66. b. .9856, strong positive relationship

68. a. 817
  b. 833

70. a. 60.68
  b. $s^2 = 31.23$; $s = 5.59$

Chapter 4

2. $\binom{6}{3} = \dfrac{6!}{3!3!} = \dfrac{6 \cdot 5 \cdot 4 \cdot 3 \cdot 2 \cdot 1}{(3 \cdot 2 \cdot 1)(3 \cdot 2 \cdot 1)} = 20$

ABC	ACE	BCD	BEF
ABD	ACF	BCE	CDE
ABE	ADE	BCF	CDF
ABF	ADF	BDE	CEF
ACD	AEF	BDF	DEF

4. b. (H,H,H), (H,H,T), (H,T,H), (H,T,T), (T,H,H), (T,H,T), (T,T,H), (T,T,T)
  c. $\frac{1}{8}$

6. $P(E_1) = .40$, $P(E_2) = .26$, $P(E_3) = .34$
  The relative frequency method was used

8. a. 4: Commission Positive—Council Approves
  Commission Positive—Council Disapproves
  Commission Negative—Council Approves
  Commission Negative—Council Disapproves

9. $\binom{50}{4} = \dfrac{50!}{4!46!} = \dfrac{50 \cdot 49 \cdot 48 \cdot 47}{4 \cdot 3 \cdot 2 \cdot 1} = 230,300$

10. a. Use the relative frequency approach
  $P(\text{California}) = 1,434/2,374 = .60$
  b. Number not from four states
  $= 2,374 - 1,434 - 390 - 217 - 112$
  $= 221$
  $P(\text{Not from 4 states}) = 221/2,374 = .09$
  c. $P(\text{Not in early stages}) = 1 - .22 = .78$

d. Estimate of number of Massachusetts' companies in early stage of development $= (.22)390 \approx 86$
  e. If we assume the size of the awards did not differ by state, we can multiply the probability an award went to Colorado by the total venture funds disbursed to get an estimate

  Estimate of Colorado funds $= (112/2374)(\$32.4)$
  $= \$1.53$ billion

  Authors' Note: The actual amount going to Colorado was \$1.74 billion

12. a. 2,869,685
  b. 1/2,869,685
  c. 1/120,526,770

14. a. $\frac{1}{4}$
  b. $\frac{1}{2}$
  c. $\frac{3}{4}$

15. a. S = (ace of clubs, ace of diamonds, ace of hearts, ace of spades)
  b. S = (2 of clubs, 3 of clubs, . . . , 10 of clubs, J of clubs, Q of clubs, K of clubs, A of clubs)
  c. There are 12; jack, queen, or king in each of the four suits
  d. For (a): $4/52 = 1/13 = .08$
  For (b): $13/52 = 1/4 = .25$
  For (c): $12/52 = .23$

16. a. 36
  c. $\frac{1}{6}$
  d. $\frac{5}{18}$
  e. No; $P(\text{odd}) = P(\text{even}) = \frac{1}{2}$
  f. Classical

17. a. (4, 6), (4, 7), (4, 8)
  b. $.05 + .10 + .15 = .30$
  c. (2, 8), (3, 8), (4, 8)
  d. $.05 + .05 + .15 = .25$
  e. .15

18. a. $P(0) = .05$
  b. $P(4 \text{ or } 5) = .20$
  c. $P(0, 1, \text{ or } 2) = .55$

20. a. .112
  b. .086
  c. .49

22. a. .40, .40, .60
  b. .80, yes
  c. $A^c = (E_3, E_4, E_5)$; $C^c = (E_1, E_4)$;
  $P(A^c) = .60$; $P(C^c) = .40$
  d. (E_1, E_2, E_5); .60
  e. .80

23. a. $P(A) = P(E_1) + P(E_4) + P(E_6)$
  $= .05 + .25 + .10 = .40$
  $P(B) = P(E_2) + P(E_4) + P(E_7)$
  $= .20 + .25 + .05 = .50$
  $P(C) = P(E_2) + P(E_3) + P(E_5) + P(E_7)$
  $= .20 + .20 + .15 + .05 = .60$

b. $A \cup B = \{E_1, E_2, E_4, E_6, E_7\}$;

$P(A \cup B) = P(E_1) + P(E_2) + P(E_4) + P(E_6) + P(E_7)$
$= .05 + .20 + .25 + .10 + .05$
$= .65$

c. $A \cap B = \{E_4\}$; $P(A \cap B) = P(E_4) = .25$

d. Yes, they are mutually exclusive

e. $B^c = \{E_1, E_3, E_5, E_6\}$;

$P(B^c) = P(E_1) + P(E_3) + P(E_5) + P(E_6)$
$= .05 + .20 + .15 + .10$
$= .50$

24. a. .05
b. .70

26. a. .30, .23
b. .17
c. .64

28. Let B = rented a car for business reasons
  P = rented a car for personal reasons
a. $P(B \cup P) = P(B) + P(P) - P(B \cap P)$
$= .540 + .458 - .300$
$= .698$

b. $P(\text{Neither}) = 1 - .698 = .302$

30. a. $P(A \mid B) = \dfrac{P(A \cap B)}{P(B)} = \dfrac{.40}{.60} = .6667$

b. $P(B \mid A) = \dfrac{P(A \cap B)}{P(A)} = \dfrac{.40}{.50} = .80$

c. No, because $P(A \mid B) \neq P(A)$

32. a.

	Yes	No	Total
18 to 34	.375	.085	.46
35 and over	.475	.065	.54
Total	.850	.150	1.00

b. 46% 18 to 34; 54% 35 and over
c. .15
d. .1848
e. .1204
f. .5677
g. Higher probability of No for 18 to 34

33. a.

	Reason for Applying			
		Cost/		
	Quality	Convenience	Other	Total
Full-time	.218	.204	.039	.461
Part-time	.208	.307	.024	.539
Total	.426	.511	.063	1.000

b. A student is most likely to cite cost or convenience as the first reason (probability = .511); school quality is the reason cited by the second largest number of students (probability = .426)

c. $P(\text{quality} \mid \text{full-time}) = .218/.461 = .473$

d. $P(\text{quality} \mid \text{part-time}) = .208/.539 = .386$

e. For independence, we must have $P(A)P(B) = P(A \cap B)$; from the table

$P(A \cap B) = .218, P(A) = .461, P(B) = .426$
$P(A)P(B) = (.461)(.426) = .196$

Because $P(A)P(B) \neq P(A \cap B)$, the events are not independent

34. a. .44
b. .15
c. .136
d. .106
e. .0225
f. .0025

36. a. .7921
b. .9879
c. .0121
d. .3364, .8236, .1764
  Don't foul Reggie Miller

38. a. .0209
b. .0141, .027
c. No
d. .0202, .0458
e. Yes

39. a. Yes, because $P(A_1 \cap A_2) = 0$
b. $P(A_1 \cap B) = P(A_1)P(B \mid A_1) = .40(.20) = .08$
  $P(A_2 \cap B) = P(A_2)P(B \mid A_2) = .60(.05) = .03$
c. $P(B) = P(A_1 \cap B) + P(A_2 \cap B) = .08 + .03 = .11$
d. $P(A_1 \mid B) = \dfrac{.08}{.11} = .7273$

$P(A_2 \mid B) = \dfrac{.03}{.11} = .2727$

40. a. .10, .20, .09
b. .51
c. .26, .51, .23

42. M = missed payment
  D_1 = customer defaults
  D_2 = customer does not default
  $P(D_1) = .05, P(D_2) = .95, P(M \mid D_2) = .2, P(M \mid D_1) = 1$

a. $P(D_1 \mid M) = \dfrac{P(D_1)P(M \mid D_1)}{P(D_1)P(M \mid D_1) + P(D_2)P(M \mid D_2)}$

$= \dfrac{(.05)(1)}{(.05)(1) + (.95)(.2)}$

$= \dfrac{.05}{.24} = .21$

b. Yes, the probability of default is greater than .20

44. a. .47, .53, .50, .45
b. .4963
c. .4463
d. 47%, 53%

46. a. .68
b. 52
c. 10

48. a. 315
  b. .29
  c. No
  d. Republicans

50. a. .76
  b. .24

52. b. .2022
  c. .4618
  d. .4005

54. a. .49
  b. .44
  c. .54
  d. No
  e. Yes

56. a. .25
  b. .125
  c. .0125
  d. .10
  e. No

58. 3.44%

60. a. .40
  b. .67

Chapter 5

1. a. Head, Head (H, H)
  Head, Tail (H, T)
  Tail, Head (T, H)
  Tail, Tail (T, T)
  b. x = number of heads on two coin tosses
  c.

Outcome	Values of x
(H, H)	2
(H, T)	1
(T, H)	1
(T, T)	0

  d. Discrete; it may assume 3 values: 0, 1, and 2

2. a. x = time in minutes to assemble product
  b. Any positive value: $x > 0$
  c. Continuous

3. Let Y = position is offered
    N = position is not offered
  a. $S = \{(Y, Y, Y), (Y, Y, N), (Y, N, Y), (Y, N, N), (N, Y, Y), (N, Y, N), (N, N, Y), (N, N, N)\}$
  b. Let N = number of offers made; N is a discrete random variable
  c.

Experimental Outcome	(Y, Y, Y)	(Y, Y, N)	(Y, N, Y)	(Y, N, N)	(N, Y, Y)	(N, Y, N)	(N, N, Y)	(N, N, N)
Value of N	3	2	2	1	2	1	1	0

4. $x = 0, 1, 2, \ldots, 12$

6. a. $0, 1, 2, \ldots, 20$; discrete
  b. $0, 1, 2, \ldots$; discrete
  c. $0, 1, 2, \ldots, 50$; discrete
  d. $0 \leq x \leq 8$; continuous
  e. $x > 0$; continuous

7. a. $f(x) \geq 0$ for all values of x
    $\Sigma f(x) = 1$; therefore, it is a valid probability distribution
  b. Probability $x = 30$ is $f(30) = .25$
  c. Probability $x \leq 25$ is $f(20) + f(25) = .20 + .15 = .35$
  d. Probability $x > 30$ is $f(35) = .40$

8. a.

x	$f(x)$
1	3/20 = .15
2	5/20 = .25
3	8/20 = .40
4	4/20 = .20
	Total 1.00

  b.

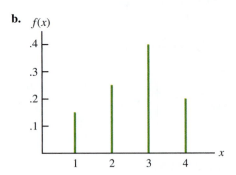

  c. $f(x) \geq 0$ for $x = 1, 2, 3, 4$
    $\Sigma f(x) = 1$

10. a.

x	1	2	3	4	5
$f(x)$	.05	.09	.03	.42	.41

  b.

x	1	2	3	4	5
$f(x)$	.04	.10	.12	.46	.28

  c. .83
  d. .28
  e. Senior executives more satisfied

12. a. Yes
  b. .65

14. a. .05
  b. .70
  c. .40

16. a.

y	f(y)	yf(y)
2	.20	.40
4	.30	1.20
7	.40	2.80
8	.10	.80
Totals	1.00	5.20

$$E(y) = \mu = 5.20$$

b.

y	y − μ	(y − μ)²	f(y)	(y − μ)²f(y)
2	−3.20	10.24	.20	2.048
4	−1.20	1.44	.30	.432
7	1.80	3.24	.40	1.296
8	2.80	7.84	.10	.784
			Total	4.560

$$\text{Var}(y) = 4.56$$
$$\sigma = \sqrt{4.56} = 2.14$$

18. a/b.

x	f(x)	xf(x)	x − μ	(x − μ)²	(x − μ)²f(x)
0	0.04	0.00	−1.84	3.39	0.12
1	0.34	0.34	−0.84	0.71	0.24
2	0.41	0.82	0.16	0.02	0.01
3	0.18	0.53	1.16	1.34	0.24
4	0.04	0.15	2.16	4.66	0.17
Total	1.00	1.84			0.79
		↑			↑
		E(x)			Var(x)

c/d.

y	f(y)	yf(y)	y − μ	(y − μ)²	y − μ²f(y)
0	0.00	0.00	−2.93	8.58	0.01
1	0.03	0.03	−1.93	3.72	0.12
2	0.23	0.45	−0.93	0.86	0.20
3	0.52	1.55	0.07	0.01	0.00
4	0.22	0.90	1.07	1.15	0.26
Total	1.00	2.93			0.59
		↑			↑
		E(y)			Var(y)

e. The number of bedrooms in owner-occupied houses is greater than in renter-occupied houses; the expected number of bedrooms is 1.09 = 2.93 − 1.84 greater and the variability in the number of bedrooms is less for the owner-occupied houses

20. a. 166

   b. −94; concern is to protect against the expense of a big accident

22. a. 445

   b. $1250 loss

24. a. Medium: 145; large: 140

   b. Medium: 2725; large: 12,400

25. a.

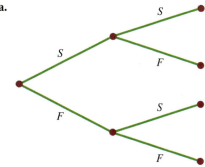

b. $f(1) = \binom{2}{1}(.4)^1(.6)^1 = \dfrac{2!}{1!1!}(.4)(.6) = .48$

c. $f(0) = \binom{2}{0}(.4)^0(.6)^2 = \dfrac{2!}{0!2!}(1)(.36) = .36$

d. $f(2) = \binom{2}{2}(.4)^2(.6)^0 = \dfrac{2!}{2!0!}(.16)(.1) = .16$

e. $P(x \geq 1) = f(1) + f(2) = .48 + .16 = .64$

f. $E(x) = np = 2(.4) = .8$
$\text{Var}(x) = np(1 − p) = 2(.4)(.6) = .48$
$\sigma = \sqrt{.48} = .6928$

26. a. $f(0) = .3487$

   b. $f(2) = .1937$

   c. .9298

   d. .6513

   e. 1

   f. $\sigma^2 = .9000, \sigma = .9487$

28. a. .2789

   b. .4181

   c. .0733

30. a. Probability of a defective part being produced must be .03 for each part selected; parts must be selected independently

   b. Let D = defective
      G = not defective

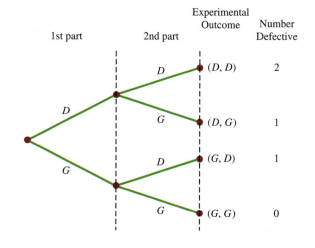

c. Two outcomes result in exactly one defect

d. P(no defects) $= (.97)(.97) = .9409$

P(1 defect) $= 2(.03)(.97) = .0582$

P(2 defects) $= (.03)(.03) = .0009$

32. a. .90

b. .99

c. .999

d. Yes

34. a. .0634

b. .0634

c. .9729

38. a. $f(x) = \dfrac{3^x e^{-3}}{x!}$

b. .2241

c. .1494

d. .8008

39. a. $f(x) = \dfrac{2^x e^{-2}}{x!}$

b. $\mu = 6$ for 3 time periods

c. $f(x) = \dfrac{6^x e^{-6}}{x!}$

d. $f(2) = \dfrac{2^2 e^{-2}}{2!} = \dfrac{4(.1353)}{2} = .2706$

e. $f(6) = \dfrac{6^6 e^{-6}}{6!} = .1606$

f. $f(5) = \dfrac{4^5 e^{-4}}{5!} = .1563$

40. a. $\mu = 48(5/60) = 4$

$f(3) = \dfrac{4^3 e^{-4}}{3!} = \dfrac{(64)(.0183)}{6} = .1952$

b. $\mu = 48(15/60) = 12$

$f(10) = \dfrac{12^{10} e^{-12}}{10!} = .1048$

c. $\mu = 48(5/60) = 4$; one can expect four callers to be waiting after 5 minutes

$f(0) = \dfrac{4^0 e^{-4}}{0!} = .0183$; the probability none will be waiting after 5 minutes is .0183

d. $\mu = 48(3/60) = 2.4$

$f(0) = \dfrac{2.4^0 e^{-2.4}}{0!} = .0907$; the probability of no interruptions in 3 minutes is .0907

42. a. $f(0) = \dfrac{7^0 e^{-7}}{0!} = e^{-7} = .0009$

b. probability $= 1 - [f(0) + f(1)]$

$f(1) = \dfrac{7^1 e^{-7}}{1!} = 7e^{-7} = .0064$

probability $= 1 - [.0009 + .0064] = .9927$

c. $\mu = 3.5$

$f(0) = \dfrac{3.5^0 e^{-3.5}}{0!} = e^{-3.5} = .0302$

probability $= 1 - f(0) = 1 - .0302 = .9698$

d.

probability $= 1 - [f(0) + f(1) + f(2) + f(3) + f(4)]$

$= 1 - [.0009 + .0064 + .0223 + .0521 + .0912]$

$= .8271$

44. a. $\mu = 1.25$

b. .2865

c. .3581

d. .3554

46. a. $f(1) = \dfrac{\binom{3}{1}\binom{10-3}{4-1}}{\binom{10}{4}} = \dfrac{\left(\frac{3!}{1!2!}\right)\left(\frac{7!}{3!4!}\right)}{\frac{10!}{4!6!}}$

$= \dfrac{(3)(35)}{210} = .50$

b. $f(2) = \dfrac{\binom{3}{2}\binom{10-3}{2-2}}{\binom{10}{2}} = \dfrac{(3)(1)}{45} = .067$

c. $f(0) = \dfrac{\binom{3}{0}\binom{10-3}{2-0}}{\binom{10}{2}} = \dfrac{(1)(21)}{45} = .4667$

d. $f(2) = \dfrac{\binom{3}{2}\binom{10-3}{4-2}}{\binom{10}{4}} = \dfrac{(3)(21)}{210} = .30$

48. a. .5250

b. .1833

50. $N = 60, n = 10$

a. $r = 20, x = 0$

$f(0) = \dfrac{\binom{20}{0}\binom{40}{10}}{\binom{60}{10}} = \dfrac{(1)\left(\frac{40!}{10!30!}\right)}{\frac{60!}{10!50!}}$

$= \left(\dfrac{40!}{10!30!}\right)\left(\dfrac{10!50!}{60!}\right)$

$= \dfrac{40 \cdot 39 \cdot 38 \cdot 37 \cdot 36 \cdot 35 \cdot 34 \cdot 33 \cdot 32 \cdot 31}{60 \cdot 59 \cdot 58 \cdot 57 \cdot 56 \cdot 55 \cdot 54 \cdot 53 \cdot 52 \cdot 51}$

$\approx .01$

b. $r = 20, x = 1$

$f(1) = \dfrac{\binom{20}{1}\binom{40}{9}}{\binom{60}{10}} = 20\left(\dfrac{40!}{9!31!}\right)\left(\dfrac{10!50!}{60!}\right)$

$\approx .07$

c. $1 - f(0) - f(1) = 1 - .08 = .92$

d. Same as the probability one will be from Hawaii; in part (b) it was equal to approximately .07

52. a. .5333

b. .6667

c. .7778

d. $n = 7$

54. a.

x	1	2	3	4	5
$f(x)$	.24	.21	.10	.21	.24

b. 3.00, 2.34

c. Bonds: $E(x) = 1.36$, $\text{Var}(x) = .23$
Stocks: $E(x) = 4$, $\text{Var}(x) = 1$

56. a. .0596
b. .3585
c. 100
d. 9.7468

58. a. .9510
b. .0480
c. .0490

60. a. 240
b. 12.9615
c. 12.9615

62. .1912

64. a. .2240
b. .5767

66. a. .4667
b. .4667
c. .0667

Chapter 6

1. a.

b. $P(x = 1.25) = 0$; the probability of any single point is zero because the area under the curve above any single point is zero

c. $P(1.0 \le x \le 1.25) = 2(.25) = .50$
d. $P(1.20 < x < 1.5) = 2(.30) = .60$

2. b. .50
c. .60
d. 15
e. 8.33

4. a.

$f(x)$

b. $P(.25 < x < .75) = 1(.50) = .50$
c. $P(x \le .30) = 1(.30) = .30$
d. $P(x > .60) = 1(.40) = .40$

6. a. .40
b. .64
c. .68

10. a. .3413
b. .4332
c. .4772
d. .4938

12. a. .2967
b. .4418
c. .3300
d. .5910
e. .8849
f. .2389

13. a. $.6879 - .0239 = .6640$
b. $.8888 - .6985 = .1903$
c. $.9599 - .8508 = .1091$

14. a. $z = 1.96$
b. $z = .61$
c. $z = 1.12$
d. $z = .44$

15. a. Look in the table for an area of $.5000 - .2119 = .2881$; $z = .80$ cuts off an area of .2119 in the upper tail; thus, for an area of .2119 in the lower tail, $z = -.80$
b. Look in the table for an area of $.9030/2 = .4515$; $z = 1.66$
c. Look in the table for an area of $.2052/2 = .1026$; $z = .26$
d. Look in the table for an area of $.4948$; $z = 2.56$
e. Look in the table for an area of .1915; because the value we are seeking is below the mean, the z value must be negative; thus, $z = -.50$

16. a. $z = 2.33$
b. $z = 1.96$
c. $z = 1.645$
d. $z = 1.28$

18. $\mu = 30$ and $\sigma = 8.2$

a. At $x = 40$, $z = \dfrac{40 - 30}{8.2} = 1.22$

$P(z \le 1.22) = .5000 + .3888 = .8888$
$P(x \ge 40) = 1.000 - .8888 = .1112$

b. At $x = 20$, $z = \dfrac{20 - 30}{8.2} = -1.22$

$P(z > -1.22) = .5000 + .3888 = .8888$
$P(x \le 20) = 1.0000 - .8888 = .1112$

c. A z-value of 1.28 cuts off an area of approximately 10% in the upper tail
$x = 30 + 8.2(1.28)$
$\quad = 40.50$
A stock price of \$40.50 or higher will put a company in the top 10%

20. a. .0885
b. 12.51%
c. 93.8 hours or more

22. a. .4194
b. \$517.44 or more
c. .0166

24. a. 902.75, 114.185
b. .1841
c. .1977
d. 1,091 million

26. a. $\mu = np = 100(.20) = 20$
$\sigma^2 = np(1 - p) = 100(.20)(.80) = 16$
$\sigma = \sqrt{16} = 4$

b. Yes, because $np = 20$ and $n(1 - p) = 80$

c. $P(23.5 \leq x \leq 24.5)$

$z = \dfrac{24.5 - 20}{4} = +1.13$ Area $= .3708$

$z = \dfrac{23.5 - 20}{4} = +.88$ Area $= .3106$

$P(23.5 \leq x \leq 24.5) = .3708 - .3106 = .0602$

d. $P(17.5 \leq x \leq 22.5)$

$z = \dfrac{17.5 - 20}{4} = -.63$ Area $= .2357$

$z = \dfrac{22.5 - 20}{4} = +.63$ Area $= .2357$

$P(17.5 \leq x \leq 22.5) = .2357 + .2357 = .4714$

e. $P(x \leq 15.5)$

$z = \dfrac{15.5 - 20}{4} = -1.13$ Area $= .3708$

$P(x \leq 15.5) = .5000 - .3708 = .1292$

28. a. .1867
b. 125
c. It's a toss-up

30. a. 220
b. .0392
c. .8962

32. a. .5276
b. .3935
c. .4724
d. .1341

33. a. $P(x \leq x_0) = 1 - e^{-x_0/3}$
b. $P(x \leq 2) = 1 - e^{-2/3} = 1 - .5134 = .4866$
c. $P(x \geq 3) = 1 - P(x \leq 3) = 1 - (1 - e^{-3/3})$
$= e^{-1} = .3679$
d. $P(x \leq 5) = 1 - e^{-5/3} = 1 - .1889 = .8111$
e. $P(2 \leq x \leq 5) = P(x \leq 5) - P(x \leq 2)$
$= .8111 - .4866 = .3245$

34. a. .3935
b. .2231
c. .3834

35. a.

b. $P(x \leq 12) = 1 - e^{-12/12} = 1 - .3679 = .6321$
c. $P(x \leq 6) = 1 - e^{-6/12} = 1 - .6065 = .3935$
d. $P(x \geq 30) = 1 - P(x < 30)$
$= 1 - (1 - e^{-30/12})$
$= .0821$

36. a. 50 hours
b. .3935
c. .1353

38. a. $f(x) = 30e^{-30x}$
b. .0821
c. .7135

40. a. \$3780 or less
b. 19.22%
c. \$8167.50

42. a. 3229
b. .2244
c. \$12,382 or more

44. a. .0228
b. \$50

46. a. 38.3%
b. 3.59% better, 96.41% worse
c. 38.21%

48. $\mu = 19.23$ ounces

50. a. Lose \$240
b. .1788
c. .3557
d. .0594

52. a. $\frac{1}{7}$ minute
b. $7e^{-7x}$
c. .0009
d. .2466

54. a. 2 minutes
b. .2212
c. .3935
d. .0821

Chapter 7

1. a. AB, AC, AD, AE, BC, BD, BE, CD, CE, DE
b. With 10 samples, each has a $\frac{1}{10}$ probability
c. E and C because 8 and 0 do not apply; 5 identifies E; 7 does not apply; 5 is skipped because E is already in the sample; 3 identifies C; 2 is not needed because the sample of size 2 is complete

2. 22, 147, 229, 289

3. 459, 147, 385, 113, 340, 401, 215, 2, 33, 348

4. a. Nasdaq 100, Oracle, Microsoft, Lucent, Applied Materials
b. 252

6. 2782, 493, 825, 1807, 289

8. Maryland, Iowa, Florida State, Virginia, Pittsburgh, Oklahoma

10. a. finite; **b.** infinite; **c.** infinite; **d.** infinite; **e.** finite

11. a. $\bar{x} = \dfrac{\Sigma x_i}{n} = \dfrac{54}{6} = 9$

b. $s = \sqrt{\dfrac{\Sigma(x_i - \bar{x})^2}{n - 1}}$

$\Sigma(x_i - \bar{x})^2 = (-4)^2 + (-1)^2 + 1^2 + (-2)^2 + 1^2 + 5^2$
$\quad = 48$

$s = \sqrt{\dfrac{48}{6 - 1}} = 3.1$

12. a. .50

b. .3667

13. a. $\bar{x} = \dfrac{\Sigma x_i}{n} = \dfrac{465}{5} = 93$

b.

x_i	$(x_i - \bar{x})$	$(x_i - \bar{x})^2$
94	+1	1
100	+7	49
85	−8	64
94	+1	1
92	−1	1
Totals 465	0	116

$s = \sqrt{\dfrac{\Sigma(x_i - \bar{x})^2}{n - 1}} = \sqrt{\dfrac{116}{4}} = 5.39$

14. a. .45

b. .15

c. .45

16. a. .10

b. 20

c. .72

18. a. 200

b. 5

c. Normal with $E(\bar{x}) = 200$ and $\sigma_{\bar{x}} = 5$

d. The probability distribution of $\bar{x}$

19. a. The sampling distribution is normal with:
$$E(\bar{x}) = \mu = 200$$
$$\sigma_{\bar{x}} = \frac{\sigma}{\sqrt{n}} = \frac{50}{\sqrt{100}} = 5$$

For $+5$, $(\bar{x} - \mu) = 5$,
$$z = \frac{\bar{x} - \mu}{\sigma_{\bar{x}}} = \frac{5}{5} = 1$$
Area $= 2(.3413) = .6826$

b. For ± 10, $(\bar{x} - \mu) = 10$,
$$z = \frac{\bar{x} - \mu}{\sigma_{\bar{x}}} = \frac{10}{5} = 2$$
Area $= 2(.4772) = .9544$

20. 3.54, 2.50, 2.04, 1.77

$\sigma_{\bar{x}}$ decreases as n increases

22. a. Normal with $E(\bar{x}) = 51,800$ and $\sigma_{\bar{x}} = 516.40$

b. $\sigma_{\bar{x}}$ decreases to 365.15

c. $\sigma_{\bar{x}}$ decreases as n increases

23. a.

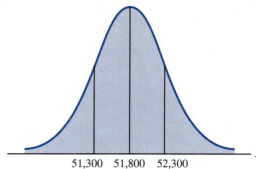

$51,300 \quad 51,800 \quad 52,300$

$\sigma_{\bar{x}} = \dfrac{\sigma}{\sqrt{n}} = \dfrac{4000}{\sqrt{60}} = 516.40$

$z = \dfrac{52,300 - 51,800}{516.40} = +.97$

Area $= 2(.3340) = .6680$

b. $\sigma_{\bar{x}} = \dfrac{\sigma}{\sqrt{n}} = \dfrac{4000}{\sqrt{120}} = 365.15$

$z = \dfrac{52,300 - 51,800}{365.15} = +1.37$

Area $= 2(.4147) = .8294$

24. a. Normal with $E(\bar{x}) = 4260$ and $\sigma_{\bar{x}} = 127.28$

b. .95

c. .5704

26. a. .5034, .6212, .7888, .9232, .9876

b. Higher probability within ± 250

28. a. Normal with $E(\bar{x}) = 687$ and $\sigma_{\bar{x}} = 34.29$

b. .9964

c. .5346

d. Increase the sample size

30. a. $n/N = .01$; no

b. 1.29, 1.30; little difference

c. .8764

32. a. $E(\bar{p}) = .40$

$\sigma_{\bar{p}} = \sqrt{\dfrac{p(1 - p)}{n}} = \sqrt{\dfrac{(.40)(.60)}{200}} = .0346$

$z = \dfrac{\bar{p} - p}{\sigma_{\bar{p}}} = \dfrac{.03}{.0346} = .87$

Area $= 2(.3078) = .6156$

b. $z = \dfrac{\bar{p} - p}{\sigma_{\bar{p}}} = \dfrac{.05}{.0346} = 1.44$

Area $= 2(.4251) = .8502$

34. a. .6156

b. .7814

c. .9488

d. .9942

e. Higher probability with larger n

35. a.

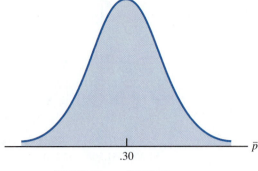

$$\sigma_{\bar{p}} = \sqrt{\frac{p(1-p)}{n}} = \sqrt{\frac{.30(.70)}{100}} = .0458$$

The normal distribution is appropriate because $np = 100(.30) = 30$ and $n(1-p) = 100(.70) = 70$ are both greater than 5

b. $P(.20 \le \bar{p} \le .40) = ?$

$$z = \frac{.40 - .30}{.0458} = 2.18$$

Area $= 2(.4854) = .9708$

c. $P(.25 \le \bar{p} \le .35) = ?$

$$z = \frac{.35 - .30}{.0458} = 1.09$$

Area $= 2(.3621) = .7242$

36. a. Normal with $E(\bar{p}) = .56$ and $\sigma_{\bar{p}} = .0287$
  b. .7062
  c. .8612, .9438

38. a. Normal with $E(\bar{p}) = .56$ and $\sigma_{\bar{p}} = .0248$
  b. .5820
  c. .8926

40. a. Normal with $E(\bar{p}) = .76$ and $\sigma_{\bar{p}} = .0214$
  b. .8384
  c. .9452

42. 112, 145, 73, 324, 293, 875, 318, 618

44. a. Normal with $E(\bar{x}) = 115.50$ and $\sigma_{\bar{x}} = 5.53$
  b. .9298
  c. .0026

46. a. 707
  b. .50
  c. .8414
  d. .9544

48. a. 625
  b. .7888

50. a. Normal with $E(\bar{p}) = .305$ and $\sigma_{\bar{p}} = .0326$
  b. .7814
  c. .4582

52. a. .9606
  b. .0495

54. a. 48
  b. Normal, $E(\bar{p}) = .25$, $\sigma_{\bar{p}} = .0625$
  c. .2119

Chapter 8

2. Use $\bar{x} \pm z_{\alpha/2}(\sigma/\sqrt{n})$
  a. $32 \pm 1.645 (6/\sqrt{50})$
    32 ± 1.4; 30.6 to 33.4
  b. $32 \pm 1.96(6/\sqrt{50})$
    32 ± 1.66; 30.34 to 33.66
  c. $32 \pm 2.576(6/\sqrt{50})$
    32 ± 2.19; 29.81 to 34.19

4. 54

5. a. $1.96\sigma/\sqrt{n} = 1.96(5/\sqrt{49}) = 1.40$
  b. 24.80 ± 1.40; 23.40 to 26.20

6. 8.1 to 8.9

8. a. Population is at least approximately normal
  b. 3.1
  c. 4.1

10. a. \$113,638 to \$124,672
  b. \$112,581 to \$125,729
  c. \$110,515 to \$127,795
  d. Width increases as confidence level increases

12. a. 2.179
  b. −1.676
  c. 2.457
  d. −1.708 and 1.708
  e. −2.014 and 2.014

13. a. $\bar{x} = \dfrac{\Sigma x_i}{n} = \dfrac{80}{8} = 10$

  b. $s = \sqrt{\dfrac{\Sigma(x_i - \bar{x})^2}{n-1}} = \sqrt{\dfrac{84}{7}} = 3.46$

  c. $t_{.025}\left(\dfrac{s}{\sqrt{n}}\right) = 2.365\left(\dfrac{3.46}{\sqrt{8}}\right) = 2.9$

  d. $\bar{x} \pm t_{.025}\left(\dfrac{s}{\sqrt{n}}\right)$
    10 ± 2.9 (7.1 to 12.9)

14. a. 21.5 to 23.5
  b. 21.3 to 23.7
  c. 20.9 to 24.1
  d. A larger margin of error and a wider interval

15. $\bar{x} \pm t_{\alpha/2}(s/\sqrt{n})$
    90% confidence: $df = 64$ and $t_{.05} = 1.669$

  $$19.5 \pm 1.669\left(\frac{5.2}{\sqrt{65}}\right)$$

    19.5 ± 1.08 (18.42 to 20.58)
    95% confidence: $df = 64$ and $t_{.025} = 1.998$

  $$19.5 \pm 1.998\left(\frac{5.2}{\sqrt{65}}\right)$$

    19.5 ± 1.29 (18.21 to 20.79)

16. a. 1.69
  b. 47.31 to 50.69
  c. Fewer hours and higher cost for United

18. a. 3.8
  b. .84

c. 2.96 to 4.64

d. Larger n next time

20. 6.28 to 6.78

22. a. 3.35

b. 2.40 to 4.30

24. a. Planning value of $\sigma = \dfrac{\text{Range}}{4} = \dfrac{36}{4} = 9$

b. $n = \dfrac{z_{.025}^2 \sigma^2}{E^2} = \dfrac{(1.96)^2(9)^2}{(3)^2} = 34.57$; use $n = 35$

c. $n = \dfrac{(1.96)^2(9)^2}{(2)^2} = 77.79$; use $n = 78$

25. a. Use $n = \dfrac{z_{\alpha/2}^2 \sigma^2}{E^2}$

$n = \dfrac{(1.96)^2(6.82)^2}{(1.5)^2} = 79.41$; use $n = 80$

b. $n = \dfrac{(1.645)^2(6.82)^2}{(2)^2} = 31.47$; use $n = 32$

26. a. 340

b. 1358

c. 8487

28. a. 343

b. 487

c. 840

d. n gets larger; no to 99% confidence

30. 81

31. a. $\bar{p} = \dfrac{100}{400} = .25$

b. $\sqrt{\dfrac{\bar{p}(1-\bar{p})}{n}} = \sqrt{\dfrac{.25(.75)}{400}} = .0217$

c. $\bar{p} \pm z_{.025}\sqrt{\dfrac{\bar{p}(1-\bar{p})}{n}}$

$.25 \pm 1.96(.0217)$

$.25 \pm .0424$; .2076 to .2924

32. a. .6733 to .7267

b. .6682 to .7318

34. 1068

35. a. $\bar{p} = \dfrac{281}{611} = .4599$ (46%)

b. $z_{.05}\sqrt{\dfrac{\bar{p}(1-\bar{p})}{n}} = 1.645\sqrt{\dfrac{4599(1-.4599)}{611}} = .0332$

c. $\bar{p} \pm .0332$

$.4599 \pm .0332$ (.4267 to .4931)

36. a. .4393

b. .3870 to .4916

38. a. .0430

b. .2170 to .3030

c. 822

39. a. $n = \dfrac{1.96^2 p^*(1 - p^*)}{E^2}$

$n = \dfrac{1.96^2(.33)(.67)}{(.03)^2} = 943.75$; use $n = 944$

b. $n = \dfrac{2.576^2(.33)(.67)}{(.03)^2} = 1630.19$; use $n = 1631$

40. .0267, (.8333 to .8867)

42. a. .0442

b. 601, 1068, 2401, 9604

44. a. 2009

b. 47,991 to 52,009

46. a. 998

b. \$24,479 to \$26,455

c. \$93.5 million

d. Yes; \$21.4 (30%) over *Lost World*

48. a. 14 minutes

b. 13.38 to 14.62

c. 32 per day

d. Staff reduction

50. 37

52. 176

54. a. .5420

b. .0508

c. .4912 to .5928

56. a. .68

b. .6391 to .7209

58. a. 1267

b. 1509

60. a. .3101

b. .2898 to .3304

c. 8219; no, this sample size is unnecessarily large

Chapter 9

2. a. $H_0: \mu \le 14$
$H_a: \mu > 14$

b. No evidence that the new plan increases sales

c. The research hypothesis $\mu > 14$ is supported; the new plan increases sales

4. a. $H_0: \mu \ge 220$
$H_a: \mu < 220$

5. a. Rejecting $H_0: \mu \le 56.2$ when it is true

b. Accepting $H_0: \mu \le 56.2$ when it is false

6. a. $H_0: \mu \le 1$
$H_a: \mu > 1$

b. Claiming $\mu > 1$ when it is not true

c. Claiming $\mu \le 1$ when it is not true

8. a. $H_0: \mu \ge 220$
$H_a: \mu < 220$

b. Claiming $\mu < 220$ when it is not true

c. Claiming $\mu \ge 220$ when it is not true

10. a. $z = \dfrac{\bar{x} - \mu_0}{\sigma/\sqrt{n}} = \dfrac{26.4 - 25}{6/\sqrt{40}} = 1.48$

    b. Area = .4306

    p-value = .5000 − .4306 = .0694

    c. p-value > .01, do not reject H_0

    d. Reject H_0 if $z \geq 2.33$

    1.48 < 2.33, do not reject H_0

11. a. $z = \dfrac{\bar{x} - \mu_0}{\sigma/\sqrt{n}} = \dfrac{14.15 - 15}{3/\sqrt{50}} = -2.00$

    b. Area = .4772

    p-value = 2(.5000 − .4772) = .0456

    c. p-value ≤ .05, reject H_0

    d. Reject H_0 if $z \leq -1.96$ or $z \geq 1.96$

    $-2.00 \leq -1.96$, reject H_0

12. a. .1056; do not reject H_0

    b. .0062; reject H_0

    c. ≈ 0; reject H_0

    d. .7967; do not reject H_0

14. a. .3844; do not reject H_0

    b. .0074; reject H_0

    c. .0836; do not reject H_0

15. a. $H_0: \mu \geq 1056$

    $H_a: \mu < 1056$

    b. $z = \dfrac{\bar{x} - \mu_0}{\sigma/\sqrt{n}} = \dfrac{910 - 1056}{1600/\sqrt{400}} = -1.83$

    p-value = .5000 − .4664 = .0336

    c. p-value ≤ .05, reject H_0. The mean refund of "last-minute" filers is less than $1056

    d. Reject H_0 if $z \leq -1.645$

    $-1.83 \leq -1.645$, reject H_0

16. a. $H_0: \mu \leq 895$

    $H_a: \mu > 895$

    b. .1170

    c. Do not reject H_0

    d. Withhold judgment; collect more data

18. a. $H_0: \mu = 4.1$

    $H_a: \mu \neq 4.1$

    b. −2.21, .0272

    c. Reject H_0

20. a. $H_0: \mu \geq 181,900$

    $H_a: \mu < 181,900$

    b. −2.93

    c. .0017

    d. Reject H_0

22. a. $H_0: \mu = 8$

    $H_a: \mu \neq 8$

    b. .1706

    c. Do not reject H_0

    d. 7.83 to 8.97; Yes

24. a. $t = \dfrac{\bar{x} - \mu_0}{s/\sqrt{n}} = \dfrac{17 - 18}{4.5/\sqrt{48}} = -1.54$

    b. Degrees of freedom = $n - 1 = 47$

    Area in lower tail is between .05 and .10

    p-value (two-tail) is between .10 and .20

    c. p-value > .05; do not reject H_0

    d. With $df = 47$, $t_{.025} = 2.012$

    Reject H_0 if $t \leq -2.012$ or $t \geq 2.012$

    $t = -1.54$; do not reject H_0

26. a. Between .02 and .05; reject H_0

    b. Between .01 and .02; reject H_0

    c. Between .10 and .20; do not reject H_0

27. a. $H_0: \mu \geq 238$

    $H_a: \mu < 238$

    b. $t = \dfrac{\bar{x} - \mu_0}{s/\sqrt{n}} = \dfrac{231 - 238}{80/\sqrt{100}} = -.88$

    Degrees of freedom = $n - 1 = 99$

    p-value is between .10 and .20

    c. p-value > .05; do not reject H_0

    Cannot conclude mean weekly benefit in Virginia is less than the national mean

    d. $df = 99$ $t_{.05} = -1.66$

    Reject H_0 if $t \leq -1.66$

    $-.88 > -1.66$; do not reject H_0

28. a. $H_0: \mu \leq 3530$

    $H_a: \mu > 3530$

    b. Between .005 and .01

    c. Reject H_0

30. a. $H_0: \mu = 600$

    $H_a: \mu \neq 600$

    b. Between .20 and .40

    c. Do not reject H_0

    d. A larger sample size

32. a. $H_0: \mu = 10,192$

    $H_a: \mu \neq 10,192$

    b. Between .02 and .05

    c. Reject H_0

34. a. $H_0: \mu = 2$

    $H_a: \mu \neq 2$

    b. 2.2

    c. .52

    d. Between .20 and .40

    e. Do not reject H_0

36. a. $z = \dfrac{\bar{p} - p_0}{\sqrt{\dfrac{p_0(1 - p_0)}{n}}} = \dfrac{.68 - .75}{\sqrt{\dfrac{.75(1 - .75)}{300}}} = -2.80$

    p-value = .5000 − .4974 = .0026

    p-value ≤ .05; reject H_0

    b. $z = \dfrac{.72 - .75}{\sqrt{\dfrac{.75(1 - .75)}{300}}} = -1.20$

    p-value = .5000 − .3849 = .1151

    p-value > .05; do not reject H_0

c. $z = \dfrac{.70 - .75}{\sqrt{\dfrac{.75(1 - .75)}{300}}} = -2.00$

p-value $= .5000 - .4772 = .0228$

p-value $\le .05$; reject H_0

d. $z = \dfrac{.77 - .75}{\sqrt{\dfrac{.75(1 - .75)}{300}}} = .80$

p-value $= .5000 + .2881 = .7881$

p-value $> .05$; do not reject H_0

38. a. H_0: $p = .64$

H_a: $p \ne .64$

b. $\bar{p} = 52/100 = .52$

$z = \dfrac{\bar{p} - p_0}{\sqrt{\dfrac{p_0(1 - p_0)}{n}}} = \dfrac{.52 - .64}{\sqrt{\dfrac{.64(1 - .64)}{100}}} = -2.50$

Area $= .4938$

p-value $= 2(.5000 - .4938) = .0124$

c. p-value $\le .05$; reject H_0

Proportion differs from the reported .64

d. Yes, because $\bar{p} = .52$ indicates that fewer believe the supermarket brand is as good as the name brand

40. a. .2702

b. H_0: $p \le .22$

H_a: $p > .22$

p-value ≈ 0; reject H_0

c. Helps evaluate the effectiveness of commercials

42. H_0: $p \le .24$

H_a: $p > .24$

p-value $= .0023$; reject H_0

44. a. H_0: $p \le .51$

H_a: $p > .51$

b. $\bar{p} = .58$, p-value $= .0026$

c. Reject H_0

46. a. H_0: $\mu = 16$

H_a: $\mu \ne 16$

b. .0286; reject H_0

Readjust line

c. .2186; do not reject H_0

Continue operation

d. $z = 2.19$; reject H_0

$z = -1.23$; do not reject H_0

Yes, same conclusion

48. a. H_0: $\mu \le 45,250$

H_a: $\mu > 45,250$

b. .0034

c. Reject H_0

50. $t = -.93$

p-value between .20 and .40

Do not reject H_0

52. $t = 2.26$

p-value between .01 and .025

Reject H_0

54. a. H_0: $p \le .50$

H_a: $p > .50$

b. .64

c. .0026; reject H_0

56. a. H_0: $p \le .50$

H_a: $p > .50$

b. .6381

c. .0023; reject H_0

58. H_0: $p \ge .90$

H_a: $p < .90$

p-value $= .0808$

Do not reject H_0

Chapter 10

1. a. $\bar{x}_1 - \bar{x}_2 = 13.6 - 11.6 = 2$

b. $z_{\alpha/2} = z_{.05} = 1.645$

$\bar{x}_1 - \bar{x}_2 \pm 1.645 \sqrt{\dfrac{\sigma_1^2}{n_1} + \dfrac{\sigma_2^2}{n_2}}$

$2 \pm 1.645 \sqrt{\dfrac{(2.2)^2}{50} + \dfrac{(3)^2}{35}}$

$2 \pm .98 \quad (1.02 \text{ to } 2.98)$

c. $z_{\alpha/2} = z_{.05} = 1.96$

$2 \pm 1.96 \sqrt{\dfrac{(2.2)^2}{50} + \dfrac{(3)^2}{35}}$

$2 \pm 1.17 \quad (.83 \text{ to } 3.17)$

2. a. $z = \dfrac{(\bar{x}_1 - \bar{x}_2) - D_0}{\sqrt{\dfrac{\sigma_1^2}{n_1} + \dfrac{\sigma_2^2}{n_2}}} = \dfrac{(25.2 - 22.8) - 0}{\sqrt{\dfrac{(5.2)^2}{40} + \dfrac{(6)^2}{50}}} = 2.03$

b. p-value $= .5000 - .4788 = .0212$

c. p-value $\le .05$; reject H_0

4. a. $\bar{x}_1 - \bar{x}_2 = 2.04 - 1.72 = .32$

b. $z_{.025} \sqrt{\dfrac{\sigma_1^2}{n_1} + \dfrac{\sigma_2^2}{n_2}} = 1.96 \sqrt{\dfrac{(.10)^2}{40} + \dfrac{(.08)^2}{35}} = .04$

c. $.32 \pm .04 \ (.28 \text{ to } .36)$

6. p-value $= .015$

Reject H_0; an increase

8. a. 1.08

b. .2802

c. Do not reject H_0; cannot conclude a difference exists

9. a. $\bar{x}_1 - \bar{x}_2 = 22.5 - 20.1 = 2.4$

b. $df = \dfrac{\left(\dfrac{s_1^2}{n_1} + \dfrac{s_2^2}{n_2}\right)^2}{\dfrac{1}{n_1 - 1}\left(\dfrac{s_1^2}{n_1}\right)^2 + \dfrac{1}{n_2 - 1}\left(\dfrac{s_2^2}{n_2}\right)^2}$

$= \dfrac{\left(\dfrac{2.5^2}{20} + \dfrac{4.8^2}{30}\right)^2}{\dfrac{1}{19}\left(\dfrac{2.5^2}{20}\right)^2 + \dfrac{1}{29}\left(\dfrac{4.8^2}{30}\right)^2} = 45.8$

c. $df = 45, t_{.025} = 2.014$

$$t_{.025}\sqrt{\frac{s_1^2}{n_1} + \frac{s_2^2}{n_2}} = 2.014\sqrt{\frac{2.5^2}{20} + \frac{4.8^2}{30}} = 2.1$$

d. 2.4 ± 2.1 (.3 to 4.5)

10. a. $t = \dfrac{(\bar{x}_1 - \bar{x}_2) - 0}{\sqrt{\dfrac{s_1^2}{n_1} + \dfrac{s_2^2}{n_2}}} = \dfrac{(13.6 - 10.1) - 0}{\sqrt{\dfrac{5.2^2}{35} + \dfrac{8.5^2}{40}}} = 2.18$

b. $df = \dfrac{\left(\dfrac{s_1^2}{n_1} + \dfrac{s_2^2}{n_2}\right)^2}{\dfrac{1}{n_1 - 1}\left(\dfrac{s_1^2}{n_1}\right)^2 + \dfrac{1}{n_2 - 1}\left(\dfrac{s_2^2}{n_2}\right)^2}$

$= \dfrac{\left(\dfrac{5.2^2}{35} + \dfrac{8.5^2}{40}\right)^2}{\dfrac{1}{34}\left(\dfrac{5.2^2}{35}\right)^2 + \dfrac{1}{39}\left(\dfrac{8.5^2}{40}\right)^2} = 65.7$

Use $df = 65$

c. $df = 65$, area in tail is between .01 and .025
two-tail p-value is between .02 and .05.

d. p-value $\leq .05$; reject H_0

12. a. $\bar{x}_1 - \bar{x}_2 = 22.5 - 18.6 = 3.9$ miles

b. $df = \dfrac{\left(\dfrac{s_1^2}{n_1} + \dfrac{s_2^2}{n_2}\right)^2}{\dfrac{1}{n_1 - 1}\left(\dfrac{s_1^2}{n_1}\right)^2 + \dfrac{1}{n_2 - 1}\left(\dfrac{s_2^2}{n_2}\right)^2}$

$= \dfrac{\left(\dfrac{8.4^2}{50} + \dfrac{7.4^2}{40}\right)^2}{\dfrac{1}{49}\left(\dfrac{8.4^2}{50}\right)^2 + \dfrac{1}{39}\left(\dfrac{7.4^2}{40}\right)^2} = 87.1$

Use $df = 87, t_{.025} = 1.988$

$$3.9 \pm 1.988\sqrt{\frac{8.4^2}{50} + \frac{7.4^2}{40}}$$

3.9 ± 3.3 (.6 to 7.2)

14. a. $H_0: \mu_1 - \mu_2 = 0$
$H_a: \mu_1 - \mu_2 \neq 0$

b. 2.18

c. Between .02 and .05

d. Reject H_0; mean ages differ

16. a. $H_0: \mu_1 - \mu_2 \leq 0$
$H_a: \mu_1 - \mu_2 > 0$

b. 38

c. $t = 1.80, df = 25$
p-value between .025 and .05

d. Reject H_0; conclude higher mean score if college grad

18. a. $H_0: \mu_1 - \mu_2 \geq 120$
$H_a: \mu_1 - \mu_2 < 120$

b. -2.10
Between .01 and .025

c. 32 to 118

d. Larger sample size

19. a. 1, 2, 0, 0, 2

b. $\bar{d} = \Sigma d_i/n = 5/5 = 1$

c. $s_d = \sqrt{\dfrac{\Sigma(d_i - \bar{d})^2}{n - 1}} = \sqrt{\dfrac{4}{5 - 1}} = 1$

d. $t = \dfrac{\bar{d} - \mu}{s_d/\sqrt{n}} = \dfrac{1 - 0}{1/\sqrt{5}} = 2.24$

$df = n - 1 = 4$
p-value is between .025 and .05
p-value $\leq .05$; reject H_0

20. a. 3, -1, 3, 5, 3, 0, 1

b. 2

c. 2.08

d. 2

e. .07 to 3.93

21. $H_0: \mu_d \leq 0$
$H_a: \mu_d > 0$
$\bar{d} = .625$
$s_d = 1.30$
$t = \dfrac{\bar{d} - \mu_d}{s_d/\sqrt{n}} = \dfrac{.625 - 0}{1.30/\sqrt{8}} = 1.36$

$df = n - 1 = 7$
p-value is between .10 and .20
p-value $> .05$; do not reject H_0

22. .16 to .35

24. $t = 1.63$
p-value between .10 and .20
Do not reject H_0

26. a. $t = -.60$
p-value greater than .40
Do not reject H_0

b. $-.103$

c. .39; larger sample size

27. a. $\bar{\bar{x}} = (30 + 45 + 36)/3 = 37$

$\text{SSTR} = \displaystyle\sum_{j=1}^{k} n_j(\bar{x}_j - \bar{\bar{x}})^2$

$= 5(30 - 37)^2 + 5(45 - 37)^2 + 5(36 - 37)^2$

$= 570$

$\text{MSTR} = \dfrac{\text{SSTR}}{k - 1} = \dfrac{570}{2} = 285$

b. $\text{SSE} = \displaystyle\sum_{j=1}^{k} (n_j - 1)s_j^2$

$= 4(6) + 4(4) + 4(6.5) = 66$

$\text{MSE} = \dfrac{\text{SSE}}{n_T - k} = \dfrac{66}{15 - 3} = 5.5$

c. $F = \dfrac{\text{MSTR}}{\text{MSE}} = \dfrac{285}{5.5} = 51.82$

From the F table (2 degrees of freedom numerator and 12 denominator), p-value is less than .01

Because p-value $\leq \alpha = 0.5$, we reject the null hypothesis that the means of the three populations are equal

d.

Source of Variation	Sum of Squares	Degrees of Freedom	Mean Square	F
Treatments	570	2	285	51.82
Error	66	12	5.5	
Total	636	14		

28. a. MSTR = 268
b. MSE = 92
c. Cannot reject H_0 because p-value is greater than .10
d.

Source of Variation	Sum of Squares	Degrees of Freedom	Mean Square	F
Treatments	536	2	268	2.91
Error	828	9	92	
Total	1364	11		

30. a. 1200, 3
300, 12
$F = 16$
b. Reject H_0 because p-value is less than .01

32.

	Mfg 1	Mfg 2	Mfg 3
Sample mean	23	28	21
Sample variance	6.67	4.67	3.33

$$\bar{\bar{x}} = (23 + 28 + 21)/3 = 24$$

$$\text{SSTR} = \sum_{j=1}^{k} n_j(\bar{x}_j - \bar{\bar{x}})^2$$
$$= 4(23 - 24)^2 + 4(28 - 24)^2$$
$$+ 4(21 - 24)^2 = 104$$

$$\text{MSTR} = \frac{\text{SSTR}}{k - 1} = \frac{104}{2} = 52$$

$$\text{SSE} = \sum_{j=1}^{k} (n_j - 1)s_j^2$$
$$= 3(6.67) + 3(4.67) + 3(3.33) = 44.01$$

$$\text{MSE} = \frac{\text{SSE}}{n_T - k} = \frac{44.01}{12 - 3} = 4.89$$

$$F = \frac{\text{MSTR}}{\text{MSE}} = \frac{52}{4.89} = 10.63$$

From the F table (2 degrees of freedom numerator and 9 denominator), p-value is less than .01

Because p-value $\leq \alpha = .05$, we reject the null hypothesis that the mean time needed to mix a batch of material is the same for each manufacturer

34. Sample means: 81, 79, 88; $F = 4.99$
p-value is between .025 and .05
Significant difference; Silicon Valley

36. Significant; $F = 3.70$
p-value is between .025 and .05

38. 8934 to 11,066

40. a. $H_0: \mu_1 - \mu_2 \leq 0$
$H_a: \mu_1 - \mu_2 > 0$
b. $t = .60$, $df = 57$
p-value greater than .20
Do not reject H_0

42. a. 15 (or $15,000)
b. 9.81 to 20.19
c. 11.5%

44. Sample means: 58.6, 48.8, 60.1; $F = 18.59$
p-value ≈ 0; significant difference

46. Sample means: 7.41, 6.11, 7.06; $F = 9.33$
p-value $< .01$; significant difference

Chapter 11

2. a. $\bar{p} = \dfrac{n_1\bar{p}_1 + n_2\bar{p}_2}{n_1 + n_2} = \dfrac{200(.22) + 300(.16)}{200 + 300} = .1840$

$$z = \frac{\bar{p}_1 - \bar{p}_2}{\sqrt{\bar{p}(1 - \bar{p})\left(\dfrac{1}{n_1} + \dfrac{1}{n_2}\right)}}$$

$$= \frac{.22 - .16}{\sqrt{.1840(1 - .1840)\left(\dfrac{1}{200} + \dfrac{1}{300}\right)}} = 1.70$$

p-value = .5000 − .4554 = .0446
b. p-value $\leq .05$; reject H_0

3. $\bar{p}_1 = 220/400 = .55$ $\bar{p}_2 = 192/400 = .48$

$$\bar{p}_1 - \bar{p}_2 \pm z_{.025}\sqrt{\frac{\bar{p}_1(1 - \bar{p}_1)}{n_1} + \frac{\bar{p}_2(1 - \bar{p}_2)}{n_2}}$$

$$.55 - .48 \pm 1.96\sqrt{\frac{.55(1 - .55)}{400} + \frac{.48(1 - .48)}{400}}$$

.07 ± .0691   (.0009 to .1391)
7% more executives are predicting an increase in full-time jobs; the confidence interval shows the difference may be from 0% to 14%

4. a. .46, .28
b. .18
c. .0777
d. .1023 to .2577, higher for Republicans

6. a. .803
b. .849
c. $H_0: p_1 - p_2 \geq 0$
$H_a: p_1 - p_2 < 0$
d. p-value = .0104
Reject H_0

8. a. $H_0: p_1 - p_2 = 0$
$H_a: p_1 - p_2 \neq 0$
b. .13

c. .0404; conclude difference exists

d. Yes; attracting younger age group

10. p-value $= .0322$

Reject H_0

11. a. Expected frequencies: $e_1 = 200(.40) = 80$

$e_2 = 200(.40) = 80$

$e_3 = 200(.20) = 40$

Actual frequencies: $f_1 = 60, f_2 = 120, f_3 = 20$

$$\chi^2 = \frac{(60 - 80)^2}{80} + \frac{(120 - 80)^2}{80} + \frac{(20 - 40)^2}{40}$$

$$= \frac{400}{80} + \frac{1600}{80} + \frac{400}{40}$$

$$= 5 + 20 + 10 = 35$$

Degrees of freedom: $k - 1 = 2$

$\chi^2 = 35$ shows p-value ≈ 0

p-value $\leq .01$; reject H_0

b. Reject H_0 if $\chi^2 \geq 9.210$

$\chi^2 = 35$; reject H_0

12. $\chi^2 = 15.33, df = 3$

p-value less than .005

Reject H_0

13. H_0: $p_{ABC} = .29, p_{CBS} = .28, p_{NBC} = .25, p_{IND} = .18$

H_a: The proportions are not

$p_{ABC} = .29, p_{CBS} = .28, p_{NBC} = .25, p_{IND} = .18$

Expected frequencies: $300(.29) = 87, 300(.28) = 84$

$300(.25) = 75, 300(.18) = 54$

$e_1 = 87, e_2 = 84, e_3 = 75, e_4 = 54$

Actual frequencies: $f_1 = 95, f_2 = 70, f_3 = 89, f_4 = 46$

$$\chi^2 = \frac{(95 - 87)^2}{87} + \frac{(70 - 84)^2}{84} + \frac{(89 - 75)^2}{75}$$

$$+ \frac{(46 - 54)^2}{54} = 6.87$$

Degrees of freedom: $k - 1 = 3$

$\chi^2 = 6.87$, p-value between .05 and .10

Do not reject H_0

14. $\chi^2 = 29.51, df = 5$

p-value ≈ 0

Reject H_0

16. a. $\chi^2 = 12.21, df = 3$

p-value is between .005 and .01

Conclude difference for 2003

b. 21%, 30%, 15%, 34%

Increased use of debit card

c. 51%

18. $\chi^2 = 16.31, df = 3$

p-value less than .005

Reject H_0

19. H_0: The column variable is independent of the row variable

H_a: The column variable is not independent of the row variable

Expected frequencies:

	A	**B**	**C**
P	28.5	39.9	45.6
Q	21.5	30.1	34.4

$$\chi^2 = \frac{(20 - 28.5)^2}{28.5} + \frac{(44 - 39.9)^2}{39.9} + \frac{(50 - 46.5)^2}{45.6}$$

$$+ \frac{(30 - 21.5)^2}{21.5} + \frac{(26 - 30.1)^2}{30.1} + \frac{(30 - 34.4)^2}{34.4}$$

$$= 7.86$$

Degrees of freedom: $(2 - 1)(3 - 1) = 2$

$\chi^2 = 7.86$, p-value between .01 and .025

Reject H_0

20. $\chi^2 = 19.77, df = 4$

p-value less than .005

Reject H_0

21. H_0: Type of ticket purchased is independent of the type of flight

H_a: Type of ticket purchased is not independent of the type of flight

Expected frequencies:

$e_{11} = 35.59$ $e_{12} = 15.41$

$e_{21} = 150.73$ $e_{22} = 65.27$

$e_{31} = 455.68$ $e_{32} = 197.32$

Ticket	Flight	Observed Frequency (f_i)	Expected Frequency (e_i)	$(f_i - e_i)^2/e_i$
First	Domestic	29	35.59	1.22
First	International	22	15.41	2.82
Business	Domestic	95	150.73	20.61
Business	International	121	65.27	47.59
Full-fare	Domestic	518	455.68	8.52
Full-fare	International	135	197.32	19.68
Totals		920		$\chi^2 = 100.43$

Degrees of freedom: $(3 - 1)(2 - 1) = 2$

$\chi^2 = 100.43$, p-value ≈ 0

Reject H_0

22. a. $\chi^2 = 7.36, df = 2$

p-value between .025 and .05

Reject H_0

b. Domestic 47.2%

24. a. $\chi^2 = 10.60, df = 4$

p-value between .025 and .05

Reject H_0; not independent

b. Higher negative effect on grades as hours increase

26. a. $\chi^2 = 7.85, df = 3$

p-value between .025 and .05

Reject H_0

b. Pharmaceutical, 98.6%

28. a. $H_0: p_1 - p_2 = 0$
$H_a: p_1 - p_2 \neq 0$
b. .31, .26
c. $z = 2.04$; p-value $= .0414$
Reject H_0; conclude difference
d. .0475, .0025 to .0975

30. $z = 2.37$; p-value $= .0178$
Reject H_0

32. a. .16
b. $H_0: p_1 - p_2 \leq 0$
$H_a: p_1 - p_2 > 0$
c. $z = 3.49$; p-value ≈ 0
Reject H_0

34. $\chi^2 = 4.64$, $df = 2$
p-value between .05 and .10
Do not reject H_0

36. $\chi^2 = 42.53$, $df = 4$
p-value ≈ 0; reject H_0

38. $\chi^2 = 23.37$, $df = 3$
p-value ≈ 0; reject H_0

40. a. $\chi^2 = 12.86$, $df = 2$
p-value less than .005
Reject H_0
b. 66.9, 30.3, 2.9
54.0, 42.0, 4.0

42. a. 24.01, 41.16, 20.46, 8.37
Last entry combines 3 and 4
b. $\chi^2 = 6.17$, $df = 3$
p-value greater than .10
Do not reject H_0; binomial

Chapter 12

1. a.

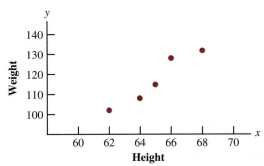

b. There appears to be a linear relationship between x and y
c. Many different straight lines can be drawn to provide a linear approximation of the relationship between x and y; in part (d) we will determine the equation of a straight line that "best" represents the relationship according to the least squares criterion

d. Summations needed to compute the slope and y-intercept:
$\Sigma x_i = 15$, $\Sigma y_i = 40$, $\Sigma(x_i - \bar{x})(y_i - \bar{y}) = 26$,
$\Sigma(x_i - \bar{x})^2 = 10$
$$b_1 = \frac{\Sigma(x_i - \bar{x})(y_i - \bar{y})}{\Sigma(x_i - \bar{x})^2} = \frac{26}{10} = 2.6$$
$b_0 = \bar{y} - b_1\bar{x} = 8 - (2.6)(3) = 0.2$
$\hat{y} = 0.2 - 2.6x$
e. $\hat{y} = .2 + 2.6x = .2 + 2.6(4) = 10.6$

2. b. There appears to be a linear relationship between x and y
d. $\hat{y} = 30.33 - 1.88x$
e. 19.05

4. a.

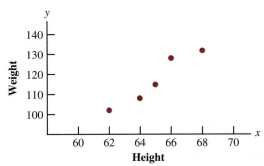

b. It indicates there may be a linear relationship between height and weight
c. Many different straight lines can be drawn to provide a linear approximation of the relationship between height and weight; in part (d) we will determine the equation of a straight line that "best" represents the relationship according to the least squares criterion
d. Summations needed to compute the slope and y-intercept:
$\Sigma x_i = 325$, $\Sigma y_i = 585$, $\Sigma(x_i - \bar{x})(y_i - \bar{y}) = 110$,
$\Sigma(x_i - \bar{x})^2 = 20$
$$b_1 = \frac{\Sigma(x_i - \bar{x})(y_i - \bar{y})}{\Sigma(x_i - \bar{x})^2} = \frac{110}{20} = 5.5$$
$b_0 = \bar{y} - b_1\bar{x} = 117 - (5.5)(65) = -240.5$
$\hat{y} = -240.5 + 5.5x$
e. $\hat{y} = -240.5 + 5.5(63) = 106$
The estimate of weight is 106 pounds

6. c. $\hat{y} = -10.16 + .18x$
e. 11.95 or approximately \$12,000

8. c. $\hat{y} = 490.21 + 204.24x$
d. \$1307

10. b. $\hat{y} = 51.82 + .145x$
c. 84.4

12. c. $\hat{y} = 1293 + .3165x$
d. 25,031

14. b. $\hat{y} = 28.30 - .0415x$
c. 26.2

15. a. $\hat{y}_i = .2 + 2.6x_i$ and $\bar{y} = 8$

x_i	y_i	$\hat{y}_i$	$y_i - \hat{y}_i$	$(y_i - \hat{y}_i)^2$	$y_i - \bar{y}$	$(y_i - \bar{y})^2$
1	3	2.8	.2	.04	-5	25
2	7	5.4	1.6	2.56	-1	1
3	5	8.0	-3.0	9.00	-3	9
4	11	10.6	.4	.16	3	9
5	14	13.2	.8	.64	6	36
				SSE = 12.40		SST = 80

$$\text{SSR} = \text{SST} - \text{SSE} = 80 - 12.4 = 67.6$$

b. $r^2 = \dfrac{\text{SSR}}{\text{SST}} = \dfrac{67.6}{80} = .845$

The least squares line provided a good fit; 84.5% of the variability in y has been explained by the least squares line

c. $r = \sqrt{.845} = +.9192$

16. a. SSE = 6.3325, SST = 114.80, SSR = 108.47
b. $r^2 = .945$
c. $r = -.9721$

18. a. The estimated regression equation and the mean for the dependent variable:

$$\hat{y} = 1790.5 + 581.1x, \quad \bar{y} = 3650$$

The sum of squares due to error and the total sum of squares:

$$\text{SSE} = \Sigma(y_i - \hat{y}_i)^2 = 85,135.14$$
$$\text{SST} = \Sigma(y_i - \bar{y})^2 = 335,000$$

Thus, SSR = SST − SSE
$$= 335,000 - 85,135.14 = 249,864.86$$

b. $r^2 = \dfrac{\text{SSR}}{\text{SST}} = \dfrac{249,864.86}{335,000} = .746$

The least squares line accounted for 74.6% of the total sum of squares

c. $r = \sqrt{.746} = +.8637$

20. a. $\hat{y} = -48.11 + 2.3325x$
b. $r^2 = .82$
c. $173,500$

22. a. $\hat{y} = -745.80 + 117.917x$
b. $r^2 = .7071$
c. $r = +.84$

23. a. $s^2 = \text{MSE} = \dfrac{\text{SSE}}{n-2} = \dfrac{12.4}{3} = 4.133$
b. $s = \sqrt{\text{MSE}} = \sqrt{4.133} = 2.033$
c. $\Sigma(x_i - \bar{x})^2 = 10$

$$s_{b_1} = \dfrac{s}{\sqrt{\Sigma(x_i - \bar{x})^2}} = \dfrac{2.033}{\sqrt{10}} = .643$$

d. $t = \dfrac{b_1 - \beta_1}{s_{b_1}} = \dfrac{2.6 - 0}{.643} = 4.04$

From the t table (3 degrees of freedom), area in tail is between .01 and .025

p-value is between .02 and .05

Actual p-value = .0272

Because p-value $\leq \alpha$, we reject H_0: $\beta_1 = 0$

e. $\text{MSR} = \dfrac{\text{SSR}}{1} = 67.6$

$$F = \dfrac{\text{MSR}}{\text{MSE}} = \dfrac{67.6}{4.133} = 16.36$$

From the F table (1 degree of freedom numerator and 3 denominator), p-value is between .025 and .05

Actual p-value = .0272

Because p-value $\leq \alpha$, we reject H_0: $\beta_1 = 0$

Source of Variation	Sum of Squares	Degrees of Freedom	Mean Square	F
Regression	67.6	1	67.6	16.36
Error	12.4	3	4.133	
Total	80	4		

24. a. 2.11
b. 1.453
c. .262
d. Significant; p-value is less than .01
e. Significant; p-value is less than .01

26. a. $s^2 = \text{MSE} = \dfrac{\text{SSE}}{n-2} = \dfrac{85,135.14}{4} = 21,283.79$

$s = \sqrt{\text{MSE}} = \sqrt{21,283.79} = 145.89$

$\Sigma(x_i - \bar{x})^2 = .74$

$$s_{b_1} = \dfrac{s}{\sqrt{\Sigma(x_i - \bar{x})^2}} = \dfrac{145.89}{\sqrt{.74}} = 169.59$$

$$t = \dfrac{b_1 - \beta_1}{s_{b_1}} = \dfrac{581.08 - 0}{169.59} = 3.43$$

From the t table (4 degrees of freedom), area in tail is between .01 and .025

p-value is between .02 and .05

Actual p-value = .0266

Because p-value $\leq \alpha$, we reject H_0: $\beta_1 = 0$

b. $\text{MSR} = \dfrac{\text{SSR}}{1} = \dfrac{249,864.86}{1} = 249,864.86$

$$F = \dfrac{\text{MSR}}{\text{MSE}} = \dfrac{249,864.86}{21,283.79} = 11.74$$

From the F table (1 degree of freedom numerator and 4 denominator), p-value is between .025 and .05

Actual p-value = .0266

Because p-value $\leq \alpha$, we reject H_0: $\beta_1 = 0$

c.

Source of Variation	Sum of Squares	Degrees of Freedom	Mean Square	F
Regression	29,864.86	1	29,864.86	11.74
Error	85,135.14	4	21,283.79	
Total	335,000	5		

28. They are related; p-value is less than .01

30. Significant; p-value is less than .01

32. a. $s = 2.033$

$\bar{x} = 3, \Sigma(x_i - \bar{x})^2 = 10$

$$s_{\hat{y}_p} = s\sqrt{\frac{1}{n} + \frac{(x_p - \bar{x})^2}{\Sigma(x_i - \bar{x})^2}}$$

$$= 2.033\sqrt{\frac{1}{5} + \frac{(4-3)^2}{10}} = 1.11$$

b. $\hat{y} = .2 + 2.6x = .2 + 2.6(4) = 10.6$

$\hat{y}_p \pm t_{\alpha/2}s_{\hat{y}_p}$

$10.6 \pm 3.182(1.11)$

10.6 ± 3.53, or 7.07 to 14.13

c. $s_{ind} = s\sqrt{1 + \frac{1}{n} + \frac{(x_p - \bar{x})^2}{\Sigma(x_i - \bar{x})^2}}$

$$= 2.033\sqrt{1 + \frac{1}{5} + \frac{(4-3)^2}{10}} = 2.32$$

d. $\hat{y}_p \pm t_{\alpha/2}s_{ind}$

$10.6 \pm 3.182(2.32)$

10.6 ± 7.38, or 3.22 to 17.98

34. Confidence interval: $-.4$ to 4.98

Prediction interval: -2.27 to 7.31

35. a. $s = 145.89, \bar{x} = 3.2, \Sigma(x_i - \bar{x})^2 = .74$

$\hat{y} = 1790.5 + 581.1x = 1790.5 + 581.1(3)$

$= 3533.8$

$$s_{\hat{y}_p} = s\sqrt{\frac{1}{n} + \frac{(x_p - \bar{x})^2}{\Sigma(x_i - \bar{x})^2}}$$

$$= 145.89\sqrt{\frac{1}{6} + \frac{(3-3.2)^2}{.74}} = 68.54$$

$\hat{y}_p \pm t_{\alpha/2}s_{\hat{y}_p}$

$3533.8 \pm 2.776(68.54)$

3533.8 ± 190.27, or $3343.53 to $3724.07

b. $s_{ind} = s\sqrt{1 + \frac{1}{n} + \frac{(x_p - \bar{x})^2}{\Sigma(x_i - \bar{x})^2}}$

$$= 145.89\sqrt{1 + \frac{1}{6} + \frac{(3-3.2)^2}{.74}} = 161.19$$

$\hat{y}_p \pm t_{\alpha/2}s_{ind}$

$3533.8 \pm 2.776(161.19)$

3533.8 ± 447.46, or $3086.34 to $3981.26

36. a. 80.86

b. 78.58 to 83.14

c. 72.92 to 88.80

38. a. $5046.67

b. $3815.10 to $6278.24

c. Not out of line

40. a. 9

b. $\hat{y} = 20.0 + 7.21x$

c. 1.3626

d. SSE $=$ SST $-$ SSR $= 51,984.1 - 41,587.3 = 10,396.8$

MSE $= 10,396.8/7 = 1485.3$

$$F = \frac{MSR}{MSE} = \frac{41,587.3}{1485.3} = 28.0$$

From the F table (1 degree of freedom numerator and 7 denominator), p-value is less than .01

Actual p-value $= .0011$

Because p-value $\le \alpha = .05$, we reject $H_0: \beta_1 = 0$

e. $\hat{y} = 20.0 + 7.21(50) = 380.5$, or $380,500

42. a. $\hat{y} = 80.0 + 50.0x$

b. 30

c. Significant; p-value is less than .01

d. $680,000

44. b. Yes

c. $\hat{y} = 37.1 - .779x$

d. Significant; p-value $= 0.003$

e. $r^2 = .434$; not a good fit

f. $12.27 to $22.90

g. $17.47 to $39.05

45. a. $\Sigma x_i = 70, \quad \Sigma y_i = 76, \quad \Sigma(x_i - \bar{x})(y_i - \bar{y}) = 200,$

$\Sigma(x_i - \bar{x})^2 = 126$

$$b_1 = \frac{\Sigma(x_i - \bar{x})(y_i - \bar{y})}{\Sigma(x_i - \bar{x})^2} = \frac{200}{126} = 1.5873$$

$b_0 = \bar{y} - b_1\bar{x} = 15.2 - (1.5873)(14) = -7.0222$

$\hat{y} = -7.02 + 1.59x$

b.

x_i	y_i	$\hat{y}_i$	$y_i - \hat{y}_i$
6	6	2.52	3.48
11	8	10.47	-2.47
15	12	16.83	-4.83
18	20	21.60	-1.60
20	30	24.78	5.22

c.

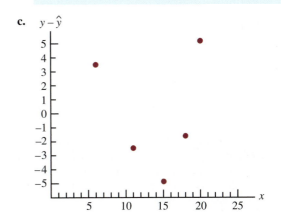

With only five observations, it is difficult to determine whether the assumptions are satisfied; however, the plot does suggest curvature in the residuals, which would indicate that the error term assumptions are not satisfied; the scatter diagram for these data also indicates that the underlying relationship between x and y may be curvilinear

46. a. $\hat{y} = 2.32 + .64x$
   b. No; the variance does not appear to be the same for all values of x

47. a. Let x = advertising expenditures and y = revenue
   $\hat{y} = 29.4 + 1.55x$
   b. SST = 1002, SSE = 310.28, SSR = 691.72

   $$MSR = \frac{SSR}{1} = 691.72$$

   $$MSE = \frac{SSE}{n-2} = \frac{310.28}{5} = 62.0554$$

   $$F = \frac{MSR}{MSE} = \frac{691.72}{62.0554} = 11.15$$

   From the F table (1 degree of freedom numerator and 5 denominator), p-value is between .01 and .025
   Actual p-value = .0206
   Because p-value $\le \alpha = .05$, we conclude that the two variables are related

   c.

x_i	y_i	$\hat{y}_i = 29.40 + 1.55x_i$	$y_i - \hat{y}_i$
1	19	30.95	−11.95
2	32	32.50	−.50
4	44	35.60	8.40
6	40	38.70	1.30
10	52	44.90	7.10
14	53	51.10	1.90
20	54	60.40	−6.40

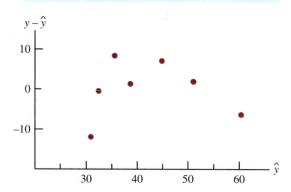

   d. The residual plot leads us to question the assumption of a linear relationship between x and y; even though the relationship is significant at the $\alpha = .05$ level, it would be extremely dangerous to extrapolate beyond the range of the data

48. b. Yes

50. a. $\hat{y} = 9.26 + .711x$
   b. Significant; p-value = .001
   c. $r^2 = .744$; good fit
   d. $13.53

52. a. Market beta = .95
   b. Significant; p-value = .029
   c. $r^2 = .470$; not a good fit
   d. Texas Instruments has a higher risk

54. a. $\hat{y} = 10.5 + .953x$
   b. Significant relationship; p-value = .000
   c. $2874 to $4952
   d. Yes

56. a. Negative linear relationship
   b. $\hat{y} = 8.10 - .344x$
   c. Significant; p-value = .002
   d. $r^2 = .711$; reasonably good fit
   e. 5.2 to 7.6 days

58. a. $\hat{y} = 5.85 + .830x$
   b. Significant; p-value = .000
   c. 84.65 points
   d. 65.35 to 103.96

Chapter 13

2. a. The estimated regression equation is
   $\hat{y} = 45.06 + 1.94x_1$
   An estimate of y when $x_1 = 45$ is
   $\hat{y} = 45.06 + 1.94(45) = 132.36$
   b. The estimated regression equation is
   $\hat{y} = 85.22 + 4.32x_2$
   An estimate of y when $x_2 = 15$ is
   $\hat{y} = 85.22 + 4.32(15) = 150.02$
   c. The estimated regression equation is
   $\hat{y} = -18.37 + 2.01x_1 + 4.74x_2$
   An estimate of y when $x_1 = 45$ and $x_2 = 15$ is
   $\hat{y} = -18.37 + 2.01(45) + 4.74(15) = 143.18$

4. a. $255,000

5. a. The Minitab output is shown in Figure D13.5a
   b. The Minitab output is shown in Figure D13.5b
   c. It is 1.60 in part (a) and 2.29 in part (b); in part (a) the coefficient is an estimate of the change in revenue due to a one-unit change in television advertising expenditures; in part (b) it represents an estimate of the change in revenue due to a one-unit change in television advertising expenditures when the amount of newspaper advertising is held constant
   d. Revenue = $83.2 + 2.29(3.5) + 1.30(1.8) = 93.56$ or $93,560

6. a. PCT = .354 + .000888 HR
   b. PCT = .865 − .0837 ERA
   c. PCT = .709 + .00140 HR − .103 ERA
   d. 54.9%

8. a. Return = 247 − 32.8 Safety + 34.6 ExpRatio
   b. 70.2

FIGURE D13.5a

```
The regression equation is
Revenue = 88.6 + 1.60 TVAdv

Predictor        Coef     SE Coef          T          p
Constant       88.638       1.582      56.02      0.000
TVAdv          1.6039      0.4778       3.36      0.015


S = 1.215     R-sq = 65.3%      R-sq(adj) = 59.5%


Analysis of Variance

SOURCE            DF          SS         MS          F          p
Regression         1      16.640     16.640      11.27      0.015
Residual Error     6       8.860      1.477
Total              7      25.500
```

FIGURE D13.5b

```
The regression equation is
Revenue = 83.2 + 2.29 TVAdv + 1.30 NewsAdv

Predictor        Coef     SE Coef          T          p
Constant       83.230       1.574      52.88      0.000
TVAdv          2.2902      0.3041       7.53      0.001
NewsAdv        1.3010      0.3207       4.06      0.010


S = 0.6426    R-sq = 91.9%      R-sq(adj) = 88.7%


Analysis of Variance

SOURCE            DF          SS         MS          F          p
Regression         2      23.435     11.718      28.38      0.002
Residual Error     5       2.065      0.413
Total              7      25.500
```

10. a. PCT $= -1.22 + 3.96$ FG%

    b. An increase of .01 in FG% will increase PCT by approximately .04

    c. PCT $= -1.23 + 4.82$ FG% $- 2.59$ Opp 3 Pt% $+ .0344$ Opp TO

    e. .6432

12. a. $R^2 = \dfrac{\text{SSR}}{\text{SST}} = \dfrac{14{,}052.2}{15{,}182.9} = .926$

    b. $R_a^2 = 1 - (1 - R^2)\dfrac{n-1}{n-p-1}$

$$= 1 - (1 - .926)\dfrac{10-1}{10-2-1} = .905$$

    c. Yes; after adjusting for the number of independent variables in the model, we see that 90.5% of the variability in y has been accounted for

14. a. .75

    b. .68

15. a. $R^2 = \dfrac{\text{SSR}}{\text{SST}} = \dfrac{23.435}{25.5} = .919$

$$R_a^2 = 1 - (1 - R^2)\dfrac{n-1}{n-p-1}$$

$$= 1 - (1 - .919)\dfrac{8-1}{8-2-1} = .887$$

    b. Multiple regression analysis is preferred because both R^2 and R_a^2 show an increased percentage of the variability of y explained when both independent variables are used

16. a. No, $R^2 = .153$

    b. Better fit with multiple regression

18. a. $R^2 = .564$, $R_a^2 = .511$

  b. The fit is not very good

19. a. $\text{MSR} = \dfrac{\text{SSR}}{p} = \dfrac{6216.375}{2} = 3108.188$

  $\text{MSE} = \dfrac{\text{SSE}}{n - p - 1} = \dfrac{507.75}{10 - 2 - 1} = 72.536$

  b. $F = \dfrac{\text{MSR}}{\text{MSE}} = \dfrac{3108.188}{72.536} = 42.85$

  From the F table (2 degrees of freedom numerator and 7 denominator), p-value is less than .01

  Because p-value $\leq \alpha$, the overall model is significant

  c. $t = \dfrac{b_1}{s_{b_1}} = \dfrac{.5906}{.0813} = 7.26$

  p-value is less than .01

  Because p-value $\leq \alpha$, β_1 is significant

  d. $t = \dfrac{b_2}{s_{b_2}} = \dfrac{.4980}{.0567} = 8.78$

  p-value is less than .01

  Because p-value $\leq \alpha$, β_2 is significant

20. a. Significant; p-value $= .000$

  b. Significant; p-value $= .000$

  c. Significant; p-value $= .002$

22. a. $\text{SSE} = 4000$, $s^2 = 571.43$,

  $\text{MSR} = 6000$

  b. Significant; p-value is less than .01

23. a. $F = 28.38$

  p-value $= .002$

  Because p-value $\leq \alpha$, there is a significant relationship

  b. $t = 7.53$

  p-value $= .001$

  Because p-value $\leq \alpha$, β_1 is significant and x_1 should not be dropped from the model

  c. $t = 4.06$

  p-value $= .010$

  Because p-value $\leq \alpha$, β_2 is significant and x_2 should not be dropped from the model

24. a. Reject H_0: $\beta_1 = \beta_2 = 0$; p-value $= .000$

  b. HR: Reject H_0: $\beta_1 = 0$; p-value $= .000$

  ERA: Reject H_0: $\beta_2 = 0$; p-value $= .000$

26. a. Significant; p-value $= .000$

  b. All of the independent variables are significant

28. a. Using Minitab, the 95% confidence interval is 132.16 to 154.15

  b. Using Minitab, the 95% prediction interval is 111.15 at 175.17

29. a. See Minitab output in Figure D13.5b.

  $\hat{y} = 83.230 + 2.2902(3.5) + 1.3010(1.8) = 93.588$ or $93,588

  b. Minitab results: 92.840 to 94.335, or \$92,840 to \$94,335

  c. Minitab results: 91.774 to 95.401, or \$91,774 to \$95,401

30. a. 58.37% to 75.03%

  b. 35.24% to 90.59%

32. a. $E(y) = \beta_0 + \beta_1 x_1 + \beta_2 x_2$

  where $x_2 = \begin{cases} 0 \text{ if level 1} \\ 1 \text{ if level 2} \end{cases}$

  b. $E(y) = \beta_0 + \beta_1 x_1 + \beta_2(0) = \beta_0 + \beta_1 x_1$

  c. $E(y) = \beta_0 + \beta_1 x_1 + \beta_2(1) = \beta_0 + \beta_1 x_1 + \beta_2$

  d. $\beta_2 = E(y \mid \text{level 2}) - E(y \mid \text{level 1})$

  β_1 is the change in $E(y)$ for a 1-unit change in x_1 holding x_2 constant

34. a. \$15,300, because $b_3 = 15.3$

  b. $\hat{y} = 10.1 - 4.2(2) + 6.8(8) + 15.3(0) = 56.1$

  Sales prediction: \$56,100

  c. $\hat{y} = 10.1 - 4.2(1) + 6.8(3) + 15.3(1) = 41.6$

  Sales prediction: \$41,600

36. a. $\hat{y} = 1.86 + 0.291\,\text{Months} + 1.10\,\text{Type} - 0.609\,\text{Person}$

  b. Significant; p-value $= .002$

  c. Person is not significant; p-value $= .167$

38. a. $\hat{y} = -91.8 + 1.08\,\text{Age} + .252\,\text{Pressure} + 8.74\,\text{Smoker}$

  b. Significant; p-value $= .01$

  c. 95% prediction interval is 21.35 to 47.18 or a probability of .2135 to .4718; quit smoking and begin some type of treatment to reduce his blood pressure

40. b. 67.39

42. a. $\hat{y} = -1.41 + .0235 x_1 + .00486 x_2$

  b. Significant

  c. $R^2 = .937$; $R_a^2 = 9.19$; good fit

  d. Both significant

44. a. Score $= 50.6 + 1.56\,\text{RecRes}$

  b. $r^2 = .431$; not a good fit

  c. Score $= 33.5 + 1.90\,\text{RecRes} + 2.61\,\text{Afford}$

  Significant

  $R_2^2 = .784$; much better fit

46. a. CityMPG $= 24.1 - 2.10\,\text{Displace}$

  Significant; p-value $= .000$

  b. CityMPG $= 26.4 - 2.44\,\text{Displace} - 1.20\,\text{Drive4}$

  c. Significant; p-value $= .016$

  d. CityMPG $= 33.3 - 4.15\,\text{Displace} - 1.24\,\text{Drive4} + 2.16\,\text{EightCyl}$

  e. Significant overall and individually

Index

Essentials of Statistics for Business and Economics Data Disk

Chapter 1

Music	Exercise 14
Hotel	Table 1.6
Minisystems	Table 1.7
Norris	Table 1.5
Shadow02	Table 1.1

Chapter 2

ApTest	Table 2.9
Audit	Table 2.5
AutoData	Exercise 38
Broker	Exercise 26
BWBooks	Exercise 6
CEOs	Exercise 9
Client	Exercise 10
Computer	Exercise 21
Comstock	Exercise 42
Concerts	Exercise 20
Crosstab	Exercise 29
Dow	Exercise 41
Fortune	Exercise 51
Frequency	Exercise 11
Golf	Exercise 40
HighLow	Exercise 46
IBD	Exercise 34
Income	Exercise 44
Marathon	Exercise 28
Names	Exercise 5
NFL	Exercise 37
OccupSat	Exercise 48
Pelican	Case Problem
Restaurant	Table 2.10
RevEmps	Exercise 49
Scatter	Exercise 30
Shadow	Exercise 43
SoftDrink	Table 2.1
Spending	Exercise 17
Stereo	Table 2.13
StockPrices	Exercise 27
TVMedia	Exercise 4
Wageweb	Exercise 18

Chapter 3

Asian	Case Problem 3
Beer	Exercise 65
Broker	Exercise 7
Cameras	Exercise 12
Cities	Exercise 64
DowS&P	Exercise 50
Health	Case Problem 2
Hotels	Exercise 5
Income	Exercise 62
Mutual	Exercise 44
NCAA	Exercise 34
Notebook	Exercise 23
Payroll	Exercise 42
PCs	Exercise 49
Pelican	Case Problem 1
Property	Exercise 40
Retainer	Exercise 59

Salary	Table 3.1
Speakers	Exercise 35
Stereo	Table 3.7
Temperature	Exercise 51
Visa	Exercise 58
WageWeb	Exercise 33
Websites	Exercise 9

Chapter 4

Judge	Case Problem

Chapter 7

EAI	Section 7.1
MetAreas	Appendix 7.2, 7.3
MutualFund	Exercise 14

Chapter 8

ActTemps	Exercise 49
Auto	Case Problem 3
Balance	Table 8.3
Bock	Case Problem 1
FastFood	Exercise 18
Flights	Exercise 48
GulfProp	Case Problem 2
Interval p	Appendix 8.2
Lloyd's	Section 8.1
Miami	Exercise 17
NYSEStocks	Exercise 47
OpenEndFunds	Exercise 22
Scheer	Table 8.4
TeeTimes	Section 8.4
TVtime	Exercise 20

Chapter 9

BLS	Case Problem 2
AirRating	Section 9.4
Coffee	Section 9.3
GolfTest	Section 9.3
Hyp Sigma Known	Appendix 9.2
Hyp Sigma Unknown	Appendix 9.2
Hypothesis p	Appendix 9.2
Orders	Section 9.4
Quality	Case Problem 1
WomenGolf	Section 9.5

Chapter 10

Cargo	Exercise 13
CheckAcct	Section 10.2
Digital	Exercise 39
Earnings	Exercise 26
ExamScores	Section 10.1
Florida	Exercise 42
Funds	Exercise 43
Golf	Case Problem 1
IDSalary	Case Problem 3
Matched	Table 10.2
Medical1	Case Problem 2
Medical2	Case Problem 2
Mutual	Exercise 40
NCP	Table 10.3

NFL	Exercise 46
Resorts	Exercise 45
SATVerbal	Exercise 16
Ships	Exercise 36
SoftwareTest	Table 10.1
Stress	Exercise 35
Technology	Exercise 34
Trucks	Exercise 44
TVRadio	Exercise 25

Chapter 11

FitTest	Appendix 11.2
Independence	Appendix 11.3
NYReform	Case Problem
TaxPrep	Section 11.1

Chapter 12

ADRs	Exercise 49
Airport	Exercise 11
Alumni	Case Problem 3
Armand's	Table 12.1
Boots	Exercise 27
Cars	Exercises 7 & 19
Cities	Exercise 20
EmpRev	Exercise 12
Hydration1	Exercise 43
IPO	Exercise 50
IRSAudit	Exercise 59
JobSat	Exercise 53
MLB	Case Problem 4
MtnBikes	Exercise 8
NAEP	Case Problem 1
OffRates	Exercise 44
Options	Exercise 51
PCs	Exercises 10, 28, & 36
Printers	Exercises 22 & 30
Safety	Case Problem 2
Salaries	Exercise 14

Chapter 13

Alumni	Case Problem 3
Backpack	Exercise 7
Brokers	Exercise 25
Butler	Tables 13.1 & 13.2
Consumer	Case Problem 1
Enquirer	Case Problem 2
Exer2	Exercise 2
Football	Exercise 37
ForFunds	Exercise 8
FuelEcon	Exercise 46
HomeValue	Exercise 44
Johnson	Table 13.6
MLB	Exercises 6, 16, & 24
NBA	Exercises 10, 18, & 26
Repair	Exercises 35 & 36
Schools	Exercises 9, 17, & 30
Showtime	Exercises 5, 15, 23, 29, & 41
SportsCar	Exercise 31
Stroke	Exercise 38
Trucks	Exercise 45